"IN CHRIST" IN PAUL

"In Christ" in Paul

*Explorations in Paul's
Theology of Union
and Participation*

edited by

Michael J. Thate, Kevin J. Vanhoozer, and Constantine R. Campbell

WILLIAM B. EERDMANS PUBLISHING COMPANY
GRAND RAPIDS, MICHIGAN

Wm. B. Eerdmans Publishing Co.
2140 Oak Industrial Drive N.E., Grand Rapids, Michigan 49505
www.eerdmans.com

First published 2014 in Germany by
Mohr Siebeck, Tübingen
© 2014 Mohr Siebeck
All rights reserved
Eerdmans edition published 2018

ISBN 978-0-8028-7394-1

Library of Congress Cataloging-in-Publication Data

Names: Thate, Michael J., 1978- editor.
Title: In Christ in Paul : explorations in Paul's theology of union and
   participation / edited by Michael J. Thate, Kevin J. Vanhoozer, and
   Constantine R. Campbell.
Description: Grand Rapids : Eerdmans Publishing Co., 2018. | Originally
   published: Tübingen : Mohr Siebeck, 2014. | Includes bibliographical
   references and index.
Identifiers: LCCN 2017031489 | ISBN 9780802873941 (pbk. : alk. paper)
Subjects: LCSH: Bible. Epistles of Paul—Theology. | Mystical union—Biblical
   teaching. | Jesus Christ—Person and offices—Biblical teaching. | Jesus
   Christ—History of doctrines.
Classification: LCC BS2655.M85 I53 2018 | DDC 227/.06—dc23
   LC record available at https://lccn.loc.gov/2017031489

Contents

Preface   viii

A Theological Introduction

From "Blessed in Christ" to "Being in Christ":
The State of Union and the Place of Participation in Paul's Discourse,
New Testament Exegesis, and Systematic Theology Today   3
    KEVIN J. VANHOOZER

Part One: Pauline Theology and Exegesis

Participation and Faith in Paul   37
    DOUGLAS A. CAMPBELL

Metaphor, Reality, and Union with Christ   61
    CONSTANTINE R. CAMPBELL

Incarnational Ontology and the Theology of Participation in Paul   87
    GRANT MACASKILL

Oneself in Another: Participation and the Spirit in Romans 8   103
    SUSAN EASTMAN

"Real Participation": The Body of Christ &
the Body of Sin in Evolutionary Perspective   127
    MATTHEW CROASMUN

Baptism and Union with Christ   157
    ISAAC AUGUSTINE MORALES, O.P.

Paul's Corporate, Cruciform, Missional *Theosis* in 2 Corinthians   181
    MICHAEL J. GORMAN

Paul and the Anxieties of (Imperial?) Succession:
Galatians and the Politics of Neglect 209
  MICHAEL J. THATE

Sharing the Heavenly Rule of Christ the King:
Paul's Royal Participatory Language in Ephesians 253
  JOSHUA W. JIPP

Paul, Φρόνησις, and Participation:
The Shape of Space and the Reconfiguration of Place
in Paul's Letter to the Philippians 281
  MICHAEL J. THATE

Part Two: Some Highlights from Reception History

Two Early Perspectives on Participation in Paul:
Irenaeus and Clement of Alexandria 331
  BEN C. BLACKWELL

Augustine and Participation:
Some Reflections on His Exegesis of Romans 357
  DARREN SARISKY

Apocalyptic Union: Martin Luther's Account of Faith in Christ 375
  STEPHEN CHESTER

The Fatherhood of God & Union with Christ in Calvin 399
  JULIE CANLIS

"One with Him in Spirit":
Mystical Union and the Humanity of Christ
in the Theology of John Owen 427
  T. ROBERT BAYLOR

Karl Barth's Reading of Paul's Union with Christ 453
  KEITH L. JOHNSON

Part Three: Theological Reflection

Fitting Participation: From the Holy Trinity to Christian Virtue 477
 ASHISH VARMA

Participating in the Body and Blood of Christ:
Christian Κοινωνία and the Lord's Supper 503
 MARY PATTON BAKER

Until We Are One? Biopolitics and the United Body 529
 DEVIN P. SINGH

List of Contributors 557

Indexes 559

Preface

This volume is intended to offer a substantial new contribution to the burgeoning discussion of union with Christ in the theology and writings of the Apostle Paul. Several scholarly works related to the theme of union with Christ have recently appeared, such as those by Gorman, Campbell, and Macaskill, yet none of those authors would claim to have said all there is to say about the theme – in fact, their essays in this volume are testament to the fact. Rather than concluding the conversation with final solutions, recent contributions have provided a fertile basis on which more exploration is possible through a variety of trajectories.

Appropriately then, the subtitle of this volume reveals its general nature: it consists of a series of *explorations* in Paul's theology of union and participation. We do not claim that this contribution, therefore, is the one to conclude the conversation either. It is exploratory; it is multifaceted and multidisciplinary; and it is but one more conversation piece for consideration within the guild.

An excellent cast has been assembled for this production, with each participant offering distinct insights. It will become clear that there is no overarching unity to the essays in the sense that the authors all agree with each other on everything. That is certainly not the case. But for such an exploratory volume, we have not attempted to achieve a fully coherent presentation with all the kinks ironed out. Nevertheless, we trust the variety of voices, topics, and approaches will offer their own rewards to the audience. The editors offer thanks to each contributor for their investment of expertise, time, andenergy.

We are indebted to our production crew, Kenny Clewett, Dan Cole, and Paul Maxwell, for their many hours of hard labour in helping to prepare the manuscript. Kevin and I particularly wish to thank our fellow editor, Mike Thate, for his tireless efforts in producing the volume. He dreamed up the project in the first place, recruited our contributors, and did a substantial amount of the editorial work. Finally, we thank Mohr Siebeck for their enthusiasm for the project. It is good to know there will always be a theatre for productions such as this.

CRC, KJV, MJT

A Theological Introduction

From "Blessed in Christ" to "Being in Christ"

The State of Union and the Place of Participation in Paul's Discourse, New Testament Exegesis, and Systematic Theology Today

KEVIN J. VANHOOZER

A. Introduction: the mystery of "in Christ"

> ...in my flesh I am completing what is lacking in Christ's afflictions. (Col. 1:24)

> I want to know Christ ... and the sharing of his sufferings by becoming like him in his death. (Phil. 3:10)

"In Christ" states the theme of the present collection of essays; "in Paul" delimits it – but not by much. For if Karl Barth was a "God-intoxicated" man, how much more can we call St. Paul a "God-in-Christ intoxicated" man. *To be or not to be in Christ* was, for Paul, the only question – new, urgent, and ever relevant. Paul considered himself "dead to sin and alive to God in Christ" (Rom. 6:11). Paul identified with Christ to the point of viewing his own story as overlapping with that of Jesus: "I have been crucified with Christ" (Gal 2:19). Indeed, Paul presses his identity thesis to the point of claiming "I carry the marks [τὰ στίγματα] of Jesus branded on my body" (Gal. 6:17). What did Paul mean by locating himself "in Christ"? To what reality does Paul's signature phrase refer? We begin our search for an answer with the Italian Renaissance, and a pictorial interpretation of what Paul meant.

I. A man in Christ? Giotto's "Stigmatization of St. Francis"

Giotto painted his famous "The Stigmatization of St. Francis" in 1300 for the church of San Francesco in Pisa, Italy (it now hangs in the Louvre). The altarpiece depicts an event in the life of Saint Francis in 1224 as recorded by Thomas of Celano, his first biographer, some years later. According to Celano, Francis had embarked on a forty day fast, during which he devoted himself to praying (for wisdom how best to please God) and to studying the Gospels, where he thrice landed on accounts of Jesus' Passion. One morning, at sunrise, he had a vision of Christ as a six-winged Seraph in the sky whose body was fixed to a cross. Francis experienced both joy and compassion at this sight. As he contemplated the meaning of the vision, he came to understand, in the words of St. Bonaventure, that he would be like Christ "not by martyrdom of body, but by enkindling of heart."[1] However, after the vision Francis discovered that he had indeed come to share in Christ's sufferings: all five of Christ's wounds (hands, feet, side) had reappeared on Francis's thirteenth-century body.

St. Francis is the first recorded stigmatic in church history (unless one counts Paul on the basis of Gal 6:17).[2] Giotto depicts Francis as kneeling on the ground, with his hands raised in a gesture of adoration and/or surrender. Giotto's innovation was to depict light beams emanating from Christ's hands and feet and leading straight to the hands and feet of St. Francis.[3] Giotto accomplishes visually, in oils and pigments, something that theologians have subsequently been trying for centuries to explain in words: the nature of a saint's participation in Christ's sufferings.[4]

Giotto's *Stigmatization* is the dominant image of his famous Pisa panel, towering over three smaller scenes from Francis's life.[5] Paul says he bore in his body the marks of Jesus, and Bonaventure says that Francis bore in his body "the image of the Crucified not made by a craftsman in wood or stone, but fashioned in his members by the hand of the living God."[6] Bonaventure suggests that just as the pope approved the rule of St. Francis, so

---

[1] Saint Bonaventura, *The Life of Saint Francis* (London: J. M. Dent, 1904), 139.

[2] See further, Edward Harrison, *Stigmata: A Medieval Phenomenon in a Modern Age* (New York: Penguin, 1994) for a critical examination of modern cases from a medical point of view. Harrison suggests that the phenomenon, though real, may be a psychosomatic manifestation of a person's identification with Christ. For another account, more indebted to Roman Catholic theology and tradition, see Michael Freze, *They Bore the Wounds of Christ: The Mystery of the Sacred Stigmata* (Huntington, Ind.: Our Sunday Visitor, 1989).

[3] I say "innovation" because there is no mention of light in Bonaventure's account of this event, in his *Legenda Maior,* which was completed in 1263.

[4] For further discussion of Giotto and his paintings of St. Francis, see Joanna Cannon, "Giotto and Art for the Friars: Revolutions Spiritual and Artistic," and William R. Cook, "Giotto and the Figure of St. Francis," in *The Cambridge Companion to Giotto* (ed. Anne Derbes and Mark Sandona; Cambridge: Cambridge University Press, 2004), 103–34 and 135–56.

[5] The three other scenes are of (1) Pope Innocent III's dream of Francis propping up a church on the verge of collapse (2) the pope approving the rule of the Franciscan order (3) Francis preaching to the birds. Giotto produced other paintings of Francis as well, including *Funeral of St. Francis and Verification of the Stigmata* in the chapel at Bardi dedicated to St. Francis.

[6] From the *Legenda Minor of St. Bonaventura - de Stigmatibus sacris,* 1–4; ed. Quaracchi, 1941, 202–4.

God places his own "seal" on Francis's body (the wounds bear a physical resemblance to a wax seal), thus providing an even greater confirmation of the Franciscan order. The stigmata were included in other images of Francis and in time became one of his distinct identifying characteristics.

II. Modern New Testament studies: recontextualizing Paul's "in Christ"

Some seven hundred years later, in an academic galaxy far from Giotto's Pisa, the German New Testament scholar Adolf Deissmann argued that that union with Christ lies at the core of Paul's theological thinking. However, instead of seeing this union manifested in physical stigmata, Deissmann linked "in Christ" to Paul's Damascus road experienced and believed it primarily to express Paul's sense of spiritual or mystical intimacy with Christ. Union is a matter of subjective perception rather than of an objective condition (i.e., the stigmata). Curiously, Deissmann nevertheless insisted on interpreting the phrase "in Christ" in consistently (and often stiltedly) locative terms: "Just as the air of life, which we breathe, is 'in' us and fills us, and yet we at the same time live in this air and breathe it, so it is also with the Christ-intimacy of the Apostle Paul: Christ in him, he in Christ."[7]

Albert Schweitzer contended that union with Christ is not only central to Paul's theology but the very core of Christianity. Since the Reformation, the doctrine of justification dominated the discussion about Paul's soteriology, but Schweitzer downsized justification to the status of a "subsidiary crater" on planet Paul, lying within the "main crater" of his understanding of union with Christ.[8] Schweitzer described this union in mystical-eschatological terms whereby believers now experience Christ's death and resurrection: "We are always in the presence of mysticism when we find a human being ... feeling himself, while still externally amid the earthly and temporal, to belong to the super-earthly and eternal."[9] Schweitzer makes two further points, each of which has launched conversations to which the present essays additionally contribute. First, Schweitzer insists that there are no Hellenistic parallels or precedents for Paul's mysticism, thus starting a race in New Testament studies to find a context that makes sense of it. Second, Schweitzer held that being in Christ incorporated believers into

---

[7] Adolf Deissman, *Paul: A Study in Social and Religious History* (London: Hodder & Stoughton, 1912), 140. Cf. James S. Stewart, who says that to be in Christ is to be "transplanted into a new soil and a new climate, and both soil and climate are Christ." *A Man in Christ: The Vital Elements of St. Paul's Religion* (New York: Harper & Row, 1935), 157.

[8] Albert Schweitzer, *The Mysticism of Paul the Apostle* (London: A & C Black, 1931), 225.

[9] Schweitzer, *Mysticism of Paul*, 1.

a new eschatological body, the church, a Christlike community. There is, then, a corporate dimension to being in Christ.

E. P. Sanders is another New Testament scholar who figures prominently in the background of the present collection inasmuch as he uses biblical exegesis to overturn what had become the received view among systematic theologians, namely, Luther's view that salvation hinges on justification by faith, understood forensically in terms of Christ's imputed righteousness. Sanders' *Paul and Palestinian Judaism* put the apostle's teaching in historical context and argued that Paul was not reacting against legalism (i.e., "works righteousness") but commending Jesus, rather than the Torah, as the way of eschatological salvation. According to Sanders, saving faith and being in Christ coincide: "righteousness by faith and participation in Christ ultimately amount to the same thing."[10] Salvation comes by participating in the age to come that has come in Jesus: "by *sharing* in Christ's death, one died to the *power* of sin or to the old aeon, with the result that one *belongs to God*."[11] Paul's basic insight, then, is that "the believer becomes one with Christ Jesus and that this effects a transfer of lordship and the beginning of a transformation which will be completed with the coming of the Lord. . . . one participates in salvation by becoming one person with Christ, dying with him to sin and sharing the promise of his resurrection. . . . It seems reasonable to call this way of thinking 'participationist eschatology.'"[12]

As to the all important question of the nature of one's participation in Christ, however, Sanders confesses himself flummoxed, even while insisting that the participatory union is "real": "But what does this mean? How are we to understand it? We seem to lack a category of 'reality' – real participation in Christ, real possession of the Spirit – which lies between naive cosmological speculation and belief in magical transference on the one hand and a revised self-understanding on the other. I must confess that I do not have a new category of perception to propose here."[13] It is precisely this paradox – that the concept of participation is central to Paul's theology but largely inaccessible to us today – that the essays in the present volume set out to address by exploring notions of union and participation in Paul through exegesis, highlights in reception history, and theological reflection. Contra Sanders, we believe there may well be a possible language that would allow us to come closer to what Paul had in mind. We therefore seek to name and navigate the various ditches, some uglier than others, that

---

[10] Sanders, *Paul and Palestinian Judaism: A Comparison of Patterns of Religion* (Minneapolis: Fortress, 1977), 506.

[11] Sanders, *Paul and Palestinian Judaism*, 467 (italics his).

[12] Sanders, *Paul and Palestinian Judaism*, 549.

[13] Sanders, *Paul and Palestinian Judaism*, 522–23.

have created divides and led to misunderstandings between biblical studies, historical theology, and systematic theology.

Richard Hays anticipates the strategy of the present volume in his "What is 'Real Participation in Christ'? A Dialogue with E. P. Sanders on Pauline Soteriology."[14] Hays identifies four complementary candidates for explaining the background behind Paul's notion of participation in Christ: belonging to a family; political or military solidarity; the *ekklesia*; "living with the Christ story." Of special importance to Hays is the last model – narrative participation – though he too is reticent when it comes to spelling out the mechanism of participation: how exactly do *I* participate in *his* story? Elsewhere Hays hints at a response, gesturing towards the East: "My own guess is that Sanders's insights would be supported and clarified by careful study of participation motifs in patristic theology, particular the thought of the Eastern fathers."[15] This is precisely the wager that Michael Gorman makes in reclaiming the notion of *theosis*: "for Paul cruciformity – conformity to the crucified Christ – is really theoformity, or theosis."[16] With this thought we have come full circle from Luther: "in Christ" no longer names a legal status (i.e., being declared righteous) but an ontological transformation (i.e., a becoming righteous).[17]

III. Systematic theology: "in Christ" in Reformation soteriology

The study of "in Christ" in Paul does not belong to New Testament scholars only. One of the surprising developments in recent years is the renewed interest in union with Christ among exegetes and theologians alike. While some of the theological interest stems from the afore-mentioned connection with *theosis* characteristic of patristic theology, many historical and systematic theologians trace their interest to the place of union with Christ in Reformation theology, and John Calvin in particular, as well as subse-

---

[14] In Fabian E. Udoh et. al., eds., *Redefining First-Century Jewish and Christian Identities: Essays in Honor of Ed Parish Sanders* (Notre Dame, Ind.: University of Notre Dame Press, 2008), 336–51.

[15] Richard B. Hays, *The Faith of Jesus Christ: The Narrative Substructure of Galatians 3:11-4:11* (2d ed.; Grand Rapids: Eerdmans, 2002), xxxii.

[16] Michael J. Gorman, *Inhabiting the Cruciform God: Kenosis, Justification, and Theosis in Paul's Narrative Soteriology* (Grand Rapids: Eerdmans, 2009), 4.

[17] For a more complete overview of participation in Christ in modern New Testament studies, see Mark Seifrid, "In Christ," in *Dictionary of Paul and his Letters* (ed. Gerald F. Hawthorne and Ralph P. Martin; Downers Grove, Ill.: InterVarsity Press, 1993), 433–36, Constantine R. Campbell, *Paul and Union with Christ: An Exegetical and Theological Study* (Grand Rapids: Zondervan, 2012), 31–58 and Grant Macaskill, *Union with Christ in the New Testament* (Oxford: Oxford University Press, 2013), 17–41.

quent Reformed soteriology.[18] To put it in Gadamerian terms: Paul's phrase "in Christ" has generated, especially through the prism of Calvin's interpretation, not only a history of reception but a history of effects (i.e., Reformed soteriology).[19]

Calvin's basic insight into union with Christ – the grace that launched a thousand soteriological ships – comes at the beginning of book III of his *Institutes* on "The Way in Which We Receive the Grace of Christ": "as long as Christ remains outside of us, and we are separated from him, all that he has suffered and done for the salvation of the human race remains useless and of no value for us."[20] According to Calvin, it is the Holy Spirit who links us to Christ, through faith, itself a work of the Spirit.[21] Indeed, instead of standing afar off, Christ engrafts believers into his body, making them "participants not only in all his benefits but also in himself."[22] Calvin had to clarify his understanding of participation in Christ to distinguish his own position from that of Osiander, who maintained that those in Christ receive a "transfusion" as it were of divine nature into their human nature.[23] For Calvin, believers participate not in Christ's nature but rather his personal history: Christ deigns to make us one with him, organically incorporating us into his life (and hence sonship) in what Calvin terms a "mystical union" (*mystica unio*). There is in this notion no mixture of natures, only a personal union, like that of husband and wife (cf. Eph. 5:31-32).

The focus of the present book is "in Christ" *in Paul*, not Calvin. We nevertheless do well to consider the conversation in Reformed soteriology, for it is at least possible that theological reflection affords as important a clue as to the meaning of "in Christ" as historical reconstruction, to the extent that the former yields the deeper ontological and soteriological implications that are ingredient to a fuller understanding.[24] It takes more than

---

[18] Five of the essays in Parts Two and Three of the present book arguably treat either Calvin himself (Canlis), a theologian in the Reformed tradition (Baylor, Johnson) or the way in which Calvin handled a particular doctrinal issue (Varma, Baker).

[19] As with Paul, so with Calvin: each has his own scholarly champions who place union with Christ at the center of his theology.

[20] John Calvin, *Institutes of the Christian Religion* (LCC 20–21; 2 vols.; ed. John T. McNeil, trans. Ford Lewis Battles Philadelphia: Westminster, 1960), III.1.1.

[21] *Inst.*, III.1.4.

[22] *Inst.* III.2.24.

[23] The context was Osiander's conviction that justification requires an actual sharing in Christ's essential righteousness (see *Inst.* III.11.5–12).

[24] Though I here focus on debates about union with Christ in recent Reformed soteriology, mention should also be made of Tuomo Mannermaa and the new Finnish interpretation of Luther, which also attempts to revise the traditional interpretation of Reformation soteriology by taking justification beyond a strict juridical understanding and moving in more mystical and ontological directions towards theosis. See further Carl E.

lexical study to grasp the reality of being in Christ. In other words, if it is true that "[t]he heart of Paul's religion is union with Christ,"[25] then it behooves us to explore this religion not only grammatically but also canonically and systematically (i.e., doctrinally); that is, in relation to the broader history of salvation. This is precisely what the succeeding generations after Calvin have done in their attempts to clarify the *ordo salutis*.

Calvin states clearly that oneness with Christ ("partaking of him") yields a double grace (*duplex gratia*): justification and sanctification.[26] These twin benefits of salvation – objective (i.e., forensic) righteousness; subjective (i.e., renovative) holiness – stem from the more basic reality of the believer's receiving Christ's very person through Spirit-effected faith.[27] Justification for Calvin is not simply a forensic fiction: rather, believers really receive Christ's righteousness (together with its status) when they receive Christ by faith. This is Calvin's basic premise, namely, that we receive the benefits of Christ's work only when we receive the person of Christ himself, through Spirit (once for all) and sacrament (repeatedly).

Those who narrate the history of subsequent Reformed theology under the rubric "Calvin vs. the Calvinists" contend that Reformed scholastics lost sight of union with Christ in their zeal for seeing justification as a benefit conferred apart from Christ himself, a result of faith's satisfaction of a covenantal (i.e., contractual) condition.[28] In this ("Calvinist") way lies forensic rather than participationist soteriology. Recent scholarship has challenged this way of telling the story, insisting that a Reformed remnant had always preserved the importance of receiving Christ himself, not simply his *presents* but his personal *presence*.[29] In any case, what is incontrovertible is the recent renaissance of scholarly interest in Calvin's doctrine of union with Christ,[30] an intriguing parallel with the current renewed interest in the same theme in Paul.

Braaten and Robert W. Jenson, *Union with Christ: The New Finnish Interpretation* (Grand Rapids: Eerdmans, 1998).

[25] James Stewart, *A Man in Christ*, 147.

[26] *Inst*. III.11.1.

[27] Mark A. Garcia refers to this model as Calvin's *unio Christi-duplex gratia* soteriology. *Life in Christ: Union with Christ and Twofold Grace in Calvin's Theology* (Milton Keynes, UK: Paternoster, 2008), 3.

[28] See esp. James B. Torrance, "Covenant or Contract? A Study of the Theological Background of Worship in Seventeenth-Century Scotland," *SJT* 23 (1970): 51–76.

[29] See Richard A. Muller, *After Calvin: Studies in the Development of a Theological Tradition* (Oxford: Oxford University Press, 2003), 63–80 and Macaskill, *Union with Christ*, 88–92, 98.

[30] In addition to Garcia, *Life in Christ*, see *inter alia* J. Todd Billings, *Calvin, Participation, and the Gift: The Activity of Believers in Union with Christ* (Oxford: Oxford University Press, 2007); William B. Evans, *Imputation and Impartation: Union with Christ in American Reformed Theology* (Eugene, Ore.: Wipf and Stock, 2009); John V. Fesko,

Whereas Pauline scholars are primarily interested in the coherence of Paul's theology and the sources behind it, Reformed theologians are primarily interested in the place of union with Christ in soteriology. Believers are not only justified in Christ but, as we shall see, elected, called, adopted, made alive, sanctified, and glorified "in Christ" as well. Where, then, might one locate "in Christ" in relation to the so-called "golden chain of salvation" – the various benefits that accrue to being in Christ – that Paul lists in Rom 8:29–30 and which has come to be known as the *ordo salutis*? Proponents of the "New Perspective on Calvin" have recently called attention to the centrality of union with Christ in Calvin,[31] but Reformed theologians like John Murray had been there, done that fifty years earlier. Murray insists that union with Christ is not merely one step in the application of redemption. Rather, "[u]nion with Christ is really the central truth of the whole doctrine of salvation."[32] Anthony Hoekema provides further specification – if something that extends "from eternity to eternity" can be said to have focus! According to Hoekema, union has its roots in eternity (divine election), its objective basis in the historical death and resurrection of Christ, and its subjective realization in believers in the present temporal flow.[33]

There is now a conflict of interpretations of what Calvin meant by union as there is with the apostle Paul. We cannot enter those debates here. What I do want to take from this conversation in Reformed soteriology is what I shall call the *simplicity* of union. In brief: union is to soteriology what the doctrine of divine simplicity is to theology proper. The doctrine of divine simplicity states that God is not a composite of his parts; rather, his being is coextensive with his attributes. For example, God does not "have" love; God is love. And now to the analogy: just as God is one, so salvation is simple. In the words of Richard Gaffin: "There is but one union, with dis-

---

Beyond Calvin: Union with Christ and Justification in Earl Modern Reformed Theology (1517-1700) (Göttingen: Vandenhoeck & Ruprecht, 2012); Richard B. Gaffin, Jr., *By Faith, Not By Sight: Paul and the Order of Salvation* (2d ed.; Phillipsburg, N.J.: P&R Publishing, 2013); Michael S. Horton, *Covenant and Salvation: Union with Christ* (Louisville, Ky.: Westminster John Knox, 2007), esp. chap. 7; Marcus Peter Johnson, *One with Christ: An Evangelical Theology of Salvation* (Wheaton: Crossway, 2013); Robert Letham, *Union with Christ: In Scripture, History, and Theology* (Phillipsburg, N.J.: P&R Publishing, 2011).

[31] See the exchange between Thomas Wenger, "The New Perspective on Calvin: Responding to Recent Calvin Interpretation," *JETS* 50 (2007): 311–28; Marcus Johnson, "New or Nuanced Perspective on Calvin? A Reply to Thomas Wenger," *JETS* 51 (2008): 545–48.

[32] John Murray, *Redemption, Accomplished and Applied* (Grand Rapids: Eerdmans, 1955), 161.

[33] Anthony A. Hoekema, *Saved by Grace* (Grand Rapids: Eerdmans, 1989), 54–55.

tinguishable but inseparable, coexisting legal and renovative aspects."[34] Just as each divine attributes gives us a perspective on God's being, so each element in the order of salvation – not only justification and sanctification but election, and glorification as well – shines a light on another aspect of our union with Christ: "Every element in the classical *ordo salutis* is thus a further perspective on the one reality of the believer's union with Christ."[35]

IV. Mapping the mystery

"So if anyone is in Christ, there is a new creation" (2 Cor. 5:17)

Our brief survey has staked the claim that union with Christ is a pervasive theme in Paul's letters and Christian tradition in general.[36] While the reality of union with Christ may be simple, attempts to describe this reality are anything but. The present volume contains interdisciplinary explorations of the fundamental mystery of salvation, namely, the nature of the believer's union with and participation in Christ. How can those who are not Jesus Christ – Paul, St. Francis, Calvin, etc. – have a share in Christ's life, death, and resurrection? The premise of the present volume is that we have a better chance of responding to this question by taking into account exegetical, historical and systematic theological perspectives.

Part One consists of contributions from biblical scholars who wrestle to understand, clarify, and explore Paul's own language and concepts in textual and historical context. A number of these essays explore particular issues in relation to particular texts (e.g., *theosis* in 2 Corinthians, Christ's kingship in Ephesians, the Spirit's mediation of Christ in Romans 8, *phronēsis* in Philippians). The intent is not to give encyclopedic coverage but to broaden the discussion by exploring passages and themes that are not always treated in works on Paul's thought about union and participation. What comes to the fore in this section is the richness and diversity of Paul's thinking about union and participation in Christ.

The essays in Part Two provide snapshots from a larger album, highlights in the history of the reception of Paul's vision. While it is true that we are presently witnessing the "second coming" of interest in union with Christ (Calvin's being the prior coming), it is also true that union and participation have been themes of perennial interest. Each of the essays

---

[34] Gaffin, *By Faith, Not By Sight*, 43.

[35] Sinclair Ferguson, *Holy Spirit* (Downers Grove, Ill.: InterVarsity Press, 1996), 106.

[36] The Johannine literature is similarly replete with images of the believer's union with Christ (the theme of reciprocal abiding is especially prominent) but beyond the scope of the present project. For an overview, see Hans Burger, *Being in Christ: A Biblical and Systematic Investigation in a Reformed Perspective* (Eugene, Ore.: Wipf & Stock, 2009), chap. 6.

demonstrates that Paul's notions of union and participation in Christ have played a key role in a number of seminal theologians from the past, from Irenaeus to Karl Barth. As I suggested earlier in connection with Reformed soteriology, reading Paul through the eyes of Augustine, Luther, Calvin, and John Owen can itself be a significant means of coming to a deeper understanding not only of these theologians, but also of the apostle Paul.

The three essays in Part Three employ the resources of systematic theology, taking soil samples of being in Christ. Each thinks through participation in Christ in light of a particular doctrine (sanctification, the Lord's Supper, ecclesiology) and vice versa. This section is in many respects the place where we confront the theological and pastoral "so what" question: if union and participation are as important as we think they are, what are the practical implications of this claim for individuals, denominations, and the church? We are happy to confront this question, especially in light of Marcus Johnson's claim that large swaths of the church (he is thinking primarily of evangelical theology) are unfamiliar with the idea of union with Christ.[37] The short answer is that these admittedly technical essays treat what is nevertheless a vitally important topic: salvation in Christ. Indeed, if we are to take Paul at his word, no subject is more important. For the apostle declares, with no hint of exaggeration, that he regards everything else as mere feces[38] in comparison to knowing Christ and being found "in him" (Phil. 3:8–9). Why that is so these essays will show.

Let me now chart the course of the rest of the present introduction. The next section briefly examines some of the issues exegetes confront in dealing with the various prepositions Paul uses for conveying the ideas of participation in Christ. I then move up a rung in the ladder of Paul's discourse from prepositions to metaphors and inquire into the meaning of some of Paul's most characteristic ways for speaking of union and participation, many of which are also stages in the history of redemption (e.g., election, adoption, baptism, etc.). Next I examine the way in which interpreters past and present move from Paul's prepositions, metaphors, and historical categories (e.g., "blessed in Christ") to their own concepts, judgments, and ontological categories (e.g., "being-in-Christ"). Where Paul sought the mind of Christ, his interpreters seek the mind of Paul. Can any scholar lay claim to recovering not only *Paulus dixit* but also *Paulus cogitatus*? Have systematic theologians found what Sanders, a New Testament scholar, could

---

[37] Johnson suggests four reasons for this contemporary neglect. *One with Christ*, 24–28).

[38] I am here following Robert Gundry's literal translation of σκύβαλα in his *Commentary on the New Testament: Verse-by-Verse Explanations with a Literal Translation* (Peabody, Mass.: Hendrickson, 2010), 791.

not, namely, categories with which to understand the nature of the reality of union with Christ?

Having raised the question, I shall then survey two recent suggestions, each involving a fourfold conceptual scheme, and make bold to suggest two more concepts that provide a potentially synthetic punch: communication and communion. I conclude by gesturing towards yet another constructive possibility for grasping the reality of union with Christ, as much theatrical metaphor as theoretical model: theodramatic participation.[39]

B. "In Christ": prepositions, history, and biblical exegesis

Luther thought that the heart of religion lies in the pronouns: "The Son of God gave himself for *me*." By way of contrast, modern evangelical theologians often give pride of place to propositions: "God is immutable." The theme of the present volume focuses attention on yet another part of speech – the preposition: "*in, into, with*, and *through* Christ." There is ancient precedent for such "prepositional" theology. Basil of Caesarea, the Great (ca.330–79) wrote an influential treatise, *On the Holy Spirit*, which refuted heretical views of the Holy Spirit largely by examining their misinterpretation of biblical prepositions. Indeed, Basil opens his treatise (written in reply to Amphilochius, a fellow bishop) by affirming the principle "that not one of the words that are applied to God in every use of speech should be left uninvestigated."[40] The heretics claimed there were three Gods on the grounds that the three divine persons were assigned different prepositions (e.g., Paul in 1 Cor 8:6 says that all things are "from" the Father but "through" the Son). Basil rebuts this claim by carefully examining biblical usage, effectively demonstrating that there is no such strict division of prepositional labor.

What Basil says of the prepositions that affect the doctrine of the Holy Spirit applies to union with and participation in Christ as well: "What you want us to examine is both little and great, little in the brevity of its utterance ... and great in the power of its meaning."[41] Indeed. Paul uses the phrase "in Christ" (ἐν Χριστῷ) seventy-three times. When we add other ways of expressing union with or participation in Christ (e.g., "in him,"

---

[39] For a helpful collection of resources on union with Christ, arranged in eleven sections, see http://philgons.com/resources/bible/bibliographies/union-with-christ/.

[40] Basil the Great, *On the Holy Spirit* tr. Stephen Hildebrand (Yonkers, N.Y.: St. Vladimir's Seminary Press, 2011), 1.1.

[41] Basil the Great, *On the Holy Spirit*, 1,2. Interestingly enough, Basil devotes chapter 26 to an examination of the preposition "in": "That 'in' is spoken of the Spirit in as many ways as 'and' is found" (26, 61).

"with Christ," "through Christ") the number of Pauline instances more than doubles, to 164 instances. The statistics are clear, their meaning less so, in large part because biblical prepositions alone are insufficient to determine meaning.[42]

A number of detailed exegetical studies of Paul's use of "in Christ" and other related phrases (e.g. "with Christ," "through Christ"), culminating with Campbell's magisterial study *Paul and Union with Christ*[43] have appeared in the past fifty years. We have time here only for a peek into these discussions.

The most obvious issue concerns the meaning and translation of ἐν. Commentators have proposed a variety of possible senses (Markus Barth mentions nine[44]), but for convenience sake we can limit the present discussion to two basic types, emphasizing either locality (*where* something is or is being done, e.g., "A is in Christ") or instrumentality (*what* is being done, e.g., "A does x through Christ") respectively.[45] As to the instrumental sense, Barth notes that in about one-half of the occurrences of "in Christ" in the book of Ephesians, "God is the subject of the decision or action made 'in Christ.'"[46] More generally, the phrase always seems to concern the relationship formed in/by/through Jesus Christ between God and God's people. However, at the end of the day Barth acknowledges the problem with trying to fix the meaning with a single definition: "Paul used the formula in more than one sense."[47] On *this* point there now seems to be a general consensus.[48] There is also broad agreement that Paul, unlike John, does not treat "in Christ" as a two-way street: that Christ dwells in believers is something that Paul affirms, but not usually in terms of ἐν Χριστῷ.

The instrumental meaning of ἐν Χριστῷ, at least, is clear. God forgives us "in Christ" by making Christ and his cross the instrument of the action by which God deals with sin. The force of the locative sense of "in Christ" is less obvious. Can we plot the coordinates of the space designated by "in

---

[42] This is perhaps the exegetical equivalent to the problem of evidential underdetermination in the philosophy of science.

[43] Other important works include Fritz Neugebauer, *In Christus: Eine Untersuchung zum paulinischen laubensverständnis* (Göttingen: Vandenhoeck & Ruprecht, 1961); Michel Bouttier, *En Christ: Étude d'exégèse et de théologie Pauliniennes* (Paris: Presses Universitaires de France, 1962).

[44] Markus Barth, *Ephesians: Introduction, Translation, and Commentary on Chapters 1-3* (AB 34A; Garden City, N.Y.: Doubleday, 1974), 69.

[45] Seifrid adds a third category, modality, which emphasizes the manner in which an action occurs ("In Christ," 433).

[46] Barth, *Ephesians*, 69.

[47] Barth, *Ephesians*, 69.

[48] See also Campbell, *Paul and Union with Christ*, 199 and Ernest Best, *One Body in Christ: A Study of the Relationship of the Church to Christ in the Epistles of the Apostle Paul* (London: SPCK, 1955), 1–7.

Christ"? Where exactly is this? One suggestion is "in his body," though whether this refers to his exalted state, his earthly church, or a new humanity of which he is the head (or all of the above) is another open question. One potentially helpful way forward is to view the locative "in" not as spatial but spherical, that is, as pertaining to the sphere or domain of Christ's lordly influence, itself coextensive with being "in the Spirit."[49] In this way, the spiritual sense (so to speak) of ἐν corresponds to its original literal/locative sense. In the words of Murray Harris: "It is used to denote the sphere within which some action occurs or the element or reality in which something is contained or consists."[50]

Harris also allows for other uses/meanings of ἐν Χριστῷ, including "incorporative union."[51] As with all difficult exegetical decisions, historical context looms large. Which context did Paul likely have in mind in speaking of what God is doing to believers in Christ? One intriguing possibility is that Paul used ἐν to signal a distinctly Hebrew conception of social solidarity according to which the "many" were viewed as incorporated into a representative "one."[52] This way of relating the one and the many is no abstract principle but is rather woven into Israel's concrete history, where individuals (e.g., Abraham, Moses, David) represent the people before God. The covenant blessing of God's presence eventually comes to focus on David's house in the figure of a future Davidic king (2 Sam. 7:14-16).[53]

Prepositions can, of course, take us only so far. N. T. Wright builds on the notion of incorporative union by arguing that we understand Paul rightly not simply by parsing his parts of speech but by relating his thought to its Old Testament background and, in particular, to the notion that *Christos* is not Jesus' last name but the title of his office: *Messiah*.[54] Wright insists that Jesus, as Messiah, "*has drawn together the identity and vocation of*

---

[49] So Stanley E. Porter, who describes Paul's use of the phrase "in Christ" as "spherical," in the sense of one being "in the sphere of Christ's control." *Idioms of the Greek New Testament* (2d ed.; Sheffield: Sheffield Academic, 1994, 159.

[50] Murray J. Harris, "Appendix: Prepositions and Theology in the Greek New Testament," in *New International Dictionary of New Testament Theology* (ed. Colin Brown; vol. 3; Carlisle: Paternoster, 1976), 1191. See also Harris, *Prepositions and Theology in the Greek New Testament: An Essential Reference Resource for Exegesis* (Grand Rapids: Zondervan, 2012), 122–26.

[51] Harris, "Prepositions and Theology," 1192.

[52] One must not confuse this more recent suggestion, which appeals to the nature of the covenant, with earlier theories of "corporate personality" such as that found in H. Wheeler Robinson, *Corporate Personality in Ancient Israel* (Philadelphia: Fortress, 1964).

[53] See Macaskill, *Union with Christ*, 103–10.

[54] See the recent study by Matthew V. Novenson, *Christ among the Messiahs: Christ Language in Paul and Messiah Language in Ancient Judaism* (Oxford: Oxford University Press, 2012).

Israel upon himself."[55] It is not necessarily that the idea of messianic incorporation was in the first-century Palestinian air (it may not have been), but rather that Paul was led to revise his understanding of the Messiah in light of Jesus' resurrection, for in raising Jesus from the dead, God had done for him what he was supposed to have done for Israel: "He was, in effect, Israel in person."[56] To be "in the Messiah" – the son of David; the "true Jew" – is to be part of the people defined and ruled by him: "*Christos* denotes ... 'the Messiah as the representative of his people,' the one *in whom* that people are summed up and drawn together."[57] In short: the Messiah does what Israel (and Adam) failed to do, and thereby receives the inheritance promised to Adam, Abraham, and David, as does anyone else who is "in" (i.e., represented by and incorporated into) the Messiah. Macaskill comes to a similar conclusion after examining the Isaianic servant songs (especially Isa 53): the servant represents Israel, fulfilling her vocation, "and through him they participate in the narrative of salvation."[58] It is to this narrative, a level of discourse beyond prepositions, that we now turn.

C. "Blessed in Christ": metaphor, redemptive history, and biblical theology

I. Redemptive history and biblical theology

After a brief opening address, Paul begins the book of Ephesians with a long, cumbersome sentence, praising God the Father "who has blessed us in Christ with every spiritual blessing in the heavenly places" (Eph. 1:3).[59] Just as Rom 8:28–29 represents the Golden Chain of salvation, so here in Eph 1:3–14 Paul gives us what we could call the Golden Chain of participation in Christ. Karl Barth, in his lectures on Ephesians in Göttingen in 1921–22, divided Paul's long opening sentence into four sections, each beginning with "in Christ":
– in Christ, we have election (vv. 4–6)
– in Christ, we have liberation and forgiveness (vv. 7–10)
– in Christ, we have an inheritance and therefore hope (vv. 11–12)

---

[55] N. T. Wright, *Paul and the Faithfulness of God* (Minneapolis: Fortress, 2013), 825 (emphasis original).
[56] N. T. Wright, *Paul and the Faithfulness of God*, 828.
[57] N. T. Wright, *Paul and the Faithfulness of God*, 834 (emphasis original).
[58] Macaskill, *Union with Christ*, 126.
[59] On Pauline authorship of Ephesians, see the essay by Joshua Jipp in the present volume.

– in Christ, we have the sealing of the Spirit, the pledge of our inheritance (vv. 13–14)

These blessings constitute one reality – all that we have "in Christ" – expressed in three tenses: past (election), present (forgiveness and the Spirit), and future (the hope of our inheritance).[60] Stated differently: "in Christ" is shorthand for the whole doctrine of salvation, and thus the whole of redemptive history. What might otherwise have been unrelated discrete events (e.g., election, atonement, sanctification) become, on this view, a single christological coat of many canonical colors. To seek to understand union with Christ in relation to redemptive history is to examine "in Christ" in the framework not of exegesis but biblical theology.[61] The key question here is not merely *what* is union with Christ (as we have seen, a preliminary answer is "incorporation into Messiah") but also *when* is union with Christ? *When* were we incorporated into the Messiah and "blessed in Christ" with every spiritual blessing?

1. Election

That Yahweh chose Abraham and his offspring, Israel, out of all the nations of the earth (Isa. 41:8) was the *cantus firmus* of the Old Testament. The Lord chose Israel to be his treasured possession (Deut 14:2) and the means by all the nations of the earth would be blessed (Gen. 26:4).[62] Paul, however, writes to the Ephesians that they were chosen in Christ "before the foundation of the world" (Eph. 1:4). On this view, God's pretemporal sovereign determination precedes an individual's temporal coming to faith and is thus the ultimate cause of the believer's incorporation into the Messiah. In the words of Richard Gaffin: "For those who are 'in Christ,' this union or solidarity is all-encompassing, extending in fact from eternity to eternity, from what is true of them 'before the foundation of the world' (Eph. 1:4, 9) to their still future glorification (Rom. 8:17; 1 Cor. 15:22)."[63]

2. Incarnation

Some theologians suggest that union with or incorporation into Christ happens when the Word who was God "became flesh" (John 1:14).[64] Accord-

---

[60] See Ross McGowan Wright, *Karl Barth's Academic Lectures on Ephesians (Göttingen, 1921-22): An original translation, annotation, and analysis* (Ph.D. diss., The University of St Andrews, 2007).

[61] For more on this approach, see Gaffin, *By Faith, Not by Sight*, 6–10.

[62] See further Joel S. Kaminsky, *Yet I Loved Jacob: Reclaiming the Biblical Concept of Election* (Nashville: Abingdon, 2007).

[63] Gaffin, *By Faith, not by Sight*, 41–42.

[64] Karl Barth, for example, sees the Son's incarnation *as* eternal election in its temporal display (i.e., Christ *is* the decree).

ing to this view, the incarnation is not simply Jesus' assumption of human nature but humanity as such. All human beings therefore participate in the Son simply by virtue of being human – call it *physical* union with Christ. There is a good deal of debate among theologians (many of them Reformed) as to whether this physical participation in Christ's humanity is intrinsically redemptive. Some view the Incarnation as a necessary (preliminary) condition of Jesus' acting on behalf of humanity. Others view the Incarnation as itself the key soteriological event (i.e., incorporation into Christ).[65] Here is the key question: is soteriology (i.e., participation in Christ) simply ontology writ large (i.e., a matter of partaking in human nature), as if being human were itself a sufficient condition for being "in Christ"?[66]

3. Death and resurrection

Most Christian theologians distinguish the (physical) union with Christ established at his incarnation from what Paul seems to highlight, namely, our participation in Jesus' death and resurrection, that is, his redemptive work: "I have been crucified with Christ" (Gal. 2:20). For Paul, the work of Christ does not establish a union with humanity in general but rather for a distinct group: "Christ loved *the church* and gave himself up *for her*" (Eph. 5:25, my emphasis). Those who place their faith in Christ share in Christ's resurrection, the "first fruits" of a great end-time resurrection harvest (1 Cor. 15:20). The "already" of believers' being raised with Christ (Eph. 2:5; Col. 2:12–13; 3:1), and the bodily resurrection yet to come, and are but two episodes of one and the same event: Christ's resurrection.[67] Incorporation into Christ's death and resurrection happens not at the believer's birth

---

[65] Robert Letham does not go as far as Torrance in stressing the universal scope of incarnational union, but he agrees that the Son's assuming human flesh has soteriological significance: "Because Christ's humanity has divine life hypostatically, we can – in union with Christ – receive divine life by grace and participation." *Union with Christ*, 32).

[66] T. F. Torrance here builds on the patristic maxim "the unassumed is the unhealed" and concludes that "incarnational union" is inherently redemptive (though he also insists that the Spirit realizes the "subjective" aspect of this union). By way of contrast, Calvin calls this incarnational union a "natural" union, distinguishing it from the "mystical" union that characterizes his soteriology. It is also significant that Paul says we are united to Christ by the Spirit who raised him a spiritual (*pneumatikon*) rather than physical (*psuchichon*) body (1 Cor 15:44; cf. Rom 8:11). See further my "The Origin of Paul's Soteriology: Election, Incarnation, and Union with Christ in Ephesians 1:4 (with special reference to Evangelical Calvinism)," in *Reconsidering the Relationship between Biblical and Systematic Theology in the New Testament: Essays by Theologians and New Testament Scholars* (ed. Benjamin Reynolds, Brian Lugioyo, and Kevin J. Vanhoozer; WUNT 2/369; Tübingen: Mohr Siebeck, 2014), 177–211.

[67] See Gaffin, *By Faith, Not by Sight*, 67–77.

(i.e., by virtue of being born human) but baptism (i.e., by virtue of saving faith): "Do you not know that all of us who have been baptized in Christ Jesus were baptized into his death?" (Rom. 6:3; cf. 6:4–5). To be blessed in Christ in this context is to be incorporated not into his nature but into his history, and baptism is the graphic public exhibit of the actualization of such incorporation. Baptism marks the moment in *our* history when we are incorporated into *Jesus'* history.[68]

4. Ascension and session

Paul says we were blessed in Christ "in the heavenly places" (Eph. 1:3) and that God has "seated us with him in the heavenly places in Christ Jesus" (Eph. 2:6). These phrases recall the ascension and heavenly session of Christ, as well as the line from the Apostles' Creed indicating the climax, and goal, of everything else in Jesus' story: "and sitteth on the right hand of God the Father Almighty."[69] Unlike all the other things the Creed mentions (e.g., born of the Virgin Mary, suffered under Pontius Pilate), the "and sits" is in the present tense and designates a *now* time that is also a *new* time: the end-time inaugurated by Jesus' death and resurrection. It is in the Lord's Supper above all that the Holy Spirit lifts our spirits up to the ascended Christ, the one who has entered the heavenly sanctuary from which he rules all as the one in whom all things are "gathered up" (Eph. 1:10). Believers have even now been incorporated into the consummation of their union with Christ in the eschaton: "future glory . . . will be nothing other than the continued unfolding of the riches of our union with Christ."[70] Union with Christ arguably spans the whole of redemptive history, from eternal election to heavenly session.

II. Metaphor and biblical theology

There is in Paul's discourse another way of speaking of union with Christ in addition to prepositions or connecting it to messianic moments in salvation history. We therefore turn from a consideration of the history of redemption (the moment of incorporation) to certain metaphors of redemption (images of incorporation).[71] Like prepositions, metaphors too call for

---

[68] See further the essay by Isaac Morales, "Baptism and Union with Christ" in the present volume.

[69] See also Joshua Jipp's essay "Sharing in the Heavenly Rule of Christ the King" in the present volume.

[70] Hoekema, *Saved by Grace*, 64.

[71] See further the discussion by Constantine Campbell, "Metaphor, Reality, and Union with Christ" in the present volume.

thought (e.g., an examination of the way in which x is and is not y), while simultaneously resisting any final conceptual closure.

1. Body

Perhaps no metaphor better conveys our incorporation into Christ, as well as the *corporate* nature of this incorporation, then the corporeal metaphor of Christ as "head" of his "body," which is to say, the church (Col. 1:18). If being in Christ means being part of his body, then it follows that union with Christ will always be corporate in nature.[72] Union with Christ entails union with other Christians – fellowship. "For as in one body we have many members ... so we, who are many, are one body in Christ, and individually we are members one of another" (Rom 12:4–5). This union with others is not uniformity, however, for Paul insists that the one body is made up of different members, each with his or her own proper gift (1 Cor. 12).[73]

2. Temple

Paul in Eph 2:21–22 creatively combines organic and inorganic images when he suggests that God's people are growing into a holy temple. "In him" (ἐν ᾧ) the whole structure [οἰκοδομὴ] is being pieced together out of the many saints into a single dwelling place for God. The figure of the people as temple picks up a number of Old Testament themes and prophecies, but what is most important for our purposes is Paul's claim that Christ is the "cornerstone" [ἀκρογωνιαίου] (Eph. 2:20; cf. Ps. 118:22; Is. 28:16). Incorporation into Christ is an ongoing building project, with each living stone sealed – cemented! – by the Spirit to Christ and hence to the rest of the structure.[74]

3. Marriage

Paul describes union with Christ in terms of marriage on several occasions (Rom. 7:1–4; 1 Cor. 6:15–17; 2 Cor. 11:2–3; Eph. 5:22–32). This nuptial metaphor describes union with Christ in much more personal and intimate terms than the previous two. First, marriage suggests an exclusive relationship, requiring faithfulness. Second, though husband and wife become "one flesh" they also remain distinct persons. The nuptial metaphor thus

---

[72] For further development of this theme, see the essay by Devin Singh in the present volume.

[73] See further, Campbell, *Paul and Union with Christ*, 268–89 and Macaskill, *Union with Christ*, 147–59.

[74] For more on the metaphor of temple (and building), see Campbell, *Paul and Union with Christ*, 289–98 and Macaskill, *Union with Christ*, 147–59.

serves as a tacit correction to the tendency to exaggerate the mystical nature of the union to the point of dissolving the distinction between Christ and Christians. Third, marriage reminds us that union with Christ is indeed mysterious, as is the ontological mystery of marriage, by which a man and a woman become one flesh (Eph. 5:31).[75] Finally, while it is not always noted, the nuptial marriage highlights not only the personal but also the *covenantal* nature of the union to the extent that marriage is, at root, a solemn promise of exclusive faithfulness to the other.[76]

4. Adoption

Though it is seldom mentioned as a metaphor for union with Christ, Paul describes the process of incorporation not only in terms of "being built together" as a temple but also as being *adopted* into a family: "for in Christ Jesus you are all children of God through faith" (Gal. 2:26).[77] Adoption is a powerful image for the way in which saints participate in Christ's sonship, which is to say, in his fellowship with the Father through the Spirit: "And because you are children, God has sent the Spirit of his Son into our hearts, crying, 'Abba! Father!'" (Gal. 4:6; cf. Rom. 8:15). To speak of being in Christ as adoption is to emphasize not only *legal* but also *familial* participation in Christ (i.e., participating in Christ's filial relationship).[78] Indeed, for this reason, adoption "in Christ" may be the epitome of what it means to be "blessed in Christ."

D. "Being in Christ": concept, reception history, and systematic theology

To this point we have examined Paul's claims about oneness with Christ in his own terms: prepositions, metaphors, and connections to key points in

---

[75] Luther locates the "wondrous exchange" just here: "for if Christ is a bridegroom, he must take upon himself all the things which are his bride's and bestow upon her the things that are his." "The Freedom of a Christian," in *Luther's Works* (vol. 31; Philadelphia: Fortress, 1957), 351.

[76] See further, Campbell, *Paul and Union with Christ*, 298–310.

[77] Campbell discusses Paul's use of new clothing, instead of adoption, in his chapter on metaphor. *Paul and Union with Christ*, 310–23. He believes that adoption is one of the blessings received through union with Christ, "but it is not what union with Christ *is*" (407, his emphasis). Hans Burger mentions adoption as a metaphor not for union with Christ but rather as a metaphor for salvation. *Being in Christ*, 252–55.

[78] "In our union with Christ ... we participate in what is most precious to him: his relationship with his Father." Johnson, *One with Christ*, 145. See also the further discussion on adoption in Johnson, *One with Christ*, 156–62 and Canlis's treatment of adoption in Calvin in the present volume.

redemptive history. Paul's epistles have generated a history of reception, an ongoing conversation in which theologians have recast Paul's thought in their own conceptual terms. The challenge is not simply to come up with new metaphors, much less prepositions, but to say what the prepositions and metaphors *mean*. The "more" in Pauline metaphor demands to be theologically thought and, as Paul Ricoeur says, interpretation is the work of concepts: "On one side, interpretation seeks the clarity of the concept; on the other, it hopes to preserve the dynamism of meaning that the concept holds and pins down."[79]

I. Reception history and historical theology

The present volume discusses some key figures in the history of reception of Paul's references to what is "in Christ": Irenaeus, Clement of Alexandria, Augustine, Luther, Calvin, John Owen, and Karl Barth all receive chapter-length treatment. That list could easily have been longer. Here I have time to mention only three others, each of which employs concepts and conceptual distinctions to say what being in Christ is (and what it is not).

1. Cyril of Alexandria

Cyril's account of union with Christ may appear to be indebted to Platonic conceptions of ontological participation, but a good case can be made that he is trying rather to think through the implications commensurate with becoming children of God.[80] Christ has by *essence* (i.e., nature) what saints have only by *adoption* (i.e., grace): sonship. What is most helpful is Cyril's distinction between a general participation in Christ, true of all creation (i.e., ontology), and "a specific dynamic dimension by which the believer participates in the fellowship of God" (i.e., soteriology).[81] In particular, Cyril insists on the necessity of the Spirit's role in adoption, and on the importance of the Eucharist for the grace to help us grow more like children of God.

2. Jonathan Edwards

Edwards put a premium on the Lord's Supper as a deepening of the covenantal union between God and his people realized in Christ through the Spirit. According to Edwards, creation exists for communion. More pre-

---

[79] Paul Ricoeur, *The Rule of Metaphor: The Creation of Meaning in Language* (London: Routledge Classics, 2003), 358.

[80] See further Ben C. Blackwell, *Christosis: Pauline Soteriology in Light of Deification in Irenaeus and Cyril of Alexandria* (WUNT 2/314; Tübingen: Mohr Siebeck, 2011).

[81] Macaskill, *Union with Christ*, 69.

cisely: "God created the world for his Son, that he might prepare a spouse of bride for him to bestow his love upon."[82] Covenant is the means by which God expands his family. What is especially noteworthy is Edwards's insistence on the deeply personal nature of the covenantal relationship: "on our part, it is giving our souls to Christ as his spouse."[83] It is faith – a deep personal trust – that relates us to Christ. This "real," mystical union, the "one flesh" symbolized by marriage, is for Edwards the foundation of what is legal.[84] Stated differently: what Edwards calls the "relative" or legal aspect of the union is grounded in the "real" or vital union.[85]

3. Herman Bavinck

The church's organic union with Christ is a central motif throughout Bavinck's systematic theology.[86] He uses it in a general sense to describe the essence of religion: fellowship with God. Yet he also works within a Reformed theological framework, viewing Christ as the organic head of the covenant of grace, and new humanity, as Adam was the organic head of the old humanity that had failed the covenant of works. Christ is the organic head of the new creation, its firstborn and first fruit. Mystical or organic union with Christ turns out to be the whole aim of creation and redemption alike. The crucial point is that we cannot have the benefits of Christ's work apart from being united to his person, "for in his person all his benefits are included."[87] Mystical union appears throughout Bavinck's

---

[82] Jonathan Edwards, *The "Miscellanies," a-500* (vol. 13 of *The Works of Jonathan Edwards*; ed. Thomas A. Schafer; New Haven, Conn.: Yale University Press, 1994), 374 (no. 271).

[83] Jonathan Edwards, *Ecclesiastical Writings* (vol. 12 of *The Works of Jonathan Edwards*; ed. David D. Hall; New Haven, Conn.: Yale University Press, 1993), 205.

[84] Jonathan Edwards, *Sermons and Discourses, 1734-1738* (vol. 19 of *The Works of Jonathan Edwards*; ed. M. X. Lesser; New Haven, Conn.: Yale University Press, 2001), 158. See also Michael J. McClymond and Gerald R. McDermott, *The Theology of Jonathan Edwards* (Oxford: Oxford University Press, 2012), chap. 26 "The Theme of Divinization."

[85] "The relative union is both begun and perfected at once, when the soul first closes with Christ by faith: the real union, consisting in the union of hearts and affections, and in the vital union, is begun in this world, and perfected in the next." Edwards, "True Saints, When Absent from the Body, Are Present with the Lord," eulogy for David Brainerd, based on 2 Cor. 5:8, preached on Oct. 12, 1747, in *Sermons and Discourses, 1743-1758* (vol. 25 of *The Works of Jonathan Edwards*; ed. Wilson H. Kimnach; New Haven, Conn.: Yale University Press, 2006), 231.

[86] Ronald N. Gleason argues that it is *the* central theological motif in his "The Centrality of the *Unio Mystica* in the Theology of Herman Bavinck" (Th.D. thesis, Westminster Theological Seminary, 2001).

[87] Burger, *Being in Christ*, 113.

theology, from election in eternity through Christ's objective actualization of the union in incarnation, crucifixion, and resurrection to its subjective realization in baptism and the sacraments and consummation at the end of time. Hans Burger therefore calls it a "narrative concept."[88] Union is "organic" because it is about believers sharing in the life of Christ through the Spirit, and because believers grow more like Christ even as they deepen their communion with one another. This is not so much divinization as an organic reality whose teleological development is set in motion by what is in Christ.

II. Concept and systematic theology

The task of systematic theology is to express biblical judgments in new conceptual idioms that both clarify the Scriptural account and make sense in the contemporary context. Faith's search for understanding is intrinsically conceptual and inextricably contextual, and has been since the each church began to transmit her faith in Christ beyond Jerusalem. Transmitting the faith cross-culturally involves using new concepts and conceptual distinctions with which to convey the meaning and reference (Christ, ultimately) of the Scriptures. Contemporary efforts to understand "in Christ" continue, modify, or revise Cyril's distinction between what Christ has by essence and believers by adoption, Edwards's distinction between "real" and "relative" union, and Bavinck's distinction between mystic-organic union and divinization respectively. What follows is a brief overview of some of the most important concepts theologians are using today to understand union and participation in Christ.

1. Formal concepts[89]

Objective/subjective/intersubjective. A first set of concepts distinguishes three aspects of being "in Christ": objective, subjective, and intersubjective. First, God has acted in Christ to bring about an objective state of affairs (i.e., a new humanity).[90] Second, believers subjectively realize this union by experiencing one or more of its blessings (e.g., sanctification). Third, union with Christ is intersubjective because union with Christ entails union with others who are in Christ.

Union/participation/identification/incorporation. Campbell concludes his magisterial study of union with Christ in Paul by proposing a conceptu-

---

[88] Burger, *Being in Christ*, 124.

[89] By "formal" I mean concepts that pertain to the structure of a thing (and the grammar for talking about it) rather than to its material content.

[90] Michael Parsons suggests that the primary connotation of "in Christ" is this objective aspect. "'In Christ' in Paul," *VE* 18 (1988), 28.

al quartet: "To do justice to the full spectrum of Paul's thought and language, the terms *union, participation, identification, incorporation* are adopted."[91] Neither "union" nor "participation" alone suffices: union, a "being" word, is static, referring to a state of affairs, and thus fails to convey the dynamic aspects of relatedness to Christ; participation, a "doing" word, is dynamic, but fails to convey the objective aspects of relatedness to Christ.[92] Hence the necessity for all four terms: "*Union* gathers up faith union with Christ, mutual indwelling, trinitarian, and nuptial notions. *Participation* conveys partaking in the events of Christ's narrative. *Identification* refers to believers' location in the realm of Christ and their allegiance to his lordship. *Incorporation* encapsulates the corporate dimensions of membership in Christ's body. Together these four terms function as 'umbrella' concepts, covering the full spectrum of Pauline language, ideas, and themes that are bound up in the metatheme of 'union with Christ.'"[93] Three of these concepts have figured prominently in the present essay, and in the general discussion. It remains to be seen whether the concept of *identification*, which describes how believer's identities are shaped by belonging to Christ's realm, will also catch on.

Representation/participation/substitution/union. Hans Burger, a systematic theologian, also proposes a conceptual quartet to describe being in Christ, though there is only partial overlap with Campbell's list. Burger begins by considering Charles Taylor's notion that the self has to inhabit a moral space, and this involves (1) a notion of the good (2) an understanding of the self (3) a narrative to live in and (4) a sense of community. Burger believes that *being in Christ* does precisely this, encapsulating what we might call the "evangelical space" that saints inhabit. Burger sets out to articulate the ontological implications of union with Christ (hence "*being in Christ*").[94]

Burger's central concepts are *representation,* a Christological concept, and *participation*, a soteriological concept. To be "in Christ" is to participate subjectively in Christ's representative (and objective) history. Burger goes on to supplement these concepts with two others: though Christ represents (and thus includes) all believers, there are some things that Christ does that we cannot do for ourselves, hence the necessity of qualifying *representation* with *substitution.* Similarly, though believers *participate* in Christ, Burger finds it necessary to qualify this ongoing sharing with *union*, the "moment of contact" between Christ and believers: "Four concepts

---

[91] Campbell, *Paul and Union with Christ*, 29.
[92] Campbell, *Paul and Union with Christ*, 413.
[93] Campbell, *Paul and Union with Christ*, 413.
[94] Burger, *Being in Christ*, 6–7.

have to structure the discourse on the relation with Christ."[95] Of special interest is his ontological parsing of participation: "This concept of participation does not imply a Platonic metaphysics of being. We do not participate in the substance of the human nature of Jesus Christ, but in his history, his identity and position."[96]

2. Material concepts

According to Campbell, union with Christ is not the center of Paul's thought but the "webbing" in which all theological things Pauline hold together.[97] What kind of a union/participation/web is it? Marcus Johnson notes that Campbell's answer ("[it] is a spiritual *reality*")[98] has the disadvantage "of understating the ontological reality of this union that includes the whole of our existence," including bodies.[99] What this brings to the fore is the need for a particular interpretive framework with which to give concrete content to what would otherwise remain merely formal concepts.

Trinitarian participation. Campbell and Burger agree that union with Christ is irreducibly Trinitarian. Campbell emphasizes union and the inner life of the Trinity: "It refers to the Father's relationship to the Son, and their union in the Spirit."[100] Burger, in contrast, stresses union and the economic Trinity: the Spirit enables the church to participate in the Son and thus in the Son's fellowship with the Father.[101] Or, in the words of Jonathan Edwards: "It seems to be God's design to admit the church into the divine family as his son's wife."[102]

Covenantal/eschatological union. Campbell and Burger similarly agree that union with Christ is both covenantal and eschatological. Burger's con-

---

[95] Burger, *Being in Christ*, 510–11. Burger himself says these concepts "test" the first pair, but I think it is more accurate to say "qualify" or "supplement" (26–27).

[96] Burger, *Being in Christ*, 521.

[97] Campbell, *Paul and Union with Christ*, 441–42.

[98] Campbell, *Paul and Union with Christ*, 411.

[99] Marcus Johnson, review of Campbell, *Paul and Union with Christ*, *JETS* 56/2 (2013): 433.

[100] Campbell, *Paul and Union with Christ*, 409 (see also 363–68. Mention should also be made of James D. Gifford's suggestion that the believer's union with Christ represents a "third type" of perichoresis, after (1) the relations that constitute the personhood of the Father, Son, and Spirit and (2) the relationship between the divine and human natures that constitute the hypostatic union of the incarnation. *Perichoretic Salvation: the Believer's Union with Christ as a Third Type of Perichoresis* (Eugene, Ore.: Wipf & Stock, 2011). The common thread is the theme of "mutual indwelling without loss of individuality" (8).

[101] Burger, *Being in Christ*, 509–10, 554.

[102] Jonathan Edwards, *The "Miscellanies" 501-832* (vol. 18 of *The Works of Jonathan Edwards*; ed. Ava Chamberlain; New Haven, Conn.: Yale University Press, 2000), 367 (no. 741).

cept of *representation* in particular acquires concrete density in relation to the biblical covenants with Adam, Abraham, Moses, and David, though Jesus Christ enacts the new covenant, and inaugurates the new creation, for the elect only.[103] Believers are caught up in Jesus' story, which is not only historical but eschatological inasmuch as it involves the resurrection, ascension, heavenly session, and second coming.[104] Macaskill too draws attention to covenant and eschatology by reminding us that Paul depicts the church as an eschatological temple built up or incorporated into the Messiah.[105]

Communication and communion. Marcus Johnson cautions against the tendency to equate salvation with the work of Christ rather than his person. *Christ* himself is our salvation, he contends, and therefore salvation means achieving "oneness" with Christ.[106] One might have thought that another obvious candidate for conceptualizing union with Christ would be *unification*. However, this term risks losing persons' individuality by emphasizing their consolidation into a single unit (think of the unification of West and East Germany). It is one thing to identify with Christ (i.e., to associate oneself with), another to be identical with him (i.e., to be the selfsame entity). Here, too, we see the difficulty of finding a single term that covers everything we want to say about union and participation with Christ – or guarding ourselves from terms that say too much. Several of the authors in the present volume wish to continue problematizing any hegemony of singular description of union in order to guard the diversity of Paul's testimony.

There is one more pair of concepts that perhaps ought to be mentioned as being particularly congenial (at least to my mind) to spelling out the ontological implications of union and participation in Christ. *Communication* means "to make common," and is especially appropriate for describing the inner-Trinitarian activity in which Father, Son, and Spirit share their light, life, and love, amongst themselves (*in se*) and with the church (*ad extra*).[107] Inasmuch as the Spirit enables believers to share in the Son's light, life, and love – which is to say, his fellowship with the Father – then we could say that being in Christ means being "communicants" in this triune fellowship.

Moreover, the ultimate aim of communication is *communion*, the successful realization of sharing resulting in a state of being in a profound

---

[103] Burger, *Being in Christ*, 35, 525.
[104] Cf. Campbell, *Paul and Union with Christ*, 410–11.
[105] Macaskill, *Union with Christ*, 103–10, 127, 169–70.
[106] Johnson, *One with Christ*, 19.
[107] See further my *Remythologizing Theology: Divine Action, Passion, and Authorship* (Cambridge: Cambridge University Press, 2010), 280–83.

personal relationship. This is also a way of speaking of the supreme covenant blessing, an intimate marriage-like relationship with God: "I will be your God, and you shall be my people" (Jer. 7:23). Being in Christ is thus a being in a triune communication (being-in-activity) leading to covenantal communion (being-in-relation). Call it, for lack of a better term, *communification*: making *commune*.

"Commune" is a felicitous term that embraces both the "doing" of participation and the "being" of union. To commune (verb) is to communicate intimately with another person. A commune (noun) is a group of people who live together in community, sharing privileges, possessions, and responsibilities. To be in Christ is to commune with Christ and other communicants in the commune that *is* Christ Jesus. This, at least, is my working hypothesis, to be tried, tested, refined, or revised by readers as they work through the essays below.

E. Conclusion: "In Christ" as eutopic theater

Where exactly is the communication and communion – the commune – indicated by "in Christ" and what exactly is going on there? With this query we return to prepositions and the original locative sense of ἐν. There is much room in the "in" of "in Christ." It is a precocious and capacious preposition, encompassing temporality (from "before the foundation of the world" to the future new creation) and spatiality (from the "heavenlies" above to the earth below).

It is somewhat surprising, given the significance of the locative, that so little work has been done connecting "in Christ" to recent literature on the concept of place.[108] To be sure: believers are not in Christ spatially the way coins are in a piggy bank, but rather *spherically*, that is, "in the sphere of Christ's control."[109] The preposition ἐν thus denotes "the sphere within which some action occurs"[110] – in other words, *theater,* like the Globe Theater in London. Better: *theater is both an interpersonal happening and the space where this communicative exchange takes place.* Like church, theater is both people and place. The church is the theater of the gospel, a local gathering in/of Christ: the interpersonal space designed for the enactment of salvation, the lived performance of/participation in the drama of redemption.[111] The drama of redemption, I submit, is the story of "com-

---

[108] The essay by Michael J. Thate in the present volume is a rare exception.
[109] Porter, *Idioms of the Greek New Testament*, 159.
[110] Harris, "Appendix: Prepositions and Theology," 119.
[111] See further my *The Drama of Doctrine: A Canonical-Linguistic Approach to Christian Theology* (Louisville, Ky.: Westminster John Knox, 2005).

munification" [from Lat. *communio + facere*] in Christ. To be "in Christ" is to be in the theater of Trinitarian and ecclesial operations.

Theater is any place where personal interaction takes place: "To exist at all . . . is to have a place – to be *implaced*."[112] To exist as a Christian is to be implaced in Christ. We are "in" Christ in a locative sense (i.e., the church as Christ's body animated by Christ's Spirit to do the Father's will) and in a participative sense inasmuch as what we *do* is enact heaven – his reign – on earth. Stated differently, the communion we have with Christ is in heaven (mystic) yet it is lived out – communicated – on earth (ethic). Moreover, the "place" where Christ is, is not simply spatial but *palatial*: Christ is at the right hand of the Father in heaven, and those who are in Christ do God's will – which is to say, to enact Christ's humanity – on earth as it is in heaven. The idea of place as a location associated with certain activities explains how being in Christ involves union, a "being" word (i.e., being *here*) and participation, a "doing" word (i.e., doing *this*) alike.[113]

Actors who make up the theater of the Christ are simultaneously "in Christ," "in the heavenlies," and "in Chicago" (to take but one earthly co-ordinate). The local church is the locale of Jesus Christ: "Where two or three are gathered in my name, I am there among them" (Matt. 18:20). The church exists in overlapping domains when, in the power of the Spirit, it presents Christ on earth as he is in heaven. To "present" Christ is to make Christ present by participating in his peacemaking and place-making activity: "The church *images* the activity of God by *performing* the activity of God of reconciling into one body – Christ's – people from all ages, nations, races, and stations."[114] Wherever two or three people "in Christ" are gathered, acting out what is in Christ in the in-between, space is transformed into place, a domain of Christ's lordship, a new outpost for citizens of heaven. Being-in-Christ gets acted out in ten thousand places, and is thus inherently dramatic. Those who are in Christ act out Christ's obedient sonship, attesting to his death and resurrection in every scene they play. Call it theodramatic participation: participation in Trinitarian communicative activity oriented toward communion "in Christ."

Those baptized in Christ have entered into his story and been transferred to his domain: "the kingdom of his beloved Son" (Col. 1:13). This king-

---

[112] Edward Casey, *Getting Back into Place: Toward a Renewed Understanding of the Place-World* (Bloomington: Indiana University Press, 1993), 13 (emphasis original).

[113] What gets "done" is the Spirit-enabled obedience of faith: "Faith for Paul is the bond of that union [with Christ], viewed from the side of the one united with Christ." Gaffin, *By Faith, Not by Sight*, 47.

[114] L. Roger Owens, *The Shape of Participation: A Theology of Church Practices* (Eugene, Ore.: Cascade, 2010), 178.

dom is not a utopia but a *eutopia*: a place where God's will is done, a place of *communification*. The people are the place where the life of Christ *is* and is *done* (i.e., acted out).[115] Indeed, every local church is to be a *eutopia*, a place in which the good news is proclaimed and exhibited in bodily form (i.e., in interpersonal interaction). In particular, the church's participation in God's life takes the shape of Jesus' cruciform participation, "the shape of a suffering servant."[116] To be in Christ is to be in a good place: *eutopia*. Better: to be "in Christ" is to be part of a eutopic theater, a place that practices and presents new humanity through communicative activity oriented to communion with the triune Creator and his new creation.

Giotto got it half right: union with Christ does indeed involve identifying with the crucified Christ through the mortification of the flesh. Yet, in the final analysis, the stigmatization of St. Francis paints too passive a picture of this participation. For Paul also says that he wants to know "the power of his resurrection" (Phil. 3:10). Becoming like Jesus in his death means giving oneself wholly, in love, for others. Theater is all about embodied persons presenting themselves to one another. Believers participate theodramatically in Jesus' death and resurrection by engaging in the same kinds of communicative activity as Jesus – truth-telling; self-giving; peacemaking – for the sake of greater communion. This too is how the "life of Jesus" is "made visible on our bodies" (2 Cor. 4:10). Where is "in Christ"? It is anywhere disciples perform scenes of his peaceable kingdom; it is anywhere Christians stage eutopic theater.

Bibliography

Barth, Markus. *Ephesians: Introduction, Translation, and Commentary on Chapters 1-3.* The Anchor Bible 34A. Garden City, N.Y.: Doubleday, 1974.
Basil, St. *On the Holy Spirit.* Tr. Stephen Hildebrand. Yonkers, NY: St. Vladimir's Seminary Press, 2011.
Best, Ernest. *One Body in Christ: A Study of the Relationship of the Church to Christ in the Epistles of the Apostle Paul.* London: SPCK, 1955.
Billings, J. Todd. *Calvin, Participation, and the Gift: The Activity of Believers in Union with Christ.* Oxford: Oxford University Press, 2007.
Blackwell, Ben C. *Christosis: Pauline Soteriology in Light of Deification in Irenaeus and Cyril of Alexandria.* Wissenschaftliche Untersuchungen zum Neuen Testament 2/314. Tübingen: Mohr Siebeck, 2011.
Bonaventura, Saint. *The Life of Saint Francis.* London: J. M. Dent, 1904.

---

[115] For further development of this theme, see my *Faith Speaking Understanding: Performing the Drama of Doctrine* (Louisville, Ky.: Westminster John Knox, 2014), ch. 7 "Staging the Play in Ten Thousand Places: How the Company of the Gospel Enacts Parables of the Kingdom."

[116] Owens, *The Shape of Participation*, 181.

Bouttier, Michel. *En Christ: Étude d'exégèse et de théologie Pauliniennes.* Paris: Presses Universitaires de France, 1962.
Braaten, Carl E. and Robert W. Jenson. *Union with Christ: The New Finnish Interpretation.* Grand Rapids: Eerdmans, 1998.
Burger, Hans. *Being in Christ: A Biblical and Systematic Investigation in a Reformed Perspective.* Eugene, Ore.: Wipf & Stock, 2009.
Calvin, John. *Institutes of the Christian Religion.* Library of Christian Classics 20–21. 2 vols. Edited by John T. McNeil. Translated by Ford Lewis Battles. Philadelphia: Westminster, 1960.
Campbell, Constantine R. *Paul and Union with Christ: An Exegetical and Theological Study.* Grand Rapids: Zondervan, 2012.
Casey, Edward. *Getting Back into Place: Toward a Renewed Understanding of the Place-World.* Bloomington: Indiana University Press, 1993.
Cannon, Joanna. "Giotto and Art for the Friars: Revolutions Spiritual and Artistic." Pages 103–34 in *The Cambridge Companion to Giotto.* Edited by Anne Derbes and Mark Sandona. Cambridge: Cambridge University Press, 2004.
Cook, William R. "Giotto and the Figure of St. Francis." Pages 135–56 in *The Cambridge Companion to Giotto.* Edited by Anne Derbes and Mark Sandona. Cambridge: Cambridge University Press, 2004.
Deissman, Adolf. *Paul: A Study in Social and Religious History.* London: Hodder & Stoughton, 1912.
Derbes, Anne and Mark Sandona, eds. *The Cambridge Companion to Giotto.* Cambridge: Cambridge University Press, 2004.
Edwards, Jonathan. *The "Miscellanies," a-500.* Vol. 13 of *The Works of Jonathan Edwards.* Edited by Thomas A. Schafer. New Haven, Conn.: Yale University Press, 1994.
———. *Ecclesiastical Writings.* Vol. 12 of *The Works of Jonathan Edwards.* Edited by David D. Hall. New Haven, Conn.: Yale University Press, 1993.
———. *The "Miscellanies" 501-832.* Vol. 18 of *The Works of Jonathan Edwards.* Edited by Ava Chamberlain. New Haven, Conn.: Yale University Press, 2000.
———. *Sermons and Discourses, 1734-1738.* Vol. 19 of *The Works of Jonathan Edwards.* Edited by M. X. Lesser. New Haven, Conn.: Yale University Press, 2001.
———. *Sermons and Discourses, 1743-1758.* Vol. 25 of *The Works of Jonathan Edwards.* Edited by Wilson H. Kimnach. New Haven, Conn.: Yale University Press, 2006.
Evans, William B. *Imputation and Impartation: Union with Christ in American Reformed Theology.* Eugene, Ore.: Wipf and Stock, 2009.
Ferguson, Sinclair. *Holy Spirit.* Downers Grove, Ill.: InterVarsity Press, 1996.
Fesko, John V. *Beyond Calvin: Union with Christ and Justification in Earl Modern Reformed Theology (1517-1700).* Göttingen: Vandenhoeck & Ruprecht, 2012.
Freze, Michael. *They Bore the Wounds of Christ: The Mystery of the Sacred Stigmata.* Huntington, Ind.: Our Sunday Visitor, 1989.
Gaffin, Richard B. Jr. *By Faith, Not By Sight: Paul and the Order of Salvation* 2nd ed. Phillipsburg, N.J.: P&R Publishing, 2013.
Garcia, Mark. *Life in Christ: Union with Christ and Twofold Grace in Calvin's Theology.* Milton Keynes: Paternoster, 2008.
Gifford, James D. *Perichoretic Salvation: the Believer's Union with Christ as a Third Type of Perichoresis.* Eugene, Ore.: Wipf & Stock, 2011.
Gorman, Michael J. *Inhabiting the Cruciform God: Kenosis, Justification, and Theosis in Paul's Narrative Soteriology.* Grand Rapids: Eerdmans, 2009.

Gundry, Robert H. *Commentary on the New Testament: Verse-by-Verse Explanations with a Literal Translation.* Peabody, Mass.: Hendrickson, 2010.

Harris, Murray J. "Appendix: Prepositions and Theology in the Greek New Testament." Pages 1171–215 in *New International Dictionary of New Testament Theology.* Vol. 3. Edited by Colin Brown. Carlisle: Paternoster, 1976.

——. *Prepositions and Theology in the Greek New Testament: An Essential Reference Resource for Exegesis.* Grand Rapids: Zondervan, 2012.

Harrison, Edward. *Stigmata: A Medieval Phenomenon in a Modern Age.* New York: Penguin, 1994.

Hays, Richard B. *The Faith of Jesus Christ: The Narrative Substructure of Galatians 3:11-4:11.* 2d ed. Grand Rapids: Eerdmans, 2002.

——. "What is 'Real Participation in Christ'? A Dialogue with E. P. Sanders on Pauline Soteriology." Pages 336–51 in *Redefining First-Century Jewish and Christian Identities: Essays in Honor of Ed Parish Sanders.* Edited by Fabian E. Udoh et. al. Notre Dame, Ind.: University of Notre Dame Press, 2008.

Hoekema, Anthony A. *Saved by Grace.* Grand Rapids: Eerdmans, 1989.

Horton, Michael S. *Covenant and Salvation: Union with Christ.* Louisville, Ky.: Westminster John Knox, 2007.

Johnson, Marcus. "New or Nuanced Perspective on Calvin? A Reply to Thomas Wenger." *Journal of the Evangelical Theological Society* 51 (2008): 545–48.

——. *One with Christ: An Evangelical Theology of Salvation.* Wheaton: Crossway, 2013.

Kaminsky, Joel S. *Yet I Loved Jacob: Reclaiming the Biblical Concept of Election.* Nashville: Abingdon, 2007.

Letham, Robert. *Union with Christ: In Scripture, History, and Theology.* Phillipsburg, N.J.: P&R Publishing, 2011.

Macaskill, Grant. *Union with Christ in the New Testament.* Oxford: Oxford University Press, 2013.

McClymond, Michael J. and Gerald R. McDermott. *The Theology of Jonathan Edwards.* Oxford: Oxford University Press, 2012.

Muller, Richard A. *After Calvin: Studies in the Development of a Theological Tradition.* Oxford: Oxford University Press, 2003.

Murray, John. *Redemption, Accomplished and Applied.* Grand Rapids: Eerdmans, 1955.

Neugebauer, Fritz. *In Christus: Eine Untersuchung zum paulinischen laubensverständnis.* Göttingen: Vandenhoeck & Ruprecht, 1961.

Novenson, Matthew V. *Christ among the Messiahs: Christ Language in Paul and Messiah Language in Ancient Judaism.* Oxford: Oxford University Press, 2012.

Owens, Roger L. *The Shape of Participation: A Theology of Church Practices.* Eugene, OR: Cascade, 2010.

Parsons. Michael. "'In Christ' in Paul." *Vox Evangelica* 18 (1988): 25–44.

Porter, Stanley E. *Idioms of the Greek New Testament* 2d ed. Sheffield: Sheffield Academic, 1994.

Ricoeur, Paul. *The Rule of Metaphor: The Creation of Meaning in Language.* London: Routledge Classics, 2003.

Sanders, E. P. *Paul and Palestinian Judaism: A Comparison of Patterns of Religion.* Minneapolis: Fortress, 1977.

Schweitzer, Albert. *The Mysticism of Paul the Apostle.* London: A & C Black, 1931.

Seifrid, Mark. "In Christ." Pages 433–36 in *Dictionary of Paul and his Letters.* Edited by Gerald F. Hawthorne and Ralph P. Martin. Downers Grove, Ill.: InterVarsity Press, 1993.

Stewart, James S. *A Man in Christ: The Vital Elements of St. Paul's Religion*. New York: Harper & Row, 1935.
Torrance, James B. "Covenant or Contract? A Study of the Theological Background of Worship in Seventeenth-Century Scotland." *Scottish Journal of Theology* 23 (1970): 51–76
Vanhoozer, Kevin J. *The Drama of Doctrine: A Canonical-Linguistic Approach to Christian Theology*. Louisville, Ky.: Westminster John Knox, 2005.
———. *Remythologizing Theology: Divine Action, Passion, and Authorship*. Cambridge: Cambridge University Press, 2010.
———. *Faith Speaking Understanding: Performing the Drama of Doctrine*. Louisville, Ky.: Westminster John Knox, 2014.
———. "The Origin of Paul's Soteriology: Election, Incarnation, and Union with Christ in Ephesians 1:4 (with special reference to Evangelical Calvinism)." Pages 177–211 in *Reconsidering the Relationship between Biblical and Systematic Theology in the New Testament: Essays by Theologians and New Testament Scholars*. Edited by Benjamin Reynolds, Brian Lugioyo, and Kevin J. Vanhoozer. Wissenschaftliche Untersuchungen zum Neuen Testament 2/369. Tübingen: Mohr Siebeck, 2014.
Wenger, Thomas. "The New Perspective on Calvin: Responding to Recent Calvin Interpretation." *Journal of the Evangelical Theological Society* 50 (2007): 311–28.
Wright, N. T. *Paul and the Faithfulness of God*. Christian Origins and the Question of God 4. Minneapolis: Fortress, 2013.

Part One: Pauline Theology and Exegesis

Participation and Faith in Paul

Douglas A. Campbell

A. Introduction

This essay will try to deepen the growing appreciation among many contemporary Pauline scholars for the nature and role of participation in, or union with, Christ in Paul's thought by scrutinizing the relationship between participation and faith. This analysis will, on the one hand, hopefully eliminate some awkward problems implicit in most discussions of faith in Paul, both conceptual and textual, and, on the other, further enrich our understanding of participation – especially the way it is positioned within any broader account of Paul's thinking. Our more detailed discussion can begin at a point of consensus.

B. Faith in Paul as confessional

Whatever else scholars think that faith in Paul was, all agree it had an overt confessional dimension, although as such it had two principal components.

Faith denotes a set of critical assertions that the first Christians[1] made about God's activity in Christ that functioned as a *sine qua non* for their identity, here highlighting the object of faith or the key things they believed in.[2] The *locus classicus* for this view is Romans 10:9–10, although the claims made there so clearly are echoed in many other texts:[3]

---

[1] Paul's preferred name for the members of his communities was ἀδελφοί, which raises complex questions of gender construction. So I will use the anachronism "Christians" deliberately to avoid begging those. I suspect it was an unflattering etic, not emic, designation for pagan converts during Paul's lifetime, only adopted by the Christian movement much later; see Acts 11:26c.

[2] This eventually gets developed as "the Faith." See, most probably, 1 Tim 1:19; 3:9 and 6:21, and hence also 1 Tim 5:8; 6:10, 12; 2 Tim 2:18; 3:8, 4:7; and perhaps Tit 1:13 and 2:2.

[3] E.g., Rom 8:11; 1 Cor 1:2; 12:3; 15:14; Phil 2:11; and 1 Thess 4:13.

[10:9] ἐὰν ὁμολογήσῃς ἐν τῷ στόματί σου κύριον Ἰησοῦν καὶ πιστεύσῃς ἐν τῇ καρδίᾳ σου ὅτι ὁ θεὸς αὐτὸν ἤγειρεν ἐκ νεκρῶν, σωθήσῃ· [10] καρδίᾳ γὰρ πιστεύεται εἰς δικαιοσύνην, στόματι δὲ ὁμολογεῖται εἰς σωτηρίαν.

It is unambiguously clear from this text that the early Christians confessed that Jesus had been raised from the dead or resurrected and was now Lord, so his ascension and heavenly enthronement are implicitly affirmed here as well (see Rom 8:34). This was the object, so to speak, of early Christian believing.

The first Christians were, however, also supposed to believe these things in the sense of holding them to be true, and presumably as firmly as possible, here identifying the subjective side of faith. They knew these things in their hearts, Rom 10:9–10 says, indicating, in a Jewish expression, a deep-seated conviction.[4] But at some point, as converts, they presumably *assented* to these claims, becoming convinced of their truth when previously they had not been, a journey Paul himself had undertaken (Gal 1:11–17), and indeed the broader argument of Rom 10 seems to be appealing for just this assent.[5] Hence the notion of "faith" or "believing" captures helpfully both the things believed in or held to be true, and the connotation of an uncoerced response of assent to their declaration, this last being something that notions like "thinking" or "knowing" do not suggest so directly, thereby possibly explaining why Paul seems to have preferred faith language over these alternatives.

Other texts in Paul broaden the objective side of the faith relation – the scope of the things believed in. It is apparent that Paul wanted his auditors to affirm Jesus' death and its atoning function (see esp. Rom 4:24; 1 Cor 15:3; also Phil 2:7–8), along with the oneness of God and the involvement of Christ within creation (Rom 3:30; 1 Cor 8:6; Col 1:15–17).[6] Belief in Christ's resurrection also seems to have entailed for Paul critical implications for the resurrection of Christians themselves. The resurrection of those Christians who had died could now be relied upon (1 Thess 4:13–14); it would be emphatically bodily, although not fleshly (1 Cor 15:12–57); and it would take place, at the least, when Christ returned in glory (1 Thess 1:10; 4:15–17; see also 1 Cor 1:2; Phil 3:20–21; 2 Thess 2:1–15).

---

[4] See Robert Jewett, *Romans: A Commentary* (assisted by Roy D. Kotansky; Hermeneia; Minneapolis: Fortress, 2007), 159.

[5] Strictly speaking, it addresses Israel; see my *Deliverance of God* (Grand Rapids: Eerdmans, 2009), 795–809, 817–21.

[6] I have recently argued that the common distinction between disputed and undisputed letters by Paul is incoherent and insufficiently substantiated; see *Framing Paul: An Epistolary Account* (Grand Rapids: Eerdmans, 2014). I have gone on to affirm the authenticity of Eph, Col, and 2 Thess, but have excluded 1 and 2 Tim, and Tit as demonstrably inauthentic.

This brief sketch is what most scholars affirm that faith in Paul denotes, something at bottom comprehended by a simple subject-object relationship.[7] But how reliable is it?

C. Faith in Paul as comprehensive, ethical, and ecclesial

Careful scrutiny of the bald data of faith in Paul suggests that while the confessional account of faith is an accurate description of much of the data, it cannot explain all of it. This occlusion is especially apparent in a series of small but strategically significant clusters of faith terminology in Rom 12–15 (see 12:3, 6; 14:1, 2, 22, 23; 15:13).

In Rom 14, as is well known, Paul makes an argument for conciliatory behavior between Christians characterized by different views of diet and time. Paul engages with a "weak" position that avoided certain foods – although probably not everything except "greens" (v 2: λάχανα) – and privileged certain days, and a "strong" position that was happy to eat everything, and that viewed all days as alike, presumably in sacredness. Most significantly for our present purposes, the "weak" who were to be "received" or "welcomed" were "weak in faith," or, rather better here, "in belief" (v. 1: Τὸν δὲ ἀσθενοῦντα τῇ πίστει προσλαμβάνεσθε). Similarly, their revilers, characterized as strong in 15:1, "believe [that they] ... can eat everything" (14:2: ὃς μὲν πιστεύει φαγεῖν πάντα).

Faith language, utilizing words with the Greek stem πιστ-, does not return after 14:2 until v. 22, but the discussion continues seamlessly between these two points using other words for the language of mental evaluation and thought: (δια/κατα)κρίνω, πληροφορέω, νοῦς, φρονέω, οἶδα, πέπεισμαι and λογίζομαι.[8] In v. 22 Paul speaks again, however, of someone possessing a πίστις about eating. This person is advised to keep his belief about eating private, "before God," to avoid possible judgment generated by what he approves (σὺ πίστιν ἣν ἔχεις κατὰ σεαυτὸν ἔχε ἐνώπιον τοῦ θεοῦ. μακάριος ὁ μὴ κρίνων ἑαυτὸν ἐν ᾧ δοκιμάζει). The discussion then turns in v. 23a to admonish someone internally debating while eating, stating that this posture is undesirable because it is not "of faith" (ὁ δὲ διακρινόμενος

---

[7] See e.g. James D. G. Dunn, *The Theology of Paul the Apostle* (Grand Rapids: Eerdmans, 1998), 371–85 (§§ 14.7–8); Thomas R. Schreiner, *Paul, Apostle of God's Glory in Christ* (Downers Grove, Ill.: InterVarsity, 2001), 209–16; Udo Schnelle, *Apostle Paul: His Life and Theology* (trans. M. Eugene Boring; Grand Rapids: Baker Academic, 2005 [2003]), 521–28 (although Schnelle is more circumspect here than most). See also Dieter Lührmann, "Faith," in *Anchor Bible Dictionary* (6 vols. New York: Doubleday, 1992), 2:749–58, esp. 2:753–54.

[8] (δια/κατα)κρίνω: vv. 3, 4, 5, [2x], 10, 13 [2x], 22, 23 [2x]; πληροφορέω: v. 5; νοῦς: v. 5; φρονέω: v. 6 [2x]; οἶδα: v. 14; πέπεισμαι: v. 14; and λογίζομαι: v. 14.

ἐὰν φάγῃ κατακέκριται, ὅτι οὐκ ἐκ πίστεως). This warning is then rounded off with a pronouncement that has vexed scholars for millennia:[9] πᾶν δὲ ὃ οὐκ ἐκ πίστεως ἁμαρτία ἐστίν (v. 23b) – literally, "everything that is not 'of faith' is sin."

Fortunately, the exact origins and details of these two different positions do not need to be determined here for us to grasp the key implications for our present discussion.[10]

Paul is using faith language to describe the different beliefs that two contrasting Christian groups hold about diet and time. One group has scruples. Its members think that not everything is legitimately eaten, and certain days are more important than others. The members of the other group believe that all food is fundamentally the same, as are all days. Hence these beliefs have direct ethical implications. Both groups will act in relation to food, time, and toward one another, in terms of their prior convictions or beliefs, which are different. And it is clear at this moment that a confessional account of faith cannot account for these beliefs. Indeed, these are not traditional "confessional" beliefs about Christ's atoning death, resurrection, and lordship at all. Are they simply different beliefs then from the important confessions that scholars usually discuss, that can safely be set to one side as marginal? Two pieces of evidence suggest that they are not but, rather, that they derive from the same important discourse of faith that characterizes so much of Paul's thinking elsewhere in Romans.

First, the weak person who dissembles or doubts while eating in v. 22 is condemned because his behavior is not ἐκ πίστεως. However we translate this phrase locally, it is a deliberate echo of Paul's key Scriptural text regarding matters of faith, Hab 2:4 (ὁ δὲ δίκαιος ἐκ πίστεως ζήσεται). Paul only uses the phrase ἐκ πίστεως in Romans and Galatians, the only two letters where, presumably not coincidentally, he cites this text from the Prophets as well (see Rom 1:17b; Gal 3:11). However, in these two letters the phrase is strikingly prominent, with twenty-one instances in total.[11] Hence the phrase ἐκ πίστεως is both deliberate and programmatic for Paul. And it follows that when it is used twice at the close of ch. 14 it is deliberately evoking Paul's entire discourse of faith as it has been developed earlier within the letter.[12]

---

[9] The options are accurately canvassed by Jewett, *Romans*, 829–73. See also esp. Mark Reasoner, *The Strong and the Weak: Romans 14.1–15.13 in Context* (SNTSMS 103; Cambridge: Cambridge University Press, 1999); and John M. G. Barclay, "'Do We Undermine the Law?' A Study of Romans 14:1–15:6," in *Paul and the Mosaic Law* (ed. J. D. G. Dunn; Tübingen: J. C. B. Mohr [Siebeck], 1996), 287–308.

[10] The options are canvassed again by Jewett; see esp. *Romans*, 837–38, 59–60.

[11] 12x in Rom; 9x in Gal. See elsewhere in the NT only Heb 10:38 and Jas 2:24.

[12] See my studies "The Meaning of Πίστις and Νόμος in Paul: A Linguistic and Structural Investigation," *JBL* 111 (1992): 91–103; and "Rom. 1:17 – a *Crux Interpretum* for

Second, the claims of v. 23b draw this discussion into the center of Paul's thinking as well. There, as we have just seen, Paul states that "everything that is not 'of faith' is sin" and uses the key faith phrase from Habakkuk for a second time. The full implications of this claim are staggering.

If everything not grounded in belief is sin it simply follows that everything that is grounded in belief is good and right. Hence, belief is not just ethical on occasion, as vv. 1–23a might suggest; the two notions *are coterminous*. Christian believing *is* Christian ethics and vice versa, just as anything that is not believing is not Christian ethics but is, rather, sin. These are two global and exclusive worlds: believing or sin.

We will not try to explain this extraordinary datum just yet. We need only note for the time being that any account of faith in Paul that limits it to the key elements within Christian confession, spoken by Christian subjects accurately about God as an object, cannot account for this. Faith in Paul is clearly more comprehensive and ethical than such an account would suggest. It is wider and deeper than mere confession, important as the latter is. And much the same situation is revealed, albeit a little more obliquely, by Rom 15:13.

Paul's discussion of the weak and the strong does not end with the pronouncement of 14:23. His exhortation to the strong continues through 15:6, while 15:7 reprises the plea that opened the entire discussion, that the two parties "receive one another." Paul then segues into an important Scriptural catena that resonates both with the concerns of the paraenesis and with some of the key issues within the letter as a whole, concluding this discussion in v. 13 with a prayer. (The transition to the letter ending in 15:14 is fairly explicit.)

Ὁ δὲ θεὸς τῆς ἐλπίδος πληρώσαι ὑμᾶς πάσης χαρᾶς καὶ εἰρήνης ἐν τῷ πιστεύειν, εἰς τὸ περισσεύειν ὑμᾶς ἐν τῇ ἐλπίδι ἐν δυνάμει πνεύματος ἁγίου.

Paul asks here, at the conclusion of his paraenesis, and of the letter body in Romans as a whole, that his auditors be filled with joy and peace, and overflow with hope through the work of the Holy Spirit – three critical aspects of the Christian life that he emphasizes repeatedly through all his letters.[13] Modern readers would probably classify joy and peace primarily as feelings or moods, and hope primarily as a set of positive expectations about the future, although joy and peace would not exclude mental content and hope should not exclude a certain feeling. But the critical implication

---

the Πίστις Χριστοῦ Dispute," *JBL* 113 (1994): 265–85; summarized in "The Faithfulness of Jesus Christ in Romans 3:22," in *The Faith of Jesus Christ: Exegetical, Biblical, and Theological Studies* (ed. Michael F. Bird and Preston M. Sprinkle; Peabody, Mass.: Hendrickson, 2009), 57–71.

[13] See §§ 73, 74, and 123, in James P. Ware, ed., *Synopsis of the Pauline Letters in Greek and English* (Grand Rapids: Baker Academic, 2010).

to grasp here is that these three mental dynamics are all aspects of Christian thinking, which Paul speaks of as Christian believing – ἐν τῷ πιστεύειν. Hence it is clear that Christian believing for Paul encompassed moods and expectations, here specifically, joy, peace, and hope. And this is basically the same picture that emerged from a consideration of faith terminology in ch. 14, where believing was focused on practices of diet, time, and interpersonal behavior.

A confessional account of faith cannot account for the presence of joy, peace, and hope, within believing in 15:13, just as it cannot account for the highly particular, ethical, and diverse nature of the beliefs apparent in 14:1–23. Advocates of the importance of confession would doubtless be happy to link these things together, trying to ground joy, peace, and hope in faith. But this is not really what the prayer says. Paul *identifies* them together, so something broader, deeper, and more integral than mere connection is going on. Romans 12 adds further evidence to this developing picture.

Paul uses faith terms within a brief account of the Christian community as a unified but diverse entity in 12:3–8 that follows his programmatic ethical statements in vv. 1 and 2. The first instance of faith, occurring at the end of v. 3, is especially significant, and it has again troubled commentators.[14]

Λέγω γὰρ διὰ τῆς χάριτος τῆς δοθείσης μοι παντὶ τῷ ὄντι ἐν ὑμῖν μὴ ὑπερφρονεῖν παρ ὃ δεῖ φρονεῖν ἀλλὰ φρονεῖν εἰς τὸ σωφρονεῖν, ἑκάστῳ ὡς ὁ θεὸς ἐμέρισεν μέτρον πίστεως.

Paul is once again concerned with correct Christian thinking. Here, however, he is focused on appropriate, prudent thinking by Christians in relation to one another over against inflated, arrogant, overly assertive thinking – an understandable concern when discussing diverse charismatic gifts in a church in the aftermath of his Corinthian difficulties. The final clause seems best read as providing an object for the infinitive φρονεῖν supplied through a dative of respect: Christians are "to think soberly with respect to each person [...]." Paul then appends that this evaluation is to take account of how [...] ὁ θεὸς ἐμέρισεν [ἑκάστῳ] μέτρον πίστεως.

Despite the stylistic similarities to 2 Cor 10:12–18, it is unlikely that Paul is referring here to a "measuring rod of faith" (or some such).[15] This makes little sense, and also ignores the information that Paul has supplied in the first parts of the sentence. There he bases his exhortation on the gift that has been given to him, moving immediately to an account of the Christian community as a body. Moreover, the discussion that follows immediately, starting in v. 4, concerns the gifting of diverse functions to dif-

---

[14] See Jewett, *Romans*, 738–42.
[15] So departing from Jewett's suggestion here in *Romans*, 741–42.

ferent Christians in accordance with the same grace that nevertheless seems to be distributing different things. In view of this evidence it seems that Paul is suggesting in v. 3b that Christians think correctly with respect to one another by recognizing "how God has distributed to each person a particular measure of faith." This measure is, he goes on to say, different from person to person, whether in the form specifically of prophecy, serving, teaching, and so on.

This interpretation of the faith data present in v. 3 accords nicely with the meaning of πίστις in v. 6, where the same term recurs in specific relation to prophecy. That is, some Christians instantiate grace in the form of prophecy,[16] and are urged to do so in accordance with an underlying gift of faith. That this is a gift of a "ratio" or "[mathematical] proportion" of faith seems unlikely, however, although this is a possible meaning of the rare ἀναλογία; neither does a reprise of "the measuring rod of/that is faith" from v. 3 make much sense.[17] But a ratio or proportion is a part of a larger quantity, line, or geometrical figure, so it seems that Paul is basically reprising here his earlier statement in v. 3 that a limited, smaller, identifiable measure of grace has been distributed, here as faith, to those prophesying. And he probably means by this that Christians who prophesy can only do so in terms of the amount that they actually know, something that has been gifted to them. As the parallels in 1 Cor suggest, prophets disclose divine secrets, literally "mysteries," to the community, whether great or small, that have been previously hidden. So they can only prophesy in accordance with the measure of understanding of these heavenly things that they have been gifted with, resulting in prophecies of different "proportion," amount, or measure.[18]

We learn from all this then that Christian faith, in the context of the community and the various forms of nurturing activity present within it, is

---

[16] The importance of grace and gift in Paul are being increasingly appreciated; see now esp. John M. G. Barclay, *Paul and The Gift* (Grand Rapids: Eerdmans, forthcoming); anticipated by (i.a.) "Manna and the Circulation of Grace: A Study of 2 Corinthians 8:1–15," in *The Word Leaps the Gap: Essays on Scripture and Theology in Honor of Richard B. Hays* (ed. J. Ross Wagner, C. Kavin Rowe, and A. Katherine Grieb; Grand Rapids: Eerdmans, 2008), 409–26.

[17] Jewett's struggles are again instructive; *Romans*, 744–47.

[18] The notion of "mystery," or the revelation of divine secrets, in Paul has now been treated definitively by T. J. Lang in "Mystery and the Making of a Christian Historical Consciousness: From Paul to the Second Century" (Ph.D. diss., Duke University, 2014). The notion of quantity in relation to morality has been explored in Matthew by Nathan Eubank, *Wages of Cross-Bearing and Debt of Sin: The Economy of Heaven in Matthew's Gospel* (BZNW 196; Berlin: de Gruyter, 2013), an analysis that is currently being extended to Paul. Also helpful here is George Lakoff's notion of "moral accounting"; see his programmatic *Moral Politics: How Liberals and Conservatives Think* (2d ed.; Chicago: University of Chicago Press, 2002).

intimately connected to, if it is not identical with, Christian knowing or thinking. Moreover, it again takes rather different shapes and forms.

As we have just seen, v. 3 exhorts Christians to recognize that each person has a different function as a result of divine grace; this will result in prudent thinking, rooted in the recognition that Christians have been gifted in different ways. There are consequently no grounds for boasting or competitive self-assertion, activities that can be destructive to Christian community. But as a result of this v. 3 suggests directly that these different forms, whether prophecy, serving, teaching, encouraging, giving, managing, or caring, are all different measures of Christian believing. These functions, it says, are all different allocations of grace, effected literally through different forms of believing that amount to different ways of thinking. Prophets, servants, teachers, encouragers, givers, managers, and carers, all think about particular things in somewhat different ways. They believe then in markedly different respects. Moreover, the sub-section thickens this commitment to what we might call diverse Christian mental description with further accompanying dispositions, seen most obviously in the association of belief with prophecy, zeal with managers or leaders, and cheerfulness or optimism with those involved in ministries of mercy. These are all further items within the Christian community's variegated mental furniture and hence all further specific instances of thinking or believing. One person believes things that have previously been hidden but now ought to be disclosed; another believes zealously in a particular leadership role or organization or direction; still another believes with great optimism that care for a certain person is necessary and salutary. And with these realizations, we are in a position to reach some important initial conclusions about faith in Paul, and possibly at variance with the way it is usually depicted.

It seems that Christian faith is largely coterminous for Paul with Christian thinking as a whole, whether about the nature of God and of Christ – these being captured by its confessional aspects – or appropriate ethical behavior and ministry, but including fundamental Christian moods and postures like joy, peace, and hope. Moreover, it is diverse. Different Christians clearly believe different things about diet, time, and community roles. As a result of this it might be clearer to speak from this point forward of Christian believing.[19] Christian believing is for Paul apparently both comprehensive and ethical, and even emotional; it is an entire mind or mentality. Only these realizations make sense of the relevant data in Rom 12–15. However, before moving on to explore some of the critical implications, we should pause to note briefly one probable cause of the difficulties in-

---

[19] I am concerned that "faith" might slightly obscure the thinking in view by suggesting, even if only subliminally, confessional and creedal data only.

terpreters have had in the past grasping these connections, namely, the pervasive influence of a presuppositional thought-act distinction, or of its close equivalents.

Perhaps modern interpreters in particular tend to assume that thoughts are not acts. To think and to act are two different things. And perhaps this distinction is made because they often assume in addition a strong distinction between rather static ontologies or notions of being (perhaps even falling back here on some underlying notion of substance), and activity – in short, a being-act distinction. Thoughts and beliefs, located in the mind, tend to be placed on the substantive side of this dichotomy as "things," not as acts. And the result of these assumptions is often a strong further distinction in Christian reflection between theology and ethics. The former concerns accurate statements about what "is," and particularly about what God is. The latter concerns appropriate behavior and hence what ought to be the case in Christian activity. And these two interpretative modes tend to occupy different realms within broader Christian writing, teaching, and speaking.

Hence, it will not be at all obvious to anyone processing Paul's data in terms of these distinctions that his account of Christian thinking is connected with his account of (further) Christian ("ethical") action; powerful subliminal forces will be at work obscuring the delicate connections here within the ancient data. Consequently most systematic accounts of Paul's thought reflect this stack of mutually reinforcing dichotomies between thought and act, being and act, and theology and ethics.[20]

But further reflection suggests that these distinctions are incoherent. Thoughts are acts, and all acts must, moreover, possess some ground in ontology or being. All thinking *is* acting. Moreover, all thoughts and any other acts presuppose embodiment. In addition, all Christian activity, whether in terms of thinking, speaking, or other acting, is ethical; it can be asked of *any* activity whether it is good and hence ethical, and this question can consequently be applied to all Christian thinking, whatever its precise focus. Hence, as Barth in particular emphasizes, theology *is* ethics and ethics *is* theology. There are not two realms here but one.[21]

---

[20] See, e.g., the basic dispositions of the three treatments noted earlier: Dunn, *Theology*; Schreiner, *Paul*; and Schnelle, *Apostle Paul*.

[21] See esp. *The Doctrine of Creation, Part 4: The Command of God and the Creator* (vol. III of *Church Dogmatics;* trans. A. T. Mackey et al.; Edinburgh: T&T Clark, 1961 [1951]). Barth also speaks of two aspects of the one Word of God – promise and command. See also Colin E. Gunton, *Enlightenment and Alienation: An Essay Toward a Trinitarian Theology* (Eugene, Ore.: Cascade, 2006 [1985]); and *Act and Being: Towards a Theology of the Divine Attributes* (London: SCM, 2002). And Stanley Hauerwas tirelessly refuses to accept this distinction and its destructive consequences.

It seems then that an accurate grasp of Paul's data of belief, and in particular of their reach beyond the confessional into concerns that modern interpreters often denote as ethical, might have been hampered in the past by the intrusion of a pervasive but incoherent set of thought-act dichotomies – dichotomies that Paul himself does not seem to have suffered from. It follows, moreover, that we must deliberately avoid introducing these categories into any further descriptions of his thought. All thinking and believing is ethical, and all ethical activity is tightly bound up with a great deal of thinking and with many beliefs, all of which are never anything other than acts. The data of believing in Paul reflect this correct account of reality.

D. Participation and believing in Paul

The agency or causality of this comprehensive, ethical account of Christian believing in Paul now cries out for explanation. How do Christians actually get this mind or mentality that spans confessional, ethical, and ecclesial behavior, and includes cognitive and affective dimensions? Fortunately, the texts we have just surveyed have already given us some clues. They point explicitly if briefly to the agency of the Holy Spirit, along with the Spirit's creation of a new mind in Christians. Romans 15:13 states that the power of the Holy Spirit will create Christian believing, while gesturing immediately toward its complexity ([...] ἐν δυνάμει πνεύματος ἁγίου). And just prior to 12:3–8, 12:2 states that Christian behavior is rooted in a changed and reconstituted mind ([...] μεταμορφοῦσθε τῇ ἀνακαινώσει τοῦ νοός [...]).[22] Some key believing texts from elsewhere in Paul can now be seen to reinforce these basic implications, although our engagement here will have to be regrettably programmatic.

The longest discussion of Christian believing by Paul is found in Rom 4:16b-22.[23] Paul asserts here in an extraordinarily convoluted sentence that Abraham believes specifically in the promise that he will be "the father of many nations" (Gen 17:5, echoed several times in this text), by way of the conception and birth of a child, despite the facts that he is ninety-nine years old and Sarah not much younger. Both therefore are sterile – as good as dead as the text puts it (v. 19). But Abraham believes this hopeless future, Paul says, in hope (v. 18a: ἐπ' ἐλπίδι), without wavering in doubt or unbelief (v. 20: οὐ διεκρίθη τῇ ἀπιστίᾳ), being, for the entire time between the promise and its fulfillment, "completely convinced" that God was

---

[22] And this raises interesting anthropological questions that cannot, unfortunately, be pursued here.

[23] More details can be found in my *Deliverance*, 715–61.

powerful enough to undertake this resurrecting act and would in fact do so (v. 21: πληροφορηθείς). Indeed, he never suffers any "weakening in belief" (v. 19: μὴ ἀσθενήσας τῇ πίστει).

It seems that the mind of Christian believers is fully on display here by way of anticipation in Paul's account of Abraham, some of the terms of mental description used in ch. 14 occurring in this discussion as well.[24] However, it is now especially clear that this new mind is utterly convinced and steadfast to an almost superhuman extent. And it is fixed on unseen truths.

The life-creating act promised to Abraham lies, at least initially, in the future, as it does for Christians, Paul observes in vv. 23–24. Isaac will in effect be constituted from nothing and born from the dead, just as Christians will be reconstituted when their bodies are resurrected. But at the moment of belief this has not happened. The truths concerning which the Christian mind is fully convinced are consequently unseen, and are generated in turn by the unseen God, a dimension within Christian believing found in other Pauline texts.

Belief is mentioned in these terms explicitly in 2 Cor 5:7 (διὰ πίστεως γὰρ περιπατοῦμεν, οὐ διὰ εἴδους). And Rom 8:24–25 is a closely parallel text to this, despite not using belief language overtly: [8:24] τῇ γὰρ ἐλπίδι ἐσώθημεν· ἐλπὶς δὲ βλεπομένη οὐκ ἔστιν ἐλπίς· ὃ γὰρ βλέπει τίς ἐλπίζει; [25] εἰ δὲ ὃ οὐ βλέπομεν ἐλπίζομεν, δι' ὑπομονῆς ἀπεκδεχόμεθα.

It can be seen here immediately that the believing mind includes endurance as well as hope. And both texts reinforce the suggestion of Rom 4:16b–22 that Christian believing is oriented toward pivotal but unseen realities. It cannot "see" the object of its convictions, as Paul puts it, and therefore includes hope and perseverance within its believing, as the example of Abraham has already suggested as well.

It seems especially clear then from this additional data that the new Christian mentality of steadfast, rock-like believing in the unseen realities of future resurrection must be a divine gift. That a sinful human being could achieve this level of mental righteousness seems prima facie absurd for the otherwise rather Augustinian Paul (see esp. Rom 5:12–14; 7:7–25), and especially for people mired in the mortality and suffering of the present, visible world, as Paul's auditors seem to be in both 2 Cor 5 and Rom 8. Left to sinful and/or oppressed human effort, who can believe in this fashion? (Mark 10:26–27!) This simply looks wildly unrealistic.[25] It is too

---

[24] In addition to those already noted – πιστ- terms, πληροφορέω, and διακρίνω – see what Abraham "knows" in v. 19 (κατενόησεν).

[25] To achieve this through human effort would also not really *create* a *new* mind; neither would it explain Paul's frequent references to giving and gift.

unwavering, too difficult (if not impossible; the objects of belief are unseen), and too comprehensive.

But it is a realistic and utterly concrete claim and exhortation if Paul views the steadfastly believing Christian mind as a gift of the Holy Spirit, as various clues in some of his texts have already suggested.[26] The Spirit can reconstitute and recreate this mentality within the midst of a sinful humanity, calling it into being where previously it was not, as happened in the miraculous conception and birth of Isaac.[27] And we might consequently dub this an "apocalyptic" account of believing in Paul. It is the result of an unconditional act of divine disclosure,[28] and is oriented, by the same token, toward (i.a.) unseen, invisible truths.[29]

But our account of the new Christian mind's causality, as a divine gift effected by the Spirit, is not yet complete. In order to complete it we will need to return to consider its ethical dimension in a little more depth.

E. Believing and ethics

We saw earlier on, when analyzing data from Rom 12–15, that an accurate account of Christian believing in Paul must include an ethical dimension. Believing Christians are to be respectful of certain differences regarding diet and time. Christian beliefs include acting steadfastly, peacefully, and hopefully. And Christians are to be prudent and humble, acting within the community in particular ways – the upbuilding of prophecy, the energy and enthusiasm of leading, the optimism of encouraging, and so on – all these disparate activities being intended, nevertheless, to build up that community constructively. And it simply needs to be appreciated at this point that in all this ethical behavior toward others, whether inside or outside the community, Paul seems to be appealing frequently to Christ.

The perception of this dimension in Paul's ethic has been greatly assisted in recent decades by a new appreciation of his use of narrative – something largely traceable to the important dissertation of Richard Hays, first

---

[26] See elsewhere in Paul, esp. 1 Cor 1:10; 2:16; and Eph 4:23; and to a lesser extent, 1 Cor 14:14, 15, and 19.

[27] Paul uses the language of (re)creation when describing the new Christian mind on occasion; see Rom 12:2.

[28] See esp. J. L. (Lou) Martyn, "Epistemology at the Turn of the Ages: 2 Corinthians 5:16," in *Theological Issues in the Letters of Paul* (Edinburgh: T&T Clark, 1997 [1967]), 89–110.

[29] See Anathea E. Portier-Young, *Apocalypse against Empire: Theologies of Resistance in Early Judaism* (Grand Rapids: Eerdmans, 2011).

published in 1983[30] – and to a complementary abandonment of an older, putatively Protestant, aversion to the *imitatio Christi*.[31] Indeed, the terms of the debate have shifted so significantly I suspect that few Pauline scholars would now dispute the suggestion that there is an appeal within Paul's ethics – at least to some extent – to a story about Christ.[32]

The case is largely inferential but the evidence is very widespread. It is clear that in Paul Christ loves the church and the rest of humanity,[33] and it is equally clear that Paul expects Christians to love others.[34] Hence it seems reasonable to infer that the love of Christ animates Christian love for others. That these two directly equivalent activities would not be connected in any way would be odd (although some have argued that it is one of mere exemplification and imitation, and hence the various Protestant protests in the past against what is perceived to be an impossible, and perhaps even an impious, ideal). But Paul, as we have already seen, speaks at times of Christians possessing the mind and thinking of Christ. Given that Christ loves it would then follow even more obviously that Christians love because they possess the loving mind of Christ. And occasionally these connections become even more explicit – for example, in Rom 15.[35]

[15:1] 'Οφείλομεν δὲ ἡμεῖς οἱ δυνατοὶ τὰ ἀσθενήματα τῶν ἀδυνάτων βαστάζειν καὶ μὴ ἑαυτοῖς ἀρέσκειν. [2] ἕκαστος ἡμῶν τῷ πλησίον ἀρεσκέτω εἰς τὸ ἀγαθὸν πρὸς οἰκοδομήν· [3] καὶ γὰρ ὁ Χριστὸς οὐχ ἑαυτῷ ἤρεσεν, ἀλλὰ καθὼς γέγραπται· οἱ ὀνειδισμοὶ τῶν ὀνειδιζόντων σε ἐπέπεσαν ἐπ' ἐμέ. [4] ὅσα γὰρ προεγράφη, εἰς τὴν ἡμετέραν διδασκαλίαν ἐγράφη, ἵνα

---

[30] *The Faith of Jesus Christ: The Narrative Substructure of Galatians 3:1–4:11* (2d ed.; Grand Rapids: Eerdmans, 2002).

[31] See, i.a., Stephen E. Fowl, *The Story of Christ in the Ethics of Paul: An Analysis of the Function of the Hymnic Material in the Pauline Corpus* (JSNTSup 36; Sheffield: JSOT Press, 1990); Michael J. Gorman, *Cruciformity: Paul's Narrative Spirituality of the Cross* (Grand Rapids: Eerdmans, 2001); and *Inhabiting the Cruciform God: Kenosis, Justification, and Theosis in Paul's Narrative Soteriology* (Grand Rapids: Eerdmans, 2009); Richard A. Burridge, *Imitating Jesus: An Inclusive Approach to New Testament Ethics* (Grand Rapids: Eerdmans, 2007), esp. 81–154 (ch. III, "Paul: Follower or Founder?"); and see also the important positional volume edited by Bruce W. Longenecker, ed., *Narrative Dynamics in Paul: A Critical Assessment* (Louisville, Ky.: Westminster John Knox, 2002). A definitive study of Rom 12 making this point well is Michael Thompson, *Clothed with Christ: The Example and Teaching of Jesus in Romans 12.1–15.13* (JSNTSup 59; Sheffield: JSOT Press, 1991).

[32] This should be distinguished but not separated dramatically from data suggesting the words or teaching of Jesus.

[33] Gal 2:20; so also 2 Cor 5:15; implicitly in 8:9 [Phil 2:5–11]; Eph 3:14–19, esp. 19; so also Rom 5:5–11; 8:35, hence 39.

[34] See of course 1 Cor 13 entire; but see also Rom 12:9–10; 13:8–10; 1 Cor 16:14; Gal 5:6, 13–15, 22–24; Eph 1:15–20; 5:1–2; Col 1:3–5; 3:14; 1 Thess 1:3; 4:9–12; 5:8; Phlm 5, 7.

[35] It is also esp. clear in Phil 2–3: see Susan Grove Eastman, "Philippians 2:6–11: Incarnation as Mimetic Participation," *JSP&L* 1 (2010): 1–22.

διὰ τῆς ὑπομονῆς καὶ διὰ τῆς παρακλήσεως τῶν γραφῶν τὴν ἐλπίδα ἔχωμεν. [5] ὁ δὲ θεὸς τῆς ὑπομονῆς καὶ τῆς παρακλήσεως δῴη ὑμῖν τὸ αὐτὸ φρονεῖν ἐν ἀλλήλοις κατὰ Χριστὸν Ἰησοῦν, [6] ἵνα ὁμοθυμαδὸν ἐν ἑνὶ στόματι δοξάζητε τὸν θεὸν καὶ πατέρα τοῦ κυρίου ἡμῶν Ἰησοῦ Χριστοῦ. [7] Διὸ προσλαμβάνεσθε ἀλλήλους, καθὼς καὶ ὁ Χριστὸς προσελάβετο ὑμᾶς εἰς δόξαν τοῦ θεοῦ.

Here in vv. 1–2 Paul exhorts his "strong" Roman auditors to act in a way that pleases their neighbors and not themselves, if necessary bearing the burdens of the "weak." In v. 3 Christ's behavior is then described in exactly the same way, and explicated quickly with the citation of Ps 69:9; Christ himself bears curses falling on others. The two benevolent postures are therefore directly parallel. A brief digression concerning the function of the Scriptures takes place in v. 4 and Paul returns to his present concern in v. 5. And here, most significantly, he prays that God will give to his auditors "the same thinking toward one another that is in accordance with [that of] Christ Jesus." So the two activities are explicitly linked together in this critical verse. Divine action will gift to Christians Christ's very thinking, which in this case is ethical and benevolent, bearing the burdens of others. Verse 6 is in effect another digression, anticipating the catena of vv. 9–12 and the wonder of a doxological unity, with diverse peoples, largely pagan, glorifying the Lord. Verse 7, however, looks back, drawing the strong and the weak into its exhortation to "receive one another" (as in 14:1), again stating that this will parallel the way that Christ "has welcomed you," and thereby reiterating the central identification in closing.

Perhaps readers could be forgiven in the past for supposing that Paul's language in these terms presupposes mere imitation; Christians are to copy or imitate the example of the benevolent Christ – a tall order admittedly. However, v. 5 explicitly grounds such exhortations in Christ's own way of thinking, and hence in effect in a christological ontology that has been gifted to Christians by God. Christians ought to love because Christ's love has been given to them and lives within them. And this is of course the gift of a new mentality or way of thinking, ergo of believing. To possess Christ's way of thinking *is* to be disposed to love others.

Once this dynamic has been grasped, various pieces of data found elsewhere in Paul become rather more comprehensible than perhaps they were previously. We now know, in particular, why Paul segues so seamlessly from believing to loving.

Scholars have long struggled to link these two activities together, knowing that Paul is deeply committed to both but not knowing quite how to combine confessional belief and ethical love organically together. However, the realization that Christians possess a reconstituted mind – the loving mind of Christ – can do so.

Love is rooted in a certain way of thinking so it is, at bottom, a particular set of beliefs and a certain believing activity. It includes, among other things, compassionate beliefs about other people, and beliefs that compassionate actions toward them are appropriate, and so on. So the believing Christian mind is, for Paul, when it acts overtly ethically, a loving mind. The two are not merely linked together; they are initially coterminous and so are indeed organically related. This interrelation is nicely summarized by Galatians 5:5–6.

[5:5] ἡμεῖς γὰρ πνεύματι ἐκ πίστεως ἐλπίδα δικαιοσύνης ἀπεκδεχόμεθα. [6] ἐν γὰρ Χριστῷ Ἰησοῦ οὔτε περιτομή τι ἰσχύει οὔτε ἀκροβυστία ἀλλὰ πίστις δι' ἀγάπης ἐνεργουμένη.

As Christians await final deliverance, Paul controversially but consistently asserts that not only will they act in belief and hope (v. 5), but that, irrespective of a circumcised or uncircumcised state (v. 6a), their believing will effect itself through love. Scholars have labored to interpret the link between believing and love effected in this text rather cryptically by a participle in the middle voice – literally, "believing effecting itself through love."[36] A confessional believing has no obviously generative role in relation to love, while getting from belief "alone" to an ethic of love requires some ingenuity. However, this brief assertion is now readily understandable in its own terms, with no additions. Christian belief is Christian believing, that is, the possession and activity of the new mind of Christ, which includes a central commitment to love *within* its understanding (see esp. Gal 2:20). So this mind would effect itself, in its concrete activities and relationships, in love; it is, indeed, primarily a disposition *of* love toward both God and humanity.

A brief perusal of one further passage in Romans should tie together all the preceding strands of evidence fairly definitively, namely, Rom 6:1–11.

Believing is mentioned explicitly in v. 8 (εἰ δὲ ἀπεθάνομεν σὺν Χριστῷ, πιστεύομεν ὅτι καὶ συζήσομεν αὐτῷ), and other terms of mental disposition stud the surrounding argument.[37] So the new Christian mind is once again fully on display, although here in an explicitly ethical discussion.

In this chapter Paul is strongly rejecting two claims. His account of Christian salvation in terms of grace is fully ethical and not libertine, he asserts – in no uncertain terms (see esp. v. 1b–2: ἐπιμένωμεν τῇ ἁμαρτίᾳ, ἵνα ἡ χάρις πλεονάσῃ; μὴ γένοιτο. οἵτινες ἀπεθάνομεν τῇ ἁμαρτίᾳ, πῶς ἔτι ζήσομεν ἐν αὐτῇ;). But his ethic is nevertheless *not* informed fundamentally

---

[36] The issues are canvassed by J. L. (Lou) Martyn, *Galatians* (AB 33A; New York: Doubleday, 1997), 472–74; I treat this text in *Deliverance*, 886–92 and notes, building on the seminal recent treatment of Hung-Sik Choi, "ΠΙΣΤΙΣ in Galatians 5:5–6: Neglected Evidence for the Faithfulness of Christ," *JBL* 124 (2005): 467–90.

[37] In Rom 6:1–11 Paul uses five verbs of knowledge, effectively hammering the thesis home that the Christian mind must understand certain things about its own state: see the appearances of ἀγνοεῖτε in v. 3; γινώσκοντες in v. 6; πιστεύομεν in v. 8; εἰδότες in v. 9; and λογίζεσθε in v. 11.

by Torah (see esp. vv. 14–15, esp. 15: Τί οὖν; ἁμαρτήσωμεν, ὅτι οὐκ ἐσμὲν ὑπὸ νόμον ἀλλὰ ὑπὸ χάριν; μὴ γένοιτο).[38] So clearly absolutely critical issues are being defended. The vital point to grasp for our present concern, however, is that Paul's trenchant rejection of Torah presupposes the reconstituted Christian mind. His claim in v. 11 is especially programmatic: οὕτως καὶ ὑμεῖς λογίζεσθε ἑαυτοὺς εἶναι νεκροὺς μὲν τῇ ἁμαρτίᾳ ζῶντας δὲ τῷ θεῷ ἐν Χριστῷ Ἰησοῦ.

This can be translated a little weakly. But I suggest that there is nothing artificial or voluntary about Paul's statement here – that Christians merely "consider" or "view themselves" as dead to sin and alive to God. His statement is indicative and factual, as the surrounding emphases on absolute knowledge noted above suggest, *and* because nothing else really makes sense of Paul's main claim that Christians are fully ethical under grace but not under Torah: "So then, you yourselves must understand yourselves to be dead, on the one hand, to sin, and alive, on the other, to God." As the rest of the argument makes clear, Paul is asserting the extraordinary claim here that Christians have been resurrected within the resurrected Christ, this being narrated in baptism. Moreover, Christ is now living in a realm of glory, beyond the reach of death, but also thereby beyond the reach of sin. Hence Christians, resurrected in Christ, *are* dead to sin and alive to God too, because they now live – at least in terms of their new minds – in this new, glorious place. Verse 8 consequently suggests that these realizations about themselves characterize a key dimension of their believing.

Hopefully then we can see at this point how this text explains programmatically the specific ecclesial and ethical flourishes in Rom 12–15 with which this essay started, along with the subsequent ethical exhortations explored in relation to Christian love. The Christian community has been gifted with the mind of the resurrected Christ. This mind is located in an eschatological place, beyond current structures like Torah (so Gal 3:26–28, not to mention 1 Cor 12:13, and Col 3:11), and beyond mental contamination by sin and corruption. It is structured, but by the interpersonal dynamics of God – dynamics of love, and of any related postures. And Christians are to understand all this – to believe in it. And it might now be worth noting briefly in passing, before we consider the broader implications of this account of Christian believing in Paul, that we have just affirmed the likelihood within Paul's account of the believing of Christ himself.

---

[38] The implication is that someone else, perhaps an opponent, is linking these two things together: to be ethical is to be informed by Torah; therefore, to be outside Torah in any sense is necessarily to lapse into unethical, libertine behavior. For more see *Deliverance*, 469–518 (ch. 13).

Christians can hardly participate in the mind of Christ if he does not (and did not) have one. And it follows directly from this that they can hardly be shaped by his beliefs and believing if he does not (and did not) possess those either. So there should now be no difficulty, in general terms, appreciating that Paul might speak on occasion of Christ's believing, in addition to his acting in other ways that have already been noted. Indeed, for Christ to act in obedience, love, or gentleness, is necessarily to affirm that he thinks and believes certain things. It is difficult to conceive of an act of obedience, for example, that involves no beliefs; such a notion is really just incoherent.

A neglected text in Paul makes many of these critical connections clear, encouraging us in the suspicion that Paul really did express things in this way explicitly on occasion – in terms, that is, of the believing Christ in whom broader Christian believing participates.

In 2 Cor 4:13 Paul states: Ἔχοντες δὲ τὸ αὐτὸ πνεῦμα τῆς πίστεως κατὰ τὸ γεγραμμένον· ἐπίστευσα, διὸ ἐλάλησα, καὶ ἡμεῖς πιστεύομεν, διὸ καὶ λαλοῦμεν.[39] Paul claims here that he speaks because he believes certain things. Specifically, he knows that God has resurrected Jesus and will resurrect him and the Corinthians (v. 14). And he acts confidently in both these respects because he possesses the same spirit of believing as the Psalmist who stated in Ps 115:10 (LXX), "I believed therefore I spoke." For this argument to work, however, it is unlikely that the spirit in question is a mere disposition; Paul's identification needs *the* Spirit. Moreover, the Psalmist really needs to be an anticipation of Christ as well, since Paul's later claims are christocentric. If the Psalmist is not believing and speaking of his resurrection, then Paul's claim to be doing the same, believing and then speaking with certainty, because he possesses the same spirit, must fall flat. However, if Paul possesses the same Spirit as the Psalmist, who is in turn anticipating the speech of Christ, then the apostle's confident believing and resultant speaking to the Corinthians are entirely fair (and not otherwise). He believes steadfastly in the resurrection and affirms it, by way of speaking, to the Corinthians, because he dwells by the Spirit in the one who has already believed, been obedient to the point of death, and been raised (see also Heb 10:38–12:2). And as a result of this we can now see that this text speaks indirectly but implicitly of Christ's believing as the ground of Paul's believing. Moreover, once we have grasped this dynamic, it can be seen that various other texts in Paul might be reproducing it as well (Rom 3:22, 26; Gal 2:16 [2x], 20; 3:22; Eph 4:13; Phil 3:9).

---

[39] See my "2 Corinthians 4:13: Evidence in Paul That Christ Believes," *JBL* 128 (2009): 337–56. Also important here is Richard Hays, "Christ Prays the Psalms: Israel's Psalter as Matrix of Early Christianity," in *The Conversion of the Imagination: Paul as Interpreter of Israel's Scripture* (Grand Rapids: Eerdmans, 2005), 101–18.

Note, however, that my argument for a christocentric, participatory understanding of believing in Paul does not stand or fall in relation to a subjective position within "the πίστις Χριστοῦ debate." The situation is the reverse of this.

A participatory understanding of believing in Paul based on other texts – more plainly apparent once its ethical dimension has been elucidated – is directly compatible with an explicit and not merely implicit christocentric emphasis within this more limited data. This emphasis now appears to be an entirely integrated and understandable part of Paul's thinking, as against some inexplicable anomaly (reproducing here Morna Hooker's angle of approach in a useful and somewhat neglected essay[40]). That is, there do not seem to be very many good objections now, in comprehensive and systematic terms, to the suggestion that Paul might have, on occasion, spoken of the believing of Christ, which is to say, of his thinking and mind; it is this, after all, that we can now see grounds his Christian ethic beyond Torah, along with all the thinking and resulting acting of the Christian community in love.

Whatever our final judgment here specifically, with this broad description of the genesis of Christian believing in Paul in place – in terms of participation, as a divine gift of the Spirit, in the mind of Christ – we can now turn in closing to a consideration of the various important implications of all this for the apostle's broader theological description.

F. The critical implications

I would suggest in conclusion that neglecting the participatory rationale for believing in Paul will severely damage any accounts of Christian believing and of participation within his theology. Indeed, the entire shape of his gospel risks being altered and disordered. We will attend first to the damage done to Christian believing. But in order to appreciate this we must first note briefly where scholars tend to position believing within Paul's theology when it is detached from its ground in participation.

If scholars have not folded believing into participation then they usually locate it at the threshold between the church and what lies outside it. Indeed, it has simply seemed obvious to most modern Pauline interpreters that believing is a, if not the, key "transfer term" for the apostle, to use E. P. Sanders's nice phrase.[41] Belief (or faith), we are told, speaks of the way

---

[40] "ΠΙΣΤΙΣ ΧΡΙΣΤΟΥ," *NTS* 35 (1989): 321–42.

[41] *Paul, the Law, and the Jewish People* (Philadelphia: Fortress, 1983). A surprising number of important recent advocates of participation in Paul repeat this consensus: see, e.g., Gorman, *Cruciformity*; and *Inhabiting the Cruciform God*; Constantine R. Camp-

people convert, and the statements of a text like Rom 10:9–10 should consequently be interpreted not just in grammatically but in soteriologically conditional terms: "if you confess with your mouth, 'Jesus is Lord,' and believe in your heart that God raised him from the dead, you will be saved" (NIV). Believing is viewed as an entry criterion, to be exercised by individuals in order to become Christians and to enter the Christian state and community.

An initial result of this definition and consequent theological location is of course that believing is separated from participation. They are not the same thing. One cannot equate the activity whereby one enters a situation with the activity that takes place in it, after this entry has taken place. This just seems confused. The ticket to get into a movie and the experience of watching a movie are not the same thing. So Christian believing is not itself understood in participatory terms. But the results of this theological distinction between believing and participation have arguably been disastrous. The first difficulty with this account is that Christian believing is really rendered impossible.

We saw at the beginning of this essay that confessional believing for Paul involves the realizations and steadfast convictions that Jesus died an atoning death, was resurrected from the dead, ascended, and is now enthroned in heaven as the cosmos's Lord. We also observed later on – especially in Rom 4:16b–22 – that these are all unseen and unseeable realities. Hence it seems fair to suggest that to ask people to believe, of their own volition, in these particular realities in order to be saved, is really to ask the impossible, and on two principal grounds.

First, contrary to much popular thinking, people cannot simply choose to believe that certain things are true – the philosophical position of belief voluntarism.[42] If one does not think that something is true, one cannot simply decide to believe that it is true even if one's life depends on it. Either one believes that little green aliens live inside one's computer or one does not. And one cannot just choose to believe the former if one is offered a million dollars to do so. (One could lie, but that would not be the same thing.) Similarly, one cannot simply choose to believe that the sun will not rise tomorrow. We all think that it will. So in asking people to choose to believe a set of propositions in order to be saved, advocates of Paul in the-

---

bell, *Paul and Union with Christ: An Exegetical and Theological Study* (Grand Rapids: Zondervan, 2012); and Grant Macaskill, *Union with Christ in the New Testament* (Oxford: Oxford University Press, 2013).

[42] A useful overview is provided by Richard Amesbury, "Fideism," in *The Stanford Encyclopedia of Philosophy* (Winter 2012 Edition; ed. Edward N. Zalta). Cited 23 January 2014. Online: http://plato.stanford.edu/archives/win2012/entries/fideism; see also Gunton, *Act and Being*.

se terms are really asking for the impossible. (People presumably believe for the usual sociological reasons, in spite of this rhetoric, suggesting the adjustment of the rhetoric.[43])

But, second, Christian belief is in unseen things that are overtly counterfactual and impossible – in the case of Abraham, in the conception and birth of a child by a ninety-nine year old father and an equally elderly mother, and in the case of Christians, in similarly bizarre notions like the recreation of the human mind on the basis of Christ's resurrection and ascended existence. Hence Christian believing is doubly impossible if it is left to human volition.

Only a revelatory rationale can make Paul's expectations here remotely realistic. Christian believing must be, in the first instance, a divine gift. It comes from revelation brought to Christians by the Spirit, at which point we are one step away from a participatory understanding if we are not already within it. (It should be noted immediately that this is emphatically not to exclude a free dimension from an appropriate response by people to revelation. But it is to avoid reducing this situation to a response alone and to one understood, moreover, in terms of choice; this would be to capitulate to a Liberal account of freedom that has done much damage to accurate Christian thinking over the years.[44])

But to understand a Christian's confessional beliefs as a gift of the Spirit is not yet to have reached a full and appropriate understanding of Christian believing. Further distortions may well remain in play, as we have already seen.

Confessional beliefs focus on accurate statements about the father and the son – on Christ's lordship and so on. Such statements are themselves conceptualized accurately as gifts of the Spirit. But we have seen that Paul's understanding stretches well beyond such beliefs to Christian believing *in toto* in all its affective and ethical dimensions. And we have also seen that these dimensions presuppose the believing of Christ. It seems then that any complete understanding of belief in Paul must encompass both the gifts of the Spirit concerning the divine father and his son, *and* the gifts of the Spirit in that son, which is really to say that the believing in which Christians participate seems to have a dynamic, Trinitarian structure. Christians sometimes stand in the Spirit over against the Lord Jesus

---

[43] See *Deliverance*, 127–36, and the literature cited there.

[44] See Stanley Hauerwas, "The Politics of Freedom: Why Freedom of Religion is a Subtle Temptation," in *After Christendom? How the Church is to Behave if Freedom, Justice, and a Christian Nation Are Bad Ideas* (Nashville: Abingdon, 1991), 69–92. An excellent critique of this notion of freedom, with a sensitive alternative based on sonic, not spatial, imagery, is Jeremy Begbie, "Room of One's Own?: Music, Space, and Freedom," in *Music, Modernity and God: Essays in Listening* (Oxford: Oxford University Press, 2013), 141–75.

Christ (so to speak), viewing Jesus in distinction, as an object; but sometimes they stand in Jesus, presumably still by way of the Spirit, over against others, whether his father or other people, with Jesus as an acting internal subject. Hence, any lingering influence from the separation of believing from participation may play out in an occlusion of just those Trinitarian dynamics that we need in order to explain key parts of Paul's data.

If believing is separated from participation and consequently limited to confession alone, this will probably be conceptualized ultimately in terms of the data speaking of Christ as an object. The work of the Spirit may be invoked but will operate on the human side of this critical relationship, where correct beliefs about God the father and his son Jesus are supplied. And the result of this will be various critical distortions. The father and his son will be viewed as distant objects – effectively a monotheistic position. And the work of the Spirit will be separated from the father and the son – effectively a tritheistic position. Hence Paul's doctrine of God will be fractured, and his account of participation in God accordingly impoverished. In particular, it will now be difficult to detect the importance for Paul of dwelling *in Christ*, and the consequent ground of his ethic. Some form of Pelagianism will beckon. Alternatively, if the importance of being in Christ for ethics is grasped, but the connection between believing, as a gift of the Spirit, and participation, as the gift of being in Christ, is not restored, then a tritheist variation will again result, played out temporally. The work of the Spirit will save Christians, and then, later, the work of Christ will make them holy (or some such) – as if the work of the one God could be compartmentalized in this fashion.

Having noted these further problems, we should turn to consider some of the broader implications flowing from the separation of believing from participation for any reconstruction of Paul's thinking as a whole.

If belief is the entry criterion into Christianity, then participation will be located strictly within the church, within a circle of people set off from the rest of humanity by the important boundary condition that is confessional belief. And the theological antecedents to the Christian condition will now be sought in the theological antecedents to believing, not to participation (setting aside here for the moment the difficulty just noted that this entry criterion is, strictly speaking, impossible). The temptation here is then that creation and non-Christian humanity will be framed theologically by notions drawn from the situation of humanity prior to believing, and hence in terms of self-evident perceptions rooted in nature. (The most common way of doing this in Pauline studies is in terms of the "Lutheran" reading.[45])

---

[45] The terminology goes back to Krister Stendahl; the tradition is analyzed in detail in my *Deliverance*.

The entire shape of Paul's gospel – of his theology – will consequently be conceptualized as a progression from nature to grace.

Concomitantly, the insights of redemption, developed in specific relation to giftedness, the presence of the Spirit, and the indwelling nature of Christ, will be limited in their application and their implications to the church. Their implications will consequently not be extended to creation (but see 1 Cor 8:6; Col 1:15–17; and so on). Consequently, redemption will be largely sundered from creation and understood as an exceptional category, at which point we are one step away from Marcionism, and are involved in a large number of other theological problems and compromises as well, not the least of which is a broad-ranging conditionality or contractualism.[46] At bottom, we will have radically curtailed here the theological influence of the information that we gain about God from participation – the insights of participating in the loving Christ by way of the Spirit in a Trinitarian dynamic. And this is surely a curious thing when what we might broadly call orthodoxy suggests that this is the place where we encounter God as God really is, united mysteriously but absolutely with creation.[47] That is, in doing this we will, in effect, have denied the importance of the incarnation, and the importance of its antecedents in the divine will, in relation to both creation and redemption, in terms of election (see Rom 8:29–30; Eph 1:3–14). We will, in other words, have undermined any fundamentally Nicene account of Paul's theology.

These are heavy prices to pay. And they all flow from something in Paul that is ultimately unnecessary, namely, the separation of Christian believing from participation. Over against this, a participatory account of believing defuses these difficulties at one stroke, and seems, moreover, to be a more accurate account of the actual data in his texts, explaining its confessional, emotional, and ethical dimensions. There seems then to be little to lose and much to gain by adopting this equation rigorously and confidently in any future explication of Paul's thought as whole. Christians believe because they respond to and participate in the understanding of the Spirit and in the believing of Christ – here at times in distinction from one another, and at times in unity. In so doing they participate in the divine communion of three persons and one God, and go on to believe, which is to say, to think and to act, as that God is constructed and acts – in unconditional and

---

[46] See esp. J. B. Torrance, "Covenant and Contract: A Study of the Theological Background of Worship in Seventeenth-Century Scotland," *SJT* 23 (1970): 51–76.

[47] Alasdair I. C. Heron, "*Homoousios* with the Father," in *The Incarnation: Ecumenical Studies in the Nicene-Constantinopolitan Creed A.D. 381* (ed. Thomas F. Torrance; Edinburgh: Handsel, 1981), 58–87; also Alan J. Torrance, "The Trinity," in *The Cambridge Companion to Barth* (ed. John Webster; Cambridge: Cambridge University Press, 2000), 72–91.

overflowing love. And this is surely the heart of Paul's understanding of believing, of participation, and of the Christian gospel.

Bibliography

Amesbury, Richard. "Fideism." *The Stanford Encyclopedia of Philosophy.* Winter 2012 Edition. Edited by Edward N. Zalta. Cited 23 January 2014. Online: http://plato.stanford.edu/archives/win2012/entries/fideism.

Barclay, John M. G. "'Do We Undermine the Law?' A Study of Romans 14:1–15:6." Pages 287–308 in *Paul and the Mosaic Law.* Edited by J. D. G. Dunn. Tübingen: J. C. B. Mohr [Siebeck], 1996.

———. "Manna and the Circulation of Grace: A Study of 2 Corinthians 8:1–15." Pages 409–26 in *The Word Leaps the Gap: Essays on Scripture and Theology in Honor of Richard B. Hays.* Edited by J. Ross Wagner, C. Kavin Rowe, and A. Katherine Grieb. Grand Rapids: Eerdmans, 2008.

———. *Paul and The Gift.* Grand Rapids: Eerdmans, forthcoming.

Barth, Karl. *The Doctrine of Creation, Part 4: The Command of God and the Creator.* Vol. III of *Church Dogmatics.* Translated by A. T. Mackey et al. Edinburgh: T&T Clark, 1961 [1951].

Begbie, Jeremy. "Room of One's Own?: Music, Space, and Freedom." Pages 141–75 in *Music, Modernity and God: Essays in Listening.* Oxford: Oxford University Press, 2013.

Burridge, Richard A. *Imitating Jesus: An Inclusive Approach to New Testament Ethics.* Grand Rapids: Eerdmans, 2007.

Campbell, Constantine R. *Paul and Union with Christ: An Exegetical and Theological Study* Grand Rapids: Zondervan, 2012.

Campbell, Douglas A. "2 Corinthians 4:13: Evidence in Paul That Christ Believes." *Journal of Biblical Literature* 128 (2009): 337–56.

———. *Deliverance of God.* Grand Rapids: Eerdmans, 2009.

———. *Framing Paul: An Epistolary Account.* Grand Rapids: Eerdmans, 2014.

Choi, Hung-Sik. "ΠΙΣΤΙΣ in Galatians 5:5–6: Neglected Evidence for the Faithfulness of Christ." *Journal of Biblical Literature* 124 (2005): 467–90.

Dunn, James D. G. *The Theology of Paul the Apostle.* Grand Rapids: Eerdmans, 1998.

Eastman, Susan Grove. "Philippians 2:6–11: Incarnation as Mimetic Participation." *Journal for the Study of Paul & his Letters* 1 (2010): 1–22.

Eubank, Nathan. *Wages of Cross-Bearing and Debt of Sin: The Economy of Heaven in Matthew's Gospel.* Beihefte zur Zeitschrift für die neutestamentliche Wissenschaft 196. Berlin: de Gruyter, 2013.

Fowl, Stephen E. *The Story of Christ in the Ethics of Paul: An Analysis of the Function of the Hymnic Material in the Pauline Corpus.* Journal for the Study of the New Testament Supplement Series 36. Sheffield: JSOT Press, 1990.

Gorman, Michael J. *Cruciformity: Paul's Narrative Spirituality of the Cross.* Grand Rapids: Eerdmans, 2001.

———. *Inhabiting the Cruciform God: Kenosis, Justification, and Theosis in Paul's Narrative Soteriology.* Grand Rapids: Eerdmans, 2009.

Gunton, Colin E. *Act and Being: Towards a Theology of the Divine Attributes.* London: SCM, 2002.

———. *Enlightenment and Alienation: An Essay Toward a Trinitarian Theology.* Eugene, Ore.: Cascade, 2006 [1985].

Hays, Richard B. "Christ Prays the Psalms: Israel's Psalter as Matrix of Early Christianity." Pages 101–18 in *The Conversion of the Imagination: Paul as Interpreter of Israel's Scripture.* Grand Rapids: Eerdmans, 2005.

———. *The Faith of Jesus Christ: The Narrative Substructure of Galatians 3:1–4:11.* 2d edition. Grand Rapids: Eerdmans, 2002.

Hauerwas, Stanley. "The Politics of Freedom: Why Freedom of Religion is a Subtle Temptation." Pages 69–92 in *After Christendom? How the Church is to Behave if Freedom, Justice, and a Christian Nation Are Bad Ideas.* Nashville: Abingdon, 1991.

Heron, Alasdair I. C. "*Homoousios* with the Father." Pages 58–87 in *The Incarnation: Ecumenical Studies in the Nicene-Constantinopolitan Creed A.D. 381.* Edited by Thomas F. Torrance. Edinburgh: Handsel, 1981.

Hooker, Morna D. "ΠΙΣΤΙΣ ΧΡΙΣΤΟΥ." *New Testament Studies* 35 (1989): 321–42.

Jewett, Robert. *Romans: A Commentary.* Assisted by Roy D. Kotansky. Hermeneia. Minneapolis: Fortress, 2007.

Lakoff, George. *Moral Politics: How Liberals and Conservatives Think.* 2d edition. Chicago: University of Chicago Press, 2002.

Lang, T. J. "Mystery and the Making of a Christian Historical Consciousness: From Paul to the Second Century." Ph.D. diss., Duke University, 2014.

Longenecker, Bruce W., ed., *Narrative Dynamics in Paul: A Critical Assessment.* Louisville, Ky.: Westminster John Knox, 2002.

Lührmann, Dieter. "Faith." Pages 2:744–60 in *Anchor Bible Dictionary.* 6 volumes. New York: Doubleday, 1992.

Macaskill, Grant. *Union with Christ in the New Testament.* Oxford: Oxford University Press, 2013.

Martyn, J. L. (Lou). "Epistemology at the Turn of the Ages: 2 Corinthians 5:16." Pages 89–110 in *Theological Issues in the Letters of Paul.* Edinburgh: T&T Clark, 1997 [1967].

———. *Galatians.* Anchor Bible 33A. New York: Doubleday, 1997.

Portier-Young, Anathea E. *Apocalypse against Empire: Theologies of Resistance in Early Judaism.* Grand Rapids: Eerdmans, 2011.

Reasoner, Mark. *The Strong and the Weak: Romans 14.1–15.13 in Context.* Society for New Testament Studies Monograph Series 103. Cambridge: Cambridge University Press, 1999.

Sanders, E.P. *Paul, the Law, and the Jewish People.* Philadelphia: Fortress, 1983.

Schnelle, Udo. *Apostle Paul: His Life and Theology.* Translated by M. Eugene Boring. Grand Rapids: Baker Academic, 2005 [2003].

Schreiner, Thomas R. *Paul, Apostle of God's Glory in Christ.* Downers Grove, Ill.: InterVarsity, 2001.

Thompson, Michael. *Clothed with Christ: The Example and Teaching of Jesus in Romans 12.1–15.13.* Journal for the Study of the New Testament Supplement Series 59; Sheffield: JSOT Press, 1991.

Torrance, Alan J. "The Trinity." Pages 72–91 in *The Cambridge Companion to Barth.* Edited by John Webster. Cambridge: Cambridge University Press, 2000.

Torrance, J. B. "Covenant and Contract: A Study of the Theological Background of Worship in Seventeenth-Century Scotland." *Scottish Journal of Theology* 23 (1970): 51–76.

Ware, James P., ed. *Synopsis of the Pauline Letters in Greek and English.* Grand Rapids: Baker Academic, 2010.

Metaphor, Reality, and Union with Christ

CONSTANTINE R. CAMPBELL

A. Introduction

One of the most compelling ways in which Paul expresses the union that believers have with Christ is through the use of corporate metaphors, such as body, temple and building, marriage, and clothing. In my monograph, *Paul and Union with Christ*,[1] I explored these metaphors with reference to Paul's conception of union, participation, identification, and incorporation ('union with Christ' is used as a shorthand for these concepts). The purpose of this essay is to explore further the ways in which Paul utilizes the phenomenon of metaphor to create, define, and evoke meaning. I will draw on the exegesis that is presented in *Paul and Union with Christ* and follow some of the trajectories coming out of that material. Rather than rehash the exegesis and conclusions of that previous work, I aim to explore some of the implications of Paul's fondness for metaphor, such as the ways in which he exploits the capacities of this creative feature of language. This will require some reflection on the nature of metaphor itself, but before turning to that it is worth reflecting briefly on the second item named in the title of this essay – "reality."

The essay title self-consciously references T. F. Torrance's *Reality and Evangelical Theology*, and while Torrance's thesis is only tangentially related to the present theme, he offers some useful insights for our investigation.[2] Torrance critiques modern biblical scholarship through his theory of

---

[1] Constantine R. Campbell, *Paul and Union with Christ: An Exegetical and Theological Study* (Grand Rapids: Zondervan, 2012).

[2] T. F. Torrance, *Reality and Evangelical Theology: The Realism of Christian Revelation* (Downers Grove: InterVarsity Press, 1982). The central thesis of Torrance's argument is based on his gleanings from modern science, that *realism* is the correct epistemological framework through which to view reality. He applies this realism to theological method, and pursues a number of its outworkings for evangelical theology, including the nature of truth, the nature of the Scriptures, and the correct principles undergirding theological formulation. With *realism*, Torrance seeks to repair "the ontological relation of the mind to reality, so that a structural kinship arises between human knowing and what is known" (p. 10). Realism is thus the rejoining of epistemology to ontology, such that it

language, arguing that the "intention of our thought does not terminate properly on ideas, far less on words or statements, but on things we intend through them."[3] This understanding of the function of language "conflicts rather sharply with that which seems to prevail widely in contemporary biblical scholarship, which is still tied up with an observationalist and phenomenalist approach."[4] Properly understood, language is a *transparent medium*, and the Scriptures are therefore "the *spectacles* through which we are brought to know the true God."[5] The signs employed by language are "ontologically controlled" by the realities they signify, but are necessarily not identical to their objects; to make such an identification would be an incorrect ultra-realism.[6] The resulting lesson for biblical scholars is that "real understanding arises where biblical statements refer us to what is true independently of them, so that in a profound sense genuine understanding begins where biblical statements leave off."[7] The relevance of Torrance to the burden of this essay is that we are concerned to study the linguistic power of metaphor for its correlation to actual reality. While metaphorical utterances are symbolic, they nevertheless bear some relation to real theological entities, while also not constituting such realities themselves.

B. The power of metaphor

Metaphor is an extraordinary feature of human language. The Greek word μεταφορά literally means "to carry over," and "refers to a particular set of linguistic processes whereby aspects of one object are 'carried over' or transferred to another object, so that the second object is spoken of as if it were the first."[8] This is the key to understanding the power of metaphor; through its use a speaker or writer can say that something *is* something it actually is not, but by doing so certain qualities of the second *something* are attributed to the first.[9] As Ricoeur claims, "metaphor is the rhetorical process by which discourse unleashes the power that certain fictions have

---

undercuts a dualist "relation between the empirical and theoretical ingredients on the structure of the real world and in our knowledge of it" (p. 60).

[3] *Reality and Evangelical Theology*, 63.
[4] *Reality and Evangelical Theology*, 63–64.
[5] *Reality and Evangelical Theology*, 64–65 [italics are original].
[6] *Reality and Evangelical Theology*, 66.
[7] *Reality and Evangelical Theology*, 68.
[8] Terence Hawkes, *Metaphor* (The Critical Idiom, volume 25; London: Methuen, 1972), 1.
[9] See J. David Sapir, "The Anatomy of Metaphor," in *The Social Use of Metaphor: Essays on the Anthropology of Rhetoric* (ed. J. David Sapir and J. Christopher Crocker; University of Pennsylvania Press, 1977), 9.

to redescribe reality."[10] Thus Paul says that the corporate fellowship of believers is the *body* of Christ. By ascribing the metaphor *body* to something that literally is *not* a physical body, certain qualities of the body are understood to define the fellowship of believers; these are "transferred" from the former to the latter. This *transference* is key to the success of metaphor.[11]

There is a long history of thinking about metaphor that is itself instructive. The diachronic development of reflection upon the phenomenon serves to undermine popular misconceptions about metaphor, thus it is helpful to survey briefly this history before further examining Paul's metaphorical language. To this end, we draw on the work of Terence Hawkes.[12]

Aristotle recognized that metaphor is the application to one thing of a name belonging to another thing.[13] While Aristotle had, on the one hand, a somewhat low view of metaphor, regarding it as a linguistic "added extra," like the "seasoning of the meat,"[14] he also recognized its capacity to convey new ideas: "strange words simply puzzle us; ordinary words convey only what we know already; it is from metaphor that we can best get hold of something fresh."[15]

According to Hawkes, the anonymous *Rhetorica ad Herennium* (c. 86 B.C.), the later works of Cicero, Quintilian, and others, reduce metaphor to a "decorative category" – a figure of speech. Thus, "it has no real claim to positive 'meaning' in its own right, since it works negatively by subverting the 'proper' meanings of words."[16] Metaphors are to be translated into "real meaning," as such they do not constitute real meaning in and of themselves.

---

[10] Paul Ricoeur, *The Rule of Metaphor: Multi-Disciplinary Studies of the Creation of Meaning in Language* (trans. Robert Czerny with Kathleen McLaughlin and John Costello; Toronto: University of Toronto Press, 1977), 7.

[11] While metaphor's cousins, *simile, synecdoche,* and *metonymy* also involve the notion of transference, these linguistic tools calibrate transference differently when compared to metaphor. *Simile* proposes transference and explains it by use of terms such as "like" or "as if." Synecdoche creates transference by taking a part of something to stand in place of the whole thing. *Metonymy* uses the name of a thing in place of something else with which it is associated. Metaphor, on the other hand, assumes that transference has already taken place. See Hawkes, *Metaphor*, 2–4. See also Ricoeur, *The Rule of Metaphor*, 55–59; Sapir, "The Anatomy of Metaphor," 4.

[12] Hawkes, *Metaphor*.

[13] Aristotle, *On the Art of Poetry*, in *Classical Literary Criticism* (trans. T. S. Dorsch; Penguin, 1965), chs. 21–25; Hawkes, *Metaphor*, 7.

[14] Aristotle, *Rhetoric* (trans. W. Rhys Roberts; Oxford, 1924), III, 1406a; Hawkes, *Metaphor*, 9.

[15] Aristotle, *Rhetoric*, III, 1410b; Hawkes, *Metaphor*, 10.

[16] Hawkes, *Metaphor*, 14. See also the classic study of Aristotle and metaphor in Ricoeur, *The Rule of Metaphor*, 9–43.

While the Middle Ages saw some formalized prescription about metaphor derived from the classical approach,[17] and the Renaissance period witnessed some interesting appropriations of metaphor through the work of Donne, Ramus, and Dryden,[18] it was the Romantic period that saw a major breakthrough in understanding the nature of metaphor. According to Hawkes, the significant shift in the appreciation of metaphor in this period is that it "is not fanciful 'embroidery' of the facts," but is "a way of *experiencing* the facts." "It is a way of thinking and of living; an imaginative projection of the truth."[19] Coleridge, in particular, conceived metaphor as "imagination in action," and in his essay on *The Tempest*, argued against the Aristotelian, mechanical, understanding of it.[20] He understood metaphor in terms of its relationship to its audience, taking into account the "imaginative response of those to whom the metaphor is addressed."[21] In the end, the mind and imagination are stretched by stretching reality through metaphor. Thus, for Coleridge, metaphor is not simply a way of conveying a pre-existent thought; it is rather a thought in its own right.[22]

This brings us to twentieth century views about metaphor. Having begun with Aristotle's somewhat low view of metaphor as an optional flavoring of language, the most recent phase of understanding has arrived at the opposite position. It is now believed that metaphor lies at the very heart of language: "*All* language, by the nature of its 'transferring' relation to 'reality' described above, is fundamentally metaphorical."[23] Metaphor is, as Ricoeur says, "the constitutive form of language."[24]

Indeed, all language consists of signs, or lexemes, and these are by and large arbitrary signs, without direct correspondence to the entities to which they point. This is illustrated by the Ogden-Richards triangle, which stresses the indirect relationship between a word and its referent.[25] As Silva summarizes, a word is a *symbol*; the mental content evoked by the symbol is the *sense*; and the *referent* is the extralinguistic thing denoted.[26] The important point here is that "the association of a particular word with a

---

[17] Hawkes, *Metaphor*, 16.
[18] Hawkes, *Metaphor*, 18–33.
[19] Hawkes, *Metaphor*, 39.
[20] Hawkes, *Metaphor*, 39.
[21] Hawkes, *Metaphor*, 49–50.
[22] Hawkes, *Metaphor*, 55.
[23] Hawkes, *Metaphor*, 60.
[24] Ricoeur, *The Rule of Metaphor*, 80.
[25] C. K. Ogden and I. A. Richards, *The Meaning of Meaning* (New York: Harcourt, Brace, 1945), 11.
[26] Moisés Silva, *Biblical Words and Their Meaning: An Introduction to Lexical Semantics* (Grand Rapids: Zondervan, 1983), 102.

particular meaning is *largely* arbitrary, a matter of convention."[27] There is no inherent connection between the symbol and its referent; the connection is made in the mind through association. The *sense* is where meaning can be found, and this sense brings together symbol and referent in the mind of the language-user.

Since the very nature of language involves the association of symbol to referent via the mentalistic process of association, all language is necessarily metaphorical. Metaphor involves the association of a thing with something that is not that thing – so too all language. As Hawkes says, "Indeed, all languages contain deeply embedded metaphorical structures which covertly influence overt 'meaning.' A language cannot be 'cleared' of metaphor without using a metaphor in the verb 'to clear.'"[28] Or, as Ricoeur says, "there is no discourse on metaphor that is not stated within a metaphorically engendered conceptual network. [...] Metaphor is metaphorically stated."[29] Rather than an embellishment of language that can be removed for the sake of "real" depiction, metaphor is an inescapable feature of language. It *is* the way language works.[30]

Furthermore, since all language operates through the linguistic-metaphorical process of association, metaphor is also the way in which new meanings are created. Again, this occurs through the mentalistic process of association. A symbol is employed in order to evoke some new referent, and consequently meaning is born. This creative power of linguistic-metaphor carries over to the literary phenomenon of metaphor. But in the latter case, metaphor employs a known symbol for a referent with which it is not normally associated. That is, a word such as *body* is used to refer to the collection of believers in Christ. That symbol, *body*, is not normally associated with that referent (that is, until Paul popularized the association). But by using the symbol for a referent other than its normal referent (or set of referents, in the case of homonyms), metaphor creates new meaning. The association of symbol with referent invents a new *sense* in the mind of the language-user.

Nevertheless, it is also true that metaphors, while always creative in the way that symbols are associated with unexpected referents, may point to material referents or irrealis referents. That is, the new sense that a meta-

---

[27] Silva, *Biblical Words*, 103–4.

[28] Hawkes, *Metaphor*, 60.

[29] Ricoeur, *The Rule of Metaphor*, 287.

[30] So Williams: "Metaphor lies at the very root of our language. All language, it seems, like the writing in which it is often expressed, began with the picture. Languages live by adding new pictures to old. It is probably true to say that most of our words started out as figures of speech that with use moved from the category of conscious metaphor into the ranks of ordinary words." David J. Williams, *Paul's Metaphors: Their Context and Character* (Peabody, Mass.: Hendrickson, 1999), 2.

phor creates can be associated with an item in reality or unreality – the latter does not refer to an actual entity; the metaphor's "creation" exists only in the mind. This second capability is what people somewhat clumsily refer to as "just a metaphor." This colloquial phrase means that the metaphor does not point to a material reality, but only an imagined, or abstract, one. The reason this is a clumsy expression is that metaphors can point to actual realities *or* imagined ones. Thus, "just a metaphor" is an idiomatic way of indicating the second type of metaphor.

One of the common questions about Paul's use of metaphor is whether or not his metaphors indicate "real" things, or are "just metaphorical." To use the example cited above, is there really such a thing as the "body of Christ," or is it "just a metaphor"? Obviously the referent of that metaphor – the church of Jesus Christ, or the people of God in Christ – is real, but is it really a *body*? In fact, this is difficult to answer. It depends on whether or not "body" is understood literally, or if the metaphorical meaning of body has become so widely used in its metaphorical capacity that it is now permanently associated with its new referent. If the latter, then the church really is a body, since "body" now refers to that corporate entity, not only an anatomical body.

This type of question, and others like it, are of interest in this essay. I am interested in what Paul is "doing" with metaphor; how his metaphors create new meaning through new associations; whether or not these new meanings refer to "real" things, or only abstract, imagined notions; and how metaphor informs and constructs his conception of union with Christ. As mentioned in the introduction, these questions will be explored by drawing on the exegesis and conclusions from *Paul and Union with Christ*, to which we now turn.

C. Paul's corporate metaphors

The Pauline metaphors examined in *Paul and Union with Christ* are "body," "temple" and "building," "marriage," and "clothing."[31] With the exception of the last, these are corporate in nature, referring collectively to the people of Christ (though "temple" can also refer to individuals). Before approaching the questions of interest in this essay, we will review the major conclusions reached about each of these metaphors in chapter 7 of *Paul and Union with Christ*.

---

[31] *Paul and Union with Christ*, chapter 7.

I. Body

From the numerous instances of the metaphorical use of σῶμα,[32] it is clear that the metaphor *body* or *body of Christ* is a rich one.[33] The body is an organic being that is one in Christ, ever growing and maturing. The oneness of the body emphasizes the fact that believers are joined to each other because they partake in Christ. Yet the diversity of the body, with its many parts, underscore the importance of differing gifts and roles among its members, all for the sake of serving the unity of the body as it grows and is built up. Christ is the head of the body, from whom and into whom the body grows by the work of God. While the body is "in Christ," he retains his own distinctiveness as its head.

II. Temple and Building

The metaphors of temple and building convey the corporate nature of the church (with one exception).[34] The people of God are regarded as the new temple, indwelt by the Holy Spirit, so that the congregation has superseded the physical construction of the temple. The people of God are also described metaphorically as a building, of which Christ is the foundation upon which Paul builds as a master builder. Temple and building are connected metaphors, explicitly so in Ephesians 2:21–22, which also depicts a trinitarian image of God's purposes for his people.

III. Marriage

At most, there are only four occasions in which Paul employs the metaphor of marriage to depict the relationship between Christ and his people.[35] In spite of its relative infrequency, Paul presses this metaphor for a profound and informative depiction of union with Christ. It is a personal metaphor due to the intimate nature of the one-flesh union of marriage. It preserves the distinctive identities of Christ and church as husband and wife, avoiding unhelpful theories of union in which identities are blurred. The metaphor underpins certain ethical constraints and underscores the grace of Christ.

---

[32] Rom 12:4–5; 1 Cor 6:15–16; 10:16–17; 11:29; 12:12–27; Eph 1:22–23; 2:14–16; 4:4; 4:11–13; 4:15–16; 5:23; 5:29–30; Col 1:18, 24; 2:19; 3:15.

[33] These summarized conclusions are from *Paul and Union with Christ*, 287–89.

[34] These summarized conclusions are from *Paul and Union with Christ*, 297–98. See 1 Cor 3:16–17; 6:19–20; 2 Cor 6:16; Eph 2:21–22; 1 Cor 3:9; 2 Cor 5:1. While employing the language involved with these metaphors, 1 Cor 9:13 and 2 Thess 2:4 are not regarded relevant (see *Paul and Union with Christ*, 294).

[35] These summarized conclusions are from *Paul and Union with Christ*, 309–10. See Rom 7:1–4; 1 Cor 6:15–17; 2 Cor 11:2–3; Eph 5:22–23.

IV. New Clothing

The metaphor of clothing has three main uses.[36] First, language of *putting on* is used in ethical contexts, referring to the adoption of appropriate characteristics. Second, the metaphor can refer to the transformation of mortal bodies into immortal at the *parousia*. Third, it sometimes refers to the permanent and current spiritual state of believers; they have put on Christ, which refers to their conversion. The first and third of these uses of the clothing metaphor can be correlated in terms of living out the spiritual reality that believers enjoy. That is, being clothed with Christ is the permanent spiritual reality of all believers, and putting on Christ is the ongoing ethical requirement that applies this reality to daily life.

D. Creating meaning

Having summarized the major conclusions of *Paul and Union with Christ* with respect to these Pauline metaphors, we turn now to the major interests of the essay. We will explore Paul's use of each metaphor through three lenses: metaphor as the creation of new meaning; metaphor as pointing to spiritual reality; metaphor as pointing to material reality. Each of these lenses will then be considered in relation to union with Christ. The first lens to be applied is metaphor as the creation of new meaning.

I. Body

In Romans 12:4–5 Paul uses the body metaphor to stress the importance of diversity and unity in the church. A body has parts, and these do not all have the same function – so too the body in Christ. The metaphor evokes a "visual image" of the church in which its oneness and its diversity are immediately obvious: a body is, by necessity, one; and yet a body includes many distinct parts within its oneness. These realities are immediately obvious upon visualization of the metaphor and do not require argumentation. The power of the metaphor in this instance, then, is that the *essential* unity and diversity of the church is asserted. One might argue for the legitimacy of both of these qualities of the church through other means, but by use of metaphor, they are simply asserted. The new thought created by metaphor is that unity and diversity are undeniable features of the church.[37]

---

[36] These summarized conclusions are from *Paul and Union with Christ*, 320–23. See Rom 13:12–14; 1 Cor 15:51–54; 2 Cor 5:1–4; Gal 3:26–27; Col 3:9–10, 12; Eph 4:20–24; 6:10.

[37] By speaking of "new thought," I do not claim that Paul has invented such thought, but that the creation of meaning is part of the power of metaphor. Indeed, Elliott and

In 1 Corinthians 12:12–27, Paul develops the body metaphor further and provides his most extended account of it. The main point of this extended discussion is again to stress the essential unity and diversity of the church, as with Romans 12:4–5, above.[38] In this use of the metaphor, however, there is yet new thought created. In 1 Corinthians 12:12, Paul equates the metaphor of the body with its oneness and many parts to *Christ himself*: "For as the body is one and has many parts, and all the parts of that body, though many, are one body – so also is Christ." He then proceeds to refer the metaphor to the church (12:13–26), and concludes the section by saying that believers are the body: "Now you are the body of Christ, and individual members of it" (12:27). In effect, Paul has assigned two referents to the same metaphor. *Christ* is "body;" and *believers* constitute the "body." By manipulating the metaphor in this way, Paul creates the thought that Christ is essentially correlated to the church. To partake in the body of the Christ – meaning the church – is to partake in Christ himself. Thus the metaphor offers a profound insight into our union with Christ and its corporate nature.

In 1 Corinthians 10:16–17 Paul states that all who share in the one bread (of the Lord's supper) are one body. In this case, there are two metaphors involved. First, the bread *is* Christ's body, and this is most likely a reference to his actual, physical body given to death on the cross (in parallel to his blood, also mentioned in this passage). Second, all who share in this one bread are one body – in this case the body refers to the church, not Christ's physical body. While the issue of unity and diversity is again in view here ("we who are many are one body"), by correlating the metaphor of body with the metaphorical nature of the bread, Paul creates a new thought: "partaking in the 'bread' that is Christ's body actually *produces* the body."[39] In this way, one symbol is used to enforce another: the communal sharing of bread is a metaphorical depiction of sharing together in the body of Christ. Thus believers who share bread metaphorically declare their union with Christ and each other.

In Ephesians 1:22–23, we witness the introduction of a new twist on the body metaphor: Christ is the *head* of the body.[40] Just as the original use of

---

Reasoner suggest that "the trope would have been instantly familiar to Paul's contemporaries, among whom the plea to act as a single body was a well-worn argument for political cohesion and cooperation." *Documents and Images for the Study of Paul* (Minneapolis: Fortress, 2011), 293–95.

[38] Though the metaphor no doubt has wider significance than this too, as Wright claims, it is "one of Paul's two or three most potent symbolic [...] statements of his entire worldview." *Paul and the Faithfulness of God* (Minneapolis: Fortress, 2013), 396.

[39] *Paul and Union with Christ*, 271.

[40] Macaskill wonders if the introduction of κεφαλή ("head") to the body metaphor might bear some relationship to the temple metaphor through an interesting connection in

the body metaphor creates an immediate visualization of oneness and diversity, so now the metaphor of "head" and "body" evokes a different visualization, and thus the creation of new thought. In fact, Christ as head creates several thoughts. First is the notion of authority – the head of the body is, well, the *head*. Second, Christ as head preserves the distinction between Christ and his people; though they are united and are one body together, nevertheless Christ remains Christ and his people remain his people. Third, though the head is distinct from the rest of the body, the head is nevertheless a member of the body, as are all other members. Thus, the introduction of "head" to the "body" metaphor enables Paul to assert the distinctive authority of Christ all the while affirming the union that believers share with him.[41]

One of the most interesting passages for the ways in which Paul uses the metaphor of body to create new meaning is found in Ephesians 4:11–16. The diversity of the body is accentuated through the list of various gifts to the church: apostles, prophets, evangelists, and pastor-teachers (4:11). These gifts are for the purpose of training the saints for service and for building the body (4:12). The next verse indicates one of the goals of this training and building: so that *we all reach unity in the faith* (4:13). Before discussing 4:15–16, it is worth pausing to reflect on what is happening. The most striking feature of Paul's use of the metaphor here is that the diversity of the body *serves* the unity of the body. That is, the various parts of the church – apostles, prophets, *et al* – function to bring about unity. This is an interesting application of the metaphor that further underscores the necessity of the diversity of the body for the sake of its unity. While I would suggest that such a notion is probably not an immediately obvious corollary of the body metaphor, once it has been suggested it becomes self-evident. Of course it is true that a human body depends upon its diversity; it cannot function without its parts. But how much does the *oneness* of a body depend upon its parts? If anything, we might reason that the situation is, in fact, the reverse: the parts of the body depend upon its oneness, since the parts can only function if connected to the whole. A foot can contribute nothing once amputated. The answer to this question, however, is indicated in 4:16, in which Paul says that the body is *fitted and knit together by every supporting ligament*. If we regard some parts of the body as "supporting ligaments," then it becomes clear that parts of the body facilitate the oneness of the body. Without such parts, the body simply cannot hang togeth-

---

LXX Psalm 118 (177):22, in which the rejected stone becomes εἰς κεφαλὴν γωνίας; Grant Macaskill, *Union with Christ in the New Testament* (Oxford: Oxford University Press, 2013), 154.

[41] For Ridderbos' objection to an anatomical correlation between head and body, and my response to his objection, see *Paul and Union with Christ*, 275, n. 16.

er. Once we grasp that (now) self-evident reality, the body metaphor causes us to visualize the essential integrity of diversity within the church.

Another striking feature of Paul's use of the body metaphor in this passage is how he describes it as being *built up* (4:12; εἰς οἰκοδομὴν τοῦ σώματος τοῦ Χριστοῦ). The strangeness of the collocation of *body* with *building* is probably missed by many readers, since we are now so familiar with Paul's language of building, interpreted as edification. We also have the modern phenomenon of *bodybuilding*. But, in actual fact, οἰκοδομή has no natural kinship with σῶμα, at least not literally. *Building* refers to the construction of a building or edifice. A body is not literally *built*. A body *grows*. It is an organic entity. By using the language of *building* with reference to the body, Paul creates new meaning in the mind of the reader. We are reminded that the reality to which the metaphor points – the people of Christ – is not fully expounded through the one metaphor. Certainly the *body* is a highly versatile and useful metaphor to get at various features of the church, but the use of building language evokes other images that contribute to the overall picture. The most obvious image is that of the temple. Paul elsewhere of course describes the church as the temple of God (which is one of the metaphors to be explored below), and the reference here to *building* the body subtly evokes such imagery.

Another image that this manipulation of the body metaphor creates is that those gifts to the church – apostles, prophets, *et al* – are workers who *build*. One of the limitations of the body metaphor is that a body is organic – it grows by itself; you cannot build it. While the church grows (by the growth given by God), it is also built. It is built by God through the work of his gifts to the church. This then causes us to visualize workers bringing about this construction or edifice through their labors. Hence the importance of these diverse gifts to the body is once again accentuated.

In Ephesians 4:15–16, Paul again manipulates the body metaphor to create yet new meaning. It is striking that he exhorts the body to grow *into* Christ, the head, while also affirming that the body grows *from* Christ. Clearly he is stretching the metaphor beyond its anatomical limits, and does so for the sake of conveying certain concepts.[42] To speak of growing *into* the head likely refers to growing in conformity to Christ. Growing *from* Christ reinforces the fact that Christ is the source of his body (see also Col 2:19). He establishes the church and stimulates its growth. The image that the reader is caused to visualize is somewhat absurd – a head with a body growing out of it, which simultaneously is growing *into* it – but the affect is to spur a profound, new thought about the body, in which its goal for growth (conformity to Christ) and its source for growth are underscored.

---

[42] *Paul and Union with Christ*, 281.

From this survey of key passages employing the body metaphor, we witness Paul's masterful capacity to create new meanings by manipulation of the metaphor. By pushing and pulling it, by stretching it beyond anatomical plausibility, and by juxtaposing it within unnatural collocations, Paul provides new insights into our corporate union with Christ. The body is one in Christ, yet distinct from him, with many essentially different parts, growing from Christ and into him, and is at once one with the head and under his authority.

II. Temple and Building

We turn now to consider the ways in which Paul uses the metaphors of temple and building to create new insights into our union with Christ.

In 1 Corinthians 3:16–17, Paul calls his readers God's temple in which the Spirit lives. From 3:10, Paul has been developing the idea of how God's servants are to "build," leading to the notion that the Corinthians are a "building," namely the temple. The designation of the temple metaphor to the Corinthians points to two corollaries. First, the Spirit of God indwells the temple of God. The Spirit is the means through whom God dwells with his people in the temple. Second, God's temple is holy, thus Paul is able to assert the Corinthians' holiness. While the fact that the Spirit indwells the Corinthian congregation is not a new thought, nor is their holiness, the temple metaphor casts a vision of the church's identity in such a way as to reinforce those notions as inevitable consequences of their identity in Christ.

Paul again refers to the Corinthians as a temple in 1 Corinthians 6:19–20, but in this instance the metaphor is assigned to individuals' bodies.[43] As Spatafora argues, this idea of each individual's body being a temple of the Spirit is not parallel to the Stoics' belief that "the individual was, in himself, the temple of God." Rather, because believers are members of the church, they "share in the nature of the whole."[44] The notion of "sharing in the nature of the whole" is conveyed by Paul's use of the temple metaphor with the twin application toward the congregation (3:16–17) and the individual (6:19–20). As suggested above with reference to the former passage, an essential element for the success of the temple metaphor is the presence of the Spirit of God. God indwells his temple by the Spirit – and

---

[43] Constantine R. Campbell, "From Earthly Symbol to Heavenly Reality: The Tabernacle in the New Testament," in *Exploring Exodus: Literary, Theological and Contemporary Approaches* (ed. Brian S. Rosner and Paul R. Williamson; Nottingham: Apollos, 2008), 185; *Paul and Union with Christ*, 291.

[44] Andrea Spatafora, *From the "Temple of God" to God as the Temple: A Biblical Theological Study of the Temple in the Book of Revelation* (Rome: Gregorian University Press, 1997), 117, n. 101.

since the Spirit indwells God's people, the people are called the temple. Having established the corporate application of the temple metaphor to the people of God because of their indwelling of the Spirit, so the metaphor is stretched to extend to individuals. It is the fact of the indwelling of the Spirit that allows the temple metaphor to be applied to individuals as well as to the corporate entity; he dwells among the people and he dwells within each person. While this might seem natural to the ears of modern individualism, and indeed to ancient Stoicism, it is not inherently natural in light of the Jewish corporate roots of Christianity. Thus we witness the temple metaphor employed for the creation of genuinely new thought.

Similar to 1 Corinthians 3:16–17, 2 Corinthians 6:16 again indicates that the corporate people of Christ constitute "the temple of the living God." The new thought evoked by this use of the temple metaphor is that Paul depicts it as the fulfillment of a catena of Old Testament texts (Lev 26:12; Jer 32:38; Ezek 37:27) that speak of God's dwelling among his people. Thus, it appears that the dwelling of God with his people is the key factor in portraying the people as a temple.[45]

In Ephesians 2:21–22, Paul speaks of God's people as growing into a holy temple in the Lord. There are three significant ways in which Paul creates new meaning through use of the temple metaphor. First, the temple metaphor explicitly conveys the incorporation of God's people into Christ. They are put together in him; they grow into a temple in the Lord; they are built together; in him they are built together. Since Christ himself is the cornerstone of this edifice (2:20), the metaphor creates the notion that believers are *built into* the dwelling place of God. The structure begins with Christ, and through union with him others become part of it. Second, the use of the metaphor is dynamic – it is a building in progress – which creates the sense that the work of incorporating into Christ is an ongoing project. Not that an individual's incorporation into Christ is unfinished, but that the collective nature of the project remains yet incomplete. More people are to be built in. Third, the metaphor evokes new meaning when Paul says that it *grows* (αὔξει; 2:21). This organic language does not literally fit the description of a temple building, but is used metaphorically to depict an organic, growing entity rather than a static, monolithic structure. In this way, Paul's use of the metaphor is a mirror-image of the body metaphor in 4:12 (discussed above), in which the body – an organic image for the people of Christ – is described as being *built up*, as though it is a building. The mixing of metaphors across both 4:12 and 2:21 indicates Paul's predilection to stretch meaning in order to convey the desired sense.

---

[45] *Paul and Union with Christ*, 292. See also Wright, *Paul and the Faithfulness of God*, 713–15.

In 1 Corinthians 3:9, Paul abruptly switches from the metaphor of a field to that of a building: "You are God's field. God's building." Having described church growth using farming imagery in 3:6–8, the switch from "field" to "building" allows Paul to explore a different perspective on the matter with reference to church "building" on the foundation of Jesus Christ. Two things stand out here. First, the abrupt switch from one metaphor to another in itself serves to create meaning. It produces a double evocation in which certain qualities of a field are attributed to the church, which are then immediately juxtaposed against certain qualities of a building. Second, the notion of incorporation is produced through the building metaphor as it is in Ephesians 2:21–22, but it is achieved differently here. Rather than relying on the prepositional phrases seen in that passage, here the very idea of building upon the foundation of Jesus Christ necessarily implies incorporation. The metaphor necessitates incorporation since a foundation must be integrated with the structure of which it is a part.[46]

Paul's usage of the temple and building metaphors demonstrates his ability as a "master builder" of meaning through metaphor. By evoking the image of the temple, Paul can assert that the Spirit of God dwells among his people, and that this people are holy – as the temple is holy. Furthermore, the metaphor can be applied corporately and individually to get at different aspects of the Spirit's indwelling. The temple can also be viewed organically as an entity that "grows." Finally, incorporation into Christ is achieved by virtue of the building being built on the foundation of Christ.

III. Marriage

We turn now to consider the ways in which Paul employs the metaphor of marriage to create new meaning.

The metaphor of marriage is arguably implied in Romans 7:1–4, in which Paul draws on the legalities of marriage to outline the believer's relationship with the Mosaic law.[47] Believers "were put to death in relation to the law through the crucified body of the Messiah so that you might belong to another" (7:4). The phrase "so that you may belong to another" most likely indicates marriage, since marriage has already been invoked in the passage (7:1–3). Paul therefore uses the metaphor of marriage to indicate the manner in which believers belong to Christ. Their belonging to him characterizes the pledge of marriage.

In Ephesians 5:22–32, we witness Paul's most explicit application of the marriage metaphor, in which he explains the nature of human marriage by

---

[46] *Paul and Union with Christ*, 295.

[47] For a discussion of the various complexities of this passage, see *Paul and Union with Christ*, 299–301.

reference to the divine marriage between Christ and the church, both of which are grounded in the prototypical marriage of Adam and Eve. This use of the metaphor conveys profound new meaning for understanding our union with Christ. It is a one-flesh union, which is personal and intimate. And yet the distinctions between Christ and the church are not obliterated, since Christ remains head of the body. Furthermore, the metaphor asserts much about how our union with Christ is mediated; contra mystical disciplines or spiritual practices, the marriage is prepared by Christ (5:25–27).[48]

Paul's use of the metaphor of marriage creates new meaning as the nature of marriage informs the nature of our relationship with Christ. Believers belong to him as a wife to her husband, and their union is intimate, personal, and prepared by Christ. Their union preserves the distinctions between husband and wife.

IV. Clothing

Paul can refer to Christ as a metaphorical garment that believers must put on. This metaphor stands out from the others surveyed in two distinct, but related, ways. First, Christ must be "put on," while the other metaphors indicate a spiritual reality that simply *is*. Second, while the other metaphors imply permanent status, the clothing metaphor is not inherently permanent.[49]

In Romans 13:12–14, Paul encourages his readers to "put on" the armor of light and to "put on" the Lord Jesus Christ, and in so doing they are to make no plans to satisfy fleshly desires. Clearly then, this use of the clothing metaphor is ethical in nature. In this way, the use of the metaphor creates the meaning that believers are to be defined in some way by their "wearing" of Christ.

In 1 Corinthians 15:53–54, Paul uses the clothing metaphor to depict the transformation of believers' bodies from corruptible to incorruptible and mortal to immortal. This remarkable use of the metaphor creates new meaning in that the old state of being is "overcome" or "swallowed up" by the new; the new garment is laid over the old. Furthermore, the context indicates that it points to a future condition rather than present, and a state of affairs rather than ethical injunction.[50]

In Galatians 3:26–27, however, the application of the metaphor is a little different. Paul says that "as many of you as have been baptized into Christ have put on Christ." So in this case putting on Christ is apparently parallel to being baptized into Christ, which is most likely a reference to

---

[48] *Paul and Union with Christ*, 306–9.
[49] *Paul and Union with Christ*, 310–11.
[50] *Paul and Union with Christ*, 313–14.

conversion. As such, the clothing metaphor does not necessarily indicate impermanence or even volition; it is a fact derived from conversion. Thus Christ defines believers as clothing defines the appearance of a person.

The clothing metaphor is used a little differently again in Colossians 3:9–10, in which Paul says that believers have put off the old self and have put on the new self, which is being renewed in according to the image of the creator. Whereas in Galatians 3:26–27 (above) it is Christ himself who has been "put on," here the "new self" most likely refers to the person reconstituted in Christ (cf. 3:3). That the believer is to be understood as "wearing" his or her "new person in Christ" is a fascinating use of the metaphor that once again creates new meaning.

Paul's employment of the clothing metaphor is more elastic than others. He can use it for ethical purposes, so that behavioral characteristics are "put on"; it can refer to the transformation of mortal to immortal; and it can refer to the permanent spiritual state of believers.[51] The metaphor is also more opaque than others, in that it is not entirely clear what Paul means by putting on Christ. He does not elaborate, which is part of the power (and difficulty) of the metaphor. While the suggestions of Wikenhauser and Wedderburn are worthy of consideration,[52] most likely Kim is correct in that the clothing metaphor is a symbol for union with Christ that entails ethical conformity to Christ.[53]

Suffice to say there is extraordinary creative power in Paul's use of metaphor. Exploration of each metaphor reveals the creation of new thought that enables Paul to envisage believers' corporate and individual union with Christ in ways that would be difficult, if not impossible, without the tool of metaphor. The creative qualities of metaphor provide a rich and fascinating account of union with Christ.

Inevitably, however, the creative facets of metaphor raise the question of reality. If metaphor is used to invent new meaning, does it correspond to reality? And if so, how? Does not the very notion of "new meaning" imply that it has no direct correlation to the real world? It is to these questions we now turn.

---

[51] *Paul and Union with Christ*, 320–21.

[52] Wikenhauser suggests that Paul is referring to Christ as a heavenly robe that enables believers to enter a new world; Alfred Wikenhauser, *Pauline Mysticism: Christ in the Mystical Teaching of St. Paul* (trans. Joseph Cunnigham; Freiburg: Herder and Herder, 1960), 32. Wedderburn argues that the imagery is taken from priestly garb of the ancient world, which symbolizes dedication and belonging; A. J. M. Wedderburn, *Baptism and Resurrection: Studies in Pauline Theology against Its Graeco-Roman Background* (WUNT 44; Tübingen: Mohr, 1987), 337.

[53] Jung Hoon Kim, *The Significance of Clothing Imagery in the Pauline Corpus* (JSNTSup 268; London: T&T Clark, 2004), 225.

E. Spiritual Reality

As discussed in §B above, a major question regarding Paul's use of metaphors and their relationship to union with Christ is whether or not it is "just metaphorical." What, if any, correspondence do such metaphors have with reality? In the following discussion of "reality," we will adhere to the distinction between *spiritual* and *material* realities. It should be uncontroversial to assert that for Paul, *spiritual* reality is no less "real" than *material* reality, if the latter is defined as whatever is pertaining to the material world. Thus, when we ask whether or not Paul's metaphors correspond to reality, this ought to be addressed in two stages – reality in the spiritual realm and reality in the material realm. We will first consider *spiritual* reality, and will proceed by exploring each metaphor again in turn.

I. Body

An interesting text with which to begin is 1 Corinthians 6:15–16. Here Paul asserts that believers' bodies are "members of Christ" (6:15; τὰ σώματα ὑμῶν μέλη Χριστοῦ ἐστιν). While he does not explicitly mention the body of Christ (but rather bodies of believers), the language of "members" (μέλη) evokes it.[54] The fascinating element that this passage contributes to our discussion is that there is a definite reality to which Paul appeals. Paul asks whether members of Christ should be made members of a prostitute (ἄρας οὖν τὰ μέλη τοῦ Χριστοῦ ποιήσω πόρνης μέλη), followed by a strong negative answer (μὴ γένοιτο). One the one hand, there is a clear reference to *material* reality, since Paul is talking about sex with a prostitute – in that respect, we will also discuss this passage in the following section of this essay. On the other hand, there is also a clear reference to *spiritual* reality, since the reality of believers' bodies being members of Christ is the reason they should not be joined to a prostitute. If the metaphor of being members of Christ's body were *merely* metaphorical, Paul's injunction here would make little sense. This passage then gives us some of the strongest evidence that the metaphor of the body of Christ is not *mere* metaphor; it corresponds to a real spiritual situation.

Another interesting example of the body metaphor indicating a spiritual reality is 1 Corinthians 10:16–17 in which Paul indicates that participation in the Lord's supper has real spiritual implications. Addressing the issue of whether or not believers should eat food sacrificed to idols, Paul argues that though idols are nothing, "the sacrifices of pagans are offered to demons, not to God, and I do not want you to be participants with demons" (10:20; NIV). He then goes on to say that they cannot drink the cup of the

---

[54] *Paul and Union with Christ*, 270.

Lord and the cup of demons too, nor have a part in the Lord's table and that of demons (10:21). This is the conclusion of Paul's ethical point here, but it is grounded in the fact that sharing in the "body of Christ" (probably referring to his physical body given in death, in 10:16) in the Lord's Supper, which constitutes the "one body" (referring to the community of Christ's people, in 10:17), points to a real spiritual situation. Participating in the body of Christ is not mere metaphor: it is a spiritual reality that has consequences for believers' actions in the physical world.

A similar, though less explicit, example is found in 1 Corinthians 11:29, in which Paul warns that whosoever eats and drinks without recognizing the body brings judgment on himself. While it is genuinely ambiguous in this context as to whether Paul is referring to Christ's physical body or to the community of believers,[55] it may in fact constitute a double entendre.[56] If so, Paul appeals to the spiritual reality of the body of Christ (as community) for the sake of proper conduct of the Lord's Supper.

In Ephesians 4:11–13, Paul lists gifts given to the church for the sake of training the saints in the work of ministry and for building the body of Christ. The building of Christ's body is until we all reach unity in the faith (4:13; μέχρι καταντήσωμεν οἱ πάντες εἰς τὴν ἑνότητα τῆς πίστεως). The fact that this unity is for *all* indicates that Paul regards the body as constituting more than just the readership of Ephesians. In other words, the body includes all believers. This, together with the reference to the body being built by works of service, seems to indicate that the body is not merely metaphorical. There is a spiritual reality to which the body of Christ refers; it is wider than one location (hence it is spiritual not only material) and yet it can be built up by real actions in the material world.

Evidently Paul's usage of the body metaphor is not only able to create new meaning, but also refers to a real spiritual entity. The body of Christ is the universal collective of Christ's people – transcending geographical location (and time). The transcendental nature of the church signals its spiritual nature. This spiritual reality is to inform believers' actions and attitudes. So, the metaphor "is yet much more than a metaphor because of the Messiah's real identification with his people, the Pauline pictures of the church as the new humanity, the true Israel, the historical and visible people of God."[57]

---

[55] Sang-Won (Aaron) Son, *Corporate Elements in Pauline Anthropology: A Study of Selected Terms, Idioms, and Concepts in the Light of Paul's Usage and Background* (AnBib 148; Rome: Editrice Pontificio Istituto Biblico, 2001), 91–92.

[56] C. F. D. Moule, *The Origin of Christianity* (Cambridge: Cambridge University Press, 1977), 73.

[57] N. T. Wright, *Pauline Perspectives: Essays on Paul 1978–2013* (Minneapolis: Fortress, 2013), 13.

II. Temple and Building

The way in which Paul uses the temple metaphor to define the identity of believers in 1 Corinthians 3:16–17 indicates the reality to which the metaphor refers. He employs the metaphor to assert the presence of the Spirit among God's people, and the fact that they are holy (see on this passage, above). Both assertions require a real referent for the metaphor. The dwelling of the Spirit would be nonsensical if the temple did not have an actual referent in reality. Likewise the claim that the temple is holy would make little sense if not for a real referent. Since the passage deals with spiritual entities – the Spirit and holiness – it is clear that the referent of the temple metaphor is also spiritual, but nonetheless real. In addition, the temple constitutes a fulfillment motif (see on 2 Corinthians 6:16, above), thus making it impossible to view it as mere metaphor. As Wright says,

> There is no mistaking the point. This is no mere metaphor, a random image culled from Paul's fertile imagination. No ex-Pharisee could write this without intending to say that the founding and building up of the church through the gospel constituted the long-awaited rebuilding of the Temple, and that *the indwelling of the spirit constituted the long-awaited return of YHWH to Zion.*[58]

The second reference in 1 Corinthians in which Paul uses the temple metaphor for God's people is found in 6:19. As noted above, however, in this instance Paul refers to individuals' bodies as a temple of the Holy Spirit. Clearly the temple metaphor has a material referent – the physical body – but it also has a spiritual dimension since the body is the abode of the Spirit. The spiritual reality of the indwelling of the Spirit in individuals' bodies is the referent of the temple metaphor, so that Wright can say, "To sin against the body is to deface the divine Temple, to ignore Shekinah who, in shocking fulfilment of ancient promises, has returned to dwell in that Temple at last."[59]

The same argument applies to Ephesians 2:21–22, in which the trinitarian nature of the temple again indicates a real spiritual referent for the metaphor. The building is being built by Christ for God's dwelling in the Spirit.[60] The fact that the temple is being built, and is the location for the indwelling Spirit, points to the spiritual reality of the referent – neither of which facts would make sense apart from reality.

As with the body metaphor, the temple and building metaphors point to a real spiritual referent, namely the dwelling of God within the people of

---

[58] Wright, *Paul and the Faithfulness of God*, 712 [italics are original]. See also p. 1074.

[59] Wright, *Paul and the Faithfulness of God*, 713.

[60] *Paul and Union with Christ*, 292–94. See also Macaskill, *Union with Christ in the New Testament*, 151.

Christ. God indwells his temple by the Spirit, and so the temple is holy, constituted of the collective people of Christ as well as each individual within it. "The spirit-filled sanctuary [...] is a metaphor of stability, abundance, and holiness. It subordinates individual liberties to the communal breath as a whole."[61]

III. Marriage

In 2 Corinthians 11:2–3, Paul uses the marriage metaphor to undergird his concern that believers remain devoted to Christ. Notwithstanding this passage's complexities,[62] it is clear that the marriage metaphor refers to a spiritual reality of betrothal to Christ. Paul's concern is that the Corinthians may be led astray by someone preaching a different Jesus, a different Spirit, or a different gospel. His concern is obviously spiritual. To be tempted away from the Jesus, Spirit and gospel they first received is spiritual adultery. Consequently, the marriage metaphor has a real spiritual referent, namely pure devotion to Christ.

In Ephesians 5:22–32, Paul's extended use of the marriage metaphor must also point to a real referent. The simple argument for this is that Paul is entirely comfortable to extrapolate out from the metaphor to provide instruction to husbands and wives. It would hardly seem appropriate to model human marriages on something that Paul did not regard as an actual reality. As Paul indicates by the citation of Genesis 2:24 in 5:31 and his comment in 5:32, Christ and the church have been joined together in a spiritual, nuptial union.

The marriage metaphor demonstrates its real spiritual referent by virtue of the fact that it is instructive for Christian living. Faithfulness to Christ, and marital responsibilities between husbands and wives are grounded in the reality of believers' spiritual union with Christ.

IV. Clothing

In Galatians 3:26, Paul sees putting on Christ as a corollary of being baptized into Christ (ὅσοι γὰρ εἰς Χριστὸν ἐβαπτίσθητε, Χριστὸν ἐνεδύσασθε). Since baptism into Christ is a likely reference to conversion,[63] which of course Paul regards as "real," then it follows that the corollary of conversion – being clothed with Christ – is also regarded as "real." The referent of "wearing Christ" is spiritual in nature, but nonetheless real.

---

[61] John R. Levison, "The Spirit and Temple in Paul's Letters to the Corinthians," in *Paul and His Theology* (ed. Stanley E. Porter; Leiden: Brill, 2006), 207.
[62] See *Paul and Union with Christ*, 304–6.
[63] See *Paul and Union with Christ*, 384–87.

Since the referent of "putting on the new self" in Colossians 3:10 is the new life in union with Christ (as described above), it follows that the clothing metaphor ("putting on," ἐνδυσάμενοι) also points to a real spiritual reality. The new person reconstituted in Christ is a spiritual entity, but no less real in Paul's mind.

In Ephesians 4:20–24, putting on the new self is conceived a little differently. Here, Paul refers to learning from Christ *to put on the new self* (ἐνδύσασθαι τὸν καινὸν ἄνθρωπον), which does not refer to a pre-existing state (cf. Col 3:10), but refers to content taught by Christ for right behaviour.[64] However, the second part of 4:24 *does* refer to the pre-existing state of the new self, which is described as having been "created according to God's likeness in righteousness and purity of the truth." In other words, 5:24 refers both to the instruction to put on the new man, and the fact that the new man has already been created. Thus, the sense of 5:24 is that believers are to *be* what they already *are*. Consequently, the referent of the clothing metaphor must be a real one; the new self to be put on has been *created*, not merely imagined.

Being clothed with Christ is a corollary of conversion. Putting on the new self refers to the new life in Christ. And this new self has been created according to God's likeness. Doubtless Paul uses the clothing metaphor to refer to actual spiritual realities.

In several different ways, Paul employs metaphor to indicate spiritual realities. As we have observed, the body, temple and building, marriage, and clothing metaphors each have referents in reality. They are spiritual referents, but they are real. This, then, leads to our next question – do these metaphors point to real things in the *material* world? Are we dealing with spiritual realities only, or are there concrete referents also to be found? It is to this question we now turn.

F. Material reality

The distinction between *spiritual* and *material* reality is discussed in §E above, and as we continue now with the *material* member of that opposition, we come to the final stage of our investigation. Do Paul's incorporative metaphors, which are so richly instructive for understanding union with Christ, point to concrete referents in the material world? Consistent with the pattern thus far, we will proceed with reference to each metaphor in turn.

---

[64] For more on this, see *Paul and Union with Christ*, 319–20.

I. Body

Perhaps the most striking example of the body metaphor in relation to this question is 1 Corinthians 6:15–16. As discussed above, Paul asks whether members of Christ should be made members of a prostitute (ἄρας οὖν τὰ μέλη τοῦ Χριστοῦ ποιήσω πόρνης μέλη), followed by a strong negative answer (μὴ γένοιτο). There is a clear reference to *spiritual* reality since the fact of believers' bodies being members of Christ is the reason they should not be joined to a prostitute (see on this passage, §E above). There is also plain reference to *material* reality, since Paul is talking about sex with a prostitute. Sexual union with a prostitute creates a physical "membership" with her that is negatively analogous with spiritual membership with Christ. Because this passage also connects to the marriage metaphor, it will be discussed one last time below. For now, however, it is sufficient to recognize that the body metaphor here is associated with a real, material referent.

As discussed in §D above, in 1 Corinthians 12:12–27 Paul equates the body metaphor – with its oneness and many parts – to *Christ himself*: "For as the body is one and has many parts, and all the parts of that body, though many, are one body – so also is Christ." He then refers the metaphor to the church (12:13–26), indicating that believers are the body: "Now you are the body of Christ, and individual members of it" (12:27). In effect, Paul has assigned two referents to the same metaphor. Christ is "body," and believers constitute the "body." Thus, Paul's use of the metaphor correlates Christ to the church. As Son argues regarding 12:12, "the analogy is made here to Christ rather than to the church…. This is significant because it indicates not only that σῶμα is more than a mere metaphor but also that there exists a special relationship between Christ and the church."[65] In fact, Son's two points are necessarily related; it is because of this relationship between Christ and the church that the body metaphor cannot be *mere* metaphor. Since the body metaphor has double referents – Christ and the church – it follows that the nature of one referent might inform the other. Christ is best categorized as spiritual *and* material, due to his ascended, yet bodily-resurrected, state. So too, therefore, we should conclude that the church belongs to spiritual and material realms. While this claim probably requires further probing, it is safe to conclude that the body metaphor is capable of (a) material referent(s).

In Ephesians 4:11–13, Paul lists gifts given to the church for the sake of training the saints in the work of ministry and for building the body of Christ. The building of Christ's body is until we all reach unity in the faith (4:13; μέχρι καταντήσωμεν οἱ πάντες εἰς τὴν ἑνότητα τῆς πίστεως). As dis-

---

[65] Son, *Corporate Elements*, 85.

cussed in §E above, the fact that this unity is for *all* indicates that Paul regards the body as constituting more than just the readership of Ephesians; there is a wider spiritual reality to which the body of Christ refers. And yet, while the unity of the body is a spiritual reality, the fact that it is growing in order to *reach* unity, indicates that the body is not only spiritual. Its literal fleshly existence in the material world means that the spiritual oneness of the body is imperfectly experienced by the worldwide church.[66] In this way, the body metaphor necessarily has a material referent.

Furthermore, Macaskill points out the image of the church as the body of Christ "is identified very specifically with the actual body of Jesus and its history" because of Ephesians 2:15–16, in which Jew and Gentile are reconciled in one body to God through the cross.[67] This observation further develops the interconnection of metaphor with material reality.

These examples demonstrate that Paul's use of the body metaphor can refer to a material referent. Being a member of Christ's body means that it is wrong to become joined to a prostitute; Christ and his body are closely correlated; and the body is in a state of growth in this world. While the metaphor is powerful in its spiritual implications, it also has much to contribute to our understanding of union with Christ in the material, physical world.

II. Temple and Building

Both 1 Corinthians 3:16–17 and 6:19–20 clearly have material referents. As discussed a couple of times now, these passages refer to the indwelling of the Spirit in and among God's people. In the first passage, this is a corporate reality; the second refers to individuals. In both cases, real referents in the material world are necessary, since Paul is discussing the spiritual reality pertaining to real, flesh and blood people. The Spirit of God lives in *people*.

III. Marriage

As anticipated above in the body metaphor section, 1 Corinthians 6:15–17 provides a powerful example of the nexus between spiritual and material realities. With the citation of Genesis 2:24 (LXX), it is evident that Paul is discussing marriage, though normal marriage terminology ("husband," "wife," etc.) is absent. His point in this passage is that believers' union with Christ means that union with a prostitute is highly inappropriate. The

---

[66] *Paul and Union with Christ*, 279–81.

[67] Macaskill, *Union with Christ in the New Testament*, 152. Macaskill thereby claims that the body of Christ "is not a general metaphor for interconnection," whereas I would counter that metaphor and reality are not mutually exclusive.

spiritual reality of being "joined to the Lord" (ὁ δὲ κολλώμενος τῷ κυρίῳ) has serious consequences for what is done in the flesh. This then means that the "marriage" relationship to Christ is not merely metaphorical, and nor is it only a spiritual reality.[68] The spiritual reality is connected to the physical so that marriage to Christ precludes any kind of ungodly physical union.

IV. Clothing

In 1 Corinthians 15:51–54, the clothing metaphor is employed to refer to the future transformation that believers will undergo. The corruptible will be clothed with incorruptibility, and what is mortal with immortality. While this use of the clothing metaphor differs from others so far observed, it is nevertheless tied to the theme of union with Christ. In 15:49, Paul refers to bearing the image of the heavenly man, which is at least suggestive of union with Christ.[69] Thus, union with Christ will lead to being clothed with incorruptibility and immortality, as Christ is so clothed. In this sense, it is apparent that the clothing metaphor refers to something material. The very nature of incorruptibility and immortality pertains to material realities; they would hardly make sense otherwise. The corrupted and mortal flesh will be transformed.

In Colossians 3:12, Paul instructs his readers to "put on" compassion, kindness, humility, gentleness, and patience. The clothing metaphor then directly corresponds to realities in the material world – the way believers are to conduct themselves in their human relations. The question here, however, is whether or not this use of the clothing metaphor is connected to union with Christ. The answer is found in 3:10, in which Paul asserts that believers have put on the *new self*, which corresponds to the believer reconstituted in Christ.[70] Thus we observe that the spiritual reality of putting on the new self leads to the putting on of godly characteristics. The spiritual reality has direct bearing on the material reality.

While the examples of metaphors that explicitly point to material referents are fewer than those with spiritual referents, nevertheless we may observe that, for Paul, the spiritual and the material are inextricably tied. Thus the metaphors of body, temple and building, marriage, and clothing are each capable of expressing referents in the material world.

---

[68] Macaskill views the use of Genesis 2:24 as "suggestive of a union within which the distinction of each party is maintained. The two do not meld or melt, their beings are not confused. They are, instead, united and any transfer of the properties of one to the other must be spoken of in terms of inter-personal communication, not hybridization." Macaskill, *Union with Christ in the New Testament*, 156.

[69] *Paul and Union with Christ*, 313–14.

[70] *Paul and Union with Christ*, 316–17.

G. Conclusion

Metaphor is a powerful tool with which Paul conveys a variety of notions related to union with Christ. The metaphors explored in this essay each correlate to different elements of union, participation, identification, incorporation. The marriage metaphor is primarily related to "union," indicating spiritual oneness. The clothing metaphor is primarily related to "identification," in that believers are no longer to identify with the old self, but to put on the new. The body, temple and building metaphors relate to "incorporation," developing the notion of corporate inclusion in Christ. Paul's conception of union with Christ is richly shaped and communicated through metaphor.

Paul's dexterity with metaphor evokes the creation of new meaning, through which he is able to further his teaching about believers' union with Christ and with each other. Through the new symbol-sense associations created with respect to body, temple and building, marriage, and clothing, these concepts become profoundly illuminating. But Paul's metaphors also point to real referents, both spiritual and material. It is simply not true that the images he employs are *mere* metaphors, since Paul insists on the implications of these realities for Christian identity and conduct. The metaphors inform Christian living precisely because they have real spiritual referents, and these spiritual realities are connected to life in the material world.

Thus, as we seek to understand the role of metaphor in understanding union with Christ, it is concluded that insofar as the metaphors convey reality, so our union with Christ is real. It is not itself "just a metaphor." It is a spiritual reality of nuptial union, conforming identification, and organic incorporation that powerfully shapes our identity, conduct, and worship.

Bibliography

Aristotle. *On the Art of Poetry*. In *Classical Literary Criticism*. Translated by T. S. Dorsch. Penguin, 1965.

———. *Rhetoric*. Translated by W. Rhys Roberts. Oxford, 1924.

Campbell, Constantine R. "From Earthly Symbol to Heavenly Reality: The Tabernacle in the New Testament." Pages 177–95 in *Exploring Exodus: Literary, Theological and Contemporary Approaches*. Edited by Brian S. Rosner and Paul R. Williamson. Nottingham: Apollos, 2008.

———. *Paul and Union with Christ: An Exegetical and Theological Study*. Grand Rapids: Zondervan, 2012.

Elliott, Neil and Mark Reasoner. *Documents and Images for the Study of Paul*. Minneapolis: Fortress, 2011.

Hawkes, Terence. *Metaphor*. Vol. 25 of *The Critical Idiom*. London: Methuen, 1972.

Kim, Jung Hoon. *The Significance of Clothing Imagery in the Pauline Corpus.* Journal for the Study of the New Testament: Supplement Series 268. London: T&T Clark, 2004.

Levison, John R. "The Spirit and Temple in Paul's Letters to the Corinthians." Pages 189–215 in *Paul and His Theology.* Edited by Stanley E. Porter. Leiden: Brill, 2006.

Macaskill, Grant. *Union with Christ in the New Testament.* Oxford: Oxford University Press, 2013.

Moule, C. F. D. *The Origin of Christianity.* Cambridge: Cambridge University Press, 1977.

Ogden, C. K. and I. A. Richards. *The Meaning of Meaning.* New York: Harcourt, Brace, 1945.

Ricoeur, Paul. *The Rule of Metaphor: Multi-Disciplinary Studies of the Creation of Meaning in Language.* Translated by Robert Czerny with Kathleen McLaughlin and John Costello. Toronto: University of Toronto Press, 1977.

Sapir, J. David. "The Anatomy of Metaphor." Pages 3–32 in *The Social Use of Metaphor: Essays on the Anthropology of Rhetoric.* Edited by J. David Sapir and J. Christopher Crocker. University of Pennsylvania Press, 1977.

Silva, Moisés. *Biblical Words and Their Meaning: An Introduction to Lexical Semantics.* Grand Rapids: Zondervan, 1983.

Son, Sang-Won (Aaron). *Corporate Elements in Pauline Anthropology: A Study of Selected Terms, Idioms, and Concepts in the Light of Paul's Usage and Background.* Analecta biblica 148. Rome: Editrice Pontificio Istituto Biblico, 2001.

Spatafora, Andrea. *From the "Temple of God" to God as the Temple: A Biblical Theological Study of the Temple in the Book of Revelation.* Rome: Gregorian University Press, 1997.

Torrance, T. F. *Reality and Evangelical Theology: The Realism of Christian Revelation.* Downers Grove: InterVarsity Press, 1982.

Wedderburn, A. J. M. *Baptism and Resurrection: Studies in Pauline Theology against Its Graeco-Roman Background.* Wissenschaftliche Untersuchungen zum Neuen Testament 44. Tübingen: Mohr, 1987.

Wikenhauser, Alfred. *Pauline Mysticism: Christ in the Mystical Teaching of St. Paul.* Translated by Joseph Cunnigham. Freiburg: Herder and Herder, 1960.

Williams, David J. *Paul's Metaphors: Their Context and Character.* Peabody, Mass.: Hendrickson, 1999.

Wright, N. T. *Paul and the Faithfulness of God.* Minneapolis: Fortress, 2013.

———. *Pauline Perspectives: Essays on Paul 1978–2013.* Minneapolis: Fortress, 2013.

Incarnational Ontology and the Theology of Participation in Paul

GRANT MACASKILL

A proper examination of Paul's participatory theology requires some consideration of his Christology, specifically in terms of the ontology of the incarnation. This is a potentially controversial statement to make.[1] The word "incarnation," of course, is potentially anachronistic and misleading when brought to the study of Paul, since it reflects the kind of language encountered in John ("the word became flesh") and developed in the Logos Christology of the patristic writings. New Testament scholars are rightly wary of such words in relation to the much earlier Christological thinking of Paul, fearful of imposing alien concepts and categories back onto his more primitive beliefs. Similarly, the use of the word "ontology" may imply an assumption about the way in which Paul considers Jesus to be "divine," an assumption that bypasses questions about whether the language of divinity is used ontologically or simply functionally. To say, then, that we must consider the ontology of the incarnation in Paul's theology if we are to understand his notions of participation is, potentially at least, to beg some serious questions.

I would suggest, however, that provided we recognize these concerns, we may use the words "ontology" and "incarnation" with appropriate critical caution, allowing them to open pathways into an investigation of Paul's theology that would otherwise remain closed because of a lack of heuristic vocabulary. As a starting point for what follows, then, I will use both words in a fairly undeveloped sense. The word "incarnation" functions as a traditional shorthand for the union of God and man that Paul understands to have taken place in Jesus – whatever that may involve – and does not necessarily indicate a "two natures" Christology. The word "ontology," meanwhile, is simply used to describe what Paul considers God and Jesus to "be," or what he understands as the constituent elements of their "being."

---

[1] I am grateful to the various participants in a seminar held at Durham University in December 2013 for their input into a discussion of these issues. Thanks are due, in particular, to Walter Moberly, John Barclay and Jane Heath.

It will become clear as I move to a conclusion, however, that I consider the more determined and traditional sense of both words to be appropriate to Paul's Christology and to be demanded by his account of participation: his theology of participation requires a Christology that is neither purely functional nor adoptionist. This conclusion will set me somewhat at odds with one of the most important modern contributions to the study of Pauline Christology, one consciously oriented towards the question of Christian participation, that of James Dunn. For this reason, I will begin this article by outlining some of the key moves in Dunn's account of pneumatological Christology. Along the way, however, my observations will also set me at odds with another significant contribution to the study of Paul's participatory theology, that of the "apocalyptic Paul" school. That school will be represented elsewhere in this volume, and does not require to be outlined with the same detail as does Dunn. I will, though, highlight points in the course of my own study of Paul that I consider to be essentially problematic for elements of the apocalyptic approach.

A. James D.G. Dunn and Pneumatological Christology

Dunn's analysis of Christology and pneumatology is developed through an extensive body of scholarly contributions that he has made to New Testament studies. The core elements in his account, however, can be seen already in his 1973 article, "Jesus – Flesh and Spirit,"[2] which has been reprinted in his collected essays,[3] and which provides a useful anchor point for our consideration of his work. The detail of the analysis, the meticulous exegesis of the text, and the sheer erudition of the study are impressive, and demand the respect of any critic. The points that I will make in response to Dunn do not represent a challenge to the findings of that article in itself, but rather a reflection on whether they can be sustained in the light of other parts of the Pauline corpus, specifically those that speak of participation in the Christ-gift.

At the heart of Dunn's Christological account is a conviction that Paul considers the "divinity" of Jesus to be constituted by the dynamic activity of the Spirit. Against readings of Paul that consider the apostle to reject earlier adoptionistic accounts, in favor of a doctrine of pre-existence, Dunn argues that Paul equates divinity with sonship, and sonship with adoption, and adoption with the gift of the Spirit:

---

[2] James D. G. Dunn, "Jesus – Flesh and Spirit: An Exposition of Romans 1:3–4," *JTS* 68 (1973): 40–68.

[3] James D. G. Dunn, *The Christ and the Spirit: Christology* (Grand Rapids: Eerdmans, 1998).

Sonship for Paul is clearly a function of the Spirit.[4]

In Paul's view the sonship of the earthly Jesus was constituted by the Holy Spirit. He was Son of God because the Holy Spirit was in him and because he lived in obedience to that Spirit.[5]

The 'deity' of the earthly Jesus is a function of the Spirit, is, in fact, no more and no less than the Holy Spirit.[6]

This means that Jesus' experience of the divinizing work of the Spirit is prototypical or archetypal for all Christians, including Paul himself. It also, of course, means that the traditional categories of two-natures Christology must be discarded, in our reading of Paul at least. As Dunn moves from his biblical work to constructive theology, these findings raise further problems for classical formulations of Trinitarian theology.

This naturally raises the question as to how appropriate it is to speak of a *Tri*nity rather than a *Bi*nity. Before the incarnation Logos and Spirit were hardly to be distinguished. After incarnation, the divinity of Jesus was a function of the Spirit. And after the resurrection the risen humanity of Jesus was a function of the Spirit.[7]

In pushing back on classical accounts of incarnation and Trinity, Dunn's work has made significant contributions to modern theology, providing biblical scholarly resources for those who consider two natures Christology to be incompatible with modern understandings of human being. Dunn's dynamically pneumatological model is seen to protect the true humanity of Jesus from being compromised by a second nature. Various species of Spirit Christology, ranging from the conservative work of Coffey and Del Colle[8] to the radically modernist accounts of MacQuarrie and Mackey,[9] have drawn on his findings as a result.

Importantly, while Dunn's account takes very seriously the historically particular identity of Jesus as a 1st Century Jew, that individual's divinizing experience of the Spirit is entirely decoupled from the story of Israel or

---

[4] "Jesus – Flesh and Spirit," 44.
[5] "Jesus – Flesh and Spirit," 57.
[6] "Jesus – Flesh and Spirit," 58.
[7] "Rediscovering the Spirit," *ExpTim* 84 (1972): 12.
[8] For example, David Coffey, *Grace: The Gift of the Holy Spirit* (Manly: Catholic Institute of Sydney, 1979); idem, "A Proper Mission of the Holy Spirit," *Theological Studies*, 47 (1986), 227–50; Ralph Del Colle, *Christ and the Spirit: Spirit-Christology in Trinitarian Perspective* (New York: Oxford University Press, 1994).
[9] John MacQuarrie, *Jesus Christ in Modern Thought* (London: SCM Press, 1990); James P. Mackey, *Jesus, the Man and the Myth: A Contemporary Christology* (London: SCM Press, 1979); idem, *Modern Theology: A Sense of Direction* (Opus; Oxford: Oxford University Press, 1987); James D. G. Dunn and James P. Mackey, *New Testament Theology in Dialogue* (London: SPCK, 1987).

from his Davidic lineage, the latter being seen as belonging to the dead world of the flesh.

> In so far as Jesus lived on the level of the flesh, was bound and determined by the weakness and inadequacy of the human condition, allowed worldly considerations to determine his conduct, he was merely Son of David and no more – Messiah indeed, but a disappointing, ineffective, irrelevant Messiah, whether judged in terms of Jewish expectations or in terms of the Christian Gentile mission. But in so far as Jesus lived on the level of the Spirit, refused to allow merely human considerations, fleshly suffering, or Jewish expectations to determine his course or deter him from his chosen ministry, he manifested that he was indeed Son of God, and thereby proved his right to be installed as Son of God in power as from the resurrection of the dead.[10]

Hence, while the particular humanity of Jesus is affirmed as the locus for the Spirit's activity, his ethnic and religious background is nullified or negated. Effectively, theologically, the importance of his humanity is generic or universal; it is simply as a human, not as an Israelite, that Jesus is redemptively significant. This contrast between the living experience of Spirit and the dead world of flesh, to which Jesus' Israelite and Davidic lineage belongs, is one that subsequently determines Paul's own experience. As Dunn wrote in a previous article:

> Paul's experience of the old covenant was of death, condemnation, and bondage; but his experience of the new covenant was of life, righteousness, and liberty.[11]

Dunn, then, represents Christ's dynamic experience of God as Spirit as a new reality, quite contrastive with the death that characterizes the experience of Israel. His rendering of the divinization of Jesus by this dynamic experience of adoption[12] is hence dislocated from any significance attached to Israel. This, indeed, is one of the reasons that Dunn's work has been taken up in much modern theology, since it allows one to speak of the humanity of Jesus in generic terms that fit with modern accounts of human nature.[13]

What I will suggest in the remainder of this article, however, is that some of the specific ways in Paul speaks of Christian participation cannot be accounted for within this model and demand a different representation of Christology and pneumatology. In order to highlight this, I will begin by looking at those places in Paul where believers are represented in terms

---

[10] Dunn, "Jesus – Flesh and Spirit," 57.

[11] James D. G. Dunn, "2 Corinthians III.17 – The Lord is the Spirit," *JTS* 21 (1970), 319.

[12] Dunn resists the claim that the label "adoptionist" may be neatly applied to the early Christian writers, including Paul; see "Jesus – Flesh and Spirit," 57–8. It is difficult to avoid attaching the label, however, to Dunn's own account.

[13] For an interesting engagement with this point, see Charles C. Hefling, "Reviving Adamic Adoptionism: the Example of John Macquarrie," *TS* 52 (1991): 476–94.

that either explicitly designate them as "participating" in Christ (i.e., that use words for participation), or describe them in terms quite evidently derived from those used by Paul of the person of Jesus (i.e., that represent their identity as *corresponding*,[14] in some sense, to him). The most obvious and explicit point where the vocabulary of participation occurs in Paul is in the Eucharistic account of 1 Cor 11, an account that is embedded into a wider section of the epistle that requires to be drawn into our discussion. The most obvious and explicit point where a correspondence is established between Christians and Jesus is in Rom 8, with its extended reflection on "sonship." By examining these two blocks of text, we can at least identify some significant issues in Paul's handling of Incarnation and participation, while modestly acknowledging that we are dealing with only a small part of the corpus of texts associated with him.

B. Paul and Participation

I. 1 Cor 10 – 12: Eucharist and Participation

Paul's accounts of the Eucharist in 1 Cor 10:16–22 and 11:17–34 are shot through with participatory language, notably the nominal κοινωνία/κοινωνός and verbal forms of μετέχω. This is anticipated by the use of similar terminology in 1 Cor 1:9 (specifically, κοινωνία), where it is deployed in relation to the themes of fraternity and filiation: Paul's addressees have been called into κοινωνία (fellowship/ participation/partnership) with God's υἱός, a fellowship that results in their enjoyment of a paternal relationship with God and a fraternal one with Jesus. Interestingly, the verse opens with the statement that God is "faithful" (πιστὸς ὁ θεός), suggestive (if not more than suggestive) of covenant conceptuality. This opening statement evokes the story of promise and covenant between God and Israel, so that the participation or partnership of the addressees with the Son is represented as a manifestation of a divine quality elsewhere associated with his relationship with Israel.

This anticipates quite strikingly the discussion of the Eucharist in 1 Cor 10. This discussion is embedded within a wider section of text in which Paul describes the problem of idolatry and does so with reference to the story of Israel's experience in the wilderness. Importantly, the way that he makes use of this story cannot be reduced to an object lesson about the

---

[14] The language of "correspondence" (Entsprechung) is widely used by Barth of the relationship between Christ and the Christian (see, e.g., *CD* IV/2, sections 64, "The Exaltation of the Son of Man," and 66, "The Sanctification of Man," where the language occurs frequently). I find it helpful and constructive for our discussion.

dangers of idolatry; rather, Paul uses language that establishes a *correspondence* between Israel in the wilderness and the Christian community. These stories concern "our fathers" (10:1), who ate "the same spiritual food and drank from the same spiritual rock," identified as Christ (10:4).[15] The precise reading strategy that Paul deploys here is a matter for another discussion, but it establishes a clear connection between Israel's wilderness experience of God and that of the Christian community, in order to stress that the same threats hang over the spirit-filled Christians as hung over the Israelites. This is more than simply a parallel: it is an identification of a common source of life held between the two, the spiritual rock of Christ. This requires some sense of correspondence between the participation in Christ experienced by Paul's addressees and the participation in Christ experienced proleptically by Israel.

The description is, I think, problematic for a linear account of salvation-history, one that considers Christ simply to fulfill the story of Israel, but it is also problematic for some treatments of the "apocalyptic Paul," particularly in their handling of participation. These treatments emphasize the invasive quality of the gospel and typically represent Torah (and the covenantal story of Israel) as part of the corrupted cosmos that requires to be invaded. Salvation entails involvement – participation – in this dramatic, invasive new work of God. While, however, this undoubtedly does justice to some of Paul's imagery, it cannot be allowed to dominate the reading of his soteriology to the exclusion of more positive representations of Israel and the Torah. For while the history of Israel – including the Exodus, the wanderings and the reception of the Law – may have been "subject to the power of sin,"[16] and permeated by the reality of death, it was also lived in the *presence* of God and, as such, permeated by life.

The theme of "presence" is, I think, a fruitful one for reflection on how the Christ-gift may relate to the history of Israel. Here, what is helpful to note is that this presence is represented in deliberately proleptic terms that identify God's life-giving presence with Christ and the Spirit. So, even in

---

[15] Richard B. Hays explores the correspondence with Israel in his commentary – *1 Corinthians* (Louisville: John Knox, 1997) – and in the opening chapter of *The Conversion of the Imagination: Paul as Interpreter of Israel's Scripture* (Grand Rapids: Eerdmans, 2005), 8–12. He agrees with Terence Donaldson that Gentiles are represented as "proselytes to an Israel reconfigured around Christ" (*Paul and the Gentiles: Remapping the Apostle's Convictional World*. Minneapolis: Fortress, 1997), 236. The point I note below is somewhat different: the truth of Israel's identity is revealed in the Christ gift.

[16] John Barclay, "Under Grace: The Christ Gift and the Construction of a Christian Habitus" in *Apocalyptic Paul: Cosmos and Anthropos in Romans 5–8* (ed. Beverley R. Gaventa; Waco: Baylor University Press, 2012), 59–76.

the time that was subject to sin, the "Christ-gift"[17] was proleptically effective, but just as *then* it could be negated by idolatry, so *now* the Corinthian church faces the very same danger. The logic here is important: it is precisely because of the identification of *salvation* in the two periods – the correspondence, the shared reality of the Christ-gift – that Paul is able to identify a common vulnerability to idolatry. This, perhaps, leads us to see the expression τύποι ἡμῶν (10:6) as pointing to a different species of correspondence or identification between Israel in the wilderness and the church than that designated with our word "typology." It is surely also significant that his account specifically describes the experience of Israel: there is no sense here of a universal encounter with divine presence. If anything is universal, it is the problem of idolatry; divine presence is specifically associated with covenant. The nation of Israel has a special status, one that demarcates it from all other nations, one that is reflected in the Passover celebrations, and is now understood in relation to the Christ gift. This recognition must be allowed to cast light on other Pauline texts that speak of the relationship between the Christ gift and the story of Israel. Notably, Paul's description of Jesus as "born of a woman, born under the law" (Gal 4:4) has a somewhat less pejorative ring than sometimes argued as it points towards his particular humanity: he is, quite specifically, a member of a privileged nation.

As well as problematizing the apocalyptic approach to Paul (in some of its forms and some of its details, at least), and speaking to particular humanity of Jesus, this insight into the participation of Israel in the Christ gift demands some reflection on the character of his divinity. I find it difficult to see how Paul could have written in such terms of the relationship between Israel and the Christ-gift if he does indeed operate with the kind of Christological beliefs that Dunn ascribes to him. Dunn's approach provides a way of understanding God's dynamic presence with Jesus, one that leaves room for the particularity of his humanity, even as it nullifies any significance in his Jewishness, but can it accommodate the way in which Paul represents *God's* particularity? For God is here *particularly* identified as Christ, even though Paul is describing the period prior to "the Christ event" within history. It was Christ who gave them life; it was Christ they put to the test (10:9).

As we move from the history of Israel to the contemporary practice of Eucharist, we are confronted by the impossibility of dual participation in the table of the Lord and the table of demons. This point is developed through Paul's use of the technical vocabulary associated with participation. In 10:16–17, for example:

---

[17] I will discuss this language later in the article, with reference to the important emergent work of John Barclay.

The cup of blessing that we bless, is it not a participation (κοινωνία) in/of the blood of Christ? The loaf that we break, is it not a participation (κοινωνία) in/of the body of Christ? Because there is one loaf, we who are many are one body, because we all of the one loaf partake (μετέχομεν).

This is followed by the contrastive statement of 10:20: "I do not wish you to be participants in the demons" (οὐ θέλω δὲ ὑμᾶς κοινωνοὺς τῶν δαιμονίων γίνεσθαι). The contrast then reaches its climax with Paul's declaration about the impossibility of dual participation: "You cannot drink the cup of the Lord and the cup of demons. You cannot partake of (μετέχειν) the table of the Lord and the table of demons" (10:21). The interplay or interchangeability of the nouns κοινωνία/κοινωνός and verbal forms of μετέχω is important and problematizes any attempt either to warrant or resist Platonic overtones according to which of the roots is used. It is striking, in fact, that the words derived from κοινων- are applied to both the Lord's Supper and the idol feasts. We must, then, push beyond the words and their lexical significance if we are to understand the nature of the participation here represented. We must look more closely at the way in which participatory language is combined with imagery.

Where applied to the Lord's Supper, the participatory language deployed has a high degree of specificity: it is not simply a matter of participation in or fellowship with the Son, as it is in 1 Cor 1:9, but rather eating the bread involves participation *in the body* and drinking the wine involves participation *in the blood* of Christ. Participation, then, is specifically in that individual and in the fatal experience that he underwent. The Eucharistic imagery hence demands a particularity of both his identity and his narrative.

How, then, is his particularity bridged with that of those who participate in the sacrament? The ritual or cultic dimension is important to this. When Paul comes to speak of the Eucharistic cup, he will designate it with a term generally seen to correspond to on element within the Passover meal: the cup of blessing (10:16).[18] Passover celebrants are expected to identify themselves imaginatively in the act of eating and drinking with those who came out of Egypt (compare Exod 12–13 and Deut 26:5ff for this). Those who partake of the Eucharist are now, in a similar way, to identify themselves with the physical death of Jesus, his broken body and shed blood. This nakedly imaginative act, though, is embedded into Paul's pneumatological account, as we will see in the next part of this article. As a result, the imaginative act of identification becomes a realistic one: a real corre-

---

[18] As I noted in my discussion of Eucharist in *Union with Christ in the New Testament* (Oxford: Oxford University Press, 2013), 204, this point does not rest on evidence for the contemporary practice of the Passover *seder*: the elements of identification are present in the biblical accounts themselves.

spondence is established between Jesus and those who share in the Eucharist. They participate in his body and his blood.

Given that the significance of Jesus' bodily death is presented in terms of the experience of his forebears, and his forebears' experience is presented in terms of the presence of Jesus, I want to suggest that Paul intends for us to understand the two as part of a singular redemptive work and that this has significance for how we understand the human element of the ontology of the Incarnation. It is, in other words, important to Paul that Christ our Passover (1 Cor 5:7) was chosen from within the flock of Israel, the people set apart. The union of God to humanity that is internal to the Incarnation involves not just any representative humanity, it involved a humanity that was derived from the nation that was in covenant with God.

If we bring this discussion and its dynamics to Paul's "apocalyptic" narratives, such as that of Gal 4, it casts into a very different light the description of Jesus being "born of a woman, born under the Law." Instead of the latter denoting the helplessness of that time and condition, its subjection to sin's power, it may function along with "born of a woman" to indicate the real and particular humanity of Jesus and its redemptive significance in relation to the will and faithfulness of the Father. The point is supported, I think, by the fact that the shackled character of the time of minority (i.e., the time of imprisonment under the law and sin) is described in terms of the administration and economy (ἐπιτρόπους ἐστὶν καὶ οἰκονόμους, stewards and managers) of the Father. That Jesus is described as coming "in the fullness of time" (τὸ πλήρωμα τοῦ χρόνου), and is further specified to have been born of a woman, under the law, is an affirmation of his particular humanity that is rendered in terms of the Father's will. Jesus is an Israelite, and that fact is important to his redemptive role.

II. Romans 8: Participating in Sonship

We turn from the Eucharistic material of 1 Corinthians to the great description of salvation and Christian life in Rom 8, a passage that will surely dominate much of the discussion in this book. It is, of course, one of the passages that establishes a clear correspondence between the Christian and Christ himself and does so with reference to the work of the Spirit, in a way that Dunn considers to support his own argument.[19] It is also part of a block of material (Rom 5–8) that has been considered to most clearly represent a mystical centre to Paul's theology, setting salvation in cosmic and pneumatological context rather than in a forensic or legal one.[20] The quest

---

[19] Dunn, "Jesus – Flesh and Spirit," 54.
[20] In the early 20th Century, Albert Schweitzer, Adolf Deissman and William Wrede challenged the idea that "justification" was the center of Paul's theology. Schweitzer, for

for a centre to Paul's theology has often been preoccupied by how the cosmic/dramatic/mystical language of these chapters relates to the more legal/forensic language of the earlier chapters of Romans, a point illustrated by Douglas Campbell's recent study, *The Deliverance of God*.[21]

I want to take as my departure point for a discussion of this text John Barclay's emergent work on "gift."[22] I choose this, in part, because of the programmatic significance that the language has in Rom 5, which is generally agreed to be pivotal to the development of the epistle and which contrasts the conditions that obtain under the trespass with those that obtain under the "gift." In part, too, I choose it because of the prominence of "receiving" language in this passage (notably in 8:15). Taking this pervasive gift-reception language seriously is vital to a proper understanding of the participatory elements in the text. Using "gift" as our departure point also allows us to enter into the discussion of soteriology in the epistle in a way that escapes some of the dichotomies that problematize the apocalyptic discussions, particularly as regards Israel. Rather than immediately miring ourselves in those discussions and their polarities, we can begin by recognizing that we are dealing here with a *given* salvation that, unlike other gifts in ancient times, was not given on the basis of worth, but did itself generate a new set of conditions and, with it, obligations. That starting point affirms some of the key points from the apocalyptic Paul reading, while also allowing us to defer the fraught discussion of Israel's place in this account.

The gift that is identified in Rom 8, as in Gal 4, is particularly developed in terms of filiation: what is "given" is a salvation that involves believers living in a filial relationship with God by the presence and activity of the Spirit and determined, in terms that we will examine momentarily, by their identification as τοῖς ἐν Χριστῷ Ἰησοῦ. The contrast between flesh and spirit that can be seen from the beginning of the chapter, and that progresses always in partnership with the identification of believers as being

---

example, famously described justification as merely a "subsidiary crater" within the "main crater" of Paul's theology of mystical union. See *The Mysticism of Paul the Apostle,* (trans. William Montgomery. London: A. & C. Black, 1931), 225. As Douglas Campbell rightly notes in *The Deliverance of God: An Apocalyptic Re-Reading of Paul* (Grand Rapids: Eerdmans, 2010), 1, this relocation of the *conceptual* center of Paul's theology resulted in a relocation of the *textual* center, from Romans 1–4 to Romans 5–8. Today, of course, discussions are more complex and the debate about whether one can speak in any sense of a center to Paul's theology continues.

[21] D. Campbell, *The Deliverance of God*.

[22] Barclay's full study of "gift" in Pauline theology – *Paul and the Gift* (Grand Rapids: Eerdmans, forthcoming) – is still to be published, but core elements have emerged already in his article, "Under Grace," the full details of which are listed above, footnote 16.

"in Christ" (see, e.g., 8:1), builds toward the designation of the Spirit as the Spirit of adoption (the πνεῦμα υἱοθεσία) in 8:15. There have, of course, been other designations for the Spirit throughout the chapter: the Spirit of Life, the Spirit of Christ and the Spirit of God. Here, though, we reach a designation that is subsequently unpacked in ways that are most strikingly participatory, in which the identity of the one led by the Spirit is most explicitly represented as corresponding to the identity of Jesus:

For you did not receive the spirit of slavery leading again to fear, but you received the Spirit of adoption, by whom we cry, "Abba, Father." The Spirit himself bears witness to our spirit that we are God's children. And if children, then heirs (namely, heirs of God and also fellow heirs with Christ)–if indeed we suffer with him so we may also be glorified with him (Rom 8:15–17, NRSV).

At this point, then, the gift is received as the Spirit who establishes a "correspondence" between the receivers and Christ himself, as the Son. The uptake of the language represented in the Synoptic tradition of Jesus' language of prayer is an important part of this: by the Spirit, believers participate in Jesus' own vocative communication with God. Alongside this, they share in his Sonly status as heirs (co-heirs, indeed: συγκληρονόμοι). Finally, they are represented as sharing in his suffering and exaltation. Leaving aside the last point of correspondence for the time being, we can see in the first two of these an outworking of the concept of filiation, presented in both its relational and its legal dimensions. The identity of Jesus as Son becomes determinative for those who receive his Spirit and are adopted into his family.

This, though, is where some caution is also required as we reflect on the "Christ event." Clearly in this gift, the identity of the Christ establishes the identity of those "in Christ." But we must enquire as to the nature of this relationship: is the Sonship of Jesus prototypical (or archetypal) for the sons who would come thereafter, or is it constitutive of their identity in a different sense? Another way to articulate this question is to ask whether the sonship of Jesus belongs to the same genus as that of the sons who come after him? The former identification underpins much of Dunn's account of Christology, and is connected to the assumption that what we encounter in the early New Testament Christologies is really a pneumatically functional divinity. Jesus receives the Spirit at his baptism and is effectively adopted at that point; the presence of the Spirit functionally divinizes him, bringing into being the new conditions of the Kingdom of God and ensuring that he serves as the paradigm and prototype for those who would follow in the kingdom. Interestingly, Dunn develops this account of Christology in heavy reliance on the myth of lost Adamic glory: in Jesus, the lost glory of Adam is restored by the indwelling of the Spirit. The application of glory language to Jesus, then, represents recovery of an Adamic property, not the recognition of a divine identity. It is, perhaps, noteworthy that Christologies of this kind have characterized much Anglican theology over the last two centuries.[23]

The significance attached to Paul's ascription of glory to Jesus is something that has been discussed elsewhere.[24] Here, the priority is to note the problems that are thrown up for Dunn's account of Christology by Paul's specific deployment of adoption/sonship language and the development of his argument, particularly when read through the lens of the Eucharist passages that we examined above, and their identification of Jesus as God. Most obviously (and as with much that is obvious, hardly originally) is the fact that while believers are represented as the beneficiaries of adoption (Rom 8:15, cf., Gal 4:5), Jesus is simply designated as the Son. His Sonship is kept out of the category of adoption while clearly being determinative or constitutive for it. It is surely important that the "Spirit of adoption" is identified as the Spirit of the Christ *to whom the vocabulary of adoption is nowhere applied*. The Spirit's activity in the experience of the believer is determined by Christ's person and narrative: that relationship is not inverted by Paul.

A less obvious point may also be noted: the identification that the Spirit establishes between the believer and Christ is never rendered in terms of Jesus' own baptism, which would be the obvious point of correspondence according to Dunn's theory. We are baptized into his death (Rom 6), we cry "Abba Father," but we are not described as being immersed in the Jordan. We would expect, if Dunn's theory were correct, to see more by way of Jordan imagery in the New Testament.

The point, in relation to the ontology of the Incarnation, is that the Sonly status of Jesus is determinative for the adoption of those who receive his Spirit, but it is nowhere represented itself as being constituted by the Spirit. We must, then, speak of his Sonship, and hence relationship with God, as belonging to a category that is distinct from that occupied by those who have subsequently received the gift. His relationship to the Father and his relationship to the Spirit are, likewise, distinct from those experienced by those who have been adopted. Adoption, though, is made possible by his Sonship and represents the Spirit's activity of generating a correspondence between recipients of the gift and the Son's identity.

---

[23] The point is noted by John Webster, in his essay on "Incarnation" in *Word and Church* (Edinburgh: T&T Clark, 2001), 120–21.

[24] I offer some criticism of the argument for a widespread myth of Adamic glory in *Union with Christ in the New Testament*, 128–43. See also Carey Newman, *Paul's Glory Christology: Tradition and Rhetoric* (Leiden: Brill, 1992) for the evidence that the glory language points to the identification of Jesus with God's own glory.

One last point on this passage will allow us to tie what we have just seen to our discussion of Eucharist. While adoption is the substance of the eschatological gift, it is also listed as a privilege of Israel in Rom 9:4, and the proximity of that statement cannot be a matter of coincidence. The Christ gift is presented in terms that explicitly correspond to the story of Israel. This is not simplistically to locate the Christ event within a salvation history in which Israel played a preparatory role: rather, it is to consider the adoption of Israel as itself belonging to the reality of divine presence constituted by the Christ event.

C. Conclusions and Further Reflections

Let me, then, draw some conclusions specific to this article, before offering some further reflections on the fruitfulness of this kind of reflection on participatory language in the New Testament. By paying attention to the ways in which Jesus' divinity and his humanity are presented in relation to salvation, particularly the participatory dimensions of salvation, we are driven to speak of his being in relation to God ("the Father" to adopt traditional language) and to the Spirit, specifically as these relations are represented as determining his Sonship. Identified as the presence of God with Israel in the wilderness (1 Cor 10:4), and as the one put to the test by their idolatry (1 Cor 10:8), and never described as the object of adoption, Jesus cannot be placed simply in a category filled by other human beings. His Sonship demands to be spoken of in a category of its own, as consequently does his relationship with the Spirit, even as it determines the category of sonship that Paul's addressees are located within. This demands an account of individuation within the being of the One True God; it is interesting that Paul, as is well known, includes Jesus within the terms of the Shema in 1 Cor 8:6. In demanding such an account of Jesus' divinity in relation to the being of God, the text demands that we move into the linguistic space occupied by later Trinitarian discussion, as we seek to articulate how the being of the Son relates to the being of the Father and of the Spirit.

Yet, Paul is also interested in the particularity of Jesus' humanity. Again, it is interesting that when he places Jesus within the divine identity in 1 Cor 8:6, it is the Shema that he employs, a text intimately connected to the identity of Israel, to the story of the Exodus, to the account of the law. As he speaks of the participation of Moses and the Israelites in Christ, proleptically, he affirms the special place of that nation from which the particular human being Jesus of Nazareth would emerge and, as such, sets the particular death of Jesus, the breaking of a particular body and particular blood into a particular narrative of election. This demands a re-evaluation of the treatment of the story of Israel that is encountered in much, at least, of the apocalyptic Paul movement.

Now, it may be that I am transgressing some scholarly expectations with this line of enquiry and with the insinuation that the Christological, incarnational and Trinitarian discussions of later Christian theology may have been doing something appropriate, rather than unacceptable, with the New Testament witness. But I think that the flourishing of interest in "participation" in recent New Testament scholarship opens some interesting new avenues for reflection on the ways in which the divinity and humanity of Jesus are presented in the New Testament literature.[25] Perhaps, just perhaps, we will find that our predecessors were rather more careful in their reading of these texts than we have given them credit for, and perhaps we will find that they were a little more mindful of the Scriptural texts when developing their theological positions than we have realized.

Bibliography

Barclay, John. *Paul and the Gift.* Grand Rapids: Eerdmans, forthcoming.

———. "Under Grace: The Christ Gift and the Construction of a Christian Habitus." Pages 59–76 in *Apocalyptic Paul: Cosmos and Anthropos in Romans 5–8.* Edited by Beverley R. Gaventa. Waco: Baylor University Press, 2012.

Campbell, Douglas. *The Deliverance of God: An Apocalyptic Re-Reading of Paul.* Grand Rapids: Eerdmans, 2010.

Coffey, David. "A Proper Mission of the Holy Spirit." *Theological Studies,* 47 (1986): 227–50.

———. *Grace: The Gift of the Holy Spirit.* Manly: Catholic Institute of Sydney, 1979.

Del Colle, Ralph. *Christ and the Spirit: Spirit-Christology in Trinitarian Perspective.* New York/ Oxford: Oxford University Press, 1994.

Donaldson, Terence. *Paul and the Gentiles: Remapping the Apostle's Convictional World.* Minneapolis: Fortress, 1997.

Dunn, James D. G. "2 Corinthians 3.17 – The Lord is the Spirit." *Journal of Theological Studies* 21 (1970): 309–20.

———. "Jesus – Flesh and Spirit: An Exposition of Romans 1:3–4." *Journal of Theological Studies* 68 (1973): 40–68.

———. "Rediscovering the Spirit," *Expository Times* 84 (1972): 7–12.

———. *The Christ and the Spirit: Christology.* Grand Rapids: Eerdmans, 1998.

Dunn, James D. G., and James P. Mackey. *New Testament Theology in Dialogue.* London: SPCK, 1987.

Hays, Richard B. *1 Corinthians.* Interpretation. Louisville: John Knox, 1997.

———. *The Conversion of the Imagination: Paul as Interpreter of Israel's Scripture.* Grand Rapids: Eerdmans, 2005.

---

[25] See chapter 1 of my *Union with Christ in the New Testament* for an overview of the scholarly interest in participatory readings.

Hefling, Charles C. "Reviving Adamic Adoptionism: the Example of John Macquarrie." *Theological Studies* 52 (1991): 476–94.
Macaskill, Grant. *Union with Christ in the New Testament*. Oxford: Oxford University Press, 2013.
Mackey, James P. *Jesus, the Man and the Myth: A Contemporary Christology*. London: SCM Press, 1979.
———. *Modern Theology: A Sense of Direction*. Opus. Oxford: Oxford University Press, 1987.
MacQuarrie, John. *Jesus Christ in Modern Thought*. London: SCM Press, 1990.
Newman, Carey. *Paul's Glory Christology: Tradition and Rhetoric*. Leiden: Brill, 1992.
Schweitzer, Albert. *The Mysticism of Paul the Apostle*. Translated by William Montgomery. London: Adam & Charles Black, 1931.
Webster, John. *Word and Church*. Edinburgh: T&T Clark, 2001.

Oneself in Another

Participation and the Spirit in Romans 8

SUSAN G. EASTMAN

By and large the crucial role of the Spirit in Paul's life and thought – as the dynamic, experiential reality of Christian life – is often either overlooked or given mere lip service.[1]

Anyone attempting to write on the topic of the Holy Spirit in Paul's letters soon learns the truth of Gordon Fee's observation: the Holy Spirit may indeed be "God's empowering presence," as Fee argues in his book of the same title, but it also is an elusive presence – at least for Pauline scholars! Considering the importance of the Spirit at certain key junctions in Paul's letters, the relative paucity of scholarly work on the Spirit is remarkable. For example, a few years ago I participated in a major conference on Romans 5–8, in which not one paper (including mine) focused on the Spirit.[2] Nor was this lacuna noted as a topic of conversation, despite the fact that Romans 8 contains one of the thickest clusters of Spirit language in Paul's letters. The Spirit slips through our grasp, and it is instructive to consider why this might be the case.[3] I suspect the experiential aspect of Paul's lan-

---

[1] Gordon D. Fee, *God's Empowering Presence: The Holy Spirit in the Letters of Paul* (Peabody, Mass.: Hendrickson, 1994), xxi.

[2] "Creation, Conflict, and Cosmos: Romans 5–8," a conference celebrating the Bicentennial of Princeton Theological Seminary, May 2–5, 2012. Papers from the conference are published in *Apocalyptic Paul: Cosmos and Anthropos in Romans 5–8* (ed. Beverly Roberts Gaventa; Waco: Baylor University Press, 2013).

[3] In addition to Fee, there are a few notable exceptions to this neglect of the Spirit. Most recently, Troels Engberg-Pedersen has argued for a Stoic notion of a material *pneuma* in *Cosmology and Self in the Apostle Paul: The Material Spirit* (Oxford: Oxford University Press, 2010). James D. G. Dunn examines the importance of the Spirit for Paul in his *The Theology of Paul the Apostle* (Edinburgh: T&T Clark, 1998); see now also Mehrdad Fatehi, *The Spirit's Relation to the Risen Lord in Paul* (WUNT 128; Tübingen: Mohr Siebeck, 2000); other sources include *The Holy Spirit and Christian Origins: Essays in Honor of James N. G. Dunn*, (ed. Graham N. Stanton, B. W. Longenecker and S. C. Barton; Grand Rapids: Eerdmans, 2004); *The Spirit and Christ in the New Testament and Christian Theology: Essays in Honor of Max Turner*, (ed. I. Howard Marshall

guage about the Spirit may be partly to blame; it is exceedingly difficult to talk about experience even in contemporary contexts, let alone across the divide of culture and time that separates us from Paul.[4] This difficulty is exacerbated by the modern tendency, at least in European and North American cultures, to think of "spiritual experience" as an individual, private and esoteric event.[5] As we shall see, however, Paul's own language about the Spirit cuts against such assumptions.

Nonetheless, Paul's language *is* experiential, and we cannot understand his theology of participation and union with Christ apart from his convictions about the empirical presence and power of God in Christ through the Holy Spirit. Throughout Paul's letters, the Spirit appears and acts as the being and action of God here and now, in human history and personal interaction rather than in some otherworldly realm. As both Fee and Paul Meyer have argued, Paul invokes the Holy Spirit to talk about the "experienced realities" of God in Christ in the midst of the community that lives together "in Christ."[6] Meyer notes that throughout the extremely varied

---

et al.; Grand Rapids and Cambridge, UK: Eerdmans, 2012); Paul Meyer, "The Holy Spirit in the Pauline Letters: A Contextual Exploration," in *The Word in This World: Essays in New Testament Exegesis and Theology* (NTL; Louisville; London: Westminster John Knox, 2004), 117–32; Finny Philip, *The Origins of Pauline Pneumatology* (WUNT 2/194; Tübingen: Mohr Siebeck, 2005).

[4] Colleen Shantz traces the resistance to investigating Paul's experiential language, labeling it "cognocentrism," in *Paul in Ecstasy: the Neurobiology of the Apostle's Life and Thought* (Cambridge: Cambridge University Press, 2009), 27–33.

[5] This individualistic and inward focus is implicit in the attempt by Shantz to provide a neurobiological account of Paul's ecstatic experiences through comparison with shamanistic trances and visions: "Paul felt himself to be 'gloriously' transformed through his religious ecstasy and . . . those experiences inspired his thinking about a corporate body of Christ. Paul's transformation is based on the distinctive pattern of religious ecstasy during which signals from the body are neurologically blocked (deafferentation) while, simultaneously, higher-level somatic processing centers remain active." *Paul in Ecstasy*, 137. Troels Engberg-Pedersen takes it as axiomatic that for Paul "religious experience" is "psychological experience," and as such is always individual and interior. "The Construction of Religious Experience in Paul," in *Experientia, Volume I: Inquiry Into Religious Experience in Early Judaism and Christianity* (ed. Frances Flannery et al.; Atlanta: SBL, 2008), 152; see also 147–58. Over against the widespread assumption that religious experience is "private," "inner," and "subjective," see Nicholas Lash, "Human Experience and the Knowledge of God," in *Theology on the Way to Emmaus* (Eugene, Ore.: Wipf & Stock, 2005), 143–47.

[6] Fee, *God's Empowering Presence*, 4; Meyer says the Holy Spirit concerns "the ways in which God and his transcendence are related to human existence and experience in the world." "Holy Spirit," 117. A. J. M. Wedderburn goes further: "Paul, sooner or later after his conversion, which in itself may well have been an ecstatic experience of some sort, and probably by no means the last in his life, found himself in a movement where ecstatic experiences were a recognized and established feature of its life." "Pauline Pneumatology and Pauline Theology," in *The Holy Spirit and Christian Origins*, 149; see also 144–56.

uses of πνεῦμα in ancient texts, the term retains its ties with "wind, breath, air" and never loses "that peculiar attachment to the world of experience or sense that comes from their application to perceived or felt phenomena of power."[7] The evidence for Meyer's claim permeates the Pauline letters. For example, in his letter to the Galatians Paul bolsters his argument that the Galatian believers already have received the Spirit, by appealing to their shared experiences of miracles worked by the Spirit (Gal 3:2–5), and of the Spirit's presence in their hearts inspiring them to cry out, "Abba! Father!" (4:6; cf., Rom 8:15b–16). The topic – more to the point, the living reality – of the Holy Spirit is central to Paul's proclamation of the gospel and his nurture of the congregations he founded. Furthermore, it is particularly central to the subject matter of this volume, Paul's language of union with Christ and participation in Christ.

Hence the focus of this essay will be the Spirit's role in mediating the experience of union with Christ. Concentrating on Romans 8, with attention to other Pauline texts as indicated, I will argue that the Spirit generates and sustains a mutually participatory bond of love between believers and God, as well as between persons "in Christ." In turn this bond has recognizable effects within the community that Paul calls "the body of Christ," as it generates a new interpersonal mode of cognition and communication through which God is glorified.

In order to get at this experiential reality, we first need to reckon with the relationship between the forensic and participatory strands of Paul's thought, which unite in Romans 8 as the climax of the first half of the letter. I shall argue that the key to these motifs, which are often wrongly opposed in Pauline scholarship, is the thoroughly participatory quality of both Paul's anthropology and his Christology. Secondly, we will attend to the qualities and characteristics of the new relational matrix generated by the Spirit, in contrast to the network generated by what Paul variously calls "the law of sin and death" and "the flesh." Thirdly, we will observe how this new relational matrix acts as the "cradle of thought" for Paul's converts – that is, as an interpersonal, interactive bond in which new modes of cognition and communication arise.[8] Finally we will reflect on the understanding of "spiritual experience" disclosed in Paul's language about the Spirit in Romans.

---

[7] Meyer, "Holy Spirit," 117.

[8] The term, "the cradle of thought" comes from Peter Hobson, *The Cradle of Thought* (London: MacMillan, 2002). Hobson argues that the human capacities for thinking and recognizing thought, intention, and emotion in others arise out of the primary interaction between infants and their parents. For a similar argument, see also Vasudevi Reddy, *How Infants Know Minds* (Cambridge, Mass.: Harvard University Press, 2008).

A. From Condemnation to Communion: Judgment and Participation in Christ and the Spirit

Romans 8 comes at a critical juncture in Paul's letter to the churches in Rome. As the climax of the first half of the letter, Rom 8:1–4 brings together the "forensic" and "participatory" themes of the preceding chapters in one dense, summative announcement of the heart of the good news:[9]

> There is therefore now no condemnation for those who are in Christ Jesus. For the law of the Spirit of Life in Christ Jesus has set you [singular] free from the law of sin and death. For what the law, rendered powerless by the weakness of the flesh, was unable to do, God has done: sending his own son in the likeness of the flesh of sin and for sin, he condemned sin in the flesh, in order that the just requirement of the law might be fulfilled in us, who walk not according to the flesh but according to the Spirit.[10]

As frequently noted, here Paul's announcement of deliverance from condemnation is addressed precisely to the "I" that cries out in 7:24: "Who will deliver me from this body of death?" This is the culmination of Paul's spiral shaped retelling of the situation of human dereliction and the salvation accomplished in Jesus Christ. In Leander Keck's words,

> [W]hat makes Romans 1–8 tick is the inner logic of having to show how the gospel deals with the human condition on three ever-deeper levels, each understood as a dimension of the Adamic condition: the self's skewed relationship to God in which the norm (law) is the accuser, the self in sin's domain where death rules before Moses arrived only to exacerbate the situation by specifying transgression, the self victimized by sin as a resident power stronger than the law.[11]

Romans 8 addresses the final situation, that of "the self victimized by sin as resident power stronger than the law," and it does this by invoking the "law of the Spirit of life in Christ Jesus." The indwelling Spirit is even stronger than indwelling sin and sin's use of the law. With the appearance of the Spirit as a major player in Christian life, Paul depicts a "changing of the guard," a coup d'état in which the ruling powers of the old age have done their worst and are dismissed from dominion. As oppressive powers, sin, the law and the flesh cease to play any significant role in Paul's argu-

---

[9] For a depiction of these interwoven but distinct strands of thought in Romans, see Martin deBoer, "Paul and Jewish Apocalyptic Eschatology," in *Apocalyptic and the New Testament: Essays in Honour of J. Louis Martyn* (ed. J. Marcus and M.L. Soards; Sheffield: JSOT Press, 1989), 169–90; and my "The Empire of Illusion: Sin and Evil in Romans," in *Comfortable Words: Essays in Honor of Paul F. M. Zahl* (ed. John D. Koch and Todd Brewer; Eugene, Ore.: Wipf & Stock, 2013) 3–21.

[10] I have used my own translations throughout.

[11] "What Makes Romans Tick?" in *Pauline Theology: Volume III: Romans* (ed. David M. Hay and E. E. Johnson; Minneapolis: Fortress, 1995), 26; see also 3–29.

ment after the victory song of Rom 8:31–39.[12] Their absence from the remaining seven chapters of the letter is striking.

Paul's argument here is dense and complex, requiring careful disentangling of the role of Christ and the role of the Spirit in setting humanity free. The Son liberates us through his full solidarity with condemned humanity, even to the point of crucifixion as a condemned criminal; the Spirit brings that liberation to fruitful experience through indwelling the new community that lives "in Christ." I suggest that Paul unites forensic and participatory themes here in Rom 8:1–4 by stressing the participation of the divine Son in human dereliction and culpability under sin, which in turn opens the way for human participation in the life of the Son. Deliverance from condemnation comes through the sending of God's Son "in the likeness of the flesh of sin and for sin (ἐν ὁμοιώματι σαρκὸς ἁμαρτίας καὶ περὶ ἁμαρτίας)." In that place – *in Christ's flesh* – God condemned and conquered sin.[13] That is, the forensic and participatory motifs of divine redemption come together in the action of God, precisely in Christ's movement into the realm of human existence as it is enmeshed in – indeed participating in! – the realm of sin and death.[14] It is in this way, via Christ's participation in the realm of bodily existence under sin's sway, that Christ also came as a sin-offering to bear and do away with the condemnation pronounced on sin.

---

[12] It is worth noting that in Paul's subsequent exhortations to the Christian community, he confidently asserts victory over evil: "Do not be conquered (νικῶ) by evil, but conquer (νίκα) evil with good" (12:21). Fee notes the disappearance of references to law: "Paul is basically done with Torah in the argument." *God's Empowering Presence*, 530, n. 174. Meyer also notes the absence of law after Rom. 8:3 "until the quite different discussion of 9:30–10:13." "Holy Spirit," 121. For sin's absence after 8:2, see "The Empire of Illusion," 8.

[13] For the translation, "flesh of sin," see Fee, *God's Empowering Presence*, 532, n. 181; Fee notes that the occurrence of the genitive qualifier rather than the adjective puts the emphasis on Christ's incarnation, but he argues that the "flesh" is still sinful human flesh in distinction from Christ's flesh. As Meyer puts it, however, "Paul is not worried about the 'sinlessness' of Jesus (Heb 4:15) because he conceives of sin as a power, not as defilement or guilt. Without fully entering the domain of that power, 'flesh,' the Son could not have broken it." "Romans: a Commentary," in *The Word in This World* (NTL; Louisville; London: Westminster John Knox, 2004), 189; see also 149–218. For an expanded defense of this argument, see Vincent Branick, "The Sinful Flesh of the Son of God (Rom 8:3): A Key Image of Pauline Theology," *CBQ* 47 (1985): 246–62; Susan Eastman, "Apocalypse and Incarnation: The Participatory Logic of Paul's Gospel," in *Apocalyptic and the Future of Theology* (ed. J. Davis and D. Harink; Eugene, Ore.: Wipf & Stock, 2012), 165–82.

[14] Similarly, "likeness" (ὁμοίωμα) also communicates divine redemptive solidarity, which in turn instigates and empowers believers' redemptive solidarity with Christ's own death; as Paul promised earlier in Rom 6:5: "If we have become united with him in the likeness (ἐν ὁμοιώματι) of his death, we will also be in [the likeness of] his resurrection."

Undergirding this interpretation of Christ's incarnation and crucifixion is a thoroughly participatory anthropology that sees all human existence as constructed in relationship to communally mediated powers. The power of sin oppresses human agents from without and subverts them from within. Space precludes a full review here of Paul's depiction of that horrific situation, particularly in the dramatization of the "I" and indwelling "sin" in Rom 7:7–20, but it is crucial to understand "the flesh of sin" in 8:3 in light of the immediately preceding performance of "sin" in Romans 7. There "sin" is not reduced to merely individual human actions, but rather is an acting subject that deceives, kills, works death, accomplishes and practices evil, even as it inhabits and overtakes the one who wants to do the good. The "flesh of sin," therefore, is not simply or primarily sinful human flesh. Rather, the term seems to signify the relational systems in which sin as a power conscripts human bodies and interactions and uses them for lethal purposes in a multitude of ways. "The flesh of sin," that is, is akin to "the body of sin" (τὸ σῶμα τῆς ἁμαρτίας –Rom 6:6). "The flesh of sin" denotes human enmeshment in a relational web possessed and ruled over by sin, just as "body of sin" denotes bodily existence as possessed and dominated by sin. Similarly, "the law of sin and death" (8:2) is the law in the grip of sin and death, used by sin to work death. "This body of death" (7:24) is the body dominated by death, in need of deliverance through incorporation into the body of Christ, who himself first initiated that incorporation by assuming a body like ours, subject to death.

If this is the case, then God's sending of his Son in "the likeness of the flesh of sin" means that Christ entered bodily into this relationally constructed existence, a corporate "living death," yet without becoming fully reduced to it. The closest parallel to this astounding claim is in 2 Cor 5:21: "For our sake he (God) made him (Christ) to be sin, who knew no sin, so that in him we might become the righteousness of God." Given such a divine assimilation to the condition of "sin" understood as the destructive relational matrix that holds all humanity hostage, the condemnation pronounced on Adam's heirs (5:16, 18) now is done away with through the condemnation pronounced on sin itself. The locus of that condemnation is the body of Jesus himself as he hangs on the cross. Yet, paradoxically, his death under condemnation, with and for humanity "under sin," is simultaneously Christ's righteous act (δικαίωμα – 5:18), through which believers are liberated from "the law of sin and death." Through this righteous act, now the "righteous requirement of the law may be fulfilled (τὸ δικαίωμα τοῦ νόμου πληρωθῇ) in us, who walk not according to the flesh but according to the Spirit" (8:4). Accordingly the liberating and empowering "law of the Spirit of life in Christ Jesus" (8:2) surely echoes the promise of 5:17: "If, because of the trespass of the one, death reigned through that one, much more will those who receive the abundance of grace and the free gift of righteousness reign in life through the one Jesus Christ." The "law of the Spirit of life in Christ Jesus" is characterized by grace and free gift, and its gifted character is central to its liberating power.[15]

Thus in Rom 8:1–4 Paul restates in experiential and pneumatically rich terms the affirmations of chapters 5–6.[16] Furthermore, the singular "you" in 8:2 must be given its due force; the deliverance from condemnation brings good news precisely to the singular "I" that laments in Rom 7:7–24, crying out, "Who will deliver me from this body of death?"[17] The lament arises from the personal experience of the full lethal and empirical force of "the law of sin and death," which with Paul Meyer I take to be the law as used and co-opted by sin (7:7–25).[18] That force demands an experiential counterforce, which for Paul is the Spirit. Just as the incarnate Christ, sent in the likeness of the flesh of sin, became assimilated to and participated in the realm of human existence "in the flesh" and "under sin," so now the Spirit unites believers in a participatory matrix of "life in Christ Jesus," indwelt by the Spirit and proceeding under the forensic banner of "no condemnation."

Paul continues to intertwine both the forensic and the participatory motifs as he limns new life in the Spirit, and he continues to keep both closely tied to the action of God in Christ. Thus later in the chapter he exclaims: "Who shall bring any charge against God's elect? It is God who rectifies: who is to condemn? Is it Christ Jesus, who died, yes, who was raised from the dead, who is at the right hand of God, who indeed intercedes for us?" (8:33b–34). This is thoroughly juridical language. At the same time, the language of the Spirit is participatory through and through. The Spirit of God indwells the community (8:9–11), countering the power of sin that "dwells in me" in 7:17, 20; nothing in all creation can separate us from the love of God in Christ Jesus our Lord" (8:39). The deadly nexus of con-

---

[15] We may note also Rom. 5:21: "as sin reigned (ἐβασίλευσεν) in death, grace also might reign (βασιλεύσῃ) through righteousness to eternal life through Jesus Christ our Lord"; and Rom. 6:14: "Sin will have no dominion (οὐ κυριεύσει) over you, because you are not under law but under grace."

[16] In Fee's words, "[T]he Spirit is the experiential, life-giving lynchpin to everything that has been argued to this point." Fee, *God's Empowering Presence*, 516.

[17] For a defense of the singular reading, see Bruce M. Metzger, *A Textual Commentary on the Greek New Testament* (2d ed.; Stuttgart: German Bible Society, 1994), 456. Stanley Stowers argues that the singular "you" addressed in Rom 8:2 is the singular "I" who cries out for deliverance in 7:24. See *A Rereading of Romans: Justice, Jews, and Gentiles* (New Haven, Conn.: Yale University Press, 1994), 282. See also my "Double Participation and the Responsible Self in Romans 5–8," in *Apocalyptic Paul: Cosmos and Anthropos in Romans 5–8* (ed. Beverly Roberts Gaventa; Waco: Baylor University Press, 2013), 93–110.

[18] Meyer, "Romans," 189.

demnation *for* sin under the law, and slavery *to* sin under the law, gives way to the dynamic presence of the life-giving Spirit through the self-giving Christ. All of this suggests that even the 'forensic' or 'juridical' language relies on participatory notions of human existence in relationship to the realm dominated by sin and death (and their lethal use of the law), along with participatory notions of God's action in Christ. It is crucial to stress that the leverage for change from the old dominion under the law of sin and death, to the new dominion animated by the Spirit of life in Christ Jesus, is precisely God's participation in humanity's condition. It is Christ's incarnation, death and resurrection in history that accomplish this cosmic power shift. It is the Spirit's ongoing participation in human existence that gives it experiential traction.

B. The Spirit-filled Community: oneself in another

But you are not in the flesh, you are in *the Spirit*, since in fact *the Spirit of God* dwells in you. If anyone does not have *the Spirit of Christ*, such a one does not belong to Him. But if *Christ* is in you, on the one hand the body is dead through sin, but on the other hand, *the Spirit* is life through righteousness. Now if *the Spirit of the one who raised Jesus from the dead* dwells in you, the one who raised Christ from the dead also will give life to your mortal bodies through *his Spirit* dwelling in you (Rom 8:9–11).

God never *starts* being in loving relationship; it's an aspect of what he is eternally.[19]

I. The Relational Spirit

Paul never talks about the Spirit as a free-standing, self-evident, or generic entity. To the contrary, Paul talks about the Spirit as always in specific relationship to God and to Christ. As Meyer puts it, notions of πνεῦμα become "distinctively Christian precisely when they are related, and by virtue of being related, to the figure of Jesus Christ."[20] Therefore this relationship, rather than widespread and varied notions of πνεῦμα in the ancient world, is the starting point for talking about the Spirit in Paul's letters.[21] Perhaps nowhere in those letters is the inter-connectedness between

---

[19] Rowan Williams, *Tokens of Trust: An Introduction to Christian Belief* (Louisville; London: Westminster John Knox, 2007), 68.

[20] Meyer, "Holy Spirit," 118.

[21] Such an approach distinguishes the present essay from the approach taken by Troels Engberg-Pedersen in *Cosmology and Self in the Apostle Paul*. Engberg-Pedersen explicitly situates his interpretation of Pauline language about the Spirit within the world-views on offer in Paul's time, specifically Stoicism. Thus his first chapter is "A Stoic Understanding of the Pneuma and Resurrection in 1 Corinthians 15." He vigorously defends

the Spirit, Christ and God more evident than in Rom 8:9–11. The relational qualification of the Spirit's identity is abundantly clear in Paul's interchangeable references to the Spirit as the indwelling "Spirit of God" (Rom 8:9), the "Spirit of Christ" (Rom 8:9), which he glosses in the next breath as simply "Christ in you" (Rom 8:10), and "the Spirit of the one who raised Jesus from the dead" which "dwells in you" (Rom 8:11). The repetition of "dwells in you" (οἰκεῖ ἐν ὑμῖν) in verses 9 and 11 forms an *inclusio* linking the Spirit with God, who in turn is known precisely as the one who raised Jesus from the dead. The central motif therefore is the indwelling of Christ through the Spirit.

In this dense and thoroughly interpersonal reference to the indwelling Spirit, Paul's proto-Trinitarian language makes explicit the connections between Christ and the Spirit that he has implied earlier in the letter. What Paul depicts in Rom 6:5–11 as union with Christ that liberates humanity from bondage to sin into new life (ζωή), he now proclaims through the indwelling Spirit of Christ.[22] Again, just as believers are to reckon themselves "dead to sin and alive to God in Christ Jesus" (6:11), through the Spirit they are to "put to death the deeds of the body" and live (8:13). In short, what Paul proclaimed Christologically in Romans 6 he now describes pneumatologically. Or in plain English, in the mutual fellowship of those "in Christ," the Spirit powerfully makes effective the reality of Christ's death and resurrection with and for humanity. Not only this (as Paul would say), but now the parallel and mutual activity between the Spirit and Christ continues: the Spirit intercedes for the saints through prayer (8:26), and the risen Christ also intercedes for the saints at the right hand of God (8:34).

All of this is to say that the Spirit is divine being-in-relationship, and as such discloses the participatory relational life at the heart of God. The action of God in raising Jesus, the action of Christ indwelling the fellowship of believers, the action of the Spirit mirroring the action of Christ, all disclose this mutuality within the divine identity. It therefore is no surprise that the Spirit animates a communal life of mutuality and interdependence among human beings as well.

II. Second-personal Identities

The first aspect of the new relational matrix animated and sustained by the Spirit is Paul's use of plural pronouns. This may seem obvious, but its importance is surprisingly neglected in discussions of the Spirit and of spir-

---

this starting point: "One idea in particular we should resist: that Paul's world-view was, as it were *beforehand*, unique and different in kind." *Cosmology and Self*, 9.

[22] See Fee, *God's Empowering Presence*, 501.

itual experience. For example, Fee's excellent exegesis of Romans 8 repeatedly alludes to the Spirit "indwelling the believer" in a formulation that easily leads the individual to look "inward" for some private knowledge or recognition of the Spirit's presence.[23] Yet such an individualistic emphasis does not reflect Paul's language. Rather, immediately after he speaks liberation to the singular second-personal "you" in 8:3, Paul enfolds his addressee into the plural, intersubjective "we" who may walk according the Spirit. After a third-person description of the contrast between the thoughts of the flesh and the thoughts of the Spirit (vv. 5–8), he returns to a second-personal address, again in the plural (vv. 9–11). The Spirit indwelling the *community* is the counterbalance to sin indwelling the singular ἐγώ in 7:17, 20. In order to bring out the sense of the plural, a paraphrase of 8:9 might read, "But together with one another, you are not in the flesh but in the Spirit, since in fact the Spirit of God dwells in the midst of your life together." As Robert Jewett rightly remarks, Paul's language "reflects a collective type of charismatic mysticism in which God's Spirit was thought to enter and energize the community as well as each member. Its primary arena of manifestation, in contrast to most later Christianity, was not individual ecstasy but social enthusiasm."[24] Jewett locates the background for this understanding in the Spirit's "indwelling" the people of Israel, citing among other passages, Ex. 29:45–46: "And I will dwell among the people of Israel and will be their God […] that I might dwell among them."[25]

Ernst Käsemann holds together both the individual and the community as the locus of the Spirit in Rom 8:9–11, by glossing "among you" (ἐν ὑμῖν) as "an anthropological reference to individual Christians and an ecclesiological reference to the whole community."[26] But ἐν ὑμῖν is not singular but plural. This is not to say that the individual person becomes lost in the collective; that such is not the case is abundantly clear from the reappearance of the singular in the exhortations of ch.14.[27] Nonetheless, here where Paul talks about the experience of the Spirit's presence and work, his focus is on that presence in the shared interaction of believers. He does

---

[23] For example, he speaks of the Spirit as the way God takes up "personal residence within the life of the believer." Fee, *God's Empowering Presence*, 554.

[24] Robert Jewett, *Romans: A Commentary* (Hermeneia; Minneapolis: Fortress, 2007), 490–91. Jewett also notes the dominance of "individualistic" interpretations of the passage. See further his "The Question of the 'Apportioned Spirit' in Paul's Letters: Romans as a Case Study," in *The Holy Spirit and Christian Origins*, 196, n. 16; see also 193–206.

[25] Jewett, *Romans*, 490.

[26] Ernst Käsemann, *Romans* (trans. G. Bromiley; Grand Rapids: Eerdmans, 1980), 219.

[27] On the relationship between personal and corporate identity in Romans, see my "Double Participation," 93–110.

not appeal to the Romans' private, inward experiences of the Holy Spirit, but to the Spirit as received and known "between ourselves."

It is worth pausing to ponder the implications of this plural language. To be "in Christ" is to be in relationship with people in the midst of whom Christ dwells through his Spirit, and thereby to share experiences not only with Christ but also with one another. It is to have an identity that is always shaped and constituted in relation to others within the bond generated and sustained by the Spirit. It is to be constituted as interpersonal beings at the very foundation of our identity, always to be oneself-in-another, never oneself in isolation or autonomy. Paul develops this insight in a number of ways, most notably through his combined use of συν-compounds and kinship imagery at two related points in the chapter: 8:14–17 and 8:26–30. The two passages parallel one another in their amplification and illumination of the workings of the Spirit in the midst of the gathered community, which in each case issues in a new kind of speech towards God (vv. 15, 26), and which in each case ends with the assurance of future glory (vv. 17, 30). The Spirit acts *with* believers so that they act *with* each other, and the depth and intimacy of that interpersonal connection is such that Paul uses familial language to express it. The result is a restructuring of the interpersonal foundations of oneself in relation to others, generating new modes of knowledge and communication.

III. The Spirit With and Between and Among Us

In Paul's deployment of συν-compound words in these passages, the Spirit is the primary actor working together with human actors. The Spirit witnesses together (συμμαρτυρεῖ) with our spirit that we are children of God (8:16). But what exactly does it mean for the Spirit to "witness together with our spirit"? In line with the dominant assumption that Paul has individual experience in view, the majority of commentators find here some sort of "inward" affirmation or personal awareness of a shift in status, a felt sense of filial relationship to God.[28] Nonetheless Paul is not addressing individuals here, but rather the community in which he includes himself with the phrase "*our* spirit" – the possessive is plural, the noun is singular.[29] Furthermore, Paul does not say the Spirit witnesses *to* our individual spirits – whatever that might mean – but *with* our spirit. Is this second

---

[28] James D. G. Dunn speaks of an "intense consciousness of sonship." *Romans 1–8* (WBC 38A; Dallas: Word, 1988), 462.

[29] Fee reads this as a distributive plural, thereby maintaining his focus on the Spirit as indwelling individual believers. But precisely because the preceding language of the Spirit's "indwelling" is addressed to the plural second person, his argument is less than persuasive. Fee, *God's Empowering Presence*, 567–68.

"spirit" anthropological?[30] Or is it, as Jewett argues, the Holy Spirit "apportioned" to the community and dwelling in its midst?[31] In support of his argument, Jewett cites the legal requirement of two witnesses to attest to the truth of any claim. Here, he claims, Paul calls the Spirit and its witnessing presence in the community as co-witnesses testifying to the truth of our identity and inheritance as children of God.[32] He further notes 1 Cor 2:11–12, where Paul says no one can understand the things of God except the Spirit of God, which indeed God has given to us. I would add that in the context of 1 Cor 2:7, among such "things of God" (τὰ τοῦ θεοῦ) is our future glorification, which surely is part of our shared inheritance as God's children (Rom 8:17).

Furthermore, in Rom 8:16–17 the shared "cry" to God as "Father" seems to refer to communal, shared acclamation or prayer.[33] So if the cry itself is the Spirit testifying "with our spirit" that we have status and inheritance as children of God, then the testimony also is a public, shared event. Is "our spirit" then the Spirit within us crying out "Abba" in an "overlay of subjects" such that we also are crying out? Such an overlay of divine and human action is typical of Paul; in Gal 4:6 *the Spirit* sent into our hearts cries out "Abba! Father!" while in Rom 8:16, inspired by the Spirit among us, *we* cry out in the same way.

All of these observations further support Jewett's suggestion that "our spirit" refers to the Spirit given by God to the gathered community. The primary argument against such a view is that God would be talking to himself, or witnessing with himself.[34] And yet when we turn our attention to Rom 8:26–29, where Paul also combines συν-compound words with familial language, such inner-divine communication is precisely what we hear. We do not know what to pray as we ought, says Paul, but in our weakness the Spirit comes to our aid (συναντιλαμβάνεται) by interceding for us with unspeakable groans, and God "who searches the hearts" knows the intention (φρόνημα) of the Spirit (8:26–27).[35] This surely is an inner-divine communication in which we bodily – indeed vocally – participate. It seems possible therefore that the earlier shared witness of the Spirit with "our spirit" expressed in the communal, public cry to God as "Father," is also such an inner-divine and yet also embodied human communication. In both

---

[30] Fee equates an anthropological spirit with "the inner person" in 2 Cor 4:16. Fee, *God's Empowering Presence*, 568–69. See also Dunn, *Romans 1–8*, 462.

[31] Jewett, *Romans*, 500–501.

[32] Jewett, *Romans*, 500–501.

[33] So Jewett, *Romans*, 499; Meyer, "Romans," 190; Käsemann, *Romans*, 227.

[34] Fee regards this as "a view that seems nearly indefensible (the Spirit is merely bearing witness to himself)." Fee, *God's Empowering Presence*, 568, n. 285.

[35] Again, I note a link with 1 Cor 2:10, where it is the Spirit who searches all things, even the depths of God.

instances, through the Spirit human beings are co-participants in an interpersonal communication between the Spirit and God. We participate in a divine-human speech-act.

That shared speech-act, I suggest, not only expresses the Spirit's presence with us, but also expresses the reality of the relationship with each other which arises from the Spirit's leading: "All who are led by the Spirit of God are children of God" (8:14). As children of God we are co-heirs (συγκληρονόμοι) with and of Christ, since we suffer together (συμπάσχομεν) that we may be glorified together (συγδοξασθῶμεν) (8:17). All of this is *with* Christ. But it is also *with* each other. That is, the compounds do not primarily denote a joint action between the individual and Christ, but rather a common experience between Christ and persons in relationship to each other. Since we join in Christ's sufferings as we share in one another's sufferings, we also will be joined together in Christ's glory. All of these compound verbs and nouns express the common reality of children of God who cry out together "Abba! Father!" (8:16–17).

Romans 8:28–29 has a similar combination of συν-compounds and familial metaphors. The translation of v. 28 is notoriously difficult.[36] It seems likely that either God or the Spirit is the subject of the verb "works together" (συνεργεῖ), depending on whether we accent the Spirit's role as intercessor, or God's role as "the one who searches the hearts" and "knows the intention of the Spirit." The first is suggested by the Spirit's placement as subject of the verb in the immediately preceding clause, but the latter is supported by God's position as subject of the verbs in vv. 29–30. Given the intimate interaction and joint activity of God and the Spirit, the question may be moot, although both Fee and Jewett mount strong arguments for the Spirit as subject, given its primary role as the subject of συν-compound verbs throughout the chapter.[37]

More to the point here is the question why Paul uses the συν prefix; he simply could have said "In all things the Spirit of God works for good." The prefix is second-personal – it assumes a second party in the action of the verb. The strong implication is that the community of those 'in Christ' is that second party; in all things the Spirit works together with and for "those who love him." In Jewett's words, Paul's language "claims a divine-human synergism in the midst of disadvantageous circumstances, because the Spirit works 'with' those who love God."[38] The purpose of this joint action is a process of shared formation, being con-formed (συμμόρφους) to the image of God's Son (8:29) and thereby glorified to-

---

[36] I join the majority of commentators in rejecting the translation of πάντα as the subject of the verb. See Jewett, *Romans*, 526–28, for discussion of the issues.

[37] Jewett, *Romans*, 526–28; Fee, *God's Empowering Presence*, 589–90.

[38] Jewett, *Romans*, 527.

gether (8:30), just as in 8:17 those in Christ share the hope of co-glorification. Again, as in 8:17, the result and indeed purpose of this shared conformation to the image of Christ is participation in a new extended family: that Christ might be the first-born among many brothers and sisters (2:29).

IV. Kinship and the Kindness of God[39]

We have seen that in both 8:14–17 and 8:26–29, the shared action of the Spirit and the community indwelt by the Spirit culminates in a new relational matrix in which believers are embedded. Paul's use of familial metaphors is striking: led by the Spirit, we are "sons of God"; crying "Abba! Father!" as "children of God," we are joint-heirs with Christ, suffering together in anticipation of being glorified together. Christ is the first-born of many siblings. Within this new "family system" the reality that follows from being adopted into God's family is co-inheritance, co-suffering, and co-glorification. Jewett gets at some of the implications of this familial language by noting how Paul's use of "children" rather than "sons" in 8:17 bypasses the competition for inheritance typical of the ancient (and modern!) world.[40] To be heirs of God and co-heirs with Christ is to be in a relationship of shared inheritance with others as well, mediated by the indwelling Spirit. Hence those whom the Spirit joins together find themselves in a new network of saving relations that surpasses and cuts through the web of deception and destructive relationships woven by sin and its use of the law to deceive and kill (7:9).

As argued earlier, Paul's word for the old relational web is "the flesh" (8:4–9, 13), which here denotes our bodily participation in and subjection to the realm of existence dominated by sin and condemned to death under the law of sin and death (8:2–3). Metaphorically it functions as a kind of "family system" that pulls us backwards into divisive and destructive behaviors.[41] Over against such an enslaving system, "all who are led by the Spirit are sons of God" (8:14), thereby sharing in a new interpersonally constituted identity that is "Christianized and broadened beyond ethnic, familial, imperial, legalistic, and educational barriers."[42] Such participation in a new primary relational matrix conveys a re-formation of personal

---

[39] This play on words, linking "kinship" with divine "kindness" or likeness to humanity, comes from Janet Martin Soskice, *The Kindness of God: Metaphor, Gender, and Religious Language* (Oxford: Oxford University Press, 2008).

[40] Jewett, *Romans*, 502.

[41] Elsewhere I have argued that in Gal 5:16–26, the "flesh" and the Spirit denote competing family systems, metaphorically speaking. See *Recovering Paul's Mother Tongue: Language and Theology in Galatians* (Grand Rapids: Eerdmans, 2007), 161–79.

[42] Jewett, *Romans*, 497.

character, motivation and relationship at the most foundational level. Paul indicates the shocking intimacy and immediacy of this re-construction of persons-in-relationship by adducing the communal cry, "Abba! Father!" We do not need to interpret "Abba" as "Daddy" to recognize the intimate, familial nuance of the term; this is language that children and adults use within the family circle.[43] And while the word translated "we cry out" (κράζομεν) occurs frequently in prayer, it also can refer to the screaming of infants, weeping, shrieking, and even Jesus' cry from the cross (Matt 27:50).[44] It is, in short, a verb expressing primitive and powerful emotions, here in the most primal of human relationships.[45] The terminology evokes the primary interaction between parent and child that human beings internalize and carry with them throughout adulthood, now transformed through the bond between the indwelling Spirit, believers and each other.

In other words, the familial metaphors of "father," "sons," "children," and "siblings" powerfully reshape the constitution of persons in Christ. They shake the foundations of personhood, conflicting with and re-narrating other interpersonal foundations, most particularly those supplied by one's family of origin, clan, ethnic group, and social status. Such was Paul's own experience in regard to his heritage as a Jew. Much as he celebrated that heritage (Rom 9:4–5), he also fought against its potentially divisive influence in his mixed congregations. And even though Paul had not founded the churches in Rome, distinctions based on Jewish or Gentile origins were a disruptive factor in those churches as well. Over against any and all originating narratives about what constitutes personal and communal identity, Paul sets forth a new, surpassing familial bond: united in calling God "Abba," the Roman Christians are united as non-competing heirs of God through their shared participation in Christ's death and in the promise of future glory (8:15–17). They are now "brothers" (8:29), and the knowledge of this new relationship is mediated through their joint experience of the Spirit.

V. The Gracious Bond of Love

Paul first speaks of the gift of the Spirit alongside his first reference to love, in Rom 5:5: "hope does not put to shame, because the love of God has been poured into our hearts through the Spirit which has been given to us."[46] Two aspects of the Spirit's presence immediately come to the fore: the Spirit mediates knowledge of God's love, and the Spirit is a gifted rela-

---

[43] Jewett, *Romans*, 499; James Barr, "*Abba* Isn't 'Daddy,'" *JTS* 39 (1988), 35–40.
[44] Jewett, *Romans*, 498–99.
[45] Dunn, *Romans 1–8*, 461.
[46] See Meyer, who notes the link between the Spirit and love in Rom. 8 as well as Rom. 5:5. "Holy Spirit," 120.

tionship. The love and the gift go together, and together they ground every other aspect of the Spirit's activity as God's empowering presence in the midst of the community. That Paul here intends to speak of God's love for us rather than our love for God is supported by 5:8: "God shows his love for us in that while we were still sinners, Christ died for us." This experience of the Spirit, as an affirmation of the love of God given to the undeserving, grounds the confidence with which Paul can say in Rom 8:15, "you did not receive a spirit of slavery [leading] again into fear, but you have received the Spirit of adoption." The Spirit-mediated experience of God's love catches Paul's auditors up into a bond of love characterized by confident belonging rather than fear and bondage.

In Rom 8:28 the theme of love returns, but here it clearly is human love towards God: "In all things God works for good with *those who love God*, who are called according to his purpose." Such human love towards God is a response of mutual engagement with the One who showed love by Christ's death for the ungodly, and who draws human beings into that love through the calling that constitutes their being. We who once were God's enemies are now caught up into an interchange of love with God. This is the interpersonal bond in which new modes of thought are born. "We do not know how to pray as we ought" but "we *do* know that in all things the Spirit works for good together with those who love God."

The triumphant affirmation of Rom 8:35–39 echoes Rom 5:3–5. Nothing, including tribulation (θλίψις), "will be able to separate us from the love of God in Christ Jesus our Lord" (8:35–39). That affirmation is the basis for the hope given in the midst of tribulation through the love of God poured into our hearts (5:5). But it also draws on the promise of 8:28, insofar as the all-encompassing list of potential threats to union with that love of God (8:35–39), simply amplifies "all things" in 8:28: in all *these* things, the Spirit works together for good with those who love God. Therefore, "affliction produces endurance, endurance produces character (δοκιμή), character produces hope, and hope does not put to shame" (5:3–5a).

Finally, Paul does not end his discussion of the bond of love with this triumphant affirmation. Later in the letter he draws out the practical, concrete implications of this divine-human interchange of love, by enjoining a similar love between human beings. In their mutual relations, the Roman Christians are to "let love be without hypocrisy" (Rom 12:9). Paul immediately expands on the effects of such love: It shows itself in the affection proper to siblings (φιλαδελφία); it honors others, it is patient in affliction, persistent in prayer, practical in showing hospitality (12:10–13). Indeed such practical service in mutual love is the only obligation now incumbent on believers (13:8–10); fulfilling the law (13:12), it enacts the fulfillment of the righteous requirement of the law in the midst of the community (8:4).

C. The Cradle of Thought

In *The Cradle of Thought*, Peter Hobson argues that human cognition, including awareness of self and of others as thinking, emoting, intending and acting beings, originates in the interaction between infants and their caregivers; this bond is the "cradle" in which thought is born. It is, one might say, precisely in loving relationships that infants are called into being as perceiving, thinking, interpersonal beings. In appropriating Hobson's title, I suggest that the relational matrix generated and sustained by the Spirit within and among believers "in Christ" is just such a "cradle" in which personal identity and social cognition are re-worked at a foundational level. The themes of cognition, intention and recognition run throughout Rom 8:1–30 and accompany the Spirit's role in generating new speech.[47] The shared witness of the Spirit generates new self-recognition in relationship to God as God's children, and to each other as siblings. The Spirit's aid with our weakness generates inarticulate groaning that also mediates a kind of knowledge of both our own limitations and God's knowledge of us and transforming work among and within us. All of this takes place in a communal life characterized by mutual love, noncompetitive kinship, shared experience, and the absence of condemnation.

Indeed, Paul foregrounds the Spirit's role in cognition in the first several verses of Romans 8. In Rom 8:4b–11 it is the Holy Spirit, in contrast with the flesh, who acts on, in and with human agents. The confusing and intriguing overlay of subjects in 8:4–8 alternates between human and divine agents doing the same things. In vv. 4–5, the δικαίωμα of the law may be fulfilled in us, who walk according to the Spirit. The passive voice leaves ambiguous the identity of the agent who fulfills the law's require-

---

[47] There is a great deal more to be said concerning the Spirit's role in speech, but space and time preclude such an investigation here. One thinks again of the "Abba" cry, the inarticulate groaning of the Spirit's intercession, the role of the Spirit in the confession of Jesus Christ as Lord (1 Cor 12:3), and of course, the Spirit's gifts of prophecy, tongues, the "word of wisdom" and the "word of knowledge" (1 Cor 12:8, 28–30; 14:2–19). The intimate link between speech and knowledge itself suggests that new speech implies and perhaps generates new modes of thought, a new grammatically structured world-view. On this see Beverly Roberts Gaventa, "From Toxic Speech to the Redemption of Doxology in Romans," in *The Word Leaps the Gap: Essays on Scripture and Theology in Honor of Richard B. Hays* (ed. J. Ross Wagner, C. Kavin Rowe and A. Katherine Grieb; Grand Rapids: Eerdmans, 2008), 392–408.

ment.⁴⁸ That ambiguity continues in the cognitive language that follows. At first Paul says that human agents possessed by the Spirit walk in line with the Spirit and indeed think the things of the Spirit, rather than deriving their identity from the flesh and thinking the things of the flesh (τὰ τῆς σαρκὸς φρονοῦσιν in 8:5). But then he names the "flesh" and the Spirit as freestanding agents with their own distinctive mindsets: "The mindset (τὸ φρόνημα) of the flesh is death, but the mindset (τὸ φρόνημα) of the Spirit is life and peace" (8:6). English translations tend to gloss over the active roles of both the flesh and the Spirit as the possessors of distinctive intentions, thoughts and attitudes, rather implying merely human activity in both cases: "To set the mind on the flesh is death, but to set the mind on the Spirit is life and peace" (RSV). Such a translation takes its cues from Rom 8:5, but it misses the significant interplay between the action of the Spirit and human action; in contrast with the deceptive, lethal and disruptive effects of sin's relational embrace of the self in the realm of "flesh," the Spirit's discernment works within and among believers, generating an attitudinal transformation that leads to life and peace.

Thus Paul here limns the first evidence of the Spirit working in and with human beings: a transformed mindset, incorporating motifs of perception, discernment and judgment that lead to peace among believers. In Rom 12:1–2 Paul amplifies this motif through the promise of transformation through the renewal of the mind, which in turn "proves, tests, and judges" in accordance with the will of God (μεταμορφοῦσθε τῇ ἀνακαινώσει τοῦ νοὸς εἰς τὸ δοκιμάζειν ὑμᾶς τί τὸ θέλημα τοῦ θεοῦ). This renewed kind of judgment that tests and performs the divine will is precisely the reverse of the base mind (ἀδόκιμος νοῦς) into which reprobate humanity was delivered by God as a result of the primal idolatry (1:28). The proof of such a transformation is in the attitudes enacted between members of the community who are not to consider themselves above others (μὴ ὑπερφρονεῖν παρ' ὃ δεῖ φρονεῖν) but rather to be wisely "minded" towards one another (φρονεῖν εἰς τὸ σωφρονεῖν) (12:3). Jewett's translation captures the four-fold word play here on φρονεῖν: "Do not be superminded above what one ought to be minded, but set your mind on being sober-minded" (12:3).⁴⁹ This is a newly minted social cognition – the practical and social outworking of the Spirit's transforming φρόνησις at work in the shared mindset of the community. Furthermore, Paul speaks emphatically here not simply to the community as a corporate entity, but to each member of the Roman congregations. He invokes a new relational quality of life, which does not erase the individual agent, but generates mutual encouragement and re-

---

⁴⁸ One may note here the parallel passive voice in Gal 5:14: "The whole law *has been fulfilled* in one word, 'You shall love your neighbor as yourself.'"

⁴⁹ Jewett, *Romans*, 736.

spect among members of the new community in Christ. The quality of interaction between believers that Paul enjoins in Rom 12:1–3 thus demonstrates the φρόνησις generated by the Spirit's presence in the midst of the community, the new family system in 8:1–29.

Throughout the Spirit's cognitive restructuring of human mindsets there is a practical, mutual demonstration of the bond of love, a distinctive mutual knowledge and understanding that draws believers into shared participation in the Christ who in turn participates in their shared life. It is just this kind of loving discernment for which Paul prays in Phil 1:9–10a: "This is what I pray: That your love (ἀγάπη) may overflow more and more in knowledge (ἐπιγνώσει) and all discernment (αἰσθήσει), so that you may approve (δοκιμάζειν) what is excellent." It would be difficult to find a more succinct and compelling expression of loving relationship as the "cradle of thought." This is the cognitive outworking of the love poured into our hearts through the gift of the Spirit.

The remainder of Romans 8 contains a tension between what "we know" and what "we do not know," and both our knowledge and our ignorance are mediated by the Spirit. "We know the whole creation groans together and travails together until now" (8:22), and indeed we share in this groaning, living in hope of a future salvation (8:23–25). "We know that in all things the Spirit works for good together with those who love God" (8:28). The Spirit gives these two objects of knowledge: the knowledge of present suffering, shared with all creation, and the knowledge of the Spirit's work in all things, including suffering, for our mutual transformation and future glorification. But in the present time between these two certainties, possession of and by the Spirit does not lead to special knowledge in prayer; to the contrary, "We do *not* know (οὐκ οἴδαμεν) how to pray as we ought, but the Spirit himself intercedes for us with inarticulate groans" (8:26). These inarticulate groans express the mindset or intention of the Spirit (τὸ φρόνημα τοῦ πνεύματος), which is known (οἶδεν) by God who searches hearts, but not by those indwelt by the Spirit.[50] The limitation suggests a degree of mystery remaining in and among Christian believers; there are depths that are not plumbed by human awareness, but are plumbed by God and articulated by the Spirit. Within this mystery, there is

---

[50] Whether the "unspeakable groaning" (στεωαγμοῖς ἀλαλήτοις) in 8:26 refers to private prayer in tongues (Fee, *God's Empowering Presence*, 580–86), silent prayer (Jewett, *Romans*, 524), public glossolalia (Käsemann, *Romans*, 240–41), or simply "the inability to use that speech which distinguishes man from animal" (Dunn, *Romans 1–8*, 479), the common strand is that the meaning of the groans is inaccessible to the mind of the one in whom and through whom the Spirit prays. Citing 1 Cor 14:14–15, Fee translates ἀλαλήτοις as "inarticulate . . . without the kind of articulation we associate with the use of words – that is, with *words that we understand with our own minds.*" *God's Empowering Presence*, 583 (emphasis original).

both union between believers and the Spirit, but also a lasting distinction between human perception and divine speech. The meaning of the Spirit's unspeakable groans exceeds our understanding, but not God's, and it leaves us in the position of trusting God at the limit of our understanding.[51] This tension between ignorance and knowledge leaves room for the mysteries of our existence, and yet the certainties of God's loving presence and powerful working with and among and between those who are in Christ, indwelt by the Spirit.

D. "Spiritual Experience" Revisited

This essay began with the observation that Paul invokes the Spirit when he talks about the experience of the presence and power of God in the midst of the community of believers. I further suggested that precisely this experiential aspect of Paul's Spirit language may contribute to its relative scarcity in studies of Paul's theology. It is just possible that what Paul means by the experience of the Spirit does not fit into some contemporary categories of either "experience" or "spiritual." For example, Nicholas Lash criticizes the unexamined assumption in many quarters that "religious experience" is by definition "private," "inner" and "subjective," and attributes that assumption in part to "the myth, at least as old as Descartes, that the *real* 'me,' the essential person, lives somewhere inside the head."[52] Within such a myth, the experience of the Holy Spirit would appear to be something individual, private, inside one's own subjective sense of oneself, and therefore elusive for some, and for others seductively susceptible to charges of psychological projection or delusional thinking.

The experience of the Spirit on display in Romans 8 simply does not fit such dualistic Cartesian categories. First, Paul's language is neither individualistic nor collective, but personal – experience occurs in our hearts, but our hearts exist in relationship with others "in Christ." So we find the bulk of Paul's references to Spirit's working located in and among people, in the midst of the community. The site of "spiritual experience" is not in private, inward sensations or thoughts, but in the relational bonds between members of Christ's body. This interpersonal experience is part and parcel

---

[51] Similarly, when Paul does adduce a personal ecstatic experience of assent to the third heaven, he declines to say what he heard, naming it rather as "words which a person may not speak (οὐκ ἐξὸν ανθρώπω λαλῆσαι)" (2 Cor 12:4). Instead he directs his auditors' attention to the concrete and visible evidence of what may be seen and heard in him: to wit, "weaknesses, insults, hardships, persecutions, and calamities" for the sake of Christ (2 Cor 12:6, 10).

[52] "Human Experience and the Knowledge of God," 144.

of Paul's participatory anthropology, which renders boundaries between self and others permeable without being fully dissolved.

Secondly, therefore, the work of the Spirit sustains a kind of "dual agency" inaugurated by God's action in Christ. As J. Louis Martyn puts it,

> When Paul speaks in Galatians 5 of the fruit of the Spirit of Christ, he refers to nothing less than God's steadfast *participation* in the moral drama itself. He refers in short to the dual agency that is a mark of the new creation. [...] Love, joy, and living at peace are deeds of human beings, to be sure, but specifically deeds carried out every day as the Spirit of Christ bears its fruit in the dual agency known in the daily life of the church, the 'body of Christ' (1 Cor 11).[53]

"Spiritual experience" in such a context is nothing other than daily reliance on the sustaining power of divine participation in mundane life together. It is acting in line with the practical outworking of love, in confidence that God also is acting in ways that exceed our ken and control.

Thirdly, therefore, all aspects of human existence are caught up into the workings of the Spirit, so that it makes no sense to talk about "spiritual experience" as distinct from daily life. As Lash puts it:

> If dependence on God, relationship with God, is simply how, as creatures, we fundamentally and ineluctably *are*, then consciousness of such relationship – what we might call the 'sense of God' – may be given, however 'dimly,' confusedly, inarticulately, in each and every area and district of our existence and activity.[54]

Paul goes further in his claims: "In *all things* the Spirit works together for good with those who love God." The "good" is our conformation to the image of the Son, which takes place through transformation from affliction to hope (5:3–5), from co-suffering to co-glorification (8:17), and from divine calling, to rectification, to glorification (8:30). Furthermore, the basis of the Spirit's claim on every aspect of life is not simply our given reliance on God, but Paul's participatory Christology and pneumatology; because Christ entered fully into human existence, there is no unclaimed or "secular" territory of the self or society; because the Spirit continues that divine participation, there is no "unspiritual" experience beyond the reach of transformation.

Therefore, far from being individualistic, hidden and inward, the mindset co-constituted by the Spirit in and between "those who are in Christ Jesus" (Rom 8:1) has practical, relational and mutual effects. Grounded in deliverance from condemnation, the new mindset issues in non-condemning attitudes towards others (8:1; 12:3). Grounded in the love of God poured out, it issues in genuine love not only towards God but to-

---

[53] "Afterword," *Apocalyptic Paul*, 164–65; see also 157–66.
[54] "Human Experience and the Knowledge of God," 152.

wards one another (12:9; 13:8–10). It is therefore the visible and verifiable public marker of the redeeming presence of God.

Bibliography

Barr, James. "*Abba* Isn't 'Daddy'." *Journal of Theological Studies* 39 (1988): 35–40.
Branick, Vincent. "The Sinful Flesh of the Son of God (Rom 8:3): A Key Image of Pauline Theology." *Catholic Biblical Quarterly* 47 (1985): 246–62.
deBoer, Martin. "Paul and Jewish Apocalyptic Eschatology." Pages 169–90 in *Apocalyptic and the New Testament: Essays in Honour of J. Louis Martyn*. Edited by J. Marcus and M. L. Soards. Sheffield: JSOT Press, 1989.
Dunn, James D. G. *Romans 1–8*. WBC 38A. Dallas: Word, 1988.
———. *The Theology of Paul the Apostle*. Edinburgh: T&T Clark, 1998.
Eastman, Susan. "Apocalypse and Incarnation: The Participatory Logic of Paul's Gospel." Pages 165–82 in *Apocalyptic and the Future of Theology*. Edited by J. Davis And D. Harink. Eugene, Ore.: Wipf & Stock, 2012.
———. *Recovering Paul's Mother Tongue: Language and Theology in Galatians*. Grand Rapids: Eerdmans, 2007.
———. "The Empire of Illusion: Sin and Evil in Romans." Pages 3-21 in *Comfortable Words: Essays in Honor of Paul F. M. Zahl* . Edited John D. Koch and Todd Brewer. Eugene, Ore.: Wipf & Stock, 2013 .
Engberg-Pedersen, Troels. *Cosmology and Self in the Apostle Paul: The Material Spirit*. Oxford: Oxford University Press, 2010.
———. "The Construction of Religious Experience in Paul." Pages 147–58 in *Experientia, Volume I: Inquiry Into Religious Experience in Early Judaism and Christianity*. Edited by Frances Flannery et al. Atlanta: SBL, 2008.
Fatehi, Mehrdad. *The Spirit's Relation to the Risen Lord in Paul*. Wissenschaftliche Untersuchungen zum Neuen Testament 1 128. Tübingen: Mohr Siebeck, 2000.
Fee, Gordon D. *God's Empowering Presence: The Holy Spirit in the Letters of Paul*. Peabody, Mass.: Hendrickson, 1994.
Gaventa, Beverly Roberts, ed. *Apocalyptic Paul: Cosmos and Anthropos in Romans 5–8*. Waco: Baylor University Press, 2013.
———. "From Toxic Speech to the Redemption of Doxology in Romans." Pages 392–408 in *The Word Leaps the Gap: Essays on Scripture and Theology in Honor of Richard B. Hays*. Edited by J. Ross Wagner, C. Kavin Rowe and A. Katherine Grieb. Grand Rapids: Eerdmans, 2008.
Hay, David M. And E. E. Johnson, eds. *Pauline Theology: Volume III: Romans*. Minneapolis: Fortress, 1995.
Hobson, Peter. *The Cradle of Thought*. London: MacMillan, 2002.
Jewett, Robert. *Romans: A Commentary*. Hermeneia. Minneapolis: Fortress, 2007.
Käsemann, Ernst. *Romans*. Translated by G. Bromiley. Grand Rapids: Eerdmans, 1980.
Lash, Nicholas. "Human Experience and the Knowledge of God." Pages 143–47 in *Theology on the Way to Emmaus*. Eugene, Ore.: Wipf & Stock, 2005.
Marshall, I. Howard, Volker Rabens and Cornelis Bennema, eds. *The Spirit and Christ in the New Testament and Christian Theology: Essays in Honor of Max Turner*. Grand Rapids: Eerdmans, 2012.

Meyer, Paul W. "Romans: A Commentary." Pages 149–218 in *The Word in This World: Essays in New Testament Exegesis and Theology*. New Testament Library. Louisville: Westminster John Knox, 2004.

———. "The Holy Spirit in the Pauline Letters: A Contextual Exploration." Pages 117–32 in *The Word in This World: Essays in New Testament Exegesis and Theology*. New Testament Library. Louisville: Westminster John Knox, 2004.

Metzger, Bruce M. *A Textual Commentary on the Greek New Testament*. 2d ed. Stuttgart: German Bible Society, 1994.

Philip, Finny. *The Origins of Pauline Pneumatology*. Wissenschaftliche Untersuchungen zum Neuen Testament 2/194. Tübingen: Mohr Siebeck, 2005.

Reddy, Vasudevi. *How Infants Know Minds*. Cambridge, Mass.: Harvard University Press, 2008.

Shantz, Colleen. *Paul in Ecstasy: the Neurobiology of the Apostle's Life and Thought*. Cambridge: Cambridge University Press, 2009.

Soskice, Janet Martin. *The Kindness of God: Metaphor, Gender, and Religious Language*. Oxford: Oxford University Press, 2008.

Stanton, Graham N., B. W. Longenecker and S. C. Barton, eds. *The Holy Spirit and Christian Origins: Essays in Honor of James N. G. Dunn*. Grand Rapids: Eerdmans, 2004.

Stowers, Stanley. *A Rereading of Romans: Justice, Jews, and Gentiles*. New Haven, Conn.: Yale University Press, 1994.

"Real Participation"

The Body of Christ & the Body of Sin in Evolutionary Perspective

MATTHEW CROASMUN

A. Introduction

E. P. Sanders, in his classic exposition of the centrality of "participation" in Paul's thought, worries about the extent to which Paul can be taken "literally." On the one hand, against Bultmann, he argues that it is "best to understand Paul as saying what he meant and meaning what he said." Among other things, "Being one body and one Spirit with Christ is not simply living out of a revised self-understanding, although that also may result... Christians really are one body and Spirit with Christ."[1] On the other hand, Sanders is nevertheless left with questions:

> But what does this mean? How are we to understand it? We seem to lack a category of "reality" – real participation in Christ, real possession of the Spirit – which lies between naive cosmological speculation and belief in magical transference on the one hand and a revised self-understanding on the other. I must confess that I do not have a new category of perception to propose here.[2]

The shadow of Bultmann looms large over this aporia. It flows naturally from Bultmann's concerns about the fundamental incompatibility of the mythological categories of the Pauline text and the scientific categories of the contemporary reader. Richard Hays proposed four (complementary) models for understanding Pauline "real participation": familial membership, military solidarity, ecclesial membership, and narrative participation – the latter two of which he takes to be in some sense primary.[3] Inasmuch as each of these models operates as a *metaphor* of

---

[1] E. P. Sanders, *Paul and Palestinian Judaism: A Comparison of Patterns of Religion* (Philadelphia: Fortress, 1977), 522.
[2] Sanders, *Paul and Palestinian Judaism*, 523.
[3] Richard B. Hays, "What is 'Real Participation in Christ'?" in *Redefining First-Century Jewish and Christian Identities: Essays in Honor of Ed Parish Sanders* (ed.

participation "in Christ" – perhaps most vividly, of participation in Christ's *body* – Hays participates, as Stanley Stowers has suggested, in "unconscious demythologizing" of an ironically Bultmannian variety.[4]

Yet, on at least one account of Pauline ecclesiology, contemporary scientific inquiry would urge us to be bolder in taking Paul's claims quite *literally*, just as Sanders desired. Evolutionary theory now suggests we might consider the unity of the church a literal, bodily reality. Of course, there are limits to what extent and in what respects such a somatic unity ought be taken seriously as an evolutionary biological reality. But within the right context and understood correctly, contemporary evolutionary theory urges us to consider the church as an adaptive unit. Indeed, evolutionary biologist David Sloan Wilson has offered a book-length treatment of this very idea.[5]

That said, let me be quite clear about what I am *not* saying. What is *not* on offer here is an unveiling of a perfect correspondence between an ancient author's intentions and contemporary Christian appropriation, much less contemporary scientific discovery. Paul does not think of bodies in terms of "adaptive units" (as contemporary evolutionary biologists do). Contemporary Christians – much less evolutionary biologists – do not imagine "spirit" to be an element of the material world (as Paul did). Nevertheless, there are resonances between Paul's deployment of the ancient discourse of social bodies and recent advances in evolutionary biology that are mutually enlightening. As Sarah Coakley noted in her 2012 Gifford Lectures, "something is now happening in contemporary evolutionary theory – indeed is imploding distractingly within it – which is set to recharge our understanding of the meaning and significance of evolutionary processes in profound ways, ways which may, in turn, affect both our moral sensibilities and choices, and our metaphysical understandings of the way the world is and what it might be *for*."[6] This

---

Fabian E. Udoh et al.; CJAS 16; Notre Dame, Ind.: University of Notre Dame Press, 2008), 347.

[4] Stanley K. Stowers, "What is "Pauline Participation in Christ"?" in *Redefining First-Century Jewish and Christian Identities: Essays in Honor of Ed Parish Sanders* (ed. Fabian E. Udoh, et al.; CJAS 16; Notre Dame, Ind.: University of Notre Dame Press, 2008), 356.

[5] David Sloan Wilson, *Darwin's Cathedral: Evolution, Religion, and the Nature of Society* (Chicago: University of Chicago Press, 2003).

[6] Sarah Coakley, "Stories of Evolution, Stories of Sacrifice," (Lecture 1 of "Sacrifice Regained: Evolution, Cooperation and God," The 2012 Gifford Lectures, Aberdeen University, 17 April, 2012), 5. Online: http://www.abdn.ac.uk/gifford/about/2012-giff/. Coakley is careful to note that by saying that this revolution is "imploding distractingly" within evolutionary theory, she by no means intends to question the validity of evolutionary theory as a whole. She is simply inviting us to pay attention to the members of the evolutionary guild rethinking the philosophical underpinnings of their discipline.

revolution in evolutionary theory describes human communities in ways so intimately familiar to the reader of Paul that it is as though Paul's texts were, in Bakhtin's words, "constructed, as it were, in anticipation of encountering this response."[7]

Because of this relationship, attentiveness to the evolutionary biological account of social bodies allows the scholar of Paul to see with new eyes some dynamics of Pauline participation that have been obscured by, for example, modernist individualism. Through engagement with multilevel selection theory, the scholar of Paul sees clearly that participation in social bodies is not a unique feature of ecclesial life, but rather a basic feature of life as a biological organism – and, in particular ways, of life as a human person. This basic feature of life opens possibilities for group-level cognition and, for intensively cognitive and *cultural* creatures like human beings, grounds individual cognition, especially what we call *moral cognition*. Furthermore, organismic boundaries at this level of biological organization are not uniform and fixed, but rather appear to change depending on the behavior under consideration. As a result, when considering something as multifaceted as the moral life, one comes to find that hybrid membership in *multiple*, competing social bodies is not only possible but perhaps inevitable.

Each of these features of group-level somatic participation is in some sense familiar to the scholar of Paul and indigenous to Paul's writings. Ancient philosophical anthropology of the sort Paul trafficked in assumed a more or less social ontology for what moderns would call the human "individual."[8] One was always already a member of a social body. Would-be members of Paul's churches were not opting out of independence and for the first time into communal life. Rather, they were transferring from membership in one social body to membership in another.[9] Paul had to argue not for the existence of social bodies, but for the peculiarity and desirability of membership in the particular social Body of Christ. So we might ask: What of the previous social-somatic allegiances of the members of Paul's churches? While of course group-level somatic participation is always multivalent, Paul does have in his letters – particularly in Romans – a discourse about a competing social body to the Body of Christ: namely, the Body of Sin. The existence and activity of this body means that, for

---

[7] Mikhail M. Bakhtin, *Speech Genres and Other Late Essays* (trans. by Vern W. McGee. Austin: University of Texas Press, 1986), 94.

[8] Dale Martin (perhaps with some degree of exaggeration) describes this in terms of the "non-existence of the individual" in the ancient world in *The Corinthian Body* (New Haven: Yale University Press, 1995), 21. (See additional discussion below.)

[9] It will be necessary to nuance this language of "transferal" below in the discussion of the possibility of multiple, overlapping participations.

Paul, ἁμαρτία does not merely threaten the unity of the Body of Christ – that is, as a force of disunity – but in fact functions as a competing unity. These two bodies function for Paul as world bodies, on roughly Stoic terms – unities that constitute κόσμοι unto themselves.[10] Using the descriptions of the social basis of cognition found in Émile Durkheim, Ludwig Fleck, and Mary Douglas, we will find that this claim of "worldmaking" is perhaps to be taken just as seriously as the claim to somatic unity – and for similar reasons.

B. The Body in Evolutionary Perspective

I. What is a Body?

Biology has long had difficulty defining its basic unit of study: the organism.[11] At its heart, the problem is mereological – a difficulty of distinguishing parts and wholes. A recent *Scientific American* article summarizes the problem well:

> The human body is not such a neatly self-sufficient island after all. It is more like a complex ecosystem – a social network – containing trillions of bacteria and other microorganisms that inhabit our skin, genital areas, mouth, and especially intestines. In fact, most of the cells in the human body are not human at all. Bacterial cells in the human body outnumber human cells 10 to one... This mixed community of microbial cells and the genes they contain... offers vital help with basic physiological processes – from digestion to growth to self-defense. So much for human autonomy.[12]

As a result, full biological description of these basic, "internal" human physiological processes necessarily requires an account of these "external" (in the sense of being genetically non-human) organisms. Restricting oneself to the human tissue itself would make a description of functions as basic as digestion and immune defense impossible. As a result, an evolutionary account of the development of human physiology requires a parallel account of the evolution of these microbial symbiotes. In other

---

[10] For the importance of Stoic cosmology to Paul's thought, see Troels Engberg-Pedersen, *Cosmology and Self in the Apostle Paul: The Material Spirit.* (Oxford: Oxford University Press, 2010).

[11] This difficulty goes back at least as far as Ernst Haeckel, *The Evolution of Man: A Popular Exposition of the Principal Points of Human Ontogeny and Phylogeny* (New York: Appleton, 1879). This is a feature common to most disciplines. It is when one most carefully focuses on a thing that its apparent givenness becomes most difficult to maintain.

[12] Jennifer Ackerman, "The Ultimate Social Network," *Scientific American* 306 (June 2012), 38.

words, *human* DNA is not the only DNA necessary for a full account of human evolution.

Even the attempt to demarcate the boundaries of the human body at the cellular level breaks down. The contemporary theory of the origin of mitochondria – one of the basic structures of all eukaryotic cells – contends that mitochondria once existed outside their eukaryotic hosts as independent prokaryotic bacteria.[13] In short, mitochondria have revealed themselves to be "aliens within": endosymbionts. They are the "outside" inside our insides, problematizing the very notion of "inside" and "outside" when it comes to the body.

II. The Parousia of Group Selection

While we struggle to come to terms with the internal "community" that is the "individual" organism, a revolution in evolutionary theory is underway that demands that – under certain conditions – we recognize communities of "individual" organisms as integrated "wholes." This revolution is the readmission of "group-level" selection into evolutionary theory – the idea that groups evolve by virtue of their competition for survival with other groups, just as individuals evolve by virtue of their competition for survival with other individuals.

While multilevel selection theory ("multilevel" in that it sees evolution as involving a dialectic between selective pressures at various levels of biological organization – e.g., cellular, individual, group) constitutes the "implosion" Coakley described above, it is, as she notes, by no means *new*.[14] Darwin himself predicted that groups would evolve in competition with other groups.[15] His prediction came from trying to solve a riddle posed to him many times in response to the inherent "selfishness" seemingly implied by the evolutionary rule "survival of the fittest" and language of evolutionary "competition": Wherefore cooperation? What is the evolutionary benefit of altruism?[16] The answer: individuals cooperate for the good of the group – that is, for the evolutionary advantage of the group.

But for a 40 year period beginning roughly with G. C. Williams' *Adaptation and Natural Selection*, "self-interest" was taken to explain even

---

[13] Lynn Margulis, *Origin of Eukaryotic Cells: Evidence and Research Implications for a Theory of the Origin and Evolution of Microbial, Plant, and Animal Cells on the Precambrian Earth* (New Haven: Yale University Press, 1970).

[14] Coakley, "Stories of Evolution, Stories of Sacrifice," 13.

[15] Charles Darwin, *The Descent of Man and Selection in Relation to Sex* (London: John Murray, 1871), 159–60.

[16] Martin A. Nowak and Roger Highfield, *Supercooperators: Altruism, Evolution and Why We Need Each Other to Succeed* (New York: Free Press, 2011), 82.

apparently "altruistic" behaviors like those Darwin was keen to describe by means of group selection. One might cooperate or even sacrifice oneself for the sake of the group and have it be in one's own evolutionary self-interest if, for instance, the "sacrifice" allowed one's kin to flourish. But, increasingly, "kin selection" and other ways of explaining away "altruism" without recourse to group selection have come up short of explaining the evidence. This is the implosion Coakley witnessed firsthand during her partnership with Martin Nowak at Harvard, one of the epicenters of the revival of multilevel selection theory.[17]

On the multilevel account, evolution – rather than being fundamentally *selfish* (that is, a story about the propagation of Dawkins' "selfish genes"[18]) – is fundamentally *cooperative*. "Without cooperation there can be neither construction nor complexity in evolution," says Nowak.[19] Indeed, there is a tendency in the evolutionary literature to find ethical significance in the dynamics of multilevel selection. Entomologist E. O. Wilson serves as a prime example:

The dilemma of good and evil was created by multilevel selection, in which individual selection and group selection act together on the same individual but largely in opposition to each other. Individual selection is the result of competition for survival and reproduction among members of the same group. It shapes instincts in each member that are fundamentally selfish with reference to other members. In contrast, group selection consists of competition between societies, through both direct conflict and differential competence in exploiting the environment. Group selection shapes instincts that tend to make individuals altruistic toward one another (but not toward members of other groups). Individual selection is responsible for much of what we call sin, while group selection is responsible for the greater part of virtue. Together they have created the conflict between the poorer and the better angels of our nature.[20]

The concession that this "altruism" extends only as far as the boundary of the group is but one indication that we ought to be careful in valuing "cooperation" as ethically *positive*. Furthermore, if multilevel selection theory does in fact describe what we might mean by "real participation" in Paul's texts, this may be our first sign that we ought not value all "participation" positively either.

---

[17] See, for instance, Nowak and Highfield, *Supercooperators*; Edward O. Wilson, *The Social Conquest of Earth* (New York: Liveright, 2012).

[18] Richard Dawkins, *The Selfish Gene* (30th Anniversary ed.; New York: Oxford University Press, 2006).

[19] Nowak and Highfield, *Supercooperators*, xix.

[20] E. O. Wilson, *Social Conquest*, 241.

III. The Body as "Adaptive Unit"

There is a mereological corollary to the resurgence of "group-level" selection in evolutionary theory: if groups evolve in their competition for survival with other groups, just as individuals evolve in their competition for survival with other individuals, then the "group" has no less a claim to the category "organism" than does the "individual." In other words, the social bodies to which "individuals" belong are just as legitimate claimants to the category "organism." Indeed, readmitting group selection to the evolutionary account suggests a striking way of understanding the mereological problem posed by the "endosymbiosis" that forms the core of any sufficiently complex organism. Within a multilevel account of evolution, the history of life becomes a story of a sequence of what John Maynard Smith and Eörs Szathmáry famously called "major transitions" in evolution in which group-level selective pressures so outweigh individual-level pressures that, from our point of view, a new type of organism at a higher level of organization emerges.[21] For example, Nowak describes the advent of multicellular life some 3.5 billion years ago as an early result of group selective forces. He cites chains of filamentous bacteria that survive because "every tenth or so cell commits suicide for the benefit of this communal thread of bacterial life."[22] This behavior is disastrous, of course, for the individual bacterium, but highly advantageous for the group. Ultimately, Nowak argues, "group"-level selective forces became so strong, and the advantages of cooperation so decisive, that these bacterial communities became the first multicellular organisms.

The advent of the endosymbiosis of mitochondria in eukaryotic cells described above fits quite neatly as an example of this process of (in this case inter-species) "group-level" fitness being so successful that what we now consider new organisms emerge. All eukaryotic cellular life is the result of one of these major transitions. All eukaryotic multicellular life is a result of these transitions at least twice-over. Multicellular life of the likes of a human individual is, diachronically, a result of these transitions recursively through evolutionary history and, synchronically, as Nowak suggests, a "Russian doll" of groups within groups.[23]

---

[21] John Maynard Smith and Eörs Szathmáry, *The Major Transitions in Evolution* (Oxford: Oxford University Press, 1997). For a recent appraisal of this important work, see John Maynard Smith and Eörs Szathmáry, *The Major Transitions in Evolution Revisited* (Cambridge: MIT Press, 2011).

[22] Nowak and Highfield, *Supercooperators*, 138.

[23] Indeed, the individual human body can be conceived of as a multi-species superorganism, given how many of our basic physiological functions are carried out in concert with our bacterial symbiotes. On multi-species superorganisms, see David Sloan

Organisms are systems all the way down. As a result, the level of the organismic "individual" is not easily determined. Indeed, through evolutionary history, what we have is a history of "individuals" becoming parts of groups, on which, in some cases, group-level selection exerts ever-increasing force until the "individuals" have become "parts" – organelles, cells, tissues, organs – and the group (e.g., Nowak's "society of cells") appears to be the "whole," the "individual" – the body. The result is that, in terms of evolutionary theory, the "organismic" level – the scale at which one is inclined to say there exists a *body* – is fundamentally *relative* to the trait or the function under consideration. This confirms the 1912 insight of William Morton Wheeler, the father of modern entomology, when he complains that an adequate definition of "organism" is difficult to give, since "the organism is neither a thing nor a concept, but a continual flux or process..."[24] The best Wheeler can offer is a functional definition: "An organism is a complex, definitely coordinated and therefore individualized system of activities..."[25] These activities – these functions – are most clearly present in a bee hive or ant colony at the level of the "group." This is particularly clear when it comes to reproduction, in which most individual bees and ants never participate, but every healthy hive and colony does. As a result, Wheeler insists, the "colony is a true organism and not merely the analogue of the person."[26]

Of course, there are other functions – metabolism, for example – for which it seems appropriate to consider the "individual" insect to be the relevant "organism." The question is: At what level of organization are entities subject to selective pressures? That is, at what level or organization do entities exhibit adaptation over time? In other words, the simplest evolutionary answer to the question, "what is a body?" is: "an adaptive unit." Nowak's strings of filamentous bacteria are functioning as adaptive units when they undertake spontaneous decimation. Other social groups may be said to function similarly with respect to certain traits – beehives

---

Wilson and Elliot Sober, "Reviving the Superorganism," *Journal of Theoretical Biology* 136 (1989): 349.

[24] This process-oriented description of the organism anticipates James W. Haag, et al., "The Emergence of Self," in *In Search of Self: Interdisciplinary Perspectives on Personhood* (ed. J. Wentzel Van Huyssteen and Erik P. Wiebe; Grand Rapids: Eerdmans, 2011), 319–37.

[25] William Morton Wheeler, "The Ant-Colony as an Organism," *Journal of Morphology* 22 (1912): 308.

[26] Wheeler, "Ant-Colony," 310. Wheeler adopts Ernst Haeckel's rather idiosyncratic, technical use of the term "person" in *Evolution of Man*. Haeckel was particularly fascinated by the question of the givenness of the organismic unit. By "person," Haeckel means "the entire body," which Wheeler takes to be the paradigmatic case of the category "organism."

and ant colonies (so-called "superorganisms") are paradigm cases. But increasingly the same biologists who are leading the charge on the revival of group selection in evolutionary theory also see no reason not to view some human social groups – under the right circumstances – as "adaptive units" – that is, as *bodies* in the most literal, biological sense.[27] In every case, the question is: What is the trait (or the *behavior*) under consideration? For this reason, David Sloan Wilson argues that group selection – and, in light of what we have said about the fundamentally combinatorial nature of life itself, *all* selection may be considered "group selection" from some lower level of biological organization – requires that we keep our group definitions tightly related to the traits with respect to which the group functions as an "adaptive unit." Thus, he says:

> I coined the term "trait-group" to emphasize the intimate relationship between traits and groups in multilevel selection theory. However, this term merely recognizes something that has always been implicit in the definition of groups, inside and outside of biology. My bowling group is the people with whom I bowl, my study group is the people with whom I study, my platoon is the group of people with whom I fight, my nation is the group of people who share the same set of laws, my church is the group of people with whom I worship. All of these groups are defined in terms of the individuals who interact with respect to a given activity. There is an infinite variety of groups, but only when we consider an infinite variety of activities. For any particular activity, there is a single appropriate grouping.[28]

The result is that "groups must be defined separately for each and every trait,"[29] which means that

> The trait-group concept conflicts with the image of an organism as a unit that is adaptive with respect to many traits. After all, an individual organism like a bird eats as a unit, flies as a unit, fights as a unit, and so on. Some animal groups such as social insect colonies are integrated with respect to many traits. Similarly, some human groups organize the lives of their members from cradle to grave. In many other cases, however, groups are adaptive only with respect to one or a few traits.[30]

Crucially, this means that, when thinking about human social groups – which *unlike* the social insects rarely are knit together so tightly that they function as adaptive units for a great many different traits – our expectation ought to be that "individuals" will belong to multiple different groups. Each of these groups is rightly said to be an organism, despite the heterogeneous nature of the overlaps between "individual" and "group" bodies. This is simply a necessary consequence of adopting a functional definition of the organism – a functional definition of the *body* from a

---

[27] D. S. Wilson, *Darwin's Cathedral*; E. O. Wilson, *Social Conquest*, 212–67.
[28] D. S. Wilson, *Darwin's Cathedral*, 15–16.
[29] D. S. Wilson, *Darwin's Cathedral*, 15.
[30] D. S. Wilson, *Darwin's Cathedral*, 17.

biological perspective. The boundaries of the body will seem to shift depending on the *function* in question. The reality is that bodies only ever exist with respect to certain functions.[31]

C. The Body of Christ as Adaptive Unit

Paul's concept of body, held in common with the (largely Stoic) philosophical common senses of his day,[32] shares much with this evolutionary view. Dale Martin's description of the ancient concept of body will sound at once counterintuitive and yet quite familiar: "the nonexistence of the 'individual,' the fluidity of the elements that make up the 'self,' and the essential continuity of the human body with its surroundings."[33] On the ancient account, far from being atomistic individuals, ancient bodies were understood to be open to influence from the outside world. As on the evolutionary account, these bodies were internally composite, whether they were composed of separated parts, like a flock, army, or senate or whether they were more unified, like a stone or a person, unified by a πνεῦμα or a ἕξις.[34] As on the evolutionary account, this mereology makes it possible to have *social* bodies, bodies made of bodies.

What an evolutionary theorist might call "group adaptive units" came in various scales. At the grandest level, the Stoics took the entire cosmos to be a living body, an idea inherited from Platonic tradition.[35] Social bodies came in smaller sizes as well. The next step down from the one, cosmic body, was the universal human body, which supplied the foundational principle for Stoic social ethics. There also existed yet smaller civic bodies

---

[31] It is simply the historically contingent fact of the many "major transitions" – more or less stable and universal victories of group-level selective forces over individual-level forces – in the history of life that has given us the common sense assumption that certain structures of biological organization obtain with respect to a great many functions. Cases where the "parts" seem to rise up against one another at the expense of the whole – cancer, for example – are reminders that none of these "major transitions" is ever so final, the bodies they construct ever so united, that we could safely allow the multilevel view to disappear from the picture. E. O. Wilson describes cancer as "an extreme example of multilevel selection." *Social Conquest*, 162.

[32] Martin, *Corinthian Body*; Michelle V. Lee, *Paul, the Stoics, and the Body of Christ* (Cambridge: Cambridge University Press, 2006).

[33] Martin, *Corinthian Body*, 21. "Non-existence of the individual" may be too strong. We might rather say that the individual in the ancient world was socially constructed, understood primarily as node in a network.

[34] Lee, *Paul, the Stoics, and the Body of Christ*, 50. Lee cites Achilles, *Isagoge 14* and Alexander of Aphrodisias, *Mixt.* 216.14–16.

[35] Lee cites Diogenes Laertius, *Vit. Phil.* 7:139. For Plato, see *Tim.* 30b, 36e, and 69c.

– the body politic. So, Seneca writes of "two commonwealths [*dues res publicas*] – the one, a vast and truly common state" (the single unified body of humanity) and "the other, the one to which we have been assigned by the accident of birth... the commonwealth of the Athenians or of the Carthiginians."[36] This political body, then, became a *topos* by which one could lobby for social unity within a particular political entity. These *homonoia* speeches were so common that they became a genre unto themselves.[37]

As on the evolutionary account, these social bodies are *literal* bodies. Seneca, in describing this body, says plainly "we are the parts [*membra*] of one great body [*corporis*]... Our relations with one another are like a stone arch, which would collapse if the stones did not mutually support each other, and which is upheld in this very way."[38] Note that Seneca says that all humanity *is* a body, but is only *like* an arch. The somatic language is not metaphor.[39] Given this background, we can be confident that Paul's invocation of corporate body language in describing participation in Christ in terms of membership in the Body of Christ is every bit as *literal*, every bit as *material* as the evolutionary language we described above. But the question of scale remains: Is the Body of Christ cosmic, universal human, or political? It is tempting to say that, for Paul, the Body of Christ is an instance only of the "political" type. There are good reasons to think so, given that political *homonoia* speeches serve as the rhetorical background for Paul's invocation of the language of the social Body of Christ 1 Cor 12–14 and Rom 12.[40] And of course Paul's language for the church – the ἐκκλησία – is borrowed from the political sphere. But Paul is also quite

---

[36] Seneca, *Otio*, 4.1.

[37] Martin, Corinthian Body, 38. See also Margaret M. Mitchell, Paul and the Rhetoric of Reconciliation: An Exegetical Investigation of the Language and Composition of 1 Corinthians (Louisville: Westminster John Knox, 1993), 60–64. The fable of Menenius Agrippa is perhaps the best known example of the homonoia genre (Livy, Hist. 2.32; Epictetus 2.10.4–5; Dionysius of Halicarnasus, Ant. Rom., 6.83–86).

[38] Seneca, *Ep.* 95.51–53.

[39] Seneca's plea to Nero in *De Clementia* to exercise restraint in dealing with the state is instructive: "if – and this is what thus far [this discourse] is establishing – you are the soul of the state and the state your body (*corpus*), you see, I think how requisite is mercy; for you are merciful to yourself when you are seemingly merciful to another." (1.5.1; translation from Lee, *Paul, the Stoics, and the Body of Christ*, 37.) Seneca's rhetoric makes it plain: this is no mere metaphor. What is merely apparently the case is the emperor and citizens' individual differentiation. This is an illusion that threatens to obscure their literal corporeal unity. The modernist instinct toward individualism in social analysis is completely inverted.

[40] Martin, *Corinthian Body*, 38. See also Margaret M. Mitchell, *Paul and the Rhetoric of Reconciliation: an Exegetical Investigation of the Language and Composition of 1 Corinthians* (Louisville: Westminster John Knox, 1993), 60–64.

happy to imagine that the Body of Christ constitutes in itself a cosmos, such that membership in Christ's Body (which he often invokes with the shorthand "in Christ") results in there being a new creation (2 Cor 5:17, cf. Gal 6:14–15). Indeed, in Rom 8:19–23, the redemption of the collective Body is said to have consequences that extend to the creation as a whole. Taken together, these two ways in which Paul appropriates ancient discourse of social bodies make Paul's point quite plain: it is in this *particular* social body – the *ecclesia* – that the new creation is breaking into the old. What appears now as a *political* body is in fact a *cosmic* body coming into being.

D. Group-Level Cognition and the Mind of Christ

I. Group-Level Cognition

If we are to understand the Body of Christ as an adaptive unit at the group level, evolutionary theory insists that it only exists as such relative to a particular *trait* or *function*. D. S. Wilson argues that a common group-level function – indeed, *the* characteristic group-level function of *human* social groups – is *cognition*. While "there is a pervasive tendency both in biology and in the human sciences to regard individuals as self-contained cognitive units," this tendency is an extension of the mistaken mereology of the body from which biology is still recovering. The assumption is that "brains are self-contained cognitive units because individuals are units of selection," but "if the individual is no longer a privileged unit of selection, it is no longer a privileged unit of cognition. We are free to imagine individuals in a social group connected in a circuitry that gives the group the status of the brain and the individual the status of the neuron."[41] Work on group-level cognitive adaptations in bee hives demonstrate the point, showing that colonies quickly adapt to changing qualities of food sources, opting for richer sources even when no individual bee has visited all of the relevant options. The comparison, rather, is done at the group level, employing the same decision-making algorithm found in neurological circuitry in the human brain in making a "best-of-n" decision.[42] Wilson concludes: "It is an important scientific achievement to show that group minds actually exist and are not just fanciful metaphors."[43] A full account of evolutionary

---

[41] D. S. Wilson, *Darwin's Cathedral*, 33.

[42] T. D. Seeley, *The Wisdom of the Hive: The Social Physiology of Honey Bee Colonies* (Cambridge: Harvard University Press, 1995); T. D. Seeley, "Honey Bee Colonies Are Group-Level Adaptive Units," *The American Naturalist* 150 (1997): 22–41.

[43] David Sloan Wilson, "Altruism and Organism: Disentangling the Themes of Multilevel Selection Theory," *The American Naturalist* 150 (1997): S122–S133.

history requires giving a full account of the *minds* of groups conceived as adaptive units.

Indeed, this scientific achievement extends to cognition performed by *human* groups.[44] Edwin Hutchins's classic example is of the traditional navigation practices of a U. S. Navy ship as it comes into port.[45] The crew of the ship – along with their various technical implements – functions together as an adaptive *unit* with regard to navigation. And, indeed, in maritime ventures, selective pressures are, of course, applied *at the group level*; a ship and its crew triumphs or sinks as a unit. Hutchins's research has become canonical for a large number of researchers working on group cognition in human social institutions, among them political theorist Philip Pettit. While denying "that our minds are subsumed in a higher form of Geist or in any variety of collective consciousness," Pettit nevertheless argues that

> There is a type of organization found in certain collectivities that makes them into subjects in their own right, giving them a way of being minded that is starkly discontinuous with the mentality of their members. This claim in social ontology is strong enough to ground talk of such collectivities as entities that are psychologically autonomous and that constitute institutional persons.[46]

Perhaps the most striking instance of group cognition in the modern world is the practice of science itself.[47] Like Hutchins's ship, large modern scientific research projects entail the development and deployment of large, distributed, and (sometimes surprisingly minimally-) coordinated collections of individual human subjects and their specialized tools. Sociologist Karin Knorr Cetina points to modern experiments in high-energy physics (HEP) like those conducted at Fermilab or CERN as examples of especially large, distributed group-level cognitive processes. In her ethnography of HEP experiments, Knorr Cetina argues that "besides building up an understanding of the deepest components of the universe,

---

[44] For a review of the substantial group mind literature: Georg Theiner and Timothy O'Connor, "The Emergence of Group Cognition," in *Emergence in Science and Philosophy* (Routledge Series in the Philosophy of Science 6; ed. Antonella Corradini and Timothy O'Connor; New York: Routledge, 2009), 78–117.

[45] Edwin Hutchins, *Cognition in the Wild* (Cambridge: MIT Press, 1995).

[46] Philip Pettit, "Groups with Minds of Their Own," in *Socializing Metaphysics* (ed. Frederick F. Schmitt; Lanham, Md.: Rowman & Littlefield, 2003), 167. Given the current political resonances of language of "institutional persons," it is perhaps worth noting that Pettit was writing before the *Citizens United* decision and, at any rate, is not arguing for granting rights to collectivities, but instead is arguing for an expansive sense of what can be demanded of them as rational interlocutors.

[47] For a cautious review of this literature, see Ronald N. Giere and Barton Moffatt, "Distributed Cognition: Where the Cognitive and the Social Merge," *Social Studies of Science* 33 (2003): 301–10.

high energy physics also builds 'superorganisms': collectives of physicists, matched with collectives of instruments, that come as near as one can get to a – post-romantic – communitarian regime."[48] Within the social structure of the experiment, "the individual has been turned into an element of a much larger unit that functions as a collective epistemic subject."[49] It is "within the experiment's conversation with itself," Knorr Cetina argues, that "knowledge is produced... The stories articulated in formal and informal reports provide the experiments with a sort of consciousness: an uninterrupted hum of self-knowledge in which all efforts are anchored and from which new lines of work follow."[50] This result would easily be recognized by D. S. Wilson as a case when "at the extreme, groups might become so integrated and the contribution of any single member might become so partial that the group could literally be said to have a mind in a way that individuals do not, just as brains have a mind in a way that neurons do not."[51] On Durkheim's terms, this is a "psychological entity of a new species."[52] The group-level mind is no "collective consciousness" in some science-fiction sense. Rather it constitutes the *mind* of a distinct body – a body that exists (like all bodies) relative to the function(s) of that particular body.[53]

---

[48] Karin Knorr Cetina, *Epistemic Cultures: How the Sciences Make Knowledge* (Cambridge, Mass.: Harvard University Press, 1999), 4. The scare-quotes on "superorganism" – which come fully equipped with a sternly-worded disclaimer in Knorr Cetina's earlier work eventually disappear in *Epistemic Cultures,* 297; cf. Karin Knorr Cetina, "How Superorganisms Change: Consensus Formation and the Social Ontology of High-Energy Physics Experiments," *Social Studies of Science* 25, no. 1 (1995): 119–47. Knorr Cetina seems more convinced of the literalness of the superorganism language and of the reality of the experiment as a collective epistemic subject: "HEP experiments, as communitarian collaborations, are fictional in the sense that they are 'contradicted' by the forms of order centered on the individual subjects. But they are very real in the sense of the integrated functioning of these experiments, without which HEP could not produce results." Knorr Cetina, *Epistemic Cultures*, 250.

[49] Knorr Cetina, *Epistemic Cultures*, 167–68.

[50] Knorr Cetina, *Epistemic Cultures*, 178.

[51] D. S. Wilson, "Altruism and Organism," 128.

[52] Émile Durkheim, *The Rules of Sociological Method and Selected Texts on Sociology and its Method* (London: Macmillan Press, 1982), 251–52.

[53] I take it that D. S. Wilson's distinction here between "mind" and "body" is more or less heuristic. It may, ultimately, be impossible to separate two so neatly. Here, "mind" is used more or less *functionally*. The "mind" is a common-sense way of describing the faculty of a body that performs cognition. The point is simply that, just as "individual" bodies perform cognition, "groups" also perform cognition.

II. The Mind of Christ

Knorr Cetina's description of HEP experiments as collective epistemic subjects sounds very much like Paul's description of the Body of Christ. Christ's Body – the Body in which the Mind of Christ resides – manifestly functions as an adaptive unit with regard to cognition. Indeed, the Body is the organ through which this Mind is realized and discerned. It is for this reason that there is an epistemology, unique and proper to the Church, that is irreducible to the Body's functioning as an adaptive unit (1 Cor 1–2). The epistemological horizons of the Body are fundamentally wider than those of the world, such that what is foolishness to the latter is power and wisdom to the former (1 Cor 1:18, 24). Participation in the very material, collective epistemic function of the Body unlocks even the interiority of God: "'For who has known the mind of the Lord so as to instruct him?' But we have the mind of Christ" (1 Cor 2:16).

That this cognition is performed at the group level is manifest in Paul's description in 1 Cor 14. This is no digression from the account of the mystical (but quite material) unity of the Body of Christ into mundane matters of liturgical order. On the contrary, these passages describe the mechanics of the collective epistemic subject emergent from the social body:

> When you come together, each one has a hymn, a lesson, a revelation, a tongue, or an interpretation. Let all things be done for building up. If anyone speaks in a tongue, let there be only two or at most three, and each in turn; and let one interpret. But if there is no one to interpret, let them be silent in church and speak to themselves and to God. Let two or three prophets speak, and let the others weigh what is said. If a revelation is made to someone else sitting nearby, let the first person be silent. For you can all prophesy one by one, so that all may learn and all be encouraged. (1 Cor 14:26b–31)

In Rom 12, before describing the Body of Christ in detail, Paul describes the transformation of the the collective mind for the purpose of enabling the adaptive unit's function as a collective epistemic subject:

> I appeal to you therefore, brothers and sisters, by the mercies of God, to present your bodies as a living sacrifice, holy and acceptable to God, which is your rational worship. Do not be conformed to this world, but be transformed by the renewing of the mind, so that you may discern what is the will of God – what is good and acceptable and perfect. (Rom 12:1–2)

The multiple individual bodies constitute a single, living sacrifice. The singular, collective mind is to be renewed so that the collective epistemic subject constituted by the Body of Christ can fulfill its adaptive function more effectively. It is here that we can become more precise about the particular function by which Paul understands this social organism to be constituted. It is not merely an issue of cognition, but specifically of *moral* cognition: discerning what is good and acceptable and perfect.[54]

Indeed, on the evolutionary account, when it comes to human social groups, the cognitive function most often performed by the adaptive unit is *moral reasoning*. D. S. Wilson argues that human groups are fundamentally "moral communities," providing a "regulatory apparatus that promotes the welfare of the group as a whole."[55] Human groups establish mores – cultural norms – that regulate the group's communal life. This regulation is not simply a matter of behavioral conformity. Rather, this regulatory power of the group's collective cognitive processes provides what Mary Douglas calls the "social basis" of even *individual* cognition.[56] Whether understood in terms of Durkheim's "collective representations," Ludwig Fleck's "*Denkkollektiv*," or Douglas's "founding analogies," human social groups constrain individual cognition in ways that create the conditions of the possibility of individual cognition by placing constraints on that cognition. This is how human individuals think, but it is also how Mary Douglas says institutions "think" – that is, through their regulation of "individual" cognition.[57]

For Durkheim, this regulation happens through what he calls "collective representations," which supply the basic categories of time, space, and causality that make human cognition possible.

> They represent the most general relations which exist between things; surpassing all our other ideas in extension, they dominate all the details of our intellectual life. If men do not agree upon these essential ideas at any moment, if they did not have the same conceptions of time, space, cause, number, etc., all contact between their minds would be impossible, and with that, all life together. Thus, society could not abandon the categories to the free choice of the individual without abandoning itself.... There is a minimum of logical conformity beyond which it cannot go. For this reason, it uses all its authority upon its members to forestall such dissidences.... The necessity with which the categories are imposed upon us is not the effect of simple habits whose yoke we can easily throw off with a little effort; nor is it a physical or metaphysical necessity, since the categories change in different places and times; it is a special sort of moral necessity which is to the intellectual life what moral obligation is to the will.[58]

---

[54] This suggests an answer to Coakley's question (below) regarding the appropriate evaluative framework for the ethics of human social adaptive units. Paul clearly sees this group cognition oriented toward discernment of divine command, hence the centrality of *obedience* in Paul's thought.

[55] D. S. Wilson, *Darwin's Cathedral*, 33.

[56] Mary Douglas, *How Institutions Think* (Syracuse: Syracuse University Press, 1986), 11.

[57] Douglas, *How Institutions Think*, 92.

[58] Émile Durkheim, *The Elementary Froms of the Religious Life* (New York: The Free Press, 1965), 30; cited in Douglas, *How Institutions Think*, 12.

Fleck, Douglas argues, pursues this Durkheimian intuition in his account of cognition in modern science. In his 1935 work on the scientific identification of syphilis, *The Genesis and Development of a Scientific Fact*, Fleck, himself a medical doctor and bacteriologist who worked on the identification of syphilis, argues that *scientific* facts have *social* histories. More than sixty years before Knorr Cetina's work on HEP experiments, Fleck highlighted the generative role of laboratory culture itself in generating scientific research. "Many workers carried out these experiments almost simultaneously, but the actual authorship is due to the collective, the practice of cooperation and teamwork."[59] This thought-collective, or *Denkkollektiv*, produces and reinforces a "thought style" that, as Douglas describes, "sets the preconditions of any cognition, and... determines what can be counted as a reasonable question and a true or false answer. It provides the context and sets the limits for any judgement about objective reality."[60] As a result of the universal presence of these constraints, Fleck argues, "the individual within the collective is never, or hardly ever, conscious of the prevailing thought style, which almost always exerts an absolutely compulsive force upon his thinking and with which it is not possible to be at variance."[61] Thus, the pressure exerted by the group mind on its constituents is at once both imperceptible and coercive – indeed, it is coercive *because* it is imperceptible. This pressure is both enabling *and* destructive, both establishing the grounds of the possibility of cognition and coercively regulating its enactment. Though they are clearly describing the same phenomenon – indeed, according to D. S. Wilson, Fleck is describing the hallmark of human social adaptive units – Fleck's account is not nearly so rosy as the evolutionary biologists' language of foundational "cooperation."

E. The Moral Ambivalence of Participation

I. Descriptive vs. Evaluative Ethics

On this account, cooperation doesn't have the positive moral force we might have assumed. Indeed, "morality" itself doesn't have the positive moral force we might have assumed. Rather, in looking at the dynamics of social bodies and group minds from evolutionary biological and anthropological points of view with Paul in mind, we have tripped over the

---

[59] Ludwik Fleck, *Genesis and Development of a Scientific Fact* (Chicago: University of Chicago Press, 1979), 78.
[60] Douglas, *How Institutions Think*, 13.
[61] Fleck, *Genesis and Development of a Scientific Fact*, 41.

crucial difference between the way that cultural anthropologists and evolutoinary biologists, on the one hand, and moral philosophers, on the other, approach "morals" and "ethics." Evolutionary biologists (like those we have seen) and cultural anthropoligists (like Mary Douglas, below) tend to talk about morals *descriptively*. They are concerend only with what is *customary*; at their best, they leave aside the evaluative questions that are the central concern of moral philosophers – questions about what is *right*.[62] But this distinction is sometimes confused. Indeed, the very words we use – "ethics" and "morals" – while they have an evaluative connotation in common usage, suffer from an etymological ambiguity, simply being Greek and Latin for "custom" or "habit." Yet what is customary is not necessarily what is right. And Paul, in placing the point of emphasis for his audience squarely on the necessity of testing and approving God's will (Rom 12:2), acknowledges the central importance of this discernment.

For her part, Coakley sees the difficulty, noting that Nowak – like we saw in the case of E. O. Wilson –

often talks carelessly as if cooperation were "good" and defection "bad." But that is to commit the so-called "naturalistic fallacy." There is nothing intrinsically good about cooperating as such, and indeed cooperating human groups are – as Darwin himself saw – capable of inflicting destruction on other groups, or of being propelled by violent or (what we might want now to call) "unethical" goals.[63]

Coakley devotes an entire lecture to considering how various evaluative perspectives might relate to the sort of evolutionary account of ethics that she offers. However, throughout, the goal is to explain "the emergence of human 'altruism'" (her evaluative term) "from pre-human 'cooperation'" (her descriptive term).[64] This focus leaves aside these *other* sorts of cooperation – unethical cooperation, "immoral ethics," if we could tolerate such tortured language.

In fact, in his account of ἁμαρτία, Paul describes precisely such an immoral ethic.[65] Parallel to Paul's clear description of participation in

---

[62] Alasdair MacIntyre argues, for example, that the distinction between descriptive and evaluative senses of key terms like ἀγαθός and ἀρετή was the condition of the possibility of moral philosophy; Alasdair MacIntyre, *A Short History of Ethics: A History of Moral Philosophy from the Homeric Age to the 20th Century* (2d ed.; New York: Routledge, 1998), 4–9.

[63] Sarah Coakley, "Cooperation, *alias* Altruism: Game Theory and Evolution Reconsidered" (Lecture 1 of "Sacrifice Regained: Evolution, Cooperation and God," The 2012 Gifford Lectures, Aberdeen University, 19 April, 2012), 20. Online: http://www.abdn.ac.uk/gifford/about/2012-giff/.

[64] Coakley, "Cooperation, *alais* Altruism," 20.

[65] In scholarship on Romans 5–8, the Greek noun ἁμαρτία is rendered variously: as "Sin" (with a capital "S"), as "sin" (with a lower-case "s"), or simply as ἁμαρτία or some transliteration thereof. I will use "Sin" when what is meant is a suprahuman power (in-

Christ, the Body of Christ, and the mind of Christ, there is an account of participation in Sin, the Body of Sin, and the "debased [ἀδόκιμον] mind" (Rom 1:28). This is a fundamental dynamic in understanding "participation" in Paul. Too often Paul scholars tend to imagine s/Sin only as a threat to the unity of the Body of Christ. Indeed, this is Paul's primary concern in 1 Cor. But s/Sin also functions as a rival unity, a perverse system of participation. By and large, this is Sin's role in Romans.[66]

II. The Body of Sin

In Romans, Sin has a social body, composed of human individuals and their sinful actions. As Anders Nygren says of the Body of Sin in Rom 6:6: "'In Adam' we all belonged to the same *organism*. As human beings we are members of one body... But now, through baptism, we have been incorporated into Christ. That means that we are henceforth not merely members in the great organism of humanity; we are members in 'the body of Christ'."[67] The Body of Sin is a social body – an adaptive unit – analogous to Paul's other social body, the Body of Christ. In Rom 6:6, as Nygren notes, we get collective language used of the addressees' former state: "We know that our [pl.] old self [sg.] [ὁ παλαιὸς ἡμῶν ἄνθρωπος] was crucified with him so that the Body of Sin [τὸ σῶμα τῆς ἁμαρτίας] might come to nothing [καταργηθῇ], and we might no longer be enslaved to Sin." The phrase ὁ παλαιὸς ἡμῶν ἄνθρωπος is obscure, but whatever its specific sense, it must be apposite "the Body of Sin." The characteristic genitive plural personal pronoun in possession of a singular noun (ὁ παλαιὸς ἡμῶν ἄνθρωπος) gives us the sense of the Body of Sin as a social body, united by the ἕξις of sin.[68]

In Rom 6:12, we find similar language. The letter's addressees are not to return to their former state: "do not let Sin reign in your [pl.] mortal body [sg.] [τῷ θνητῷ ὑμῶν σώματι], to make you [pl.] obey its [sg.]

---

cluding social entities understood as collective subjects), "sin" when what is meant is a concrete action (or aggregate of actions), and the neologism "s/Sin" when the contested meaning is especially foregrounded.

[66] The distinction I am making here is one of degree only. Sin functions as a competing unity in 1 Cor – by and large, described in terms of the wisdom (3:19), immorality (5:10), and form (7:31) of "this world." (One sees a "powers" sort of function for Sin in 15:56.) And s/Sin functions as a threat to the unity of the Body of Christ in Romans 12 in terms of the dangers of haughtiness (16) and vengeance (19–21).

[67] Anders Nygren, *Commentary on Romans* (trans. C. C. Rasmussen; Philadelphia: Fortress, 1949), 232–33. *Contra* Nygren, I am not persuaded that this "organism" – or "our old self" – ought to be identified precisely with Adam.

[68] So Tannehill says that both of these terms, "Body of Sin" and "our old self," are corporate entities. Robert C. Tannehill, *Dying and rising with Christ: A study in Pauline theology* (Berlin: Töpelmann, 1967), 29.

passions." This singular "mortal body" does not refer to each individual's body.[69] When Paul uses this phrase to refer to the constituent individual bodies, he is quite happy to use the plural for the exact same phrase in 8:11: "he who raised Christ from the dead will give life to your mortal bodies [τὰ θνητὰ σώματα ὑμῶν]." Rather, the body referred to in 6:12 is the collective, social body of Sin, of which they are members. It is "mortal" inasmuch as it is subject to Sin, and therefore subject, at the mythological level, to Death, the consort of Sin.[70] The collective nature of this Body is made explicit in 6:13, where Paul invokes language of *members* (μέλη), often an image in Paul for the constituent bodies of a collective (save for in Rom 7:23–24, in which the macrocosm of the Body of Sin has become a microcosm within the constituent's individual body).[71] "No longer present your members [τὰ μέλη ὑμῶν] to Sin as weapons of wickedness, but present yourselves [ἑαυτοὺς] to God as those who have been brought from death to life – that is, present your members [τὰ μέλη ὑμῶν] to God as weapons of righteousness. For Sin will not rule over you, since you are not under law but under grace."[72] This is martial language reminiscent of the Stoic social body of separated parts, of which an army is a chief example.[73] The recipients of Romans are being recruited into two armies, each of which constitutes a collective body. Their individual bodies are enlisted as members of these collective bodies and deployed as weapons to two very different ends – either wickedness or righteousness. These two armies constitute two different dominions. Here we see the structure of the dominion of Sin (5:21, 6:12, 14): Sin rules over those members of its own social body through legally encoded social customs, the legal expressions of the regnant thought style that "sets the preconditions of any cognition, and... determines what can be counted as a reasonable question and a true or false answer."[74] In 1:28, Paul writes of the gentiles that "God handed them [pl.] over to a [sg.] debased mind.

---

[69] Smyth describes the "distributive singular," but notes that it is rare with concrete substantives like σῶμα; Herbert Weir Smyth, *Greek Grammar* (rev. Gordon M. Messing; Cambridge, Mass.: Harvard University Press; 1963 [1920]), §998.

[70] Beverly Roberts Gaventa, "The Cosmic Power of Sin in Paul's Letter to the Romans: Toward a Widescreen Edition," *Int* (2004): 234.

[71] The use of τοῖς μέλεσιν ἡμῶν in Rom 7:5 is a liminal case, the pivot point around which Paul makes the turn from the macrocosm to the microcosm.

[72] I take the καὶ in 6:13 as epexegetical or explicative. See also Rom 6:19–20 where Paul switches seamlessly from "your members" to "you." For ὅπλα as "weapons" in this verse, see Robert Jewett, *Romans: A Commentary* (Hermeneia; Minneapolis: Fortress, 2007), 410.

[73] Lee, *Paul, the Stoics, and the Body of Christ*, 50. Lee cites Achilles, *Isagoge* 14 (SVF 2.368) and Alexander of Aphrodisias, *Mixt.* 216.14–16.

[74] Douglas, *How Institutions Think*, 13.

(παρέδωκεν αὐτοὺς ὁ θεὸς εἰς ἀδόκιμον νοῦν)." The moral degradation of "the gentiles" results in a social body with a debased corporate mind. This is a social body – a *Denkkollektiv* on Fleck's terms – unified by a common ἕξις: sinful rebellion against God.[75]

III. The Dominion of Sin

As Durkheim, Fleck, and Douglas predict, Sin rules through a socially-mediated control over the moral psychology of its members. Liberationist Franz Hinkelammert describes the dynamic well:

> The text speaks of sin, but it is not a question of the violation of any law. It is in the law, it acts through the law, it uses the law. In the fulfilled [or enforced] law, sin acts. Now, Saint Paul speaks of a law and of commandments institutionalized in structures. It is enforceable law, which is the other face of a structure. Sin operates through the structure and its enforceable law, and not through the transgression of the law. This Sin is a substantive being [*un ser sustantivado*], from which the law derives its own existence and which is present in this law. It is a structural sin [*un pecado estructural*].[76]

Sin is a substantive being – this is no matter of "mere personification" or "mere metaphor" – precisely as a social power embedded in institutional structures. Sin's usurpation of law, therefore, has real, material impact for how we think about life in institutions. Ethics are rendered suspect. Institutional norms cannot be taken for granted. Even (or *especially*) law enforcement cannot be trusted: "Paul is faced with the fact that law enforcement [*el cumplimiento de la ley*] leads to death."[77]

In fact, law is revealed as a *sine qua non* of the life of Sin: "apart from the law, sin lies dead" (7:8). What follows in Romans is an analysis of the psychology of s/Sin. Through the law, Sin's dominion has reached its peak. The ἐγώ is unable to carry out that which it wills (v. 15). The conclusion is obvious; there is an enemy within: "Now if I do what I do not want, I agree that the law is good. But in fact it is no longer I that do it, but Sin who dwells within me" (vv. 17–18). The cosmic power, Sin, is a "foreign" presence embedded deep within the individual mind itself. Of course, the "foreignness" of this presence is not so straight-forward, as it is

---

[75] We might also imagine this in terms of Bourdieu's *habitus* as does Engberg-Pedersen in *The Material Spirit*, 141–42.

[76] Franz J. Hinkelammert, *La Fe de Abraham y el Edipo Occidental* (2. ampliada ed. San José, Costa Rica: Editorial DEI, 1991), 28 (all translations mine, following my own capitalization convention for s/Sin, described above).

[77] Hinkelammert, *La Fe de Abraham*, 28. "*El cumplimiento de la ley*" (literally, "the fulfillment of the law") is the technical term for "law enforcement" (i.e., the police). So, for Hinkelammert, it is a straightforward exegetical matter that "law enforcement leads to death." Hinkelammert's flagship example is the crucifixion of Jesus at the hands of Roman law enforcement.

the presence of a power that has emerged from the participation of the human self in sinful systems and is now deeply embedded within the socially-conditioned cognition of the self. Its presence is a puzzle that must be reasoned out. As Fleck predicts is the case in any *Denkkollektiv*, the regular experience of the self embedded in the Body of Sin, suffering as a slave under its dominion, is precisely *not* to recognize this constraint. In its usurpation of law, Sin takes up the normative ethics of a society, which mask Sin's dominion. Distinguishing between "The Sin" as structural Sin which has a substantive being and "many sins" (or "*pecaditos*"), Hinkelammert writes:

there are sins in the sense of transgressions of some law, and there is Sin, a being who kills through its own law enforcement... There is a big difference between this Sin and the many sins. The many sins are transgressions, and whoever commits them is conscious of having done that which is transgressing a normal ethic. Sin is distinct. The ethic confirms it, it demands that it be committed. You have to do it, because any ethics demands fulfillment [or enforcement] and orients the consciousness of sin around transgressions. For the normative ethic, only sins exist; The Sin as structural sin does not exist. Since it is located within the ethic and its fulfillment, the ethic cannot denounce it. It can only denounce transgressions. For this reason, The Sin consisting in the identification with structural sin is necessarily committed without consciousness of sin. Its own character brings about the elimination of the consciousness of The Sin. This sin is committed with a clean conscience, which is to say, with consciousness of complying with the current ethics.[78]

Hinkelammert's analysis confirms Fleck's prediction that "the individual within the collective is never, or hardly ever, conscious of the prevailing thought style, which almost always exerts an absolutely compulsive force upon his thinking and with which it is not possible to be at variance."[79] The law serves both as a tool and as a cover for Sin's dominion over its subjects – its material constituents.

If Paul's and Hinkelammert's critiques of law evoke defensiveness, Mary Douglas has a theory as to why. It has everything to do with our "sacred" commitment to our theories of justice:

[Hume's] idea that justice is a necessary social construct is exactly parallel to Durkheim's idea of the sacred, but Hume clearly refers to us, ourselves. He brings our idea of the scared under scrutiny. Our defensive reaction against Hume is exactly what Durkheim would predict. We cannot allow our precepts of justice to depend on artifice. Such teaching is immoral, a threat to our social system with all its values and classifications. Justice is the point that seals legitimacy. For this very reason, it is difficult to think about it impartially. In spite of a wide belief in the modern loss of mystery, the idea of justice still remains to this day obstinately mystified and recalcitrant

---

[78] Hinkelammert, *La Fe de Abrabam*, 29.
[79] Fleck, *Genesis and Development of a Scientific Fact*, 41.

to analysis. If we are ever to think against the pressure of our institutions, this is the hardest place to try, where the resistance is strongest.[80]

This is only more so the case when it comes to life and death decisions, says Douglas – precisely the sorts of stakes Paul is talking about.[81] In such cases, "individuals normally off-load such decisions on to institutions. No private ratiocination can find the answer. The most profound decisions about justice are not made by individuals as such, but by individuals thinking within and on behalf of institutions."[82] Indeed, this is precisely how Paul describes the situation: moral reasoning takes place within the constraints of one or the other social body. If moral reasoning takes place "in Christ" and with the aid of the Spirit (8:1–2), conclusions will be sound. If moral reasoning takes place in the Body of Sin – that is, with Sin ruling within – it turns into tortured convolutions (7:17, 20, 23). The major question then becomes: in which Body should we participate? Properly engaging the νοῦς (7:23, 25), or "choosing rationally, on this argument, is not choosing intermittently among crises or private preferences, but choosing continuously among social institutions."[83] Taken together with what we gleaned from D. S. Wilson, Philip Pettit, and Karin Knorr Cetina regarding group minds, institutional persons, and collective epistemic subjects respectively – all of which give us every reason to take these institutions seriously as *persons* – Douglas summarizes the dynamics of participation in the social bodies of one of these two corporate persons quite elegantly.

The result is the ironic "law of Sin," namely "that when I want to do what is good, evil lies close at hand. For I delight in the law of God in my inmost self, but I see in my members another law at war with the law of my mind (νοός), making me captive to the law of Sin that dwells in my members" (7:21–23). As a result, there is an experience of conflict between the "inmost self" and this foreign presence that invades through the members, through the flesh, the material interface with the adaptive unit.[84] The distinction between these two cognitive faculties is expressed in

---

[80] Douglas, *How Institutions Think*, 113.
[81] Douglas, *How Institutions Think*, 124.
[82] Douglas, *How Institutions Think*, 124.
[83] Douglas, *How Institutions Think*, 124.
[84] Of course, our modern conceptions of the mind-body relation make it hard to cleanly divide the flesh and the members – if we understand them as synonymous with the body – from the mind. Instead, my practice in this reading is to read the flesh and members as the material interfaces with the broader Body of Sin. In many respects, this is a struggle that ancient Stoics, as ontological monists, faced in appropriating popular dualist Platonic ideas of moral psychology, as described in Stanley K. Stowers, *A Rereading of Romans: Justice, Jews, and Gentiles* (New Haven, Conn.: Yale University Press, 1997), 262.

8:7: There exists both a φρόνημα – a pattern of thought – of the flesh and a φρόνημα of the Spirit. The first yields death, the second brings life and peace. As the cognitive pattern of the self dominated by the foreign power because it is the material interface with the social body that constitutes this foreign power, "the φρόνημα of the flesh is hostile to God; it does not submit to the law of God, for it cannot," with the result that "those who are in the flesh cannot please God" (8:7–8). Rescue comes in the form of the Spirit of God, available to those "in Christ" (8:1–2), which grants victory to the mind, which serves the law of God (v. 25), restoring its natural freedom and power.[85] This is nothing less than the transfer of the self from one cosmic body to another: from the Body of Sin to the Body of Christ, from enslavement to the law of Sin to enslavement to the law of God (7:25). Since Sin depends for its existence on the members that comprise its social body, once these members of the Body of Sin are put to death with Christ in baptism, the Body of Sin comes to nothing (6:6). When this happens, "Sin can no longer keep itself alive by leading the body toward death, but rather the death of sin now enables the body to live in freedom..."[86] Sin has been put to death; the self is free to choose the good.

In short, "participation," for Paul, is not a category unique to participation in Christ. One is always already a "participant." As Käsemann notes, when "Paul speaks of our members, or even our bodies themselves are called members, it is clear that we are never autonomous, but always participate in a definite world and stand under lordship."[87] Rather than the modernist assumption of an "original" individuality only later joined into a communal identity through participation in Christ, one rather gets the sense, as Troels Engberg-Pedersen has noted, that "there is no self-conscious notion of 'the self' in Paul... he thinks in terms of membership of groups: Jews, Gentiles, Christ followers."[88] We ought to add to this list "sinners": those who constitute the Body of Sin by their submission to Sin's rule through their cooperation in committing sins. The Body of Sin in this sense is a *cosmic* body, that is, it constitutes a *cosmos* within itself, a degraded version of the cosmos God established and through which God's true nature is revealed (Rom 1:20). The cosmic consequences of Sin are evident not just in human sinners but in the

---

[85] Plato, *Laws*, 875c. The natural connection between νοῦς and πνεῦμα is a commonplace in ancient philosophical cosmological reflection in which νοῦς is materially composed of πνεῦμα. (Though see Martin, *Corinthian Body*, 96–102.)

[86] Franz J. Hinkelammert, *The Ideological Weapons of Death: A Theological Critique of Capitalism* (trans. Phillip Berryman; Maryknoll, N.Y.: Orbis Books, 1986), 137. He goes on to cite Rom 6:11–14.

[87] Ernst Käsemann, *Commentary on Romans* (trans. Geoffery William Bromiley; Grand Rapids: Eerdmans, 1980), 176.

[88] Engberg-Pedersen, *Cosmology and Self*, 142.

natural world around them (Rom 8:19–23). The creation itself is in slavery (δουλείας), under the reign of Sin, to whom, like the Gentiles in Rom 1, God has subjected it, allowing the natural consequence of human sin: the emergence of the cosmic agent, the collective epistemic subject, corporate person, Sin. Only through the redemption of the (always already-)social Body will creation be set free.

F. Overlapping Worlds

What we have, then, in these two locutions – "Body of Sin" and "Body of Christ" – is a Pauline syncretism: Paul's apocalyptic dualism meets a popular philosophical doctrine of a world body and we get *two* world bodies.[89] Each of these world bodies is constituted by the particular set of practices, or in ancient terms, ἕξις – disobedience in the case of the Body of Sin, obedience in the case of the Body of Christ. Each of these bodies involves a group mind: in the case of the Body of Sin, the debased mind of 1:28, in the case of the Body of Christ, the renewed mind of 12:2.

Each of these minds emerges from and in turn coercively regulates a particular *Denkkollektiv* among its members. And, indeed, Douglas argues, these thought collectives might more accurately be called thought *worlds*.[90] Inasmuch as they supply, as Durkheim insisted, essential categories like space and time, cause and effect, "worldmaking" hardly seems like a stretch in describing what the group-level cognition of these adaptive units accomplishes.[91] Douglas's "founding analogies" (her synthesis of Durkheim's collective representations and Fleck's *Denkkollektiv*) share this worldmaking function. For Douglas, these lists of opposites provide a framework for the foundational concepts of distinction and sameness. For example:

female	male
left	right
people	king[92]

Louis Martyn suggests that Paul is actively engaged with ancient traditions like Sirach that understood the κόσμος to be founded on precisely such pairs of opposites: "…all the works of the Most High are in pairs, one the

---

[89] Whether this is good Stoic philosophy is no matter; Paul wasn't a Stoic. He is seeing what he can get away with from the scraps of philosophy he has heard in the *agora* for the sake of his apostolic mission to the Gentiles.

[90] Douglas, *How Institutions Think*, 16.

[91] Douglas cites Nelson Goodman, *Ways of Worldmaking* (Indianapolis: Hackett Publishing, 1978).

[92] Douglas, *How Institutions Think*, 49.

opposite of the other."[93] Therefore, when Paul declares in Gal 3:28 that "in Christ Jesus" – that is, in Christ's Body – "there is no longer Jew or Greek, there is no longer slave or free, there is no longer male and female," Paul is describing the end of old κόσμος in the Body of Sin and the arrival of a new κόσμος in the Body of Christ. The shift from one mode of participation to another is a shift from one κόσμος to another. Especially revelatory of this apocalyptic turn is the third antinomy – what Martyn calls "the erasure of the distinction of male from female."[94] In declaring that "*in Christ* there is no longer... male and female," Paul precisely declares that participation in Christ entails the undoing of the sensible κόσμος, the κόσμος created in Gen 1, in which "male and female" is one of the distinctions established at the outset.[95] In this sense, participation in Sin or in Christ has everything to do with Paul's ever-generative eschatological framework.

Inasmuch as the shift from participating in Sin to participating in Christ is an eschatological action, it is never complete in this world. The believer who participates "in Christ" and in the new creation constituted in Christ's Body nevertheless continues to participate in "this world" in which the categories of the Gal 3:28 baptismal formula continue to obtain. This forces Paul in 1 Cor 7 to give one of his most tortured teachings[96]:

I mean, brothers and sisters, the appointed time has grown short; from now on, let even those who have wives be *as though* they had none, and those who mourn *as though* they were not mourning, and those who rejoice *as though* they were not rejoicing, and those who buy *as though* they had no possessions, and those who deal with the world *as though* they had no dealings with it. For the present form of this world is passing away. (1 Cor 7:29–31)

The eschatological displacement of "this world" with the new creation *in Christ* is in process – "the present form of this world is passing away" – and so Paul and his community live in substantial tension. On the one hand, there are those who have wives, but, given the fact that the present form of the world is passing away (a world which in part constituted by the dichotomy between male and female), "even those who have wives" ought to "be as though they had none." Paul's advice is not to divorce; he has a

---

[93] J. Louis Martyn, Galatians: A New Translation with Introduction and Commentary (New York: Doubleday, 1997), 403–6.

[94] Martyn, *Galatians*, 381.

[95] Krister Stendahl is instructive: "If one counters that this would lead to a conflict with the order of creation, and hence must be wrong we must say that it does indeed lead to such a conflict, and that is precisely what it should do and intends to do." *The Bible and the Role of Women: A Case Study in Hermeneutics* (Philadelphia: Fortress, 1966), 34.

[96] Martyn notes 1 Cor 7:29 as the place where Paul takes up the tension between old- and new-creation arguments, neglected in Galatians; Martyn, *Galatians*, 381.

saying of Jesus that prevents him from saying so (7:10–11). The ethic in the overlap of worlds is an "as though" ethic.

This possibility of overlap, is, of course, a constant threat to the cleanest articulation of Paul's participation ethic. Recall from the start what we said about the possibility – even *likelihood* – of hybrid identities, memberships in overlapping social bodies. Given that social bodies are constituted functionally as trait-groups, bodily boundaries can vary with different traits – especially in the case of human groups.[97] Indeed, Paul's ardent rhetoric regarding the impossibility of hybrid allegiance to Sin and to Christ is proof positive of the *practical* reality of such hybrid allegiances. What might these hybrid allegiances look like? Most simply, we might imagine wavering allegiances. In one circumstance, one's moral reasoning takes place "in Christ" – that is, within the *Denkkollektiv* of the social Body of Christ. In another, one reasons from different principles, and, therefore, within a different social body. But this sort of "double-mindedness" only begins to capture the possibilities.

Engaging a bit more honestly with the nuance of the world in which we live, we might question the unity we have presumed for "moral reasoning" as a function of various adaptive units at the social level. Might we instead imagine that "moral reasoning" is itself fundamental *composite* such that trait groups might have to be determined with respect to whatever component functions one might find under the "moral reasoning" umbrella? Perhaps various fields of ethics – sexual, economic, medical – constitute different enough functions that different trait groups might be organized around each of these different fields. This fragmentation of moral reasoning opens up substantial opportunity for hybrid identities. One's sexual ethics might be reasoned within the Church, while one's economics are instead reasoned within The Market, which most certainly functions as a well-integrated adaptive unit – a somatic unity – with respect to financial reasoning.[98] Yet more insidiously, we might imagine that the Church may itself from time to time function as a member of social bodies Paul would describe as worlds that are now passing away. We could imagine ecclesial structures functioning in the perverse ways Hinkelammert describes, standardizing sin and outlawing the good. Presumably, this would require relying on the common theological distinction between the Church as a social entity or collection of social entities and the Body of Christ as a theological ideal. Regardless, the picture we get is one of overlapping and conflicting identities –

---

[97] D. S. Wilson, *Darwin's Cathedral*, 15–17.

[98] I have given an superorganismic description of The Market in Matthew Croasmun, "The Body of Sin: An Emergent Account of Sin as a Cosmic Power in Romans 5–8" (PhD diss., Yale University, 2014), 313–22.

overlapping and conflicting corporate memberships or even world-participations – as they relate to different *functions,* different *traits,* different *adaptive behaviors*. This is simply a consequence of the way the world is – what it means to engage in "real participation" as organisms under selective pressure at multiple levels.

G. Conclusion

Contrary to any Bultmannian fears that may still linger, modern scientific description ends up helping us take Pauline participation language quite literally – at least in the case of somatic union. Indeed, not only does the evolutionary biological account of the body as an "adaptive unit" lend credence to a more literal appropriation of Paul's thought, such an account leads us to consider some of the nuances we might otherwise miss in our description of participation. On this description, "participation" is quite clearly morally ambivalent. Participation in complex social systems – even "cooperation" of a certain sort within such systems – can be morally problematic. The primary moral choice then becomes the choice between systems – on Paul's description, between the Body of Sin and the Body of Christ. This choice between bodies is also a choice between worlds, between this world and the world that has now come upon us (1 Cor 10:11). But even this fundamental choice has to be nuanced, as the evolutionary model demands that we consider convoluted memberships in overlapping group-level bodies that pertain to various adaptive behaviors. An account of the redemption of embodied humanity necessarily entails these sorts of complexities, indigenous as they are to embodied existence.

Bibliography

Ackerman, Jennifer. "The Ultimate Social Network," *Scientific American* 306 (June 2012), 36–43.

Bakhtin, Mikhail M. *Speech Genres and Other Late Essays*. Translated by Vern W. McGee. Austin: University of Texas Press, 1986.

Coakley, Sarah. "Sacrifice Regained: Evolution, Cooperation and God." The 2012 Gifford Lectures, Aberdeen University, 17 April – 3 May, 2012. Online: http://www.abdn.ac.uk/gifford/about/2012-giff/.

Croasmun, Matthew. "The Body of Sin: An Emergent Account of Sin as a Cosmic Power in Romans 5–8." PhD diss., Yale University, 2014.

Darwin, Charles. *The Descent of Man and Selection in Relation to Sex*. London: John Murray, 1871.

Dawkins, Richard. *The Selfish Gene*. 30th Anniversary ed. New York: Oxford University Press, 2006.

Douglas, Mary. *How Institutions Think*. Syracuse: Syracuse University Press, 1986.
Durkheim, Émile. *The Elementary Forms of the Religious Life*. New York: The Free Press, 1965.
———. *The Rules of Sociological Method and Selected Texts on Sociology and its Method*. London: Macmillan Press, 1982.
Engberg-Pedersen, Troels. *Cosmology and Self in the Apostle Paul: The Material Spirit*. Oxford: Oxford University Press, 2010.
Fleck, Ludwik. *Genesis and Development of a Scientific Fact*. Chicago: University of Chicago Press, 1979.
Gaventa, Beverly Roberts. "The Cosmic Power of Sin in Paul's Letter to the Romans: Toward a Widescreen Edition," *Interpretation* (2004): 229–40.
Giere, Ronald N., and Barton Moffatt. "Distributed Cognition: Where the Cognitive and the Social Merge." *Social Studies of Science* 33 (2003): 301–10.
Goodman, Nelson. *Ways of Worldmaking*. Indianapolis: Hackett, 1978.
Haag, James W., et al. "The Emergence of Self." Pages 319–37 in *In Search of Self: Interdisciplinary Perspectives on Personhood*. Edited by J. Wentzel Van Huyssteen and Erik P. Wiebe. Grand Rapids: Eerdmans, 2011.
Haeckel, Ernst. *The Evolution of Man: A Popular Exposition of the Principal Points of Human Ontogeny and Phylogeny*. New York: Appleton, 1879.
Hays, Richard B. "What is 'Real Participation in Christ'?" Pages 336–51 in *Redefining First-Century Jewish and Christian Identities: Essays in Honor of Ed Parish Sanders*. Edited by Fabian E. Udoh et al. Christianity and Judaism in Antiquity Series 16. Notre Dame, Ind.: University of Notre Dame Press, 2008.
Hinkelammert, Franz J. *La Fe de Abraham y el Edipo Occidental*. 2. ampliada ed. San José, Costa Rica: Editorial DEI, 1991.
———. *The Ideological Weapons of Death: A Theological Critique of Capitalism*. Translated by Phillip Berryman. Maryknoll, N.Y.: Orbis, 1986.
Hutchins, Edwin. *Cognition in the Wild*. Cambridge: MIT Press, 1995.
Jewett, Robert. *Romans: A Commentary*. Hermeneia. Minneapolis: Fortress, 2007.
Käsemann, Ernst. *Commentary on Romans*. Translated by Geoffrey William Bromiley. Grand Rapids: Eerdmans, 1980.
Knorr Cetina, Karin. *Epistemic Cultures: How the Sciences Make Knowledge*. Cambridge, Mass.: Harvard University Press, 1999.
Knorr Cetina, Karin. "How Superorganisms Change: Consensus Formation and the Social Ontology of High-Energy Physics Experiments." *Social Studies of Science* 25, no. 1 (1995): 119–47.
Lee, Michelle V. *Paul, the Stoics, and the Body of Christ*. Cambridge: Cambridge University Press, 2006.
MacIntyre, Alasdair. *A Short History of Ethics: A History of Moral Philosophy from the Homeric Age to the 20th Century*. 2d ed. New York: Routledge, 1998.
Margulis, Lynn. *Origin of Eukaryotic Cells: Evidence and Research Implications for a Theory of the Origin and Evolution of Microbial, Plant, and Animal Cells on the Precambrian Earth*. New Haven, Conn.: Yale University Press, 1970.
Martin, Dale. *The Corinthian Body*. New Haven, Conn.: Yale University Press, 1995.
Martyn, J. Louis. *Galatians: A New Translation with Introduction and Commentary*. New York: Doubleday, 1997.
Mitchell, Margaret M. *Paul and the Rhetoric of Reconciliation: An Exegetical Investigation of the Language and Composition of 1 Corinthians*. Louisville: Westminster John Knox, 1993.

Nowak, Martin A., and Roger Highfield. *Supercooperators: Altruism, Evolution and Why We Need Each Other to Succeed.* New York: Free Press, 2011.
Nygren, Anders. *Commentary on Romans.* Translated by C. C. Rasmussen. Philadelphia: Fortress, 1949.
Pettit, Philip. "Groups with Minds of Their Own," Pages 167–93 in *Socializing Metaphysics.* Edited by Frederick F. Schmitt. Lanham, Md.: Rowman & Littlefield, 2003.
Sanders, E. P. *Paul and Palestinian Judaism: A Comparison of Patterns of Religion.* Philadelphia: Fortress, 1977.
Seeley, T. D. "Honey Bee Colonies Are Group-Level Adaptive Units." *The American Naturalist* 150 (1997): 22–41
———. *The Wisdom of the Hive: The Social Physiology of Honey Bee Colonies.* Cambridge: Harvard University Press, 1995.
Smith, John Maynard, and Eörs Szathmáry. *The Major Transitions in Evolution.* Oxford: Oxford University Press, 1997.
Smith, John Maynard, and Eörs Szathmáry. *The Major Transitions in Evolution Revisited.* Cambridge: MIT Press, 2011.
Smyth, Herbert Weir. *Greek Grammar.* Revised by Gordon M. Messing. Cambridge, Mass.: Harvard University Press, 1963 [1920].
Stendahl, Krister. *The Bible and the Role of Women: A Case Study in Hermeneutics.* Philadelphia: Fortress, 1966.
Stowers, Stanley K. *A Rereading of Romans: Justice, Jews, and Gentiles.* New Haven: Yale University Press, 1997.
———. "What is "Pauline Participation in Christ"?" Pages 352–71 in *Redefining First-Century Jewish and Christian Identities: Essays in Honor of Ed Parish Sanders.* Edited by Fabian E. Udoh, et al. Notre Dame, Ind.: University of Notre Dame Press, 2008.
Tannehill, Robert C. *Dying and Rising with Christ: A Study in Pauline Theology.* Berlin: Töpelmann, 1967.
Theiner, Georg, and Timothy O'Connor. "The Emergence of Group Cognition." Pages 78–117 in *Emergence in Science and Philosophy.* Routledge Series in the Philosophy of Science 6. Edited by Antonella Corradini and Timothy O'Connor. New York: Routledge, 2009.
Wheeler, William Morton. "The Ant-Colony as an Organism." *Journal of Morphology* 22 (1912): 307.
Wilson, David Sloan. "Altruism and Organism: Disentangling the Themes of Multilevel Selection Theory." *The American Naturalist* 150 (1997): S122-S133.
———. *Darwin's Cathedral: Evolution, Religion, and the Nature of Society.* Chicago: University of Chicago Press, 2003.
Wilson, David Sloan, and Elliot Sober. "Reviving the Superorganism." *Journal of Theoretical Biology* 136 (1989): 337–56.
Wilson, Edward O. *The Social Conquest of Earth.* New York: Liveright, 2012.

Baptism and Union with Christ[1]

ISAAC AUGUSTINE MORALES, O.P.

At least since the publication of E. P. Sanders's landmark study *Paul and Palestinian Judaism*, participation in Christ – the notion that in some sense Christians take part in the saving events of Christ's death and resurrection – has played a prominent role in Pauline scholarship.[2] A steady stream of English-speaking scholars has followed Sanders in putting participation at the center of Paul's thought, and though Germans have been less quick to embrace Sanders's approach, more recently some German scholars have begun to acknowledge the importance of participatory categories for Paul's thought.[3] Amidst this renewed interest in participation in Christ, one area

---

[1] Research for this essay was made possible by a fellowship from the Alexander von Humboldt Foundation. An earlier version of the essay was presented at the May, 2012 meeting of the Academy of Catholic Theology. I am grateful for the feedback of those who attended. I would also like to thank Nathan Eubank and Chad Pecknold for reading and commenting on earlier drafts of the essay.

[2] E. P. Sanders, *Paul and Palestinian Judaism: A Comparison of Patterns of Religion* (Philadelphia: Fortress, 1977).

[3] See Richard B. Hays, *The Faith of Jesus Christ: The Narrative Substructure of Galatians 3:1–4:11* (2d ed.; Grand Rapids: Eerdmans, 2002), xxix–xxxiii; James D. G. Dunn, *The Theology of Paul the Apostle* (Grand Rapids: Eerdmans, 1997), 390–441 *et passim*; Michael J. Gorman, *Inhabiting the Cruciform God: Kenosis, Justification, and Theosis in Paul's Narrative Soteriology* (Grand Rapids: Eerdmans, 2009); Douglas A. Campbell, *The Deliverance of God: An Apocalyptic Rereading of Justification in Paul* (Grand Rapids: Eerdmans, 2009); idem, *The Quest for Paul's Gospel: A Suggested Strategy* (London: T&T Clark, 2005); Daniel G. Powers, *Salvation through Participation: An Examination of the Notion of the Believers' Corporate Unity with Christ in Early Christian Soteriology* (CBET 29; Leuven: Peeters, 2001); Constantine R. Campbell, *Paul and Union with Christ: An Exegetical and Theological Study* (Grand Rapids: Zondervan, 2012); more recently, and covering all of the New Testament, Grant Macaskill, *Union with Christ in the New Testament* (Oxford: Oxford University Press, 2013). Among German scholars, see particularly Udo Schnelle, *Apostle Paul: His Life and Theology* (trans. M. Eugene Boring; Grand Rapids: Baker Academic, 2005); idem, "Transformation und Partizipation als Grundgedanken paulinischer Theologie," *NTS* 47 (2001): 58–75; Folker Blischke, *Die Begründung und die Durchsetzung der Ethik bei Paulus* (Arbeiten zur Bibel und ihrer Geschichte 25; Leipzig: Evangelische Verlagsanstalt, 2007); Christian Strecker, *Die liminale Theologie des Paulus: Zugänge zur paulinischen Theologie aus kulturanthropologischer Perspektive* (FRLANT 185; Vandenhoeck & Ruprecht: Göttingen,

of Pauline theology has remained for the most part on the margins, particularly in Anglophone scholarship: the role of baptism and the Lord's Supper. Sanders himself devotes precious little space to these rituals, other than to dismiss Albert Schweitzer's explication of the efficacy of baptism as *ex opere operato*.[4]

Those who have followed Sanders in emphasizing participation in Christ as a central category for Paul have, for the most part, also followed his lead in downplaying or ignoring the significance of baptism and the Lord's Supper for Paul's thought. To take one example among many, consider Michael Gorman's stimulating work on theosis in Paul, *Inhabiting the Cruciform God*. To his credit, Gorman devotes a few pages to Romans 6, connecting participation in Christ, justification, and baptism. It is all the more striking, then, that baptism and Eucharist do not even appear in his list of areas for further research.[5] If this is true of a work that actually ascribes some significance to baptism, it is all the more so in the case of those works that either make fleeting reference to baptism or reinterpret much of Paul's baptismal language as metaphorical – and there are many.[6]

1999), 189–211 *et passim*; though see the critical comments of Michael Wolter, *Paulus: Ein Grundriss seiner Theologie* (Neukirchen-Vluyn: Neukirchener Theologie, 2011), 227–59.

[4] As Hays has noted, there are only four entries for baptism in the index of *Paul and Palestinian Judaism*, and no extended discussion of the topic. See Richard B. Hays, "What Is 'Real Participation in Christ'?" in *Redefining First-Century Jewish and Christian Identities: Essays in Honor of Ed Parish Sanders* (ed. Fabian E. Udoh et al.; CJAS 16; Notre Dame: University of Notre Dame Press, 2008), 336–51, here 344. It should be noted that Schweitzer's lone use of the phrase *opus operatum* in *Paul and his Interpreters* has little in common with the traditional theological definition of the concept: "The sacramental is therefore non-rational. The act and its effect are not bound together by religious logic, but laid one upon the other and nailed together. With that is connected the fact that in Paul we find the most prosaic conception imaginable of the *opus operatum*." Albert Schweitzer, *Paul and His Interpreters: A Critical History* (trans. W. Montgomery; 1912; repr., Eugene: Wipf and Stock, 2004), 213. Traditional theology does not pose a sharp divide between the sacraments and faith as Schweitzer does, nor does it treat the sacraments as "magical" or "non-rational." It is unfortunate that his misuse of a well-known theological term has helped to marginalize the role of baptism and the Lord's Supper in many treatments of Paul's writings and thought.

[5] Gorman, Inhabiting the Cruciform God, 8 n. 22.

[6] See, e.g., D. Campbell, *The Deliverance of God*, 213, which devotes a single paragraph to the question of the sacraments, along with isolated comments here and there, but no sustained discussion of the topic in a monograph of over 1,000 pages; Dunn, *The Theology of Paul the Apostle, passim*; C. Campbell, *Paul and Union with Christ*, 384–87. A rare, but refreshing, example to the contrary is the recent work of Macaskill, which devotes an entire chapter to the role of the sacraments (*Union with Christ in the New Testament*, 192–218). Since the work covers the entire New Testament, however, Macaskill offers only a cursory discussion of Paul's baptismal texts (195–97).

The picture is somewhat different in German scholarship. German exegetes such as Eduard Lohse, Udo Schnelle, and Christian Strecker, among others, ascribe a greater role to baptism than their English-speaking counterparts.[7] The most robust formulation of the significance of baptism for Paul is that of Lohse. In his classic essay "Taufe und Gerechtigkeit bei Paulus," he asserts: "If one considers the exceedingly frequent use of the formula 'in Christ' in Paul, with which the apostle shows that the transfer to the Lord effected in baptism and the claim of the baptized by his Lord associated with it actually extends to all areas of life and puts the human being under the control of the Lord in his entire thinking, working, and action, then one can rightly characterize the whole of Paul's theology as an exposition of baptism."[8] Lohse's characterization no doubt goes too far – certainly Paul's understanding of God, of the mission of Christ, and of the role of the Spirit, to name but a few examples, are not derived from baptism. Nevertheless, Lohse's emphasis on the importance of baptism is refreshing.

In this essay I will examine a few key texts in Romans, 1 Corinthians, and Galatians in order to substantiate the basic thrust of Lohse's assertion.[9] Being "in Christ" is indeed closely connected to baptism, as a careful consideration of some of the most explicit participatory texts in the Pauline corpus will show. For Paul, baptismal participation in Christ empowers the baptized to lead a life of holiness in the present ordered to eternal life. This

---

[7] Eduard Lohse, "Taufe und Rechtfertigung bei Paulus," *KD* 11 (1965): 308–24; repr. in *Die Einheit des Neuen Testaments: Exegetische Studien zur Theologie des Neuen Testaments* (Göttingen: Vandenhoeck & Ruprecht, 1973), 228–44; Udo Schnelle, *Apostle Paul*; idem, "Transformation und Partizipation"; Christian Strecker, *Die liminale Theologie des Paulus*; cf. Friedrich Lang, "Das Verständnis der Taufe bei Paulus," in *Evangelium, Schriftauslegung, Kirche: Festschrift für Peter Stuhlmacher aum 65 Geburtstag* (ed. Jostein Ådna et al.; Göttingen: Vandenhoeck & Ruprecht, 1997), 255–68.

[8] Lohse, "Taufe und Rechtfertigung bei Paulus," 238, my translation: "Faßt man die überaus häufige Verwendung der Formel. In Christus' bei Paulus ins Auge, mit der der Apostel anzeigt, daß die in der Taufe erfolgte Übereignung an den Kyrios und die damit geschehene Beschlagnahme des Getauften durch seinen Herrn sich tatsächlich auf alle Bereiche des Lebens erstreckt und den Menschen in seinem gesamten Denken, Wirken und Handeln dem Kyrios unterstellt, so kann man mit Recht geradezu die ganze Theologie des Paulus als Taufauslegung bezeichnen."

[9] In restricting myself to these texts, I do not intend to come down one way or the other on the question of the disputed Pauline epistles. The decision is one primarily of space constraints and of common scholarly practice. Whatever the provenance of the disputed epistles, there is much to be gained from a broader, canonical approach to Paul, as a number of recent studies have suggested. See, e.g., C. Campbell, *Paul and Union with Christ*; Frank Matera, *God's Saving Grace: A Pauline Theology* (Grand Rapids: Eerdmans, 2012); Brevard Childs, *The Church's Guide for Reading Paul: The Canonical Shaping of the Pauline Corpus* (Grand Rapids: Eerdmans, 2008).

holiness is manifested, among other ways, in the unity that baptism brings about."

A. Baptized into Christ's Death

Few texts in the Pauline corpus have a higher concentration of language often described as "participatory" than Rom 6:1–11. In a brief span of five verses, the apostle says believers were "buried with (συνετάφημεν)" Christ (v. 4), that they have been "joined to (σύμφυτοι γεγόναμεν) the likeness of his death" (v. 5), that their "old human being was co-crucified (συνεσταυρώθη) [with him]" (v. 6), that they "died with Christ (σὺν Χριστῷ)," and that they "will live together with him (συζήσομεν αὐτῷ)" (v. 8).[10] Moreover, Paul rounds out this section by exhorting the Romans to consider themselves "dead to sin but alive to God *in Christ Jesus* (ἐν Χριστῷ Ἰησοῦ)" (v. 11).[11] If ever there were a text rife with the idea that believers are in some sense united to the saving events of Christ's death and resurrection, this is the one.[12]

Despite the explicit description of baptism as a co-burial with Christ and a long history of interpretation that sees Rom 6:1–11 at least in part as an exposition of baptism, some scholars have recently marginalized the rite's significance, portraying vv. 3–4 as a digression or an illustration. James Dunn and Robert Tannehill, to take but two examples, argue that the primary thrust of the passage is death to sin rather than baptism.[13] While there is a grain of truth to this argument – the passage is indeed hortatory, though this does not settle the question of the importance of baptism – there are problems with marginalizing baptism in this way.

Scholars such as Tannehill argue that the co-crucifixion Paul describes in Rom 6:6 took place at Golgotha. In other words, it was on the cross itself rather than in baptism that we were co-crucified with Christ. Such a reading runs up against at least two difficulties. As Strecker has argued,

---

[10] Unless otherwise noted, translations of the NT are my own.

[11] C. Campbell (*Paul and Union with Christ*, 115–16) rightly argues that the "in Christ" language of 6:11 refers to the realm the believer now inhabits.

[12] Cf. Dunn, *The Theology of Paul the Apostle*, 403–4.

[13] James D. G. Dunn, "Baptism as Metaphor," in *Baptism, the New Testament and the Church: Historical and Contemporary Studies in Honour of R.E.O. White* (ed. Stanley E. Porter and Anthony R. Cross; JSNTSup 171; Sheffield: Sheffield Academic, 1999), 294–310, here 307 n. 42: "It needs to be recalled that the real theme of 6.2–11 is not baptism but death to sin (6.2)." Cf. Robert C. Tannehill, *Dying and Rising with Christ: A Study in Pauline Theology* (BZNW 32; Berlin: de Gruyter, 1967), 7: "in Rom. 6 also Paul is not primarily concerned to set forth an interpretation of baptism." See also, more recently, C. Campbell, *Paul and Union with Christ*, 386.

the consistency of the verbal forms in vv. 3–4 and v. 6 (all in the aorist tense) suggests that all these verbs point to the same event.[14] Indeed, one wonders whether Paul's audience would be able to track the argument if it jumps back and forth between baptism and Golgotha. Similarly, the various compound forms and uses of the preposition "with" in the passage ("co-buried," "co-crucified," "died with") make much more sense if they point to the same event, namely baptism. Again, it is hard to follow Paul's argument if he asserts that believers were crucified with Christ at Golgotha but buried with him in baptism. Much more likely both events (i.e. crucifixion and burial) are actualized in baptism, and baptism is the moment Paul has in mind throughout when he speaks of dying with Christ (Rom 6:6, 8).[15]

Having suggested that baptism does in fact play a central role for Paul in this passage, we must ask the question: what exactly does baptism do? Most basically, the repeated use of compound verbs and the preposition "with" suggests that it actualizes the saving events of Christ's death and resurrection for the baptized, but in what sense and to what end? In the rest of this section, I will argue that baptism makes possible a life of holiness in the present that leads to eternal life. The connection between holiness and hope can be seen both in the structure of Rom 6:5–10 and in the way this structure reflects the penultimate verse of Romans 6.

As already noted, the primary thrust of Rom 6:1–11, indeed of Romans 6 as a whole, is hortatory. Paul begins with the rhetorical question, "We who died to sin, how can we continue to live in it?" To substantiate the presumed answer to the question (we must not continue in sin), he appeals to baptism as the moment when the baptized initially died to sin: "Or don't you know that as many of us as were baptized into Christ Jesus were baptized into his death?" (Rom 6:3). Baptism brings about a death to sin because it is a baptism into Christ's own death, which in a (no doubt quite different) sense was also a death to sin (cf. 6:10). As v. 4 (together with the rest of the chapter) makes clear, this death to sin is meant to lead to holiness: "therefore we were buried with him through baptism into his death in order that, just as Christ was raised from the dead, so also we might walk in newness of life" (6:4).

It is not uncommon to contrast this language of "walking in newness of life" with explicit resurrection language in order to argue that Paul never speaks of a present resurrection for believers.[16] Such a reading, however, fails adequately to account for the way v. 5 develops and grounds v. 4.

---

[14] Strecker, *Die liminale Theologie des Paulus*, 253.
[15] Strecker, *Die liminale Theologie des Paulus*, 253.
[16] See, e.g., James D. G. Dunn, *Romans 1–8* (WBC 38A; Dallas: Word Books, 1988), 316, 330.

That v. 5 serves as the basis of v. 4 should be clear from the conjunction that binds the two verses.[17] Verse 5 explains why it is that the baptized may now "walk in newness of life": "For if we have been joined to a death like his, we shall also be [joined to the likeness] of [his] resurrection." Some scholars take the future tense in the second part of the verse as an eschatological future, that is, as pointing to the future resurrection.[18] The context, however, suggests otherwise. The parallel structure of vv. 4 and 5 suggests that both verses are hortatory in nature, or at least that they both refer to present life in Christ:

v. 4: We were buried with him through baptism...
    in order that we might walk in newness of life
v. 5: *For* if we have been joined to the likeness of his death,
    we shall also be [joined to the likeness] of [his] resurrection

These parallels alone need not imply that the language of v. 5 refers to a present resurrection. It is possible that Paul inserts a reference to the eschatological hope in order to give his readers the motivation for his exhortation, and, to be sure, this is ultimately where his argument leads (note the sequence holiness-eternal life in Rom 6:22). The continuation of the argument in v. 6, however, further supports a reading of v. 5 as referring to an inaugurated participation in Christ's resurrection.

Just as v. 5 is closely related to v. 4, so also v. 6 continues the line of thought in v. 5. Like vv. 4 and 5, the first part of v. 6 uses death imagery: "knowing this, that our old human being was co-crucified [with him] in order that the body of sin might be destroyed" (6:6a). The second part of the verse speaks again of the present life: "so that we might no longer be enslaved to sin" (6:6b). The parallel structure just noted thus extends to v. 6:

v. 4: We were buried with him through baptism... (a)
    in order that we might walk in newness of life (b)
v. 5: For if we have been joined to the likeness of his death, (a')

---

[17] Cf. Eduard Lohse, *Der Brief an die Römer* (KEK 4; Göttingen: Vandenhoeck & Ruprecht, 2003), 190: "Obwohl in V. 5ff. spezifische Taufterminologie nicht mehr verwendet wird, bleibt doch der Sache nach der Bezug auf die Taufe im Blick." Anders Klostergaard Petersen, "Shedding New Light on Paul's Understanding of Baptism: A Ritual-Theoretical Approach to Romans 6," *ST* 52 (1998): 3–28, here 17: "V.5a is simultaneously developing the point of the incorporation of the baptised into an order of being determined by the Christ event and maintaining the difference between the death of Christ and the baptismal death." Hans Dieter Betz, "Transferring a Ritual: Paul's Interpretation of Baptism in Romans 6," in *Paul in his Hellenistic Context* (ed. Troels Engberg-Pedersen; Minneapolis: Fortress, 1995), 84–118, here 113–14.

[18] See Dunn, *Romans 1–8*, 318, 331; C. K. Barrett, *The Epistle to the Romans* (rev. ed.; BNTC; London: Adam & Charles Black, 1991), 116; Douglas J. Moo, *The Epistle to the Romans* (NICNT; Grand Rapids: Eerdmans, 1996), 371. Contrast Joseph A. Fitzmyer, *Romans* (AB 33; New York: Doubleday, 1992), 435–36.

We shall also be [joined to the likeness] of [his] resurrection (b')
v. 6: knowing this, that our old human being was co-crucified [with him] in order that the body of sin might be destroyed (a")
so that we might no longer be enslaved to sin (b")

Given these parallels, it seems most natural to take the second half of each verse to refer to the same reality. In other words, walking in newness of life corresponds to being joined to a resurrection like Christ's, and both correspond to liberation from sin.[19]

This emphasis on release from sin continues in v. 7, which rounds out the first part of the discussion: "For the one who died has been justified from sin." The context of the passage suggests that this dying relates in some way to baptism.[20] It is through baptism that believers have died and so are freed from sin. In the verses that follow, Paul shifts from sin to immortality and from the present life to eternal life.

Over forty years ago, Günther Bornkamm proposed an outline of Rom 6:5–10 that shows clear structural parallels between vv. 5–7 and vv. 8–10:[21]

vv. 5–7: Holiness	vv. 8–10: Eternal Life
For if we have been joined to a death like his	Now if we died with Christ
We shall also be joined to a resurrection like his	We believe that we shall also live with him
Because we know that	Knowing that
Our old human being has been co-crucified in order that the body of sin might be destroyed so that we might no longer be enslaved to sin	Christ raised from the dead no longer dies, because death no longer reigns over him

---

[19] Cf. Bo Frid, "Römer 6,4–5: εἰς τὸν θάνατον und τῷ ὁμοιώματι τοῦ θανάτου αὐτοῦ als Schlüssel zu Duktus und Gedankengang in Röm 6,1–11," *BZ* 30 (1986): 188–203, esp. 198–200.

[20] Conleth Kearns sees the language of "the one who died" functioning on three levels: "when Paul says 'The one who has died has been justified from sin' he is thinking and speaking on three levels simultaneously, as he is throughout the whole passage. He is thinking (1) on the level of Christ's own experience of death and resurrection or justification; (2) on the level of the Christian's mystical union with Christ in that resurrection or justification, effected by baptism; (3) on the level of the Christian's consequent duty in the moral order to live henceforth as one who has died to sin and who has risen, by justification, to a new life of virtue for God." "The Interpretation of Romans 6,7," *Studiorum paulinorum congressus internationalis catholicus 1961* (AnBib 17–18; Rome: Biblical Institute, 1961), 1.301–07, 307

[21] The following table is adapted from Günther Bornkamm, "Taufe und neues Leben (Röm 6)," in *Das Ende des Gesetzes: Paulusstudien* (Theologische Abhandlungen 16; München: Chr. Kaiser, 1952), 34–50, here 39.

| For the one who died has been freed from sin | For what he died, he died once for all to sin, but what he lives, he lives to God. |

Though Bornkamm himself does not draw this conclusion, I suggest that this parallelism demonstrates the close relationship in Paul's thought between holiness and eternal life, both of which find their starting point in baptism. Considering vv. 5–7 and vv. 8–10 side-by-side, one notes both the structural similarities and the slight but significant shift in emphasis. Verses 5–7 focus primarily on liberation from sin; vv. 8–10 place the accent on eternal life. That these two consequences of baptism are closely related can be seen toward the end of Romans 6. Developing the slavery imagery introduced in v. 6, Paul exhorts his audience, "But now that you have been freed from sin and enslaved to God, you have your fruit leading to holiness, and as its end eternal life" (Rom 6:22). For Paul, freedom from sin has both present and future consequences, and these two are intimately related. Liberation from sin results in a life of holiness, which in turn has as its end eternal life. All of this stems initially from baptism, in which the baptized first die with Christ to sin and thus are empowered to live out the holiness that leads ultimately to the same eternal life Christ attained through his death and resurrection.

B. "But you were washed, you were sanctified, you were justified"

Were Romans 6 the only baptismal text in the Pauline corpus, one might get the impression that baptism has significance primarily, perhaps even exclusively, for the individual. A consideration of texts in 1 Corinthians and Galatians shows that the holiness Paul associates with baptism has corporate as well as personal dimensions. We begin with 1 Corinthians.

Despite the way Paul qualifies his baptismal activity at the beginning of 1 Corinthians ("For Christ did not send me to baptize, but rather to preach the gospel," 1:17a), the rite plays a significant role throughout the letter. Paul refers to baptism directly or indirectly five times, and each time in connection with significant Pauline themes (1:13 – the cross, church unity; 6:11 – sanctification and justification; 10:2 – idolatry and sexual immorality; 12:13 – church unity; 15:29 – the resurrection).[22] Though Paul does not

---

[22] Assuming the language of "being washed" in 6:11 is a baptismal reference, for which I will argue presently. A number of scholars interpret 1 Cor 1:17 to suggest that Paul minimized the importance of ritual baptism (see, e.g., C. Campbell, *Paul and Union with Christ*, 336; Dunn, *Theology of Paul the Apostle, passim*). Indeed, Campbell suggests that most of Paul's references to baptism are metaphorical, rather than physical, but given the practices of the early Church, such an interpretation strains credulity. Of the nineteen occurrences of the verb βαπτίζω in the Acts of the Apostles, seventeen refer to

expound on baptism as extensively in this letter as he does in Romans 6, the references to baptism in 1 Corinthians nevertheless share a number of themes with Romans. The clearest connections between the two letters in this regard appear in a passage that does not actually use the word βαπτίζω.

Halfway through 1 Corinthians 6 Paul reminds his audience, "But you were washed, but you were sanctified, but you were made righteous in the name of the Lord Jesus Christ and in the Spirit of our God" (1 Cor 6:11). Scholars have long taken this language of being "washed" as a baptismal reference for two reasons. First, the reference to "the name of the Lord Jesus Christ" and "the Spirit of our God" suggests a baptismal context, particularly in light of the connection between the "name" and baptism in 1 Cor 1:13 on the one hand and the Spirit and baptism in 12:13 on the other.[23] Second, other early Christian texts describe baptism in terms of washing, most explicitly Acts 22:16, where Ananias exhorts Paul: "Arise, be baptized and wash away your sins, calling upon [Jesus'] name."[24] Though the most obvious, these are not the only elements of 1 Corinthians 6 that suggest a baptismal interpretation.

Shortly before the reference to washing, Paul warns the Corinthians against sins that exclude one from the kingdom of God: "Or don't you know that the unrighteous will not inherit the kingdom of God?" (1 Cor 6:9a). A vice list follows, at the end of which the apostle reiterates that none of those who commit the sins enumerated "will inherit the kingdom of God" (6:10b). This reference to "inheritance," like the language of

---

physical baptism (see Acts 2:38, 41; 8:12–13, 16, 36, 38; 9:18; 10:47–48; 16:15, 33; 18:8; 19:3–5; 22:16). It is highly unlikely that the baptism referred to in Eph 4:4–5 is a metaphorical one. With respect to 1 Corinthians, see the section on 1 Cor 12:13 below. See also the helpful comments of N. T. Wright, *Paul and the Faithfulness of God* (Vol. 4 of Christian Origins and the Question of God; Minneapolis: Fortress, 2013), 417–27, esp. 425.

[23] See Lars Hartman, *Auf den Namen des Herrn Jesus: Die Taufe in den neutestamentlichen Schriften* (SBS 148; Stuttgart: Verlag katholischer Bibelwerk, 1992), 64–66; Udo Schnelle, *Gerechtigkeit und Christusgegenwart: Vorpaulinische und paulinische Trauftheologie* (GTA 24; Göttingen: Vandenhoeck & Ruprecht, 1983), 179 n. 61; Jakob Kremer, *Der Erste Brief an die Korinther* (RNT; Regensburg: Verlag Friedrich Pustet, 1997), 117; G. R. Beasley-Murray, *Baptism in the New Testament* (London: Macmillan, 1962/3), 163; C. K. Barrett, *A Commentary on the First Epistle to the Corinthians* (BNTC; London: Adam & Charles Black, 1968), 141. The classic study of the variant forms of the phrase "in the name" is Wilhelm Heitmüller, „*Im Namen Jesu*": *eine Sprach- und religionsgeschichtliche Untersuchung zum Neuen Testament, speziell zur altchristlichen Taufe* (FRLANT I:2; Göttingen: Vandenhoeck & Ruprecht, 1903); see also Gerhard Delling, *Die Zueignung des Heils in der Taufe: Eine Untersuchung zum neutestamentlichen taufen auf den Namen* (Berlin: Evangelische Verlagsanstalt, 1961).

[24] See also Eph 5:22; Tit 3:5; Heb 10:22.

washing, also suggests a baptismal context. In Galatians, Paul closely connects baptism with inheritance, noting that those who belong to Christ because of baptism (Gal 3:26–29) are now "heirs according to the promise" (Gal 3:29b).[25] Later in the same letter, he specifies the content of the inheritance in the context of another vice list: "Those who do such things [i.e. the vices enumerated in Gal 5:19–21a] will not inherit the kingdom of God" (Gal 5:21b). The close connection between baptism, a vice list, and becoming heirs of the kingdom in Galatians suggests a similar connection in 1 Corinthians 6.[26] By being washed by the Spirit through baptism, the Corinthians have become heirs of the kingdom of God.

Another important feature of v. 11 is the close connection it implies between baptism and being made righteous. The parallelism of the verbs in 1 Cor 6:11b ("But you were washed, but you were sanctified, but you were made righteous in the name of the Lord Jesus Christ and in the Spirit of our God") suggests that all three should be read together, and by implication that being made holy and righteous are related to being "washed."[27] Such a connection further supports a baptismal interpretation of the washing language, as Paul elsewhere connects baptism with "righteousness" language. As we have already seen, in Rom 6:7 he writes, "The one who died has been justified [δεδικαίωται] from sin." Given the baptismal context and the interpretation of baptism as dying and being buried with Christ (Rom 6:3–4), this verse seems to suggest that justification is in some sense a consequence of baptism. Thus, when Paul closely aligns "being washed" with "being made righteous," a baptismal reading of the former phrase is at the very least plausible.[28]

Thus we see that a number of features in 1 Cor 6:9–11 point to a baptismal reference in the language of being "washed," and that this brief section implies a number of theological interpretations of the rite that are laid out more explicitly in Romans. If we read 1 Cor 6:9–11 in conjunction with the verses that follow, we find further support for a baptismal interpretation of the washing language.

Though most commentaries divide the chapter between vv. 11 and 12, there are good reasons to read vv. 9–20 – and indeed all of 1 Corinthians 6

---

[25] See below on baptism in Galatians.

[26] Cf. Hans Halter, *Taufe und Ethos: paulinische Kriterien für das Proprium christlicher Moral* (Freiburger theologische Studien; Freiburg: Herder, 1977), 148–49.

[27] Gordon Fee argues that all three verbs should be read together, though he finds an allusion to baptism unlikely. *The First Epistle to the Corinthians* (NICNT; Grand Rapids: Eerdmans, 1987), 245–47.

[28] Cf. Halter, *Taufe und Ethos*, 149–50; Christian Wolff, "Abwaschung – Heiligung – Rechtfertigung: Zur Interpretation von 1. Kor 6,11," in *Der Wahrheit Gottes verpflichtet: Theologische Beiträge aus dem Sprachenkonvikt Berlin für Rudolf Mau* (ed. Matthias Köckert; Berlin: Wichern, 1993), 298–303, here 300.

– as a unit. The first vice listed in 1 Cor 6:9b is sexual immorality (πορνεία), the very subject of vv. 12–20.²⁹ Moreover, Paul's appeal to the resurrection in vv. 13–14 fits with the reference to the kingdom of God in vv. 9–10, particularly given the close connection he makes toward the end of the letter between resurrection and the kingdom (1 Cor 15:50).³⁰

In addition to this connection between resurrection and the kingdom, appeal to the resurrection at the service of exhortation makes sense in a baptismal context. As we have seen, in Romans 6 Paul closely associates baptism, walking in newness of life, and participating in Christ's resurrection, both in the here and now and at the eschaton. Though the connection is not as explicit in 1 Corinthians 6, the underlying logic seems to be similar: baptism and holiness lead ultimately to eternal life. This connection is not, however, automatic. As 1 Corinthians 6 and 10 both show (see esp. 1 Cor 10:1–13), baptism does not guarantee that one will participate in the resurrection.

Thus far, everything we have seen in this text seems to suggest a personal understanding of baptism similar to the one we have seen in Romans 6. One additional aspect of 1 Corinthians 6, however, supports a baptismal reading of v. 11 in a way that also connects it to baptismal texts that emphasize a more communal understanding of the rite. Immediately following his appeal to the resurrection, Paul introduces the imagery of the Corinthians as members of Christ's body: "Don't you know that your bodies are members of Christ? Shall I therefore take away Christ's members and join them to a prostitute? Of course not!" (1 Cor 6:15). As many scholars note, this imagery anticipates the fuller discussion of the church as the Body of Christ in 1 Corinthians 12.³¹ In both texts Paul refers to the Corinthians as

---

[29] It is also worth noting that the second vice listed is idolatry. If the "food" referred to in 6:13 is temple food – and there are good reasons for thinking so – then there may be an implicit critique of idolatry in vv. 12–20, as well (note also the reference to the baptized as temples of the Holy Spirit in 6:19). With the exception of the metaphorical usage of βρῶμα in 1 Cor 3:2, every occurrence of the word in the letter has some kind of cultic association (cf. 1 Cor 8:8, 13; 10:3). Cf. Brian S. Rosner, "Temple Prostitution in 1 Corinthians 6:12–20," *NovT* 40 (1998): 336–51, here 346. Joseph A. Fitzmyer also sees *porneia* as the theme connecting chapters 5–6. *First Corinthians: A New Translation with Introduction and Commentary* (AYBC 32; London: Yale University Press, 2008), 251.

[30] On the connection between 1 Cor 6:13–20 and the discussion of the resurrection in 1 Corinthians 15, see Dale B. Martin, *The Corinthian Body* (New Haven, Conn.: Yale University Press, 1995), 176.

[31] See, e.g., Gerd Häfner, "Taufe und Einheit: paulinische Tauftheologie in Gal 3,26–29," in *Paul et L'Unité des Chrétiens* (ed. Jacques Schlosser; Colloquium Oecumenicum Paulinum 19; Löwen: Peeters, 2010) 105–39, here 132; Fitzmyer, *First Corinthians*, 266. For a reading of Paul's use of the Body of Christ image in the context of other ancient descriptions of society as a body, see Martin, *The Corinthian Body*, 92–96.

members of Christ (6:15; 12:12). Moreover, both texts appeal to the Spirit (6:19; 12:13).

Less often noted is the fact that both texts also relate to baptism.[32] In 1 Corinthians 12, the baptismal language is explicit: "for by one Spirit we all were baptized into one body" (1 Cor 12:13). While 1 Corinthians 6 does not use the actual word "baptism," we have seen that a number of aspects of the text suggest a baptismal interpretation of the "washing" language in 1 Cor 6:11. Moreover, it is worth repeating that Paul attributes the efficacy of this washing to the Spirit: "But you were washed [...] in the name of the Lord Jesus Christ and in the Spirit of our God" (1 Cor 6:11). That this washing reference is followed closely by an argument based on union with Christ (1 Cor 6:17) and on being a part of the body of Christ (6:15) further confirms the baptismal interpretation of 6:11. Sanders begins his discussion of Paul's participatory Christology with the exhortation of 1 Cor 6:13–18, noting that Paul's argument rests on the mutual exclusiveness of union with Christ and union with a prostitute, and that Paul's exhortation simply presumes an underlying understanding of union with Christ.[33] It is striking that this appeal to union with Christ appears amidst so many images closely related to baptism.[34] Here we see further evidence that participation in Christ is rooted, though not exhausted, in baptism.

For Paul, then, the misdeeds of the baptized are not merely private or personal matters. Rather, as the language of union with Christ suggests, the sins of one member of the body of Christ affect the entire body (cf. 1 Cor 12:26). Thus we see in 1 Corinthians 6, at least implicitly, that the holiness baptism brings about and requires has both personal and communal dimensions. These dimensions are grounded in the union with Christ that baptism brings about and are ultimately ordered toward hope in the resurrection.

---

[32] A rare exception is Renate Kirchhoff, *Die Sünde gegen den eigenen Leib: Studien zu πόρνη und πορνεία in 1 Kor 6,12–20 und dem sozio-kulturellen Kontext der paulinischen Adressaten* (SUNT; Göttingen: Vandenhoeck & Ruprecht, 1994), 125–27, 156–57. Surprisingly, Kirchhoff does not make an explicit connection with a baptismal reference in 6:11, though she comes close (129 n. 77): "Der Hinweis auf die Gerechtmachung durch Christus in 6,11 betont ebenfalls die sich daraus ergebende Verpflichtung, nicht mehr zu tun, was sie nach Darstellung des Paulus vor der Taufe getan haben (V.10.11a). Auch hier ist Gott der Handelnde (vgl. Schrage, 1Kor, 433f.), und er ist es, dem die Getauften gehorsam sein sollen." Kirchhoff does not interpret the imagery of the community as the body of Christ in terms of union with Christ, but rather as a metaphor (see pp. 154–58).

[33] Sanders, *Paul and Palestinian Judaism*, 454–55.

[34] Cf. Søren Agersnap, *Baptism and the New Life: A Study of Romans 6:1–14* (Aarhus: Aarhus University Press, 1999), 169–70.

C. Baptized by one Spirit into one Body

Whereas the baptismal allusion in 1 Corinthians 6 focuses primarily on holiness, 1 Corinthians 12 emphasizes unity. Some scholars have argued that 1 Cor 12:13 refers to a metaphorical baptism in the Spirit rather than to ritual baptism, but several factors speak against this reading, both in 1 Corinthians itself and in the Pauline corpus more broadly.[35]

Within 1 Corinthians, Paul uses the language of baptism in four passages (1 Cor 1:13–17; 10:1–13; 12:13; 15:29). In the first and last instances, the language clearly refers to a ritual of some kind. In 1 Corinthians 10, Paul describes the Israelites being baptized "into Moses" (10:2). Though this text does not refer to a rite the Israelites underwent, the way Paul sets up his telling of the exodus story presupposes the rituals of the Lord's Supper and baptism, as the latter half of the chapter makes clear. Given that each of these other instances of baptismal language in the letter relate in some way to ritual baptism, one would expect clearer indications of the metaphorical nature of the language in 1 Cor 12:13 if that were Paul's intention.[36]

The parallels with other instances of baptismal language in the Pauline corpus further undermine a metaphorical reading of 1 Cor 12:13. In Galatians, Paul appeals to baptism to underscore the unity of the baptized across ethnic, social, and sexual differences: "For as many of you as were baptized into Christ have put on Christ. There is neither Jew nor Greek, there is neither slave nor free, there is no male and female; for you are all one in Christ Jesus" (Gal 3:27–28).[37] Colossians includes a similar formula: "Where there is neither Greek nor Jew, circumcision or uncircumcision, barbarian, Scythian, slave, free, but Christ is all and in all" (Col 3:11). Though the phrase does not appear directly in connection with baptism, the

---

[35] In addition to Dunn, see Fee, *First Corinthians*, 604; Richard B. Hays, *First Corinthians* (Interpretation; Louisville: John Knox, 1997), 214; Anthony C. Thiselton, *The First Epistle to the Corinthians: A Commentary on the Greek Text* (NIGTC; Grand Rapids: Eerdmans, 2000), 454. Contrast Fitzmyer, who finds Fee's denial of any connection between baptism and reception of the Spirit "baffling." *First Corinthians*, 478.

[36] Häfner's observation is apt: "1 Kor 12,13 wäre die einzige Stelle in diesem Brief, in dem Paulus metaphorisch von Taufe sprechen würde. Um eine solche Annahme zu begründen, wären stärkere Argumente nötig als die Täufertradition der Evangelien." "Taufe und Einheit," 110. Cf. the similar assessment of Wolfgang Schrage, *Der Erste Brief an die Korinther: 1 Kor 11,17–14,40* (EKK 7/3; Zürich: Benziger, 1999), 216 n. 607. Hence, C. Campbell's suggestion that most of Paul's uses of baptismal language are metaphorical fails to convince. *Paul and Union with Christ*, 336.

[37] So also Beasley-Murray, *Baptism in the New Testament*, 169; cf. Andreas Lindemann, *Der Erste Korintherbrief* (HNT 9/1; Tübingen: Mohr Siebeck, 2000), 272, who also offers some possible reasons for the absence of the male-female pair in 1 Corinthians.

entire context can be taken as part of a baptismal exhortation (cf. the imagery of being buried with Christ in baptism in 2:12 and putting to death the earthly members in 3:5).[38] Finally, Ephesians predicates unity at least in part on baptism: "There is one body and one Spirit, just as you also were called in the one hope of your calling, one Lord, one faith, one baptism" (Eph 4:4–5). It beggars belief to suggest that this baptism is a metaphorical one, particularly given the widespread witness to the ritual practice in the NT. Given this repeated connection of unity with ritual baptism, 1 Cor 12:13 most likely also refers to a ritual that derives its efficacy from the action of the Spirit.[39]

One more factor speaks in favor of reading the baptismal language in 1 Cor 12:13 as a reference to the ritual. First Corinthians 8–14 deals largely with liturgical abuses in the Corinthian churches. In the first half of 1 Corinthians 10 Paul retells the exodus story in such a way that presupposes the Christian rituals of baptism and the Lord's Supper. In the second half of that chapter, as well as in 1 Corinthians 11, he both appeals to and corrects the Corinthians' practice of the Lord's Supper. Given that Paul's retelling of the exodus story leads to discussions of the rite of the Lord's Supper and given the liturgical context of this larger section of the letter, the baptismal reference makes most sense as a reference to the rite. If Paul intended to contrast baptism in the Spirit with water baptism, he could have made it much clearer at the outset of the letter by noting that it is baptism in the Spirit rather than water baptism at the hands of one's favorite minister that matters. As the letter stands, 1 Corinthians 1 establishes the primary reference of baptismal language as the rite, not a metaphorical reception of the Spirit.

It is hardly surprising, then, that Paul should appeal to baptism in order to foster unity among the Corinthians. This unity seems to be one of the primary purposes and fruits of baptism,[40] and it is the theme he underscores in 1 Corinthians 12, indeed, in much of 1 Corinthians as a whole.

---

[38] Cf. Friedrich Lang, *Die Briefe an die Korinther* (NTD 7; Göttingen: Vandenhoeck & Ruprecht, 1986), 172: "Die Aufzählung der Gruppen und Stände der alten Welt begegnet immer im Zusammenhang mit dem Taufgeschehen (1. Kor 12,13; Gal 3,27f.; vgl. Das Ablegen des alten Menschen in Kol 3,10ff.), und das Taufgeschehen wird in Röm 6,4–11 verankert im Heilsgeschehen von Tod und Auferweckung Jesu Christi."

[39] So also Barrett: "There is no reason to think that *we were baptized* refers to anything other than baptism in water (together with all that this outward rite signified)." *First Corinthians*, 289.

[40] It is worth noting that in critiquing the Corinthians' loyalty to the figures who baptized them (1 Corinthians 1), he implies that baptism should be a source of unity rather than of division. Cf. Wright, *Paul and the Faithfulness of God*, 425: "Paul's main concern is to offer a preliminary challenge to the factionalism that has emerged in Corinth, and he does so by appealing, again merely preliminarily, to baptism itself."

This unity does not, however, flatten out differences, but rather constitutes the church as a union of members given diverse gifts, all for the building up of the body of Christ (1 Cor 12:7). Through baptism the Corinthians have become interdependent members of the body of Christ: "For by one Spirit we all were baptized into one body, whether Jews or Greeks, whether slaves or free, and we all were given to drink of one Spirit" (1 Cor 12:13).[41] Paul thus makes explicit what remained implicit in 1 Corinthians 6: baptism brings about a union with Christ that affects not only the one being baptized, but the whole body of Christ, such that the deeds of the one affect the many (1 Cor 6:15; 12:26).

D. Crucifying the Flesh through Baptism for the sake of Unity[42]

"I have been crucified with Christ; I live, yet no longer I, but Christ lives in me" (Gal 2:19b–20a). This statement, one of the most striking in Paul's letters, is the only other one besides Rom 6:6 to use the imagery of being "crucified with Christ," and though Galatians 2 does not use the language of baptism, Paul does refer to baptism in the next chapter of the letter.[43] The baptismal language in Gal 3:27 (εἰς Χριστὸν ἐβαπτίσθητε) resembles that of Romans 6 (ὅσοι ἐβαπτίσθημεν εἰς Χριστὸν Ἰησοῦν), though the imagery Paul uses to interpret the ritual differs. Whereas in Romans he de-

---

[41] In favor of an instrumental reading of the phrase ἐν ἑνὶ πνεύματι see Lindemann, *Der erste Korintherbrief*, 271–72; Schrage, *Der erste Brief an die Korinther*, 216; J. W. McGarvey, "A Note on 1 Corinthians 12:13," *ResQ* 2 (1958), 45–47.

[42] I have made a similar argument in a bit more detail in Rodrigo J. Morales, "Baptism, Unity, and Crucifying the Flesh," in *A Man of the Church: Honoring the Theology, Life, and Witness of Ralph Del Colle* (ed. Michel René Barnes; Eugene: Wipf and Stock, 2012), 249–62.

[43] Many scholars have read Gal 2:19–20 as a reference to baptism. See Marie-Joseph Lagrange, *Saint Paul Épître aux Galates* (EBib; Paris: Gabalda, 1918), 51; Heinrich Schlier, *Der Brief an die Galater* (4th ed.; KEK 7; Göttingen: Vandenhoeck & Ruprecht, 1965), 99–100; Franz Mussner, *Der Galaterbrief* (5th ed.; HTK 9; Freiburg: Herder, 1988), 180–81; Ragnar Bring, *Commentary on Galatians* (trans. Eric Wahlstrom; Philadelphia: Muhlenberg, 1961), 99–100; Thomas Söding, "Kreuzestheologie und Rechtfertigungslehre: Zur Verbindung von Christologie und Soteriologie im Ersten Korintherbrief und im Galaterbrief," in *Das Wort vom Kreuz: Studien zur paulinischen Theologie* (WUNT 93; Tübingen: Mohr Siebeck, 1997), 153–82, here 170; cf. recently Wilfried Eckey, *Der Galaterbrief: Ein Kommentar* (Neukirchen-Vluyn: Neukirchener, 2010), 147. Rudolf Schnackenburg (*Das Heilsgeschehen bei der Taufe nach dem Apostel Paulus: Eine Studie zur paulinischen Theologie* [München: K. Zink Verlag, 1950], 57–61) interprets the verses as a baptismal reference based on the aorist verb ἀπέθανον, but reads the verb συνεσταύρωμαι on three levels: Christ's death on the cross, the Christian's death in baptism, and the continuing state of being crucified with Christ (cf. 2:19b; 6:14).

scribes baptism in terms of dying and rising with Christ, here he interprets the ritual as "being clothed with Christ." On the basis of this being clothed with Christ, all who have been baptized are united in Christ (Gal 3:28). Whereas the baptismal language refers to the ritual, the clothing imagery is to be taken metaphorically, and the question naturally follows: how ought one to interpret the metaphor?[44]

In seeking to answer this question, it is worth noting that the baptismal language of Gal 3:27 is not the only imagery this letter shares with Romans 6. Again, both letters also use the imagery of being "co-crucified with Christ" (Gal 2:19; Rom 6:6), as well as the related notions of "crucifying the flesh" (Gal 5:24) and "destroying the body of sin" (Rom 6:6).[45] Though some scholars resist drawing the conclusion that the co-crucifixion imagery in Galatians relates to baptism, there are good reasons to do so.[46] While it is true that the connection is not explicit in Galatians, it is hard to believe that Paul had not reflected on the significance and meaning of baptism before he wrote Romans.[47] Indeed, the way Paul talks about his own crucifixion and the Galatians' crucifixion of the flesh seems to suggest a

---

[44] Dunn's suggestion that not only the clothing imagery, but also the technical language of baptism is metaphorical, fails to convince. *The Epistle to the Galatians* (BNTC; Peabody, Mass.: Hendrickson, 1993), 203–5. Häfner rightly notes that it is much more natural for a ritual (baptism) to be illustrated by a metaphor (clothing) than that a metaphor should illustrate another metaphor. "Taufe und Einheit," 112 n. 24.

[45] While the language is not identical, the basic idea is quite similar. Note especially the relationship between sin and the flesh in Romans 7.

[46] Hans Dieter Betz, for example, points out that in Gal 3:27, the only verse in the letter to mention baptism explicitly, Paul does not connect the rite to the crucifixion. Moreover, the verses in Galatians that do apply crucifixion imagery to Paul and the Galatians (5:24; 6:14) do not explicitly mention baptism. Additionally, unlike Romans, in none of these texts does Paul refer to the resurrection. On the basis of this evidence, Betz concludes that Romans 6 represents a later development in Paul's understanding of baptism. *Galatians: A Commentary on Paul's Letter to the Churches in Galatia* (Hermeneia; Philadelphia: Fortress, 1979), 123. Other scholars are skeptical or noncommittal on the question. See also Dunn, *The Epistle to the Galatians*, 144 n. 1; Udo Borse, *Der Brief an die Galater* (RNT; Regensburg: Pustet, 1984), 117; Joachim Rohde, *Der Brief des Paulus an die Galater* (THK 9; Berlin: Evangelische Verlagsanstalt, 1989), 116 n. 80. Richard N. Longenecker does not address the question. *Galatians* (WBC 41; Nashville: Thomas Nelson, 1990), 92. F. F. Bruce tentatively connects the saying with baptism, but is quick to suggest that for Paul the experience of co-crucifixion occurred on the road to Damascus rather than in baptism. *The Epistle of Paul to the Galatians: A Commentary on the Greek Text* (NIGTC; Exeter: Pater Noster, 1982), 144.

[47] One might even argue that the ἀγνοεῖτε of Romans 6:2 suggests that on some level Paul presumed such an interpretation of baptism even on the part of believers he had not yet visited.

decisive event at which this crucifixion took place. The most obvious candidate for such an event is baptism.[48]

Another aspect of Galatians supports a reading of the clothing imagery in Gal 3:27 in terms of crucifixion. With the exception of Gal 1:1, which refers to God as the one who raised Christ from the dead, Paul's description of Christ in the letter is fundamentally cross-centered. He refers to Christ as the one "who gave himself for our sins" (Gal 1:4); with similar language he calls Christ the one "who gave himself for me" (2:20); when Paul came to the Galatians he graphically presented Christ crucified (3:1); his discussion of the curse of the law focuses on Christ's crucifixion (3:13–14); those who belong to Christ are said to have crucified the flesh (5:24); those advocating circumcision do so to avoid persecution for the sake of the cross (6:12); Paul has been crucified to the world through the cross of Christ (6:14). From the perspective of this letter, then, the Christ with whom the Galatians have been clothed in baptism is primarily the crucified Christ. Thus, particularly in the context of the cross-centered Christology of Galatians, the idea of being clothed with Christ and being co-crucified with him naturally belong together.[49]

If this is the case, one might ask: why does Paul not make the connection more explicit? Though one cannot know for certain, one possible answer is that he could presume the connection and that his audience would recognize it as well. Whereas Paul founded the churches in Galatia, he had not even visited the churches in Rome. Thus, it makes sense that he would lay out his understanding of baptism more explicitly in Romans than in his other letters.[50] As we saw above, 1 Corinthians similarly hints at some of the theological significance of baptism without explicitly laying out the connections.

Another feature of Galatians suggests that baptism is the moment when one is "co-crucified" with Christ. In Gal 3:26–29, Paul uses a number of images in conjunction with baptism: becoming "sons of God"; being

---

[48] Cf. Alastair Campbell, "Dying with Christ: The Origin of a Metaphor?" in *Baptism, the New Testament and the Church: Historical and Contemporary Studies in Honour of R. E. O. White* (ed. Stanley E. Porter and Anthony R. Cross; JSNTSup 171; Sheffield: Sheffield Academic, 1999), 273–93, here 282.

[49] Jung Hoon Kim (, asks regarding the clothing imagery: "[W]ho is 'Christ' with whom the baptized has been clothed; in other words, with whom he has been united?" *The Significance of Clothing Imagery in the Pauline Corpus* (JSNTSup 268; London: T&T Clark, 2004), 122. Kim fails, however, to consider the importance of the cross for Paul's portrayal of Christ in Galatians. Macaskill rightly draws a close connection between baptism, death and resurrection, and clothing imagery. *Union with Christ in the New Testament*, 196–97.

[50] Though again, even in Romans he seems to presume some understanding on the part of his audience.

"clothed with Christ"; belonging to Christ (εἰ δὲ ὑμεῖς Χριστοῦ); being "Abraham's seed" and, as a result, "heirs." Two of these images recur in Galatians 5. First, at the end of the vice list in Gal 5:19–21, Paul notes that those who commit such sins "will not *inherit the kingdom of God*" (5:21b).[51] Second, following his enumeration of the "fruit of the Spirit," he refers to "those who belong to Christ" (οἱ δὲ τοῦ Χριστοῦ).[52]

On its own, the appearance of these two ideas might seem unremarkable. But when we compare Galatians 5 with 1 Corinthians 6 again, a baptismal interpretation of the former text becomes more plausible. As we saw above, in 1 Corinthians 6 Paul combines a vice list, a warning about inheriting the kingdom of God, and a reference to being washed by the Spirit through baptism, all in the service of exhortation. In Galatians 5, we see a similar conjunction of a vice list with a warning about inheriting the kingdom and references to the Spirit (Gal 5:22, 25). Moreover, these elements are ordered toward an exhortation (cf. Gal 5:25). The only element missing is a clear reference to baptism, though again, the overlap of images of inheritance and belonging to Christ recall Gal 3:26–29. In light of the description of baptism as "being clothed with Christ" and the cross-centered portrayal of Christ in the letter, the idea of "crucifying the flesh" (5:24) would easily be connected with baptism.[53] Indeed, such a connection dovetails with the more explicit description of baptism in Romans as being for the destruction of "the body of sin" (Rom 6:6).

If Gal 5:24 is in fact a reference to baptism, then we see a further connection between baptism and unity. In addition to being open to all irrespective of ethnicity, social status, or sex, the ritual also empowers the baptized to live out the unity that comes from the Spirit. As some have noted, the vice list of Gal 5:19–21 contains a high concentration of sins against unity (Gal 5:20b: "hatred, strife, jealousy, anger, selfishness, dissension, division").[54] Surely these vices are among the "passions and desires" that the Galatians crucified through baptism. Moreover, the fruit of

---

[51] This reference to the kingdom of God, along with the special vocabulary of "doing" (πράσσω as opposed to ποιέω, the verb Paul more commonly uses in Galatians) and the usage of inheritance language, leads Longenecker to conclude that this section reflects a pre-baptismal catechetical tradition. *Galatians*, 258. Betz makes a similar observation, but nevertheless contests a baptismal reading of Gal 5:24. *Galatians*, 281.

[52] On both these points, see Strecker, *Die liminale Theologie des Paulus*, 254–55.

[53] Among the commentators who interpret the verse as a baptismal reference, see Mussner, *Galaterbrief*, 390 n. 4; Schnackenburg, *Heilsgeschehen*, 61; surprisingly also Dunn, *Galatians*, 315, though given his other comments, it is difficult to know for certain whether he means ritual baptism or a metaphorical baptism.

[54] John M. G. Barclay, *Obeying the Truth: Paul's Ethics in Galatians* (Studies of the New Testament and Its World; Edinburgh: T&T Clark, 1988), 152–53; cf. Bruce, *Galatians*, 250.

the Spirit brings about qualities that foster concord (5:22–23a: "love, joy, peace, patience, kindness, goodness, faith, meekness, self-control"). Crucifying the flesh through baptism demands that the baptized live out the unity that the rite symbolizes by the power of the Spirit: "If we live by the Spirit, let us also order our lives by the Spirit" (5:25). Life in the Spirit, the life of those who through baptism belong to Christ, is incompatible with boasting and jealousy (5:26).

E. Conclusion

As noted at the outset, Schweitzer's exaggerated claims about baptism and the Lord's Supper have had the unfortunate effect of marginalizing the role of these rituals even further in NT scholarship, with the exception of a few Catholic scholars.[55] Many scholars relegate baptism to a secondary position, placing the emphasis on faith in Christ, in part, perhaps, as a reaction against Schweitzer's minimization of the role of faith.[56] As I hope to have shown, the ritual of baptism plays a significant, though not exclusive, role in Paul's understanding of union with Christ. Indeed, some of the clearest examples of Paul's "participatory Christology" closely connect union with Christ to baptism.

This is not to say that baptism exhausts the meaning of dying and rising with Christ, or that it is the only way in which the baptized participate in the saving events of Christ's life.[57] Nevertheless, the way Paul appeals to baptism highlights some of the essential elements of union with Christ, showing the close connection between this union, holiness, and the unity of the body of Christ. Baptism creates a bond between believers such that when one member sins, the whole body suffers (cf. 1 Cor 12:26). This is

---

[55] See, e.g., Alfred Wikenhauser, *Pauline Mysticism: Christ in the Mystical Teaching of St. Paul* (trans. Joseph Cunningham; New York: Herder & Herder, 1960). It should be noted, as we saw above, that this marginalization is predominant in English-speaking scholarship, less so in German scholarship.

[56] See, e.g., Albert Schweitzer, *The Mysticism of Paul the Apostle* (trans. William Montgomery; 2d ed.; 1953; repr.; Baltimore: Johns Hopkins University, 1998), 220–21: "Another point, which tells strongly in favour of the doctrine of righteousness by faith being merely a fragment of a doctrine of redemption, is that Paul does not bring into connection with it the other blessings of redemption, the possession of the spirit, and the resurrection."

[57] In this regard, see the helpful corrective of Thomas Söding, "Taufe, Geist und neues Leben," in *Das Wort vom Kreuz* (WUNT 93; Tübingen: Mohr Siebeck, 1997), 335–45, here 342: "Innerhalb der Ekklesia erweist sich der Geist Gewiß nicht nur in der Taufe (und anderen Sakramenten), aber hier doch in besonderer Dichte und mit besonderer Wirkung." Later, on baptism and faith: "Soteriologisch entscheidend ist gerade *die Verbindung* von Glaube und Taufe." (344, emphasis added).

true not only of sins that directly attack unity, such as strife and contention (Gal 5:19–21), but also of sins against one's own body (1 Cor 6:13–18). Union with Christ and union with other believers are of a piece precisely because the former is ordered, at least in part, to the latter (Gal 3:27–28; 1 Cor 12:13).[58] Baptism thus initiates a life patterned on Christ's own death and resurrection (cf. Rom 8:17) that empowers and obligates the baptized to live out the holiness that builds up the body of Christ (1 Cor 12:25), and will one day fully bloom to eternal life (Rom 6:22–23).

Bibliography

Agersnap, Søren. *Baptism and the New Life: A Study of Romans 6:1–14*. Aarhus: Aarhus University Press, 1999.
Barclay, John M. G. *Obeying the Truth: Paul's Ethics in Galatians*. Studies of the New Testament and Its World. Edinburgh: T&T Clark, 1988.
Barrett, C. K. *A Commentary on the First Epistle to the Corinthians*. Black's New Testament Commentaries. London: Adam & Charles Black, 1968.
———. *The Epistle to the Romans*. Rev. ed. Black's New Testament Commentaries. London: Adam & Charles Black, 1991.
Beasley-Murray, G. R. *Baptism in the New Testament*. London: Macmillan, 1962/3.
Betz, Hans Dieter. *Galatians: A Commentary on Paul's Letter to the Churches in Galatia*. Hermeneia. Philadelphia: Fortress, 1979.
———. "Transferring a Ritual: Paul's Interpretation of Baptism in Romans 6." Pages 84–118 in *Paul in his Hellenistic Context*. Edited by Troels Engberg-Pedersen. Minneapolis: Fortress, 1995.
Blischke, Folker. *Die Begründung und die Durchsetzung der Ethik bei Paulus*. Arbeiten zur Bibel und ihrer Geschichte 25. Leipzig: Evangelische Verlagsanstalt, 2007.
Bornkamm, Günther. "Taufe und neues Leben (Röm 6)." Pages 34–50 in *Das Ende des Gesetzes: Paulusstudien*. Theologische Abhandlungen 16. München: Chr. Kaiser, 1952.
Borse, Udo. *Der Brief an die Galater*. Regensburger Neues Testament. Regensburg: Pustet, 1984.
Bring, Ragnar. *Commentary on Galatians*. Translated by Eric Wahlstrom. Philadelphia: Muhlenberg, 1961.
Bruce, F. F. *The Epistle of Paul to the Galatians: A Commentary on the Greek Text*. New International Greek Testament Commentary. Exeter: Pater Noster, 1982.
Campbell, Alastair. "Dying with Christ: The Origin of a Metaphor?" Pages 273–93 in *Baptism, the New Testament and the Church: Historical and Contemporary Studies in Honour of R. E. O. White*. Edited by Stanley E. Porter and Anthony R. Cross. Journal for the Study of the New Testament: Supplement Series 171. Sheffield: Sheffield Academic, 1999.
Campbell, Constantine R. *Paul and Union with Christ: An Exegetical and Theological Study*. Grand Rapids: Zondervan, 2012.

---

[58] Cf. the similar assessment of Barrett, *First Corinthians*, 288.

Campbell, Douglas A. *The Deliverance of God: An Apocalyptic Rereading of Justification in Paul.* Grand Rapids: Eerdmans, 2009.

———. *The Quest for Paul's Gospel: A Suggested Strategy.* London/New York: T&T Clark, 2005.

Childs, Brevard. *The Church's Guide for Reading Paul: The Canonical Shaping of the Pauline Corpus.* Grand Rapids: Eerdmans, 2008.

Delling, Gerhard. *Die Zueignung des Heils in der Taufe: Eine Untersuchung zum neutestamentlichen taufen auf den Namen.* Berlin: Evangelische Verlagsanstalt, 1961.

Dunn, James D. G. "Baptism as Metaphor." Pages 294–310 in *Baptism, the New Testament and the Church: Historical and Contemporary Studies in Honour of R. E. O. White.* Edited by Stanley E. Porter and Anthony R. Cross. Journal for the Study of the New Testament: Supplement Series 171. Sheffield: Sheffield Academic, 1999.

———. *Romans 1–8.* Word Biblical Commentary 38a. Dallas: Word Books, 1988.

———. *The Epistle to the Galatians.* Black's New Testament Commentaries. Peabody, Mass.: Hendrickson, 1993.

———. *The Theology of Paul the Apostle.* Grand Rapids: Eerdmans, 1997.

Eckey, Wilfried. *Der Galaterbrief: Ein Kommentar.* Neukirchen-Vluyn: Neukirchener, 2010.

Fee, Gordon. *The First Epistle to the Corinthians.* New International Commentary on the New Testament. Grand Rapids: Eerdmans, 1987.

Fitzmyer, Joseph A. *First Corinthians: A New Translation with Introduction and Commentary.* Anchor Yale Bible Commentary 32. London/New Haven: Yale University, 2008.

———. *Romans.* Anchor Bible 33. New York: Doubleday, 1992.

Frid, Bo. "Römer 6,4–5: εἰς τὸν θάνατον und τῷ ὁμοιώματι τοῦ θανάτου αὐτοῦ als Schlüssel zu Duktus und Gedankengang in Röm 6,1–11." *Biblische Zeitschrift* 30 (1986): 188–203.

Gorman, Michael J. *Inhabiting the Cruciform God: Kenosis, Justification, and Theosis in Paul's Narrative Soteriology.* Grand Rapids: Eerdmans, 2009.

Häfner, Gerd. "Taufe und Einheit: paulinische Tauftheologie in Gal 3,26–29." Pages 105–39 in *Paul et L'Unité des Chrétiens.* Edited by Jacques Schlosser. Colloquium Oecumenicum Paulinum 19. Löwen: Peeters, 2010.

Halter, Hans. *Taufe und Ethos: paulinische Kriterien für das Proprium christlicher Moral.* Freiburger theologische Studien. Freiburg: Herder, 1977.

Hartman, Lars. *Auf den Namen des Herrn Jesus: Die Taufe in den neutestamentlichen Schriften.* Stuttgarter Bibelstudien 148. Stuttgart: Verlag katholischer Bibelwerk, 1992.

Hays, Richard B. *First Corinthians.* Interpretation. Louisville: John Knox, 1997.

———. *The Faith of Jesus Christ: The Narrative Substructure of Galatians 3:1–4:11.* 2d ed. Grand Rapids: Eerdmans, 2002.

———. "What Is 'Real Participation in Christ'?" Pages 336–51 in *Redefining First-Century Jewish and Christian Identities: Essays in Honor of Ed Parish Sanders.* Edited by Fabian E. Udoh et al. Christianity and Judaism in Antiquity Series 16. Notre Dame: University of Notre Dame, 2008.

Heitmüller, Wilhelm. „Im Namen Jesu": *eine Sprach- und religionsgeschichtliche Untersuchung zum Neuen Testament, speziell zur altchristlichen Taufe.* Forschungen zur Religion und Literatur des Alten und Neuen Testaments I:2. Göttingen: Vandenhoeck & Ruprecht, 1903.

Kearns, Conleth. "The Interpretation of Romans 6,7." Section 1.301–07 in *Studiorum paulinorum congressus internationalis catholicus 1961*. Analecta biblica 17–18. Rome: Biblical Institute, 1961.

Kim, Jung Hoon. *The Significance of Clothing Imagery in the Pauline Corpus*. Journal for the Study of the New Testament: Supplement Series 268. London/New York: T&T Clark, 2004.

Kirchhoff, Renate. *Die Sünde gegen den eigenen Leib: Studien zu πόρνη und πορνεία in 1 Kor 6,12–20 und dem sozio-kulturellen Kontext der paulinsichen Adressaten*. Studien zur Umwelt des Neuen Testaments. Göttingen: Vandenhoeck & Ruprecht, 1994.

Klostergaard Petersen, Anders. "Shedding New Light on Paul's Understanding of Baptism: A Ritual-Theoretical Approach to Romans 6." *Studia theologica* 52 (1998): 3–28.

Kremer, Jakob. *Der Erste Brief an die Korinther*. Regensburger Neues Testament. Regensburg: Verlag Friedrich Pustet, 1997.

Lagrange, Marie-Joseph. *Saint Paul Épître aux Galates*. Etudes bibliques. Paris: Gabalda, 1918.

Lang, Friedrich. "Das Verständnis der Taufe bei Paulus." Pages 255–68 in *Evangelium, Schriftauslegung, Kirche: Festschrift für Peter Stuhlmacher aum 65 Geburtstag*. Edited by Jostein Ådna et al. Göttingen: Vandenhoeck & Ruprecht, 1997.

———. *Die Briefe an die Korinther*. Das Neue Testament Deutsch 7. Göttingen: Vandenhoeck & Ruprecht, 1986.

Lindemann, Andreas. *Der Erste Korintherbrief*. Handbuch zum Neuen Testament 9/1. Tübingen: Mohr Siebeck, 2000.

Lohse, Eduard. *Der Brief an die Römer*. Kritisch-exegetischer Kommentar über das Neue Testament (Meyer-Kommentar) 4. Göttingen: Vandenhoeck & Ruprecht, 2003.

———. "Taufe und Rechtfertigung bei Paulus," *Kerygma und Dogma* 11 (1965): 308–24. Repr. in pages 228–44 in *Die Einheit des Neuen Testaments: Exegetische Studien zur Theologie des Neuen Testaments*. Göttingen: Vandenhoeck & Ruprecht, 1973.

Longenecker, Richard N. *Galatians*. Word Biblical Commentary 41. Nashville: Thomas Nelson, 1990.

Macaskill, Grant. *Union with Christ in the New Testament*. Oxford: Oxford University, 2013.

Martin, Dale B. *The Corinthian Body*. New Haven/London: Yale University Press, 1995.

Matera, Frank. *God's Saving Grace: A Pauline Theology*. Grand Rapids: Eerdmans, 2012.

McGarvey, J. W. "A Note on 1 Corinthians 12:13." *Restoration Quarterly* 2 (1958), 45–47.

Moo, Douglas J. *The Epistle to the Romans*. New International Commentary on the New Testament. Grand Rapids: Eerdmans, 1996.

Morales, Rodrigo J. "Baptism, Unity, and Crucifying the Flesh." Pages 249–62 in in *A Man of the Church: Honoring the Theology, Life, and Witness of Ralph Del Colle*. Edited by Michel René Barnes. Eugene, Ore.: Wipf and Stock, 2012.

Mussner, Franz. *Der Galaterbrief*. 5th ed. Herders theologischer Kommentar zum Neuen Testament 9. Freiburg: Herder, 1988.

Powers, Daniel G. *Salvation through Participation: An Examination of the Notion of the Believers' Corporate Unity with Christ in Early Christian Soteriology*. Contributions to Biblical Exegesis and Theology 29. Leuven: Peeters, 2001.

Rohde, Joachim. *Der Brief des Paulus an die Galater*. Theologischer Handkommentar zum Neuen Testament 9. Berlin: Evangelische Verlagsanstalt, 1989.

Rosner, Brian S. "Temple Prostitution in 1 Corinthians 6:12–20." *Novum Testamentum* 40 (1998): 336–51.
Sanders, E. P. *Paul and Palestinian Judaism: A Comparison of Patterns of Religion.* Philadelphia: Fortress, 1977.
Schnackenburg, Rudolf. *Das Heilsgeschehen bei der Taufe nach dem Apostel Paulus: Eine Studie zur paulinischen Theologie.* München: K. Zink Verlag, 1950.
Schlier, Heinrich. *Der Brief an die Galater.* 4th ed. Kritisch-exegetischer Kommentar über das Neue Testament (Meyer-Kommentar) 7. Göttingen: Vandenhoeck & Ruprecht, 1965.
Schnelle, Udo. *Apostle Paul: His Life and Theology.* Translated by M. Eugene Boring. Grand Rapids: Baker Academic, 2005.
———. *Gerechtigkeit und Christusgegenwart: Vorpaulinische und paulinische Tauftheologie.* Göttinger theologischer Arbeiten 24. Göttingen: Vandenhoeck & Ruprecht, 1983.
———. "Transformation und Partizipation als Grundgedanken paulinischer Theologie." *New Testament Studies* 47 (2001): 58–75.
Schrage, Wolfgang. *Der Erste Brief an die Korinther: 1 Kor 11,17–14,40.* Evangelisch-Katholischer Kommentar zum Neuen Testament 7/3. Zürich: Benziger, 1999.
Schweitzer, Albert. *Paul and His Interpreters: A Critical History.* Translated by W. Montgomery. 1912. Repr., Eugene, Ore.: Wipf and Stock, 2004.
———. *The Mysticism of Paul the Apostle.* Translated by William Montgomery. 2d ed. 1953. Repr., Baltimore: Johns Hopkins University, 1998.
Söding, Thomas. "Kreuzestheologie und Rechtfertigungslehre: Zur Verbindung von Christologie und Soteriologie im Ersten Korintherbrief und im Galaterbrief." Pages 153–82 in *Das Wort vom Kreuz: Studien zur paulinischen Theologie.* Wissenschaftliche Untersuchungen zum Neuen Testament 93. Tübingen: Mohr Siebeck, 1997.
———. "Taufe, Geist und neues Leben." Pages 335–45 in *Das Wort vom Kreuz.* Wissenschaftliche Untersuchungen zum Neuen Testament 93. Tübingen: Mohr Siebeck, 1997.
Strecker, Christian. *Die liminale Theologie des Paulus: Zugänge zur paulinischen Theologie aus kulturanthropologischer Perspektive.* Forschungen zur Religion und Literatur des Alten und Neuen Testaments 185. Vandenhoeck & Ruprecht: Göttingen, 1999.
Tannehill, Robert C. *Dying and Rising with Christ: A Study in Pauline Theology.* Beihefte zur Zeitschrift für die neutestamentliche Wissenschaft 32. Berlin: de Gruyter, 1967.
Thiselton, Anthony C. *The First Epistle to the Corinthians: A Commentary on the Greek Text.* New International Greek Testament Commentary. Grand Rapids: Eerdmans, 2000.
Wikenhauser, Alfred. *Pauline Mysticism: Christ in the Mystical Teaching of St. Paul.* Translated by Joseph Cunningham. New York: Herder and Herder, 1960.
Wolff, Christian. "Abwaschung – Heiligung – Rechtfertigung: Zur Interpretation von 1. Kor 6,11." Pages 298–303 in *Der Wahrheit Gottes verpflichtet: Theologische Beiträge aus dem Sprachenkonvikt Berlin für Rudolf Mau.* Edited by Matthias Köckert. Berlin: Wichern, 1993.
Wolter, Michael. *Paulus: Ein Grundriss seiner Theologie.* Neukirchen-Vluyn: Neukirchener Theologie, 2011.
Wright, N. T. *Paul and the Faithfulness of God.* Vol. 4 of Christian Origins and the Question of God. Minneapolis: Fortress, 2013.

Paul's Corporate, Cruciform, Missional *Theosis* in 2 Corinthians

MICHAEL J. GORMAN

One of the most significant developments in the recent study of Paul has been the (re)turn to participation, with the present collection of essays being both evidence of that claim and an important contribution to its ongoing development. Space does not permit a review of the literature that has brought about and then given expression to this phenomenon.[1] Of course it was simulated by the revolutionary work of E. P. Sanders,[2] but unlike other aspects of Sanders's work, this theme, though controversial in its de-centering of justification, has been explored by a wide variety of Pauline scholars who might fervently disagree about, say, the meaning and role of "works of the law" in Second Temple Judaism and in Paul. It is nearly impossible to engage Paul seriously today without recognizing the centrality of participation to his lived experience ("spirituality") and his theology. Participation is not merely one aspect of Pauline theology and spirituality, or a supplement to something more fundamental; rather, it is at the very heart of Paul's thinking and living. Pauline soteriology is inherently participatory and transformative.[3]

The present essay will further develop my own contributions to this conversation by both expanding upon a general thesis that has appeared in

---

[1] For one such survey, see Grant Macaskill, *Union with Christ in the New Testament* (Oxford: Oxford University Press, 2013), 17–41.

[2] E. P. Sanders, *Paul and Palestinian Judaism: A Comparison of Patterns of Religion* (Philadelphia: Fortress, 1977), esp. 447–74.

[3] In addition to the contributions of the various writers in this volume, special mention should be made of Daniel G. Powers, *Salvation through Participation: An Examination of the Notion of the Believers' Corporate Unity with Christ in Early Christian Soteriology* (CBET 29; Leuven: Peeters, 2001); Udo Schnelle, *Apostle Paul: His Life and Theology* (trans. M. Eugene Boring; Grand Rapids: Baker Academic, 2005); and N. T. Wright, *Paul and the Faithfulness of God* (Minneapolis: Fortress; London: SPCK, 2013). Constantine Campbell calls union with Christ the "webbing" that holds Paul's thought together; Constantine R. Campbell, *Paul and Union with Christ: An Exegetical and Theological Study* (Grand Rapids: Zondervan, 2012), 441.

previous work and presenting some specific theses that have been implied or briefly noted, but not developed at length.[4]

The general claim to be further developed is this: Paul's spirituality and soteriology should be characterized as transformative participation in Christ, who is the image of God, and for Paul this transformative participation is inherent to his understanding of justification. Moreover, because justification is transformative participation in the life of the God who is revealed in Christ, justification is itself what the Christian tradition has called theosis, or deification. Furthermore, because this God is revealed in a Messiah who was *crucified* before being glorified, theosis in a Pauline context means "transformative participation in the kenotic, cruciform character of God through Spirit-enabled conformity to the incarnate, crucified, and resurrected/glorified Christ."[5] Moreover, I have argued that for Paul theosis is a communal or corporate, not merely an individual, experience,[6] and that it constitutes the goal of Paul's mission because he believes it is the mission of God.[7] Finally, I have argued that theosis – specifically sharing in God's glory and justice (δόξα and δικαιοσύνη) – is central to Paul's concerns in Romans, which (I suggested) elaborates on theotic texts in 2 Corinthians. In sum, theosis in Paul is corporate, cruciform, and missional.[8]

The more specific theses to be further developed (though of course not fully) here are (1) that 2 Corinthians is a rather comprehensive expression of this Pauline theology of theosis as justification, participation, and transformation; and (2) that 2 Cor 5:21 in particular contains all three aspects of this Pauline soteriology and forms a bridge between the rather general presentation of theosis in 2 Cor 3:18 as δόξα and its concrete expression as the praxis of δικαιοσύνη in 2 Cor 8:9. Thus I will argue that 2 Corinthians as a whole, like Romans, tells us that Paul sees salvation as theosis in the specific sense of humans coming to share in two divine attributes, divine

---

[4] See my *Cruciformity: Paul's Narrative Spirituality of the Cross* (Grand Rapids: Eerdmans, 2001); *Inhabiting the Cruciform God: Kenosis, Justification, and Theosis in Paul's Narrative Soteriology* (Grand Rapids: Eerdmans, 2009); "Romans: The First Christian Treatise on Theosis," *JTI* 5 (2011): 13–34. In addition, see my forthcoming book *Becoming the Gospel: Paul, Participation, and Mission* (Grand Rapids: Eerdmans, forthcoming 2015) and my forthcoming THNTC commentary on 2 Corinthians (Grand Rapids: Eerdmans, forthcoming 2016). For participation in the New Testament more broadly, see my *The Death of the Messiah and the Birth of the New Covenant: A (Not So) New Model of the Atonement* (Eugene, Ore.: Cascade, 2014).

[5] *Inhabiting*, 7.

[6] E.g., *Inhabiting*, 38, 56, 70, 91, 106, 112.

[7] *Inhabiting*, 38; "Romans."

[8] The third of these aspects (missional) is the least developed in my previously published work and the emphasis in this essay.

glory and divine justice; that is, they can and must be both glorified and "justice"-ified. With respect to 5:21 in particular, I will continue to argue not merely that three distinct but closely related Pauline themes (justification/reconciliation, participation, and transformation) appear in that verse and its context, but also that these three aspects of the passage are best understood as expressing three aspects of one reality: corporate, cruciform, missional theosis. Justification takes place in the crucified and exalted Messiah; it is the community's participatory transformation in the life of God such that those who are in the Messiah take on one of the primary divine attributes and activities: justice (δικαιοσύνη). And with respect to 2 Cor 8:9 and its context, including its links to the other two main texts, I will argue that theosis finds concrete expression in the collection for Jerusalem as an act of participating in the grace-filled justice of God manifested in Christ. This part of the argument addresses the concerns some have raised about what participation actually means "on the ground" – what practices it generates.[9]

But is "theosis" the right language to describe this transformative, missional participation in Christ?[10]

A. Is "Theosis" the Right Language?

Theosis, or deification, is back on the theological table across the Christian traditions and in the study of the New Testament.[11] It is a word with numerous uses and nuances of meaning, but most would agree that it signifies a soteriology of sharing in the divine nature that is grounded in the incar-

---

[9] See especially Richard B. Hays, "What Is 'Real Participation in Christ'? A Dialogue with E. P. Sanders on Pauline Soteriology," in *Redefining First-Century Jewish and Christian Identities: Essays in Honor of Ed Parish Sanders* (ed. Fabian E. Udoh et al; Notre Dame, IN: University of Notre Dame Press, 2008), 336–51. Hays's suggestions are important but still a bit general: belonging to a family; political or military solidarity with Christ (as in Romans 6); participating in the *ekklēsia*; and living within the Christ story ("narrative participation") – what I refer to as Paul's narrative spirituality of cruciformity.

[10] Campbell (*Paul and Union*) says most recent interpreters say "no" (63), while he gives a qualified "yes" (368). See also Stephen Finlan, "Can We Speak of *Theosis* in Paul?," in *Partakers of the Divine Nature: The History and Development of Deification in the Christian Traditions* (ed. Michael J. Christensen and Jeffery A. Wittung; Grand Rapids: Baker Academic, 2007), 68–80 (yes).

[11] On theosis see, *inter alia*, Christensen and Wittung, eds., *Partakers*, and Stephen Finlan and Vladmir Kharlamov, eds., *Theōsis: Deification in Christian Theology* (Eugene, Ore.: Pickwick, 2006). In addition to the scholars discussed below, Finlan has written significantly on theosis in the NT, and several other scholars have presented conference papers in recent years.

nation and death of God's Son – "He became what we are, so that we could become what he is" [12] – and the transforming work of the Spirit, i.e., the indwelling presence of the risen Christ. This transformation is a process of healing and restoration to God's intention for humanity that includes, but is not limited to, sanctification, for its eschatological end is bodily resurrection and transformation. Although theosis is most commonly associated with the Eastern church Fathers and with Eastern Orthodoxy, it is not unknown in the West (e.g., Augustine, Aquinas) and it is, according to some interpreters, at the heart of the soteriology of Calvin, Luther, Wesley, and Torrance.[13]

In an important new book, Grant Macaskill argues that the term "theosis" is not helpful for interpreting or describing the New Testament; it is, in fact, "potentially misleading."[14] He rightly insists that the New Testament is replete with language of union, participation, and transformation, and that this language is related to the theology of the new covenant.[15] I agree with the basic thrust of what Macaskill affirms, and I have myself recently written on the same themes in relation to the new covenant.[16] I take Macaskill's criticisms of my work seriously, but this is not the place to engage them at length.[17] I would contend, however, that neither Macaskill's positive contributions nor his criticisms of my work necessarily negate the claim that various New Testament writers, including Paul, witness to what later theologians call theosis. Theosis, is, however, as Macaskill indicates, a "theologically plastic" – I would say "fluid" – term,[18] and we must allow for ongoing exploration of its meaning(s). I would argue, in fact, that a reading of Paul and of the theological tradition can assist in the interpretation of each, and that Paul may actually help us

---

[12] This is the spirit of, e.g., Irenaeus, *Against Heresies* 5.Preface ("the Lord Jesus Christ... did, through his transcendent love, become what we are, that he might bring us to be even what he is himself"); cf. Athanasius, *Incarnation of the Word* 54.

[13] See, e.g., the articles in Christensen and Wittung, eds., *Partakers*.

[14] Macaskill, *Union with Christ*, esp. 42–76. "Potentially misleading" is from p. 75. Macaskill does allow, however, that some of the theological elements associated with "theosis" are significant for NT studies.

[15] See his summary in Macaskill, *Union with Christ*, 297–99.

[16] Gorman, *Death of the Messiah*.

[17] See Macaskill, *Union with Christ*, 25–28, 75–76. He is particularly concerned that I have blurred the creator-creature distinction by speaking of participation in the divine essence. My theological rationale for using the traditional but debated term "essence" was to keep divine act and being together while speaking of believers participating in the narrative identity of God in Christ. Like all orthodox Christian proponents of theosis, I do not intend to blur the creator-creature distinction. I do wonder, however, whether Macaskill underestimates (though he notes it [p. 26]), both for me and for the New Testament, my fundamental claim that cruciformity is theoformity.

[18] Macaskill, *Union with Christ*, 27.

shape an appropriate contemporary understanding of participation, and specifically theosis.[19]

I would submit, therefore, and will now argue with respect to a particular letter, that we should not abandon the term "theosis" when describing Paul's theology. I would suggest, however, that the term's fluidity means that, for the moment, we need to take a minimalist approach to the definition of theosis and its identification in the New Testament. Three exegetical and theological guidelines present themselves as candidates for the contours of this minimalist position.

(1) First of all, no interpretation of theosis can compromise the creator-creature distinction. To share in certain divine attributes is not to cease being a creature and to become the creator.

(2) Secondly, a text that is theotic will identify, implicitly or explicitly, either one or more divine attributes or else a general divine likeness that is the goal of transformation. This desired likeness can be a present, ethical goal or a future, eschatological one, or both. This proposal means that although there are certain theological grammars that will be especially important for identifying and examining theosis in the New Testament (e.g., exchange or interchange texts such as 2 Cor 5:21 and 8:9: "Christ became... so that we could become..."), the presence of theosis is not limited to those particular grammars.

(3) Thirdly, since the New Testament is inherently Christocentric (concerned with the identity and significance of Jesus), there normally needs to be a Christological assumption in a potentially theotic text (or its co-text), whether explicit or implicit, that Christ participates in the divine identity. This assumption leads inexorably to the conclusion that, at least in such texts, participation in Christ and/or becoming like Christ mean participation in God and/or becoming like God. (Hence my argument that *cruci*formity is *theo*formity.[20]) Further, I would suggest that since the New Testament writers reconfigure theology proper (the doctrine of God) Christologically, this assumption undergirds each of the Christologies of the New

---

[19] Lewis Ayres has said of Gregory of Nyssa, "While I cannot but agree that Gregory actually seems to avoid some of the basic terminology for deification... his account of the ways in which Christians become 'like' God actually points to some of the most fruitful ways of giving density to the idea of deification." "Deification and the Dynamics of Nicene Theology: The Contribution of Gregory of Nyssa," *SVTQ* 49 (2005): 377. Similarly, we should not expect Paul to use the same language as subsequent theologians.

[20] *Inhabiting*, 4. I do not mean that all Christological texts claim that Christ participates in the divine identity, only that such a claim must be at least implicit for a text about participation in Christ to be theotic. There may also, of course, be texts about participation in Christ that are not clearly theotic, as well as texts about participation in God that are not directly linked to participation in Christ (e.g., 2 Pet 1:4, though even there the context makes Christological connections).

Testament (though I realize that claim would be debated[21]), which means that theosis, in this Christological sense, should be a common rather than a rare New Testament theme. But what about Paul in particular?

B. Why We Should Expect Theosis in Paul, and Specifically in 2 Corinthians

In a paper delivered in the Theological Interpretation of Scripture Seminar of SBL at the 2013 annual meeting,[22] Ben Blackwell delineated three current approaches to identifying theosis in the New Testament, especially in Paul: (1) textual logic (with particular attention to the present writer); (2) history of religions, or the comparative approach (especially David Litwa[23]); and (3) history of interpretation, meaning especially patristic interpretations of Paul (especially Blackwell himself).[24] The convergence of these three approaches constitutes an argument that (1) there is an internal logic to Paul's Christology and participationist spirituality that supports understanding Paul's soteriology in terms of theosis; (2) there is historical context and precedent (both Jewish and pagan) for understanding Paul's soteriology in terms of theosis; and (3) there is an early reception history of understanding Paul's soteriology in terms of theosis.

As for 2 Corinthians, there are three key texts that potentially have theotic significance: 3:18, 5:21, and 8:9.[25] Each of these texts has been noted as theotic by virtue of its textual logic, its historical context, and/or its patristic reception.[26]

---

[21] Though the issues are complex, I think that the work of people like Richard Bauckham and Chris Tilling is generally persuasive.

[22] "Theosis in the New Testament?" forthcoming in the *Journal of Theological Interpretation*.

[23] M. David Litwa, *We are Being Transformed: Deification in Paul's Soteriology* (BZNW 187; Berlin: de Gruyter, 2012); "Transformation through a Mirror: Moses in 2 Cor 3.18," *JSNT* 34 (2012): 286–97.

[24] Ben C. Blackwell, *Christosis: Pauline Soteriology in Light of Deification in Irenaeus and Cyril of Alexandria* (WUNT 2/314; Tübingen: Mohr Siebeck, 2011).

[25] These three do not exhaust the theme. See, for example, Joseph Gordon, "Deification by Ascent: Paul's Ascent (2 Cor 12:1–10) in its Historical and Theological Contexts," unpublished paper, Marquette University. In addition, the language of being in Christ, κοινωνία with/of the Spirit, cruciform existence, etc. is arguably all part of theosis.

[26] My brief discussion of the Fathers here is meant only to be representative of larger themes and additional writers. For convenience, all references are taken from Gerald Bray, ed., *1–2 Corinthians* (ACCS NT 7; ed. Thomas C. Oden; Downers Grove, Ill.: InterVarsity Press, 1999).

Stephen Finlan calls 2 Cor 3:18 "the most frankly theotic passage in Paul."[27] It figures in the textual approaches of Litwa, Blackwell, and myself; in Litwa's comparative work; and in some patristic texts noted by Blackwell and others.[28] Gregory of Nyssa, for example, concludes his work *On Perfection* with an argument for the value of change in humans, which is how they will have a share in Christ. The work ends with an interpretation of 2 Cor 3:18:

> Therefore let no one be grieved if he sees in his nature a penchant for change. Changing in everything for the better, let him exchange "glory for glory," becoming greater through daily increase, ever perfecting himself and never arriving too quickly at the limit of perfection. For this is truly perfection: never to stop growing toward what is better and never placing any limit on perfection.[29]

The other two texts from 2 Corinthians have a different format and focus, that of the "marvelous exchange" (O admirabile commercium), or what Morna Hooker has called "interchange" texts. She explains what she means by "interchange" by appealing to the words of Irenaeus ("Christ became...") and then identifying 2 Cor 5:21 and 8:9 as "the clearest examples" of interchange, understood à la Irenaeus, in Paul's letters: "Here we see the basic pattern of the interchange between Christ and the believer: Christ is identified with the human condition in order that we might be identified with his."[30] Both of these texts figure briefly in the previous textual work I have done, as well as in Litwa's historical work, while 5:21 figures prominently in Blackwell's.[31]

As for the Fathers, they also saw theosis in these two passages. The complexity and richness of 5:21 are on display in their various treatments of it: comments on God's benevolence; the incarnation; the means of justification (grace not works – in Chrysostom, for example); Jesus' sinless-

---

[27] Finlan, "Can We Speak," 75.

[28] Litwa, "2 Corinthians 3:18 and its Implications for *Theosis*," *JTI* 2 (2008): 117–34; idem, *We are being Transformed*, esp. 216–25; idem, "Transformation"; Blackwell, *Christosis*, 179–93 et passim; Gorman, *Inhabiting*, passim. Blackwell notes, however, that the two Fathers he investigates use 3:18 either not at all (Irenaeus) or sparingly (Cyril of Alexandria).

[29] Cited in Bray, *1–2 Corinthians*, 224.

[30] Morna D. Hooker, *From Adam to Christ: Essays on Paul* (Cambridge: Cambridge University Press, 1990), 26. The entire first part of the book is relevant (pp. 13–69). See also her article "On Becoming the Righteousness of God: Another Look at 2 Cor 5:21," *NovT* 50 (2008): 358–75. Hooker does not use the term "theosis" or "deification," probably because she does not think Paul implies "ontological" change; Hooker, *From Adam to Christ*, 22.

[31] Gorman, *Inhabiting*, 63 n.57, 80, 87–90, 91 n.140, 95; Litwa, *We are being Transformed*, 223–24; Blackwell, *Christosis*, 226–32 et passim. (Blackwell's treatment of 2 Corinthians includes only chapters 3–5.)

ness, his assumption of our sins, and his willingness to die; and theosis. Theodoret of Cyrus wrote that "Christ was called what we are in order to call us to be what he is."[32] Cyril of Alexandria proclaimed, "[W]e do not say that Christ became a sinner. Far from it, but being just, or rather in actuality justice, for he did not know sin, the Father made him a victim for the sins of the world."[33] In addition, some Fathers connected this text to the Pauline idea of Christ's becoming a curse for us (Gal 3:13–14), another instance of the interchange (and thus potentially theosis) texts identified by Morna Hooker.[34]

The Fathers also sometimes see 2 Cor 8:9 as a text about theosis. Ambrosiaster, for instance, comments as follows: "Paul is saying that Christ was made poor because God deigned to be born as man, humbling the power of his might so that he might obtain for men the riches of divinity and thus share in the divine nature, as Peter says."[35] Augustine echoes Ambrosiaster with a similar sentiment, explaining 2 Cor 8:9 in terms of Phil 2:6–8:

> When he assumed our mortality and overcame death, he manifested himself in poverty, but he promised riches though they might be deferred.... To make us worthy of this perfect gift, he [Christ], equal to the Father in the form of God, became like to us in the form of a servant and refashions us into the likeness of God.[36]

With these brief textual, comparative, and patristic considerations in mind, we are ready to proceed expectantly into our three texts from 2 Corinthians, with the goal of seeing what Paul might have to say about theosis – about sharing in the divine life.

C. Theosis as Future Resurrection Glory and Present Cruciform Glory: 2 Cor 3:18

We begin by setting out the Greek text and the NRSV translation:

ἡμεῖς δὲ πάντες ἀνακεκαλυμμένῳ προσώπῳ τὴν δόξαν κυρίου κατοπτριζόμενοι τὴν αὐτὴν εἰκόνα μεταμορφούμεθα ἀπὸ δόξης εἰς δόξαν καθάπερ ἀπὸ κυρίου πνεύματος.

---

[32] Theodoret of Cyr, *Commentary on the Second Epistle to the Corinthians 318*, cited in Bray, *1–2 Corinthians*, 249. See also Gregory of Nazianzus, *Theological Oration 5*; Bray, *1–2 Corinthians*, 250.
[33] Cyril of Alexandria *Letter 41*, cited in Bray, *1–2 Corinthians*, 250.
[34] E.g. Eusebius, *Proof of the Gospel* 4.17 and Gregory of Nazianzus, *Theological Oration 5*, both cited in Bray, *1–2 Corinthians*, 250.
[35] *Commentary on Paul's Epistles*, cited in Bray, *1–2 Corinthian*, 269.
[36] *Feast of the Nativity* 194.3, cited in Bray, *1–2 Corinthians*, 269.

And all of us, with unveiled faces, seeing the glory of the Lord as though reflected in a mirror, are being transformed into the same image from one degree of glory to another; for this comes from the Lord, the Spirit.

David Litwa has been at the forefront of interpreting this passage in terms of deification, and while I do not concur with every aspect of his approach or arguments, I do find his general thesis persuasive, and in what follows I rely in part on his work, as well as Blackwell's. I wish to make five main points.

First, this is obviously a text about transformation, whether or not we call that transformation "theosis." The verb that indicates the process, which appears also in Rom 12:1–2, is in the passive voice (μεταμορφούμεθα); the agent of the transformation is the Spirit: "this comes from the Lord, the Spirit."[37] The human action that permits this transformation to occur is "looking," or better "seeing," specifically "seeing the glory of the Lord (τὴν δόξαν κυρίου) as though reflected in a mirror," and even more specifically, doing so "with unveiled faces." It was a commonplace of antiquity that gazing on a deity could effect transformation,[38] but Paul makes it clear here that even this ability to gaze at the Lord's glory in an unveiled state (unlike Moses under the old covenant) is the result of grace, indicated by another divine passive: "when one turns to the Lord, the veil is removed" (3:16).[39] Though it is possible that Paul is here referring to unique visions/revelations of the Lord that he has had (perhaps specifically the one narrated in 2 Cor 12:1–10), the main point is that this transformation is not unique to Paul, even if his visions are unusual. Indeed, no matter how we translate the tricky participle κατοπτριζόμενοι (beholding? reflecting?), the overall sense of the passage in context is that both Paul and the Corinthians are enabled by the Spirit, in Christ, both to

---

[37] The famously confusing language about the Spirit and the Lord here need not detain us; the point is that this transformation is the work, not merely of the self or the community, but of "the Spirit of the Lord" (3:17). This is implied also in Rom 12:2. The only other occurrences of the verb μεταμορφοῦσθαι are in the transfiguration narrative (Mark 9:2; Matt 17:2), which may have influenced Paul, perhaps as oral tradition.

[38] This phenomenon is documented and assessed with respect to Paul by numerous commentators, including Victor Paul Furnish, *II Corinthians* (AB 32A; Garden City, N.Y.: Doubleday, 1984), 240–42. See especially J. M. F. Heath, *Paul's Visual Piety: The Metamorphosis of the Beholder* (Oxford: Oxford University Press, 2013).

[39] To be sure, the removal of the veil is predicated on turning to the Lord, which is expressed as an active verb. There is an interesting dynamic of human and divine activity at work here, but the emphasis falls on divine action.

see and to *be* (i.e., participate in) the glory of God revealed in Christ, and they are doing so *all together* (πάντες).⁴⁰

Second, Paul specifies the content of this transformation in two closely related phrases: "into the same image" (τὴν αὐτὴν εἰκόνα) and "from one degree of glory to another" (NRSV; ἀπὸ δόξης εἰς δόξαν). The first part of the latter phrase is better rendered simply "from glory," and the second part "to," "toward," or "into glory." The meaning of these two phrases is warmly debated, but I would suggest that Paul himself provides the most basic interpretation in the context, beginning especially with his description of the content of the gospel as "the glory of Christ, who is the image of God" (4:4; εὐαγγελίου τῆς δόξης τοῦ Χριστοῦ, ὅς ἐστιν εἰκὼν τοῦ θεου). That is, the transformation is into the likeness of Christ, the image of God (cf. 8:29; συμμόρφους τῆς εἰκόνος τοῦ υἱοῦ αὐτου). It is a process of becoming more Christlike and hence more Godlike. Logically (and theologically), then, if we are to speak here of Christification or Christosis (Ben Blackwell's term), we would have to mount a very strong case indeed for not also speaking about deification or theosis.

Yet the content of this Christlikeness still needs to be unpacked (whether here or in the parallel text of Rom 8:29). Does it refer primarily, or even only, to "moral transformation," or does it also include – or perhaps even refer solely – to something else, even something transcendent or ontological? What does "from glory to glory mean?" I would suggest that the primary meaning is the transition from a present, paradoxical, cruciform glory to a future, eschatological, fully anastiform (resurrection-shaped) glory.⁴¹ The process of becoming more Christlike and Godlike is a process of glorification, and it is glorification with both present and future aspects.

Third, then, and to begin with the easier aspect of glorification, the transformation involves *future* glory.

– In Romans, Paul speaks about the "hope of sharing [so NRSV] the glory of God" (5:2; cf. 8:17–21), meaning (at least) conformity to the resurrected and immortal Christ and thereby to share in the glory – the radiant splendor – of God. Paul also speaks of the necessity of co-suffering with Christ as a condition of co-glorification with him (8:17).

---

⁴⁰ How this "beholding" or "reflecting" occurs is implicit in the context: in lives of Christlike power-in-weakness. See the discussion below. The word πάντες is missing from p⁴⁶, but its absence is likely accidental; see Hooker, "On Becoming," 365 n.14.

⁴¹ The term "anastiform" is Stephen Finlan's ("Can We Speak?," 78–79), who rightly claims that the anastiform aspect begins in the present as new life. Future resurrection and glory are, for Paul, somatic, as we will see below, but in an important sense present glory is also "somatic" (involving the body), as we will also see. I do not deny the reality of a theotic process, but I think Paul's main point, in this specific phrase, is to highlight the move from present, partial to future, full glory.

- In Philippians, Paul writes that Christ "will transform the body of our humiliation that it may be conformed to the body of his glory, by the power that also enables him to make all things subject to himself" (3:21).
- In 1 Corinthians, Paul says that "we will all be changed" (πάντες δὲ ἀλλαγησόμεθα, another divine passive; 15:51),[42] and he speaks of continuity yet discontinuity with present embodied existence in a "spiritual body" that has been changed from perishability, dishonor, and weakness into imperishability, glory, and power (15:42b–44; cf. 15:51–54). We might refer to this glory as "embodied" or "somatic" immortality.

This condition of future glory appears also in 2 Corinthians, summarized in the claim that "we know that the one who raised the Lord Jesus will raise us also with Jesus, and will bring us with you into his presence" (4:14), a claim developed in the subsequent verses (4:16–5:11).[43] But the previous verses make it equally clear that the *present* situation is one of suffering, of "always carrying in the body the death of Jesus" (4:10b; cf. all of 4:5–12).

But is this present reality also glory? For Paul, it seems to be. Fourth, then, is what Paul says about *present* glory. In each of the texts just mentioned from the various letters, the context makes it clear that the promised future glory is in stark contrast to present existence, which is characterized by suffering, weakness, and death – by cruciform existence. Yet the description of humanity's condition in Rom 3:23 – "all… fall short of the glory of God" – and the offer of salvation from that condition in Christ *may imply* the possibility of experiencing something of divine glory in the present. But 2 Cor 3:18 speaks of a process that *requires* us to acknowledge, for Paul, a present experience of glory. It is almost certainly the theological foundation of the similar (but even more debated) text in Rom 8:29, where Paul claims that those whom God called and justified, God also glorified. The context of 2 Cor 3:18 speaks of a paradox, namely that God's power is manifested in human weakness and that Christ's life is demonstrated in human death, meaning death-like existence in our mortal bodies (4:10–11). In other words, there is real participation in divine power

---

[42] The similarity of πάντες δὲ ἀλλαγησόμεθα in 1 Cor 15:51 to ἡμεῖς δὲ… μεταμορφούμεθα in 2 Cor 3:18 is worthy of note, the former being a good summary of the future dimension of the latter.

[43] Contra Litwa (*We are Being Transformed*, 221), I see no evidence in 2 Cor 3:18 or its context (or anywhere else) that Paul thinks that *physical* transformation begins to take place in the present. Blackwell (*Christosis*, 191) rightly calls the transformation "noetic, moral, and somatic embodiment," meaning "inward renewal in the midst of present sufferings and outward renewal in glorified, resurrected bodies in the future"; he designates this "a full christoformity… directly in line with the new covenant hope." That is, bodily *activity* is transformed in the present, but the body itself only in the future.

and Christic life – the glory of God *and of Christ* – in the present, but that participation is paradoxically marked by what appears to be the opposite of power, life, and glory. Present glory is power in weakness, life in death, glory in suffering, but it is nonetheless glory, nonetheless participation in the life and power of God in Christ. The apostolic practices of being afflicted and persecuted (4:8–9), of non-retaliation and blessing when cursed (1 Cor 4:11–13), and so on are fundamentally, then, experiences of glory, the glory of the cross; they are spiritual practices, cruciform practices, theotic practices.

This experience of cruciform glory appears in living, metaphorical color slightly earlier in 2 Corinthians, when Paul speaks of God always leading "us" (perhaps primarily a reference to him and his colleagues) "in triumphal procession" – "in Christ" (2:14). There is both irony and paradox in this claim, for although Paul likely portrays himself here as the conquered captive, he locates himself in Christ – the living, victorious Christ. In union with Christ, he is both defeated and victorious, dying and living. That Christ was crucified by Rome means that Paul is a conquered victim; that God raised Christ from the dead means that Paul is both alive and a source of life for others (2:16). Although this passage in 2 Corinthians 2 focuses on Paul, who is explaining and defending his ministry, it cannot and does not exclude other believers, for they too are "in Christ," and that is what is determinative of this paradoxical experience and practice of cruciform glory – not apostolicity per se.

The connection of 2 Cor 3:18 to Rom 12:1–2, noted above, suggests that the transformation Paul has in mind involves both the mind and the body, both ways of perceiving and ways of acting, within the community. In Rom 12 the presentation of the many bodies of believers as one living sacrifice (παραστῆσαι τὰ σώματα ὑμῶν θυσίαν ζῶσαν; cf. Rom 6:13, 16, 19) is contrasted with being conformed to the present age and equated with (or at least linked to) being transformed. Romans 12 takes up a theme already introduced in Rom 6, where the self-presentation of bodily members that Paul calls for is an offering to God and to "righteousness" (NRSV), or justice, and as weapons and slaves of righteousness/justice:

... παραστήσατε ἑαυτοὺς τῷ θεῷ ὡσεὶ ἐκ νεκρῶν ζῶντας καὶ τὰ μέλη ὑμῶν ὅπλα δικαιοσύνης τῷ θεῷ....
... παραστήσατε τὰ μέλη ὑμῶν δοῦλα τῇ δικαιοσύνῃ εἰς ἁγιασμόν. (Rom 6:13b, 19c)

Is this passage an echo of the text in 2 Cor 5:21 (discussed below) that speaks of becoming the righteousness/justice of God?

In both Rom 6 and Rom 12 there is a clear human role in the process of sanctification (Rom 6:19) or transformation (Rom 12:1–2). But Rom 12 identifies the means to this transformation implicitly as God's Spirit (with another divine passive) and explicitly as the renewal of the corporate mind:

μεταμορφοῦσθε τῇ ἀνακαινώσει τοῦ νοός. It is likely, then, that in 2 Cor 3:18 Paul has the transformation of both perception and action in mind. Indeed, this is probably what Paul means when he refers, with either νοῦς or φρον-, to "the mind of Christ" (1 Cor 2:16; Phil 2:5): a Christlike, cruciform mindset and its corollary practices.

Fifthly and finally, this transformation is more than an individual, and more than an apostolic, experience; it is, as noted earlier, a communal reality ("all of us"),[44] shared by the believers at Corinth with one another, with Paul and his colleagues, and with "all those who in every place call on the name of our Lord Jesus Christ, both their Lord and ours," as Paul describes the church universal in 1 Cor 1:2. Furthermore, if theosis means cruciform missional praxis for Paul and his colleagues, then it will mean fundamentally the same thing for the entire church. Theosis is not static but dynamic, and it is not merely about personal transformation in a privatistic sense, but personal transformation into the service of God and others. David Litwa argues that glorification in 2 Cor 3:18 is "moral assimilation to God."[45] The contexts we have examined support that interpretation, but greater clarity and specificity are needed. The God Paul knows has a certain character expressed in particular kinds of acts. And that leads us naturally to 2 Cor 5:21.

D. Theosis as Becoming the Cruciform Justice of God in Christ: 2 Cor 5:21

It will again be valuable to set out the Greek text and the NRSV translation:

τὸν μὴ γνόντα ἁμαρτίαν ὑπὲρ ἡμῶν ἁμαρτίαν ἐποίησεν, ἵνα ἡμεῖς γενώμεθα δικαιοσύνη θεοῦ ἐν αὐτῷ.

For our sake he made him to be sin who knew no sin, so that in him we might become the righteousness of God.

I wish to make six critical exegetical points about this "interchange" text. In doing so I assume, without space to argue, that the first-person-plural pronouns in this verse are inclusive of all believers, not restricted to Paul and his colleagues.[46]

---

[44] So also Blackwell, *Christosis*, 183–84.
[45] Litwa, *We are Being Transformed*, 216–23.
[46] So also A. Katherine Grieb, "'So That in Him We Might Become the Righteousness of God' (2 Cor 5:21): Some Theological Reflections on the Church Becoming Justice," *Ex Auditu* 22 (2006): 58–80. Wright ("On Becoming the Righteousness of God: 2 Corinthians 5:21," in *Pauline Theology; Volume 2: 1 and 2 Corinthians* [ed. David M. Hay;

The first point should be relatively uncontroversial, though it is not. This is a text about being "in Christ." The preposition "in" (ἐν) should be taken locatively, as describing the sphere within which something happens to "us." That is, this something (a "becoming") occurs in the sphere of the crucified and resurrected Messiah.[47] Thus, although the language of the verse is not "transfer language" per se, which is most clearly expressed with the preposition "into" (εἰς),[48] it presumes that such a transfer has occurred: that "we" have moved from being outside Christ to being inside Christ.[49]

This in/inside idiom has itself been the subject of much debate. Suffice it to say here that being "in Christ" has multiple levels of significance for Paul. The language is clearly not meant to describe an impersonal location but rather a deeply personal relationship.[50] Yet this intimacy is not well

---

Minneapolis: Fortress, 1993], 200–208) and Hooker ("On Becoming," 364–75), both read 5:21 as referring to Paul and his ministry team, but Hooker, looking ahead to chaps. 8–9, also thinks others are implicitly included as participants in Paul's, and therefore God's, mission.

[47] In addition to debate about the meaning of "in," there is also debate about the meaning of "Christ." I generally agree with Wright (*Paul and the Faithfulness of God*) that when Paul says *Christos*, he means "Messiah," so I use the terms interchangeably.

[48] See especially Gal 2:16 (εἰς Χριστὸν Ἰησοῦν ἐπιστεύσαμεν) and 3:27 (εἰς Χριστὸν ἐβαπτίσθητε).

[49] Constantine Campbell (*Paul and Union*, 185–87) proposes three strong candidates for the interpretation of "in Christ" here: locative ("the sphere or realm of Christ," p. 185), instrumental, and unitive (my term) – indicating union with Christ. He rightly rejects the instrumental interpretation but dismisses the locative interpretation because, unlike the nearby text 2 Cor 5:17, where "realm transfer is in view" (p. 185), in our verse "believers are not described as passing into the realm of God's righteousness but as *becoming* the righteousness of God" (p. 186). I would note, however, that 5:17 does not speak explicitly of "realm transfer" any more than does 5:21; each verse *assumes* that such transfer has occurred, with the result being that the transferees are now in Christ. Campbell therefore opts for a rather vague "union with Christ" interpretation that allegedly expresses Paul's understanding of justification as being "made righteous by sharing in his [Christ's] right standing" by virtue of Christ's "sharing in the plight of the sinful" (pp. 186–87). Paul, however, does not here speak of union per se, but of location. To be sure, this implies participation, and the language of "becoming" in the context of "location" underscores that. However, although Campbell rightly points out that Paul here speaks about believers "becom[ing] righteous" (p. 187), this does not mean "sharing in his right standing" (p. 187), as we will see below. Thus Campbell's decision against a locative interpretation and for a unitive interpretation seems to be controlled by his prior theological understanding of justification as sharing in Christ's right standing. The same seems to be the case in his treatment (pp. 114–15) of the somewhat parallel text Gal 2:17 (discussed briefly below).

[50] "In Christ" language is of course complemented by "Christ within" language. Together this complementary language communicates a relationship of mutual indwelling, or reciprocal residence.

described by the term "mystical" (at least as that term is commonly used) because Paul's "in Christ" language, both here and elsewhere, also suggests both a corporate reality and an arena of power, not merely a private love affair or something similar.[51] To be in Christ is to be in a community of people who have come under the influence of this crucified but resurrected (and thus living) Messiah. Thus, the language of "location" is not static but dynamic; it indicates being in the presence of something/someone possessing the ability to re-orient and reshape one's existence. It implies, in other words, participation. For this reason, Paul elsewhere employs the imagery of being clothed with Christ (Rom 13:14; Gal 3:27). To be in Christ is to wear him. And since Christ is the δικαιοσύνη of God (1 Cor 1:30), those in him wear (participate in, become), that δικαιοσύνη; they can and will take on that essential divine attribute.

The second point about 2 Cor 5:21 is that this also is a text about transformation, about people becoming (either once and for all, or through a process) something they previously were not. The use of the verb γίνομαι makes this clear; also clear, due to the specific way Paul deploys the verb – in a purpose clause – is that this transformation is both the intended purpose and the desired result of a prior transformation: namely, Christ's having been made sin by the action of God.

Whether our "becoming" refers to a once-for-all event or an ongoing reality is a question whose answer may well be dependent on the way we read the "in Christ" reference. The verbs and their tenses alone will not suffice. One could argue that since the aorist active indicative verb ἐποίησεν refers to the one-time event of Jesus' death, the aorist active subjunctive verb γενώμεθα must refer to the corresponding one-time event of initial righteousness, or rectification. This interpretation would follow the traditional Protestant understanding of justification as declaration, resulting in a change of status.

But this kind of interpretation ignores several important aspects of the text and its context. First of all, it ignores the presupposition of the "in Christ" language discussed above: that the process of becoming is predicated on the prior (one-time) act of transfer into Christ. That is, we cannot *become* something in Christ until we are actually *in* Christ. This suggests, then, that the purpose of Christ's death was not merely to effect a *status* change in people but to effect an *existential* change among those who have entered the realm of Christ. This suggestion is confirmed by the immediate context of 5:21, which must also be ignored in order to arrive at a merely status-change interpretation of becoming the righteousness of God. For one thing, Paul has just spoken about "new creation," and whether we take that

---

[51] This is how Albert Schweitzer's Pauline "mysticism" is often understood, though Schweitzer himself had sensitivities to the corporate dimensions of Paul's spirituality.

as a reference to each individual or to the new reality in which all who are in Christ participate, it is hardly the language of status change; it is the idiom of transformation. Furthermore, in an earlier sentence that is semantically parallel to 5:21, Paul has already expressed the purpose of Christ's death in terms of transformation: "And he died for all, so that those who live might live no longer for themselves, but for him who died and was raised for them" (5:15). The parallel with 5:21 is clear:

Text	Main clause: the death of Christ narrated	Purpose conjunction	Purpose clause: the goal of Christ's death indicated
5:15	And he died for all	so that (ἵνα)	those who live might live (ζῶσιν) no longer for themselves, but for him who died and was raised for them
5:21	For our sake he [God] made him to be sin who knew no sin	so that (ἵνα)	in him we might become (γενώμεθα) the righteousness of God

Accordingly, the *aorist* subjunctive verb γενώμεθα in 5:21 is semantically parallel to the *present* subjunctive verb ζῶσιν in 5:15. It would be contextually inappropriate to interpret 2 Cor 5:21 as anything less than a reference to new life in Christ. To "become the righteousness of God" is materially parallel to "no longer living for themselves but for the one who died and was raised for them."

Richard Hays is therefore absolutely right to make the following strong assertion about our text:

[Paul] does not say "that we might *know about* the righteousness of God," nor "that we might *believe in* the righteousness of God," nor even "that we might *receive* the righteousness of God." Instead, the church is to *become* the righteousness of God: where the church embodies in its life together the world-reconciling love of Jesus Christ, the new creation is manifest. The church incarnates the righteousness of God.[52]

Morna Hooker has written similarly, reflecting on another aspect of the context, Paul's language of reconciliation:

Becoming God's righteousness is not just a matter of being acquitted in God's court or of sharing Christ's status before God. If God's righteousness is a restorative power, bringing life and reconciliation, then those who "become righteousness" will be the means of manifesting that power in the world.[53]

---

[52] Richard B. Hays, *The Moral Vision of the New Testament: Community, Cross, New Creation; A Contemporary Introduction to New Testament Ethics* (San Francisco: HarperCollins, 1996), 24.

[53] Hooker, "On Becoming," 374–75.

We will return later to the precise meaning of becoming the righteousness of God, looked at from various angles. For now we simply stress that this text is about transformation, about existential change, not status change.

The third point about 2 Cor 5:21 is that if it is an interchange text about participation and transformation, we should at least consider using the term "theosis" to characterize what Paul is describing. Indeed, the term theosis, or something similar, is arguably the only sort of term that can adequately express what Paul is describing.

Although the christological emphasis in the doctrine of theosis has often been on the incarnation, the doctrine does not exclude the death of Christ, as the patristic evidence indicates.[54] Similarly, the emphasis in Paul's theology of interchange may be on the death of Christ, but it does not exclude his incarnation (cf. esp. 2 Cor 8:9). The point of theosis is that human beings can share in God's attributes because God has shared in humanity's situation. In the famous image of the seventh-century Byzantine theologian Maximus the Confessor, theosis is like the placing of an iron sword in a fire: it remains an iron sword but also takes on certain properties of the fire – light and heat – by "participating" in it.[55] To put the words of the Fathers in slightly more Pauline language:

In Christ's self-emptying, self-humbling, and self-impoverishment in incarnation and crucifixion, God's fullness, power, wisdom, abundance, holiness, and righteousness (or justice) were revealed in human form so that we might share in that incarnate and cruciform fullness, power, wisdom, abundance, holiness, and justice of God.

To be sure, the doctrine of theosis is about more than moral transformation, or what is often called "sanctification" in the West.[56] It includes both present and eschatological transformation, understood as a single and continuous salvific reality, the former dimension corresponding largely to moral transformation, the latter to the eschatological resurrection and glorification of the body. (We have already seen this in discussing 2 Cor 3:18.) That is, the primary divine attributes in which humans can participate are holiness (i.e., moral character, which includes righteous-

---

[54] See, e.g., Blackwell (*Christosis*, 111), who notes that patristic exchange formulas even refer to the "whole of Christ's work."

[55] *Ambiguum* 7; cf. Opuscule 16.

[56] Respondents to those who have been proposing that we return to the language of theosis in describing Pauline soteriology have rightfully been quick to point out that limiting theosis to sanctification is to transform the doctrine almost beyond recognition. This was perhaps Edith Humphrey's main criticism in her response to papers on theosis in the New Testament, and to the scholarly development of using theosis language more generally, in the 2013 session of SBL's Theological Interpretation of Scripture Seminar.

ness/justice) and immortality.[57] The paradox of theosis is that when humans become "divine" (in this sense of sharing in these particular divine attributes), they become most fully human. Surely this is a sentiment with which Paul would agree: to become like Christ is to become reshaped into the image of God that God originally intended for humans to embody, as 2 Cor 3–4 certainly suggests by using the language of "image." This Christification, in both its moral and its eschatological senses, as I have elsewhere suggested and wish now to re-emphasize, is both deification and humanization.[58]

This topic leads naturally to a discussion of 3:18 in connection with 5:21. Our fourth point, then, is that 5:21 is materially reminiscent of, and theologically connected to, Paul's earlier theotic text, 3:18, and also to Paul's later presentation of the theotic themes of justification and glorification in Romans.

In my essay "Romans: The First Christian Treatise on Theosis," I contended that Romans tells the story of humanity's restoration to the two divine attributes that it has, in some profound sense, "lost" – δόξα and δικαιοσύνη. These two come together in Rom 8:30, where Paul says, "those whom he [God] justified he also glorified." For Paul, the restoration of justice/righteousness and glory has happened, is happening, and will happen to believers. Paul wants the house churches in Rome to embody the (cruciform) glory and justice/righteousness that they have received in Christ. These same two lost (or, perhaps to be more theologically precise, diminished) elements of the human condition are also named in 2 Cor 3:18 and 5:21; the veil has been lifted by God so that believers can gaze on Christ and become what he is: the δόξα of God; the Messiah has been made sin by God so that people can enter into him and, once in him, become what he is: the δικαιοσύνη of God (cf. 1 Cor 1:30). The two verses complement each other and need to be read in tandem, even joined, as they essentially are in Rom 8:30; glorification means also "justice-ification," which then needs to be worked out in concrete manifestations of justice.[59]

Fifthly, and finally, then, 2 Cor 5:21 is undoubtedly about justification – by grace. That is one "traditional" reading of this text, and there is support for it going back to the Fathers.[60] Although the verb δικαιόω is not present,

---

[57] Or, in the Fathers, "incorruption and sanctification" (Blackwell, *Christosis*, 100). Litwa (*We are Being Transformed*, 223–24) finds a parallel in Plato's notion of participation in Justice as sharing in the divine nature.

[58] *Inhabiting*, 37.

[59] On justification as incorporation into the community of the just, see 1 Cor 6:1–11, discussed in my "Justification and Justice in Paul, with Special Reference to the Corinthians," *Journal for the Study of Paul and His Letters* 1 (2011): 23–40.

[60] See, e.g., Chrysostom, *Homilies on the Epistles of Paul to the Corinthians* 11.5, cited in Bray, ed., *1–2 Corinthians*, 249.

most interpreters read the reference to δικαιοσύνη as an indication that the subject is justification. Paul's theological claims here and elsewhere in his corpus support that contention. The language of reconciliation (5:18–20), for instance, clearly anticipates Paul's discussion of justification as reconciliation in Rom 5:1–11. Furthermore, the language of dying and living a new life for Christ (5:14–15) is reminiscent of Paul's discussion of justification as co-crucifixion and co-resurrection in Gal 2:15–21, especially 2:19–21. Galatians 2 also makes it clear that justification occurs *in* Christ: δικαιωθῆναι ἐν Χριστῷ (Gal 2:17), a phrase parallel to γενώμεθα δικαιοσύνη θεοῦ ἐν αὐτῷ in 2 Cor 5:21. Indeed, 2 Cor 5:14–21 looks like both a *restatement* of Gal 2:15–21 for a new audience and a *foreshadowing* of the central affirmations of Romans on justification. Finally, the reference to the love of Christ in 2 Cor 5:21 is surely the same love that is the divine source of justification (Rom 5:8; 8:32–39).

If 2 Cor 5:21 is about justification, however, it is a text, like Gal 2:15–21,[61] which demonstrates that for Paul justification is inherently participatory and transformative. Everything we have considered so far points to this reality. Justification is in Christ; it is a death and resurrection; it is reconciliation; it is becoming the righteousness/justice of God. It is – to the unnecessary chagrin of some interpreters – theosis.[62] This second text under consideration, then, is about the church becoming the justice of God, and it therefore anticipates concrete practices of justice that are, in turn, concrete practices of participation: practices of, corporate, cruciform, missional theosis. That is, *2 Cor 5:21 is a bridge from the heavenly glory of 3:18 to its practical, even mundane, embodiment in 8:9.*

John Wesley, heavily influenced by the Greek Fathers, defined salvation as follows:

By salvation I mean, not barely (according to the vulgar notion) deliverance from hell, or going to heaven, but a present deliverance from sin, a restoration of the soul to its primitive health, its original purity; a recovery of the divine nature; the renewal of our souls after the image of God in righteousness and true holiness, in justice, mercy, and truth.[63]

Wesley, I submit, was thinking Paul's thoughts.

---

[61] On which, see my *Inhabiting*, 63–85.

[62] E.g., Campbell, *Paul and Union*, 394–95 ("Gorman has gone too far"). Wright, though open to theosis as a post-justification reality (e.g., *Paul and the Faithfulness of God*, 955, 1021–23), finds transformative understandings of justification "dangerous" in their effects (913; cf. 1031).

[63] John Wesley, *The Works of John Wesley, Vol. 11: The Appeals to Men of Reason and Religion and Certain Related Open Letters* (ed. Gerald R. Cragg; Nashville: Abingdon, 1987), 106, para. 1.3.

E. Theosis on the Ground: Cruciform Economic Justice in 2 Corinthians 8–9

Chapters 8 and 9 of 2 Cor contain Paul's appeal to the believers in Corinth for their support of the collection for the Jerusalem church. Specifically, Paul is urging them to fulfill their previous commitment to that effort. The Greek language supplies Paul with a strategic opportunity for a word play as he seeks to call the justified/justice-ized community at Corinth (cf. 1 Cor 6:1–11) to practice justice. In 2 Cor 8–9 Paul uses the word χάρις, often translated "grace," ten times,[64] with various but interconnected senses: benefaction, generosity, generous act, gratitude. Paul likely draws on both the scriptural sense of God's benefaction (expressed by the Hebrew word *hesed* and cognates) and the contemporary Greco-Roman usage of χάρις, which could refer to a generous disposition, a generous gift, or the response of gratitude and subsequent indebtedness to the giver.[65] In addition, Paul uses the cognate εὐχαριστία, "thanksgiving," twice, and he quotes Psalm 112:9 (LXX 111:9) in 9:9, which refers to the manifestation of justice (δικαιοσύνη) in generosity to the poor.

Portions of this eloquent piece of rhetoric are worth quoting here. I again cite the NRSV but replace "righteousness" with "justice." Occurrences of "justice," "grace" (variously translated by the NRSV), and "thanksgiving" are underlined:

8 ¹We want you to know, brothers and sisters, about the <u>grace</u> [χάριν] of God that has been granted to the churches of Macedonia.... ³For, as I can testify, they voluntarily gave according to their means, and even beyond their means, ⁴begging us earnestly for the <u>privilege</u> [χάριν] of sharing in this ministry to the saints... ⁶so that we might urge Titus that, as he had already made a beginning, so he should also complete this <u>generous undertaking</u> [χάριν] among you. ⁷Now as you excel in everything – in faith, in speech, in knowledge, in utmost eagerness, and in our love for you – so we want you to excel also in this <u>generous undertaking</u> [χάριτι].... ⁹For you know the <u>generous act</u> [χάριν] of our Lord Jesus Christ, that though [or perhaps "because"[66]] he was rich, yet for your sakes he became poor, so that by his poverty you might become rich.... ¹⁶But <u>thanks</u> [χάρις] be to God who put in the heart of Titus the same eagerness for you that I myself have.... ¹⁹ ...he has also been appointed by the churches to travel with us while we are administering this <u>generous undertaking</u> [χάριτι] for the glory of the Lord himself and to show our goodwill.... 9 ... ⁸And God is able to provide you with every <u>blessing</u> [χάριν] in abun-

---

[64] 8:1, 4, 6, 7, 9, 16, 19; 9:8, 14, 15.

[65] Thus English translations, unfortunately, do not always reveal all the linguistic and theological connections in the text. The cluster of occurrences of χάρις in these two chapters is rivaled only by Romans 5. Helpful is John M. G. Barclay, "Manna and the Circulation of Grace: A Study of 2 Corinthians 8:1–15," in *The Word Leaps the Gap: Essays on Theology and Scripture in Honor of Richard B. Hays* (ed. J. Ross Wagner, C. Kavin Rowe, and A. Katherine Grieb; Grand Rapids: Eerdmans, 2008), 409–26.

[66] See discussion below.

dance, so that by always having enough of everything, you may share abundantly in every good work. ⁹As it is written, "He scatters abroad, he gives to the poor; his justice [δικαιοσύνη] endures forever." ¹⁰He who supplies seed to the sower and bread for food will supply and multiply your seed for sowing and increase the harvest of your justice [δικαιοσύνης]. ¹¹You will be enriched in every way for your great generosity, which will produce thanksgiving [εὐχαριστίαν] to God through us; ¹²for the rendering of this ministry not only supplies the needs of the saints but also overflows with many thanksgivings [εὐχαριστιῶν] to God. ¹³Through the testing of this ministry you glorify God by your obedience to the confession of the gospel of Christ and by the generosity of your sharing with them and with all others [εἰς πάντας], ¹⁴while they long for you and pray for you because of the surpassing grace [χάριν] of God that he has given you. ¹⁵Thanks [χάρις] be to God for his indescribable gift!

Laced with the word χάρις and additional rich theological and theocentric language, artfully mixed with the idiom of honor and shame, the appeal for generosity has as its goal something approximating equality (so NIV, NAB in 8:13–14 for ἰσότης; NRSV "fair balance"), or what we would describe as economic justice.[67] Four key exegetical and theological points about 2 Cor 8:9 and its immediate context (chaps. 8–9) need to be made, all of which demonstrate the intermingling of divine justice and human justice that are each "located" ἐν Χριστῷ. *This suggests that 2 Cor 8:9 in particular, and all of chapters 8 and 9 in general, constitute a gloss on 2 Cor 5:21* – indicating in one situation what becoming the justice of God means and looks like.

First, Paul's appeal to the Corinthians is grounded in what Katherine Grieb has labeled the "generous justice of God,"[68] which has been manifested concretely in Christ, but also in the Macedonian believers located in Christ. The "generous justice of God in Christ," then, appropriately summarizes what Paul conveys through multiple occurrences of the word χάρις and related terms in conjunction with the two occurrences of δικαιοσύνη (9:9, 10). In 2 Cor 8–9 as a unit, Paul speaks of Christ both as the generous, "indescribable gift" of God (δωρεᾷ; 9:15) and as the gracious self-gift of Christ himself (χάρις; 8:9). The latter text narrates Christ's self-emptying, or kenosis, probably referring to both his incarnation and his death (as in Phil 2:6–8), in the metaphorical economic language of self-impoverishment for the benefit of others. Paul calls the Corinthians, as beneficiaries of this greatest gift, to participate in it more fully and responsibly – yet freely, cheerfully, and without worry – by sharing in the grace of Christ, which is summarized in 8:7–9, and the justice of God, which is summarized in 9:9–10.

---

[67] So also Grieb, "'So That in Him,'" 69 et passim. Gordon Zerbe (*Citizenship: Paul on Peace and Politics* [Winnipeg: CMU Press, 2012], 82–87) argues that "economic mutualism" was a consistent part of Paul's teaching in the various assemblies.

[68] Grieb, "'So That in Him,'" 59, 74, et passim.

Second, the translation of 2 Cor 8:9 requires some attention. That 2 Cor 8:9 is an "exchange" or "interchange" text is quite clear: Christ became poor so that we could become rich. As I and others have argued, the verse echoes the poem in Phil 2, and it seems even to have a similar underlying semantic structure: although he was [x], he did not do [y (the natural corollary of x)], but he did do [z (the opposite of x)].[69] The standard translations of both Phil 2:6 and 2 Cor 8:9 render the participles ὑπάρχων and ὤν (respectively) concessively, with words like "though" or "although." John Barclay has recently argued, however, that here in 2 Cor 8:9 the better interpretation of the participle is as an indicator of cause, not concession, and thus the preferred translation is "because he was rich...."[70] Barclay summarizes the two possible readings in the phrases "'wealth' as possession, lost and gained" ("because") versus "'wealth' as generosity, gained in loss" ("although"). His point, then, is that "'wealth' consists not in possession but in generosity," and that "it is precisely in Christ becoming poor that we see in what his 'wealth' consists."[71] Barclay continues: "Paul is less interested here in what Christ gave up than in what he gave out, a momentum of generosity that is not tied solely to one form of giving (giving away) but could be expressed in a variety of forms (including sharing and mutual participation)."[72]

Third, if Barclay is right, then the hortatory point of 2 Cor 8:9 is as follows: "If Christ's 'wealth' consists of his generosity, then the purpose of this momentum is to make 'you' rich... not in the sense of what you acquire as possessions, but in the sense of becoming *rich in generosity*.... [T]he purpose of 'enrichment' or 'abundance' is not that believers may possess more, but give more."[73] In my view, this reading (though it may need some nuancing) is correct, and it does not deny but rather enhances a theotic interpretation of 2 Cor 8:9. Because Christ is by nature gracious and generous, he has acted generously toward us both to enrich us and to enable us to enrich others. Soteriology is inherently ethical; theosis is missional. This is a fully participatory understanding of salvation, ethics, and

---

[69] To be sure, the [y] element is not explicit in 2 Cor 8:9, as it is in Phil 2:6–8, probably because Paul abbreviates the structure of the Philippians poem as he changes the emphasis from kenosis itself to the soteriological purpose (interchange).

[70] John M. G. Barclay, "'Because he was rich he became poor': Translation, Exegesis and Hermeneutics in the Reading of 2 Cor 8.9," in *Theologizing in the Corinthian Conflict: Studies in the Exegesis and Theology of 2 Corinthians* (ed. Reimund Bieringer et al.; Biblical Tools and Studies 162; Leuven: Peeters, 2013), 331–44. As Barclay notes (340 n. 19; 343–44), I have made an argument for translating Phil 2:6 with both the causal and the concessive senses; *Inhabiting*, 9–39.

[71] Barclay, "'Because he was rich he became poor,'" 340, 341.

[72] Barclay, "'Because he was rich he became poor,'" 341.

[73] Barclay, "'Because he was rich he became poor,'" 342.

mission. Because of the larger context, I would amend Barclay's proposal to include *justice* as inseparably part of the grace/generosity of God, Christ, and believers. The Corinthians are being called to a similar kind of ministry (διακονία)[74] to that of Paul and his team, who enrich others (2 Cor 6:10; "as poor, yet making many rich'; ὡς πτωχοὶ πολλοὺς δὲ πλουτίζοντες).

Throughout the Corinthian correspondence Paul wants the Corinthians' life in Christ and the Spirit to be marked not only by χαρίσματα (charismatic gifts; 1 Cor 1:7; 12:4, 9, 28–31) but also by Christlike, cruciform χάρις. In 2 Cor 8–9 that means that their life in the Spirit given to them in justice-ification (1 Cor 6:11) needs to be expressed in a "harvest of [their] justice" (9:10) – which is ultimately the justice of God (9:9; cf., again, 1 Cor 6:1–11). "The Corinthians," writes Barclay elsewhere, "are being invited not just to *imitate* God's dynamic of grace [and, we should add, "justice"] toward the world but to *embody* it, to continue and extend it in their own giving to meet the needs of others."[75] Indeed, what is remarkable is that Paul sees such a close relationship between grace and justice, first as the characteristic of God (including Christ and the Spirit) and then as the characteristic of God's people. As an extension of 2 Cor 5:21, 2 Cor 8:9 could have said, "The grace of God appeared in Christ's self-impoverishing so that you, in turn, might become the grace of God for others." The church participates in God's gracious, justice-creating mission, and Paul indicates this by using the common Greek word for sharing, κοινωνία (8:4; 9:13), giving it a profound theological twist.

Fourth, in chapter 9 Paul use a common image – the sowing of seed – to further emphasize that God is the ultimate source of generosity and justice for the poor, while the church participates in that generous justice. Paul invites believers to "sow" bountifully and cheerfully, knowing that God provides abundantly for the doing of good (9:6–11). This point raises the question of the grammatical subject in 9:9, which quotes Psalm 112:9. Is the one who "scatters abroad" and "gives to the poor," whose "justice endures forever," God, or is it the just and faithful person? In Psalm 112 itself, the subject is the one who fears the Lord, but Paul's use is less clear; the subject may be God. In either case, however, God is the ultimate benefactor who provides and multiplies the seed, blessing the sower to bless others. Thomas Stegman suggests that Paul's thought reflects the flow of Psalms 111 and 112 (LXX 110 and 111): Psalm 111 describes the generous, merciful, and just God who feeds those who fear him, while Psalm 112 describes the one who fears and imitates that God by doing justice and

---

[74] See 5:18; 6:3–4; 8:4, 19, 20; 9:1, 12, 13.
[75] Barclay, "Manna," 420 (emphasis added).

giving to the poor.[76] Both are characterized by justice (δικαιοσύνη in LXX 110:3; 111:3, 9). Accordingly, for Paul, "those who give generously to the needy should know that their charitable act is a part of that larger righteousness of God by which they themselves live and in which they shall remain forever."[77] This is a text about *missional* participation.

Having made these four main points about 2 Cor 8:9, we turn briefly to the text in connection with the letter as a whole. The overall participatory thrust of Paul's gentle but prophetic argument and the presence of δικαιοσύνη language suggest that it is no coincidence that we find another "interchange" text following 5:21. Christ became sin so that we might become just(ice) (5:21), and, similarly, he became poor so that we might become rich (8:9). His generous self-gift to us in our spiritual poverty translates into the generous gift of our material possessions to others in their material poverty.[78] Again, this is not a mere summons to imitation, but rather "the *identification of a divine momentum in which believers are caught up*, and by which they are empowered to be, in turn, richly self-sharing with others."[79] Together the two interchange texts in 2 Cor suggest that Paul's addressees will be on their way to becoming the justice of God when they are conformed to the cruciform grace of Christ expressed in selfless generosity to the poor. Although Paul's primary concern is the collection for the Jerusalem church, in chapter nine, at least, the poor to be cared for are not only believers ("the saints"; 9:1, 12) but "all" (9:13; πάντας; NRSV "all others") – probably meaning outsiders.[80]

It is significant that Paul refers to this generous justice as ministry (διακονία; 8:4 [cf. 8:19–20]; 9:1, 12, 13), the same word he uses in 2 Cor to describe his own ministry; that is, of embodied gospel proclamation (3:8–9; 4:1; 5:18; 6:3; 11:8). Moreover, he refers to his own ministry as a "ministry of justice" (δικαιοσύνης; 3:9), of reconciliation (5:18), and of enrich-

---

[76] Thomas D. Stegman, *Second Corinthians* (CCSS; Grand Rapids: Baker Academic, 2009), 214.

[77] Furnish, *II Corinthians*, 449.

[78] "The ultimate goal is not a reversal of fortunes through some kind of class warfare, but 'equality' through the establishment of new economic relationships under the sign of Messiah's economic divestment for the sake of the other." Zerbe, *Citizenship*, 81–82.

[79] Barclay, "Manna," 421 (emphasis added). Barclay does not use the language of justice, but he describes it in characterizing Paul's vision of equality as the "redistribution of surplus" that is "bilateral" and "reciprocal" because all parties have different sorts of riches to give and needs to be met (423).

[80] See Zerbe, *Citizenship*, 80; Bruce W. Longenecker, *Remember the Poor: Paul, Poverty, and the Greco-Roman World* (Grand Rapids: Eerdmans, 2010), 291–94. "All," as distinguished from the direct addressees in a letter, is normally Paul's way of referring to, or including, those outside the church. Translations express this interpretation of 9:13 in various ways: CEB, NET, and Wright, *Kingdom New Testament:* "everyone"; NIV: "everyone else"; NKJV: "all men." The NLT has "all believers," which seems unlikely.

ing others (6:10). More precisely, Paul participates in God's ministry, in Christ, of justice, reconciliation, and enrichment – and so do the Corinthians. As Morna Hooker writes,

> Paul's appeal to the Corinthians in chapters 8–9 can also be seen as a logical continuation from the conviction that Christians are agents of righteousness.... Since God's righteousness abides for ever, he will increase the yield of *their* righteousness (9:8–10): once again, we see the link between God's righteousness and that of Christians – and this righteousness is demonstrated in bringing assistance to those in need. It is certainly no accident that the key appeal in this section is made on the basis of another of Paul's "interchange" statements... (8:9). The Corinthians, too, must in their turn bring riches to others. By doing so, they will be sharing in Paul's ministry, and God's saving power will work through them.[81]

In speaking of justice, neither Paul nor I have left either glory or justification behind. As I have noted above and elsewhere, for Paul the inseparability of justification and justice is critical, though few contemporary Pauline scholars have adequately noted or explored this connection.[82] The community of the justified is the community of the just, which is the community of those being transformed and glorified and recreated – all in Christ. *These are not different, competing soteriologies or even quasi-independent slices of one soteriological pie. Rather, they are intimately interconnected dimensions of one soteriological reality, such that one aspect cannot be fully or adequately articulated without reference to the others.* A comprehensive term or phrase is needed, or at least helpful, to keep these dimensions integrated. "Participatory transformation" might work, or simply "union with Christ," "life in the crucified and resurrected Messiah," or "life in the Spirit." But not to be missed are the benefits of using "corporate, cruciform, missional theosis," or "Christosis," or simply, with the ecumenical Christian tradition, "theosis."

F. Conclusion

So what have we discovered in this investigation? First, we have found that the three main texts we have considered – 2 Cor 3:18, 5:21, and 8:9 – were seen by the Fathers as witnesses to theosis and have been treated as such by several significant recent interpreters of Paul. Second, we have seen that the theosis to which Paul bears witness in 2 Cor, at least with respect to its present (as opposed to its eschatological) expression, is corporate, cruciform, and missional. Its corporate (communal) character is clear from the first- and second-person-plural verbs in each verse: "all of us...

---

[81] Hooker, "On Becoming," 374.
[82] See my "Justification and Justice."

are being transformed" (3:18); "so that in him we might become the righteousness of God" (5:21); and "so that by his poverty you [plural] might become rich" (8:9). Its cruciform and missional character is evident in the texts themselves, and also in the context of each passage and of the letter as a whole. The glory into which apostles and all believers are being transformed is manifested, paradoxically, in cruciform, life-giving activity; to become the righteousness/justice of God means to share in Christ's gracious self-impoverishment for the benefit of others. These aspects of Paul's understanding of theosis, I would submit, are absolutely fundamental to the apostle's soteriology and ought to be seen as dimensions of theosis that are critical to contemporary appropriation of both Paul's theology and the church's tradition of theosis.

A third finding has been that theosis is not something distinct from justification. Justification is itself the event of initial and ongoing sharing in the justice of God revealed in Christ by the power of the Spirit, and thus of being made just – of being "justice-ified." For believers, the process of justice-ification and glorification has begun already and will be consummated with bodily resurrection and transformation in the future. In the meantime, believers share in the divine attributes of glory and righteousness/justice (δόξα and δικαιοσύνη) manifested in Christ in a partial but real way such that they become more like Christ, more like God, and more fully human, all by the working of grace and the Spirit of God.[83]

In this regard, 2 Corinthians is much like Romans, which also focuses on Spirit-generated δόξα and δικαιοσύνη. In my article on theosis in Romans, I argued that it was the first Christian treatise on theosis, building on theotic hints in 2 Corinthians. I stand by the thesis of that article except for the presence of the words "the first." That honor, I now suggest, belongs to 2 Corinthians; its witness to theosis is just as weighty as that of Romans, and slightly earlier.[84]

Bibliography

Ayres, Lewis. "Deification and the Dynamics of Nicene Theology: The Contribution of Gregory of Nyssa." *St. Vladimir's Theological Quarterly* 49 (2005): 375–94.

---

[83] Indeed, because believers live in the Christ who is the justice of God, and he lives in them, *"the church's participation in God is none other than Christ's practicing himself as the embodied practices of the church, in the Spirit, on behalf of the world."* L. Roger Owens, *The Shape of Participation: A Theology of Church Practices* (Eugene, Ore.: Cascade, 2010), 183.

[84] I use "treatise" of 2 Corinthians somewhat loosely, but not without reason. For ongoing, stimulating conversation about 2 Corinthians, I am grateful to my colleague Brent Laytham, and for assistance with this essay, to my research assistant, Daniel Jackson.

Barclay, John M. G. "'Because he was rich he became poor': Translation, Exegesis and Hermeneutics in the Reading of 2 Cor 8.9." Pages 331–44 in *Theologizing in the Corinthian Conflict: Studies in the Exegesis and Theology of 2 Corinthians*. Edited by Reimund Bieringer et al. Biblical Tools and Studies 162. Leuven: Peeters, 2013.

———. "Manna and the Circulation of Grace: A Study of 2 Corinthians 8:1–15." Pages 409–26 in *The Word Leaps the Gap: Essays on Theology and Scripture in Honor of Richard B. Hays*. Edited by J. Ross Wagner, C. Kavin Rowe, and A. Katherine Grieb. Grand Rapids: Eerdmans, 2008.

Blackwell, Ben C. *Christosis: Pauline Soteriology in Light of Deification in Irenaeus and Cyril of Alexandria*. Wissenschaftliche Untersuchungen zum Neuen Testament 2/314. Tübingen: Mohr Siebeck, 2011.

———. "Theosis in the New Testament?" *Journal of Theological Interpretation*. Forthcoming.

Bray, Gerald, ed. *1–2 Corinthians*. Volume VII of Ancient Christian Commentary on Scripture. Edited by Thomas C. Oden. Downers Grove, Ill.: InterVarsity Press, 1999.

Campbell, Constantine R. *Paul and Union with Christ: An Exegetical and Theological Study*. Grand Rapids: Zondervan, 2012.

Christensen, Michael J., and Jeffery A. Wittung, eds. *Partakers of the Divine Nature: The History and Development of Deification in the Christian Traditions*. Grand Rapids: Baker Academic, 2007.

Finlan, Stephen. "Can We Speak of Theosis in Paul?" Pages 68–80 in *Partakers of the Divine Nature: The History and Development of Deification in the Christian Traditions*. Edited by Michael J. Christensen and Jeffery A. Wittung. Grand Rapids: Baker Academic, 2007.

Finlan, Stephen and Vladmir Kharlamov, eds. *Theōsis: Deification in Christian Theology*. Eugene, Ore.: Pickwick, 2006.

Furnish, Victor Paul. *II Corinthians*. Anchor Bible 32A. Garden City, N.Y.: Doubleday, 1984.

Gordon, Joseph. "Deification by Ascent: Paul's Ascent (2 Cor 12:1–10) in its Historical and Theological Contexts." Unpublished paper, Marquette University.

Gorman, Michael J. *Becoming the Gospel: Paul, Participation, and Mission*. Grand Rapids: Eerdmans, forthcoming.

———. *2 Corinthians*. Two Horizons New Testament Commentary. Grand Rapids: Eerdmans, forthcoming.

———. *Cruciformity: Paul's Narrative Spirituality of the Cross*. Grand Rapids: Eerdmans, 2001.

———. *Inhabiting the Cruciform God: Kenosis, Justification, and Theosis in Paul's Narrative Soteriology*. Grand Rapids: Eerdmans, 2009.

———. "Justification and Justice in Paul, with Special Reference to the Corinthians." *Journal for the Study of Paul and His Letters* 1 (2011): 23–40.

———. "Romans: The First Christian Treatise on Theosis," *Journal of Theological Interpretation* 5 (2011): 13–34.

———. *The Death of the Messiah and the Birth of the New Covenant: A (Not So) New Model of the Atonement*. Eugene, Ore.: Cascade, 2014.

Grieb, A. Katherine. "'So That in Him We Might Become the Righteousness of God' (2 Cor 5:21): Some Theological Reflections on the Church Becoming Justice." *Ex Auditu* 22 (2006): 58–80.

Hays, Richard B. *The Moral Vision of the New Testament: Community, Cross, New Creation; A Contemporary Introduction to New Testament Ethics*. San Francisco: HarperCollins, 1996.

———. "What Is 'Real Participation in Christ'? A Dialogue with E. P. Sanders on Pauline Soteriology." Pages 336–51 in *Redefining First-Century Jewish and Christian Identities: Essays in Honor of Ed Parish Sanders*. Christianity and Judaism in Antiquity Series 16. Edited by Fabian E. Udoh et al. Notre Dame, Ind.: University of Notre Dame Press, 2008.

Heath, J. M. F. *Paul's Visual Piety: The Metamorphosis of the Beholder*. Oxford: Oxford University Press, 2013.

Hooker, Morna D. *From Adam to Christ: Essays on Paul*. Cambridge: Cambridge University Press, 1990.

———. "On Becoming the Righteousness of God: Another Look at 2 Cor 5:21." *Novum Testamentum* 50 (2008): 358–75.

Litwa, M. David. "2 Corinthians 3:18 and its Implications for *Theosis*." *Journal of Theological Interpretation* 2 (2008): 117–34.

———. "Transformation through a Mirror: Moses in 2 Cor 3.18." *Journal for the Study of the New Testament* 34 (2012): 286–97.

———. *We are Being Transformed: Deification in Paul's Soteriology*. Beihefte zur Zeitschrift für die nuetestamentliche Wissenschaft 187. Berlin: de Gruyter, 2012.

Longenecker, Bruce W. *Remember the Poor: Paul, Poverty, and the Greco-Roman World*. Grand Rapids: Eerdmans, 2010.

Macaskill, Grant. *Union with Christ in the New Testament*. Oxford: Oxford University Press, 2013.

Owens, L. Roger. *The Shape of Participation: A Theology of Church Practices*. Eugene, Ore.: Cascade, 2010.

Powers, Daniel G. *Salvation through Participation: An Examination of the Notion of the Believers' Corporate Unity with Christ in Early Christian Soteriology*. Contributions to Biblical Exegesis and Theology 29. Leuven: Peeters, 2001.

Sanders, E. P. *Paul and Palestinian Judaism: A Comparison of Patterns of Religion*. Philadelphia: Fortress, 1977.

Schnelle, Udo. *Apostle Paul: His Life and Theology*. Translated by M. Eugene Boring. Grand Rapids: Baker Academic, 2005.

Stegman, Thomas D. *Second Corinthians*. Catholic Commentary on Sacred Scripture. Grand Rapids: Baker Academic, 2009.

Wesley, John. *The Works of John Wesley, Vol. 11: Farther Appeals to Men of Reason and Religion and Certain Related Open Letters*. Edited by Gerald R. Cragg. Nashville: Abingdon, 1987.

Wright, N. T. "On Becoming the Righteousness of God: 2 Corinthians 5:21." Pages 200–208 in *Pauline Theology; Volume 2: 1 and 2 Corinthians*. Edited by David M. Hay. Minneapolis: Fortress, 1993.

———. *Paul and the Faithfulness of God*. Minneapolis: Fortress; London: SPCK, 2013.

Zerbe, Gordon. *Citizenship: Paul on Peace and Politics*. Winnipeg: CMU Press, 2012.

Paul and the Anxieties of (Imperial?) Succession

Galatians and the Politics of Neglect

MICHAEL J. THATE

> For God's sake, let us sit upon the ground
> And tell sad stories of the death of kings;
> William Shakespeare[1]

> ... every politics is grounded in a "theological" view of reality,
> it is also that every theology is inherently political,
> an ideology of a new collective space.
> Slavoj Žižek[2]

> Who cares about politics if you are burning with desire for life?
> Karl Ove Knausgaard[3]

Questions of Paul's political participations with and relationship toward the Roman Empire have been hotly contested in recent years. Positions tend to fall along a spectrum of Paul as counter-imperial polemicist or apolitical salvation historian. This essay attempts to trouble this spectrum by reading two scripts of succession anxiety alongside each other: viz., the tenuous times following Claudius' final years between his natural son Britannicus and his adopted son Nero, and Paul's adoption theology explicated in Galatians. This essay argues that Paul is neither a counter-imperial polemicist nor an apolitical salvation historian. It argues, rather, via Agamben and Badiou, for a subtle yet deeper politic in Paul's refusal to attend to Empire's dominant scripts and narrations by busily constructing his own. It is this *politics of neglect* where Paul, ironically, can be read as most pointed against Empire.

---

[1] Shakespeare, "The Life and Death of Richard the Second," Act III, Scene 2.
[2] Slavoj Žižek, *Living in the End Times* (New York: Verso, 2011), 18.
[3] Karl Ove Knausgaard, *My Struggle* (Book 1; New York: Farrar, Straus & Giroux, 2012 [2009]), 158.

A. Introduction

Over the course of the last twenty-five years or so there has been a steady increase in reading New Testament texts within the spaces of imperial ideology. These studies have ranged from general *Ideologiekritik* and continental philosophical readings,[4] to more particular investigations of beliefs and practices of early Christianity within wider Roman scripts.[5] Within this latter category, there appears to be somewhat of a continuum. Some scholars see Caesar, his empire, and his cult as significant – if not the main – targets of Paul's polemics.[6] Others in response to this position see an al-

---

[4] See, e.g., Giorgio Agamben, *The Time that Remains: A Commentary on the Letter to the Romans* (Stanford: Stanford University Press, 2005); Alain Badiou, *Saint Paul: The Foundation of Universalism* (Stanford: Stanford University Press, 2003); Stanislas Breton, *A Radical Philosophy of Saint Paul* (trans. Ward Banton; New York: Columbia University Press, 2011 [1988]); and Jacob Taubes, *The Political Theology of Paul* (Stanford: Stanford University Press, 2004). See P. Travis Kroeker, "Recent Continental Philosophers," in *The Blackwell Companion to Paul* (ed. Stephen Westerholm; Oxford: Wiley-Blackwell, 2011), 450–54; John D. Caputo and Linda Martin Alcoff, eds., *St Paul among the Philosophers* (Bloomington: University of Indiana Press, 2009); Ward Blanton, *A Materialism for the Masses: Saint Paul and the Philosophy of Undying Life* (Insurrections; New York: Columbia University Press, 2014); and Ward Blanton and Hent de Vries, eds., *Paul and the Philosophers* (New York: Fordham University Press, 2013). Rarely mentioned are the important majority-world readings which engage the text from similar critical reflexes. For, e.g., African readings, see Grant LeMarquand, "African Readings of Paul," in *The Blackwell Companion to Paul* (ed. Stephen Westerholm; Oxford: Wiley-Blackwell, 2011), 488–503, especially his important bibliography on 500–503.

[5] Note Barclay on the complexities surrounding the term "Christian" in "Pauline Churches, Jewish Communities and the Roman Empire," in *Pauline Churches and Diaspora Jews* (WUNT 276; Tübingen: Mohr Siebeck, 2011), 3 n. 1.

[6] N. T. Wright, e.g., sees at every point the confession that "Jesus is Lord" implicitly negates the imperial boast of Caesar. See, e.g., N. T. Wright, *Paul: Fresh Perspectives* (Minneapolis: Fortress, 2009) 69. Cf., N. T. Wright, *Paul and the Faithfulness of God* (Minneapolis: Fortress, 2013) 1.279–347; 2.1271–1353. At one point, Richard A. Horsley states that Paul's gospel opposed the Roman imperial order *not Judaism*. See *idem.*, ed., *Paul and the Roman Imperial Order* (Harrisburg: Trinity Press International, 2004) 3. See Horsley, ed., *Paul and Politics: Ekklesia, Israel, Imperium, Interpretation* (London: T&T Clark, 2000); Horsley, ed., *Paul and Empire: Religion and Power in Roman Imperial Society* (London: T&T Clark, 1997). Note, too, the impressive studies of Neil Elliot, *The Arrogance of Nations: Reading Romans in the Shadow of Empire* (Minneapolis: Fortress, 2008); Brigitte Kahl, *Galatians Re-Imagined: Reading with the Eyes of the Vanquished* (Minneapolis: Fortress, 2010); Davina C. Lopez, *Apostle to the Conquered: Reimagining Paul's Mission* (Minneapolis: Fortress, 2008); Klaus Wengst, *Pax Romana and the Peace of Christ* (trans. J. Bowden; London: SCM Press, 1987 [1986]); D. Georgi, *Theocracy in Paul's Practice and Theology* (trans. D. E. Green; Minneapolis: Fortress, 1991 [1987]). Cf., too, the entire fascicle of *JSNT* 27 (2005) which was dedicated to the imperial cult.

together *apolitical* Paul – at least *apolitical* with respect to Rome.⁷ Somewhere in the middle – or, perhaps, asymmetrical to these poles – are those who suggest that "to give the Roman empire particular significance is to misconstrue the terms with which Paul addressed the political (and other) dimensions of human life."⁸ In other words, Paul is neither for nor against Rome *qua* Rome as he is on about something else altogether.

When Paul is read within a Roman context, most of the studies tend toward comparing the conflict between the cult of Christ and the cult of Caesar – to borrow from the slightly dated phrasing from Adolf Deissmann.⁹ These studies emphasize "the prominence of the imperial cult in the social, political and religious context of the early Christian churches."¹⁰ The imperial cult, of course, was no singular nor simple phenomenon.¹¹ The image and reception of the emperor "on the (post)colony" was a negotiation,¹² and the cult itself often took on regional significance and assimilation.¹³ It is therefore difficult to say in general terms what it looked like on

---

⁷ Seyoon Kim, e.g., in looking at 1 Thessalonians, Philippians, Romans, and 1 Corinthians, sees "no warning about the imperial cult and no message subversive to the Roman Empire." *Christ and Caesar: The Gospel and the Roman Empire in the Writings of Paul and Luke* (Grand Rapids: Eerdmans, 2008), 66. And, again, "there is no anti-imperial intent to be ascertained in the Pauline Epistles" (p. 68).

⁸ John M. G. Barclay, "Why the Roman Empire Was Insignificant to Paul" in *Pauline Churches and Diaspora Jews* (WUNT 276; Tübingen: Mohr Siebeck, 2011), 363.

⁹ Adolf Deissmann, *Light from the Ancient East* (trans. L. R. M. Strachan from the 4th rev. ed.; London: Hodder & Stoughton, 1927 [1922]), 338–78.

¹⁰ John M. G. Barclay, "Paul, Roman Religion and the Emperor: Mapping the Point of Conflict," *Pauline Churches and Diaspora Jews* (WUNT 276; Tübingen: Mohr Siebeck), 345. For a survey of classicists who have worked on the imperial cult, see Barclay, "Paul, Roman Religion and the Emperor," 345 n. 2. In addition, see Simon Price and Emily Kearns, eds., *The Oxford Dictionary of Classical Myth and Religion* (Oxford: Oxford University Press, 2003), 481–83 on the roman ruler cult; and pp. 111–17 on Christianity.

¹¹ See, generally, Ittai Gradel, *Emperor Worship and Roman Religion* (Oxford: Clarendon, 2002), esp. 1–26, 73–108.

¹² See Fergus Millar, *The Emperor in the Roman World* (London: Duckworth, 2003). The phrase "on the (post)colony," refers to the fascinating work of Achille Mbembe, *On the Postcolony* (Berkeley: University of California Press, 2001).

¹³ "It was precisely because it was incorporated into local interpretations of this pervasive divine order that the imperial cult became so successful so quickly." Barclay, "Paul, Roman Religion and the Emperor," 355. For an intriguing study of particularly North African incarnations of *pater* and *patria* manifestations of the emperor's image, see Alain Cadotte, *La romanisation des diex: L'interpretatio romana en Afrique du Nord sous le Haut-Empire* (Religions in the Graeco-Roman World 158; Leiden: Brill, 2007). On the 'romanization' of foreign gods, see Robert Turcan, *The Cults of the Roman Empire* (trans. Antonia Nevill; Oxford: Blackwell, 1996 [1992]), 12–15. On western negotiations, see Greg Woolf, *Becoming Roman: The Origins of Provincial Civilization in Gaul* (Cambridge: Cambridge University Press, 2000); for the east, see Susan E. Alcock, ed., *The Early Roman Empire in the East* (Oxbow Monographs 95; Oxford: Oxbow,

the ground in its rituals, symbols, and beliefs – to say nothing of what it would look like to be against such practices.[14] Nevertheless, in favor of such approaches, it is difficult to think that the social dynamics of the imperial cult in all their complexity and varieties would not have encroached upon Paul's missionary priorities at some points.[15] Or, more generally, how the complex sprawling of Roman "religion" constructed and enforced spaces and boundaries through which Paul often traversed.[16] He was well travelled throughout the Empire and surely did not walk around blindly.[17] "Imperial images were ubiquitous,"[18] be they on coins, statues, busts, do-

---

1997); Guy Rogers, *The Sacred Identity of Ephesos: Foundation Myths of a Roman City* (London: Routledge, 1991); Simon Swain, *Hellenism and Empire, Classicism and Power in the Greek World, A.D. 50–250* (Oxford: Oxford University Press, 1998); and, generally, Susan E. Alcock et. al., *Empires: Perspectives from Archaeology and History* (Cambridge: Cambridge University Press, 2001).

[14] See M. Beard, J. North and S. Price, *Religions of Rome: A History* (Cambridge: Cambridge University Press, 1998), 1.348–65; J. B. Rives, *Religion of the Roman Empire* (Oxford: Blackwell, 2006), 148–56; and Barclay, "Paul, Roman Religion and the Emperor," 345. Note, too, Ulrike Egelhaaf-Gaiser and Alfred Schäfer, *Religiöse Vereine in der römischen Antike: Untersuchungen zu Organisation, Ritual und Raumordnung* (STAC 13; Tübingen: Mohr Siebeck, 2002). See, too, Oliver Hekster, Sebastian Scmidt-Hofner, and Christian Witschel, eds., *Ritual Dynamics and Religious Change in the Roman Empire: Proceedings of the Eight Workshop of the International Network Impact of Empire* (Leiden: Brill, 2009).

[15] See, e.g., the interesting study of Justin K. Hardin, *Galatians and the Imperial Cult* (WUNT 2/237; Tübingen: Mohr Siebeck, 2008). Hardin is most interested in what the "Galatians were actually doing at the time of Paul's letter" (p. 15) and favors reading Galatians in light of the imperial cult as opposed to rural folk religion in Anatolia or other scenarios (see p. 16 and esp. p. 47). Though Hardin mentions that this question is rarely asked, one should keep in mind J. Louis Martyn, "Events in Galatia," in *Pauline Theology* (vol. 1; ed. J. Bassler; Minneapolis: Fortress, 1991), 160–79. Cf. the interesting set of studies noted in John M. G. Barclay, "Why the Roman Empire Was Insignificant to Paul," in *Pauline Churches and Diaspora Jews* (WUNT 276; Tübingen: Mohr Siebeck), 365 nn. 8–12; as well as N. T. Wright's approach (p. 368 n. 17; pp. 368–73) and Barclay's reading of Wright. Note, too, Judy Diehl, "Empire and Epistles: Anti-Roman Rhetoric in the New Testament Epistles," *CBR* 10.2 (2012): 217–63; and Colin Miller, "The Imperial Cult in the Pauline Cities of Asia Minor and Greece," *CBQ* 72 (2010): 314–32.

[16] On the control of space in terms of communication and boundaries, see Jörg Rüpke, *Religion of the Romans* (trans. Richard Gordon; Cambridge: Polity, 2007 [2001]) 174–85. See, too, Jörg Rüpke, ed., *A Companion to Roman Religion* (Oxford: Blackwell, 2007). On Paul's traveling, see the excellent study of Timothy L. Marquis, *Transient Apostle: Paul, Travel, and the Rhetoric of Empire* (New Haven, Conn.: Yale University Press, 2013).

[17] Cf. Deissmann, *Light from the Ancient East*, 340.

[18] Barclay, "Paul, Roman Religion and the Emperor," 351.

mestic frescos,[19] or paintings.[20] The cult was entangled with everyday elements of religious life,[21] as well as with the cosmic order.[22] At points Paul does seem at least to be received as speaking against Caesar (cf. Acts 17:7),[23] and it is difficult not to hear the similarities of certain vocabularies in addresses to Christ and Caesar.[24] But as Barclay has pointed out, the peculiarity of Paul is that despite the many different kinds of cults he must have encountered, he never seems to differentiate "between one cult and another, and never names the various deities which he undoubtedly encountered."[25]

What is more, at the level of ostensive reference, Paul rarely even names the Roman Empire.[26] The way this "virtual silence"[27] is parsed, of

---

[19] See, e.g., Alex Butterworth and Ray Laurence, *Pompeii: The Living City* (New York: St Martin's Press, 2005) plates 23a–b of Apollo Citarista from Murecine wall frescoes, where Apollo's face is the face of Nero. The identification of the emperor with Apollo was then common in the Roman *domus* where Christians would have lived, worked and worshiped.

[20] On imperial images, see S. R. F. Price, *Rituals and Power: The Roman Imperial Cult in Asia Minor* (Cambrdige: Cambridge University Press, 1985), 170–206; Clifford Ando, *Imperial Ideology and Provincial Loyalty in the Roman Empire* (Berkeley: University of California Press, 2000), 206–73; and Paul Zanker, *The Power of Images in the Age of Augustus* (Ann Arbor: University of Michigan Press, 1990). In a slightly later period, cf. Laura Salah Nasrallah, *Christian Responses to Roman Art and Architecture: The Second-Century Church Amid the Spaces of Empire* (Cambridge: Cambridge University Press, 2010). See, generally, Alan K. Bowman, Peter Garnsey, and Bominic Rathbone, eds., *The High Empire, AD 70–192* (CAH 11; 2d ed.; Cambridge: Cambridge University Press, 2000).

[21] See Beard, North, and Price, *Religions of Rome*, 1.348, cf. 318; and Robert E. A. Palmer, *Roman Religion and Roman Empire* (Philadelphia: University of Pennsylvania Press, 1974).

[22] Barclay, "Paul, Roman Religion and the Emperor," 354.

[23] Note Kim, *Christ and Caesar*, 65. On issues of the Paul of Acts, see Stanley E. Porter, "The Portrait of Paul in Acts," in *The Blackwell Companion to Paul* (ed. Stephen Westerholm; Oxford: Wiley-Blackwell, 2011), 124–38; Porter, *Paul in Acts* (Grand Rapids: Baker Academic, 2000); John Clayton Lentz Jr., *Luke's Portrait of Paul* (Cambridge: Cambridge University Press, 1993); and, Daniel Marguerat, *Paul in Acts and Paul in His Letters* (WUNT 310; Tübingen: Mohr Siebeck, 2013).

[24] Here, see John Dominic Crossan and Jonathan L. Reed, *In Search of Paul: How Jesus' Apostle Opposed Rome's Empire with God's Kingdom* (New York: HarperOne, 2005). Seyoon Kim notes *kyrios, soter/soteria, euangelion, dikaiosyne, pistis, eirene, eleutheria, elpis, parousia, apantesis* in *Christ and Caesar*; Kim, *Christ and Caesar*, 65.

[25] Barclay, "Paul, Roman Religion and the Emperor," p. 355; cf. Kim, *Christ and Caesar*, p. 66. On Roman religion in general, see, *inter alia*, Clifford Ando, ed., *Roman Religion* (Edinburgh: Edinburgh University Press, 2003). Particularly relevant are the studies of Jonathan Z. Smith "On Comparison," pp. 23–38; Greg Woolf, "*Polis*-Religion and Its Alternatives in the Roman Provinces," pp. 39–54; and Richard Gordon, "From Republic to Principate: Priesthood, Religion and Ideology," pp. 62–83.

[26] Cf. Rom 5:1; 13:1–7; 1 Thess 5:3; Phil 1:13; 4:22; 2 Thess 2:1–12.

course, is contested.²⁸ Some suggest that there is indeed much to be read off script while others think such off-script reading is indeed reading too much *into* the script.²⁹ To be sure, lack of ostensive reference hardly constitutes lack of proof. Sometimes the really big political questions are often precisely the ones which people dare not speak in public performances – or, when they do, they speak it in a different kind of way.³⁰ Shakespeare's historical plays, for example, take on a rather political bite when read within the tenuous times of Elizabethan succession.³¹ It is difficult to read the infamous deposition scene in Richard II (Act IV, Scene 1) without feeling the force of the 1571 Treason Act which made it fatal to discuss the succession and particularly the title of any potential successor to Elizabeth; or the 1581 Act which reinforced the need for silence on matters of succession.³² Indeed, in early February of 1601, the Earl of Essex used the performance of the play at the Globe as the public rallying cry against what would prove to be his unsuccessful rebellion against the monarchy. Somewhat similarly, Richard Horsley has edited a collection of essays which look at the ways in which Paul's silence vis-à-vis Rome is actually a coded "hidden transcript."³³ Whether or not Paul's letters are best described as "public" or "private" performances, Barclay is right to stress that just as

---

²⁷ John M. G. Barclay, "Pauline Churches, Jewish Communities and the Roman Empire: Introducing the Issues," in *Pauline Churches and Diaspora Jews* (WUNT 276; Tübingen: Mohr Siebeck), 31.

²⁸ N. T. Wright, for example, has argued for cryptic allusions to "echoes of Caesar." *Paul: Fresh Perspectives*, 61–62, 70, 71. Barclay calls his method "hardly valid." See, Barclay, "Why the Roman Empire Was Insignificant to Paul," 380.

²⁹ E.g., Barclay, "Why the Roman Empire Was Insignificant to Paul," 383 and his clever turn of phrase on Hans Christian Andersen's short tale, "The Emperor's New Clothes" in n. 69.

³⁰ Here, of course, the key figure is that of James C. Scott, *Domination and the Arts of Resistance: Hidden Transcripts* (New Haven, Conn.: Yale University Press, 1990).

³¹ See, e.g., Wolfgang Iser, *Staging Politics: The Lasting Impact of Shakespeare's Histories* (trans. David Henry Wilson; New York: Columbia University Press, 1993).

³² On the complex issues of Elizabeth and succession, see the many works of Susan Doran. Shakespeare's deposition scene, of course, has a complicated history of being removed and re-inserted. On the complexities surrounding the censorship and reinsertion of the deposition scene, see the interesting article by Jean-Christophe Mayer, "The 'Parliament Sceane' in Shakespeare's *King Richard III*," *Bulletin de la société d'études anglo-ameéricaines des XVIIe et SVIIIe siècles* 59.59 (2004): 27–42. See, too, the recent BBC *Shakespeare Uncovered* where Sir Derek Jacoby discusses the latent politics of "Richard II."

³³ Richard A. Horsley, ed., *Hidden Transcripts and the Arts of Resistance: Applying the Work of James C. Scott to Jesus and Paul* (Semeia Studies 48; Atlanta: SBL, 2004); William R. Herzog, "Dissembling, A Weapon of the Weak: The Case of Christ and Caesar in Mark 12:13–17 and Romans 13:1–7," *Journal of the NABPR* 21 (1994): 339–60; and other studies from the likes of Neil Elliot, Warren Carter, and Monya Stubbs.

there is "a danger of modernization in separating 'religion' from 'politics,' there is also a danger of allowing the fusion of these domains to be governed by modern expectations and perceptions."[34] Indeed, Barclay suggests that "proper exegetical method requires us to read precisely what is on the lines" as opposed to "tracing a hidden 'code'." And if this "does not fit what we imagine Paul *must have* said," Barclay states, "it is not Paul's texts that need revision, but our preformed expectations of his political theology."[35]

In what follows I would like to work with this "virtual silence" and challenge the various positions on the continuum of a political Paul or an *apolitical* Paul with respect to Rome as outlined above through a reading of Paul's letter to the Galatian assembly.[36] Though sympathetic with aspects from all positions, I think some nuance may be in order which both reads "what is on the lines" while at the same time allowing for the hermeneutical complexity in any text where an infinite space behind and between the lines is present. I suggest that in reading Galatians within its sprawling contexts of "life on the (post)colony,"[37] within the assembly's fledgling negotiations with its regional environs, Judaism(s) and the Scriptures,[38] and the coming to terms with – and indeed coming up with terms to grammaticalize – the Christ-event, Paul's imperial "silence" gestures toward a most radical politics. My approach is comparative in that it looks at the way imperial ideology and the epistemology which informs Pauline theology resonate over the complicated – and sometimes deadly – issues of fathers, sons, and successions in antiquity. In what follows I would like to tell the tale of two succession narratives which transpired concurrently somewhere in Rome's mapping of the world. The first is about the most powerful *pater* in the empire: the *pater patriae*, Caesar himself. With the passing of any Caesar, however, there were surrounding anxieties of succession. This essay particularly tracks the tenuous times of Claudius and

---

[34] Barclay, "Paul, Roman Religion and the Emperor," 367.

[35] Barclay, "Paul, Roman Religion and the Emperor," 383.

[36] On the use of "assembly" here, see Barclay, "Pauline Churches, Jewish Communities, and the Roman Empire," 3; and the literature cited in n. 1.

[37] Again, see Mbembe, *On the Postcolony*. Cf. D. J. Mattingly, ed., *Dialogues in Roman Imperialism: Power, Discourse, and Discrepant Experience in the Roman Empire* (JRASup 23; Portsmouth: JRA, 1997).

[38] "Diaspora Jews negotiated their identities in different ways, depending on context, circumstance and social level, and Pauline churches differed amongst themselves, and developed variously in the following generations." Barclay, "Pauline Churches, Jewish Communities and the Roman Empire," 12. It was in Paul's attempt to construct and maintain a "durable identity" for early Christian assemblies which best makes sense of his letter-writing practices. See, Barclay, "Pauline Churches, Jewish Communities and the Roman Empire," 8.

his two conflicting sons: his natural son Britannicus and his adopted son Nero.

In this sense, Galatians represents an intriguing test case in the ways Paul directed life lived on the colony for the Galatian assembly.[39] Comparisons, of course, are "complex."[40] Beyond the usual challenges,[41] what I am attempting is further complicated in that my argument is at its strongest if the letter was written sometime around 54 CE. The setting and date of Galatians, however, is contested.[42] Nevertheless, the imperial anxieties I am chronicling were on display as early as 49CE, so any date between 49–54 is conducive for this study. The location of the addresses is not entirely relevant to my argument. Brigitte Kahl stated in her own study, wherever "Galatia was – South or North, East or West – it was a *Roman* location, as much as were Jerusalem or Judea."[43] Indeed, there was imperial presence in Roman Galatia under Claudius (CE 41–54) with several cities adopting the Emperor's name (e.g., Claudiconium, Claudioderbe).[44] In this sense,

---

[39] "Paul's letter to the Galatians affords a fascinating insight into the development of the early Christian movement." John M. G. Barclay, *Obeying the Truth: A Study of Paul's Ethics in Galatians* (Studies in the New Testament and Its World; Edinburgh: T&T Clark, 1988), 1. Elsewhere, Barclay states that Galatians was "Paul's most revolutionary pamphlet." See John M. G. Barclay, "Paul and the Philosophers: Alain Badiou and the Event," *New Blackfriars* 91.1032 (2010), 176; also 171–84. It is therefore not only owing to space constraints that we will limit our investigation here to Paul's letter to the Galatian assembly.

[40] Stanley K. Stowers calls them "a complex, multitaxonomic activity." "Does Pauline Christianity Resemble a Philosophical School?" in *Beyond the Judaism/Hellenism Divide* (ed. Engberg-Pedersen; Louisville: Westminster John Knox, 2001), 89.

[41] E.g., Jonathan Z. Smith, *Drudgery Divine: On the Comparison of Early Christianities and the Religions of Late Antiquity* (Chicago: University of Chicago Press, 1990); and Luke Timothy Johnson, *Among the Gentiles: Greco-Roman Religion and Christianity* (New Haven, Conn.: Yale University Press, 2009), 1–14.

[42] See, generally, Mark D. Nanos, ed., *The Galatians Debate: The Contemporary Issues in Rhetorical and Historical Interpretation* (Grand Rapids: Baker Academic, 2002).

[43] Brigitte Kahl, *Galatians Re-Imagined*, 7. Kahl slightly overstates her case in continuing, "To perceive these places only as sites of 'Judaism' is historically naïve. And whatever the subject of contention between Paul and his 'stupid Galatians' regarding *Jewish* law and *Jewish* affiliation, it was *Roman* law that ultimately defined and enforced what was licit or illicit" (p. 7). On matters of administrative arrangement in regional environments, see Stephen Mitchell, *Anatolia: Land, Men, and Gods in Asia Minor* (2 vols.; Oxford: Clarendon, 1993), 1.199. On matters of indigenous law and Roman intervention in judicial matters, see, too, Andrew Lincott, *Imperium Romanum: Politics and Administration* (London: Routledge, 1993), 11–67. For Roman administration in Egypt, see Alan Bowman and Dominic Rathbone, "Cities and Administration in Roman Egypt," *JRS* 82 (1992): 107–27. These works balance well the seeming optimism of Pliny, *Ep.* 10.112–13.

[44] On the north (Celtic)/south (Roman province) debate, see F. Müssner, *Der Galaterbrief* (HTKNT 9; Freiburg: Herder & Herder, 1974), 3–9; and A. Oepke, *Der Brief des*

this essay only listens to half of Simon R. F. Price's advice to NT scholars engaging with Paul and politics:

> The important intellectual issue in thinking about Paul and politics is to get two things straight: what politics are at issue, and how we are to consider the relationship between Paul and that context.[45]

Price rightly states that "the context in which Paul should be set is not that of Rome" but within his local communities."[46] Though this is a wise corrective to sloppy associations with Paul and the Capital, it is difficult to imagine Paul *only* writing from his Galatian experience while writing to Galatia, or from his Corinthian experience while writing to Corinth. Surely the destination of his communication would weigh his writing with provincial accents. But Paul's cosmopolitan exposure throughout the Mediterranean surely informed his writings in ways in which perhaps even he was unaware. This essay is therefore firm on its political examination – viz., *pater* imagery and succession anxieties – but flexible on the complex issues of context.

The essay is an exploratory test case in Paul's political theology with its argument developing through three main sections. The first looks at the evolving political ideology of *pater* with respect to the Emperor and the desire for a stable line. The second considers the awkward and sometimes dangerous negotiation between adopted and natural heirs with special attention given to the catastrophe of Claudius' vying adopted and natural sons: Nero and Britannicus respectively. The third section will consider Paul's radical recast of Father, Son(s), and Heirs in his letter to the Galatians. We will conclude with some (theo)(political) reflections.

B. The Political Ideology of Pater

Ovid states in his *Metamorphoses* that, "Jupiter governs the heavenly citadels and the kingdoms of the tri-formed world, but the earth is under Augustus' rule; *each is father and ruler*" (15.855–60).[47] Nevertheless, during

---

Paulus an die Galater (THKNT 9; Berlin: Evangelische Verlagsanstalt, 1955), 5–8. See, too, James M. Scott, *Paul and the Nations: The Old Testament and Jewish Background of Paul's Mission to the Nations with Special Reference to the Destination of Galatians* (WUNT 84; Tübingen: Mohr Siebeck, 1995), 181–215; cf., too, the relevant sections in J. P. Lémonon, *L'Épître aux Galates* (Paris: Cerf, 2008).

[45] Simon R. F. Price, "Response," in *Paul and Politics: Ekklesia, Israel, Imperium, Interpretation* (ed. Horsley, Richard A.; London: T&T Clark, 2000), 175–84.

[46] Price, "Response," 175–76.

[47] The italic portion translates *pater est et rector uterque*. Horace addressed Jupiter as "father and guardian of the human race...with [Augustus] next in power" (Horace *Carm.*

the reign of Augustus there was a kind of "honored insignificance" developing toward Jupiter with respect to the language of *pater* which allowed for a new political ideology to immerge.[48] This had far-reaching effects. With perhaps a touch of overstatement, Michael Peppard has written that on 5 February 2 BCE, "the Roman family changed forever."[49] This was the day when Augustus was declared *pater patriae* – father of the fatherland.[50] According to the *Res Gestae*, Augustus is to have claimed, "In my thirteenth consulship the Senate, the equestrian order, and the whole people of Rome gave me the title of *pater patriae*, and resolved that this should be inscribed in the porch of my house in the *Curia Julia* and in the *Forum Augustum* below the chariot that had been set there in my honor by decree of the Senate" (*Res gest. divi Aug.* 35.1; cf. Seutonius, *Aug.* 58).[51] Augus-

---

1.12.49–60; cf. 3.5.1; and Ovid *Met.* 15.858–60. Horace hints that Augustus should have used the title *pater* prior to when he assumed it (*Carm.* 1.2.49–52). Indeed, a whole mythology began to grow around Augustus as *pater* of Rome and the world. See Ando, *Imperial Ideology*, 399.

[48] See J. Rufus Fears, "Jupiter and Roman Imperial Ideology," *ANRW* 17.1:20; cf. Michael Peppard, *The Son of God in the Roman World: Divine Sonship in its Social and Political Context* (Oxford: Oxford University Press, 2011,) 61. "The Augustan revolution ensured that the emperor, as the figurehead and representative of Roman power, was everywhere received with honours that integrated his person at an elevated level into the cosmic hierarchy." Alan K. Bowman, Peter Garnsey, et al., eds., *The Augustan Empire, 43 BC–AD 69* (CAH 10; 2d ed.; Cambridge: Cambridge University Press, 1996). See, too Barclay, "Paul, Roman Religion and the Emperor," 351. Ando states, "An ideology as a lived system is dynamic, determined and defined through the evolution and manipulation, no less than the internalization and iteration, of the ruling order's normative script." *Imperial Ideology*, 398. See, generally, D. Kienast, *Augustus, Prinzeps und Monarch* (3d ed.; Darmstadt: Wissenschaftliche Buchgesellschaft, 1999).

[49] Peppard, *The Son of God in the Roman World*, 60.

[50] See, generally, Anthony Everitt, *Augustus: The Life of Rome's First Emperor* (New York: Random House, 2006); and, especially, Ronald Syme, *The Roman Revolution* (Oxford: Oxford University Press, 2002); and the fine collection of essays in Karl Galinsky, ed., *The Cambridge Companion to the Age of Augustus* (Cambridge: Cambridge University Press, 2005).

[51] See Alison E. Cooley, *Res Gestae Divi Augusti: Text, Translation, and Commentary* (Cambridge: Cambridge University Press, 2009). The consequences of this are reaching in that archaeologists have excavated his *domus* and the Temple of Apollo that Octavian built immediately adjacent and connected by a ramp. One of Apollo's important attributes was the god who defeated the Gauls. See here David L. Balch, "Cult Statues of Augustus' Temple of Apollo on the Palatine in Rome: Artemis' / Diana's Birthday in Ephesus, and Revelation 12:1–5a," in *Contested Spaces: Houses and Temples in Roman Antiquity and the New Testament* (ed. David L. Balch and Annette Weissenrieder; WUNT 285; Tübingen: Mohr Siebeck, 2005), 415–16, 419–20, 423, 425–27, 431, with nn. 31, 42, 64, 70, 87, and Figs. 9–13. Augustus' temple of Apollo celebrated the defeat of the Gauls as did the temple of Sosius' (also in Rome) which had a Galatomachia. See Steven Rutledge, *Ancient Rome as a Museum: Power, Identity, and the Culture of Collecting*

tus only reluctantly received this honor after initially refusing its offer.[52] Messalla Corvinus would not hear of his refusal and spoke up in the Senate: "The Senate, in *consensus* with the people of Rome, salutes you as *pater patriae*." An overwhelmed and opportunistic Augustus responded, "Having realized the object of my prayers, Conscript Fathers, for what am I now to pray to the immortal gods, other than that it be permitted to me to retain this your *consensus* until the end of my life?"[53]

The title *pater patriae* was not uncommonly awarded during the Republic for "saving the city from invaders or conspirators, or for saving the lives of many citizens."[54] The appellation could be associated with the founder of Rome, Romulus – whose name the Senate considered using as an honorific title in 27 BCE for Octavian instead of "Augustus."[55] One who "saved the city," therefore, could be viewed as founding Rome a second time.[56] Augustus was viewed as the second-founder of Rome in this respect through what Diane Favro describes as his treating "Rome as his *domus*."[57] A "whole world exhausted by civil wars" was "received into his control."[58] Suetonius claimed that Augustus was given a city built in brick but left a city built in marble (Suetonius, *Augustus*, 28).[59] He restored some eighty-two temples (*Res Gestae* 20), and reformed municipality legislation by giving attention to fire prevention, the preservation of the existing fab-

---

(Oxford: Oxford University Press, 2012), 249, Fig. 7.10; cf. Figs. 7.22–23. See, too, G. Nachtergael, *Les Galates en Grèce et la Sotèria de Delphes: recherches d'histoire et d'épigraphie hellénistiques* (Mémoires de la Classe des lettres, Académie royal de Belgique, serie 2, tome 63.1; Bruxelles: Georges Nachtergael, 1975).

[52] This act of "refusal" became a significant political trope in subsequent imperial political performances.

[53] Suetonius, *Augustus* 58.1–2; cf. Ovid *Fasti* 2.126–28. See Ando, *Imperial Ideology*, 146.

[54] Cf. the literature cited in Ando, *Imperial Ideology*, 399 n. 292.

[55] On the complexities relating to the power and religion of the senators and senate, see Zsuzsanna Várhelyi, *The Religion of Senators in the Roman Empire: Power and the Beyond* (Cambridge: Cambridge University Press, 2010). See, too, D. S. Potter and Cynthia Damon, "Senatus Consultum de Cn. Pisone Patre," *The American Journal of Philology*. Special Issue: "The Senatus Consultum de Cn. Pisone Patre": Text, Translation, Discussion 120.1 (1999): 13–42; Miriam Griffin, "The Senate's Story," *JRS* 87 (1997): 249–63; and, Werner Eck, Antonio Caballos and Fernando Fernández, *Das senatus consultum de Cn. Pisone patre* (Vestigia 48; Munich: C. H. Beck, 1996). Note, generally, Richard J. A. Talbert, *The Senate of Imperial Rome* (Princeton: Princeton University Press, 1984).

[56] E.g., Camillus in Livy 5.49.7. See Ando, *Imperial Ideology*, 399 and n. 293.

[57] Diane Favro, "*Pater urbis*: Augustus as City Father of Rome," *Journal of the Society of Architectural Historians* 51.1 (1992): 72.

[58] Tacitus *Annales* 1.1.1.

[59] See the intriguing work of Paul Rehak, *Imperium and Cosmos: Augustus and the Northern Campus Martius* (Madison: University of Wisconsin Press, 2006), 3–8.

ric of the city, as well as the promotion of building restoration.[60] His provision for "fire fighting, water distribution, building maintenance, and urban safety reflect a consistent policy of social control."[61] Collectively, his civic planning beguiles a "disguised centralization."[62] Tacitus reflected that "step by step [Augustus] began to make his ascent and to unite in his own person the functions of the Senate, the magistracy, and the legislature" (*Annals* 1.2).[63] The second-century jurist, Paulus, wrote that Augustus believed that "the business of looking after the public safety was [...] suited for no one so well as the Emperor himself, nor was anyone else equal to the duty" (*Digesta* 1.15.3).[64] Augustus' "efforts to create a functional, attractive, and enduring urban environment were both paternal and calculated."[65] As *pater patriae*, Augustus could justify this centralization as a "good Roman father direct[ing] the lives of his offspring and improv[ing] the family *domus*."[66] *Pater patriae* during and subsequent to Augustus' reign became less a title, not quite an office, and more a role.[67] As Favro suggests, "beyond the improvement of administration and legal provisions for urban care, Augustus' most effective legacy was a paternal attitude toward the city."[68] Ovid would say of Augustus that "our fatherland is safe and secure with you as its parent," and named him "father of our country" (Ovid, *Tristia* 2.157, 181). Indeed, after his death, Augustus was commemorated as *Divus Augustus pater* on coins distributed throughout the empire.[69]

As stated above, the conferring of the honors *parens patriae* or *pater patriae* was not without precedent. Cicero received the honors for his defense against the Catilinarian conspirators. The Senate also conferred the

---

[60] Favro, "*Pater urbis*," 62; Kitty Chisholm and John Ferguson, eds., *Rome: The Augustan Age. A Sourcebook* (Oxford: Oxford University Press, 1981), 187–212; 446–88.

[61] Favro, "*Pater urbis*," 61.

[62] Favro, "*Pater urbis*," 83.

[63] There was an attempt to name Augustus *curator legum et morum*. See Ando, *Imperial Ideology*, 399.

[64] Quoted in Favro, "*Pater urbis*," 84; see, too, Strabo, *Geography*, 6.4.2.

[65] Favro, "*Pater urbis*," 61.

[66] Favro, "*Pater urbis*," 83–84. Augustus seems to boast as much in *Res Gestae* 8.5.

[67] See Meret Strothmann, *Augustus: Vater der res publica. Zur Funktion der drei Begriffe restitutio – saeculum – pater patriae im augusteischen Principat* (Stuttgart: Franz Steiner, 2000), esp. 73–108.

[68] Favro, "*Pater urbis*," 84.

[69] See Harold Mattingly, ed., *Coins of the Roman Empire in the British Museum* (3 vols.; London: British Museum, 1965), Tiberius no. 155, plate 26.5; and others cited in Charles Brian Rose, *Dynastic Commemoration and Imperial Portraiture in the Julio-Claudian Period* (Cambridge: Cambridge University Press, 1997), 225 n. 15.

title upon Julius Caesar in 44 BCE,⁷⁰ a month before he would be assassinated, and also stamped the name along with his image on coins (see Dio 64.4.4).⁷¹ But as Clifford Ando has shown, there appears to be a decided shift from honorific title to *role* with Augustus.⁷² This set a precedent in the way the emperor was both viewed and portrayed.⁷³ Seneca, for example, would write, in an attempt to instruct the young Nero, that any good *princeps* should resemble a good parent.⁷⁴ He lists some honorific titles for the *princeps* but states, "But we have given the name *pater patriae* so that he should know that a father's power has been given to him, constraining him to think of his children's interests and placing his after theirs" (*Clem.* 1.14.2).⁷⁵ The "father-son relationship appears frequently in Julio-Claudian texts as an ameliorative paradigm for the emperor's relationship to his free subjects, particularly the aristocracy."⁷⁶ This is especially on display in Seneca's *De Clementia*.⁷⁷ Seneca begins by establishing and articulating the reaches of young Nero's power: he is the agent of *deus* on earth and the mouthpiece of *fortuna* (1.1.2); he is in control of the status and wealth of persons, kings, cities, and nations (1.2–3); even the "judge of life and death over whole peoples" (1.2; 14.2; 21.2).⁷⁸ Seneca follows his earlier explication of Nero's powers "with setting forth schematically two contrasting modes in which such power can be deployed" (See, esp., 1.11–13).⁷⁹ These contrasting modes are his distinction between *rex* and *tyrannus*. Seneca argues at great length for the father-son model (cf. 1.14.1–16.1), with "the *paterfamilias*, in his dual roles as *pater* and *dominus*, [as]

---

⁷⁰ Sarah A. Nix has argued for an assimilation of the character of Caesar to Jupiter in Lucan's *Bellum Civile*; Sarah A. Nix, "Caesar as Jupiter in Lucan's 'Bellum Civile,'" *CJ* 103.3 (2008): 281.

⁷¹ See J. M. C. Toynbee, "Portraits of Julius Caesar," *Greece & Rome* (*Second Series*) 4.1 (1957): 2–9.

⁷² See Ando, *Imperial Ideology*, 400; cf. 398–404.

⁷³ See, esp., Matthew B. Roller, *Constructing Autocracy: Aristocrats and Emperors in Julio-Claudian Rome* (Princeton: Princeton University Press, 2001), 233–46, 247–64.

⁷⁴ On the *princeps* in relation to Augustus, see Wilhelm Weber, *Princeps: Studienzur Geschichte des Augustus* (Stuttgart: Scientia Verlag Aalen, 1969).

⁷⁵ Here note that Nero is an agent of *deus* on earth. In the Octagonal Room of his Goden House, Nero placed the statue of the dying Gaul. See David L. Balch, *Roman Domestic Art and Early House Churches* (WUNT 228; Tübingen: Mohr Siebeck, 2008), 101–3, place 9, CD 198.

⁷⁶ Roller, *Constructing Autocracy*, 236.

⁷⁷ See J. Osgood, "The *vox* and *verba* of an Emperor: Claudius, Seneca and Le Prince Ideal" *CJ* 102.4 (2007): 329–53.

⁷⁸ Cf. Roller, *Constructing Autocracy*, 236–40.

⁷⁹ Roller, *Constructing Autocracy*, 241.

the obvious social paradigm for the authority of the emperor."[80] Indeed, the ability to govern a household was often seen as equivalent to governing a city.[81] And some would point to one's household as grounds both for promotion and demotion in public affairs.[82] In §14.2–3, Seneca points out that the father-son relationship "has been institutionalized as a model for the emperor through the title *pater patriae*."[83]

Pliny's *Panegyric* to Trajan urged him to view his office as that of "a father and not a master" (*non de domino sed de parente*).[84] Moreover, the abbreviated *p.p.* was in the titular from Augustus to Theodosius.[85] Claudius himself was conferred the title *pater patriae* by the Senate on 42 CE. At first he refused the title,[86] but later took it "when news broke of Appius Silanus' 'conspiracy'."[87] The lobbying for the father-son paradigm reveals a competition over the social and political ordering and development of the principate. Here both aristocracy and emperors themselves "participated in this debate, setting and rejecting different paradigms as appropriate or inappropriate, desirable or undesirable, and so were collectively involved in a continuing negotiation about the nature and limits of the emperor's authority" – and indeed his image.[88]

Clifford Ando has shown how these ideas were translated into "concrete symbols of Roman power" with both "immediate and long-term relevance."[89] Though coins and inscriptions communicating the *pater* imagery of the emperor were cast far and wide, the readers of these inscriptions and spenders of these coins most likely did not understand the political ideologies in every respect. But it was the collection of imperial statues, coins,

---

[80] Roller, *Constructing Autocracy*, 243. Noteworthy, too, is Clifford Ando, "From Republic to Empire," in *Oxford Handbook to Social Relations in the Roman World* (ed. Michael Peachin; Oxford: Oxford University Press, 2011), 37–66.

[81] Euripides *El.* 386–87; Isocrates *Ad Nic.* 19, *Or.* 2; Plutarch *Dinner of Seven Wise Men* 12, *Mor.* 155D.

[82] Isocrates *Ad. Nic.* 41, *Or.* 3.35; Diodorus Siculus *Bib. Hist.* 12.12.1; Marcus Aurelius *Med.* 1.16.4; Diogenes Laertius *Vit.* 170; cf. *Sipre Deut* 32.5.12.

[83] Roller, *Constructing Autocracy*, 244.

[84] Pliny *Pan.* 2.3; 7.4.

[85] Tiberius appears to be the exception. Tacitus states that he only accepted the term with "cold condescension." See Ando, *Imperial Ideology*, 402. See, too, Barbara Levick, *Claudius* (New Haven: Yale University Press, 1990), 41. On Augustus' changing titulature and his claims to power, see Theodor Mommsen, *Römisches Staatsrecht* (2 vols.; Akademische Druck-u: Verlagsanstalt, 1952), 2.818–22; and 2.1139–43. See, too, Ronald Syme, "Imperator Caesar: A Study in Nomenclature," *Historia* 7 (1958): 172–88.

[86] He seems to have suggested that the title had been worn out, especially since it had been give to others such as Gaius. See Levick, *Claudius*, 102.

[87] Levick, *Claudius*, 41.

[88] Roller, *Constructing Autocracy*, 262.

[89] Ando, *Imperial Ideology*, 8; cf. 206–73.

inscriptions and their diffusion "throughout the empire [which] gave to its inhabitants a universal symbolic language that operated across linguistic boundaries."[90] The "idea" of the emperor as *pater* became, to appropriate from Max Weber, an effective force in history.[91] And central to this idea of *pater patriae* is stable succession.[92] Indeed, according to Ando, nothing "illustrates the multiple influences that shaped the evolution and reception of imperial ideology so well as an examination of attitudes toward dynastic succession in the early Principate."[93] One of the primary motivations in the practice of diplomacy under the Roman empire was the spreading the 'good news'; that is; "a victory over an enemy of *res publica*, or the gift of some benefaction to the citizens of empire," or, of course, "the succession of an emperor or the adoption of an heir."[94] One of the strategies emperors employed to communicate stable succession was adoption.[95] Even when the line was clearly arranged, however, as in the case with Augustus and Tiberius,[96] the moment of succession was "fraught with tension."[97] This

---

[90] Ando, *Imperial Ideology*, 8–9. Ando notes that a series of inscriptions from Asia Minor post 2 BCE reflect the titulature form a Greek perspective: e.g., πατὴρ τῆς πατρίδος (father of his country), "that title could imply a distinction between Augustus's role at Rome and his role in the provinces." Others rendered the title: πατὴρ τῆς πατρίδος καὶ τοῦ σύμπαντος τῶν ἀνθρώπων γένους: (father of his fatherland and of the entire human race). Ando, *Imperial Ideology*, 403.

[91] Max Weber, *The Protestant Ethic and the Spirit of Capitalism* (trans. Talcott Parsons: New York: Routledge Classics, 2001), 48.

[92] See Greg Rowe, "*Omnis spes futura paternae stationis*: Public Responses to the Roman Imperial Succession," D.Phil. thesis, The Queen's College, Oxford University, 1997. See, too, Rose, *Dynamic Commemoration and Imperial Portraiture*.

[93] Ando, *Imperial Ideology*, 31–32. Note, too, the important treatment of Augustus' imperial philosophy in Dietmar Kienast, *Augustus: Prinzeps und Monarch*.

[94] Ando, *Imperial Ideology*, 175–76.

[95] None of the Julio Claudian emperors were natural sons of previous emperors. All were adopted except Claudius who was the uncle of Gaius Caligula and himself adopted Nero. Augustus (31 BCE–CE14); Tiberius (14–37); Gaius Caligula (37–41); Claudius (41–54); Nero (54–68).

[96] See Peter Michael Sawn, *The Augustan Succession: An Historical Commentary on Cassius Dio's* Roman History *Books 55–56 (9BC–AD14)* (Oxford: Oxford University Press, 2004). Note, too, Rose's comments on Augustus' establishment of his dynasty; Rose, *Dynastic Commemoration*, 11–21.

[97] See Ando, *Imperial Ideology*, 32 n. 65. On succession in general, though after Nero, see M. Hammond, "The Transmission of the Powers of the Roman Emperor from the Death of Nero in AD 68 to that of Alexander Severus in AD 235," *MAAR* 24 (1956): 61–133. Note, too, C. Simpson, "The Julian Succession and Its Claudian Coda: A Different Perspective on the So-called 'Julio-Claudian' Dynasty," *Latomus* 67 (2008): 253–65; and G. Rowe, *Princes and Political Cultures: The new Tiberian Senatorial Decrees* (Ann Arbor: University of Michigan Press, 2002).

was particularly the case in the anxieties surrounding the succession of Claudius – to which we now turn.[98]

C. Fictive or Familial Continuity? The Example of Britannicus and Nero

The complexities of succession revolve around the awkward tension inherent to notions of the hereditability of the Principate.[99] Constitutional powers as such could not be passed onto successors but social standing and political influence were often enacted by appointed heirs in accordance with Republican custom.[100] In other words, succession was less a legality and more of an enactment of fictive continuity.[101] Though neither the ruling emperor nor the heir-apparent in principle could give legal claim to succession, in practice the threat of civil war left the establishment of fictive continuity in their hands – especially if the heir "had already exercised in the lifetime of the late Princeps the constitutional powers requisite for the Principate."[102] This was the functional significance of adoption – viz., it addressed the anxiety of producing a fitting heir. Nevertheless, as in the cases of Augustus or Claudius, though adoption did not give full security to the fictive line,[103] it allowed the Princeps to proclaim and enact a stable continuity of authority.[104]

---

[98] See, esp., Rose, *Dynamic Commemoration and Imperial Portraiture*, 39–45.

[99] See the final section in Anton von Premerstein, *Vom Werden und Wesen des Prinzipats* (Aus dem Nachlass herausgegeben von Hans Volkmann; Abhandlungen der Bayerischen Akademie der Wissenschaften, Ph.-h. Abt., N.F., Heft 15; Munich: Beck, 1937).

[100] The literature on "succession" is both everywhere and nowhere. That is, there are very few concentrated studies on the phenomenon but it is fairly diffuse. This is owing, in part, to the uncertain relationship between succession of the purely biological kind (along with its related laws of inheritance) and the underdetermined nature of adoptive strategies regarding imperial power in the Roman Principate.

[101] This tension between the law of testamentary succession and definitions of office in public law is on display in the opening of Tacitus' *Annals*. See Anthony J. Woodman, *Tacitus Reviewed* (Oxford: Clarendon Press, 1998) 40–69.

[102] J. G. C. Anderson, "Review of A. von Premerstein, *Vom Werden und Wesen des Prinzipats*," *JRS* 29.1 (1939): 97. Roller states that "legal texts often provide poor and misleading evidence for actual social practices and attitudes." See Matthew B. Roller, *Constructing Autocracy*, 237.

[103] Note especially the literature in Woodman, *Tacitus Reviewed*, 40 n. 2. On Tacitus and Claudius, see D. W. T. C. Vessey, "Thoughts on Tacitus' Portrayal of Claudius," *AJPh* 92 (1971): 385–409.

[104] An important issue for modern scholars is when the principate began. It is one thing for Augustus to be the *de facto* monarch but to assume that his status and position could be "inherited" is complicated by the fact that for such a "succession" to be possible

In the case of Claudius, an added measure of anxiety was introduced to matters of succession when he married his niece, Agrippina, after the execution of his third wife, Messalina.[105] The marriage to Agrippina on New Year's Day in CE 49 put the status of his children with Messallina, Octavia and Britannicus, in jeopardy.[106] In the following year, Agrippina convinced Claudius to adopt Nero into the Claudian *gens*.[107] On several occasions, Claudius appears to have re-arranged his household in order to promote Nero,[108] arranging the marriage with his daughter Octavia in CE 53, and granting Nero the *toga virilis* ahead of his fourteenth year.[109] Claudius worked with the Senate to allow Nero the consulship in his twentieth year. "In the meantime [the Senate] granted him proconsular *imperium*, the power of a general, outside of the city, along with the title *princeps iuventutis*, leader of the youth of Rome, an honor sometimes held by princes of blood relation. A cash donative was given in his name to the soldiers, along with largesse to civilians, and he led a parade of the Praetorian Guard with a shield in his hand."[110] In the realms of religion and *imperium*, "Nero officially was second only to Claudius."[111] Moreover, there was a stated attempt to set Nero's priority over Britannicus in the popular mind. At the games of the circus held to win him popular favor, Britannicus was dressed in the garments of boyhood while Nero wore the *Triumphali veste*

---

there would need to be a permanent change in the constitutional order. The question becomes when this was acknowledged (14, 41, 68 CE?). Tacitus believes the year was 14; on which see Ronald Syme, *Tacitus* (2 vols.; Oxford: Oxford University Press, 1980); Wiseman thinks the death of Caligula was key; T. P. Wiseman, *Flavius Josephus, Death of an Emperor: Translated, with Introduction and Commentary* (Exeter: University of Exeter Press, 1991); which deals with Josephus' *Antiquities of the Jews* (XIX 1–273); see, too, Arthur Ferrill, *Caligula* (London: Thames & London, 1991).

[105] He had earlier married and divorced Plautia Urgulanilla and Aelia Paetina – the former was divorced for adultery and suspicions of murdering her sister-in-law while the latter was divorced owing to have become a political liability. See S. Wood, "Messalina, Wife of Claudius: Propaganda Successes and Failures of His Reign," *JRA* 5 (1992): 219–34.

[106] The birth of Britannicus, especially, gave Messallina immense influence, yet despite Britannicus' birth, her position was not without rivals. See Levick, *Claudius*, 56–57. Indeed, Messallina appeared to have attempted an assassination plot on the young Nero. See, Levick, *Claudius*, 70.

[107] Tacitus *Annals* 12.9.1–2; Seutonius *Claudius* 27.2; 39.2; *Nero* 7; Dio 60.33.2.

[108] See Miriam T. Griffin, *Nero: The End of a Dynasty* (London: Routledge, 2000 [1984]), 29–30; and Levick, *Claudius*, 70–75.

[109] See Tacitus *Annals* 12.41.1; Dio 60.33. Cf. John Aveline, "The Death of Claudius," *Historia: Zeitschrift für Alte Geschichte* 53.4 (2004): 462; also 453–75.

[110] Champlin, *Nero*, 215. Champlin notes that though Nero was never to see an army in peace or in war, "militarism and triumphalism marked Nero's life as a prince in Rome." *Nero*, 215.

[111] Aveline, "The Death of Claudius," 463.

(Tacitus 12.1–4; Suetonius 7.2). "The people would thus behold the one with the decorations of a general, the other in a boy's habit, and would accordingly anticipate their respective destinies."[112]

Complete "data on the reasons why Claudius advanced his adopted older son, [Nero], over his natural son, Britannicus" is missing.[113] Britannicus was born after Claudius' succession by less than three weeks on 12 February 41. He was dubbed the hope of the dynasty, *Spes Augusta*, on coins.[114] Seneca wrote from exile in CE 43, expressing his "will that Britannicus would be Claudius' consort long before he became his successor, attributing to Claudius the plan devised by Augustus for Tiberius" in 9 BCE.[115] With respect to jurisprudence, "Claudius neither broke tradition, nor introduced any new precedent when he designated his adopted son as his principal heir" – the issue is the uncertainty as to why he did so.[116]

Though the sources are somewhat conflicted as to the particulars,[117] added uncertainty appears to surround the succession when Claudius began showing favor to his natural son in the early 50s. He granted Britannicus the *toga virilis* a year prior to the usual fourteenth birthday so that the Roman people might finally have "a real Caesar."[118] This caused some to think that the natural heir was being favored over the adopted son.[119] As Britannicus grew closer to his fourteenth year, however, Claudius "conven-

---

[112] Champlin, *Nero*, 215–16.

[113] Vincent M. Scramuzza, *The Emperor Claudius* (Cambridge: Harvard University Press, 1940), 92.

[114] Note Levick, *Claudius*, 207 n. 6, for references.

[115] Levick, *Claudius*, 92.

[116] Scramuzza, *The Emperor Claudius*, 92. The likely explanation, however, appears to be a political move on Claudius' part to circumvent the fallout of the Messallina scandal as well as Agrippina's political maneuverings. On these "Roman women," see the two volumes of Diana E. E. Kleiner and Susan B. Matheson, *I, Claudia II: Women in Roman Art and Society* (Austin: University of Texas Press, 2000); and Annelise Freisenbruch, *The First Ladies of Rome: The Women Behind the Caesars* (London: Jonathan Cape, 2010), 119–57. It should be noted that there is enough "convenient" gendered history of "good" emperors (e.g., Augustus and Claudius) being exonerated from their "bad" heirs by placing the blame of their succession on their scheming wives to make one suspicious of the veracity of such claims.

[117] "The main resistance to Agrippina's plans for the sole succession of Nero is attributed by Tacitus to Claudius' freedman Narcissus, while Suetonius and Dio see Claudius himself battling for his son." Levick, *Claudius*, 75.

[118] Suetonius *Claudius*, 43; cf. Dio 60.34.1; Tacitus *Annals* 12.65.3. Tacitus, however, differs slightly from these accounts – most pointedly in that the reconciliation of the two had yet to happen. Indeed, the very reason that Agrippina did not slowly poison Claudius was so that he would not recognize the plot and renew affections with his natural son (12.66.1). On all of this, see Aveline, "The Death of Claudius," 455.

[119] On the politics within court from 48–54 with respect to Nero and Britannicus, see Levick, *Claudius*, 72–79.

iently" died.[120] The untimely death of Claudius – or, perhaps, timely from the perspective of Agrippina and her son, Nero – increased succession anxieties. All three major ancient sources agree that Agrippina poisoned Claudius,[121] and she appears both to have attempted to cover up Claudius' death as well as keep Britannicus out of sight owing to his threat as natural offspring (Tacitus *Annals* 12.68.2).[122] Moreover, the suppression of Claudius' will may have stoked these fires.[123] Some theorize that Agrippina was involved owing to the possibility of Claudius changing his will to favor Britannicus over Nero (see Tacitus *Annals* 12.69.3).[124] Levick, based upon Claudius' final speech to the Senate in which he admonishes them to look after both his sons (Suetonius *Claudius* 46), thinks that the will had made them joint-heirs.[125]

Whatever the case may have been, what followed was a struggle over the succession.[126] There also appears to be some instances of rallying be-

---

[120] On the complexities surrounding the poisoning of Claudius, see Edward Champlin, *Nero* (Cambridge: The Balknap Press of Harvard University Press, 2003), 44–46.

[121] Though see, generally, Aveline, "The Death of Claudius." Aveline suggest this agreement reveals a common source: viz., Pliny the Elder; Aveline, "The Death of Claudius," 467.

[122] On the deserting of Britannicus, see Levick, *Claudius*, 210 n. 13.

[123] Levick states that "Tacitus tells us that the will was not read in public, to prevent the fact that Nero had been preferred to Britannicus causing an upset. He is wrong about this reason. Nero's position depended heavily on a favorable will. What the public must not know was that Britannicus and Nero had been instituted equal heirs in it. In his last address to the senate Claudius had commended both youths to them." *Claudius*, 78.

[124] From 51 CE onward, however, "the Roman mint, so sensitive to the realities of power, looked to Agrippina and Nero, as did Balkan and other provincial mints; ignored at Rome, Britannicus still kept a place alongside Nero in provincial issues, and at Sinope even took an obverse, Nero appearing on the reverse. Time proved this a misreading of the situation." Levick, *Claudius*, 73; see also, 210 n. 15. Images of Britannicus appear in Thessaloniki as well. See A. Burnett and M. Amandry, eds., (1992–), *Roman Provincial Coinage*. London and Paris: British Museum Press and Bibliothèque Nationale. Vol. I (1992): *From the Death of Caesar to the Death of Vitellius* (44 BC–AD 69) by A. Burnett, M. Amandry, and P. P. Ripollès. Supplement 1 (1998). See *RPC* I: 1588ff.

[125] See Levick, *Claudius*, 78. See, too, A. A. Barrett, *Agrippina: Sex, Power and Politics in the Early Empire* (New Haven, Conn: Yale University Press, 1996), 139. Aveline, however, cautions that we should exercise caution in "assuming that merely because the will was not read that its provisions were not honoured." See Aveline, "The Death of Claudius," 467.

[126] Britannicus was not the only rival to Nero's throne: so were Faustus Cornelius Sulla, Rubellius Plautus, Marcus Junius Silanus, Decimus Silanus Torquatus, Lucius Junius Silanus Torquatus, Annius Pollio and Annius Vinicianus. See Robert Samuel Rogers, "Heirs and Rivals to Nero," *Transactions and Proceedings of the American Philological Association* 86 (1955): 190–212, esp. 195–96. See, too, Eugen Cizek, *L'Époque de Néron et ses Controverses Idéologiques* (Leiden: Brill, 1972), 80–83, 88–92; Isabelle Cogitore, *La Légitimité Dynastique D'Auguste à L'épreuve des Conspirations* (Rome: École Fran-

hind Britannicus as in the case of the equestrian Julius Densus (Tacitus *Annals* 13.10.3).[127] Tensions began to manifest themselves between Nero and Britannicus as well. There is an interesting report of the celebration of Saturnalia in December of 54 CE where Nero "was chosen by lot from among his friends to play" *Rex Saturnalicius*. Britannicus is said to have been ordered to give an oration extemporaneously by Nero in order to shame him but Britannicus turned the tables by crafting his poem in a way "in which it was indicated that he had been turned out of his paternal abode and the supremacy" (Tacitus *Annals* 13.15.2). This slight caused Nero to have "redoubled his hatred' (Tacitus *Annals* 13.15.3), and, if Tacitus can be trusted, began plotting his poisoning (Tacitus *Annals* 13.15.3–5).[128] Tacitus further suggests that several "writers of those times" reported Nero's sexual molestation of Britannicus "on frequent days" before he was poisoned (13.17.2). The issues involved were not related to sexual attraction "but violent humiliation of a political rival before a society familiar with the idea of sexual assault as punishment."[129] These tensions only grew as Agrippina's power began to shrink after her falling out with Nero (Tacitus *Annals* 13.12.1).[130] In an apparent last-ditch effort to regain control, she denounced and threatened Nero. And in a bizarre political *mea culpa*, Agrippina is reported by Tacitus to have said that

> Britannicus was now old enough for the throne, the true and worthy heir to his father's power, now wielded by the engrafted adopted son through the wrongs herself had committed; she would willingly reveal all the woes of the unhappy house, including her marriage to Claudius and her poisoning of him; the gods and she had taken one precaution – her stepson still lived; she and Britannicus would go to the praetorian camp; the Guard would listen to her, Germanicus' daughter (*Annals* 13.14.3–6).[131]

Nero, proving himself to be his mother's son, responded by poisoning Britannicus in the beginning of 55 CE (Tacitus *Annals* 13.15–17; Dio 61.7.4;

çaise de Rome, 2002), 14, 205, 209, 235. See, too, Vasily Rudich, *Political Dissidence Under Nero: The Price of Dissimulation* (London: Routledge, 1993).

[127] The indictment was rejected.

[128] We should, however, show some suspicion of Tacitus' account. Recent commentators are more skeptical of this account, seeing it as the replication of a common trope within anti-Nero myth-making. The claim itself is questioned by Seneca – though, of course, here we should question Seneca's reasons for this disputation. Cf. Barrett, 171.

[129] Champlin, *Nero*, 165. Champlin refers readers to T. P. Wiseman, "A World Not Ours," in *Catullus and His World: A Reappraisal* (Cambridge: Cambridge University Press, 1986), 11–12.

[130] Cf. Rogers, "Heirs and Rivals to Nero," 198, for a discussion of the fallout of Nero and Agrippina.

[131] Rogers, "Heirs and Rivals to Nero," 198.

Suetonius 33.2).[132] As Ovid might have said, "even brothers show scant love and faith" (*Metamorphoses* 1.205).

Even in death, however, Britannicus figured in the imaginary of the public.[133] Titus, Vespasian's son, had been educated alongside Britannicus in his youth. Suetonius states that the "Flavians made every effort to identify Titus with Britannicus, even propagate the story that Titus had been sitting near Britannicus at the fatal banquet in 55 when he was poisoned; he had even taken a sip of the poison himself."[134] The Flavians viewed Britannicus as the legitimate successor of Claudius whose rightful place was usurped by Nero.[135] In an effort to keep the memory of Britannicus alive and further his own claim, Titus had statues of Britannicus erected: one made of gilt in the Palatium; the other of ivory equestrian "which was still being carried in procession at the Circus in Suetonius' day."[136] Moreover, during Titus' reign (79–81), coins were minted in Britannicus' honor.[137] These political posturings on the part of Titus to further his own claim belies an attempt to mitigate the instabilities of succession by grafting himself into the stable line of rightful power.

To what degree Paul was aware of the particulars of this succession squabble is difficult to venture a guess. Even more difficult is to discern how much he would have known, or how much would have been possible to know at the writing of his epistle to the Galatian assembly. The aim of the previous two sections has been to form a narrative of the thriving *pater* imagery on display in Rome's imperial ideology and offer a near-contemporary example of succession anxieties which were being played out on the widest stage possible. In what follows I would like to attempt a brief reading of Galatians by giving special attention first to Paul's own "father" imagery; and, then, second, to his imagery of "adoption," "sons," and "heirs." I am not arguing for any kind of dependence or originating cause, or offering some new theory of the Galatian "crisis."[138] The aim is

---

[132] Cf. Champlin, *Nero*, 85.

[133] See P. Murgatroyd, "Tacitus on the Deaths of Britannicus and Claudius," *Eranos* 103.2 (2005): 97–100.

[134] Cf. Levick, *Claudius*, 190–91.

[135] Suetonius also discusses the rehabilitation of Narcissus in the Flavian period. In his biography of Titus, "the freedman is made to prophecy that he, unlike Britannicus, would succeed his father." See, Levick, *Claudius*, 190–91.

[136] Levick, *Claudius*, 191.

[137] See, esp., Levick, *Claudius*, 237 n. 13.

[138] Though, cf. J. Louis Martyn, *Galatians* (AB 33A; New Haven, Conn.: Yale University Press, 2004), 302–6 and 377–78 where he comments on Paul's engagement with the "Teachers" precisely on who are the rightful heirs of Abraham. I follow Martyn here and see Paul and the "agitators" as engaging in some sort of succession squabble regarding the heirs of Abraham. See, too, Martyn, *Galatians*, 84, with 117–26. See, too, James C. Walters, "Paul, Adoption, and Inheritance," in *Paul in the Greco-Roman World: A*

more modest: viz., to show how similar tropes were told in radically *indifferent* ways to each other. What is more, there is no attempt to separate Jewish or Roman "influences" into neat separable entities.[139] Paul's reaction to or his inhabitation within the Roman world cannot be divorced from his complex relationship with Judaism or the peculiarities of his own person. Paul's sources of his "self" are a negotiation between and within these worlds. My aim in this section, therefore, is to discern Paul's peculiar epistemology which coordinates the rhetorical, political, and meaning-making web which is spun in this letter by placing his succession narrative next to the dominant script described above.

D. Paul's Radical Recast? Father, Son(s), and Heirs

Within Galatians, there appear to be four referents to Paul's father imagery: God (1:1, 3, 4; 4:6 cf. 1:16; 2:20; 3:26; 4:4, 7),[140] Abraham (3:7–9, 16, 29; cf. 3:14; 4:22), to whomever τῶν πατρικῶν μου παραδόσεων refers (1:14),[141] and Paul himself (4:19).[142] In the Hebrew scriptures, God as father is a key metaphor in the episodes of exodus and exile. The Lord said to Pharaoh, "Israel is my firstborn son [Υἱὸς πρωτότοκός], and I told you let my people [τὸν λαόν μου] go, so he may worship me" (Exod 4:22–23; cf. Jer 31:9; Isa 63:16). God as father and Israel as son – or God as parent and Israel as child – provides a tensive trope through which to reflect upon

---

Handbook (ed. J. Paul Sampley; London: Trinity Press International, 2003), 65. This seems to make good historical sense in asking what from the "past made possible the traces that now remain, what were the conditions of their production?" On which, see Elizabeth A. Clark, *History, Theory, Text: Historians and the Linguistic Turn* (Cambridge, Mass.: Harvard University Press, 2004), 157.

[139] This, of course, is not a new discovery. Note D. E. H. Whiteley, *The Theology of St Paul* (Blackwell: Oxford, 1964), 5; Cyrus H. Gordon, *Before the Bible: The Common Background of Greek and Hebrew Civilizations* (London: Harper & Row, 1963), 7; and, of course, Martin Hengel, *Judaism and Hellenism: Studies in Their Encounter in Palestine During the Early Hellenistic Period* (trans. John Bowden; Philadelphia: Fortress, 1974).

[140] See Mary Rose D'Angelo, "Abba and 'Father': Imperial Theology and the Jesus Traditions," *JBL* 111 (1992): 611–30.

[141] J. Louis Martyn suggests that this phrase "is one of the typical expressions by which virtually any Jew of the time referred to the Law, the venerable tradition studied under the guidance of senior scholars." *Galatians*, 155.

[142] Paul uses paternal imagery elsewhere and explicit maternal imagery in places like Gal 4:19 and 1 Thess 2:7. See Abera M. Mengestu, *God as Father in Paul: Kinship Language and Identity Formation in Early Christianity* (Eugene, Ore.: Pickwick, 2013). On the "maternity of Paul," see Beverly Roberts Gaventa, *Our Mother Saint Paul* (Louisville: Westminster John Knox, 2007), 29–39.

God's relationship with Israel largely through themes of care and punishment (e.g., Deut 1:31–32; 8:5; 32:18; Isa 1:2; 43:6–7; Hos 11:1).[143] Writers through the second-temple period continued this trajectory as well, reflecting on the imagery of God as father to Israel (e.g., Sir 4:10; 36:17; *Jos. Asen.* 6:3; 18:11; 21:4; 23:10; *Jub.* 1:24–25; 2:19–20; *4 Ezra* 6:58; cf. *Pss. Sol.* 17:30; 18:4).[144] There are also instances in which God is portrayed as father to the king of Israel – many times through adoption formulae (e.g., 2 Sam 7:14; 1 Chron 17:13; 22:10; 28:6).[145] Most well-known, of course, is LXX Psalm 2:7,

The king says, "I will announce the Lord's decree. He said to me:
'You are my son!' This very day I have become your father! (Υἱός μου εἶ σύ ἐγὼ σήμερον γεγέννηκά σε)

Abraham is also referred to as "father" throughout the Hebrew scriptures.[146] He is referred to as "the father of a multitude of nations" (πατέρα πολλῶν ἐθνῶν; Gen 17:5; cf. 26:3; Josh 24:2; Isa 51:2).[147]

Galatians opens with a salutation naming God as father (πατήρ, 1:1). Paul himself can use the image of πατήρ in various ways which can both strengthen his solidarity with his hearers or construct a sense of distance – be it Paul's authority within the assembly or to highlight outright opposition between groups. Abraham is significant in this respect in that he remains the paternal pincer of the promise.[148] In Paul's imaginative scriptural exegesis of Gen 15:5–6,[149] what T. R. Glover has called in a different con-

---

[143] See, too, Mal 2:10; Ps 103:13; and the issues of loving orphans in, e.g., Deut 10:18; Ps 68:5.

[144] Israel as an only child is on display in such texts as 4Q504 as well. God is noted as "Father" in Philo's (*Sobr.* 56); and as "the primal God and Father of all" (*Abr.* 75).

[145] Gerald Cooke, "The Israelite King as Son of God," *ZAW* 73.2 (2012): 202–25.

[146] On the promises to Abraham, see Gen 12:1–3; 15:5, 18–21; 17:4–8; Exod 6:6–8. Interestingly, Philo refers to him as God's adopted son (*Sobr.* 56).

[147] Abraham proved a useful figure to "think with" in texts from the DSS – some eighty occurrences with three extended treatments in 4Q252; 1QapGen, 1Q20; and 4Q225. Note, too, the Damascus Document.

[148] Here see Bruce W. Longenecker, *The Triumph of Abraham's God: The Transformation of Identity in Galatians* (London: T&T Clark, 2001); and, Francis Watson, *Paul and the Hermeneutics of Faith* (London: T&T Clark, 2004) and his first two chapters on Genesis.

[149] Worth comparing is Paul's reading of Abraham with Philo's in *Heres*, particularly in his transforming of Abraham's question into "can this blood-life be the heir of higher things?" And God's answer of what comes out of his seed will be his heir. See, especially, Watson, *Paul and the Hermeneutics of Faith*, 63–68; and, Richard B. Hays, *The Conversion of the Imagination: Paul as Interpreter of Israel's Scripture* (Grand Rapids: Eerdmans, 2005).

text, Paul's "curious way of playing with the text of Scripture,"[150] he appears to be (re)focusing the identity of the assembly around those who are and those who are not υἱοί εἰσιν Ἀβραάμ (3:7, 9).[151] Those who are, are οἱ ἐκ πίστεως, which Martyn translates as "those whose identity is derived from faith,"[152] with the demonstrative pronoun οὗτοι serving as a marker of contrast between "Law-people" and "faith-people."[153]

It is in Paul's construction of Abraham as a paternal pincer which sets his own intrigue of succession in motion: viz., who are the legitimate heirs of Abraham?[154] Paul himself locates his prior way-of-being as formerly rooted within the natural heirs of Abraham (1:14),[155] but introduces a pronounced break with Ὅτε δέ in v. 15 referring to how God καλέσας [με] διά τῆς χάριτος αὐτος.[156] Paul even sets up a distinction between natural and adoptive imagery with respect to his apostleship (1:1; 11–12, 16). This break begins to present itself within the assembly where Peter and οἱ λοιποὶ Ἰουδαῖοι are reported to have συνυπεκρίθησαν (2:13).[157] Paul proleptically introduces the rival heirs with the contrasting φύσις and πίστις (2:15–16) –

---

[150] T. R. Glover, *The Conflict of Religions in the Early Roman Empire* (London: Methuen, 1909), 155.

[151] Martyn argues that here (and in 3:29) we can see Paul taking "pains to connect his exegetical argument in 3:6–4:7 with the Teachers' theme of descent from Abraham." *Galatians*, 306.

[152] Martyn, *Galatians*, 299.

[153] Martyn, *Galatians*, 299; cf. Richard B. Hays, "The Letter to the Galatians," in *The New Interpreter's Bible: Second Corinthians–Philemon* (vol. 11; Nashville: Abingdon, 2000), 255. Hays prefers "circumcision people."

[154] It should be stressed that to reduce this reading of Galatians to a tired rerun of the so-called "parting of the ways" is to miss the point. Such simplistic understandings of the "parting of the ways" confuses beliefs, practices, and the multiplicity of disagreement: e.g., theological, socio-culture, and institutional. See, e.g., Barclay, "Pauline Churches, Jewish Communities and the Roman Empire," 23 n. 53.

[155] See Jörg Frey, "Paul's Jewish Identity," in *Jewish Identity in the Greco-Roman World: Jüdische Identität in der griechische-römischen Welt* (AJEC 71; ed. Jörg Frey, Daniel R. Schwartz, and Stephanie Gripentrog; Leiden: Brill, 2007), 285–322; Daniel Boyarin, *A Radical Jew: Paul and the Politics of Identity* (Berkeley: University of California Press, 1994).

[156] Throughout Paul is quite careful to differentiate his calling and new identity as originating with God and the Spirit as opposed to flesh and natural origins (e.g. 1:1, 16, 17, 19; 2:1, 6; cf. 2:8).

[157] Worth noting is Walter Schmithals, *Paulus, die Evangelien und das Urchristentum: Beiträge von und zu Walter Schmithals von Walter Schmithals* (ed. Cilliers Breytenbach; Leiden: Brill, 2004), esp. 5–38. See, too, James D. G. Dunn, "What was the Issue between Paul and 'Those of the Circumcision'?" in *Paulus und das antike Judentum* (WUNT 58; ed. Martin Hengel and Ulrich Heckel; Tübingen: Mohr Siebeck, 1991), 295–318.

which is further expanded into πνεῦμα and σάρξ (3:2–3).¹⁵⁸ Again in 3:9, Paul speaks of οἱ ἐκ πίστεως as the progeny of promise and rehearses the logic of his (re)reading of Gen 15:6–7 in 3:16 and 3:29,¹⁵⁹ and illustrates it further in 4:21–31. The comments in 3:7 are thus a remarkable claim with respect to the true heirs of Abraham: οἱ ἐκ πίστεως.¹⁶⁰ The way Paul justifies this statement is by claiming that the scriptural promises to Abraham and his "offspring" consisted of a singular heir which is Christ (3:16).¹⁶¹ In this sense, ἡ εὐλογία τοῦ Ἀβραὰμ γένηται ἐν Χριστῷ Ἰησοῦ (3:14) as does ἡ κληρονομία (3:18).¹⁶²

This, of course, puts Paul in a pickle with respect to the law: Τί οὖν ὁ νόμος (3:19)?¹⁶³ On the surface of Paul's argument the law and promise seem contrary (cf. 3:21). Paul irons away this wrinkle by reading the law as somehow preparatory (3:21–4:7).¹⁶⁴ Whatever the mechanics of this preparatory relationship might be, for Paul – now that faith has come (ἐλθούσης δὲ τῆς πίστεως) – those characterized by πίστις are υἱοὶ θεοῦ (3:24–26); viz., κατ' ἐπαγγελίαν κληρονόμοι (3:29).¹⁶⁵ Paul extends his argument – and, perhaps, confuses his metaphors – by loosely incorporating

---

[158] See Jörg Frey, "Die paulinische Antithese von Fleisch un Geist und die palästinisch-jüdische Weisheitstradiction," *ZNW* 90 (1999): 45–77; cf. too, Jörg Frey, "The Notion of 'Flesh' in 4QInstruction and the Background of Pauline Usage," in *Sapiential, Poetical and Liturgical Texts: Published in the Memory of Maruice Baillet* (STJD 35; ed. D. Falk, F. García Martínez, and E. Schuller; Leiden: Brill, 2000), 197–226.

[159] See John Riches, *Galatians through the Centuries* (Oxford: Blackwell, 2008), 204–13; and Martin Meiser, *Galater* (Göttingen: Vandenhoeck & Ruprecht, 2007), 175–77.

[160] Hans Dieter Betz sees this construction intentionally crafted in opposition to οἱ ἐξ ἔργων νόμου in 3:1; Hans Dieter Betz, *Galatians* (Hermeneia; Minneapolis: Fortress, 1989), 141–42.

[161] Martyn is keen to point out Paul's following of a midrashic form of reading scripture where one reading is negated by a second reading; Martyn, *Galatians*, 338–39.

[162] Cf. Brendan Byrne, *'Sons of God' – 'Seed of Abraham': A Study of the Idea of the Sonship of God of All Christians against the Jewish Background* (AnBib 83; Rome: Biblical Institute, 1979). Note, too, James Hester, "The Heir and *Heilsgeschichte*: A Study of Galatians 4:1ff.," in *OIKONOMIA: Heilsgeschichte als Thema der Theologie* (Festschrift für Oscar Cullmann; ed. Felix Christ; Hamburg: Herbert Reich, 1967), 118–25. Hester sees inheritance as a metaphor which functions to preserve unity through elements of discontinuity.

[163] See, e.g., Terence L. Donaldson, *Paul and the Gentiles: Remapping the Apostle's Convictional World* (Minneapolis: Fortress, 1997), 165–86; James D. G. Dunn, *The Theology of Paul the Apostle* (Grand Rapids: Eerdmans, 1998), 22, 719–22; Arland J. Hultgren, "Paul and the Law," pp. 202–15 in Stephen Westerholm, ed., *The Blackwell Companion to Paul* (Oxford: Wiley-Blackwell, 2011); and, of course, E. P. Sanders, *Paul, the Law, and the Jewish People* (Philadelphia: Fortress, 1983), *inter alia*.

[164] See David Lull, "'The Law was Our Pedagogue': A Study in Galatians 3:19–25," *JBL* 105 (1986): 481–98.

[165] The trope Children of Abraham "is one of the ways of naming the church of God." Martyn, *Galatians*, 306.

Roman laws surrounding the tutelage of heirs (4:1–7).[166] The "fundamental theme" of 4:1–7 is "the believer as 'heir'" – picking up the earlier discussion of those who belong to Christ as heirs according to promise (3:29) and not on the basis of Law observation (3:18).[167] The twist, however, is that the identity of those characterized by πίστις are no longer referred to as descendents of Abraham but as the adopted sons (υἱοθεσίαν) and heirs (κληρονόμος) of God (4:5–7).[168] The Galatians are "taken by God into his own family."[169] The fatherhood of God here harkens back to the beginning of the letter (1:1–5), where its functional significance is revealed in Paul's language of adoption and inheritance.[170] God alone, for Paul, is Father, and in opposition to the teaching of the "agitators,"[171] he develops "the notion

---

[166] See specifically, Betz, *Galatians*, 202–4. See David Ibbetson and Andrew Lewis, eds., *The Roman Law Tradition* (Cambridge: Cambridge University Press, 1994). For a helpful introduction to the problematics surrounding matters of method and the sources themselves, see David Johnston, *Roman Law in Context* (Cambridge: Cambridge University Press, 1999), 2–29; and Franz Wieacker, *Römische Rechtsgeschichte: Quellenkunde, Rechtsbildung, Jurisprudenz und Rechtsliteratur* (Munich: C. H. Beck, 1988), 63–182. Here cf. Walters, "Paul, Adoption and Inheritance," 42–76.

[167] Martin C. de Boer, "The Meaning of the Phrase τὰ στοιχεῖα τοῦ κοσμοῦ in Galatians," *NTS* 53 (2007): 204–24; here at 208–09. See, too, Hans Hübner, "Paulusforschung seit 1945: Ein kritischer Literaturbericht," *ANRW* 25.4:2691–94; cf. James M. Scott, *Adoption as Sons of God: An Exegetical Investigation into the Background of ΥΙΟΘΕΣΙΑ in the Corpus Paulinium* (WUNT 2/48; Tübingen: J. C. B. Mohr, 1992), 157–61.

[168] "Does Paul here rescind the formula of 3:28 with its affirmation of the erasure of sexual distinctions in Christ? No. He uses the word 'sons' inclusively in order to draw the link between God's Son and God's family, the members of which are sons by being incorporated into the Son." Martyn, *Galatians*, 391. See Walters, who claims that "Paul's use of the word 'inheritance' is unparalleled in Greco-Roman usage outside of Judaism." "Paul, Adoption, and Inheritance," 42. For Roman law contexts, see, alternatively, Francis Lyall, *Slaves, Citizens, Sons: Legal Metaphors in the Epistles* (Grand Rapids: Zondervan, 1984), 98; and David Williams, *Paul's Metaphors: Their Context and Character* (Peabody, Mass.: Hendrickson, 1999), 64–65. On 4:7, see Meiser, *Galater*, 175–77.

[169] Martyn, *Galatians*, 391.

[170] Cf. Betz, *Galatians*, 39 n. 27. The complex issue of adoption cannot detain us here owing to space and for the reason that the issues has been thoroughly worked through by others. See, e.g., Scott, *Adoption*; and Charles A. Wanamaker, "The Son and the Sons of God: A Study in Elements of Paul's Christological and Soteriological Thought," (Ph.D. diss., University of Durham, 1980). Scott argues that υἱοθεσία in the Hellenistic period "always denotes 'adoption as sons' and never merely, as commonly supposed, 'sonship'" (xiv). Elsewhere he intimates that this is a "sure conclusion" (267).

[171] There have been many intriguing works on the influence and identity of the "agitators" by the likes of Bruce W. Longenecker (*The Triumph of Abraham's God*, 25–34), and especially the mirror-reading efforts of J.M.G. Barclay ("Mirror-Reading a Polemical Letter: Galatians as a Test Case," *JSNT* 31 [1987]: 73–93); and now Nijay K. Gupta ("Mirror-Reading Moral Issues in Paul's Letters," *JSNT* 34.4 [2012]: 361–81). Susan Elliott is right to suspect such readings in light of the fact that "Paul addresses his audience, not his adversaries." *Cutting Too Close for Comfort: Paul's Letter to the Galatians*

that the Galatians are the liberated children of the God who is the gracious Father."[172] This puts the fatherhood of Abraham in a somewhat "distinctly secondary place,"[173] while making fragile questions of ethnicity and the natural heir.[174] "In Paul's perspective the grace of God, experienced in Christ, relativizes all such human traditions, including Judaism."[175]

The rhetorical effect of Paul's fictive line is the construction of a clear wedge between, from his perspective, οἱ σὺν ἐμοὶ πάντες ἀδελφοί (1:2),[176] and the ψευδάδελφος (2:4).[177] It is through his genealogy of the succession of promise,[178] as it were, that Paul constructs the space of οἰκείους τῆς πίστεως (6:10) – which he later terms καινὴ κτίσις (6:15).[179] To appropriate from the words of Knausgaard, he "combats fiction with fiction."[180] As

---

in its Anatolian Cultic Context (JSNTSup 248; London: T&T Clark, 2003), 3. Elliott is correct to stress the "turn to the audience" as opposed to hypothetical mirror readings (1–6). She sees the world of the audience as the "central matter" (349).

[172] Martyn, *Galatians*, 84. For a different view, see, generally, Scott J. Hafemann, "Paul and the Exile in Galatians 3–4," in *Exile: Old Testament, Jewish, and Christian Conceptions* (JSJSup 56; ed. James M. Scott; Leiden: Brill, 1997), 329–62.

[173] Martyn, *Galatians*, 84.

[174] Though it is unlikely that Paul or his readers had an extensive knowledge of Greek or Roman law regarding inheritance and adoption, it is worth noting that in matters of adoption, "Roman jurists were concerned almost entirely with succession rights to property." Walters, "Paul, Adoption, and Inheritance," 52. See, generally, Jane F. Gardner, *Family and Familia in Roman Law and Life* (Oxford: Clarendon, 1998); and Marek Kurylowicz, *Die adoptio im klassischen römischen Recht* (Studia antiqua 6; Warsaw: University of Warszawskeigo, 1981). In this sense, it could be configured that the metaphorical reading of the land of promise is given a physical dimension in property rites. Walters sees "four points of contact between Greco-Roman adoption and inheritance practices" reflected in Galatians: the association of adoption and inheritance; if a son, then an heir; certainty of the adoptee's right to inherit; adoption as a metaphor for status change" (p. 56).

[175] Barclay, *Obeying the Truth*, 241.

[176] Paul repeatedly addresses the assembly as ἀδελφοί (1:11; 3:15; 4:12, 28, 31; 5:11, 13; 6:1; 6:18).

[177] On the complex issues of anti-semitism, see Michael Bachmann, *Anti-Judaism in Galatians? Exegetical Studies on a Polemical Letter and on Paul's Theology* (trans. Robert L. Brawley; Grand Rapids: Eerdmans, 2008 [1999]). Noteworthy, too, is the discussion of flesh and spirit as "two family trees" in Susan Eastman, *Recovering Paul's Mother Tongue: Language and Theology in Galatians* (Grand Rapids: Eerdmans, 2007), 161–79. Though in no way should we attempt to minimize the barbarism which has attended the reception of such language in Galatians, space should be allowed for strong intra-polemical language *within* Judaism to remain 'within its own environment' before thoughtlessly read with anachronistic categories of "Christian" vs. "Jew."

[178] See Herman Ridderbos, *Paul: An Outline of His Theology* (trans. John Richard de Witt; London: SPCK, 1977 [1966]), 197–204.

[179] For the linking of these two images, see Martyn, *Galatians*, 554.

[180] Knausgaard, *My Struggle*, 222.

such, relationality is restructured as is what we may call the *statio* of the people of God. The "natural" sons characterized by φύσις are passed over by those characterized by πίστις in Paul's succession narrative.[181] Paul's "strong relativising statements" in Gal 3:28 places constructed ethnic difference under erasure in light of the *novum*.[182] The adopted children characterized by faith are thus in the place of succession over the natural heirs (cf. 4:21–5:1). The central antitheses introduced in the letter are therefore not necessarily Christ and law, cross or circumcision, slave or free, natural heir or adopted heir – or Christ and Caesar! – but new creation and cosmos. Everything else is resituated within this mapping (cf. 6:15).[183]

E. Some (Theo)(Political) Conclusions

It is difficult to know what precisely to make of these two narratives of fathers, sons, and succession squabbles. Any similarities of the imperial political ideology of *pater* and Paul's theology of God as πατήρ on display in Gal 1:1–5, e.g., are equally overwhelmed with difference. And, if Paul wrote his letter sometime between or after 49CE–54, there was a public narrative regarding succession struggles into which Paul could have anchored his, or, at least, with which his would have resonated. Despite these similarities the rest is silence. How should one interpret this silent nearness?[184] One way is to "read after the lines of Paul" the inference that all

---

[181] Cf. the work of C. Johnson Hodge, *If Sons, then Heirs: A Study of Kinship and Ethnicity in the Letters of Paul* (Oxford: Oxford University Press, 2007); note, too, Love L. Sechrest, *A Former Jew: Paul and the Dialectics of Race* (London: T&T Clark, 2009), 111–64.

[182] Cf. Barclay, "Pauline Churches, Jewish Communities and the Roman Empire," 13. Cf., too, his important discussion on ethnic and non-ethnic communities; Barclay, "Pauline Churches, Jewish Communities and the Roman Empire," 12–15. It could be argued that in light of the widespread visual representation of the Gauls in Rome, Athens, and asia Minor as barbarians/Asians defeated by the Romans, opponents who die when faced by Greco-Roman power, Gal 3:28 offers the Gauls a radical revision of the visual image projected onto them by the colonizing power, Rome, which they would have likely to have seen – and internalized.

[183] See Beverly Roberts Gaventa, "The Singularity of the Gospel: A Reading of Galatians," pp. 147–59 in *Pauline Theology* (vol. 1; ed. Jouette Bassler; Minneapolis: Fortress, 1991) 149. See Jerome H. Neyrey, *Paul, In Other Words: A Cultural Reading of His Letters* (Louisville: Westminster John Knox, 1990) and his comments on "maps of people" (32–33) and "God's different maps" and issues of divine "disorder" (58–65).

[184] In many respects this silence is precisely the point. In the foregoing discussion we briefly outlined two contemporaneous succession narratives: one imperial and one Pauline. They have some interesting similarities and differences, but ultimately neither interacts with the other nor shows any direct concern. But there are many parallel practices

that Christ *is*, Caesar is *not*. God is the true πατήρ; the true *pater patriae* and Caesar is not.[185] God is the true benefactor, the true giver of grace and Caesar is not; the true giver of peace and Caesar is not, and so on. Another way is to take the route of postcolonial "mimicry."[186] Homi K. Bhabha describes "mimicry" as the desire "for a reformed, recognizable Other, *as a subject of a difference that is almost the same, but not quite.*" A discourse of "mimicry emerges as the representation of a difference that is itself a process of disavowal."[187] In this sense, Paul's theology of God as πατήρ, then, is almost the same as imperial political ideology of *pater*...but not quite. The succession squabbles between Paul and the "agitators" are almost the same as those between Nero and Britannicus...but not quite.

Yet it is at this point where I actually think that Paul was doing something far more radical than "subverting" empire, or "mimicking" empire as a form of disavowal, or composing "hidden transcripts" on empire's public stage. At least in Galatians, Paul's "politics of inheritance"[188] altogether neglected to attend to empire's ideologies, narratives of rationality, and cosmologies while busily constructing his own. To call this "neglect," of course, is an interpretive move as indifference assumes some measure of Paul's awareness of the *pater* imagery and succession squabbles surveyed above. A more measured approach might be to explore the political space created by Paul's ignorance of these tropes. In other words, what does Paul's ignorance of *Roman* politics – so far as we can tell – reveal of *his* politics? My articulation of Paul's politics of *neglect*, however, is an extension of and informed by Agamben's complex notion of "inoperativi-

---

and beliefs between Paul and surrounding religions which never explicitly intersect or interact: e.g., the beliefs of the Cybele cult of the Galli on circumcision or penis-cutting. These could have been included as well to prove the underlying point of Paul's fundamental disinterest in such realities.

[185] The challenge in this comparison, however, is over the complexities of *patriae*. The Christian is not one with a fatherland. In this regard, one should note interesting reflections in the *Epistle to Diognetus* 5.

[186] See Christopher D. Stanley, ed., *The Colonized Apostle: Paul through Postcolonial Eyes* (Minneapolis: Fortress, 2011); Davina C. Lopez, "Visualizing Significant Otherness: Reimagining Paul(ine Studies) through Hybrid Lenses," in *The Colonized Apostle: Paul through Postcolonial Eyes* (ed. Christopher D. Stanley; Minneapolis: Fortress, 2011), 74–94.

[187] Homi K. Bhabha, *The Location of Culture* (London: Routledge, 1994), 86.

[188] See Mark Forman, *The Politics of Inheritance in Romans* (SNTSMS 148; Cambridge: Cambridge University Press, 2011). Cf., too, L. T. Lincoln, "The Stories of Predecessors and Inheritors in Galatians and Romans," in, *Narrative Dynamics in Paul: A Critical Assessment* (ed. Bruce W. Longenecker; Louisville: Westminster John Knox, 2002), 172–203.

ty."[189] The term is "rich in associations," ranging from the radical Italian worker's groups in the 60s and 70s "refusal to work,"[190] Georges Bataille's notion of *désoeuvrement*, the *voyou désoeuvré* of Raymond Queneau, and the "Shabbat of man" of Alexandre Kojève.[191] *Désoeuvrement*, for Bastaille, was the name he gave to the response to society's totalizing tendency of "forming a homogenous body politic."[192] It was the form of negativity that would escape the dialectic of historical progress's reabsorption.[193] Bastaille thus sees *désoeuvrement* as a refusal to participate within the work (the *oeuvre* or *oeuvres*) of one's society. Agamben's movement of "inoperativeness" or *désoeuvrement* becomes a "fundamental extension" of Bastaille. "It refers not only to a refusal to do the work of a coercive society, but also to something quite different – an ontological reflection on the modalities of being."[194] Inoperativity stresses potentiality which cannot be exhausted;[195] and refuses to pass from the possible to the actual.[196] It is this drive to loose political theory from the bounds of sovereignty while conceiving of a new politics and a new idea of community which is very much the vocation of Agamben.[197] This new politic and configuration of community is fueled by the energies of an "openness of inactivity, of *disengagement* from one's environment, and perhaps from one's world."[198] This inoperativity is not an inertia but *katargesis*, an operation of the *as if* which replaces the *that* "in which formless life and lifeless form coincide in a form of life."[199] Inoperativity within sovereignty's *that* allows for an existence of the *as if* and opens up space for an authentic politics of possi-

---

[189] Leland de la Durantaye states that "[n]o single term in Agamben's writing is so easty to misunderstand as *inoperativeness* [*inoperosità*]." *Giorgio Agamben: A Critical Introduction* (Stanford: Stanford University Press, 2009), 18.

[190] See Mario Troni, "The Strategy of Refusal," *Semiotext(e). Special Issue: Autonomia: Post-Political Politics* 3 (1980): 28–34.

[191] See de la Durantaye, *Agamben*, 18. Agamben is followed and in conversation with Marucie Blanchot, *La communaeté inavouable* (Paris: Minuit, 1983) and Jean-Luc Nancy, *La communauté désœuvrée* (Paris: C. Bourgois, 1986); Jean-Luc Nancy, *The Inoperative Community* (ed. Peter Connor; Minneapolis: University of Minnesota Press, 1991).

[192] de la Durantaye, *Agamben*, 18–19.

[193] Giorgio Agamben, *Language and Death: The Place of Negativity* (trans. Karen E. Pinkus with Michael Hardt; Minneapolis: University of Minnesota Press, 1991), 49.

[194] de la Durantaye, *Agamben*, 19.

[195] Giorgio Agamben, *Homo Sacer: Sovereign Power and Bare Life* (trans. Daniel Heller-Roazen; Stanford: Stanford University Press, 1998), 62.

[196] de la Durantaye, *Agamben*, 19.

[197] de la Durantaye, *Agamben*, 233.

[198] de la Durantaye, *Agamben*, 330. Cf. Giorgio Agamben, *The Open: Man and Animal* (trans. Kevin Attell; Stanford: Stanford University Press, 2004).

[199] de la Durantaye, *Agamben*, 331. This is near Alain Badiou's reading of Paul in *Paul* and the relativizing statements of 1 Cor 7:29–31.

bility outside the absorption of actualizing dialectics. It is this "neglect" which Agamben calls "the paradigm for the coming of politics."[200]

Near this reading is Alain Badiou's differentiation between the *site* of the event (the socio-economic, linguistic location in which Paul's discourse is constructed), and the *event itself* along with its truth-effects.[201] The *event* – for Badiou this is Paul's (mis)reading of resurrection – introduces a deep environmental fracture from which emerges a radical discourse of the *novum*;[202] a discourse which arises out of a space which is "unplugged from the organic community" in which Paul was situated.[203] Though not necessarily the polemical target of the *novum*, all else is reduced to the inferior. The *novum* does not keep easy company. This is Paul's revolution: his *politics of neglect*. Within Galatians, his theology of God as πατήρ, his succession narrative, and his recasting of the οἰκείους τῆς πίστεως (6:10),[204] together bear witness to a nascent *doxa* which informs a developing and fledgling *habitus* in the assembly.[205] This tacit and unarticulated logic governing such practices as circumcision and table manners for the "provincial" Paul reveals itself to be the most fundamental postures within the new creation.[206] Paul's focalized forms of being – what it means in practice to be "heirs" – are guided by this new and deeper symbol system. As such Paul is not and cannot be politically targeting Rome; his epistemology prevents him from doing so.[207] In this new cosmology,[208] the

---

[200] Giorgio Agamben, *The Coming Community* (trans. Michael Hardt; Minneapolis: University of Minnesota Press, 1993), 93.

[201] See Badiou, *Paul*, 23, 70–71. Note, too, the more recent Alain Badiou, *Logiques des Mondes* (Paris: Seuill, 2006). Barclay sees *Logiques des Mondes* as a watering down of his early work on Paul; Barclay, "Paul and Philosophers," 181.

[202] For a critique of Badiou's reading, see Larry Welborn, "Extraction from the Mortal Site: Badiou on the Resurrection in Paul," *NTS* 55 (2008): 295–314.

[203] Cf. Žižek, who is referring to Paul's notion of love in 1 Cor 13: Žižek, *Living in the End Times*, 106.

[204] Betz has suggested, in comparison with the universalism of 6:10a, 6:10b "seems a rather tiny entity." Betz continues, however, in considering if just maybe "this contrast is intended." *Galatians*, 311.

[205] See, esp., Pierre Bourdieu, *Outline of a Theory of Practice* (Cambridge Studies in Social and Cultural Anthropology; Cambridge: Cambridge University Press, 1977), 72–95; Pierre Bourdieu, *The Logic of Practice* (Stanford: Stanford University Press, 1990), 52–65.

[206] Price terms Paul's world as the "lower and more peripheral." "Response," 182.

[207] On Paul's epistemology, see the brief but fertile essay of J. Louis Martyn, "Epistemology at the Turn of the Ages: 2 Corinthians 5:16," in *Theological Issues in the Letters of Paul* (Edinburgh: T&T Clark, 1997), 89–110.

[208] Robert Hall argues that texts such as Gal 3:1–5; 3:7–29; 4:1–11; 4:21–5:1 and 5:16–6:10 reflect similar themes and arguments which appear in Jewish apocalypses; namely, the revelation of a cosmic order under the rule of God. See Robert Hall, "Argu-

contrasting elements are καινὴ κτίσις (6:15) and αἰῶνος τοῦ ἐνεστῶτος πονηροῦ (1:4), and are played out "on an apocalyptic stage newly configured by the Christ-event."[209] Of utmost importance for Paul are the ecclesial effects of this reality. The conflict is therefore not between Christ and Caesar,[210] but in conflicting constructions of reality and the population of that reality with a different set of relationships.[211]

The ethical and political implications of this position are both difficult to discern and fascinating to consider. If anything, I hope that this essay might trouble the easy movement between Paul's "politics" (or whatever) and current ecclesial practices and direction.[212] In other words, the perlocutions of this essay are not necessarily a-political postures. If anything, I think this reading of Paul provides a radical politics for the post-political "silent majority" that "is not stupid, but it is cynical and resigned."[213] This majority is not necessarily unsure of what they want, but "cynical resignation prevents them from acting upon it, with the result that a weird gap opens up between what people think and how they act (or vote)."[214] Thucydidies spoke, with respect to Athenian public life, "the man who refuses

---

ing Like and Apocalypse: Galatians and an Ancient *Topos* outside the Greco-Roman Rhetorical Tradition," *NTS* 42 (1996): 434–53.

[209] Barclay, "Pauline Churches, Jewish Communities and the Roman Empire," 33. Cf., too, the study on notions of "cosmic war" by J. B. Rives, "Christian Expansion and Christian Ideology," in *The Spread of Christianity in the First Four Centuries* (ed. W. V. Harris; Leiden: Brill, 2005), 15–41.

[210] Cf. Barclay's excellent discussion in "Why the Roman Empire Was Insignificant to Paul," 386–87.

[211] "[N]ot to place oneself within the set of relationships between emperor, gods, élite and people was effectively to place oneself outside the mainstream of the whole world and the shared Roman understanding of humanity's place within that world. Maintenance of the social order was seen by the Romans to be dependent on maintenance of this agreed set of symbolic structures, which assigned a role to people at all levels." Beard, North and Price, *Religions of Rome*, 1.361. See, too, Rives, "Christian Expansion and Christian Ideology," 16.

[212] In this respect, Barclay's critique of Badiou slightly misses the point; see Barclay, "Paul and the Philosophers," 182–83. Badiou is not trying to read Paul within any kind of tradition or sense of authorial intention. Badiou, along with Žižek, are interested in the revolutionary potential of (mis)readings which make them still relevant for the revolutionary task of articulating a space "for a revolt which will not be captured by one or another version of the discourse of the Master." On this, see Slavoj Žižek, *Less than Nothing: Hegel and the Shadow of Dialectical Materialism* (New York: Verso, 2012), 19. See, esp., Žižek, *Living in the End Times*, 140. This is Žižek's continued interest in Hegel as read through Lacan. Similarly: "If theology is again emerging as a point of reference for radical politics, it is so not by way of supplying a divine 'big Other' who would guarntee the final success of our endeavors, but on the contrary, as a token of our radical freedom in having no big Other to rely on." *Living in the End Times*, 401.

[213] Žižek, *Living in the End Times*, 390.

[214] Žižek, *Living in the End Times*, 390.

to participate in public life is useless" (*Peloponnesian War*, 2.40.2). This "uselessness," or inopertivity, however, introduces the possibility of a real negation outside the actualizing dialectic of sovereignty. Paul's refusal to participate in the public of political life, his deep *dis*interest in empire, and his accordant politics of neglect might well prove to be the revolutionary potential which awakens, in an ironic way, the revolutionary spirit within our current world of hyperpolitics.

In any case, the aim in this essay has been to listen to the tale of two succession stories regarding two powerful fathers and their natural and adopted sons. In both cases, the adopted son succeeds their powerful fathers instead of the natural sons (esp. 4:30). The dynamics of the succession are, of course, remarkably different, but the narratives share similar vocabulary. No one, of course, is surprised by the Emperor's neglect of attending to Paul's "provincial" narrative.[215] But maybe it is time we are no longer surprised by Paul's neglect to attend to the Emperor's. Paul was not sitting upon the ground telling sad tales of the death of kings. He was telling the world of a king who died, rose, and not only re-mapped the cosmos but brought a new creation (Gal 6:14–15; cf 1 Cor 1:18–2:16). Paul's Christological cartography of this new cosmos, of this new creation, does not merely flip the script on empire in terms of shifting center and periphery. Rather, Paul's inoperative political theology develops in such a way that empire is neglected altogether as it is reduced to irrelevance. This is Paul's radical politics; his *politics of neglect*. For Paul, it is not that Jesus is Lord and Caesar is not; it is that Jesus is Lord [*punkt!*].

Bibliography

Agamben, Giorgio. *Homo Sacer: Sovereign Power and Bare Life*. Translated by Daniel Heller-Roazen. Stanford: Stanford University Press, 1998.

———. *Language and Death: The Place of Negativity*. Translated by Karen E. Pinkus with Michael Hardt. Minneapolis: University of Minnesota Press, 1991.

———. *The Coming Community*. Translated by Michael Hardt. Minneapolis: University of Minnesota Press, 1993.

---

[215] Price is only half right when he says Paul's politics are local and that they "encompassed broader aspects of local social and religious values." "Response," 183. Moreover, Claudius' expulsion of the Jews/Christians(?) from Rome in 49CE (Suetonius, *Claudius* 25.4 and acts 18.2) cannot necessarily be in response to Paul's activity as he did not reach Rome until *after* 49. Though, cf. Udo Schnelle, *Apostle Paul: His Life and Theology* (trans. M. Eugene Boring; Grand Rapids: Baker Academic, 2012), 48–50. See, too, the related letter of Claudius to Alexandria in V. A. Tcherikover, A. Fuks, and M. Stern, *Corpus Papyrorum Judaicarum* (3 vols.; Cambridge, Mass.: Harvard University Press, 1957–1964), 2.42–43.

———. *The Open: Man and Animal.* Translated by Kevin Attell. Stanford: Stanford University Press, 2004.

———. *The Time that Remains: A Commentary on the Letter to the Romans.* Stanford: Stanford University Press, 2005.

Alcock, Susan E., ed. *The Early Roman Empire in the East.* Oxbow Monographs 95. Oxford: Oxbow, 1997.

Alcock Susan E., et. al. *Empires: Perspectives from Archaeology and History.* Cambridge: Cambridge University Press, 2001.

Anderson, J. G. C. "Review of A. von Premerstein, *Vom Werden und Wesen des Prinzipats*" *The Journal of Roman Studies* 29.1 (1939): 93–97; p. 97

Ando, Clifford. "From Republic to Empire." Pages 37–66 in *Oxford Handbook to Social Relations in the Roman World.* Edited by Michael Peachin. Oxford: Oxford University Press, 2011.

———. *Imperial Ideology and Provincial Loyalty in the Roman Empire.* Berkeley: University of California Press, 2000.

Aveline, John. "The Death of Claudius." *Historia: Zeitschrift für Alte Geschichte* 53.4 (2004): 453–75.

Bachmann, Michael. *Anti-Judaism in Galatians? Exegetical Studies on a Polemical Letter and on Paul's Theology.* Translated by Robert L. Brawley. Grand Rapids: Eerdmans, 2008 [1999].

Badiou, Alain. *Logiques des Mondes.* Paris: Seuill, 2006.

———. *Saint Paul: The Foundation of Universalism.* Stanford: Stanford University Press, 2003.

Balch, David L. "Cult Statues of Augustus' Temple of Apollo on the Palatine in Rome: Artemis' / Diana's Birthday in Ephesus, and Revelation 12:1–5a." Pages 413–34 in *Contested Spaces: Houses and Temples in Roman Antiquity and the New Testament.* Edited by David L. Balch and Annette Weissenrieder. Wissenschaftliche Untersuchungen zum Neuen Testament 285; Tübingen: Mohr Siebeck, 2005.

———. *Roman Domestic Art and Early House Churches.* Wissenschaftliche Untersuchungen zum Neuen Testament 228; Tübingen: Mohr Siebeck, 2008.

Barclay, J.M.G. "Mirror-Reading a Polemical Letter: Galatians as a Test Case." *Journal for the Study of the New Testament* 31 (1987): 73–93.

———. *Obeying the Truth: A Study of Paul's Ethics in Galatians.* Studies in the New Testament and Its World. Edinburgh: T&T Clark, 1988.

———. "Paul and the Philosophers: Alain Badiou and the Event," *New Blackfriars* 91.1032 (2010), 171–84.

———. *Pauline Churches and Diaspora Jews.* Wissenschaftliche Untersuchungen zum Neuen Testament 276; Tübingen: Mohr Siebeck, 2011

Barrett, A. A. *Agrippina: Sex, Power and Politics in the Early Empire.* New Haven, Conn: Yale University Press, 1996.

Beard, M., J. North and S. Price. *Religions of Rome: A History.* Cambridge: Cambridge University Press, 1998.

Betz, Hans Dieter. *Galatians.* Hermeneia. Minneapolis: Fortress, 1989.

Bhabha, Homi K. *The Location of Culture.* London: Routledge, 1994.

Blanchot, Marucie. *La communaeté inavouable.* Paris: Minuit, 1983.

Blanton, Ward. *A Materialism for the Masses: Saint Paul and the Philosophy of Undying Life.* Insurrections. New York: Columbia University Press, 2014.

Blanton, Ward, and Hent de Vries, eds., *Paul and the Philosophers.* New York: Fordham University Press, 2013.

Bourdieu, Pierre. *Outline of a Theory of Practice*. Cambridge Studies in Social and Cultural Anthropology. Cambridge: Cambridge University Press, 1977.

———. *The Logic of Practice*. Stanford: Stanford University Press, 1990 .

Bowman, Alan K., Peter Garnsey, et al., eds., *The Augustan Empire, 43 BC–AD 69*. Cambridge Ancient History 10. 2d ed. Cambridge: Cambridge University Press, 1996.

Bowman. Alan K., Peter Garnsey, and Dominic Rathbone, eds. *The High Empire, AD 70–192*. Cambridge Ancient History 11. 2d ed. Cambridge: Cambridge University Press, 2000.

Bowman, Alan, and Dominic Rathbone, "Cities and Administration in Roman Egypt," *Journal of Roman Studies* 82 (1992): 107–27.

Boyarin, Daniel. *A Radical Jew: Paul and the Politics of Identity*. Berkeley: University of California Press, 1994.

Breton, Stanislas. *A Radical Philosophy of Saint Paul*. Translated by Ward Banton. New York: Columbia University Press, 2011 [1988].

Byrne, Brendan. *'Sons of God' – 'Seed of Abraham': A Study of the Idea of the Sonship of God of All Christians against the Jewish Background*. AnBib 83. Rome: Biblical Institute, 1979.

Burnett, A., M. Amandry, and P. P. Ripollès, *From the Death of Caesar to the Death of Vitellius (44 BC–AD 69)*. Volume I of *Roman Provincial Coinage*. Edited by A. Burnett and M. Amandry. London: British Museum Press, 1992

———, *Roman Provincial Coinage Supplement I*. Edited by A. Burnett and M. Amandry. London: British Museum Press, 1998.

Butterworth, Alex, and Ray Laurence. *Pompeii: The Living City*. New York: St Martin's Press, 2005.

Cadotte, Alain. *La romanisation des diex: L'interpretatio romana en Afrique du Nord sous le Haut-Empire*. Religions in the Graeco-Roman World 158. Leiden: Brill, 2007.

Caputo, John D., and Linda Martin Alcoff, eds., *St Paul among the Philosophers*. Bloomington: University of Indiana Press, 2009.

Champlin, Edward. *Nero*. Cambridge: The Balknap Press of Harvard University Press, 2003.

Chisholm, Kitty, and John Ferguson, eds. *Rome: The Augustan Age. A Sourcebook*. Oxford: Oxford University Press, 1981.

Cizek, Eugen. *L'Époque de Néron et ses Controverses Idéologiques*. Leiden: Brill, 1972.

Clark, Elizabeth A. *History, Theory, Text: Historians and the Linguistic Turn*. Cambridge, Mass.: Harvard University Press, 2004.

Cogitore, Isabelle. *La Légitimité Dynastique D'Auguste à L'épreuve des Conspirations*. Rome: École Française de Rome, 2002.

Cooke, Gerald. "The Israelite King as Son of God." *Zeitschrift für die Alttestamentliche Wissenschaft* 73.2 (2012): 202–25.

Cooley, Alison E. *Res Gestae Divi Augusti: Text, Translation, and Commentary*. Cambridge: Cambridge University Press, 2009.

Crossan, John Dominic, and Jonathan L. Reed. *In Search of Paul: How Jesus' Apostle Opposed Rome's Empire with God's Kingdom*. New York: HarperOne, 2005.

D'Angelo, Mary Rose. "Abba and 'Father': Imperial Theology and the Jesus Traditions," *Journal of Biblical Literature* 111 (1992): 611–30.

De Boer, Martin C. "The Meaning of the Phrase τά στοιχεῖα τοῦ κοσμοῦ in Galatians." *New Testament Studies* 53 (2007): 204–24.

Deissmann, Adolf. *Light from the Ancient East*. Translated by L. R. M. Strachan from the 4th rev. ed. London: Hodder & Stoughton, 1927 [1922].

De la Durantaye, Leland. *Giorgio Agamben: A Critical Introduction*. Stanford: Stanford University Press, 2009.

Diehl, Judy. "Empire and Epistles: Anti-Roman Rhetoric in the New Testament Epistles," *Currents in Biblical Research* 10.2 (2012): 217–63.

Donaldson, Terence L. *Paul and the Gentiles: Remapping the Apostle's Convictional World*. Minneapolis: Fortress, 1997.

Dunn, James D. G. *The Theology of Paul the Apostle*. Grand Rapids: Eerdmans, 1998.

———. "What was the Issue between Paul and 'Those of the Circumcision'?" Pages 295–318 in *Paulus und das antike Judentum*. Wissenschaftliche Untersuchungen zum Neuen Testament 58. Edited by Martin Hengel and Ulrich Heckel. Tübingen: Mohr Siebeck, 1991.

Eastman, Susan. *Recovering Paul's Mother Tongue: Language and Theology in Galatians*. Grand Rapids: Eerdmans, 2007.

Eck, Werner, Antonio Caballos, and Fernando Fernández. *Das senatus consultum de Cn. Pisone patre*. Vestigia 48; Munich: C. H. Beck, 1996).

Egelhaaf-Gaiser, Ulrike, and Alfred Schäfer. *Religiöse Vereine in der römischen Antike: Untersuchungen zu Organisation, Ritual und Raumordnung*. Studien und Texte zu Antike und Christentum 13. Tübingen: Mohr Siebeck, 2002.

Elliot, Neil. *The Arrogance of Nations: Reading Romans in the Shadow of Empire*. Minneapolis: Fortress, 2008.

Elliot, Susan, *Cutting Too Close for Comfort: Paul's Letter to the Galatians in its Anatolian Cultic Context*. Journal for the Study of the New Testament: Supplement Series 248. London: T&T Clark, 2003.

Everitt, Anthony. *Augustus: The Life of Rome's First Emperor*. New York: Random House, 2006.

Favro, Diane. "*Pater urbis*: Augustus as City Father of Rome." *Journal of the Society of Architectural Historians* 51.1 (1992): 61–84.

Ferrill, Arthur. *Caligula*. London: Thames & Hudson, 1991.

Forman, Mark. *The Politics of Inheritance in Romans*. Society for New Testament Studies Monograph Series 148. Cambridge: Cambridge University Press, 2011.

Freisenbruch, Annelise. *The First Ladies of Rome: The Women Behind the Caesars*. London: Jonathan Cape, 2010

Frey, Jörg. "Die paulinische Antithese von Fleisch un Geist und die palästinisch-jüdische Weisheitstradiktion," *Zeitschrift für die neutestamentliche Wissenschaft und die Kunde der älteren Kirche* 90 (1999): 45–77.

———. "Paul's Jewish Identity" Pages 285–322 in *Jewish Identity in the Greco-Roman World: Jüdische Identität in der griechische-römischen Welt*. Ancient Judaism and Early Christianity 71. Edited Jörg Frey, Daniel R. Schwartz, and Stephanie Gripentrog. Leiden: Brill, 2007.

———. "The Notion of 'Flesh' in 4QInstruction and the Background of Pauline Usage." Pages 197–226 *Sapiential, Poetical and Liturgical Texts: Published in the Memory of Maruice Baillet*. Studies on the Texts of the Desert of Judah 35. Edited by D. Falk, F. García Martínez, and E. Schuller. Leiden: Brill, 2000.

Galinsky, Karl, ed., *The Cambridge Companion to the Age of Augustus*. Cambridge: Cambridge University Press, 2005.

Gardner, Jane F. *Family and Familia in Roman Law and Life*. Oxford: Clarendon, 1998.

Gaventa, Beverly Roberts. *Our Mother Saint Paul*. Louisville: Westminster John Knox, 2007.

———. "The Singularity of the Gospel: A Reading of Galatians." Pages 147–59 in *Pauline Theology*. Vol. 1. Edited by Jouette Bassler. Minneapolis: Fortress, 1991.

Georgi, D. *Theocracy in Paul's Practice and Theology*. Translated by D. E. Green. Minneapolis: Fortress, 1991 [1987].
Glover, T. R. *The Conflict of Religions in the Early Roman Empire*. London: Methuen, 1909.
Gordon, Cyrus H. *Before the Bible: The Common Background of Greek and Hebrew Civilizations*. London: Harper & Row, 1963.
Gradel, Ittai. *Emperor Worship and Roman Religion*. Oxford: Clarendon, 2002.
Griffin, Miriam T. *Nero: The End of a Dynasty*. London: Routledge, 2000 [1984].
———. "The Senate's Story," *The Journal of Roman Studies* 87 (1997): 249–63.
Gupta, Nijay K. "Mirror-Reading Moral Issues in Paul's Letters." *Journal for the Study of the New Testament* 34.4 (2012): 361–81.
Hafemann, Scott J. "Paul and the Exile in Galatians 3–4." Pages 329–71 in *Exile: Old Testament, Jewish, and Christian Conceptions*. Supplements to the Journal for the Study of Judaism 56. Edited by James M. Scott. Leiden: Brill, 1997.
Hall, Robert. "Arguing Like and Apocalypse: Galatians and an Ancient *Topos* outside the Greco-Roman Rhetorical Tradition." *New Testament Studies* 42 (1996): 434–53.
Hammond, M. "The Transmission of the Powers of the Roman Emperor from the Death of Nero in AD 68 to that of Alexander Severus in AD 235." *Memoirs of the American Academy in Rome* 24 (1956): 61–133.
Hardin, Justin K. *Galatians and the Imperial Cult*. Wissenschaftliche Untersuchungen zum Neuen Testament 2/237. Tübingen: Mohr Siebeck, 2008.
Hays, Richard B. *The Conversion of the Imagination: Paul as Interpreter of Israel's Scripture*. Grand Rapids: Eerdmans, 2005.
———. "The Letter to the Galatians." Pages 183–348 in *The New Interpreter's Bible: Second Corinthians–Philemon*. Vol. 11. Nashville: Abingdon, 2000.
Hekster, Oliver, Sebastian Scmidt-Hofner, and Christian Witschel, eds. *Ritual Dynamics and Religious Change in the Roman Empire: Proceedings of the Eight Workshop of the International Network Impact of Empire*. Leiden: Brill, 2009.
Hengel, Martin. *Judaism and Hellenism: Studies in Their Encounter in Palestine During the Early Hellenistic Period*. Translated by John Bowden. Philadelphia: Fortress, 1974.
Herzog, William R. "Dissembling, A Weapon of the Weak: The Case of Christ and Caesar in Mark 12:13–17 and Romans 13:1–7," *Journal of the NABPR* 21 (1994): 339–60.
Hester, James. "The Heir and *Heilsgeschichte*: A Study of Galatians 4:1ff.," Pages 118–25 in *OIKONOMIA: Heilsgeschichte als Thema der Theologie*. Festschrift für Oscar Cullmann. Edited by Felix Christ. Hamburg: Herbert Reich, 1967.
Hodge, C. Johnson *If Sons, then Heirs: A Study of Kinship and Ethnicity in the Letters of Paul*. Oxford: Oxford University Press, 2007.
Horsley, Richard A., ed. *Hidden Transcripts and the Arts of Resistance: Applying the Work of James C. Scott to Jesus and Paul*. Semeia Studies 48. Atlanta: SBL, 2004.
———. *Paul and Empire: Religion and Power in Roman Imperial Society*. London: T&T Clark, 1997.
———. *Paul and Politics: Ekklesia, Israel, Imperium, Interpretation*. London: T&T Clark, 2000.
———. *Paul and the Roman Imperial Order*. Harrisburg: Trinity Press International, 2004.
Hultgren, Arland J. "Paul and the Law." Pages 202–15 *The Blackwell Companion to Paul*. Edited by Stephen Westerholm. Oxford: Wiley-Blackwell, 2011.

Ibbetson, David, and Andrew Lewis, eds. *The Roman Law Tradition.* Cambridge: Cambridge University Press, 1994.
Iser, Wolfgang. *Staging Politics: The Lasting Impact of Shakespeare's Histories.* Translated by David Henry Wilson. New York: Columbia University Press, 1993.
Johnson, Luke Timothy. *Among the Gentiles: Greco-Roman Religion and Christianity.* New Haven, Conn.: Yale University Press, 2009.
Johnston, David. *Roman Law in Context.* Cambridge: Cambridge University Press, 1999
Kahl, Brigitte. *Galatians Re-Imagined: Reading with the Eyes of the Vanquished.* Minneapolis: Fortress, 2010.
Kienast, Dietmar. *Augustus: Prinzeps und Monarch.* 3d ed. Darmstadt: Wissenschaftliche Buchgesellschaft, 1999.
Kim, Seyoon. *Christ and Caesar: The Gospel and the Roman Empire in the Writings of Paul and Luke.* Grand Rapids: Eerdmans, 2008.
Kleiner, Diana E. E., and Susan B. Matheson. *I, Claudia II: Women in Roman Art and Society.* Austin: University of Texas Press, 2000.
Knausgaard, Karl Ove. *My Struggle.* Book 1. Translated by Don Bartlett. New York: Farrar, Straus & Giroux, 2012 [2009].
Kroeker, P. Travis. "Recent Continental Philosophers" Pages 450–54 in *The Blackwell Companion to Paul.* Edited by Stephen Westerholm. Oxford: Wiley-Blackwell, 2011.
Kurylowicz, Marek. *Die adoptio im klassischen römischen Recht.* Studia antiqua 6. Warsaw: University of Warszawskeigo, 1981.
LeMarquand, Grant. "African Readings of Paul." Pages 488–503 in *The Blackwell Companion to Paul.* Edited by Stephen Westerholm. Oxford: Wiley-Blackwell, 2011.
Lémonon, J. P. *L'Épître aux Galates.* Paris: Cerf, 2008.
Lentz, John Clayton, Jr. *Luke's Portrait of Paul.* Cambridge: Cambridge University Press, 1993.
Levick, Barbara. *Claudius.* New Haven, Conn.: Yale University Press, 1990.
Lincoln, L. T. "The Stories of Predecessors and Inheritors in Galatians and Romans." Pages 172–203 in *Narrative Dynamics in Paul: A Critical Assessment.* Edited by Bruce W. Longenecker. Louisville: Westminster John Knox, 2002.
Lincott, Andrew. *Imperium Romanum: Politics and Administration.* London: Routledge, 1993.
Lopez, Davina C. *Apostle to the Conquered: Reimagining Paul's Mission.* Minneapolis: Fortress, 2008.
———. "Visualizing Significant Otherness: Reimagining Paul(ine Studies) through Hybrid Lenses." Pages 74–94 in *The Colonized Apostle: Paul through Postcolonial Eyes.* Edited by Christopher D. Stanley. Minneapolis: Fortress, 2011.
Longenecker, Bruce W. *The Triumph of Abraham's God: The Transformation of Identity in Galatians.* London: T&T Clark, 2001.
Lull, David. "'The Law was Our Pedagogue': A Study in Galatians 3:19–25." *Journal of Biblical Literature* 105 (1986): 481–98.
Lyall, Francis. *Slaves, Citizens, Sons: Legal Metaphors in the Epistles.* Grand Rapids: Zondervan, 1984.
Marguerat, Daniel. *Paul in Acts and Paul in His Letters.* Wissenschaftliche Untersuchungen zum Neuen Testament 310. Tübingen: Mohr Siebeck, 2013.
Marquis, Timothy L. *Transient Apostle: Paul, Travel, and the Rhetoric of Empire.* New Haven, Conn.: Yale University Press, 2013.
Martyn, J. Louis. "Epistemology at the Turn of the Ages: 2 Corinthians 5:16." Pages 89–110 in *Theological Issues in the Letters of Paul.* Edinburgh: T&T Clark, 1997.

———. "Events in Galatia." Pages 160–79 in *Pauline Theology*. Volume 1. Edited by J. Bassler. Minneapolis: Fortress, 1991.
———. *Galatians*. Anchor Bible 33A. New Haven, Conn.: Yale University Press, 2004.
Mattingly, D. J. ed. *Dialogues in Roman Imperialism: Power, Discourse, and Discrepant Experience in the Roman Empire*. Journal of Roman Archaeology Supplement Series 23; Portsmouth: *JRA*, 1997.
Mattingly, Harold, ed. *Coins of the Roman Empire in the British Museum*. 3 vols. London: British Museum, 1965.
Mayer, Jean-Christophe. "The 'Parliament Sceane' in Shakespeare's *King Richard III*," *Bulletin de la société d'études anglo-ameéricaines des XVIIe et SVIIIe siècles* 59.59 (2004): 27–42.
Mbembe, Achille. *On the Postcolony*. Berkeley: University of California Press, 2001.
Meiser, Martin. *Galater*. Göttingen: Vandenhoeck & Ruprecht, 2007.
Mengestu, Abera M. *God as Father in Paul: Kinship Language and Identity Formation in Early Christianity*. Eugene, Ore.: Pickwick, 2013.
Millar, Fergus. *The Emperor in the Roman World*. London: Duckworth, 2003.
Miller, Colin. "The Imperial Cult in the Pauline Cities of Asia Minor and Greece," *Catholic Bible Quarterly* 72 (2010): 314–32.
Mitchell, Stephen. *Anatolia: Land, Men, and Gods in Asia Minor*. 2 vols. Oxford: Clarendon, 1993.
Mommsen, Theodor. *Römisches Staatsrecht*. 2 vols. Akademische Druck-u: Verlagsanstalt, 1952.
Murgatroyd, P. "Tacitus on the Deaths of Britannicus and Claudius." *Eranos* 103.2 (2005): 97–100.
Müssner, F. *Der Galaterbrief*. Herders theologischer Kommentar sum Neuen Testament 9. Freiburg: Herder & Herder, 1974.
Nachtergael, G. *Les Galates en Grèce et la Sotèria de Delphes: recherches d'histoire et d'épigraphie hellénistiques* .Mémoires de la Classe des lettres, Académie royal de Belgique, serie 2, tome 63.1. Bruxelles: Georges Nachtergael, 1975.
Nancy, Jean-Luc. *La communauté désœuvrée*. Paris: C. Bourgois, 1986.
———. *The Inoperative Community*. Edited by Peter Connor. Minneapolis: University of Minnesota Press, 1991.
Nanos, Mark D., ed. *The Galatians Debate: The Contemporary Issues in Rhetorical and Historical Interpretation*. Grand Rapids: Baker Academic, 2002.
Nasrallah, Laura Salah. *Christian Responses to Roman Art and Architecture: The Second-Century Church Amid the Spaces of Empire*. Cambridge: Cambridge University Press, 2010.
Neyrey, Jerome H. *Paul, In Other Words: A Cultural Reading of His Letters*. Louisville: Westminster John Knox, 1990.
Nix, Sarah A. "Caesar as Jupiter in Lucan's 'Bellum Civile'." *Classical Journal* 103.3 (2008): 281–94.
Oepke, A. *Der Brief des Paulus an die Galater*. Theologischer Handkommentar zum Neuen Testament 9. Berlin: Evangelische Verlagsanstalt, 1955.
Osgood, J. "The *vox* and *verba* of an Emperor: Claudius, Seneca and Le Prince Ideal" *Classical Journal* 102.4 (2007): 329–53
Palmer, Robert E. A. *Roman Religion and Roman Empire*. Philadelphia: University of Pennsylvania Press, 1974.
Peppard, Michael. *The Son of God in the Roman World: Divine Sonship in its Social and Political Context*. Oxford: Oxford University Press, 2011..
Porter, Stanley E. *Paul in Acts*. Grand Rapids: Baker Academic, 2000.

———. "The Portrait of Paul in Acts." Pages 124–38 in *The Blackwell Companion to Paul*. Edited by Stephen Westerholm. Oxford: Wiley-Blackwell, 2011.

Potter, D. S., and Cynthia Damon. "Senatus Consultum de Cn. Pisone Patre," *The American Journal of Philology*. Special Issue: "The Senatus Consultum de Cn. Pisone Patre": Text, Translation, Discussion 120.1 (1999): 13–42.

Premerstein, Anton von. *Vom Werden und Wesen des Prinzipats*. Aus dem Nachlass herausgegeben von Hans Volkmann; Abhandlungen der Bayerischen Akademie der Wissenschaften, Ph.-h. Abt., N.F., Heft 15. Munich: Beck, 1937

Price, Simon, and Emily Kearns, eds. *The Oxford Dictionary of Classical Myth and Religion*. Oxford: Oxford University Press, 2003.

Price, S. R. F. *Rituals and Power: The Roman Imperial Cult in Asia Minor*. Cambrdige: Cambridge University Press, 1985.

Rehak, Paul. *Imperium and Cosmos: Augustus and the Northern Campus Martius*. Madison: University of Wisconsin Press, 2006.

Riches, John. *Galatians through the Centuries*. Oxford: Blackwell, 2008.

Ridderbos, Herman. *Paul: An Outline of His Theology*. Translated by John Richard de Witt. London: SPCK, 1977 [1966].

Rives, J. B. "Christian Expansion and Christian Ideology." Pages 15–41 in *The Spread of Christianity in the First Four Centuries*. Edited by W. V. Harris. Leiden: Brill, 2005.

———. *Religion of the Roman Empire*. Oxford: Blackwell, 2006.

Rogers, Guy. *The Sacred Identity of Ephesos: Foundation Myths of a Roman City*. London: Routledge, 1991.

Rogers, Robert Samuel. "Heirs and Rivals to Nero." *Transactions and Proceedings of the American Philological Association* 86 (1955): 190–212.

Roller, Matthew B. *Constructing Autocracy: Aristocrats and Emperors in Julio-Claudian Rome*. Princeton: Princeton University Press, 2001.

Rose, Charles Brian. *Dynastic Commemoration and Imperial Portraiture in the Julio-Claudian Period*. Cambridge: Cambridge University Press, 1997.

Rowe, Greg. "*Omnis spes futura paternae stationis*: Public Responses to the Roman Imperial Succession," D.Phil. thesis, The Queen's College, Oxford University, 1997.

———. *Princes and Political Cultures: The new Tiberian Senatorial Decrees*. Ann Arbor: University of Michigan Press, 2002.

Rudich, Vasily. *Political Dissidence Under Nero: The Price of Dissimulation*. London: Routledge, 1993.

Rüpke, Jörg. *Religion of the Romans*. Translated Richard Gordon; Cambridge: Polity, 2007 [2001].

Rüpke, Jörg, ed. *A Companion to Roman Religion*. Oxford: Blackwell, 2007.

Rutledge, Steven. *Ancient Rome as a Museum: Power, Identity, and the Culture of Collecting*. Oxford: Oxford University Press, 2012.

Sanders, E. P. *Paul, the Law, and the Jewish People*. Philadelphia: Fortress, 1983.

Sawn, Peter Michael. *The Augustan Succession: An Historical Commentary on Cassius Dio's Roman History Books 55–56 (9BC–AD14)*. Oxford: Oxford University Press, 2004.

Schmithals, Walter. *Paulus, die Evangelien und das Urchristentum: Beiträge von und zu Walter Schmithals von Walter Schmithals*. Edited by Cilliers Breytenbach. Leiden: Brill, 2004.

Schnelle, Udo. *Apostle Paul: His Life and Theology*. Translated by M. Eugene Boring. Grand Rapids: Baker Academic, 2012.

Scott, James C. *Domination and the Arts of Resistance: Hidden Transcripts*. New Haven, Conn.: Yale University Press, 1990.

Scott, James M. *Adoption as Sons of God: An Exegetical Investigation into the Background of ΥΙΟΘΕΣΙΑ in the Corpus Paulinium*. Wissenschaftliche Untersuchungen zum Neuen Testament 2/48. Tübingen: J. C. B. Mohr, 1992.

———. *Paul and the Nations: The Old Testament and Jewish Background of Paul's Mission to the Nations with Special Reference to the Destination of Galatians*. Wissenschaftliche Untersuchungen zum Neuen Testament 84. Tübingen: Mohr Siebeck, 1995.

Scramuzza, Vincent M. *The Emperor Claudius*. Cambridge: Harvard University Press, 1940.

Sechrest, Love L. *A Former Jew: Paul and the Dialectics of Race*. London: T&T Clark, 2009.

Simpson, C. "The Julian Succession and Its Claudian Coda: A Different Perspective on the So-called 'Julio-Claudian' Dynasty." *Latomus* 67 (2008): 253–65.

Smith, Jonathan Z. *Drudgery Divine: On the Comparison of Early Christianities and the Religions of Late Antiquity*. Chicago: University of Chicago Press, 1990.

Stanley, Christopher D. ed. *The Colonized Apostle: Paul through Postcolonial Eyes*. Minneapolis: Fortress, 2011.

Stowers, Stanley K. "Does Pauline Christianity Resemble a Philosophical School?" Pages 81–102 in *Beyond the Judaism/Hellenism Divide* (ed. Engberg-Pedersen; Louisville: Westminster John Knox, 2001).

Strothmann, Meret. *Augustus: Vater der res publica. Zur Funktion der drei Begriffe* restitutio – saeculum – pater patriae *im augusteischen Principat*. Stuttgart: Franz Steiner, 2000.

Swain, Simon. *Hellenism and Empire, Classicism and Power in the Greek World, A.D. 50–250*. Oxford: Oxford University Press, 1998.

Syme, Ronald. "Imperator Caesar: A Study in Nomenclature." *Historia* 7 (1958): 172–88.

———. *Tacitus*. 2 vols. Oxford: Oxford University Press, 1980.

———. *The Roman Revolution*. Oxford: Oxford University Press, 2002.

Talbert, Richard J. A. *The Senate of Imperial Rome*. Princeton: Princeton University Press, 1984.

Taubes, Jacob. *The Political Theology of Paul*. Stanford: Stanford University Press, 2004.

Tcherikover, V. A., A. Fuks, and M. Stern. *Corpus Papyrorum Judaicarum*. 3 vols. Cambridge, Mass.: Harvard University Press, 1957–1964.

Toynbee, J. M. C. "Portraits of Julius Caesar," *Greece & Rome (Second Series)* 4.1 (1957): 2–9.

Troni, Mario. "The Strategy of Refusal." *Semiotext(e). Special Issue: Autonomia: Post-Political Politics* 3 (1980): 28–34.

Turcan, Robert. *The Cults of the Roman Empire*. Translated by Antonia Nevill. Oxford: Blackwell, 1996 [1992].

Várhelyi, Zsuzsanna. *The Religion of Senators in the Roman Empire: Power and the Beyond*. Cambridge: Cambridge University Press, 2010.

Vessey, D. W. T. C. "Thoughts on Tacitus' Portrayal of Claudius" *American Journal of Philology* 92 (1971): 385–409

Walters, James C. "Paul, Adoption, and Inheritance." Pages 42–76 *Paul in the Greco-Roman World: A Handbook*. Edited by J. Paul Sampley. London: Trinity Press International, 2003.

Wanamaker, Charles A. "The Son and the Sons of God: A Study in Elements of Paul's Christological and Soteriological Thought." Ph.D. diss., University of Durham, 1980.

Watson, Francis. *Paul and the Hermeneutics of Faith.* London: T&T Clark, 2004.
Weber, Max. *The Protestant Ethic and the Spirit of Capitalism.* Translated by Talcott Parsons. New York: Routledge Classics, 2001.
Weber, Wilhelm. *Princeps: Studienzur Geschichte des Augustus.* Stuttgart: Scientia Verlag Aalen, 1969.
Welborn, Larry. "Extraction from the Mortal Site: Badiou on the Resurrection in Paul." *New Testament Studies* 55 (2008): 295–314.
Wengst, Klaus. *Pax Romana and the Peace of Christ.* Translated by J. Bowden. London: SCM Press, 1987 [1986].
Whiteley, D. E. H. *The Theology of St Paul.* Blackwell: Oxford, 1964.
Wieacker, Franz. *Römische Rechtsgeschichte: Quellenkunde, Rechtsbildung, Jurisprudenz und Rechtsliteratur.* Munich: C. H. Beck, 1988.
Williams, David. *Paul's Metaphors: Their Context and Character.* Peabody, Mass.: Hendrickson, 1999.
Wiseman, T. P. "A World Not Ours." Pages 1–14 in *Catullus and His World: A Reappraisal.* Cambridge: Cambridge University Press, 1986.
——. *Flavius Josephus, Death of an Emperor: Translated, with Introduction and Commentary.* Exeter: University of Exeter Press, 1991.
Wood, S. "Messalina, Wife of Claudius: Propaganda Successes and Failures of His Reign," *Journal of Roman Architecture* 5 (1992): 219–34
Woodman, Anthony J. *Tacitus Reviewed.* Oxford: Clarendon Press, 1998.
Woolf, Greg. *Becoming Roman: The Origins of Provincial Civilization in Gaul.* Cambridge: Cambridge University Press, 2000.
Wright, N. T. *Paul and the Faithfulness of God.* Minneapolis: Fortress, 2013.
——. *Paul: Fresh Perspectives.* Minneapolis: Fortress, 2009.
Zanker, Paul. *The Power of Images in the Age of Augustus.* Ann Arbor: University of Michigan Press, 1990.
Žižek, Slavoj. *Less than Nothing: Hegel and the Shadow of Dialectical Materialism.* New York: Verso, 2012.
——. *Living in the End Times.* New York: Verso, 2011.

Sharing in the Heavenly Rule of Christ the King

Paul's Royal Participatory Language in Ephesians

JOSHUA W. JIPP

One of the puzzles that continues to perplex interpreters of Paul is how a theme that dominates Paul's soteriological discourse, namely the participation of Christians in the narrative and identity of Messiah Jesus, defies attempts to locate its religious-historical antecedent(s).[1] While no one would deny Paul's innovative articulation of his participatory soteriology, most would also agree that the motif was not created *ex nihilo* out of Paul's own mind. A search for precedents and analogous speech patterns, however, has simply not been met with much success in terms of bringing scholarship to anything near a consensus. To make matters more difficult, finding an ap-

---

[1] For recent explications of Paul's participatory soteriology, see Michael J. Gorman, *Inhabiting the Cruciform God: Kenosis, Justification, and Theosis in Paul's Narrative Soteriology* (Grand Rapids: Eerdmans, 2009); Douglas A. Campbell, *The Quest for Paul's Gospel: A Suggested Strategy* (London: T&T Clark, 2005); Constantine R. Campbell, *Paul and Union with Christ: An Exegetical and Theological Study* (Grand Rapids: Zondervan, 2012). On conceptual precedents for Paul's participatory soteriology, Rudolf Bultmann describes Paul's participatory language as deriving from the mystery religions wherein "participating in the fate of the mystery-divinity through baptism and sacramental communion grants the *mystes* (initiate) participation in both the dying and the reviving of the divinity; such participation, that is, by leading the *mystes* into death delivers him from death." *Theology of the New Testament* (trans. Kendrick Grobel; New York: Charles Scribner's Sons, 1951–55), 298. Albert Schweitzer, *The Mysticism of Paul the Apostle* (trans. William Montgomery; Baltimore: The Johns Hopkins University Press, 1998), argued, to the contrary, that Paul's "eschatological doctrine of redemption" remained untouched by Hellenistic influence (139–40) and was rather the result of Paul's "conception of the predestined solidarity of the Elect with one another and with the Messiah" which gave birth to "Paul's resurrection mysticism the conception of the common possession of a corporeity" (117). See Matthew V. Novenson, *Christ Among the Messiahs: Christ Language in Paul and Messiah Language in Ancient Judaism* (Oxford: Oxford University Press, 2012), 124–26, who argues that Paul's "in-Christ" language should be understood as analogous to the many biblical phrases along the lines of "in your seed," as seen particularly in God's promises to fulfill his purposes in the seed of Abraham (cf. LXX Gen 12:3; 18:18; 22:18; Gal 3:8–9, 14).

propriate analogical discourse, or, as E.P. Sanders has argued, a "category of perception" whereby modern contemporary interpreters might understand how it is that Christians "really are one body and Spirit with Christ" by virtue of their union with the Messiah has not been successfully accomplished.[2]

In his essay for E. P. Sanders' *Festschrift*, Richard B. Hays makes an important attempt to rectify this lack by identifying four complementary models for conceptualizing what Paul means by his participatory discourse: "participation as belonging to a family," "participation as political or military solidarity with Christ," "participation in the *ekklēsia*," and "participation as living within the Christ story."[3] Hays' four models are not only helpful for enabling us to think about contemporary categories of perception, but they also enable us to see the predominant (not to say the only) conceptual resource that Paul employs to develop his participatory soteriology – royal messianism.[4] Royal messianism, that is, the linguistic and conceptual resources rooted in reflections upon Israel's *ideal coming king*, best explains Paul's articulation of the narrative of Messiah Jesus *and* his mapping of the same narrative identity onto the Messiah's people.[5] Paul

---

[2] E. P. Sanders, *Paul and Palestinian Judaism* (Minneapolis: Fortress, 1977), 522–23. Similarly, see the discussion in C. F. D. Moule, *The Origin of Christology* (Cambridge: Cambridge University Press, 1977), 47–54.

[3] Richard B. Hays, "What is 'Real Participation in Christ'?: A Dialogue with E. P. Sanders on Pauline Soteriology," in *Redefining First-Century Jewish and Christian Identities: Essays in Honor of Ed Parish Sanders* (ed. Fabian E. Udoh et al.; CJAS 16; Notre Dame: University of Notre Dame Press, 2008), 336–51.

[4] Here I must insert an important methodological caveat. My use of "royal messianism," "messianic discourse," "royal christology," and other such terms does not indicate a belief that Jewish messianic expectation was of a single form, or that Paul's language depends upon conforming to a Jewish messianic ideal or the psychological messianic expectation of Paul's hearers. On the diversity of messianic language among different Jewish communities, see John J. Collins, *The Scepter and the Star: The Messiahs of the Dead Sea Scrolls and Other Ancient Literature* (ABRL; New York: Doubleday, 1995); Andrew Chester, *Messiah and Exaltation: Jewish Messianic and Visionary Traditions and New Testament Christology* (WUNT 207; Tübingen: Mohr-Siebeck, 2007), 355–63. Rather, as Matthew V. Novenson has argued persuasively, Paul's messianic language is messianic "because it was deployed in the context of a linguistic community whose members shared a stock of common linguistic resources," namely, the Scriptures of Israel that refer to an ideal coming king; Novenson, *Christ Among the Messiahs*, 47.

[5] I speak of royal messianism as a lexical and conceptual way of expressing hope for an eschatological royal human agent of God who would deliver his people and establish God's rule. So while speculation upon messianic agents often involved conceptions of his kingly rule it is not the same thing as ancient reflections upon the ideal king. Deuteronomy 17:14–20, for example, depicts the Deuteronomist's conception of Israel's ideal king, but there are no explicitly eschatological and therefore messianic signals in the text. The depiction of Josiah as Torah-observant and the statement that no king has arisen like him

conceptualizes the relationship between Christ and his people as the relationship between king and subjects with the Messiah's people, however, sharing in the rule and the benefits of the resurrected-enthroned Messiah's heavenly rule. As participants in the Messiah's lordship, the king's subjects share in the benefits of his royal rule, foremost of which are: participation in the Messiah's election, participation in the Messiah's assembly where the Messiah nourishes and gives gifts to his people, and participating in the Messiah's establishment of ethnic peace and reconciliation. Thus, the models Hays articulates for conceptualizing Pauline participation, I hope to show, are actually pieces of this larger pattern, a pattern that stems from Paul's innovative re-reading of Israel's royal ideology around Messiah Jesus. In what follows I restrict my argument to Paul's (or one of his disciple's) letter to the Ephesians[6] and leave it to the reader to decide the argument's merit with respect to the rest of Paul's corpus.[7]

A. Χριστός as a Royal Figure in Ephesians

Paul's letter to the Ephesians is dominated by a figure referred to as Χριστός who acts and rules on God's behalf.[8] Though some have argued

---

(2 Kgs 23:25) presents an ideal depiction of Israel's king but it is not messianic or eschatological. Nevertheless, whether certain Hebrew scriptural passages that reflect upon an ideal king such as Gen 49:8–12; Isa 9; Pss 2, 110, are messianic or not, *once the belief that the Messiah has come* is present these passages easily lend themselves to retrospective messianic interpretations. The royal messiah has come, and this now makes almost any reflection upon the ideal king susceptible to a messianic interpretation. On the distinction between "Messiah" and idealistic royal ideology, see Sigmund Mowinckel, *He That Cometh: The Messiah Concept in the Old Testament and Later Judaism* (trans. G. W. Anderson; Grand Rapids: Eerdmans, 2005); Joseph A. Fitzmyer, *The One Who Is to Come* (Grand Rapids: Eerdmans, 2007).

[6] I maintain Pauline authorship for Ephesians, *but even if* it is pseudonymous all scholars agree that the Deutero-Pauline letters were written shortly after Paul's death, within the sphere of Paul's missionary network, and by someone of the Pauline school. Even on these assumptions, the author would provide invaluable evidence for the roots and use of "Paul's" participatory soteriology. For those accepting Pauline authorship of both Ephesians and Colossians, see Luke Timothy Johnson, *The Writings of the New Testament: An Interpretation* (Minneapolis: Fortress, 1999), 393–95, 407–12; N. T. Wright, *Paul and the Faithfulness of God* (Christian Origins and the Question of God 4; Minneapolis: Fortress, 2013), 56–61.

[7] I believe my argument does have serious explanatory power for the rest of Paul's epistles, but I restrict my argument to Ephesians for the sake of space constraints. I develop the claims in this essay more fully and with respect to all of Paul's epistles in my forthcoming *Christ Is King: Paul's Royal Christology* (Minneapolis: Fortress, forthcoming 2016).

[8] There are 46 occurrences in Ephesians.

that Paul's use of the articular ὁ Χριστός indicates that Paul refers to this figure as Israel's Messiah (e.g., Eph 1:10; 1:20; 2:5; 4:20), grammatical arguments regarding the presence or absence of the article and their indication of Χριστός as an honorific or, alternatively, a proper name have proved unconvincing one way or the other.[9] Rather, the meaning of Χριστός can best be determined by specific contextual features such as the literary role of the Christ-figure, influence from Israel's Scriptures on the use of the term, and confessional statements.[10]

We see, first, that "the Christ" is spoken of as, along with God, having his own kingdom (τῇ βασιλείᾳ τοῦ Χριστοῦ καὶ θεοῦ, Eph 5:5b), a kingdom that is marked, here described with what is likely an early hymnic fragment, by the Messiah's bestowal of resurrection light upon the dead (5:14).[11] Second, in significant portions of his argument Paul develops his articulation of the Messiah's activity through marked quotations and allusions to Israel's scriptural royal ideology. Thus, the Messiah's resurrection and enthronement by God is thus understood through the lens of Pss 8 and 110 (Eph 1:20–23), the Messiah's defeat of his hostile enemies through Ps 2 and Dan 7 (Eph 1:21; 2:1–3), the Messiah's establishment of peace for his people through Isaiah (Isa 9:5–6; 52:7; 59:17; Eph 2:14–18), and the Messiah's giving of gifts to his people with the help of Ps 68 (Eph 4:7–11). Paul's deployment of these royal texts from Israel's scriptures to refer to "the Christ" in Ephesians suggests Paul uses Χριστός to mean Messiah.

The third contextual feature is worth developing with a bit more detail. In ancient Israel the king was installed by means of anointing such that he received the title and office of "Messiah," an office that marked him out "not merely [as] 'the Messiah' but 'the Messiah of Yahweh.'"[12] Tryggve Mettinger notes that the term "'Messiah' denotes the king as very definite-

---

[9] See the discussion in Julien Smith, *Christ the Ideal King: Cultural Context, Rhetorical Strategy, and the Power of Divine Monarchy in Ephesians* (WUNT 2/313; Tübingen: Mohr-Siebeck, 2011), 76–82.

[10] So M. de Jonge, "The Use of the Word 'Anointed' in the Time of Jesus," *NovT* 8 (1966): 147; see also 132–48.

[11] The hymn begins with the quotation formula διὸ λέγει: "wake up you sleeper, and rise up from the dead, and the Messiah will shine light upon you" (ἔγειρε, ὁ καθεύδων, καὶ ἀνάστα ἐκ τῶν νεκρῶν, καὶ ἐπιφαύσει σοι ὁ Χριστός). The hymnic fragment appears to provide evidence for the early Christian belief that ὁ Χριστός, as the first to be raised from the dead, shines his light upon the dead who are in a state of darkness (Eph 5:8) thereby communicating resurrection and light (cf. 1 Cor 15:20–22). As the first to be raised from the dead, the Messiah is able to shine resurrection light upon the dead, thereby bringing them into a realm of "light in the Lord" (Eph 5:8b) and procuring for them "an inheritance in the kingdom of the Messiah and God" (5:5b).

[12] Aubrey Johnson points to such texts as Judg 9:7–21; 1 Sam 16:1–13; 2 Sam 2:1–7; 5:1–5; 1 Kgs 1:28–40; 2 Kgs 9:1–13; 11:4–20; Aubrey R. Johnson, *Sacral Kingship in Ancient Israel* (Cardiff: University of Wales Press, 1967), 14–15.

ly set apart from the rest of the people, since it signifies his status *as linked with God and thus inviolable*" (italics mine).[13] As God's own son, Israelite royal ideology viewed the Lord's Messiah as invested with God's authority and power to rule (Ps 2:6–9; 89:26–28; 110:1–4; cf. 2 Sam 7:12–14).[14] It was this relationship between king and God that enabled the anointed Messiah to operate as a channel for God's Spirit (1 Sam 16:13; Isa 11:1–2; 61:1–3; *Pss. Sol.* 17:22, 37; 18:5–7), to share in and represent God's rule (e.g., Ps 89:20–37), and to shepherd God's people with righteousness and peace (Ps 72:1–3; Ezek 34; *Pss. Sol.* 17:32).[15] The king's participation in God's rule was thought to result in the bestowal of God's gifts to his people, foremost of which included righteousness, rule over one's enemies, and internal peace and prosperity.[16] The investiture of Israel's anointed king with God's authority and rule was not unique to Israel, but is an element of royal ideology that characterizes Ancient Near Eastern and Hellenistic-Roman notions of kingship.[17] The important point here, for our purposes, is that the royal figure is the subordinated vicegerent of God whose job it is *to rule and act on God's behalf by bestowing divine benefits to his subjects*.[18] He is the royal agent who *shares in God's rule* and acts as the channel through whom God acts.

When we turn, then, to Ephesians we encounter a figure consistently referred to as Χριστός who is subordinated to the plans, purposes, and acts of God. In almost every instance, when Paul speaks of God as the acting sub-

---

[13] Tryggve N. D. Mettinger, *King and Messiah: The Civil and Sacral Legitimation of the Israelite Kings* (Coniectanea Biblica Old Testament 8; Lund: Gleerup, 1976), 199.

[14] See John H. Eaton, *Kingship and the Psalms* (SBT 32; London: SCM Press, 1976), 146–49. Mowinckel, who, speaking of Israelite kingship within the context of its Ancient Near Eastern counterparts, states: "The king is thus the representative of the gods on earth, the steward of the god or the gods. Through him they exercise their power and sovereignty, and he is the channel through which blessing and happiness and fertility flow from the gods to me." *The Psalms in Israel's Worship* (rev. ed.; trans. D. R. Ap-Thomas; 2 vols.; Grand Rapids: Eerdmans, 2004), 1:51.

[15] On the Messiah as receiving God's Spirit, see Johnson, *Sacral Kingship in Ancient Israel*, 15–19.

[16] For justice and righteousness, see Ps 72:1–4a; Isa 11:4–5; *Pss. Sol.* 17:32. For defeat over one's enemies, see Gen 49:10–12; Num 24:17–19; Pss 72:4b, 8–11; *2 Bar.* 39–40, 70–72. For peace and prosperity, see Pss 72:15–16; 132:15; 144:11–14; Isa 11:6–9.

[17] On this, see the excellent and comprehensive study of J. Rufus Fears, *PRINCEPS A DIIS ELECTUS: The Divine Election of the Emperor as Political Concept at Rome* (Rome: American Academy at Rome, 1977). See also Christian Habicht, *Gottmenschentum und griechische Städt* (Zetemata 14; München: Beck, 1956).

[18] "The ideal state of humanity is to be ruled by God, the supreme sovereign. This ideal state of peace, harmony, and virtue is enjoyed when God rules through his human agent, the king. That is to say, sharing in God's rule places the king in the position of distributing to humanity the benefits of God's rule." Smith, *Christ the Ideal King*, 175.

ject he portrays God acting by the channel of the Messiah.[19] God's acting through the Messiah is often indicated through the use of the phrase ἐν Χριστῷ and related prepositional constructions; so, one frequently finds the pattern of God as the subject of a verbal idea that is put into effect "in/by Christ."[20] The syntactical sense of many of these "in Christ" prepositional phrases is, on first blush, instrumental,[21] though, I suggest, a locative or participatory sense is also likely for most of these phrases. So, for example, "God has forgiven you in/by the Messiah" (ὁ θεὸς ἐν Χριστῷ ἐχαρίσατο ὑμῖν, Eph 4:32).[22] God the Father has blessed "us with every spiritual blessing in the heavenly places in/by the Messiah (ἐν τοῖς ἐπουρανίοις ἐν Χριστῷ, 1:3; cf. 1:4).[23] God will sum up all of his cosmic purposes on heaven and earth "in/by the Messiah" (ἐν τῷ Χριστῷ, 1:10).[24] God demonstrated his great power "in/by the Messiah" (Ἣν ἐνέργησεν ἐν τῷ Χριστῷ) by seating the Messiah at God's right hand (1:20). Believers are God's workmanship "created in/by Messiah Jesus" (κτισθέντες ἐν Χριστῷ Ἰησοῦ) for good works that God has ordained (2:10).

The Messiah is, then, as John Allan has argued, God's agent "through whom God works his will, elects, redeems, forgives, blesses, imparts new life, builds up his church."[25] Allan accurately recognizes the use of ἐν Χριστῷ and its correlates to mark out the Messiah as the agent of God who accomplishes his purposes; however, Allan is wrong to deny that the "in

---

[19] This has been argued by Smith, who concludes by suggesting that God's consistent activity in the Messiah "coheres well with the concept of the ideal king in antiquity, who served as the vicegerent of the High God." Smith, *Christ the Ideal King*, 195; see also 185–95.

[20] Scholars frequently describe this as "God does or gives X for his people in/by the Messiah." See Smith, *Christ the Ideal King*, 183. Campbell says that the phrase is frequently used to indicate that "God's acts towards believers are performed through Christ or are in some way conditioned or associated with Christ." *Paul and Union with Christ*, 94. Cf. Te-Li Lau, *The Politics of Peace: Ephesians, Dio Chrysostom, and the Confucian Four Books* (NovTSup 133; Leiden: Brill, 2010), 53–54.

[21] John A. Allan, "The 'In Christ' Formula in Ephesians," *NTS* 5 (1958–59): 54–62.

[22] For an example of trying to convey the instrumental and locative force of the preposition in 4:32, see Lau: "God forgave you through Christ and brought you into Christ." *The Politics of Peace*, 53–54.

[23] While not wishing to deny an instrumental sense of ἐν Χριστῷ the preceding ἐν τοῖς ἐπουρανίοις, which is certainly locative, suggests that here the in-Christ formula refers to the location or position of those in-Christ. They are "in Christ," namely, with him "in the heavens." This is further bolstered by the fact that Paul portrays Christ as raised and enthroned in heaven, and those in Christ as sharing in this heavenly enthronement (1:20–23 and 2:5–6). For an interpretation that argues for a primarily instrumental sense of the prepositional phrase, see Campbell, *Paul and Union with Christ*, 82–84.

[24] Campbell prefers a locative rendering of the prepositional phrase; Campbell, *Paul and Union with Christ*, 146.

[25] Allan, "The 'In Christ' Formula in Ephesians," 59.

Messiah" formula *often* has a locative sense, and thereby participatory connotations, in many of these constructions, for Paul clearly uses the formula to refer to believers as sharing in the identity of the Messiah.²⁶ The Messiah's heavenly exaltation (1:20–23), for example, is the basis for the church's co-resurrection and co-exaltation "in the heavenly places in Messiah Jesus" (ἐν τοῖς ἐπουρανίοις ἐν Χριστῷ Ἰησοῦ, 2:6b).²⁷ The Messiah's resurrection is the foundation, then, for God's act of "making [the church] alive together *with him*" (συνεζωοποίησεν τῷ Χριστῷ, 2:5b). So when Paul begins his epistle by blessing God for granting the church "every spiritual blessing in the heavenly places in/by the Messiah (ἐν τοῖς ἐπουρανίοις ἐν Χριστῷ, 1:3)," it is likely that ἐν Χριστῷ has both an instrumental (i.e. the Messiah as the agent of these blessings) and local sense (i.e. the church shares in the identity of the Messiah). The σύν- prefixes, which indicate association between Messiah and his people, further suggest that the ἐν prepositional phrases do not exclude a locative force.²⁸ Believers, then, are not only the recipients of God's actions *by means of the Messiah*, but they are also said to share with the Messiah in his identity and, as I will soon suggest, in his rule. How should one account for Paul's diverse employment of the ἐν Χριστῷ formula and its use to connote both the Messiah's agency for the sake of his people *and* the people's location with, or participation in, the Messiah? May it be that the formula retains both connotations precisely because when God acts *by means of* the Messiah, God acts to *incorporate the people into* the identity and rule of the Messiah (cf. 5:5)? That is, the way in which God rules, saves, and forgives is by the agency of the Messiah in whose rule they participate. Since the Messiah is the agent of salvation *and* the location where salvation is found, I suggest

---

²⁶ "It should now be clear that there is an entire absence in Ephesians of the deeper and more striking features of Paul's use of the formula, and little or no trace of the intense personal emotion it expresses in Paul. The epistle is marked by a very extensive use of the formula, but its use is predominantly, if not exclusively, in the instrumental sense ... '[i]n Christ' is no longer for this Writer the formula of incorporation into Christ, but has become the formula of God's activity through Christ." Allan, "The 'In Christ' Formula in Ephesians," 59. Lau is nearer to the mark in arguing that "in Christ" is "not a formula with a single meaning" and that the prepositional phrase often carries both instrumental and locative connotations; Lau, *The Politics of Peace*, 52; see also 52–57. Similarly, with respect to Ephesians, see Moule, *The Origin of Christology*, 62–63.

²⁷ See here Thomas G. Allen, "Exaltation and Solidarity with Christ: Ephesians 1:20 and 2:6," *JSNT* 28 (1986): 103–20.

²⁸ Campbell states with respect to the σύν-prefixed verbs in Eph 2:5–6 that they "express accompaniment and association, including participation with Christ in his being made alive, his ascension, and his being seated in the heavens." *Paul and Union with Christ*, 233. Further locative senses of the formula can be found in Eph 1:1, 4, 13; 2:15; 3:11; 4:21.

we retain both instrumental and locative connotations of ἐν Χριστῷ.[29] Thus, if the ἐν Χριστῷ formula has both connotations, then God, for example, gives resurrection life to his people *by means of the Messiah*, that is, *by means of enabling them to share in the Messiah's resurrection life* (2:5–6).[30] God forgives his people ἐν Χριστῷ, that is, by Christ and by incorporating them into his rule.

B. Pauline Participation as Sharing in the Messiah's Royal Rule in Ephesians

Having established that within Ephesians Χριστός is God's royal vicegerent who acts on God's behalf to bring his subjects within the sphere of his rule, we are now in a position to see that Paul's participatory soteriological discourse is constructed such that the church shares in the Messiah's rule and its benefits. What is true of the king and his rule is applied to the king's subjects such that the church shares in the messianic king's rule over the evil powers and thereby participates in all of the benefits of the king's rule. Paul develops his participatory soteriology, then, through a creative and innovative rereading of Israel's royal ideology through the lens of its fulfillment in God's resurrection and heavenly enthronement of the Messiah.

I. God's Enthronement of His Anointed King in Israel's Psalter

One of the central hopes of the royal psalms within Israel's Psalter is that God will establish his kingdom by extending his worldwide dominion over his people through his "chosen," elected king (Pss 89:3, 20; 132:11) – often described as Χριστός/*Mashiah* (Pss 2:2; 18:51; 20:8; 89:35, 39; 132:17).[31] These royal psalms frequently portray intense opposition to the king and his rule, with God's and the king's enemies often described in cosmic-mythical language (e.g., Pss 2:1–3; 45:5; 69:9–10; 72:9; cf. Pss

---

[29] Similarly, see Ernest Best, *One Body in Christ: A Study in the Relationship of the Church to Christ in the Epistles of The Apostle Paul* (London: SPCK, 1955), 5. Cf. Moule, *The Origin of Christology*, 54–56, 62.

[30] Best, *One Body in Christ*, 29.

[31] On the generic categorization of royal psalms, see Eaton, *Kingship and the Psalms*, 1–86; Mowinckel, *Psalms in Israel's Worship*, 1:42–80. On the Davidic king as God's elected chosen one, see Hans-Joachim Kraus, *Theology of the Psalms* (Minneapolis: Fortress, 1992), 109. Scott Starbuck argues that the royal psalms are united by the simple fact that they use the term *Mashiah* and center upon him; Scott R. A. Starbuck, *The Court Oracles in the Psalms: The So-Called Royal Psalms in their Ancient Near Eastern Context* (SBLDS 172; Atlanta: SBL, 1999), 121.

46:3–6; 48:4–8).³² The king's enemies are further described as political rulers themselves, as those "kings of the earth" (οἱ βασιλεῖς τῆς γῆς) and "rulers" (οἱ ἄρχοντες) who try to destroy "the Lord and his anointed" (κατὰ τοῦ κυρίου καὶ κατὰ τοῦ χριστοῦ, Ps 2:2–3).³³ God's response to these rebels is to rescue the king out of his persecutions (Pss 18:4–6, 43–48; 20–21),³⁴ and to enthrone the king by giving him a share in God's own royal rule.³⁵ So in Ps 110 God exalts the king over his enemies by inviting the king to share his throne:

"The Lord says to my lord, 'Sit at my right hand until I make your enemies a footstool under your feet (Κάθου ἐκ δεξιῶν μου, ἕως ἂν θῶ τοὺς ἐχθρούς σου ὑποπόδιον τῶν ποδῶν σου).' The Lord sends out from Zion your mighty scepter. Rule in the midst of your enemies" (Ps 110 [109]:1–2).³⁶

Again, in Ps 2 God's response to the political rebels is the enthronement of his son:

"I have set my king on Zion my holy hill," and "You are my son; today I have begotten you. Ask of me, and I will make the nations your heritage, and the ends of the earth your possession" (Ps 2:6, 7b–8).

As a result of the king's enthronement, at least three elements are made to characterize God's anointed king: a) The king is elected as God's earthly representative such that he shares God's throne and is installed as God's

---

³² J. J. M. Roberts, "The Enthronement of Yhwh and David: The Abiding Theological Significance of the Kingship Language of the Psalms," *CBQ* 64 (2002): 675–86; Jerome F. D. Creach, *The Destiny of the Righteous in the Psalms* (St. Louis: Chalice Press, 2008), 54–69. Eaton states: "The impression we gain is of the king as the unique representative of God and of God's people, and hence the target for all the evil forces which assault earthly society." *Kingship and Psalms*, 137.

³³ Speaking of Ps 2:1–3, James L. Mays states: "The question [of v. 3] gathers up the entire scene of governments and rulers, grasping and consolidating power, working out their destiny in terms of force; and it interprets the machinations of the whole thing theologically as rebellion against the Lord and his Anointed." *The Lord Reigns: A Theological Handbook to the Psalms* (Louisville: Westminster John Knox, 1994), 109.

³⁴ On the king's sufferings and his persecution by his enemies, see Johnson, *Sacral Kingship in Ancient Israel*, 22–26.

³⁵ On God's enthronement of the king, see Kraus, *Theology of the Psalms*, 112–13.

³⁶ For detailed analyses of the Septuagintal context, tradition history, and use in the NT of Ps 110:1, see David M. Hay, *Glory at the Right Hand: Psalm 110 in Early Christianity* (SBLMS 18; Nashville: Abingdon, 1973); Martin Hengel, "'Sit at My Right Hand!': The Enthronement of Christ at the Right Hand of God and Psalm 110:1" in *Studies in Early Christology* (Edinburgh: T&T Clark, 1995), 119–225; W. R. G. Loader, *Sohn und Hoherpriester: Eine traditionsgeschichtliche Untersuchung zur Christologie des Hebräerbriefes* (WMANT 53; Neukirchen–Vluyn: Neukirchener, 1981); Loader, "Christ at the Right Hand: Ps cx.1 in the New Testament," *NTS* 24 (1977–78): 199–217; Donald Juel, *Messianic Exegesis: Christological Interpretation of the Old Testament in Early Christianity* (Philadelphia: Fortress, 1988), 135–50.

son (Pss 2:7; 89:26–27 cf. 2 Sam 7:12–14);[37] b) the king is rescued out of a situation of distress, is exalted over his enemies (Pss 2:8–9; 110:2; cf. Dan 7:14), and is invited to rule over them; and, c) the enthroned king ushers in a time of righteous rule characterized by peace and prosperity for his people.

There is an inextricable relationship between the rule of God's royal son and the good of the people. The king's rule over his people and his concomitant defeat of his enemies, it was believed, would usher in a period of peace and prosperity for his subjects.[38] The life and rule of the king (Ps 72:5–6, 15), it was hoped, would result in "prosperity for the people" (v. 3), "peace abounding" (v. 7), and an "abundance of grain in the land" (v. 16). Thus, the psalmist prays that the king would "have dominion from sea to sea and from the River to the ends of the earth. May his foes bow down before him and his enemies lick the dust" (Ps 72:8; cf. Gen 49:8–12; Num 24:17–19; Zech 9:10). God's establishment of the king's throne enables the king to "crush his foes before him and strike down those who hate him" (Ps 89:23). The rule of this righteous king will result in "all nations [being] blessed in him" (Ps 72:17). The end of Ps 2 declares that those who "take refuge in him" (Ps 2:11), that is, those who submit to the king's rule, will find blessing and will not perish (Ps 2:9–10). The king will protect and defend the righteous from evildoers (Ps 101:5–8). The king defends his people and delivers them from their enemies (Ps 72:1–4, 12–14). The king's rule over his people is characterized by God's own "faithfulness and steadfast love" (Ps 89:24). In Ps 144 the king prays for his deliverance from his enemies so that his people may enjoy protection, peace, and fertility in the land (Ps 144:11–14).[39] God's granting of life and deliverance to the king (Ps 22:20–25) will result in food for the poor (22:26) and service and worship of God (22:27–31). The king even stabilizes and rules the cosmos as God sets "his hand on the sea and his right hand on the rivers" (Ps 89:25).

---

[37] On the significance of God's invitation to the king to share his throne and its significance for early Christian Christology, see Richard Bauckham, *Jesus and the God of Israel: God Crucified and other Studies on the New Testament's Divine Identity Christology* (Grand Rapids: Eerdmans, 2008), 152–81.

[38] "God's gift of life to his king brings life also to his people." Eaton, *Kingship and the Psalms*, 156. On the saints sharing in God's rule in pre-Christian Judaism, see M. David Litwa, *We are Being Transformed: Deification in Paul's Soteriology* (BZNW 187; Berlin: Walter de Gruyter, 2012), 179–82. See also Franz Mussner, who points to Jewish apocalyptic to explain the conceptual precedent for the ruled sharing in the rule of a transcendent figure; Franz Mussner, *Christus das All und die Kirche: Studien zur Theologie des Epheserbriefes* (Trier: Paulinus, 1955), 91–97.

[39] See Eaton, *Kingship and the Psalms*, 166.

II. Participating in the Rule of the Resurrected-Enthroned King in Ephesians

The central contention of my argument is that Paul develops his participatory soteriology by rereading Israel's royal-messianic ideology, particularly (but not exclusively) Ps 110, such that the Messiah's people not only benefit from, but also participate in the Messiah's resurrection from the dead, enthronement and rule over his enemies, and heavenly-cosmic blessings.[40] Paul's participatory metaphors and language thereby declares that what has happened to the Messiah in his resurrection and enthronement is true, by participation, of the Messiah's people.[41]

Israelite royal ideology, and particularly Ps 110, supplies the narrative movement and categories for God's resurrection and enthronement of the Messiah in Eph 1:20–23.[42] Though assumed in Paul's retelling of the event, the Messiah is under opposition from hostile political-cosmic powers (Eph 1:21) not unlike the anointed figure in Ps 2, and they have managed to bring about the Messiah's death (cf. ἐκ νεκρῶν, Eph 1:20a). That the "rulers of this age" (1 Cor 2:8) are, at least indirectly, responsible for the death of the Messiah is something Paul's readers are familiar with from his other epistles (cf. 1 Cor 2:8; 15:24–25). So too the Messiah's people were formerly in a state of death as they were beholden to their transgressions and sins (ὑμᾶς ὄντας νεκρούς, Eph 2:1; ὄντας ἡμᾶς νεκρούς, 2:5). Those responsible for humanity's state of "death" are the same political enemies of the Messiah (cf. Eph 1:21); namely, the hostile rulers of "the age of this world" (τὸν αἰῶνα τοῦ κόσμου τούτου, 2:2), and "the ruler of the authority of the air" (τὸν ἄρχοντα τῆς ἐξουσίας τοῦ ἀέρος, 2:2).[43] Given Paul's direct citation of Pss 110:1 (Eph 1:20) and 8:7 (Eph 1:22), it is likely that the enemies of God and his anointed are understood by Paul through

---

[40] I agree here with the claim of Bauckham that "early Christian theology developed mainly through the exegesis of the Scriptures." See Bauckham, *Jesus and the God of Israel*, 173.

[41] Litwa argues similarly, though he is arguing for a version of deification in Paul, that "[W]hat makes Paul's promise of eschatological sovereignty distinctive, however, is that the rule he envisions is a rule believers receive *as siblings and co-heirs of a divine being (Christ)*." *We are Being Transformed*, 182.

[42] This is clearly articulated by Douglas A. Campbell, "The Story of Jesus in Romans and Galatians," in *Narrative Dynamics in Paul: A Critical Assessment* (ed. Bruce W. Longenecker; Louisville: Westminster John Knox, 2002), 116; see also 97–124; cf. Timo Eskola, *Messiah and the Throne: Jewish Merkabah Mysticism and Early Christian Exaltation Discourse* (WUNT 2/142; Tübingen: Mohr-Seibeck, 2001), 158–204.

[43] On the connections between 1:20–23 and 2:1–6, see Allen, "Exaltation and Solidarity with Christ," 103–4.

the lens of the Psalms' portrait of opposition to the anointed (Pss 2:2–3; 110:2–3; cf. Dan 7:27).[44]

God responds, however, to the enemies of his Messiah by demonstrating his great power "at work *in the Messiah* by raising him from the dead" (Ἣν ἐνήργησεν ἐν τῷ Χριστῷ ἐγείρας αὐτόν ἐκ νεκρῶν, Eph 1:20a). God not only raises the Messiah but also, echoing the language of Ps 110:1, "seats him at his right hand, that is, in the heavenly places" (καθίσας ἐν δεξιᾷ αὐτοῦ ἐν τοῖς ἐπουρανίοις, Eph 1:20b).[45] The opposition against the Messiah is thereby overcome, as it is in Ps 2, by God's act of giving resurrection life to his anointed and sharing his heavenly throne with his vicegerent.[46] The resurrected-enthroned Messiah, having taken his royal seat at God's right hand, now receives the subjection of all things underneath his feet (Eph 1:22a; cf. Ps 8:7).[47] God's enthronement of his king is cosmic in scope in that the Messiah is exalted over every imaginable heavenly power, that is, "above all rule, authority, power, lord, and every name that is named, not only in this age but also in the coming age" (ὑπεράνω πάσης ἀρχῆς καὶ ἐξουσίας καὶ δυνάμεως καὶ κυριότητος καὶ παντὸς ὀνόματος ὀνομαζομένου οὐ μόνον ἐν τῷ αἰῶνι τούτῳ ἀλλὰ καὶ ἐν τῷ μέλλοντι, Eph 1:21). These rulers over which the Messiah now reigns are the same hostile rulers of "the age of this world" (τὸν αἰῶνα τοῦ κόσμου τούτου, 2:2), namely, "the ruler of the authority of the air" (τὸν ἄρχοντα τῆς ἐξουσίας τοῦ ἀέρος, 2:2) that have held humanity in a state of death and bondage to sin (2:1, 5). The Messiah's enthronement over the evil powers results in the

---

[44] See also, Novenson, *Christ Among the Messiahs*, 144–45.

[45] Timothy Gombis argues that Paul "echoes the movement of the entire psalm, especially the manner in which the conquering activity of God and Christ in Eph 2 reflects the subjecting activity of Yahweh and his appointed king in Ps. 110." "Ephesians 2 as a Narrative of Divine Warfare," *JSNT* 26 (2004): 408–9; see also 403–18. See also, Gordon D. Fee, *Pauline Christology: An Exegetical-Theological Study* (Grand Rapids: Baker Academic, 2007), 353.

[46] On the early church's interpretation of Jesus' resurrection as his royal enthronement, see John H. Hayes, "The Resurrection as Enthronement and the Earliest Church Christology," *Int* 22 (1968): 333–45; Lidija Novakovic, *Raised from the Dead According to the Scripture: The Role of Israel's Scripture in the Early Christian Interpretation of Jesus' Resurrection* (Jewish and Christian Texts in Contexts and Related Studies Series; London: Bloomsbury T&T Clark, 2012), 133–46.

[47] The link between Ps 110:1 and Ps 8:7 appears to have developed at the very beginning stages of early Christian Christology (see 1 Cor 15:23–28; Heb 2:5–18; 1 Pet 3:22). See Aquila H. I. Lee, *From Messiah to Preexistent Son: Jesus' Self-Consciousness and Early Christian Exegesis of Messianic Psalms* (WUNT 2/192; Tübingen: Mohr-Siebeck, 2005), 216–23.

salvation and rescue of the king's subjects (χάριτί ἐστε σεσωμένοι, 2:5; Τῇ γὰρ χάριτί ἐστε σεσωμένοι, 2:8; αὐτὸς σωτὴρ τοῦ σώματος, 5:23).[48]

But Paul sees the resurrection and enthronement of the Messiah as having more than positive and prosperous implications for the Messiah's subjects; those who are "in Messiah Jesus" (ἐν Χριστῷ 'Ιησοῦ, Eph 2:6b, 7b) actually participate in the Messiah's resurrection and enthronement. Thus, God has "made them alive together with the Messiah" (συνεζωοποίησεν τῷ Χριστῷ, 2:5), "raised them together," (συνήγειρεν) and "seated them together in the heavenly places in Messiah Jesus" (συνεκάθισεν ἐν τοῖς ἐπουρανίοις ἐν Χριστῷ 'Ιησοῦ, 2:6).[49] The three σύν- prefixed compound verbs in Eph 2:5–6 recall Paul's use of Ps 110 in Eph 1:20–23,[50] but here he applies the royal notion of resurrection and enthronement to all who are in Messiah Jesus thereby royal-izing the king's subjects.[51] As God rescued his Messiah "from the dead" (Eph 1:20a) and "seated him at his right hand in the heavenly places" (1:20b), so he has rescued the Messiah's subjects from "death" (2:1, 5) and seated them with him "in the heavenly places; namely, in Messiah Jesus" (ἐν τοῖς ἐπουρανίοις ἐν Χριστῷ 'Ιησοῦ, 2:5b). The locative force of the preceding prepositional phrases should not be missed as they indicate the messianic-royal realm where believers now rule – in the heavenly realm with the Messiah himself.[52] The Messiah's resurrection life and heavenly rule are now realities that the Messiah's people participate in by virtue of their incorporation into Messiah Jesus and his rule. That is, the royal promises made to the king in Israel's Psalter, particularly the promises of resurrection and enthronement, now belong *both* to the Messiah *and his people*.

The peoples' sharing in the Messiah's resurrection and enthronement is the foundation for their active participation in the Messiah's triumph over

---

[48] On the good king as the savior of his people and "Savior" as a typical honorific for many of the Hellenistic kings, see Donald Dale Walker, *Paul's Offer of Leniency (2 Cor 10:1): Populist Ideology and Rhetoric in a Pauline Letter Fragment* (WUNT 2/152; Tübingen: Mohr-Siebeck, 2002), 127–28, n. 138. The good king was frequently portrayed as rescuing his subjects and fighting their battles out of his love or φιλανθρωπία for his subjects (*Let. Aris.* 289–90; Plutarch, *Alex.* 21.3; Dio Chrysostom, *1 Regn.* 20). See further Celsus Spicq, "La philanthropie hellénistique, vertu divine et royale (à propos de Tit 3:4)" *ST* 12 (1958): 169–91.

[49] See Campbell, *Paul and Union with Christ*, 84–86.

[50] The three σύν- prefixed verbs stress the relational solidarity between the Messiah and his people. So Allen, "Exaltation and Solidarity with Christ," 105; Campbell, *Paul and Union with Christ*, 232–33. On the significance of the relationship between 1:20–23 and 2:5–6, see A. T. Lincoln, "A Re-Examination of 'the Heavenlies' in Ephesians," *NTS* 19 (1972–73): 472–74; see also 468–83.

[51] Gombis, "Ephesians 2 as a Narrative of Divine Warfare," 410–11; Markus Barth, *Ephesians 1 – 3* (AB 34A; Garden City, N.Y.: Doubleday, 1974), 164–65.

[52] Allen, "Exaltation and Solidarity with Christ," 106.

the evil powers as they do battle against the powers of evil (Eph 6:10–20). When Paul says "be empowered in the Lord and by the might of his strength" (ἐν<u>δυ</u>ναμοῦσθε ἐν κυρίῳ καὶ ἐν τῷ κράτει τῆς ἰσχύος αὐτοῦ, 6:10), it is difficult to determine whether the prepositional phrases "in the Lord" and "in the strength of his might" refer to God's strength *or* the Messiah's.[53] Yet based on Paul's previous mention of power language, I suggest Paul is referring to *God's powerful agency* that has been climactically displayed in his resurrection of the Messiah. So in Eph 1:19–20 he has prayed that the saints might know "the surpassing greatness of [God's] power (μέγεθος <u>τῆς δυνάμεως</u> αὐτοῦ) for us who believe, which is according to the mighty power of his strength (κατὰ τὴν ἐνέργειαν <u>τοῦ κράτους τῆς ἰσχύος αὐτοῦ</u>) *which he worked* ("Ην ἐνήργησεν) *when he raised the Messiah from the dead and seated him at his right hand.*" Thus, Paul's language of divine power is inextricably tied to God's mighty act of raising and enthroning his Son to his right hand. When Paul prays to this powerful God (Τῷ δὲ δυναμένῳ, 3:20a) as the one who works about his will for his people *according to the power which is at work within us*" (κατὰ τὴν δύναμιν τὴν ἐνεργουμένην ἐν ἡμῖν, 3:20b), based on the parallel with 1:19–20, Paul is declaring that *God's resurrection power* is intrinsic to the life of the church. Thus, by virtue of its union with the resurrected-enthroned Messiah (1:20–23; 2:5–6), the church is strengthened with God's resurrection power to do battle against its enemies. There is no need, however, for the church to triumph over its enemies but rather simply a need to resist them (6:11, 13), given that they are the same enemies the Messiah has already defeated (6:12). They are the same "rulers" (τὰς ἀρχάς, 6:12; cf. πάσης ἀρχῆς, 1:21), "authorities," (τὰς ἐξουσίας, 6:12; cf. πάσης...ἐξουσίας, 1:21; τὸν ἄρχοντα τῆς ἐξουσίας τοῦ ἀέρος, 2:2b), and "cosmic powers of this darkness" (τοὺς κοσμοκράτορας τοῦ σκότους τούτου, 6:12; τὸν αἰῶνα τοῦ κόσμου τούτου, 2:1) that the Messiah subjected to his rule when he was enthroned "in the heavenly places" (ἐν τοῖς ἐπουρανίοις, 1:20b) thereby ending their evil dominion "in the heavenly places" (ἐν τοῖς ἐπουρανίοις, 6:12b).

III. Participating in the Benefits of the Messiah's Rule

The people's share in the cosmic rule of God's resurrected and enthroned Messiah is the foundation for their participation in the royal benefits of his rule. As Israel's Psalter held forth the hope that God's enthronement of his king would lead to a period of peace and prosperity for Israel, so the people's participation in the enthroned king's rule enables them to share in the benefits of the Messiah's rule. At least three royal benefits for the Messi-

---

[53] Campbell, *Paul and Union with Christ*, 151–54.

ah's people are taken up by Paul in Ephesians as ways of articulating the people's participation in the Messiah's rule.

1. Participating in the Messiah's Election

God's election of his people to adoptive sonship is founded upon their participation in God's election of his royal son. We have seen that in Israelite royal ideology God's election of the king involves the adoption of him as his son (Pss 2:7; 89:25–27; 1 Sam 16:1–13; 1 Chr 17:13–14).[54] As God's anointed, the king is imbued with the rule, authority, and Spirit of God (1 Sam 10:6–11; 11:6–7; 16:13; Pss 2:2; 89:21–22, 27–28). Foundational here, of course, is God's promise in 2 Sam 7 where God chooses to establish the house of David to rule over Israel thereby creating the Father-Son relationship between God and David: "I will be a father to him, and he will be a son to me" (ἐγὼ ἔσομαι αὐτῷ εἰς πατέρα, καὶ αὐτὸς ἔσται μοι εἰς υἱόν, 2 Sam 7:14a).[55] Thus, one of the honorifics for God's enthroned king is his elect or chosen one (e.g., LXX Pss 88:4, 20). This royal context between God/Father and King/Son is the appropriate context for understanding Paul's election language in Eph 1:3–14 where the Messiah's people participate in the Son's election.

Within Eph 1:3–14 Paul speaks of the Messiah as God *the Father's* elected son in whose election the church shares by participation.[56] Thus, Paul declares that "God *the Father's*" (ὁ θεὸς καὶ πατήρ, 1:3; cf. ἀπὸ θεοῦ πατρὸς ἡμῶν, 1:2) *electing grace* bestowed upon the adoptive sons "is gifted to us *in the beloved*" (ἐχαρίτωσεν ἡμᾶς ἐν τῷ ἠγαπημένῳ, 1:6). The Father's bestowal of electing love upon his son (1:6) is the foundation here for God's choosing the church "in love" (ἐν ἀγάπῃ, 1:4b) and "by means of Messiah Jesus" (1:5).[57] Some significant witnesses (D*, F, G) even read "is gifted to us *in his beloved son*" (ἐν τῷ ἠγαπημένῳ υἱῷ αὐτοῦ), a reading that makes explicit the relationship between the Messiah's sonship and the

---

[54] Mowinckel, *The Psalms in Israel's Worship*, 1:53–55, 64–65; J. Randall Short, *The Surprising Election and Confirmation of King David* (HTS 63; Cambridge, Mass.: Harvard University Press, 2010), 129–92.

[55] On Israel's king as God's Son, see Gerald Cooke, "The Israelite King as Son of God," *ZAW* 73 (1961): 202–25; Mettinger, *King and Messiah*, 259–68; Eaton, *Kingship and the Psalms*, 146–49; James M. Scott, *Adoption as Sons of God: An Exegetical Investigation into the Background of ΥΙΟΘΕΣΙΑ in the Pauline Corpus* (WUNT 2/48; Tübingen: Mohr-Siebeck, 1992), 88–117.

[56] There are 40 occurrences of "Father" as language for God in the Pauline corpus and eight of them occur in Ephesians. This is rightly emphasized by Trevor J. Burke, *Adopted into God's Family: Exploring a Pauline Metaphor* (NSBT 22; Downers Grove, Ill.: InterVarsity Press, 2006), 74–75.

[57] I am taking ἐν ἀγάπῃ as modifying προορίσας in 1:5. See Burke, *Adopted into God's Family*, 77–78.

adoptive sonship of his people.[58] This statement may allude to David's response to God's electing love demonstrated in God's bestowal of sonship upon David: "what is my house that *you have loved me* in this way?" (ἠγάπηκάς με ἕως τούτων, 2 Sam 7:18).[59] The allusion to Israelite royal ideology is further established by the parallel in Col 1:13 where Paul speaks of God's redemptive purposes as centering upon τοῦ υἱοῦ τῆς ἀγάπης αὐτοῦ ("his beloved son," 1:13b).[60] The relationship between God "the Father" (τῷ πατρί, Col 1:12) and "the son of his love" echoes Ps 2:6–8 and 2 Sam 7:12–14 where the king is spoken of as God's son. Thus, Paul's description of the Messiah as "the beloved one" recalls God's election of him as his chosen son. Paul speaks explicitly of God's election of the Messiah when he refers to God's "kind choice that he set forth in him" (τὴν εὐδοκίαν αὐτοῦ ἣν προέθετο ἐν αὐτῷ, Eph 1:9) to provide reconciliation of all things in him (1:10). Just as the Messiah's accomplishment of reconciliation is according to the Father's "kind choice" (τὴν εὐδοκίαν αὐτοῦ, 1:9b), so is God's election of his people to sonship through the Messiah "*according to the kind choice* of his will" (κατὰ τὴν εὐδοκίαν τοῦ θελήματος αὐτοῦ, 1:5b). The language of εὐδοκ- is also used to describe God's election of David: "My brothers were handsome and tall, but the Lord *did not choose them*" (οὐκ εὐδόκησεν ἐν αὐτοῖς); God's rescue of David is the result of his electing delight in the king (ὅτι εὐδόκησεν ἐν ἐμοί, 2 Sam 22:20).[61]

Thus, God "elects us *in him*" (ἐξελέξατο ἡμᾶς ἐν αὐτῷ, Eph 1:4a); God "foreordains us for adoption *through Messiah Jesus*" (προορίσας ἡμᾶς εἰς υἱοθεσίαν διὰ Ἰησοῦ Χριστοῦ, 1:5a); God's electing adoption of his people is a manifestation of "his grace which he gifted to us *in the beloved*" (1:6b); "we have been called *in him* having been foreordained" (Ἐν ᾧ καὶ ἐκληρώθημεν προορισθέντος, 1:11). Leslie Allen has argued that many of the occurrences of (προ)ὁρίζω in the NT reflect Ps 2:7 and God's "decree" to elect the king as his son.[62] So, in Rom 1:4 Paul, in interaction with Ps 2,

---

[58] Michael Peppard makes the intriguing suggestion that Eph 1:4–6 alludes to Mk 1:11 and the Father's declaration of Jesus as his chosen son; Michael Peppard, *The Son of God in the Roman World: Divine Sonship in Its Social and Political Context* (Oxford: Oxford University Press, 2011), 112.

[59] Cf. 1 Chron 17:16: ὅτι ἠγάπησάς με ἕως αἰῶνος. See also the song of Moses in LXX Deut 33:5a, in which Moses prophesies of a time when there "will be a ruler in the beloved one" (ἔσται ἐν τῷ ἠγαπημένῳ ἄρχων).

[60] Christopher A. Beetham, *Echoes of Scripture in the Letter to the Colossians* (Biblical Interpretation Series 96; Leiden: Brill, 2008), 97–112.

[61] For more detail, and with detailed attention to Mk 1:11, see Peppard, *The Son of God in the Roman World*, 106–12.

[62] Leslie C. Allen, "The Old Testament Background of (προ)ὁρίζειν in the New Testament," *NTS* 17 (1970): 104–8. This is not, however, borne out by the witness of the Sep-

declares that Jesus was "destined as God's Son" (τοῦ ὁρισθέντος υἱοῦ θεοῦ) by his resurrection from the dead.[63] Much of the (προ)ὁρίζω language in the NT, in fact, occurs in contexts where the Messiah is enthroned in power to rule and judge (ὁ ὡρισμένος ὑπὸ τοῦ θεοῦ κριτὴς ζώντων καὶ νεκρῶν, Acts 10:42; κρίνειν τὴν οἰκουμένην ἐν δικαιοσύνῃ, ἐν ἀνδρὶ ᾧ ὥρισεν, 17:31; cf. Rom 8:29; 1 Cor 2:7). Thus, Paul's application of election language to the church (Eph 1:4, 5, 11) whereby it shares in adoptive sonship (1:5) and "every spiritual blessing" (1:3) through their participation in the Messiah is (in part) the result of Paul's distinctive application of Ps 2 to the peoples' share in the Messiah's election.

Paul articulates the foundation for the people's election to share in the Messiah's sonship, however, in Eph 1:3 where he gives it as an example (καθώς, 1:4) of God's blessings for those who are "in the heavenly places, in the Messiah" (ἐν τοῖς ἐπουρανίοις ἐν Χριστῷ, 1:3b). Both prepositional phrases refer here to the location of the Messiah's people, namely, "in heaven with the Messiah," and provide the ground for God's bestowal to them of "every spiritual blessing" (1:3). The people's heavenly participation in the Messiah's heavenly enthronement (ἐν δεξιᾷ αὐτοῦ ἐν τοῖς ἐπουρανίοις, 1:20; ἐν τοῖς ἐπουρανίοις ἐν Χριστῷ Ἰησοῦ, 2:6) is the ground that establishes their election to sonship, a blessing that has been given to them "in the heavenly places in the Messiah" (1:3b).[64] The Father's love for his beloved and elect Son (1:6) is the same love (2:4) that stands behind God's decision to extend the Messiah's rule to his people (2:5–6).[65]

2. Participating in the Messiah's Body

Paul conceptualizes the church's participation in the Messiah's heavenly rule through the royal imagery of "head" and "body."[66] As Campbell notes, "If the church is Christ's body, of which he is head, the metaphor must convey connotations of union [i.e., with Christ]."[67] But these "connotations

---

tuagint which reads πρόσταγμα κύριου (Ps 2:7a LXX), and it depends upon a possible earlier rendering of *haq* with (προ)ὁρίζω.

[63] With respect to Rom 1:3–4, see Christopher G. Whitsett, "Son of God, Seed of David: Paul's Messianic Exegesis in Romans 2:3–4," *JBL* 119 (2000): 661–81; Joshua W. Jipp, "Ancient, Modern, and Future Interpretations of Romans 1:3–4: Reception History and Biblical Interpretation," *JTI* 3 (2009): 241–59.

[64] See Lincoln, who states that the blessings of 1:3ff "are to be found both ἐν τοῖς ἐπουρανίοις and ἐν Χριστῷ, the latter phrase signifying that believers partake of the benefits because they are incorporated into the ascended Christ as their representative who is himself in the heavenlies." "A Re-Examination of 'the Heavenlies' in Ephesians," 471.

[65] Allen, "Exaltation and Solidarity with Christ," 109–12.

[66] There are many complex issues related to this metaphor into which we cannot enter. See the sage treatment of Moule, *The Origin of Christology*, 69–89.

[67] Campbell, *Paul and Union with Christ*, 268.

of union" are precisely that of participating in the king's lordship, given that God makes the Messiah "head over all things" by means of his royal enthronement *and* by the fact that the metaphor is frequently deployed in royal contexts. And this should not be an entirely surprising claim given the frequent depiction of the commonwealth as body-politick.[68]

The first occurrence of the metaphor is in Eph 1:22–23 where God's enthronement of his Son to a position of cosmic rule is the prior event that enables God's "subjection of all things underneath his feet" (πάντα ὑπέταξεν ὑπὸ τοὺς πόδας αὐτοῦ, 1:22a). The statement is a quotation of Ps 8:7 (LXX), a psalm that celebrates God's gift of dominion over creation to Adam/humanity as his royal vicegerent(s).[69] Thus, God's heavenly enthronement of the Messiah enables him to enter into the task given to Adam; namely, the subjugation of "all things" (πάντα). It is God's enthronement of his Messiah that results in God "appoint[ing] him [i.e., the Messiah] to be head over all things for the church" (αὐτὸν ἔδωκεν κεφαλὴν ὑπὲρ πάντα τῇ ἐκκλησίᾳ, Eph 1:22b)[70] and establishes the church as the Messiah's body (ἥτις ἐστὶν τὸ σῶμα αὐτοῦ, 1:23a).[71]

Both the context of the metaphor and its primary conceptual field of discourse indicate that, for Paul, to speak of the Messiah as head is to portray him as *ruler* and to speak of the church as his body is to portray it as *ruled*.[72] Paul's use of ἡ κεφαλή has spawned an enormous amount of literature, but for my purposes it is enough to demonstrate how the metaphor of "the head" can be, and here is, language that stresses Christ's regal au-

---

[68] See, for example, Plato, *Rep.* 8.556e; Livy 2.32.12–33.1; Dionysius of Halicarnassus, *Ant. Rom.* 6.83.2; Aristotle, *Pol.* 3.6.4; Dio Chrysostom, *Oration* 33.16; 34.10–20; Aelius Aristides, *Oration* 24.38–39. Also, see Dale B. Martin, *The Corinthian Body* (New Haven, Conn.: Yale University Press, 1995), 38–47; Margaret M. Mitchell, *Paul and the Rhetoric of Reconciliation: An Exegetical Investigation of the Language and Composition of 1 Corinthians* (Louisville: Westminster John Knox, 1991), 157–64.

[69] That Adam was believed to have been God's prototypical king is a frequent theme in Jewish traditions as well (Sir 49:16; *Jub.* 2:13–15; *4 Ezra* 6:53–54; *2 En.* 30:12; 31:3). See Robin Scroggs, *The Last Adam: A Study in Pauline Theology* (Philadelphia: Fortress, 1966), 25; John R. Levison, *Portraits of Adam in Early Judaism: From Sirach to 2 Baruch* (JSPSS 1; Sheffield: Sheffield Academic Press, 1988).

[70] Barth notes that within political contexts the verb frequently has the sense of "to appoint" or "to install." *Ephesians 1–3*, 157–58; cf. 1 Sam 8:5–6; Lev 17:11; Num 14:4; Isa 42:6; Eph 4:11.

[71] I understand τῇ ἐκκλησίᾳ here as signifying that the Messiah's enthronement is the event that creates his corporate solidarity with the church (cf. 2:5–6).

[72] That Col 2:10 and Eph 1:20–23 use the term "head" in the sense of enthroned ruler is rightly recognized by Gottfried Nebe, "Christ, the Body of Christ and Cosmic Powers in Paul's Letters and the New Testament as a Whole," in *Politics and Theopolitics in the Bible and Postbiblical Literature* (ed. Henning Graf Reventlow, Yair Hoffman and Benjamin Uffenheimer; JSOTSup 171; Sheffield: JSOT Press, 1994), 114–16; see also 100–118.

thority over his assembly. For example, in 2 Samuel 22 David praises God for providing "salvation for his king and steadfast love for his anointed" (LXX 2 Sam 22:51a). David sings: "you kept me as the head over the nations (φυλάξεις με εἰς κεφαλὴν ἐθνῶν); people whom I had not known served me" (22:44).[73] Similarly, Philo says of Ptolemy II Philadelphus that "as the head takes the ruling part in a living body, so [the king] may be said to be head over the kings" (ἐν ζώῳ τὸ ἡγεμονεῦον κεφαλὴ τρόπον τινὰ τῶν βασιλέων, *Moses* 2.30). Paul's metaphor finds an obvious parallel with imperial panegyrists who exalt Caesar as head and ruler of his imperial body.[74] In *De Clementia*, Seneca repeatedly refers to Nero as the "head" and "mind" over the body of the empire and as the one who stabilizes the empire and unites his people: "the whole body (*corpus*) is the servant of the mind" and "the vast multitude of men surrounds one man as though he were its mind, ruled by his spirit, guided by his reason" (1.3.5); the emperor is "the bond by which the commonwealth is united, the breath of life which these many thousands draw," for the empire would be prey were the "mind of the empire to be withdrawn" (1.4.1); the emperor stabilizes the body, and for this reason "the commonwealth needs the head" (1.4.2–3); "the gentleness of your mind will be transmitted to others [...] it will be diffused over the whole body of the empire, and all will be formed in your likeness for health springs from the head (2.2.1)."[75] For Seneca, the function of the head (emperor)/body (empire) metaphor is to stress *the remarkable connection between the ruler and the ruled* such that Nero will care for and not harm his own body.

Given that Paul's head/body metaphor is found within a context dominated by royal language, it is almost certain that Paul's employment of the metaphor in Eph 1:22–23 portrays the Messiah as the cosmic ruler of the universe.[76] But the church as the Messiah's body does not sit passively under the rule of its head; rather, Paul claims that *the church shares in the Messiah's rule by extending his dominion in all places*. Such a claim is both the essence and function of the church – to fill the created world with the presence of its king. This is the force of Paul's claim that the church is "the fullness *of the one filling* all things in all places" (τὸ πλήρωμα τοῦ τὰ

---

[73] See, for example, Judg 10:18; 11:11; 1 Kgs 20:12 (LXX); Isa 7:8–9; 11:10–11; Jer 38:7 (LXX).

[74] On the head as the *ruling* part of the body, see Plato, *Tim.* 44d.

[75] Cf. Harry Maier, "A Sly Civility: Colossians and Empire," *JSNT* 27 (205): 335 n. 29; see also 323–49. See also, Michelle V. Lee, *Paul, the Stoics, and the Body of Christ* (SNTSMS 37; Cambridge: Cambridge University Press, 2006), 35–39.

[76] Smith, *Christ the Ideal King*, 218.

πάντα ἐν πᾶσιν πληρουμένου, 1:23b).⁷⁷ The language of πλήρωμα frequently has connotations of God's glorious dominion, often associated with creation and/or temple, in both the Greek Old Testament (e.g., Pss 23:1; 49:12; 88:12; Isa 6:1–3; Jer 23:24) and in Paul (Col 1:19; 2:9–10), and its employment here speaks of the worldwide dominion of the Messiah ("the head") extended by means of the church ("his body").⁷⁸ The Messiah fills his body with his presence, thereby establishing a deep union between Christ and church that is extended, by means of the body, to "all things in all places."⁷⁹

Paul portrays Christ-the-head as a beneficent king who rules his body by bestowing to it health, nourishment, peace, and salvation.⁸⁰ As the victorious heavenly king who "fills all things" (πληρώσῃ τὰ πάντα, Eph 4:10), the Messiah gives gifts to his church "for the edification of the Messiah's body" (εἰς οἰκοδομὴν τοῦ σώματος τοῦ Χριστοῦ, 4:12b). In his role as "the head, the Messiah" (ἡ κεφαλή, Χριστός) is the source of nourishment for the body (ἐξ οὗ πᾶν τὸ σῶμα) and the enabler of its growth (τὴν αὔξησιν τοῦ σώματος) (4:15–16). Christ's rule over the body (ὁ Χριστὸς κεφαλὴ τῆς ἐκκλησίας, 5:22b) is manifested not in tyrannical rule but, rather, in his role as "savior of the body" (αὐτὸς σωτὴρ τοῦ σώματος, 5:22c), further defined as self-giving love, service, and nourishment (5:25, 29).⁸¹ As a good king's legislation and character was thought to have produced domestic concord, so the portrayal of the loving messianic king has as its goal the production of peaceful and harmonious households and assemblies that reflect the rule of their king.⁸²

3. Participating in the Messiah's Reconciliation and Peace

Those who are united with the Messiah also participate in the Messiah's reconciled, peaceful body politic, a sacred assembly where the Messiah's peaceful reconciliation, accomplished through his death, has eradicated all

---

⁷⁷ I understand τοῦ ... πληρουμένου as middle, hence with an active meaning stressing the subject's involvement (i.e. the Messiah) in his cosmic filling by means of his body/church. See also, Moule, *The Origin of Christology*, 76–77.

⁷⁸ On the use of "fullness"-language in Ephesians and its historical-religious context, see Mussner, *Christus das All und die Kirche*, 45–64.

⁷⁹ Similarly, see Lau, *The Politics of Peace*, 58–59.

⁸⁰ Both notions of sovereignty and the nourishing union between head and body are emphasized by Best, *One Body in Christ*, 146–48.

⁸¹ For more exegetical detail on these verses, see Campbell, *Paul and Union with Christ*, 277–83. Best rightly argues that Paul's emphasis in these verses is less on the rule of the body by the head as much as on the head's nourishment to and organic unity with the body; Best, *One Body in Christ*, 150–51.

⁸² For a similar reading of Eph 5:22–33, see Smith, *Christ the Ideal King*, 235–38.

ethnic dissension (Eph 2:11–22).[83] One of the most foundational and widely recognized tasks of any ancient king was the creation of a peaceful body politic.[84] In his *Precepts of Statecraft*, Plutarch says that "peace, liberty, plenty, abundance of men, and concord are the greatest blessings that cities can enjoy," and therefore a primary responsibility of the ruler is to "instill concord and friendship in those who dwell together with him and to remove strifes, discords, and all enmity" (*Mor.* 824D). Thus, the language of (making-)peace, reconciliation, and communal harmony are frequently spoken of as a necessity for successful kings and rulers.[85] The successful king usually brought about this peace and harmony *through* the violent pacification of the king's enemies. J. Rufus Fears refers to this aspect of royal ideology as "the theology of victory."[86] Peace through pacification or reconciliation of one's enemies was often situated in a cosmic context where the peace and harmony was thought to be a gift of the gods.[87] Thus, forms of καταλάσσω and διαλάσσω are frequently used in royal and diplomatic contexts to indicate a leader's pacification of enemies thereby resulting in peace and harmony.[88] Andrew Wallace-Hadrill summarizes it succinctly when he states that the king's legitimacy to rule over a people depends upon his "power to conquer, to save, to bring harmony and stability, and to distribute benefits."[89] This depiction of the king's legitimacy to rule

---

[83] See especially here the fine work of Lau, *The Politics of Peace*, 81–97.

[84] This often took the form of reconciliation and peace through military pacification. See Philip de Souza, "*Parta Victoriis Pax*: Roman Emperors as Peacemakers," in *War and Peace in Ancient and Medieval History* (ed. Philip de Souza and John France; Cambridge: Cambridge University Press, 2008), 76–106.

[85] Augustus' *Res Gestae* boasts of his "making of peace on land and sea" (εἰρηνευομένης ... πάσης γῆς τε καὶ θαλάσσης, 13.1; cf. θάλασσα[ν] [εἰ]ρήνευσα-, 25.1; εἰρήνη κατέστησα, 26.2; θαλάσσης εἰρηνεύεσθαι πεπόηκα, 26.3). For text and translation, see Alison E. Cooley, *Res Gestae Divi Augusti: Text, Translation, and Commentary* (Cambridge: Cambridge University Press, 2009). Philo of Alexandria summarizes Augustus' accomplishments in this way (*Embassy* 145–47): "This is he who exterminated wars both of the open kind and of the covert which are brought about by the raids of brigands. This is he who cleared the sea of pirate ships and filled it with merchant vessels. This is he who reclaimed every state to liberty, who led disorder into order (ὁ τὴν ἀταξίαν εἰς τάξιν ἀγαγών) and brought gentle manners and harmony to all unsociable and brutish nations, who enlarged Hellas by many a new Hellas and Hellenized the outside world, in its most important regions – the guardian of peace (ὁ εἰρηνοφύλαξ)."

[86] Fears, *PRINCEPS A DIIS ELECTUS*, 45–46.

[87] E.g., see Pliny, *Pan.* 4.4; 5.6–9; Calpurnius Siculus, *Eclogue* 4.142–46.

[88] E.g., see Dio Cassius 1.5.6; 5.18.9; 41.35.3; 46.1.3; 48.10.2; 48.20.1.

[89] Andrew Wallace-Hadrill, "The Emperor and his Virtues," *Historia* 30 (1981): 316; see also 298–323. This ideology is stated clearly in much of the recounting of Alexander the Great's kingship. E.g., "But, as he believed that he came as a heaven-sent governor to all, and as a reconciler for the whole world (διαλλακτὴς τῶν ὅλων), those whom he could not persuade to unite with him, he conquered by force of arms, and he brought together

conforms nicely with Paul's narration of the Messiah's activity in Eph 1:20–2:22.[90] Paul has portrayed the Messiah's powerful conquering of his enemies (1:20–23), his act of saving and rescuing his subjects (2:1–8), and now proceeds to demonstrate how those in the Messiah benefit by sharing in his establishment of a sacred assembly that is marked by the king's peace.

Paul engages in ethnic stereotyping as a means of highlighting the state of ethnic discord between Jew and Gentile as he refers to the *former* (μνημονεύετε ὅτι ποτέ, Eph 2:11) animosity between the "Gentiles in the flesh" (τὰ ἔθνη ἐν σαρκί, 2:11a), namely, "those called the uncircumcision" (οἱ λεγόμενοι ἀκροβυστία, 2:11a) and "the so-called circumcision in the flesh with human hands" (τῆς λεγομένης περιτομῆς ἐν σαρκὶ χειροποιήτου, 2:11b).[91] The former state of the Gentiles was one of alienation (ἀπηλλοτριωμένοι) from Israel's *politeia*, as they are excluded outsiders (ξένοι, 2:12) from God's covenants and have no knowledge of God (2:12). They are both "far off" from God and the covenantal blessings of Israel (οἵ ποτε ὄντες μακράν, 2:13a; τοῖς μακράν, 2:18). Furthermore, there is a "dividing wall" (τὸ μεσότοιχον τοῦ φραγμοῦ, 2:14) that separates the two groups and perpetuates their enmity and hostility toward one another.

Thus, it is no surprise that Paul portrays the Messiah as an ideal king who eradicates the ethnic hostility between Jew and Gentile and transforms the two groups into one peaceful body. What is remarkable, however, is that the messianic king conquers and kills the "hostility" between Jew and Gentile, not through the usual weapons of political warfare, but by means of his bloody death on the cross: "but now in Messiah Jesus, you who were far off have been brought near by the Messiah's blood" (2:13). Paul speaks of the Messiah as a conquering king who defeats and destroys the social enmity: he "destroys ... the enmity in his flesh" (λύσας, τὴν ἔχθραν ἐν τῇ σαρκὶ αὐτοῦ, 2:14); "he tears down (καταργήσας) the law with its decrees and commands" (2:15a); "he reconciles (ἀποκαταλλάξῃ) both groups into one body for God through the cross" (2:16a); and "he kills the enmity by

---

into one body all men everywhere, uniting and mixing in one great loving-cup, as it were, men's lives, their characters, their marriages, their very habits of life" (*On the Fortune of Alexander* 329C).

[90] For a similar proposal and one that emphasizes an Ancient Near Eastern context, see Gombis, "Ephesians 2 as a Narrative of Divine Warfare."

[91] The adjective χειροποίητος is most frequently found in anti-idol polemic and is never used in a positive sense in the LXX or the NT (see, for example, Isa 2:18; 10:11; 16:12; 19:1; 21:9; 31:7; 46:6; Dan 5:4, 23; 6:28; Mk 14:58; Acts 7:48; 17:24; Heb 9:11, 24). On ethnic stereotyping of non-Jews as "the uncircumcised," see Joel Marcus, "The Circumcision and the Uncircumcision in Rome," *NTS* 35 (1989): 67–81. On ethnic stereotyping of Jews in antiquity, see Benjamin Isaac, *The Invention of Racism in Classical Antiquity* (Princeton, N.J.: Princeton University Press, 2004), 440–91.

[the cross]" (ἀποκτείνας τὴν ἔχθραν ἐν αὐτῷ, 2:16). Paul's language of the Messiah as "destroying," "tearing down," "reconciling," and "killing" conforms well with depictions of conquering kings who pacify and reconcile through violence, as we have seen, and yet Paul transforms this trope by declaring that the Messiah has created a new people by absorbing their enmity and hostility in his flesh, that is, through his bloody death on a cross.

Paul is emphatic that the result of the Messiah's death is the accomplishment of peace between Jew and Gentile thereby creating a unified body politic. And his portrait of the Messiah as a peaceful king echoes Isaiah's own *peaceful depiction of the Davidic King and God's eschatological kingdom* (Isa 9:5–6; 52:7; 57:19).[92] Peter Stuhlmacher has argued that within these verses, "the author offers a Christological exegesis of Isa 9:5–6; 52:7; and 57:19" based on the catchword of "peace."[93] In Isa 9:5–6 (LXX) God declares that through his royal Davidic Son he will "bring peace upon the rulers, peace and health to him" (εἰρήνην ἐπὶ τοὺς ἄρχοντας, εἰρήνην καὶ ὑγίειαν αὐτῷ) and that "his peace has no boundary" (τῆς εἰρήνης αὐτοῦ οὐκ ἔστιν ὅριον). Paul sees the enthroned Messiah as the Isaianic agent who "heralds the announcement of peace" (εὐαγγελιζομένου ἀκοὴν εἰρήνης, Isa 52:7).[94] Likewise, Paul speaks of the Messiah as an agent of peace: "he is our peace" (Αὐτὸς γάρ ἐστιν ἡ εἰρήνη ἡμῶν, Eph 2:14); he "makes peace" (ποιῶν εἰρήνην, 2:15b); he "comes and proclaims the good news of peace to you who are far and peace to those who are near" (ἐλθὼν εὐηγγελίσατο εἰρήνη ὑμῖν τοῖς μακρὰν καὶ εἰρήνην τοῖς ἐγγύς, 2:17). This latter statement is almost certainly an allusion to Isa 57:19 where the Lord declares "peace, peace, to the far and the near" (εἰρήνην ἐπ' εἰρήνην τοῖς μακρὰν καὶ τοῖς ἐγγὺς οὖσιν).

The result of the Messiah's establishment of peace is the eradication of the social "enmity" between Jew and Gentile (Eph 2:14b, 16b) and the creation of "one new people," (ἕνα καινὸν ἄνθρωπον, 2:15), that is, a peaceful unified "single body" (ἑνὶ σώματι, 2:16).[95] Thus, the defining marker of

---

[92] Smith provides further references for the Davidic king as an agent of peace in Jewish thought (see *Pss. Sol.* 17:24, 35; 1QSb V, 20–29; 4Q285 5 1–6; 4Q161 8–10 III, 18–25); Smith, *Christ the Ideal King*, 211.

[93] Peter Stuhlmacher, *Reconciliation, Law, & Righteousness: Essays in Biblical Theology* (Philadelphia: Fortress, 1986), 187.

[94] Stuhlmacher, *Reconciliation, Law, & Righteousness*, 187–88.

[95] It is possible to understand "one body," however, as a reference to the Messiah's bodily death rather than a corporate entity. See, however, Col 3:15; Ign. *Smyrn.* 1.2; Moule, *The Origin of Christology*, 77. See Sang-Won (Aaron) Son, *Corporate Elements in Pauline Anthropology: A Study of Selected Terms, Idioms, and Concepts in the Light of Paul's Usage and Background* (Rome: Editrice Pontificio Istituto Biblico, 2001), 95–96.

this new community is no longer ethnic or religious but is rather union with the messianic king. Those who belong to this peaceful new corporate body are singularly defined by their participation "in Messiah Jesus" (ἐν Χριστῷ Ἰησοῦ, 2:13; ἐν αὐτῷ, 2:15; ἐν ᾧ, 2:21; ἐν ᾧ, 2:22).[96] Paul uses a variety of political metaphors to portray the Messiah's peaceful and harmonious corporate community: a) it is a community of people transformed from "strangers and outsiders" into "fellow citizens with the saints" (2:19); b) "God's own household" (2:19); and, c) a "sacred temple in the Lord" (2:21) having "Messiah Jesus himself as the cornerstone" (2:20b). Thus, those who are in the Messiah share in his rule as they benefit from his act of reconciliation which has eradicated ethnic dissension and results in a peaceful, harmonious, sacred community belonging to the Messiah.

But not only does the Messiah *establish* a unified peaceful community, he also provides gifts to its members which enable them to actively share in "the edification of the Messiah's body" (4:12) for the establishment of "the unity of faith" (4:13).[97] The language of the Messiah's gift-giving is redolent in 4:7–11: "to each one of us the gift has been given according to the measure of the Messiah's gift" (Ἑνὶ δὲ ἑκάστῳ ἡμῶν ἐδόθη ἡ χάρις κατὰ τὸ μέτρον τῆς δωρεᾶς τοῦ Χριστοῦ, 4:7); "he gave gifts to people" (ἔδωκεν δόματα τοῖς ἀνθρώποις, 4:8b); and "he has gifted to some..." (αὐτὸς ἔδωκεν τούς, 4:11a).[98] The Messiah's giving of gifts to his people is predicated upon his defeat of the evil powers by means of his heavenly enthronement. Paul quotes Ps 68:19, the details of which need not concern us here, to explain (διό, Eph 4:8a) the ground of the Messiah's giving of gifts to his people: "when he rose up on high he took captivity captive" (ἀναβὰς εἰς ὕψος ᾐχμαλώτευσεν αἰχμαλωσίαν, 4:8a). Note that this is, then, followed by *another* statement about the bestowal of gifts upon humanity (4:8b).[99] Though Paul does not define ᾐχμαλώτευσεν αἰχμαλωσίαν, it is almost surely a reference to the Messiah's triumph over the evil powers based upon Paul's elaboration of the meaning of ἀναβὰς εἰς ὕψος as the Messiah's ascension "above all the heavens" (ὑπεράνω πάντων τῶν οὐρανῶν, 4:10). The reference to the Messiah's descent to the lowers regions of the earth

---

[96] The prefixed compound participle and verb also convey union between the believer and Messiah Jesus (συναρμολογουμένη, 2:21; συνοικοδομεῖσθε, 2:22).

[97] On the good king as giver of gifts and as benefactor, see Klaus Bringmann, "The King as Benefactor: Some Remarks on Ideal Kingship in the Age of Hellenism," in *Images and Ideologies: Self-definition in the Hellenistic World* (ed. Anthony Bulloch et al., Hellenistic Culture and Society 12; Berkeley: University of California Press, 1993), 7–24.

[98] Smith, *Christ the Ideal King*, 217–21.

[99] This is the central difficulty of explaining Paul's use of Ps 68:18 (LXX 67:19), namely Paul's transformation of the text from saying God *received* gifts to the Messiah as the one now giving the gifts.

(κατέβη αὐτός εἰς τὰ κατώτερα τῆς γῆς, 4:9b), then, is likely a reference to the Messiah's death. We have already seen that preceding God's seating of the Messiah at his right hand, the event enabling him to rule his enemies is God's resurrection of the Messiah "from the dead" (1:20), and in 2:13–16 Paul will speak of the Messiah's death as the surprising means whereby the Messiah triumphs over the hostility that divides Jew and Gentile.[100] Therefore, the Messiah's resurrection and exaltation over his enemies enables him to give gifts to his people that produce peace, harmony, and moral growth within the corporate community (4:11–16).[101]

C. Conclusion: The Royal Roots of Paul's Participatory Soteriology in Ephesians

I have argued that Paul develops his participatory discourse, at least within Ephesians, through a creative and innovative re-interpretation of Israelite royal ideology and reflections upon Israel's ideal and messianic king. The narrative of the Messiah, who he is and what he does, can be situated neatly against this framework: election to sonship, defeat of one's enemies, resurrection, enthronement/exaltation, the creation of a harmonious and peaceful body politic, the giving of gifts to one's subjects, and of course the honorific "Messiah" itself – all point to Israel's royal ideology as the framework for Paul's understanding of Jesus as Messiah. Paul has taken the major step, however, in describing the subjects of the Messiah as not simply benefitting from the Messiah's rule but as *sharing in the rule of the Messiah by virtue of their union with the Messiah*. This framework allows us to account for the four models articulated by Richard Hays for conceptualizing Paul's participatory soteriology. Those *in Christ*: a) belong to a family by virtue of their participation in the Messiah's sonship; b) share in the Messiah's political/military victory precisely by virtue of the Davidic Messiah's defeat of his and his peoples' political enemies; c) participate in the church/assembly as the relation between ruler (head) and ruled (body); and d) participate in the story of Christ precisely as by sharing in the messianic royal events of death, resurrection, and heavenly enthronement. My intent in this essay has simply been to show the conceptual resources and framework with which Paul is working. How Paul took the step of *apply-*

---

[100] See also Timothy G. Gombis, "Cosmic Lordship and Divine Gift-Giving: Psalm 68 in Ephesians 4:8," *NovT* 47 (2005): 277–78; see also 367–80.

[101] Moule states that "the various Christian services bestowed by the risen and ascended Christ ... are intended to complete the process of creating a Christian community, which is spoken of as Christ's body and which is to grow progressively, by virtue of the vitality derived from Christ." *The Origin of Christology*, 78.

ing this royal and messianic framework to the messiah's subjects by virtue of real participation or union is a question for another time.[102]

Bibliography

Allan, John A. "The 'In Christ' Formula in Ephesians." *New Testament Studies* 5 (1958–59): 54–62.
Allen, Leslie C. "The Old Testament Background of (προ)ὀρίζειν in the New Testament." *New Testament Studies* 17 (1970): 104–8.
Allen, Thomas G. "Exaltation and Solidarity with Christ: Ephesians 1:20 and 2:6." *Journal for the Study of the New Testament* 28 (1986): 103–20.
Barth, Markus. *Ephesians 1–3*. Anchor Bible 34A. Garden City, N.Y.: Doubleday, 1974.
Bauckham, Richard. *Jesus and the God of Israel: God Crucified and other Studies on the New Testament's Divine Identity Christology*. Grand Rapids: Eerdmans, 2008.
Beetham, Christopher A. *Echoes of Scripture in the Letter to the Colossians*. Biblical Interpretation Series 96. Leiden: Brill, 2008.
Best, Ernest. *One Body in Christ: A Study in the Relationship of the Church to Christ in the Epistles of The Apostle Paul*. London: SPCK, 1955.
Bringmann, Klaus. "The King as Benefactor: Some Remarks on Ideal Kingship in the Age of Hellenism." Pages 7–24 in *Images and Ideologies: Self-definition in the Hellenistic World*. Edited by Anthony Bulloch et al. Hellenistic Culture and Society 12. Berkeley: University of California Press, 1993.
Bultmann, Rudolf. *Theology of the New Testament*. Translated by Kendrick Grobel. New York: Charles Scribner's Sons, 1951–55.
Burke, Trevor J. *Adopted into God's Family: Exploring a Pauline Metaphor*. New Studies in Biblical Theology 22. Downers Grove, Ill.: InterVarsity Press, 2006.
Campbell, Constantine R. *Paul and Union with Christ: An Exegetical and Theological Study*. Grand Rapids: Zondervan, 2012.
Campbell, Douglas A. *The Quest for Paul's Gospel: A Suggested Strategy*. London: T&T Clark, 2005.
———. "The Story of Jesus in Romans and Galatians." Pages 97–124 in *Narrative Dynamics in Paul: A Critical Assessment*. Edited by Bruce W. Longenecker. Louisville: Westminster John Knox, 2002.
Chester, Andrew. *Messiah and Exaltation: Jewish Messianic and Visionary Traditions and New Testament Christology*. Wissenschaftliche Untersuchungen zum Neuen Testament 207. Tübingen: Mohr-Siebeck, 2007.
Collins, John J. *The Scepter and the Star: The Messiahs of the Dead Sea Scrolls and Other Ancient Literature*. Anchor Bible Reference Library. New York: Doubleday, 1995.
Cooke, Gerald. "The Israelite King as Son of God." *Zeitschrift für die alttestamentliche Wissenschaft* 73 (1961): 202–25.
Cooley, Alison E. *Res Gestae Divi Augusti: Text, Translation, and Commentary*. Cambridge: Cambridge University Press, 2009.
Creach, Jerome F. D. *The Destiny of the Righteous in the Psalms*. St. Louis: Chalice Press, 2008.

---

[102] And one I take up in my forthcoming *Christ Is King: Paul's Royal Christology*.

de Jonge, M. "The Use of the Word 'Anointed' in the Time of Jesus." *Novum Testamentum* 8 (1966): 132–48.
de Souza, Philip. "*Parta Victoriis Pax*: Roman Emperors as Peacemakers." Pages 76–106 in *War and Peace in Ancient and Medieval History*. Edited by Philip de Souza and John France. Cambridge: Cambridge University Press, 2008.
Eaton, John H. *Kingship and the Psalms*. Studies in Biblical Theology 32. London: SCM Press, 1976.
Eskola, Timo. *Messiah and the Throne: Jewish Merkabah Mysticism and Early Christian Exaltation Discourse*. Wissenschaftliche Untersuchungen zum Neuen Testament 2/142. Tübingen: Mohr-Seibeck, 2001.
Fears, J. Rufus. *PRINCEPS A DIIS ELECTUS: The Divine Election of the Emperor as Political Concept at Rome*. Rome: American Academy at Rome, 1977.
Fee, Gordon D. *Pauline Christology: An Exegetical-Theological Study*. Grand Rapids: Baker Academic, 2007.
Fitzmyer, Joseph A. *The One Who Is to Come*. Grand Rapids: Eerdmans, 2007.
Gombis, Timothy G. "Cosmic Lordship and Divine Gift-Giving: Psalm 68 in Ephesians 4:8." *Novum Testamentum* 47 (2005): 367–80.
———. "Ephesians 2 as a Narrative of Divine Warfare." *Journal for the Study of the New Testament* 26 (2004): 403–18.
Gorman, Michael J. *Inhabiting the Cruciform God: Kenosis, Justification, and Theosis in Paul's Narrative Soteriology*. Grand Rapids: Eerdmans, 2009.
Habicht, Christian. *Gottmenschentum und griechische Städt*. Zetemata 14. München: Beck, 1956.
Hay, David M. *Glory at the Right Hand: Psalm 110 in Early Christianity*. Society of Biblical Literature Monograph Series 18. Nashville: Abingdon, 1973.
Hayes, H. "The Resurrection as Enthronement and the Earliest Church Christology." *Interpretation* 22 (1968): 333–45.
Hays, Richard B. "What is 'Real Participation in Christ'?: A Dialogue with E. P. Sanders on Pauline Soteriology." Pages 336–51 in *Redefining First-Century Jewish and Christian Identities: Essays in Honor of Ed Parish Sanders*. Christianity and Judaism in Antiquity Series 16. Edited by Fabian E. Udoh et al. Notre Dame: University of Notre Dame Press, 2008.
Hengel, Martin. "'Sit at My Right Hand!': The Enthronement of Christ at the Right Hand of God and Psalm 110:1." Pages 119–225 in *Studies in Early Christology*. Edinburgh: T&T Clark, 1995.
Isaac, Benjamin. *The Invention of Racism in Classical Antiquity*. Princeton, N.J.: Princeton University Press, 2004.
Jipp, Joshua W. "Ancient, Modern, and Future Interpretations of Romans 1:3–4: Reception History and Biblical Interpretation." *Journal for Theological Interpretation* 3 (2009): 241–59.
———. *Christ Is King: Paul's Royal Christology*. Minneapolis: Fortress, forthcoming.
Johnson, Aubrey R. *Sacral Kingship in Ancient Israel*. Cardiff: University of Wales Press, 1967.
Johnson, Luke Timothy. *The Writings of the New Testament: An Interpretation*. Minneapolis: Fortress, 1999.
Juel, Donald. *Messianic Exegesis: Christological Interpretation of the Old Testament in Early Christianity*. Philadelphia: Fortress, 1988.
Kraus, Hans-Joachim. *Theology of the Psalms*. Minneapolis: Fortress, 1992.
Lau, Te-Li. *The Politics of Peace: Ephesians, Dio Chrysostom, and the Confucian Four Books*. Supplements to Novum Testamendum 133. Leiden: Brill, 2010.

Lee, Aquila H. I. *From Messiah to Preexistent Son: Jesus' Self-Consciousness and Early Christian Exegesis of Messianic Psalms.* Wissenschaftliche Untersuchungen zum Neuen Testament 2/192. Tübingen: Mohr-Siebeck, 2005.

Lee, Michelle V. *Paul, the Stoics, and the Body of Christ.* Society for New Testament Studies Monograph Series 37. Cambridge: Cambridge University Press, 2006.

Levison, John R. *Portraits of Adam in Early Judaism: From Sirach to 2 Baruch.* Journal for the Study of the Pseudepigrapha Supplement Series 1. Sheffield: Sheffield Academic Press, 1988.

Litwa, M. David. *We are Being Transformed: Deification in Paul's Soteriology.* Beihefte zur Zeitschrift für die neutestamentliche Wissenschaft 187; Berlin: de Gruyter, 2012.

Lincoln, A. T. "A Re-Examination of 'the Heavenlies' in Ephesians." *New Testament Studies* 19 (1972–73): 468–83.

Loader, W. R. G. "Christ at the Right Hand: Ps cx.1 in the New Testament." *New Testament Studies* 24 (1977–78): 199–217.

———. *Sohn und Hoherpriester: Eine traditionsgeschichtliche Untersuchung zur Christologie des Hebräerbriefes.* Wissenschaftliche Monographien zum Alten und Neuen Testament 53. Neukirchen–Vluyn: Neukirchener, 1981.

Maier, Harry. "A Sly Civility: Colossians and Empire." *Journal for the Study of the New Testament* 27 (205): 323–49.

Marcus, Joel. "The Circumcision and the Uncircumcision in Rome." *New Testament Studies* 35 (1989): 67–81.

Martin, Dale B. *The Corinthian Body.* New Haven, Conn.: Yale University Press, 1995.

Mays, James L. *The Lord Reigns: A Theological Handbook to the Psalms.* Louisville: Westminster John Knox, 1994.

Mettinger, Tryggve N. D. *King and Messiah: The Civil and Sacral Legitimation of the Israelite Kings.* Coniectanea Biblica Old Testament 8. Lund: Gleerup, 1976.

Mitchell, Margaret M. *Paul and the Rhetoric of Reconciliation: An Exegetical Investigation of the Language and Composition of 1 Corinthians.* Louisville: Westminster John Knox, 1991.

Moule, C. F. D. *The Origin of Christology.* Cambridge: Cambridge University Press, 1977.

Mowinckel, Sigmund. *He That Cometh: The Messiah Concept in the Old Testament and Later Judaism.* Translated by G. W. Anderson. Grand Rapids: Eerdmans, 2005.

———. *The Psalms in Israel's Worship.* Revised edition. Translated by D. R. Ap-Thomas. 2 vols. Grand Rapids: Eerdmans, 2004.

Mussner, Franz. *Christus das All und die Kirche: Studien zur Theologie des Epheserbriefes.* Trier: Paulinus, 1955.

Nebe, Gottfried. "Christ, the Body of Christ and Cosmic Powers in Paul's Letters and the New Testament as a Whole." Pages 100–118 in *Politics and Theopolitics in the Bible and Postbiblical Literature.* Edited by Henning Graf Reventlow, Yair Hoffman and Benjamin Uffenheimer. Journal for the Study of the Old Testament: Supplement Series 171. Sheffield: JSOT Press, 1994.

Novakovic, Lidija. *Raised from the Dead According to the Scripture: The Role of Israel's Scripture in the Early Christian Interpretation of Jesus' Resurrection.* Jewish and Christian Texts in Contexts and Related Studies Series. London: Bloomsbury T&T Clark, 2012.

Novenson, Matthew V. *Christ Among the Messiahs: Christ Language in Paul and Messiah Language in Ancient Judaism.* Oxford: Oxford University Press, 2012.

Peppard, Michael. *The Son of God in the Roman World: Divine Sonship in Its Social and Political Context.* Oxford: Oxford University Press, 2011.

Roberts, J. J. M. "The Enthronement of Yhwh and David: The Abiding Theological Significance of the Kingship Language of the Psalms." *Catholic Biblical Quarterly* 64 (2002): 675–86.
Sanders, E. P. *Paul and Palestinian Judaism*. Minneapolis: Fortress, 1977.
Schweitzer, Albert. *The Mysticism of Paul the Apostle*. Translated by William Montgomery. Baltimore: The Johns Hopkins University Press, 1998.
Scott, James M. *Adoption as Sons of God: An Exegetical Investigation into the Background of ΥΙΟΘΕΣΙΑ in the Pauline Corpus*. Wissenschaftliche Untersuchungen zum Neuen Testament 2/48. Tübingen: Mohr-Siebeck, 1992.
Scroggs, Robin. *The Last Adam: A Study in Pauline Theology*. Philadelphia: Fortress, 1966.
Short, J. Randall. *The Surprising Election and Confirmation of King David*. Harvard Theological Studies 63. Cambridge, Mass.: Harvard University Press, 2010.
Smith, Julien. *Christ the Ideal King: Cultural Context, Rhetorical Strategy, and the Power of Divine Monarchy in Ephesians*. Wissenschaftliche Untersuchungen zum Neuen Testament 2/313. Tübingen: Mohr-Siebeck, 2011.
Son, Sang-Won (Aaron). *Corporate Elements in Pauline Anthropology: A Study of Selected Terms, Idioms, and Concepts in the Light of Paul's Usage and Background*. Rome: Editrice Pontificio Istituto Biblico, 2001.
Spicq, Celsus. "La philanthropie hellénistique, vertu divine et royale (à propos de Tit 3:4)." *Studia theologica* 12 (1958): 169–91.
Starbuck, Scott R. A. *The Court Oracles in the Psalms: The So-Called Royal Psalms in their Ancient Near Eastern Context*. Society of Biblical Literature Dissertation Series 172. Atlanta: SBL, 1999.
Stuhlmacher, Peter. *Reconciliation, Law, & Righteousness: Essays in Biblical Theology*. Philadelphia: Fortress, 1986.
Walker, Donald Dale. *Paul's Offer of Leniency (2 Cor 10:1): Populist Ideology and Rhetoric in a Pauline Letter Fragment*. Wissenschaftliche Untersuchungen zum Neuen Testament 2/152. Tübingen: Mohr-Siebeck, 2002.
Wallace-Hadrill, Andrew. "The Emperor and his Virtues." *Historia* 30 (1981): 298–323.
Whitsett, Christopher G. "Son of God, Seed of David: Paul's Messianic Exegesis in Romans 2:3–4." *Journal of Biblical Literature* 119 (2000): 661–81.
Wright, N. T. *Paul and the Faithfulness of God*. Volume 4 of Christian Origins and the Question of God. Minneapolis: Fortress, 2013.

Paul, Φρόνησις, and Participation

The Shape of Space and the Reconfiguration of Place in Paul's Letter to the Philippians[*]

MICHAEL J. THATE

> O God, I could be bounded in a nutshell and count myself a king of infinite space [...]
> William Shakespeare[1]

> Life is a matter of form – that is the hypothesis we associate with the venerable philosophical and geometric term "sphere." It suggests that life, the formation of spheres and thinking are different expressions of the same thing.
> Peter Sloterdijk[2]

A. Thieving Spaces and Placing this Study

In Markus Zusak's magical novel, *The Book Thief*, the unlikeliest of narrators, Death, shares the haunting tale of the young orphan Liesel and her newly constructed life with her adopted parents, Hans and Rosa Hubermann, on 33 Himmel Street in the small town of Molching outside of Munich.[3] The story flows through a kind of experiment in normalization and youth: viz. the innocence and play of friendship, which we would expect, and the invasive presences of bullies and cruelty. These presences are orchestrated around responses to words,[4] the intensification of Nazism in Molching during the years 1939–43, and the spatial re-shaping of Himmel

---

[*] I am grateful for the generous and insightful feedback from and conversations with Devin Singh and Mary Farag on this essay.
[1] William Shakespeare, *Hamlet*, Act 2, Scene 2.
[2] Peter Sloterdijk, *Bubbles* (Spheres 1; trans. Wieland Hoban; Semiotext(e); Cambridge: MIT Press, 2011 [1998]), 10–11.
[3] Markus Zusak, *The Book Thief* (New York: Alfred A. Knopf, 2005).
[4] Cf., in particular, the conflict of words between Hitler and *The Word Shaker* in Zusak, *The Book Thief*, 405–55. Cf., too, the final words of Liesel, "I have hated the words and I have loved them, and I hope I have made them right." Zusak, *The Book Thief*, 528.

Street. It is a curious narrative of presences and absences, which becomes particularly pointed when the Hubermanns put their lives at risk by hiding Max Vandenburg during the Jewish purge. Max's father had helped save Hans's life in WWI, and Hans swore to assist the family whenever that time should arise.

Of particular interest for this essay is the gift Max makes for young Liesel: a book he entitles *The Standover Man*.[5]

<blockquote>During that week, Max had cut out a collection of pages from *Mein Kampf* and painted over them in white. He then hung them up with pegs on some string, from one end of the basement to the other. When they were all dry, the hard part began. He was educated well enough to get by, but he was certainly no writer and no artist. Despite this, he formulated the words in his head till he could recount them without error. Only then, on the paper that had bubbled and humped under the stress of drying paint, did he begin to write the story.[6]</blockquote>

In Max's gift to Liesel, the "desecrated pages of *Mein Kampf*" become a site of contest and transvaluation.[7] The struggle of the one is constructed over the struggle of the other. In the basement of 33 Himmel Street, the wretched of the earth blanks the pronouncement of Power's declarations and fills them over with the revolutionary ink of self-narration. Over its very own pages of propaganda, the spatial boasts of the *Reich* are made fragile, painted over, by the creations of love from the Hubermann's humble cellar, and envelop the entire village of Molching. But even so, the pages "bubbled and humped under the stress," showing the faint traces of their ideology through Max's painted pages.

This is the curiosity driving this essay: What does it mean to construct within (or over) spaces that have already been constructed? There may well be a finite lump of clay upon which we all tread, but this spatial finitude shatters in the kiln by the infinite array of social formations. How do spaces change – both in the sense of their own mutations and in their mutating effects upon subjectivities – when different conceptualities emerge within the same geography?

This curiosity in multiplicity within spatiality is applied to the familiar territory of Paul's letter to the Philippians. What if we ask of this familiar letter what it means for the "pages" of Philippi to be painted over and the letter to the Philippians to be written over them? When Paul addresses πᾶσιν τοῖς ἁγίοις ἐν Χριστῷ Ἰησοῦ τοῖς οὖσιν ἐν Φιλίπποις (1:1), how do these two localities interact and affect each other? How and where do the pages "bubble and hump"? These questions guide the experimental reading of the letter in this brief essay, which will in turn suggest a (re)reading of

---

[5] Zusak, *The Book Thief*, 223–38.
[6] Zusak, *The Book Thief*, 223.
[7] Zusak, *The Book Thief*, 277.

φρόνησις in Paul's letter to the Philippians as Paul's civic direction within a reconceived spatiality: a kind of spatial reasoning. Before unpacking this reading, however, I wish to place my proposed reading within five key studies from which I see my proposal both drawing as well as extending.

I. Φρόνησις and an Alternative Civic Template: Wayne Meeks

The first is the important sketch of Wayne Meeks.[8] Meeks follows Helmut Koester's interest in the "exuberance" of the early followers of Jesus which created "the wildest diversity of mythic portraits" of him within the first decades of the movement.[9] The subject of this early Christian mythopoesis was the astonishing development of a "Jewish man from Galilee who died early and in public shame."[10] Many years prior, Meeks traced this development through the Gospel of John,[11] suggesting that through the narrative presentation of Jesus, the Fourth Gospel gives the community a "template for interpreting their own experience."[12] Meeks sees a similar movement at work in Paul's use of the so-called "Christ hymn" in Phil 2:6–11: viz., the use of the "christological motif to interpret the experience of the community and thus to shape and reinforce certain attitudes and patterns of behavior in that community."[13] For Meeks, the "hymn" thus extends vertically along a christological axis as well as horizontal along a communal axis.[14]

The force of Meeks' argument comes to bear most directly upon this essay in his insistence on seeing the "most comprehensive purpose" of the letter to the Philippians as "the shaping of a Christian [φρόνησις], a practical moral reasoning that is 'conformed to [Christ's] death' in hope of his resurrection."[15] The community-forming letter is one of friendship and ranging parenetic aims,[16] which are all read through the centering

---

[8] Wayne Meeks, "The Man from Heaven in Paul's Letter to the Philippians," in Birger A. Pearson, ed., *The Future of Early Christianity* (Minneapolis: Fortress, 1991), 329–36.

[9] Meeks, "Man from Heaven," 329.

[10] Meeks, "Man from Heaven," 329.

[11] Wayne Meeks, "The Man from Heaven in Johannine Sectarianism," *JBL* 91 (1972): 44–72.

[12] Meeks, "Man from Heaven," 331.

[13] Meeks, "Man from Heaven," 331.

[14] Cf. Martin Hengel, "Hymns and Christology," in *Between Jesus and Paul: Studies in the Earliest History of Christianity* (Philadelphia: Fortress, 1983), 96; see also 78–96; cf. Meeks, "Man from Heaven," 331.

[15] Meeks, "Man from Heaven," 333.

[16] Meeks, "Man from Heaven," 331. See, recently, Joseph A. Marchal, *Hierarchy, Unity, and Imitation: A Feminist Rhetorical Analysis of Power Dynamics in Paul's Letter to the Philippians* (Leiden: Brill, 2006), 24–29; 35–50; and, Stanley K. Stowers, "Friends and Enemies in the Politics of Heaven: Reading Theology in Philippians," in *Thessaloni-*

parenesis: Τοῦτο φρονεῖτε ἐν ὑμῖν ὃ καὶ ἐν Χριστῷ Ἰησοῦ (2:5). The verb φρονεῖν occurs ten times throughout Philippians, and, according to Meeks, issues an accordant civic existence (πολιτεύεσθαι) which troubles the geopolitical sovereignty of the πόλις in light of the heavenly πολίτευμα (3:20).[17] Meeks proceeds by suggesting that Paul communicates this new existence through two models: "his own experience and the myth of Christ."[18] The hymn itself dramatizes Christ as "the master model" which "underlies Paul's characterization of his career and of the mediating Epaphroditus" (2:30), and through which the Philippians are to think and act in the face of internal conflict and external hostility.[19] Meeks thus gathers two important elements: first, the dynamic effects of 2:6–11 for the shaping of a communal identity; and, second, Paul's development of moral / practical reasoning as appropriate civic action within a newly conceived πόλις with Christ as the "master model."

II. Paul's 'Mixed' Messages of Christic Being: Adela Yarbro Collins

Significant for this essay is also the two important studies from Adela Yarbro Collins.[20] In the first study, Yarbro Collins argues for the "major role" κύριος plays in 2:6–11, and shrewdly suggests the composition of the so-called "Christ hymn" may well be dependent on Jewish tradition, but "features of Greek, Hellenistic and Roman religion are also crucial for its interpretation."[21] The text cannot be parceled into neat categories of "Jewish" and "non-Jewish" influences. The wide range of "cultural experiences" from the members of these early Christian groups must be kept in mind,[22] as they surely "adapted non-Jewish religious traditions deliberately and consciously as a way of formulating a culturally meaningful system of belief and life."[23] Yarbro Collins follows the "plot and logic" of the so-called hymn through what we might call the three stages of Christic being: first, the originary being in the form of God; second, the emptying of this being and taking on the form/being of a slave; and, third, God restoring

---

ans, Philippians, Galatians, Philemon (Pauline Theology, vol. 1; ed. Jouette M. Bassler; Minneapolis: Fortress, 1991), 105–21.

[17] Meeks, "Man from Heaven," 333.

[18] Meeks, "Man from Heaven," 333.

[19] Meeks, "Man from Heaven," 335.

[20] Adela Yarbro Collins, "The Worship of Jesus and the Imperial Cult," in *The Jewish Roots of Christological Monotheism: Papers from the St Andrews Conference on the Historical Origins of the Worship of Jesus* (ed. Carey C. Newman, James R. Davila, and Gladys S. Lewis; Leiden: Brill, 1999); and, Adela Yarbro Collins, "Psalms, Philippians 2:6–11, and the Origins of Christology," *BibInt* 11.3 (2002): 361–72.

[21] Yarbro Collins, "The Worship of Jesus and the Imperial Cult," 240.

[22] Yarbro Collins, "The Worship of Jesus and the Imperial Cult," 241.

[23] Yarbro Collins, "The Worship of Jesus and the Imperial Cult," 242.

this being in the exaltation.[24] These are read as the dynamics of a "daring" poetic composition where the worship of Christ is legitimated by "closely associat[ing] him" with the being and activity of God.[25] This daring move is read as an implicit and subtle "alternative" to imperial worship.[26]

In her second study,[27] the long-held assumption of 2:6–11 as a "hymn" is questioned.[28] Yarbro Collins follows the important study of Samuel Vollenweider, who says that ἁρπαγμός in v. 6 should be understood as *res rapienda* within a history of religions context about "the typical ruler who is violent and who presumes to take a divine role."[29] Verse 6 is thus a point of cutting contrast: although Christ had divine form (ὃς ἐν μορφῇ θεοῦ ὑπάρχων), this was not something he "seized by force" like the typical arrogant ruler.[30] The so-called "hymn" is thus less a pre-existent hymn worked over by Paul as it is Paul's "rhythmic prose," or "prose hymn," or his "brief encomium" to Christ as the ideal king.[31] Quintilian, the fist-century rhetorician who suggests rules for composing prose hymns to deities, states that gods may be praised either for being born immortal or because they attained immortality by means of their merit or excellence.[32] Intriguingly, Paul praises Christ for both. He is the one *who is divine* (ὃς ἐν μορφῇ θεοῦ ὑπάρχων), *and the one who became divine* (vv. 9–11), marking him off as the ideal king and ruler.[33] Paul is, according to Yarbro Collins, a kind of Χριστολόγος, after the pattern of the θεολόγοι and σεβαστολόγοι, adapting "the form of the Greek prose hymn in order to instruct the Philippians in cultural terms familiar to them."[34]

From Yarbro Collins, we again see the identity formation of the community through her provocative reading of 2:6–11. I also wish to extend

---

[24] Yarbro Collins, "The Worship of Jesus and the Imperial Cult," 243.

[25] Yarbro Collins, "The Worship of Jesus and the Imperial Cult," 250.

[26] Yarbro Collins, "The Worship of Jesus and the Imperial Cult," 250.

[27] Yarbro Collins, "The Origins of Christology."

[28] Cf. Ernst Lohmeyer, *Kyrios Jesus: Eine Untersuchung zu Phil. 2,5–11* (Darmstadt: Wissenschaftliche Buchgesellschaft, 1961 [1928]).

[29] Yarbro Collins, "The Origins of Christology," 367. Here she follows Samuel Vollenweider, "Der 'Raub' der Gottgleichheit: Ein religionsgeschichtlicher Vorschlag zu Phil 2.6(11)," *NTS* 45 (1999): 413–33.

[30] Cf. Vollenweider, "Der 'Raub' der Gottgleichheit," 429.

[31] Yarbro Collins, "The Origins of Christology," 368; cf., too, Yarbro Collins, "The Worship of Jesus and the Imperial Cult," 257.

[32] Quintilian, *Institutio Oratoria* 3.7.9; cf. Adela Yarbro Collins, "The Origins of Christology," 370. Philo's *Life of Moses* is also worth being brought into this discussion. Yarbro Collins refers to it, but does not discuss its shared logic with Phil 2:6–11; cf Yarbro Collins, The Origins of Christology," 371.

[33] Here we await the important study of Joshua W. Jipp, *Christ is King: Paul's Royal Christology* (Minneapolis: Fortress, forthcoming).

[34] Yarbro Collins, "Origins of Christology," 372.

the nature of innovation developing not only "in dialogue" – whether implicitly or explicitly – with other "religious traditions," but also within other conceptions of spatiality.[35] Paul is therefore not only a Χριστολόγος, but also a kind of τοπολόγος; not only placing the identity / being of the assemblies in Christ (as has often been pointed out), but placing Christic being *in Philippi*.

III. The Christ-Pattern: Luke Timothy Johnson

A third tributary which flows into this essay is the work of Luke Timothy Johnson.[36] Though not engaging the letter to the Philippians in any extended fashion,[37] elements of his interest in the "two kinds of language in Paul's letter about the way human behavior is directed" is significant. These languages are those which he terms "explicitly and obviously religious," and "moral and paraenetic" in character.[38] I would certainly want to quibble with what he terms "obviously religious" language,[39] but his interest in the alignment of human agency with "transcendental spiritual power" gestures toward the τέχνη operative in appropriate action which is very much at the heart of this essay. Moreover, his placing of this language within the contextual milieu of Aristotle's discussion of φρόνησις in the *Nicomachean Ethics* is also suggestive.

After surveying Romans,[40] Johnson surmises that "Paul shares the logic of ancient moralists,[41] who assume that moral behavior follows upon right perception, enabling ancient polemic to argue that just as good perceptions lead to proper behavior, so also wicked deeds suffice to demonstrate a derangement in thinking."[42] Moreover, he sees the language of Paul informed by the role of φρόνησις in moral discernment and is "programmatic for

---

[35] Yarbro Collins, "The Worship of Jesus and the Imperial Cult," 251.

[36] Luke Timothy Johnson, "Transformation of the Mind and Moral Discernment in Paul," in *Early Christianity and Classical Culture: Comparative Studies in Honor of Abraham J. Malherbe* (ed. John T. Fitzgerald, Thomas H. Olbricht, and L. Michael White; Leiden: Brill, 2003), 215–36.

[37] Though see Johnson, "Mind and Moral Discernment," 232–34.

[38] Johnson, "Mind and Moral Discernment," 215.

[39] On the problematics of this designation, see Brent Nongbri, *Before Religion: A History of a Modern Concept* (New Haven, Conn.: Yale University Press, 2013).

[40] Johnson, "Mind and Moral Discernment," 216–21.

[41] Cf. Abraham J. Malherbe, *Paul and the Popular Philosophers* (Minneapolis: Fortress, 1989).

[42] Johnson, "Mind and Moral Discernment," 220; cf. Luke Timothy Johnson, "II Timothy and the Polemic Against False Teachers: A Reexamination," *JRS* 6/7 (1978–79): 1–26; and, Luke Timothy Johnson, "The New Testament's Anti-Jewish Slander and the Conventions of Ancient Polemic," *JBL* 108 (1989): 419–41.

Paul's entire moral argument concerning life in the community."[43] Johnson turns to Aristotle,[44] not because he thinks Paul necessarily had the *Nicomachean Ethics* in hand,[45] but because he sees "Paul's language about moral discernment follow[ing] a strikingly similar kind of logic."[46] In both Paul and Aristotle, the capacity to test or proximate moral measures comes from a νοῦς, a mindset or framework.[47] For Paul, this framework is patterned after Christ (Rom 3:21–26; 5:12–21; cf. *N.E.* VI 5.1);[48] what we might call *the Christ pattern*.[49] Philippians 2:6–11 is thus seen as an exemplary pattern through which Timothy (2:19–24), Epaphroditus (2:25–30), and Paul himself (3:1–16) not only participate, but also become proximate models for the assemblies at Philippi.[50]

IV. Ideological Re-mapping at Philippi: Peter Oakes

Another significant study for this essay is the intriguing work of Peter Oakes.[51] Oakes charts the four varying ways 1 Thess 4:15–17; 5:3 and Phil 2:9–11 have been understood in relation to Roman imperial ideology and terminology. First, Roman and early Christian discourses exemplify independent uses of common sources.[52] Second, early Christian expressions and practices follow Roman expressions and practices.[53] Third, early

---

[43] Johnson, "Mind and Moral Discernment," 221.
[44] Johnson, "Mind and Moral Discernment," 221–25.
[45] Johnson, "Mind and Moral Discernment," 225.
[46] Johnson, "Mind and Moral Discernment," 225.
[47] Johnson, "Mind and Moral Discernment," 225. See Norman O. Dahl, *Practical Reason, Aristotle, and Weakness of the Will* (Minneapolis: University of Minnesota Press, 1984).
[48] Johnson, "Mind and Moral Discernment," 225–29.
[49] "[T]he Holy Spirit may be seen as the effective cause of this transformation, and the messianic pattern as the formal cause." Johnson, "Mind and Moral Discernment," 231.
[50] Here see J. Paul Sampley, *Pauline Partnership in Christ* (Philadelphia: Fortress, 1980); L. Michael White, "Morality between Two Worlds: A Paradigm of Friendship in Philippians," in *Greeks, Romans, and Christians: Essays in Honor of Abraham J. Malherbe* (ed. D. L. Balch, E. Ferguson, and W. A. Meeks; Philadelphia: Fortress, 1990), 201–15; John T. Fitzgerald, "Philippians in the Light of Some Ancient Discussions of Friendship," in *Friendship, Flattery, and Frankness of Speech: Studies on Friendship in the New Testament World* (NovTSup 82; ed. J. T. Fitzgerald; Leiden: Brill, 1996), 141–62; W. S. Kurz, "Kenotic Imitation of Paul and Christ in Phil 2 and 3," in *Discipleship in the New Testament* (ed. F. Segovia; Philadelphia: Fortress, 1985), 103–26; M.D. Hooker, "Philippians 2:6–11," in *Jesus und Paulus* (ed. E. Ellis and E. Grasser; Goettingen: Vandenhoeck & Ruprecht, 1975), 151–64.
[51] Peter Oakes, "Re-mapping the Universe: Paul and the Emperor in 1 Thessalonians and Philippians," *JSNT* 27.3 (2005): 301–22.
[52] Oakes, "Re-mapping the Universe," 303.
[53] Oakes, "Re-mapping the Universe," 303–4.

Christian expressions and practices valorize in reaction to conflict with Rome.[54] And, fourth, "Christians use Roman terminology because they want to oppose something Roman."[55] Oakes suggests that at least 1 Thess 5:3 and Phil 2:9–11 should be seen in conflict with Roman ideology at the levels of Rome's domination and violence, Paul's developed eschatology and Christology, and specific aspects of discourse and behavior from the scattered presences of the imperial cult in Thessalonica and Philippi.[56]

Rather intriguingly, Oakes alludes to the complex settlement history of Philippi within his mapping of imperial presences,[57] and the shared suffering of Paul and Philippi at the hands of colonizing power.[58] Though I am not convinced Oakes keeps these movements together as consistently as he could have,[59] his notion that Christ becomes "emperor of the universe" (2:9–11),[60] resulting in *an alternative state* in both civic (πολίτευμα) and ethical dimensions, takes on added subversive shades when these spatial dynamics are kept in mind. The apparent "accession to imperial authority" in vv. 9–11 *abnormalizes* the Caesar pattern by *normalizing* the Christ pattern for societal direction.[61]

This is what Oakes sees as Paul's re-mapping of society:[62] Paul's rearranging center and periphery in both Christological (2:6–11) and communal (2:15–16) dimensions. Though I would like to challenge notions of "center" and "periphery" later, what I hope to develop further in this essay is Oakes's stunning observation regarding Paul's alternative cartography and the christic reorganization of space and the consequent outcome of

---

[54] Oakes, "Re-mapping the Universe," 304–5.

[55] Oakes, "Re-mapping the Universe," 305; see also 305–7.

[56] Oakes points to the studies of M. Sève and P. Weber, 'Un monument honorifique au forum de Philippes,' *Bulletin de Correspondance Hellénique* 112 (1988): 467–79; Christoph vom Broke, *Thessaloniki: Stadt des Kassander und Gemeinde des Paulus* (WUNT 2/125; Tübingen: Mohr Siebeck, 2001); and, I. Touratsoglou, *Die Münzstätte von Thessaloniki in der römischen Kaiserzeit (32/31 v. Chr. Bis 268 n. Chr.)* (Antike Münzen und geschnittene Steine 12; Berlin: de Gruyter, 1998).

[57] Oakes cites the excellent studies of Lawrence Keppie, *Colonization and Veteran Settlement in Italy, 47–14 B.C.* (London: British School at Rome, 1983), 60; E. T. Salmon, *Roman Colonization under the Republic* (London: Thames & Hudson, 1969), 137–38; cf. Peter Oakes, *Philippians: From People to Letter* (SNTSMS 110; Cambridge: Cambridge University Press, 2001), 26–27. Cf. Oakes, "Re-mapping the Universe," 308–09; see also 310–21 and esp. 310–15.

[58] See Oakes, "Re-mapping the Universe," 318–21.

[59] Cf. Oakes, *Philippians*, 1–54.

[60] Oakes, "Re-mapping the Universe," 318.

[61] Oakes, "Re-mapping the Universe," 320; cf. Oakes, *Philippians*, 201–10. On normalization and abnormalization, see Michel Foucault, *Abnormal: Lectures at the Collège de France 1974–1975* (trans. Graham Burchell; New York: Picador, 2003 [1999]).

[62] Oakes, "Re-mapping the Universe," 320.

time (eschatology).⁶³ What I find most intriguing about Oakes's reading is his suggestion that Paul's spatial rearrangement of the universe secures a *place* for the assemblies in Philippi.⁶⁴

V. A Place for civitas: Steven J. Kraftchick

Following the observation of Troels Engberg-Pedersen that scholars tend to latch on to a "fairly restricted motif as *the* theme" of Philippians on the one hand, or, on the other, "fix on a single, specific, but very general motif (like 'the gospel')" on the other,⁶⁵ Kraftchick offers an "overarching task for the letter" as a way of mediating these two poles.⁶⁶ That task is Paul's correction of the "Philippians' communal self-understanding" by explicating his own identity in Christ."⁶⁷ The self-presentation of Paul has been noted by others,⁶⁸ and, of particular note, are those studies which place this trope within the friendship epistolary genre.⁶⁹ Kraftchick extends these discussions by placing Paul as the revealed cipher through which the assemblies are to imitate not only the actions of Paul, but also his way of thinking: viz., his "practical wisdom."

> Paul made use of the letter to provide the Philippians with a communal 'constitution' by which they can guide themselves in both their internal life and in their relationships to those outside their communion. In doing this he prepares them to be a self-sufficient and mature community capable of responding faithfully to the vicissitudes of everyday life up to and including their current suffering.⁷⁰

The significance of the latter of these two moves – viz., the desire to clarify external communal relations – is highlighted in Kraftchick's recourse to

---

⁶³ Oakes, "Re-mapping the Universe," 321. On eschatology, see "Re-mapping the Universe," 315. Oakes stresses the temporal reconfiguration of the cosmos in 1 Thessalonians; cf. "Re-mapping the Universe," 315–18.

⁶⁴ Oakes, "Re-mapping the Universe," 322. He goes on to locate this "place close to the real central power." Again, I would like to problematize these notions of center and periphery later, but I see the move from space to place in Oakes as theoretically significant to my understanding of space and place.

⁶⁵ Troels Engberg-Pedersen, *Paul and the Stoics* (Louisville: Westminster John Knox, 2000), 86.

⁶⁶ Steven J. Kraftchick, "Self-Presentation and Community Construction in Philippians," in *Scripture and Traditions: Essays on Early Judaism and Christianity in Honor of Carl R. Holladay* (ed. Patrick Gray and Gail R. O'Day; Leiden: Brill, 2008), 239–62.

⁶⁷ Kraftchick, "Self-Presentation and Community Construction," 241.

⁶⁸ E.g., Robert Fortna, "Paul's Most Egocentric Letter," in *The Conversation Continues* (ed. Beverly Gaventa and Robert Fortna; Philadelphia: Fortress, 1999), 219–30; cited in Kraftchick, "Self-Presentation and Community Construction," 242 n. 10.

⁶⁹ Cf. Kraftchick, "Self-Presentation and Community Construction," 242 n. 12.

⁷⁰ Kraftchick, "Self-Presentation and Community Construction," 245.

Kathryn Tanner. External relationships are negotiated through a series of fragile boundaries.

> [And the] distinctiveness of a Christian way of life is not so much formed *by* the boundary as *at* it; Christian distinctiveness is something that emerges in the very cultural processes occurring at the boundary, processes that construct a distinctive identity for Christian social practices through the distinctive use of cultural materials shared by others.[71]

These boundaries, for Kraftchick, are therefore less issues of *what* than *how*: that is to say, "the differences between the Christian community and its wider context are not found in the practices of each *per se* but in how those practices are understood." We should stress, however, that it is not so much that cultural practices remain the same while the understanding of them changes. For it is within changing contexts and understandings where practices themselves are transformed.[72] Paul must therefore provide the assemblies with a kind of "constitution."[73] It is within this dynamic which Kraftchick suggests Paul's citizenship language of 1:27–30 and 3:20 should be understood. There is thus a contrasting presence between licit and illicit constitutions (cf. 3:2, 18–19). These are conflicting models, or templates. The true template or model is that of Christ (2:6–11), and Paul can refer both to himself and others as models and templates in so far as they participate within the structural dynamics of the Christ pattern.[74] The Philippians are therefore not only to imitate Paul but *together with Paul* (συμμιμητής) the contours of this Christ pattern.

Most helpful for the purposes of this essay is Kraftchick's insightful explication of the contrasts in 3:17–21.[75] The first of which is signaled by the presence of the participial φρονοῦντες in v. 19. The ἐχθροὺς τοῦ σταυροῦ τοῦ Χριστοῦ (v. 18) have accorded to the pattern of οἱ τὰ ἐπίγεια, where the assemblies in Philippi are to accord (2:2, 5) to the Christ pattern (2:6–11). The second contrast has to do with the "spatial shift" between ἐπίγεια (v. 19) and πολίτευμα (v. 20).[76] On the face of it, it might seem that what we have here are two simple contrasts of localities: those on the earth and those in heaven. The spatial shift, however, is not the movement from one square mileage to another, as it were, *but in the actual conception of space*. Those characterized by οἱ τὰ ἐπίγεια and those characterized by a

---

[71] Kathryn Tanner, *Theories of Culture: A New Agenda for Theology* (Minneapolis: Fortress, 1997), 115; cited in Kraftchick, "Self-Presentation and Community Construction," 246.

[72] I am grateful to Devin Singh for talking this point through with me.

[73] Kraftchick, "Self-Presentation and Community Construction," 246.

[74] Kraftchick, "Self-Presentation and Community Construction," 248–49.

[75] Kraftchick mentions four, but we will focus only the first two. See Kraftchick, "Self-Presentation and Community Construction," 258–59.

[76] Kraftchick, "Self-Presentation and Community Construction," 258.

πολίτευμα ἐν οὐρανοῖς live within the same square mileage. The difference is that the latter await *from within* (ἐξ) these shared square miles (v. 20) a Savior and Lord (ἀπεκδεχόμεθα [...] σωτῆρα κύριον Ἰησοῦν Χριστόν) who will not only transform (μετασχηματίσει) the "lowly assembly into the likeness of his glorious body" (σύμμορφον τῷ σώματι τῆς δόξης αὐτοῦ),[77] but do so "by the effective force which enables him to subject all things to himself" (κατὰ τὴν ἐνέργειαν τοῦ δύνασθαι αὐτὸν καὶ ὑποτάξαι αὐτῷ τὰ πάντα; v. 21). The "effective force" here recalls God's "exaltation" (ὑπερυψόω) of Jesus and "bestowing upon him the name which is above every name" (ἐχαρίσατο αὐτῷ τὸ ὄνομα τὸ ὑπὲρ πᾶν; 2:9). The effect of this act cannot therefore simply be the placement of the assemblies into the spatial re-shaping of the cosmos. It is *from within* (ἐξ) these overlapping square miles of those living in accordance to the earthly pattern and those after the Christ pattern that Christ's spatial re-shaping of the cosmos particularizes itself in the reconfiguration of the assemblies sense of place.

Kraftchick's final move is reading Aristotle's discourse on proofs from character (ἦθος) in his *Rhetoric* so as to discern what he calls Paul's "implied constitution" for the assemblies.[78] He sees an inversion of Aristotle's argument that the "community's ethos determined the shape of the speaker's character proofs," while in Philippians "the community's ethos is to be determined and developed on the basis of Paul's character presentation."[79] Following the fascinating study of Michael J. Hyde on the ways discourses of ἦθος transform space and time into "dwelling places,"[80] Kraftchick suggests that Paul's reversal of "Aristotle's calculus" created a "living space" for the deliberation of the identities of the assemblies as "citizens of heaven."[81] Whereas Kraftchick may see this "living space" as figurative, I suggest extending Paul's "implied constitution" as part of a developing *civitas* within the reconfigured sense of place of the assemblies.

---

[77] My translation of σώματι here as "assembly" is informed by Troels Engberg-Pedersen's plea for reading the physical into (or out of?) the metaphorical. See Troels Engberg-Pedersen, *Cosmology and the Self in the Apostle Paul: The Material Spirit* (Oxford: Oxford University Press, 2010), 1.

[78] Kraftchick, "Self-Presentation and Community Construction," 259–61; Kraftchick notes, esp., *Rhet.* 1.2.3–5; 2.1.5–7.

[79] Kraftchick, "Self-Presentation and Community Construction," 261.

[80] Michael J. Hyde, ed., *The Ethos of Rhetoric* (Columbia: University of South Carolina Press, 2004), xiii; Kraftchick also lists the study of Calvin O. Schrag, *Communicative Praxis and the Space of Subjectivity* (Bloomington: Indiana University Press, 1986).

[81] Kraftchick, "Self-Presentation and Community Construction," 261.

B. Theorizing Space and Place in Philippians

Though surely others could (and perhaps should) have been considered,[82] these particular studies prove intriguing candidates through which to extend a spatial (re)reading of Paul's letter to the Philippians. The challenge of reading a first-century letter through any theory of spatiality is that the social contingencies which gave rise to the so-called "spatial turn" within architectural theory,[83] geography,[84] or the wider humanities in general,[85] were geo-political pressures exerted by capitalist economies formulated centuries later. Charges of anachronism could therefore be easily – and perhaps rightly – levied against my approach here. What follows, however, is a suggestive reading strategy and not some official report of recovery. The stubborn placement of anachronism in this study of "history" is intended not only to place an intentional fragility into our present recourses to "history," but also what I hope will be the production of a different "historical" question: viz., what does it mean to be both ἐν_Χριστῷ and ἐν Φιλίπποις? And how might these patterns of questioning be appropriated into current discourses of human geography within religious imaginaries?

---

[82] Of particular note are the intriguing studies of Paul A. Holloway, *Consolation in Philippians* (Cambridge: Cambridge University Press, 2001); Holloway, "*Alius Paulus*: Paul's Promise to Send Timothy at Philippians 2.19–24," *NTS* 54 (2008): 542–65; Holloway, "*Bona Cogitare*: An Epicurean Consolation in Phil 4:8–9," *HTR* 91.1 (1998): 89–96; Holloway, "Thanks for the Memories: On the Translation of Phil 1.3," *NTS* 52.3 (2006): 419–32; and, Holloway, "Paul as Hellenistic Philosopher: The Evidence of Philippians," in *Paul and the Philosophers* (ed. Ward Blanton and Hent De Vries; New York: Fordham University Press, 2013), 52–68. In many ways, I consider this present essay to be a kind of spatial bridge between the five studies listed above and the fascinating work of Holloway on "Paul's appropriation of contemporary philosophical consolation." "Paul as Hellenistic Philosopher," 58.

[83] See, esp., Gaston Bachelard, *The Poetics of Space* (trans. Maria Jolas; Boston: Beacon Press, 1969 [1958]).

[84] Edward W. Soja, *Postmodern Geographies: The Reassertion of Space in Critical Social Theory* (2d ed.; London: Verso, 2011).

[85] See, generally, P. Hubbard et al. eds., *Thinking Geographically: Space, Theory and Contemporary Human Geography* (London: Continuum, 2002); S. Holloway, S. Rice, and G. Valentine, eds., *Key Concepts in Geography* (London: Sage, 2003); N. Clifford, and G. Valentine, eds., *Key Methods in Geography* (London, Sage, 2003); P. Hubbard, R. Kitchin, and G. Valentine, eds., *Key Thinkers on Space and Place* (London: Sage, 2004); and the helpful bibliographical essay by Thomas F. Gieryn, "A Space for Place in Sociology," *Annual Review of Sociology* 26 (2000): 463–96. See, too, Barney Warf and Santa Arias, eds., *Spatial Turn: Interdisciplinary Perspectives* (London: Routledge, 2009); and, Robert T. Tally, Jr., *Spatiality* (London: Routledge, 2012).

I. Spatial Imaginaries and Contested Places: Laura S. Narallah

A useful travel way from the studies surveyed above to the eclectic theorizing of spatiality to follow is the important essay by Laura S. Nasrallah.[86] Though our theorizing of space and place are slightly different,[87] Nasrallah rightly insists upon and usefully demonstrates the significance of spatial and archeological readings for Paul's letter to the assemblies in Philippi. To venture ahead of ourselves for a moment, a key to my theorizing of spatiality is a trialectics of space which sees spaces as both *socialized* and *socializing* forces. These first two elements of the trialectic focus on the modes of spatial production in the sense in which Baudrillard explicated how to produce (*pro-ducere*) is to make appear or move forward. The third element of my trialectic considers the seductive forces which lead astray and make disappear (*se-ducere*).[88] This trialectic thus pays attention both to the modes of production as well as to the modes of disappearance – what remains and what has been erased. But even these *seduced* spaces, like Max's "bubbled and humped" pages warping under "the stress of drying paint,"[89] haunt and bend the *produced* spaces with the chills of their absences which are never fully absent.[90] The rocks themselves cry out and testify to specters unseen by human histories – unseen but not necessarily unfelt. For these seduced spaces complicate themselves back into the productive forces of spatiality. "The relationship of a thought to space and movement is complicated."[91] These "complicated" spatial relationships of Philippi – in all their guises and by all their names – must therefore be considered in any spatial reading of Paul's letter to the Philippians.[92]

Located near the silver and gold mines of Mount Pangaion and the port of Neapolis, Philippi "had been a site of conflict long before Paul and his

---

[86] Laura S. Nasrallah, "Spatial Perspectives: Space and Archaeology in Roman Philippi," in *Studying Paul's Letters: Contemporary Perspectives and Methods* (ed. Joseph A. Marchal; Minneapolis: Fortress, 2012), 53–74.

[87] See Nasrallah, "Spatial Perspectives," 53–58.

[88] Cf. Jean Baudrillard, *Seduction* (trans. B. Singer; London: Macmillan, 1979).

[89] Zusak, *The Book Thief*, 223.

[90] Again, the best illustration of this is in Zusak, *The Book Thief*, 224–36. The formatting of the printed pages is such that you can actually detect the faint text of *Mein Kampf* through painted pages of *The Standover Man*. The irony, of course, is that it is precisely *Mein Kampf* which had painted over all the stories and *The Standover Man* is an instance of reifying that which had been seduced or erased.

[91] Alain Badiou with Nicolas Truong, *In Praise of Love* (trans. Peter Bush; New York: The New Press, 2012 [2009]), 85.

[92] Clearly, such a complex narration cannot take place here. See the excellent discussion in Oakes, *Philippians*, 1–54, and the literature cited there.

coworkers arrived there."[93] The land and peoples had been serially colonized;[94] its pages thick with the paint of rivaling painters. Beginning with the settlers from Thasos colonizing the Pieri and Edoni – those peoples we have come to designate as "Thracians" – Philip II of Macedonia (382–336BCE) established "Philippi" in 356BCE, leaving heavy garrisons to protect and pilfer the mines.[95] In 167BCE, while Mattathias and his five sons were liberating Jerusalem from Antiochus IV Epiphanes, the Romans had concluded the so-called Third Macedonian War,[96] dissolving the Macedonian kingdom into four republics (Livy, *History*, 45.29.5).[97] Andriscus (or Pseudo-Philip), claiming to be a son of Perseus, was at the time merely the ruler of Adramyttium but set in motion a plan to recoup Macedonia

---

[93] Nasrallah, "Spatial Perspectives," 58. She goes on to cite the important study of Paul Collart, *Philippes: Ville de Macédoine, depuis ses origins jusqu' à la fin de l'époque romaine* (2 vols. Paris: E. de Boccard, 1937); cf. Oakes, *Philippians*, 1–54.

[94] See Markus Bockmuehl, *The Epistle to the Philippians* (BNTC; Peabody, Mass.: Hendrickson, 1998), 2–9; P. T. O'Brien, *The Epistle to the Philippians* (NIGTC; Grand Rapids: Eerdmans, 1991), 3–4; Charles B. Cousar, *Philippians and Philemon* (NTL; Louisville: Westminster John Knox, 2009), 3–7; Bonnie B. Thurston and Judith M. Ryan, *Philippians and Philemon* (Sacra Pagina Series 10; Collegeville: Liturgical Press, 2005), 7–10; Lukas Bormann, *Philippi: Stadt und Christengemeinde zur Zeit des Paulus* (Leiden: Brill, 1995); Peter Pilhofer, *Philippi: Die erste christliche Gemeinde Europas* (vol. 1; Tübingen: Mohr, 1995); note, too, the relevant sections in Efraín Agosto, "The Letter to the Philippians," in *A Postcolonial Commentary on the New Testament* (ed. Ferdando F. Segovia and R. S. Sugirtharajah; Sheffield: Sheffield Academic Press, 2007), 281–93.

[95] Cf. N. G. L. Hammond, *Philip of Macedon* (London: Duckworth, 1994); René Ginouvès, *Macedonia: From Philip II to the Roman Conquest* (trans. David Hardy; Princeton: Princeton University Press, 1994 [1993]); Alfred S. Bradford, ed., *Philip II of Macedon: A Life from the Ancient Sources* (Westport: Praeger, 1992); Miltiades B. Hatzopoulos, and Louisa D. Loukopoulos, eds., *Philip of Macédon* (Paris: Bibliothèque des Arts, 1982); John R. Ellis, *Philip II and Macedonian Imperialism* (London: Thames and Hudson, 1976); Eugene N. Borza, *Before Alexander: Constructing Early Macedonia* (Claremont: Regina Books, 1999); and, Richard A. Billows, *Kings and Colonists: Aspects of Macedonian Imperialism* (Leiden: Brill, 1995).

[96] The key was the Battle of Pydna (168BCE). See Polybius, *History*, 31.29.

[97] The Romans were suspicious of the remnants of Philip V's (221–179BCE) son, Perseus, owing to Philip's treaty with Hannibal during the Second Punic War (cf. Polybius, *History*, 7.9). The role of the king of Pergamum, an enemy of Perseus, cannot be overstated in this move either. On Philip V, see F. W. Walbank, *Philip V of Macedon* (Cambridge: Cambridge University Press, 1940); cf. Michael L. Barré, *God-list in the Treaty between Hannibal and Philip V of Macedonia: A Study in Light of the Ancient Near Eastern Treaty Tradition* (Baltimore: Johns Hopkins University Press, 1983). On Perseus, cf. Piero Meloni, *Perseo e la fine della monarchia Macedone* (Roma: "L'Erma" di Bretschneider, 1953); Paul Hermann Heiland, *Untersuchungen zur Geschichte des Königs Perseus von Makedonien, 179–168BCE* (Jena: Neuenhahn, 1913); and, Sviatoslav Dmitriev, *The Greek Slogan of Freedom and Early Roman Politics in Greece* (Oxford: Oxford University Press, 2011), 283–312.

from Rome. The Romans met his brief reunification with the Fourth Macedonian War (150–148BCE), and shattered it at the Second Battle of Pydna (148BCE). Two years later, the Romans moved toward annexation, creating the *Provincia Macedoniae* in 148BCE.[98] Bruce suggests that in a move of consolidating "their hold on the new province, the Romans built the *Via Egnatia* from Apollonia and Dyrrhachium on the Adriatic to Thessalonica; it was in due course extended eastward to Philippi and its port Neapolis."[99] Macedonia was made a senatorial province by Augustus in 27BCE, transferred to imperial control in 15CE, and then returned to senate control in 44CE. The land thus served not only as a stage, but also a bridge "for the further expansion of Roman power" for the rest of the colonies.[100]

The presence(s) of *res republica*, however, introduced its/their own unsettling forces. A significant series of events culminated in Philippi in 42 BCE during the battles in the low plains to the southwest of Philippi between the forces of Mark Antony and Octavian and those of Brutus and Cassius (Appian, *Civil Wars*, 4.105–38; Plutarch, *Life of Brutus*).[101] Veterans and farmers of the area, according to some,[102] feuded over land rights. Some historians depicted "veterans as dispossessed, suffering from the lies and political machinations of the leaders they had served."[103] Appian, however, depicted "a contestation over space and the chaos wreaked by soldiers and veterans upon the 'ordinary' Italians whose lives the military disrupted" (cf. Appian, *Bell. Civ.* 5.12–13).[104] Though veterans wanted their promised due – land in Italy – Nasrallah conjectures that those veterans from the legion XXVIII and of the Praetorian cohorts which eventually settled at Philippi must have been "more disgruntled, disenfranchised, and ruthless than those sent back to their Italian homeland."[105] Keppie suggests that these veterans could be unruly and politically dangerous (cf. Dio,

---

[98] See Craig Champion, "Empire by Invitation: Greek Political Strategies and Roman Imperial Interventions in the Second Century BCE," *TAPA* 137.2 (2007): 255–75.

[99] F. F. Bruce, "St. Paul in Macedonia," *Bulletin of the John Rylands Library* 63 (1981) 337–54, here, 338.

[100] Bruce, "St. Paul in Macedonia," 338–39.

[101] To the victors went the spoils of further civil wars, ending in the triumph of Octavian over Antony and Cleopatra at Actium (31BCE). Cf. Marie-Laure Freyburger-Galland, "Political and Religious Propaganda between 44 and 27BC," *Vergilius* 55 (2009): 17–30.

[102] Lawrence Keppie, *Colonisation and Veteran Settlement*.

[103] Nasrallah, "Spatial Perspectives," 61.

[104] Nasrallah, "Spatial Perspectives," 61.

[105] Nasrallah, "Spatial Perspectives," 61. Cf. Keppie, *Colonisation and Veteran Settlement*, 60; and, Collart, *Philippes*, 1.233–35. The community of Philippi was largely made up of Antony's veterans and then Augustus' (Strabo 8.331; Appian, *B. Civ.* 5.3.11, 13; Dio Cassius 51.4.6).

Rom. Hist. 48.4–14),[106] and Nasrallah states their "impact upon the city" would have been certainly felt.[107] The spaces of Philippi could thus be "contested and imagined in various ways" within Roman society itself: "fissures defined by war, by wealth, by loyalties."[108]

After defeating Antony at Actium in 31 BCE, Augustus began painting over (*se-ducere*) Antony's presence form, e.g., their joint victory at Philippi in 42 BCE in his series of bronze coins associating the goddess of Victory with *himself*.[109] Moreover, numismatic evidence from Italy and Philippi reflect the disputed land divisions which followed occupation and veteran resettlement. Coins "depicting military standards with a plough and a surveyor's rod" jingled in pockets in Italy just as the coffers of Philippi clanged with coins "depicting the rituals of groove-making and the plow that marked the borders of the colony."[110] Philippi would again figure within wider spatial memory when, according to Dio (54.9) and Suetonius (14.3), the altars at Philippi burst ablaze into awareness of Tiberius' passing through the region. Philippi's spatial imaginary could thus be construed as a site which recognized and affirmed *auctoritas* "even for the generation after the triumvirate, and after the *imperium* of Augustus."[111]

The *Via Egnatia* was important not only as a technology of transporting trade and military presences, but it also, as Nasrallah suggests, "dictated" the "spatial organization" of Philippi.[112] Though Nasrallah expresses caution over drawing too many hard and fast conclusions about Julio-Claudian Philippi owing to the majority of the archeological remains dating to the

---

[106] Keppie, *Colonisation and Veteran Settlements*, 68; first noted in Nasrallah, "Spatial Perspectives," 73 n. 16.

[107] Nasrallah, "Spatial Perspectives," 61. Cf. Edgar M. Krentz, "Military Language and Metaphors in Philippians," in *Origins and Method: Towards a New Understanding of Judaism and Christianity* (ed. Bradley H. McLean; Sheffield: JSOT Press, 1993), 105–27; and, Joseph H. Hellerman, *Reconstructing Honor in Roman Philippi: Carmen Christi as Cursus Pudorum* (Cambridge: Cambridge University Press, 2005), 64–97 (Nasrallah, "Spatial Perspectives," 73 n. 19).

[108] Nasrallah, "Spatial Perspectives," 61.

[109] Nasrallah notes that "earlier numismatic evidence shows that Antony, not Octavian, was the primary founder of Philippi, and that Antony used Philippi to settle not only military personnel but also civilians. Later coinage tells a different story, depicting the laurel-wreathed head of Augustus with the legend *COL(onia) AFG(usta) IVL(ia) PHIL(ippensis) IVSSV AVG(usti)*. That is, the colony is named in relation to Augustus and the Julian family, and with the word *iussus* – an order, command, or decree – Octavian claims that it was *he* who founded the colony." "Spatial Perspectives," 62–63. Cf., too, Peter Pilhofer, *Philippi: Katalog der Inschriften von Philippi* (Band 2; WUNT 119; Tübingen: Mohr Siebeck, 2000).

[110] Nasrallah, "Spatial Perspectives," 63; cf. Collart, *Philippes*, 1.226–27.

[111] Nasrallah, "Spatial Perspectives," 63. "Spatial imaginary" first occurs on 56.

[112] Nasrallah, "Spatial Perspectives," 58.

second century,[113] she suggests that "running from the southeast to the northwest," the *Via Egnatia* "divides the three temples of the Capitolium from the forum to the south."[114] The *curia* of the Roman *colonia* stood on the western side, and the eastern side "was associated with the imperial cult."[115] The *Via Egnatia* spilled several "religious options" into the city: Sylvanus, Isis, various Thracian, Roman, and Greek idioms of Artemis – each with their own "ethnic affiliations," none of which precluded the other.[116] Philippi, like other cities throughout the colonies, was a *contact zone* "in which racial, ethnic, and imperial conflicts and negotiations occurred."[117] And the redistributed military presences cluttered this contact zone further.[118]

Jonathan Z. Smith, in the spirit of Kant, stated that "the relationship to the human body, and our experience of it," is the dynamic which "orients us in space," and confers meaning to place. "Human beings are not placed, they bring place into being." As such, place "is best understood as a locus of meaning."[119] These orientations and loci, of course, are set by power: "authority produces space."[120] Kant's analysis of space, via Smith's reformulation, is therefore incomplete. Bodies *are* placed in the sense that spaces are constructed so as to manipulate bodies.[121] Humans may "bring place into being," but not *all* humans bring places into being in the same ways or to the same degrees. Authority produces place *for others* just as it also *se-*

---

[113] See Chaido Koukouli-Chrysantaki, "Colonia Iulia Augusta Philippensis," in *Philippi at the Time of Paul and After His death*, ed., Charalambos Bakirtzis and Helmut Koester (Harrisburg: Trinity Press International, 1998) 5–35; Michel Sève, "Le coté nord du forum de Philippes," *BCH* 112.1 (1988): 467–79; cited in Nasrallah, "Spatial Perspectives," 72 n. 10.

[114] Nasrallah, "Spatial Perspectives," 58.

[115] Nasrallah, "Spatial Perspectives," 60.

[116] Nasrallah, "Spatial Perspectives," 60.

[117] Nasrallah, "Spatial Perspectives," 60. On "contact zones," see 72 n. 14.

[118] See J. Helgeland, "Roman Army Religion," *ANRW* 2 16.2:147–505; R. MacMullen, *Romanization in the Time of Augustus* (New Haven: Yale University Press, 2000); F. Vittinghoff, *Römische Kolonisation und Bürgerrechtspolitikunter Caesar und Augustus* (Mainz, Akademie der Wissenschaft und der Literatur, Abhandlungen der Geistes- und Socialwissenschaftlichen Klasse Jahrgang 1951, Nr 14; Wiesbaden: Steiner Verlag, 1952).

[119] Jonathan Z. Smith, *To Take Place: Toward Theory in Ritual* (Chicago: Chicago University Press, 1987), 28; cited in Nasrallah, "Spatial Perspectives," 57.

[120] Steve Pile, "Introduction: Opposition, Political Identities, and Spaces of Resistance," in *Geographies of Resistance* (ed. Steve Pile and Michael Keith; London: Routledge, 1997), 3.

[121] See here Nasrallah's excellent discussion of Vitruvius (*De arch.* 6.1.10–11) in Nasrallah, "Spatial Perspectives," 65–66. See, too, Laura Salah Nasrallah, *Christian Responses to Roman Art and Architecture: The Second-Century Church Amid the Spaces of Empire* (Cambridge: Cambridge University Press, 2010), 10–12.

duces. But precisely here Nasrallah rightly sees in Steve Pile's analysis of space "no simple binary of resister and empire, dominated and dominator." She appropriates Pile's notion of surveillance, borders, and parcels of space into her defining imperial technologies of domination as the "surveying, cutting up, and surveilling" of occupied territories.[122] "At the heart of questions of resistance lie questions of spatiality – the politics of lived space."[123]

Paul was thus among those classical writers who, like Max's *Standover Man*, "constructed the spaces of the world through words" and invited/conscripted his audiences into a "spatial imaginary" through his explication of τὸ πολίτευμα ἐν οὐρανοῖς (Phil 3:20).[124] Paul was a maker of space, and placed the Philippians among others within that space.[125] Nasrallah's reading of Paul and space is read through "the human body as the means from which we perceive space."[126] Her focus is on the bodily perceptions of Paul, Paul's partners, and Christ's (2:6–11).[127] A "broader trend" in Philippians is suggested by Nasrallah in which people's relations to each other are mapped vertically according to "spatial organizations in which people knew where they stood on a social map." She continues:

> The Philippians who heard or read Paul's letter would have empire and its spatial expansion to Philippi in mind, as well as (likely) the empire's vertical spatial expansion in terms of the divinization of the imperial family [...] Those who heard and debated Paul's letter would not be ignorant of their city's own history as a site of contestation in the very late republican period, and then its site as the eventual triumph of one who would become emperor, and then its imagined status as a site of omen that confirmed Tiberius's rule.[128]

Though I do not share her confidence in what readers would have heard, Nasrallah is an important bridge in linking the studies on φρόνησις above with my attempted spatial (re)reading of Philippians to follow. I will at-

---

[122] Nasrallah, "Spatial Perspectives," 64.

[123] Pile, "Introduction," 27. Pile's strong language on "resistance" should be tempered with the mounting literature on "resilience."

[124] Nasrallah, "Spatial Perspectives," 64. Among other classical writers on space, we would add Strabo (*Geography*), Vitruvius (*On Architecture*), and Claudius Ptolemy (*Almagest, Geography, Tetrabiblos*); cf. Daniela Duerk, *Geography in Classical Antiquity* (Cambridge: Cambridge University Press, 2012); Claude Nicolet, *Space, Geography, and Politics in the Early Roman Empire* (Ann Arbor: University of Michigan Press, 1991 [1988]); Michael Scott, *Space and Society in the Greek and Roman Worlds* (Cambridge: Cambridge University Press, 2012); and, James S. Romm, *The Edges of the Earth in Ancient Thought* (Princeton: Princeton University Press, 1994).

[125] Nasrallah, "Spatial Perspectives," 68. See, generally, "Spatial Perspectives," 66–68.

[126] Nasrallah, "Spatial Perspectives," 66.

[127] Nasrallah, "Spatial Perspectives," 66–69.

[128] Nasrallah, "Spatial Perspectives," 69.

tempt to synthesize these two together in the next section in what I am calling "spatial reasoning," but, before that, I must first explicate what I mean by "space" and "place."

II. Definition and Imagination: Space and Place

Nigel Thrift has rightly stressed that space is not some "commonsense external background to human and social action."[129] Space is the *result* of "highly problematic temporary settlements that divine and connect things up into different kinds of collectives which are slowly provided with the means which render them durable and sustainable."[130] Though the earth's 197 million square miles of land may be relatively fixed,[131] the *spaces* of these relatively fixed square miles are not. Humans "live constructivistically,"[132] arranging the world with, for, and in opposition to others.[133] As Henri Lefebvre has pointed out, absolute space cannot exist owing to the relativizing and historicizing effects of these colonial "arrangements." Deleuze noted how "the world is constantly being territorialized, de-territorialized and re-territorialized in unexpected [and unnoticed?] ways."[134] Doreen Massey and others have argued that it is also being temporalized, de-temporalized, and re-temporalized. Space and time are thus "inseparable."[135] They have been sutured.

Rejecting notions of absolute space led Lefebvre to his initial explication of the "trialectics of spatiality": viz., the bundled complex of cultural practices, representations and imaginaries operative within spatiality. Lefebvre distinguishes between the "perceived space" (*le perçu*) of everyday popular action and outlook,[136] the "conceived space" (*le conçu*) of the professional and the official, and the "third space" of "lived space" (*le vécu*). This third space is the habitation of *l'homme totale*, the site wherein

---

[129] Nigel Thrift, "Space: The Fundamental Stuff of Geography," in *Key Concepts in Geography* (ed. S. L. Holloway, S. Rice, and G. Valentine; London: Sage, 2003), 95.

[130] Thrift, "Space," 95.

[131] Though with the realities of climate change, even this is hardly as fixed as it might initially seem.

[132] Sloterdijk, *Bubbles*, 84.

[133] Sloterdijk, *Bubbles*, 85.

[134] See Hubbard et. al., *Key Thinkers on Space and Place*, 9.

[135] Doreen B. Massey, "Politics and Space/Time," *New Left Review* 196 (1992): 65–84; cf. Nigel Thrift, "Time and Theory in Human Geography Part One," *Progress in Human Geography* 1 (1977): 65–101; and, Nigel Thrift, "Time and Theory in Human Geography Part Two," *Progress in Human Geography* 1 (1977): 415–57.

[136] Cf. Henri Lefebvre, *Critique of Everyday Life* (3 vols.; London: Verso, 2014).

both the "perceived space" of the ordered masses and the officiality of "conceived spaces" are threatened by a power of potential refiguration.[137]

This "third space" has been understood and appropriated in numerous ways,[138] but here I simply stress the possibility within spatiality for the potentialities of emergence. Even within the (en)forced contours of the everyday, *lived space* allows for a rupture both within the soul-destroying everydayness of *perceived space*,[139] and within the official designations of *conceived space*. Inquiries into social locations are therefore "productive" insofar as they examine the places "humans create in order to have somewhere they can appear as those who they are."[140] This "somewhere" is what Peter Sloterdijk has termed "spheres": those "effective forms of the real,"[141] both as "an enlivened space and as the imagined and virtual orb of being,"[142] in all its "world-creating formal potencies."[143] Space-time is thus a plurality of folds of selves in negotiation.[144] It is alive. Identities-in-space become cork-like, "floating on a tempestuous ocean," no longer moving on their own but as an "element that moves."[145] Space is thus an active milieu that both influences and is influenced by social interactions.[146] In any reading of spatial theory, then, space must be viewed as both a socializing force and a *product* of socializing forces.[147] To appropriate from

---

[137] Henri Lefebvre, *The Production of Space* (trans. Donald Nicholson-Smith; Oxford: Wiley-Blackwell, 1992). Cf. Kanishka Goonewardena, et. al., eds., *Space, Difference, Everyday Life: Reading Henri Lefebvre* (London: Routledge, 2008).

[138] See, e.g., Edward W. Soja, *Thirdspace: Journeys to Los Angeles and Other Real-and-Imagined Places* (Oxford: Blackwell, 1996), 53–82; and, Kevin Bruyneel, *Third Space of Sovereignty: The Postcolonial Politics of U.S. Indigenous Relations* (Minneapolis: University of Minnesota Press, 2007).

[139] Lefebvre, *Critique of Everyday Life*; cf., too, Michel de Certeau, *Practice of Everyday Life* (trans. Steven Rendall; Berkeley: University of California Press, 1984); and, Inigo Bocken, ed., *Spiritual Spaces: History and Mysticism in Michel de Certeau* (Leuven: Peeters, 2013).

[140] Sloterdijk, *Bubbles*, 28.
[141] Sloterdijk, *Bubbles*, 61.
[142] Sloterdijk, *Bubbles*, 67.
[143] Sloterdijk, *Bubbles*, 77.

[144] Gillians Rose, *Feminism and Geography* (Minneapolis: University of Minnesota Press, 1993). On folds, I mean something near to Gilles Deleuze, *The Fold: Leibniz and the Baroque* (trans. Tom Conley; Minneapolis: University of Minnesota Press, 1993); cf. Sjoerd van Tuinen and Niamh McDonnell, eds., *Deleuze and the Fold: A Critical Reader* (New York: Palgrave Macmillan, 2010).

[145] Gilles Deleuze, *Essays Critical and Clinical* (trans. Daniel W. Smith and Michael A. Greco; Minneapolis: University of Minnesota Press, 1997), 26.

[146] Cf. Anthony Giddens, *The Constitution of Society: Outline of the Theory of Structuration* (Berkeley: University of California Press, 1986).

[147] Cf. Doreen B. Massey, *Spatial Divisions of Labor: Social Structures and the Geography of Production* (New York: Methuen, 1984).

Sloterdijk, "spaces have their own histories."[148] In other words, space is both *socializing* and *socialized*.[149] But as we anticipated above, these first two elements of the trialectic I am developing here focus on the modes of spatial production in the sense in which Baudrillard explicated how to produce (*pro-ducere*) is to make appear or move forward. The third element of my trialectic considers the seductive forces which lead astray and make disappear (*se-ducere*). Painting over pages, effacing monuments, producing coins with truncated storylines. The trialectic suggested here pays attention both to the modes of *production* as well as the modes of *disappearance* – what remains and what has been erased; what has been painted and what has been painted over.

It is here that "place emerges as a particular form of space."[150] Place is the particular and peculiar of space animated by the "lived experiences of people."[151] A place's specificity is "constructed out of a particular constellation of social relations, meeting and weaving together at a particular locus."[152] Important for my reading of Philippians will be appropriating from Benedict Anderson's notion of the "imagined community"[153] into this conceptualizing of spatiality. Anderson has not passed without criticisms,[154] particularly from post-colonial theorists,[155] but I am most intrigued by his explication of the "deep, horizontal comradeship" of imagined communities with those "fellow members" who will never meet.[156] Space, of course, never comes all at once. It is contested, negotiated, subverted, enforced,

---

[148] Sloterdijk, *Bubbles*, 90.

[149] Here I should stress that my appropriation of Sloterdijk's "history" has received a Baudrillardian texture in viewing history as not only narrations which *produce* (*pro-ducere*) but also *seduce* (*se-ducere*). That is to say, my understanding of the "histories of spaces" confronts those silencing modes of disappearance which lay dispersed and buried around the modes of production. Cf. Jean Baudrillard, *Seduction*, Jean Baudrillard, *Forget Foucault* (Semiotext[e] / Foreign Agents; Cambridge, Mass.: MIT Press, 2007).

[150] For a helpful bibliographical essay, see Gieryn, "A Space for Place in Sociology."

[151] Hubbard et. al., *Key Thinkers on Space and Place*, 5.

[152] Doreen B. Massey, "A Global Sense of Place," *Marxism Today* June (1991):28; see also 24–29.

[153] Benedict Anderson, *Imagined Communities: Reflections on the Origin and Spread of Nationalism* (rev. ed.; London: Verso, 1991).

[154] E.g., T. Mayer, "Gender Ironies of Nationalism: Setting the Stage," in *Gender Ironies of Nationalism: Sexing the Nation* (ed. T. Mayer; London: Routledge, 2000), 1–22; L. McDowell, *Gender Identity, and Place: Introducing Feminist Geographies* (Minneapolis: University of Minnesota Press, 1999); A. McClintock, *Imperial Leather: Race, Gender and Sexuality in the Colonial Contest* (London: Routledge, 1995); and, D. Mitchell, *Cultural Geography: A Critical Introduction* (Oxford: Blackwell, 2000).

[155] Edward Said, *Culture and Imperialism* (New York: Vintage, 1993); and, Partha Chatterjee, *The Nation and Its Fragments: Colonial and Postcolonial Histories* (Princeton: Princeton University Press, 1993).

[156] Anderson, *Imagined Communities*, 6–7.

reinforced, produced, erased. But it is in the *imagining* of a shared community, a shared space, localized in the particularity of place,[157] where a social network allows not only for worn versions of "unity and diversity" to emerge, but what Walter D. Mignolo has called "border thinking," and "pluriversality as a universal project."[158]

We will return to Mignolo in the final part of this essay, but I would like to appropriate a final element into our developing spatial theory before turning to Philippians: viz., the role of the newspaper in Anderson's *Imagined Community*. Intriguingly, Anderson drew on the works of Erich Auerbach and Walter Benjamin in theorizing newspapers as the media and technology which "made it possible for rapidly growing numbers of people to think about themselves, and relate themselves to others, in profoundly new ways."[159] Disparate experiences were thus published as the diverse expressions of a common identity. Here again, we must remind ourselves that Anderson is discussing the "convergence of capitalism and print technology," not universal practices across time and space.[160] Some might (rightfully) claim that his understanding of the newspaper as de-centered dispersal is fundamentally at odds with Paul's centralized direction of the assemblies. But Anderson provides helpful theoretical language for understanding Paul as a letter-writer.[161] The distribution of his letters and their recitation across multiple sites (1 Thess 5:27; cf. Col 4:16) wraps the disparate experiences of the scattered assemblies into a shared imaginary of the diverse expressions of an ἐκκλησία that is ἐν Χριστῷ. It is not insignificant that Paul says πᾶσιν τοῖς οὖσιν ἐν Ῥώμῃ ἀγαπητοῖς θεοῦ (Rom 1:7): ἡ πίστις ὑμῶν καταγγέλλεται ἐν ὅλῳ τῷ κόσμῳ (Rom 1:8; cf. 16:19). Or τῇ

---

[157] Related here is Lefebvre's notion of rhythmanalysis. Place is made through the rhythms of being which naturalize and normalize certain spaces. Henri Lefebvre, *Rythmanalysis: Space, Time and Everyday Life* (New York: Bloomsbury Academic, 2004).

[158] Walter D. Mignolo, *Local Histories / Global Designs: Coloniality, Subaltern Knowledges, and Border Thinking* (2d ed.; Princeton Studies in Culture/Power/History; Princeton: Princeton University Press, 2012); and Walter D. Mignolo, "On Pluriversality," *Walter Mignolo* (blog), October 20, 2013, http://waltermignolo.com/on-pluriversality/.

[159] Anderson, *Imagined Communities*, 36.

[160] Anderson, *Imagined Communities*, 46; cf. Uriya Shavit, *The New Imagined Community: Global Media and the Construction of National and Muslim Identities of Migrants* (Eastbourne: Sussex Academic Press, 2009).

[161] Stanley E. Porter and Sean A. Adams, eds., *Paul and the Ancient Letter Form* (Pauline Studies 6; Leiden: Brill, 2010); M. Luther Stirewalt, *Paul, the Letter Writer* (Grand Rapids: Eerdmans, 2003); cf. Stanley K. Stowers, *Letter Writing in Greco-Roman Antiquity* (LEC 5; Louisville: Westminster John Knox, 1986); Lutz Doering, *Ancient Jewish Letters and the Beginnings of Christian Epistolography* (WUNT 298; Tübingen: Mohr Siebeck, 2012); and, Neil Elliot and Mark Reasoner, eds., *Documents and Images for the Study of Paul* (Minneapolis: Fortress, 2011), 63–118, 303–15.

ἐκκλησίᾳ Θεσσαλονικέων (1 Thess 1:1): ἐν παντὶ τόπῳ ἡ πίστις ὑμῶν ἡ πρὸς τὸν θεὸν ἐξελήλυθεν (1 Thess 1:8). Or, in Phil 1:12, as Stephen Fowl suggests, while "engaging in the conventional sharing of news characteristic of letters of friendship," Paul is shaping "the way the Philippians view that news."[162] It is through the epistle, akin to Anderson's newspaper within the *Imagined Community*, then, that we can construct a Pauline instillation of a global sense of the local, and a global sense of place throughout the assemblies.[163] It is this reading strategy which will guide my reading of Philippians.

III. Paul's Spatial Imaginary

It is perhaps most intriguing to begin at the end of Philippians to explicate what I mean by the spatial imaginary of Paul's *imagined community*. Paul concludes his final greetings to the assemblies in Philippi by charging them to "greet every saint *in Christ*" (Ἀσπάσασθε πάντα ἅγιον ἐν Χριστῷ Ἰησοῦ; 4:21), then passes general greetings from "all the saints" (πάντες οἱ ἅγιοι), followed by the more localized greetings from the "brethren" (ἀδελφοί) with Paul and "those of Caesar's household" (οἱ ἐκ τῆς Καίσαρος οἰκίας). There is a subtle spatial movement at work in Philippians from the particular in 1:1 (πᾶσιν τοῖς ἁγίοις ἐν Χριστῷ Ἰησοῦ τοῖς οὖσιν ἐν Φιλίπποις) to the more general and again to its local reverberations in 4:21–23. The assemblies are given Paul's thanks for their "partnership" (κοινωνία) in the gospel (εὐαγγέλιον) in 1:5, and called "participants" (συγκοινωνοί) with Paul in "grace" (χάρις) in 1:7.[164] They are described as being with Paul "in the beginning of the gospel" (ἐν ἀρχῇ τοῦ εὐαγγελίου), entering into a partnership with him when others would not (4:15). And they are designated as being part of the "same conflict" (τὸν αὐτὸν ἀγῶνα) they first saw and heard in Paul (1:30). The particular participation of the assemblies is thus sutured within Paul's wider geographical mapping. This mapping is triangulated by the "one spirit, one mind and [one] faith of the gospel" (ἑνὶ πνεύματι, μιᾷ ψυχῇ [...] τῇ πίστει τοῦ εὐαγγελίου, 1:27; cf. Eph. 4:5–6).

---

[162] Stephen E. Fowl, *Philippians* (THNTC; Grand Rapids: Eerdmans, 2005), 37. Cf. Troels Engberg-Pedersen, *Paul and the Stoics*, 107.

[163] Here I attempt to place this reading into the call of Massey, "A Global Sense of Place," 29. Cf. Anna Tsing, "The Global Situation," in *The Anthropology of Globalization: A Reader* (2d ed.; ed. Jonathan Xavier Inda and Renato Rosaldo; Oxford: Blackwell, 2008), 66–98.

[164] See James R. Harrison, *Paul's Language of Grace in its Graeco-Roman Context* (WUNT 2/172; Tübingen: Mohr Siebeck, 2003); and, John M. G. Barclay, *Paul and The Gift* (Grand Rapids: Eerdmans, forthcoming); John M. G. Barclay, "Manna and the Circulation of Grace: A Study of 2 Corinthians 8:1–15," in *The Word Leaps the Gap: Essays on Scripture and Theology in Honor of Richard B. Hays* (ed. J. Ross Wagner, C. Kavin Rowe, and A. Katherine Grieb; Grand Rapids: Eerdmans, 2008) 409–26.

These spatial contours are also set by a temporal directive in two directions: ἡ ἡμέρα τοῦ Χριστοῦ Ἰησοῦ (1:6, 10; 2:16; 4:5; cf. 3:20) and the "arrival" (παρουσία) of Paul (1:26–27; cf. 2:12, 24).[165]

Whether it is language of εἰς τὸ εὐαγγέλιον (1:5; 2:22; 4:3), τῆς χάριτος (1:7), τῆς πίστεως (1:25), τοῦ εὐαγγελίου τοῦ Χριστοῦ (1:27), κοινωνία πνεύματος (2:1), ἐν κυρίῳ (3:1; 4:1, 2, 4), οἱ πνεύματι θεοῦ λατρεύοντες (3:3), εὑρεθῶ ἐν αὐτῷ (3:9), or whatever, it all reflects the ways in which those *placed* ἐν Φιλίπποις are set within Paul's wider communal imaginary of being ἐν Χριστῷ. Paul's communal imaginary, as it were, is thus the sphereic locality of a *being* that is ἐν Χριστῷ (1:1). Being ἐν Χριστῷ is to be within the *spatiality* of Christ, which is shorthand for the complex relational dynamics of being within a new spatio-temporality. As Nasrallah has stated, "what you see depends upon where you stand, and where you stand depends in part on who you are and how you are formed socially, economically, politically by the culture that surrounds you."[166] Paul's radical move is to place those in Philippi ἐν Χριστῷ, and *from* that place call for new orientations and expressions of being. A being that is ἐν Χριστῷ thus not only produces new spatial perspectives and orientations, but it is also the place of a new sociality – a place where *being* is transformed socially, economically, and politically by the spatiality of Christ, and from the perspective of *his body*. The saints in Philippi are charged by Paul στήκετε ἐν κυρίῳ (4:1), and it is this new "standing" which introduces naturalizing and normalizing practices and perspectives (e.g., 4:6–7, 13) from which place is reconfigured.

It is important to stress that this "standing" and perspective take place not merely in some figurative spirit, but *in a body* – not just any body, of course (cf. 3:3), but the body of Christ. Paul's imperative στήκετε ἐν κυρίῳ follows the remarkable claim that this same Lord μετασχηματίσει τὸ σῶμα τῆς ταπεινώσεως ἡμῶν σύμμορφον τῷ σώματι τῆς δόξης αὐτοῦ κατὰ τὴν ἐνέργειαν τοῦ δύνασθαι αὐτὸν καὶ ὑποτάξαι αὐτῷ τὰ πάντα (3:21). But this "transformation" (μετασχηματίζω) has an oddly effective absence. As I have been suggesting, it is the *body* of the κυρίου Ἰησοῦ Χριστοῦ (3:20) that sets the spatio-temporal perspective of the assemblies *over* other spatio-temporal perspectives.[167] But *where* and *when* is this body? Clearly there is delay within Paul's schema (ἀπεκδέχομαι) as well as distance (ἐξ), yet in many respects the somatic *where* and *when* remain immaterial. It is that there was-is-will-be a body that issues forth an effective spatio-temporal perspective. This subjection (ὑποτάσσω) therefore not only includes the

---

[165] Cf. Bockmuehl, *Philippians*, 246.
[166] Nasrallah, "Spatial Perspectives," 57.
[167] Here we await the promising work of Melanie Johnson-DeBaufre, *I'll Fly Away: Making Space in the Letters of Paul* (Place: Publisher, forthcoming).

transvaluation of Paul's pedigree (3:4–11) and its *seduction* (3:13), but the shape of space and reconfiguration of place in Philippi.

To be placed ἐν Χριστῷ is thus to be placed within a new body politic (Rom 12:5; 1 Cor 12:27; cf. Eph 5:30) – or, as Paul will call it, τὸ πολίτευμα ἐν οὐρανοῖς (3:20).[168] Paul's imperatival use of πολιτεύομαι in 1:27 – which, I suggest, heads all his ethical directives – carries clear civic overtones.[169] Brewer has noted how πολιτεύομαι was a thought which communicated the obligations of a citizen.[170] Bockmuehl suggests that Paul "goes on to hijack the language of citizenship" (1:27; 3:20; 4:15),[171] and argues that πολιτεύομαι should be read as "live as citizens;"[172] or, as Heil suggests, "citizens of the gospel."[173] Reumann highlights the political, military, and ecclesial tone to 1:27–30,[174] and glosses 1:27 as the charge to "be citizens in Philippi and Christ."[175] De Vos sees in this civic language of Paul a call to renounce Roman citizenship and live as Christ did in renouncing his privileges (2:6–11).[176] Whether one should go as far as De Vos in seeing a call for an outright renunciation is debatable. It is clear, however, that the fundamental issue is that of allegiance (cf. Philo *Conf.* 17; *Gig.* 61).[177] Paul's constructed body politic was not the only one in

---

[168] See the excellent analysis of Paul's body-politic topos in Dale B. Martin, *The Corinthian Body* (New Haven, Conn.: Yale University Press, 1995), 92ff. Cf. Peter T. O'Brien, *Philippians*, 458–63.

[169] Celsas Spicq, "πολιτεύομαι," 3.124–33; Bauer, "πολιτεύομαι," *BDAG*, 846; and, G. W. H. Lampe, *A Patristic Greek Lexicon*, 1113–14.

[170] R. Brewer, "The Meaning of *Politeuesthe* in Philippians 1:27," *JBL* 71 (1952): 227–31.

[171] Bockmuehl, *Philippians*, 53.

[172] Bockmuehl, *Philippians*, 97. Ralph Martin suggests "behave as citizens" or "Let your life as citizens." *The Epistle of Paul to the Philippians* (Grand Rapids: Eerdmans, 1959), 83. Cf. Gerald F. Hawthorn, *Philippians* (rev. ed.; WBC 43; Waco: Word Books, 2004), 56; Charles B. Cousar, *Philippians and Philemon*, 42–44; G. Walter Hansen, *The Letter to the Philippians* (PNTC; Grand Rapids: Eerdmans, 2009), 93–190; Bruce Winter, *Seek the Welfare of the City: Christians as Benefactors and Citizens* (Grand Rapids: Eerdmans, 1994), 81–104.

[173] John Paul Heil, *Philippians: Let Us Rejoice in being Conformed to Christ* (ECL 3; Atlanta: SBL, 2010), 69–72.

[174] John Reumann, *Philippians* (AB 33B; New Haven, Conn.: Yale University Press, 2008), 279–82.

[175] Reumann, *Philippians*, 284–89.

[176] Craig Steven De Vos, *Church and Community Conflicts: The Relationships of the Thessalonian, Corinthian, and Philippian Churches with their Wider Civic Communities* (Atlanta: Scholars Press, 1999), 282–86; Gordon D. Fee, *Paul's Letter to the Philippians* (NICNT; Grand Rapids: Eerdmans, 1995), 19, 161, 162, 378.

[177] On the full range of options, see Reumann, *Philippians*, 264–68. Cf. Thurston and Ryan, *Philippians and Philemon*, 138. Cf. the LXX usages in Es 8:31; 2 Macc 6:1; 11:25; *3 Macc* 3:4; *4 Macc* 2:8, 23; 4:23; 5:16; cf. Jos. *Vita* 1.2; *Letter of Aristeas* 31.

town.[178] Cicero, for example, warned Marcellus that wherever he is he will be in the "power of him whom [he seeks] to flee." And that the "power of [Caesar] whom we fear stretches so far that it embraces the entire world."[179]

Reconciliation to Roman rule took place at the level of the individual, as each person incorporated the Roman emperor into his personal pantheon and accommodated himself to the bureaucratic rituals and ceremonial forms that endowed membership in the Roman community with meaning.[180]

The efficacy of Roman rule was thus in its bureaucratic conscription of their subjects as "active participants in their own subjugation by urging them to iterate the principles of the ruling order."[181] It was the publication of this bureaucracy through varying media which constructed for others and conscripted others into a rationality which in turn became a kind of capital from which provincials could leverage in varying ways and directions of social mobility. Provincials enacted their faith in the "truth value" of these media "when they constructed personal and institutional histories based on their contents and chronology."[182] These administrative and bureaucratic practices "operated in harmony with, even as they helped to constitute, the rhythms of daily life" providing a "field in which people could 'practice the rituals of ideological recognition.'"[183] It was through "participation in its bureaucratic procedures and not simply by coincidental habitation within the boundaries of the empire" that communal membership was defined and recognized.[184]

Ando posits that Tatian (120–180 CE) "became one of the earliest participants within a debate that would divide Christians from pagans" by "positing the Christian community as an alternative political structure."[185]

---

[178] Here see the excellent chapter "The King Is a Body Politick...for that a Body Politique Never Dieth" in Clifford Ando, *Imperial Ideology and the Provincial Loyalty in the Roman Empire* (Berkeley: University of California Press, 2000), 336–412.

[179] Cicero *Ep. ad fam.* 4.7.4. First cited in Ando, *Imperial Ideology*, 336–37.

[180] Ando, *Imperial Ideology*, 337.

[181] Ando, *Imperial Ideology*, 338; cf. 131–205.

[182] Ando, *Imperial Ideology*, 338; cf. 73–130.

[183] Ando, *Imperial Ideology*, 352, citing F. Jameson, *The Ideologies of Theory: Essays 1971–1986* (Minneapolis: University of Minnesota Press, 1988), 2.54

[184] Ando, *Imperial Ideology*, 352. Here we could fruitfully consider these dynamics in relation to the theoretical framework of Henri Lefebvre, *Rhythmanalysis*.

[185] Ando, *Imperial Ideology*, 344. Ando goes on to cite E. Peterson, "Das Problem des Nationalismus im alten Christentum," pp. 51–63 in *Frühkirche, Judentum und Gnosis* (Freiburg: Herder, 1959); A. Momigliano, "Some Preliminary Remarks on the 'Religious Opposition' to the Roman Empire," in *Opposition et resistances à l'empire d'Auguste à Trajan* (ed. A. Giovannini and K. A. Raaflaub; Entretiens sur l'Antiquité classique 33; Vandoeuvres-Genève: Foundation Hardt, 1987): 103–33; cf. A. Momigliano, *On Pagans, Jews, and Christians* (Middletown: Wesleyan University Press, 1987), 142–58.

We might also consider Clement of Alexandria (e.g., *Strom.* 4.26.166.1; cf. 7.12.78.3, 79.4),[186] or the *Epistle to Diognetus* (e.g., 5.5ff.). Yet "buried there in the 'foundations'" of the "alternative political structure" of later Christianity/ies of the likes of Tatian is Paul's intervention into this banal participation of imperial ideology with the construction of his own body politic.[187] In a manner similar to the ubiquitous emperor who managed,[188] according to Aristides, "the entire civilized world by letters, which arrive almost as soon as they are written, as if they were carried by winged messengers" (*Or.* 26.33), Paul policed and shaped his own body politic through the epistolary genre. It is within the body politic of Christ which, as Paul directs the assemblies, "constitutes the present sphere of their new existence":[189] a *being* which "means living within the realm of Christ's rule,"[190] and a reconceived spatiality from the perspective of his *body*.

Paul's body politic, his communal imaginary, is thus a christic reconfiguration of space. This spatiality of Christ fashions a *being* that is ἐν Χριστῷ, reordering the "common life" of the assemblies from this new embodied relationality.[191] The appropriate civic action which Paul calls for in 1:27 is to live in accord with the εὐαγγέλιον – to this reconfigured space. It both "establishes the relationship between Paul and the Philippians and provides a space or context within which that relationship will grow." This "space" or locality of the εὐαγγελίου "provides the body of shared convictions and social and ecclesial conventions."[192] It forms a "living arena" for a new civic way of being in the world.[193] Perhaps the referencing to Epaphroditus as a συστρατιώτης (2:25) receives a contrasting shade in this light.[194] Whatever the case, "their allegiance is to a polity completely outside the reaches of the Roman Empire, even though they remain spatially

---

[186] Cf. Brian E. Daley, *The Hope of the Early Church: A Handbook of Patristic Eschatology* (Grand Rapids: Baker Academic, 2002), 45.

[187] Cf. Ward Blanton, *A Materialism for the Masses: Saint Paul and the Philosophy of the Undying Life* (New York: Columbia University Press, 2014), 37.

[188] On the ubiquity of the emperor through imperial portraits and other images, see Ando, *Imperial Ideology*, 73–130; 206–76, 368–70; cf. Paul Zanker, *The Power of Images in the Age of Augustus* (trans. Alan Shapiro; Ann Arbor: University of Michigan Press, 1988); and, Nasrallah, *Christian Responses to Roman Art and Architecture*.

[189] Fee, *Corinthians*, 65.

[190] Gerhard Lohfink, *Jesus and Community: The Social Dimensions of Christian Faith* (trans. John P. Galvin; Philadelphia: Fortress, 1984 [1982]), 127.

[191] Fowl, *Philippians*, 61.

[192] Fowl, *Philippians*, 24. Being "in Christ" for Fowl thus stands "for a body of convictions about Christ." 38–39.

[193] Cf. Lohfink, *Jesus and Community*, 62. Lohfink calls this a "contrast society" (see 121–32, 146, 157–63), which is near Bockmuehl's notion of a contrasting vision; see Bockmuehl, *Philippians*, 98.

[194] Cf. Fowl, *Philippians*, 135.

located within it."[195] Paul's address in 1:1 now comes into fuller view: πᾶσιν τοῖς ἁγίοις ἐν Χριστῷ Ἰησοῦ relativizes the priority of life on the colony for τοῖς οὖσιν ἐν Φιλίπποις. The polity of τοῦ εὐαγγελίου τοῦ Χριστοῦ (1:27) paints a "cruciform common life" as the communal imaginary over the bureaucratic pages of Roman rule. Space is reconfigured, and a new sense of place, a new sense of being ἐν Φιλίπποις, emerges.[196]

C. Φρόνησις as Spatial Reasoning

Though our analysis of φρόνησις takes into account only Paul's letter to the Philippians,[197] a brief comparison of its distribution in Paul's letters shows that it is most evenly distributed in Philippians than in any other letter. Its forms show up fifteen times in Romans,[198] five times throughout the Corinthian correspondence,[199] and once in Galatians.[200] (It also occurs three times in the disputed letters.)[201] The word appears in clusters in Romans, whereas in Philippians Paul consistently deploys and develops the concept. As Meeks suggested, the shaping of a "Christian" φρόνησις appears to be the letter's "most comprehensive purpose."[202] In what follows I do not want to set my suggested (re)reading of φρόνησις in opposition to Meeks or Kraftchick or the other fine studies on φρόνησις in Philippians; rather, I hope that my experimental explication of this complex concept as "spatial reasoning" adds a measure of texture and dimensionality.

I. Revisiting the Archive

A natural place to begin any (re)reading of φρόνησις is Book VI of Aristotle's *Nicomachean Ethics*.[203] As C. D. C. Reeve has noted, φρόνησις "is not simply a central topic of the *Ethics* but its crowning glory and most valua-

---

[195] Fowl, *Philippians*, 173.

[196] Cf. Fowl, *Philippians*, 187; and, of course, the excellent work of Michael J. Gorman, *Cruciformity: Paul's Narrative Spirituality of the Cross* (Grand Rapids: Eerdmans, 2001), 349–67; Michael J. Gorman, *Apostle of the Crucified Lord: A Theological Introduction to Paul and His Letters* (Grand Rapids: Eerdmans, 2003), 412–53; and, Michael J. Gorman, *Inhabiting the Cruciform God: Kenosis, Justification, and Theosis in Paul's Narrative Soteriology* (Grand Rapids: Eerdmans, 2009), 9–39.

[197] Phil 1:7; 2:2 [2x], 5; 3:15 [2x], 19; 4:2, 10 [2x].

[198] Rom 8:5 [4x], 27; 11:20, 25; 12:3 [2x], 16 [3x]; 14:6 [2x]; and 15:5.

[199] 1 Cor 4:10; 10:15; 13:11; 2 Cor 11:19; 13:11.

[200] Gal 5:10.

[201] Eph 1:8; Col 3:2; Titus 3:8.

[202] Meeks, "Man from Heaven," 333.

[203] Translations will come from Aristotle, *The Nicomachean Ethics* (trans. H. Rackham; Cambridge, Mass.: Harvard University Press, 1934 [1926]).

ble legacy."[204] Excellent studies have been carried out in this terrain,[205] so there is no need to rework Book VI here in any exhaustive fashion. But of significance for my reading, and as has often been pointed out, is the way in which Book VI attempts to define a relevant ὀρθός λόγος – "a certain mark to aim at, on which the [one] who knows the principle involved fixes [their] gaze, and increases or relaxes the tension accordingly" (VI.1). But what is that ὀρθός λόγος and how does one access it? "Outside the sphere of the necessary and scientifically explicable lies the sphere of what admits of being otherwise where things happen by luck [τύχη]. This is the sphere within which production [ποίησις] and action [πρᾶξις] – and thus practical wisdom – operate."[206] Reeve's reading φρόνησις within language of "spheres" here, I suggest, is not insignificant. He goes on to suggest that appropriate practical reasons are thus either *architectonic* or *deliberative*.[207] And, with respect to the latter, "what alerts us to the need for deliberation is the situation in which we perceive ourselves to be."[208] Deliberation thus cannot be subject merely to "time constraints," but *environmental* and *spatial* perceptions as well. Though no clear perception is associated with φρόνησις, it "is clearly identified as a practical state rather than a productive one, dealing with perceptible objects rather than simply intelligible ones" (I.34 1196^{b}27–28, 1197^{a}3–16, 1198^{a}32–^{b}8). Yet φρόνησις also "exerts architectonic control over the virtues of character, so that to be in accord with reason they must do the actions it prescribes."[209] And, more often than not, "the laws of the city" or one's "practical perception" will inform one in what to do, minimizing the need for deliberation.[210]

---

[204] C. D. C. Reeve, *Aristotle on Practical Wisdom: Nicomachean Ethics VI* (Cambridge, Mass.: Harvard University Press, 2013), 41.

[205] E.g., Kraftchick, "Self-Presentation and Community Construction"; Reeve, *Aristotle*, pp. 1–42, 89–264 (cf., too, pp. xiii–xiv for a listing of editions, translations, and commentaries); Reeve, *Action, Contemplation, and Happiness: An Essay on Aristotle* (Cambridge: Harvard University Press, 2012); Olav Eikeland, *The Ways of Aristotle: Aristotelian Phrónēsis, Aristotelian Philosophy of Dialogue, and Action Research* (Bern: Peter Lang, 2008); Daniel C. Russel, "Phronesis and the Virtues (*NE* vi 12–13)," in *The Cambridge Companion to Aristotle's* Nicomachean Ethics (ed. Ronald M. Polansky; Cambridge: Cambridge University Press, 2014), 203–20; cf., in general, Polansky, ed., *The Cambridge Companion to Aristotle's* Nicomachean Ethics; and, Paul Studtmann, "Aristotle's Categorial Scheme," pp. 63–80 in Christopher Shields, ed., *The Oxford Handbook of Aristotle* (Oxford: Oxford University Press, 2012). Note, too, Troels Engberg-Pedersen, *Aristotle's Theory of Moral Insight* (Oxford: Oxford University Press, 1983).

[206] Reeve, *Aristotle*, 6.
[207] Reeve, *Aristotle*, 10.
[208] Reeve, *Aristotle*, 13.
[209] Reeve, *Aristotle*, 24–25.
[210] Reeve, *Aristotle*, 37.

In a roundabout sort of way, then, φρόνησις as "ethically correct reason" involves a target (VI.1/1138ᵇ20–34) and is the virtue of the soul which forms beliefs and perceptions (VI.5/1140ᵇ25–28). And these beliefs and perceptions cannot be separated from the individual, the household, *or the πόλις* (VI.8/1141ᵇ23–33). Φρόνησις is a "truth-attaining rational quality, concerned with action in relation to things that are good and bad for human beings" (VI.5).[211] And, again, the measure of what is appropriate is the ὀρθός λόγος. It is the ὀρθός λόγος which sets a sphere of rationality in which φρόνησις perceives, situates, and reasons. It is φρόνησις as both architectonic and deliberative, then, which in its "truth attaining" becomes a kind of rationality within the sphere; or, to put it differently, *spatial reasoning*.[212]

The concept of φρόνησις has been picked up in many ways throughout the history of philosophy.[213] During the summer semester of 1923 at Marburg, for example, the young Heidegger held an influential seminar devoted to the anti-rationalistic potential of this ἄλλο γένος γνώσεως.[214] One of the participants in that seminar was Hans-Georg Gadamer,[215] who made great use of φρόνησις in his own philosophical hermeneutics through its deployment in such concepts like *sensus communis*, taste, tact, and *cognitio sensitive*.[216] Gadamer builds off of Heidegger's understanding of

---

[211] The Greek reads: λείπεται ἄρα αὐτὴν εἶναι ἕξιν ἀληθῆ μετὰ λόγου πρακτικὴν περὶ τὰ ἀνθρώπῳ ἀγαθὰ καὶ κακά (*NE* VI 5–6 [336–37]).

[212] Worth comparing would be Aristotle's notion of φρόνησις within *NE* VI and his explications of space in *Phys* IV. On the *Physics*, see David Bostock, *Space, Time, Matter, and Form: Essays on Aristotle's* Physics (Oxford: University of Oxford Press, 2006); Helen S. Lang, *The Order of Nature in Aristotle's* Physics: *Place and the Elements* (Cambridge: Cambridge University Press, 1998). See, too, Keimpe Algra, *Concepts of Space in Greek Thought* (Leiden: Brill, 1994), 121–91; H. Mendell, "*Topoi* on *topos*: The development of Aristotle's concept of space," *Phron* 32 (1987): 206–31; and, Keimpe Algra, "Space," *Brill's New Pauly Encyclopaedia of the Ancient World* (15 vols.; Leiden: Brill, 2008), 13.685–87.

[213] Cf., e.g., L. Cortella, "Prudenza," *Enciclopedia Filosofica*, 9091–93; E. Vimercati, "Phronesis," *Enciclopedia Filosofica*, 8595–96; Onora O'Neill, "Practical Reason and Ethics," *Routledge Encyclopedia of Philosophy*, 7.613–20.

[214] See Theodore J. Kisiel, *The Genesis of Heidegger's "Being and Time"* (Berkeley: University of California Press, 1995), 269; James Van Buren, *The Young Heidegger: Rumor of a Hidden King* (Studies in Continental Thought; Bloomington: Indiana University Press, 1994), 220–34.

[215] Hans-Georg Gadamer, *Philosophical Hermeneutics* (trans. David E. Linge; Berkeley: University of California Press, 1976), 201; cf. Hans-Georg Gadamer, *Heidegger's Ways* (trans. John W. Stanley; Albany: SUNY Press, 1994). See, too, Robert J. Dostal, "Gadamer's Relation to Heidegger and Phenomenology," in *The Cambridge Companion to Gadamer* (ed. Robert J. Dostal; Cambridge: Cambridge University Press, 2002), 247–66.

[216] One can clearly hear allusion to Giambattista Vico. Cf. Hans-Georg Gadamer, *Truth and Method* (London: Continuum, 2011 [1975]), 17–26.

φρόνησις as not only a *practical* reasoning of our being-in-the-world, but also as constituting one's insight into a concrete situation. For Gadamer, this "mode of insight" has its "own rationality irreducible to any simple rule or set of rules, that cannot be directly taught, and that is always oriented to the particular case at hand."[217] Each concrete situation, then, has its own kind of rationality.

Pierre Bourdieu picks up some of these points as well in his important work on *Practical Reason*.[218] He notes how his philosophy is *relational* in its accord with the "primacy of relations" as well as *dispositional* which "notes the potentialities inscribed in the body of agents and in the structure of the situations where they act, or, more precisely, in the relations between them."[219] These converge into the fundamental concepts of habitus, field, and capital – its cornerstone being the "two-way relationship between objective structures (those of social fields) and incorporated structures (those of the habitus)."[220] For Bourdieu, space thus becomes a "set of distinct and coexisting positions which are exterior to one another and which are defined in relation to one another through their *mutual exteriority* and their relations of proximity, vicinity, or distance, as well as through relations of order, such as above, below, and *between*."[221] The spatiality of social positions gets "retranslated" into a spatiality of position-takings via a negotiation of habitus.[222] To be within social space is thus to differ, "to be different."[223]

Social space, for Bourdieu, is a "space of differences;" a space in which "classes exist in some sense in a state of virtuality," not as something given all at once, but as a project.[224] But this space is also structured by the distribution of different forms of capital which can function as "weapons," commanding "the representations of this space and the position-takings in the struggles to conserve or transform it."[225] All societies appear as "social

---

[217] Quote taken from the online Stanford Encyclopedia of Philosophy: Jeff Malpas, "Hans-Georg Gadamer," in *The Stanford Encyclopedia of Philosophy* (Winter 2013 Edition; ed. Edward N. Zalta). Cited 8 June 2014. Online: http://plato.stanford.edu/entries/gadamer/#DiaPhr. On φρόνησις in Gadamer, *Truth and Method*, see 19–20, 324, 327, 331–33, 558, 560, 581.

[218] Pierre Bourdieu, *Practical Reason: On the Theory of Action* (Stanford: Stanford University Press, 1998).

[219] Bourdieu, *Practical Reason*, vii.

[220] Bourdieu, *Practical Reason*, vii

[221] Bourdieu, *Practical Reason*, 6; cf. Pierre Bourdieu, *Distinctions: A Social Critique of the Judgment of Taste* (trans. Richard Nice; Cambridge, Mass.: Harvard University Press, 1984).

[222] Bourdieu, *Practical Reason*, 7.

[223] Bourdieu, *Practical Reason*, 9.

[224] Bourdieu, *Practical Reason*, 12.

[225] Bourdieu, *Practical Reason*, 12.

spaces."[226] Social space is therefore "the first and last reality" as it commands the representations of social agents. And this spatiality contains in and of itself "the principle of a *relational* understanding of the social world."[227] The result is a *field* of forces "whose necessity is imposed on agents who are engaged in it, and as a field of struggles within which agents confront each other, with differentiated means and ends according to their position in the structure of the field of forces."[228] Rules develop in the field which work like a kind of market; that is, they are constructed according to underlying *nomoi* – fundamental principles of vision and division which govern practices and imaginaries.[229] One gets a "feel" for the rules with respect to and by participating within the dynamics of the field. Practical reason, then, is a rationality with respect to social space – which, is another way of reading Bourdieu reading φρόνησις as *spatial reasoning*: viz., a rationality in accord to this concrete situation/place.

II. Paul's Spatial Reasoning

"Spatial reasoning" is a phrase I borrow from A.I. theory and computer science. Escrig, for example, begins his work on applications for robot navigation by stating that "spatial reasoning is present in our everyday interactions with the world. In particular we use orientation information or approximated distances to locate places in space."[230] This spatio-temporal calculus coordinates the complexities of φρόνησις at which I am driving for its appearance in Philippians. From Aristotle we emphasize that φρόνησις acts as both temporal and environmental and spatial perception. The πόλις and its laws form this perception in accordance with the ὀρθός λόγος. As such, each concrete situation has its own kind of rationality in which φρόνησις is operative (Gadamer). But these concrete situations are constituted as a set of distinctions and differences (Bourdieu). The relational / perception side of φρόνησις and the dispositional live within a field and its capital which sets a social space of *difference*.

By now my suggested reading strategy should be clear: within Paul's spatial imaginary (§B.3), φρόνησις acts as a spatial reasoning *of difference.* In other words, the rationality Paul describes for πᾶσιν τοῖς ἁγίοις ἐν Χριστῷ Ἰησοῦ is *different* than the rationality for τοῖς οὖσιν ἐν Φιλίπποις. In his excellent commentary on Philippians, Stephen Fowl argues that φρονεῖν

---

[226] Bourdieu, *Practical Reason*, 32.
[227] Bourdieu, *Practical Reason*, 31.
[228] Bourdieu, *Practical Reason*, 32.
[229] Cf. Pierre Bourdieu, *The Field of Cultural Production* (New York: Polity Press, 1993).
[230] M. T. Escrig, *Qualitative Spatial Reasoning: Theory and Practice* (Frontiers in Artificial Intelligence and Applications 47; Amsterdam: IOS Press, 1998), 1.

is a "comprehensive pattern of thinking, feeling, and acting."[231] And that 1:27 presents "a pattern of life" which is framed by 1:3–8,[232] and, of course, with 2:6–11 as its "decisive display."[233] To call for a "common perspective or way of thinking about things and for a common pattern of action flowing from that pattern of thinking," is therefore near to my reading of spatial reasoning.[234] Spatial reasoning is concerned with perception, deliberation, living in accord with the rationality of the πόλις – viz., to live appropriately with respect to one's πολιτεία (cf. 1:27). The contrast operative within 3:2–16 becomes a spatial contrast, detailing spatialities of difference, conflicting rationalities,[235] and alternative perceptions from a different *body*.[236] The Philippians' πολίτευμα ἐν οὐρανοῖς (3:20) is an alternative body politic with an alternative rationality,[237] and from which an alternative perspective issues. Paul's spatial reasoning is thus constitutive of a set of distinctives, differences, and alternatives.[238]

The dynamic realities of a *being* that is ἐν Χριστῷ, within the spatiality of Christ, is thus the ὀρθός λόγος which sets the field and its appropriate perceptions within the overlapping pages and spaces of life in Philippi. Spatial reasoning is about everyday interactions with the world, and orientating information which locates a sense of place within reconfigured space.[239] The spatial imaginary of Christ gives "force and intelligibility" to these everyday interactions and orientating information.[240] It temporally orders (1:6, 10; 2:16; 3:20; 4:5; cf. 1:26–27; 2:12, 24) and spatially directs (1:27; 2:2, 5; 3:1, 3; 4:1–4),[241] it naturalizes and normalizes (4:6–7, 13). "Little events, ordinary things, smashed and reconstituted. Imbued with new meaning," until suddenly "they become the bleached bones of a story."[242] A different story. A story of difference. A story painted over the "bubbled and humped" pages of ideology masquerading as the only narrative in town. But a φρόνησις operative ἐν Χριστῷ (2:5),[243] is the orientating

---

[231] Stephen E. Fowl, *Philippians*, 6.

[232] Fowl, *Philippians*, 31; cf. R. Brewer, "The Meaning of *Politeuesthe* in Philippians 1:27," 227–31.

[233] Fowl, *Philippians*, 90, 100.

[234] Fowl, *Philippians*, 83; cf. 126.

[235] Cf. Fowl, *Philippians*, 107–8.

[236] See Veronica Koperski, *The Knowledge of Jesus Christ My Lord: The High Christology of Philippians 3:7–11* (CBET 16; Kampen: Pharos, 1996), 232.

[237] Cf. Fowl, *Philippians*, 181.

[238] Though perhaps a bit strong for my argument, cf. Fowl, *Philippians*, 175–76.

[239] Here again, cf. M. T. Escrig, *Qualitative Spatial Reasoning*.

[240] Cf. Fowl, *Philippians*, 210.

[241] Cf. Bockmuehl, *Philippians*, 246.

[242] Arundhati Roy, *The God of Small Things* (London: Fourth Estate, 1997), 32–33.

[243] There is some debate within the literature to which the demonstrative pronoun in 2:5 refers: viz., that which precedes or follows. See, e.g., Hawthorne, *Philippians*, 80;

information to ἀξίως τοῦ εὐαγγελίου τοῦ Χριστοῦ πολιτεύεσθε (1:28). Paul's call to being of the same mind (αὐτὸ φρονῆτε) and having one mind (ἓν φρονοῦντες) in 2:2 is a call to live within the spatiality of Christ (cf. 4:2) *while being placed in Philippi*. To participate within this re-shaped space and reconfigured place (cf. τοῦτο φρονῶμεν) is to be among the τέλειοι (3:15; cf. v. 19) – a judgment which only makes sense within the spatial reasoning of the spatial imaginary of Paul's imagined community.

D. Conclusions

The aim of this essay has been to wonder aloud about the relationality of two overlapping localities: viz., ἐν Χριστῷ and ἐν Φιλίπποις. How do these two spatialities which occupy a shared square mileage, as it were, interact and affect each other? And what does it mean for Paul to construct space within a place that has already been spatially constructed?[244] What does it mean for the pages of Philippians to be painted over the pages of Philippi? This essay has not been interested in producing some official report of recovery; rather, it has attempted to offer a reading strategy which might allow an "appropriated Paul" into current discourses of human geography within religious imaginaries, particularly as it relates to the global and the local. I would like to conclude this essay by briefly returning to the five studies worked through in §A.1–5, and suggest ways each can be extended through the spatial reading explicated above.

I. Φρόνησις as Spatial Reasoning

Wayne Meeks rightly saw the significance of φρόνησις within Philippians and Christ as the template for civic action within a newly conceived πόλις. I have been suggesting a gloss for conceiving φρόνησις as "spatial reasoning." As Escrig argues, "spatial reasoning is present in our everyday interactions with the world. In particular we use orientation information or approximated distances to locate places in space."[245] This "orientating information" or approximating calculus is done with respect to an ὀρθός λόγος. Judgments thus make sense within a rationality set by the ὀρθός λόγος, with

---

Fowl, *Philippians*, 89. My reading is that the demonstrative pronoun acts as a pivot in both directions.

[244] With respect to other loci, note the studies of A. H. Cadwallader and M. Trainor, eds., *Colossae in Space and Time: Linking to an Ancient City* (Göttingen: Vandenhoek & Ruprecht, 2011); and, Jorunn Økland, J. Cornelis de Vos, and Karen J. Wenell, *Constructions of Space III: Biblical Spatiality and the Sacred* (LHBOTS; London: T&T Clark, 2014).

[245] M. T. Escrig, *Qualitative Spatial Reasoning*, 1.

φρόνησις acting as reasoning within concrete situations. Moreover, beliefs and perceptions cannot be separated from the individual, the household, *or the πόλις* (*N.E.* 8/1141^{b}23–33). With Christ as an alternative template, then, and the participation of the assemblies within that template, the resulting spatial reasoning not only becomes one of *difference*, or an alternative rationality to the one on offer in Philippi, but a different conceptuality of *place* in Philippi within a reconfigured spatiality.

II. Christic Being and the Spatiality of Christ

Adela Yarbro Collins introduced a provocative reading of the "mixed messages" of 2:6–11 along with their identity forming effects. Paul is, according to Yarbro Collins, a kind of Χριστολόγος, after the pattern of the θεολόγοι and σεβαστολόγοι, adapting "the form of the Greek prose hymn in order to instruct the Philippians in cultural terms familiar to them."[246] In addition, I suggested that not only is Paul a Χριστολόγος, but also a kind of τοπολογός; not only placing the identity / being of the assemblies ἐν Χριστῷ, but placing Christic being ἐν Φιλίπποις. This new *being* within the spatiality of Christ contains within itself multiplicity – or at least the possibility of it – owing to the diversity of resources from which Paul draws and the complex realities of Philippi as a "contact zone."

But how does one understand this mixing of familiar scripts? One route, of course, and which has been picked by numerous studies on Paul, is through the framework of Homi Bhabha's postcolonial mimicry and hybridity.[247] As far as adopting a Pauline reading strategy, however, I suggest that mimicry and hybridity might mismatch chances for appropriation within our current moment. On the one hand, though discursive resources available to marginalized subjects are "provided by the hegemonic regime,"[248] Paul himself must be held accountable for his replication of "strategies of domination in his own leadership tactics."[249] Moreover, as Katharyne Mitchel has brilliantly demonstrated, hybrid subject positions are easily absorbed within capital accumulation.[250] Subtle alternatives have sprung up from the likes of Rey Chow,[251] Anne McClintock,[252] Meyda

---

[246] Yarbro Collins, "Origins of Christology," 372.

[247] Homi K. Bhabha, *The Location of Culture* (2d ed.; London: Routledge, 2004 [1991]), 121–31.

[248] Timothy L. Marquis, *Transient Apostle: Paul, Travel, and the Rhetoric of Empire* (New Haven, Conn.: Yale University Press, 2013), 17.

[249] Marquis, *Transient Apostle*, 11.

[250] Katharyne Mitchel, "Different Diasporas and the Hype of Hybridity," *Environment and Planning D: Society and Space* 15 (1997): 533–53.

[251] See Paul Bowman, ed., *Rey Chow Reader* (New York: Columbia University Press, 2010).

Yeğenoğlu,[253] and others.[254] Of particular interest is the fascinating work of Walter D. Mignolo.[255] Mignolo argues that in order to make visible the "perverse logic" within "the philosophical conundrum of modernity/coloniality and the political and economic structure of imperialism/colonialism, we must consider how to decolonize the 'mind' (Thiongo) and the 'imaginary' (Gruzinski) – that is, knowledge and being."[256] He calls the "de-colonial shift" a project of "de-linking;" and "post-colonial criticism and theory" a project of "scholarly transformation within the academy."[257] De-linking is to *desprenderse* from "the coloniality of knowledge controlled and managed by the theo-, ego- and organo-logical principles of knowledge and its consequences."[258] It seeks to write *nuevas corónicas*,[259] and let loose a "pluriversality as a universal project."[260]

My reading strategy is to see the imagined community and a being that is ἐν Χριστῷ differentiate itself from "the colonial matrix" of a being that empire historicizes ἐν Φιλίπποις.[261] To be within the body politic of Christ – the spatiality of Christ – is to *delink* from the body politic of Philippi. The being that is ἐν Φιλίπποις, that space and people which have been serially colonized, becomes a particularization of that imagined community, of Christic being, in its own idiom and with its own leadership (ἐπίσκοπος καὶ διάκονος; 1:1). Paul's voice is thus but one within a multiplicity of idiomatic expressions of being in the spatiality of Christ. His call to be imitated (3:17; cf. 1 Cor 4:16) is authoritative only insofar as it itself accords to the Christ pattern (cf. 1 Cor 11:1; 1 Thess 1:6). Paul as τοπολογός, then, allows for a placing of the identity / being of the assemblies ἐν Χριστῷ while also placing Christic being ἐν Φιλίπποις. It is the introduction of a "global sense of the local," and a "global sense of place;" or, to put it differently, the translation of the *city of God* into *cities of God*.

---

[252] Anne McClintock, *Imperial Leather*; and, Anne McClintock, *Double Crossings: Madness, Sexuality, and Imperialism* (Vancouver: Ronsdale Press, 2001).

[253] Meyda Yeğenoğlu, *Colonial Fantasies: Towards a Feminist Reading of Orientalism* (Cambridge: Cambridge University Press, 1998).

[254] See, e.g., the work of Kwok Pui-lan and Musa Dube.

[255] Walter D. Mignolo, "Delinking: The Rhetoric of Modernity, the Logic of Coloniality, and the Grammar of De-coloniality," *Cultural Studies* 21.2–3 (2007): 449–514.

[256] Mignolo, "Delinking," 450.

[257] Mignilo, "Delinking," 452.

[258] Mignilo, "Delinking," 463.

[259] Mignilo, "Delinking," 484.

[260] Mignilo, "Delinking," 453, 63, 98.

[261] Cf. Mignilo, "Delinking," 476.

III. The Field of Christ

From Luke Timothy Johnson we can see the formation of a Christ pattern or field through which power is leveraged,[262] and from which space is perceived. Place, as Nigel Thrift suggests, is linked with *embodiment*.[263] Space and place are made from the perspective of a body. The embodied existence of the assemblies ἐν Φιλίπποις, along with measures of right perspective, issues from a participation and union in Christ's body. To be ἐν Χριστῷ is to be within the spatiality of Christ. The spatiality of Christ reconfigures place ἐν Φιλίπποις. And φρόνησις is a spatial reasoning or "feel for the field" within this embodied disposition.[264]

IV. Alternatives to Center and Periphery

With Peter Oakes, the reading strategy on offer here suggests a spatial rearrangement which secures a place for the assemblies in Philippi. Where Oakes suggests rearrangement of center and periphery in both Christological (2:6–11) and communal (2:15–16) dimensions, however, I think there might be a subtler polemic on offer. Though there are clearly temporal dynamics which must be taken into account (cf. 2:9–11 with 3:20–21), how can Paul's language of suffering (1:29; 3:10; cf. 2 Cor 1:5) make sense within a rearrangement of center and periphery?[265] Paul's language of suffering is a place of marginalization *from which* a diversity of identities is produced. Drawing on the work of bell hooks, this marginality becomes more than a mere "site of deprivation." It also becomes the "site of radical possibility, a space of resistance." For hooks, then, marginality is not something one wishes to lose as such, but, rather, "a site one stays in." To be placed in the margins offers to those oppressed "the possibility of radical perspective from which to see and create, to imagine alternatives, new worlds."[266] The task of imagining alternatives grows out of these places of marginalization.[267] Being placed on the margins – the periphery – creates a "politics of location" from which issues an alternative way of being in the world that abnormalizes the center. Space and place, again, are issued from

---

[262] This field creates the varying forms of capital which are leveraged by, e.g., Timothy (2:19–24), Epaphroditus (2:25–30), and Paul himself (3:1–16). Again, see Bourdieu, *Distinction*.

[263] Thrift, "Space."

[264] Bourdieu, *Distinction*.

[265] On suffering in Philippi, see L. Gregory Bloomquist, *The Function of Suffering in Philippians* (JSNTSup 78; Sheffield: Sheffield Academic Press, 1992).

[266] bell hooks, *Yearning: Race, Gender and Cultural Politics*, (Boston: South End Press, 1990), 149–50.

[267] See Arturo Escobar, *Encountering Development: The Making and Unmaking of the Third World* (Princeton: Princeton University Press, 2012 [1995]), 14.

embodied perspectives. And it is from the perspective of the marginalized body of Christ (e.g., 2:7–8) that an alternative spatiality exists. To be ἐν Χριστῷ is to be in a place of marginality. The spatiality of Christ is a marginal existence that by its persistence abnormalizes centers and from which reconfigures place ἐν Φιλίπποις.

V. The Social Body

Steven Kraftchick helpfully suggests an "overarching task" of Paul's letter to the assemblies in Philippi as a correction of their "communal self-understanding by explicating his own identity in Christ."[268] Paul thus provides a "living space" for the deliberation of the identities of the assemblies in Philippi as "citizens of heaven."[269] This "living space" troubles the conceived spaces of power and the perceived spaces of the banality of the everyday. This corrective is an enlivening to the serial colonizing and seduction of their land and histories, and a theoretical space from which to paint over and write their own narrations. It provides not merely a new way of being ἐν Φιλίπποις, but, through participating within the perspective of the body of Christ, *a new Φίλιπποι*. To be ἐν Χριστῷ, the king of infinite space (cf. Eph 3:18), is to be within an alternative social body which can "offer a retrospective narration of the self's becoming what it is," and wherever it is, outside of the bounded nutshells of colonial conscriptions.[270]

Bibliography

Agosto, Efraín. "The Letter to the Philippians." Pages 281–93 in *A Postcolonial Commentary on the New Testament*. Edited by Ferdando F. Segovia and R. S. Sugirtharajah. Sheffield: Sheffield Academic Press, 2007.

Algra, Keimpe. "Space." Pages 13.685–87 in *Brill's New Pauly Encyclopaedia of the Ancient World*. 15 vols. Leiden: Brill, 2008.

———. *Concepts of Space in Greek Thought*. Leiden: Brill, 1994.

Anderson, Benedict. *Imagined Communities: Reflections on the Origin and Spread of Nationalism*. Rev. ed. London: Verso, 1991.

Ando, Clifford. "The King Is a Body Politick...for that a Body Politique Never Dieth." Pages 336–412 in *Imperial Ideology and the Provincial Loyalty in the Roman Empire*. Berkeley: University of California Press, 2000.

Aristotle. *The Nicomachean Ethics*. Translated by H. Rackham. Cambridge, Mass.: Harvard University Press, 1934 [1926].

---

[268] Kraftchick, "Self-Presentation and Community Construction," 241.

[269] Kraftchick, "Self-Presentation and Community Construction," 261.

[270] Here cf. the lyrical work of Peter Brooks, *Enigmas of Identity* (Princeton: Princeton University Press, 2011), 167.

Bachelard, Gaston. *The Poetics of Space*. Translated by Maria Jolas. Boston: Beacon Press, 1969 [1958].
Badiou, Alain, with Nicolas Truong. *In Praise of Love*. Translated by Peter Bush. New York: The New Press, 2012 [2009].
Barclay, John M. G. "Manna and the Circulation of Grace: A Study of 2 Corinthians 8:1–15." Pages 409–26 in *The Word Leaps the Gap: Essays on Scripture and Theology in Honor of Richard B. Hays*. Edited by J. Ross Wagner, C. Kavin Rowe, and A. Katherine Grieb. Grand Rapids: Eerdmans, 2008.
———. *Paul and The Gift*. Grand Rapids: Eerdmans, forthcoming.
Barré, Michael L. *God-list in the Treaty between Hannibal and Philip V of Macedonia: A Study in Light of the Ancient Near Eastern Treaty Tradition*. Baltimore: Johns Hopkins University Press, 1983.
Baudrillard, Jean. *Forget Foucault*. Semiotext[e] / Foreign Agents; Cambridge, Mass.: MIT Press, 2007.
Baudrillard, Jean. *Seduction*. Translated by B. Singer. London: Macmillan, 1979.
Bhabha, Homi K. *The Location of Culture*. 2d ed. London: Routledge, 2004 [1991].
Billows, Richard A. *Kings and Colonists: Aspects of Macedonian Imperialism*. Leiden: Brill, 1995.
Blanton, Ward. *A Materialism for the Masses: Saint Paul and the Philosophy of the Undying Life*. New York: Columbia University Press, 2014.
Bloomquist, Gregory. *The Function of Suffering in Philippians*. Journal for the Study of the New Testament: Supplement Series 78. Sheffield: Sheffield Academic Press, 1992.
Bocken, Inigo, ed. *Spiritual Spaces: History and Mysticism in Michel de Certeau*. Leuven: Peeters, 2013.
Bockmuehl, Markus. *The Epistle to the Philippians*. Baker New Testament Commentary. Peabody, Mass.: Hendrickson, 1998.
Bormann, Lukas. *Philippi: Stadt und Christengemeinde zur Zeit des Paulus*. Leiden: Brill, 1995.
Borza, Eugene N. *Before Alexander: Constructing Early Macedonia*. Claremont: Regina Books, 1999.
Bostock, David. *Space, Time, Matter, and Form: Essays on Aristotle's* Physics. Oxford: University of Oxford Press, 2006.
Bourdieu, Pierre. *Distinctions: A Social Critique of the Judgment of Taste*. Translated by Richard Nice. Cambridge, Mass.: Harvard University Press, 1984.
———. *Practical Reason: On the Theory of Action*. Stanford: Stanford University Press, 1998.
———. *The Field of Cultural Production*. New York: Polity Press, 1993.
Bowman, Paul, ed. *Rey Chow Reader*. New York: Columbia University Press, 2010.
Bradford, Alfred S. ed. *Philip II of Macedon: A Life from the Ancient Sources*. Westport: Praeger, 1992.
Brewer, R. "The Meaning of *Politeuesthe* in Philippians 1:27." *Journal of Biblical Literature* 71 (1952): 227–31.
Broke, Christoph vom. *Thessaloniki: Stadt des Kassander und Gemeinde des Paulus*. Wissenschaftliche Uuntersuchungen zum Neuen Testament 2/125. Tübingen: Mohr Siebeck, 2001.
Brooks, Peter. *Enigmas of Identity*. Princeton: Princeton University Press, 2011.
Bruyneel, Kevin. *Third Space of Sovereignty: The Postcolonial Politics of U.S. Indigenous Relations*. Minneapolis: University of Minnesota Press, 2007.

Cadwallader, A. H., and M. Trainor, eds. *Colossae in Space and Time: Linking to an Ancient City*. Göttingen: Vandenhoek & Ruprecht, 2011.
Certeau, Michel de. *Practice of Everyday Life*. Translated by Steven Rendall. Berkeley: University of California Press, 1984.
Champion, Craig. "Empire by Invitation: Greek Political Strategies and Roman Imperial Interventions in the Second Century BCE." *Transactions of the American Philological Association* 137.2 (2007): 255–75.
Chatterjee, Partha. *The Nation and Its Fragments: Colonial and Postcolonial Histories*. Princeton: Princeton University Press, 1993.
Collart, Paul. *Philippes: Ville de Macédoine, depuis ses origins jusqu' à la fin de l'époque romaine*. 2 vols. Paris: E. de Boccard, 1937.
Cortella, L. "Prudenza." Pages 9091–93 in *Enciclopedia Filosofica*. Edited by Virgilio Melchiorre. Milano: Bompianii, 2006.
Cousar, Charles B. *Philippians and Philemon*. New Testament Library. Louisville: Westminster John Knox, 2009.
Dahl, Norman O. *Practical Reason, Aristotle, and Weakness of the Will*. Minneapolis: University of Minnesota Press, 1984.
Daley, Brian E. *The Hope of the Early Church: A Handbook of Patristic Eschatology*. Grand Rapids: Baker Academic, 2002.
Danker, Frederick William. *A Greek-English Lexicon of the New Testament and other Early Christian Literature*. 3d ed. Chicago: University of Chicago Press, 2000.
De Vos, Craig Steven. *Church and Community Conflicts: The Relationships of the Thessalonian, Corinthian, and Philippian Churches with their Wider Civic Communities*. Atlanta: Scholars Press, 1999.
Deleuze, Gilles. *Essays Critical and Clinical*. Translated by Daniel W. Smith and Michael A. Greco. Minneapolis: University of Minnesota Press, 1997.
———. *The Fold: Leibniz and the Baroque*. Translated by Tom Conley. Minneapolis: University of Minnesota Press, 1993.
Dmitriev, Sviatoslav. *The Greek Slogan of Freedom and Early Roman Politics in Greece*. Oxford: Oxford University Press, 2011.
Doering, Lutz. *Ancient Jewish Letters and the Beginnings of Christian Epistolography*. Wissenschaftliche Uuntersuchungen zum Neuen Testament 298. Tübingen: Mohr Siebeck, 2012.
Dostal, Robert J. "Gadamer's Relation to Heidegger and Phenomenology." Pages 247–66 *The Cambridge Companion to Gadamer*. Edited by Robert J. Dostal. Cambridge: Cambridge University Press, 2002.
Duerk, Daniela. *Geography in Classical Antiquity*. Cambridge: Cambridge University Press, 2012.
Eikeland, Olav. *The Ways of Aristotle: Aristotelian Phrónēsis, Aristotelian Philosophy of Dialogue, and Action Research*. Bern: Peter Lang, 2008.
Elliot, Neil, and Mark Reasoner, eds. *Documents and Images for the Study of Paul*. Minneapolis: Fortress, 2011.
Ellis, John R. *Philip II and Macedonian Imperialism*. London: Thames and Hudson, 1976.
Engberg-Pedersen, Troels. *Aristotle's Theory of Moral Insight*. Oxford: Oxford University Press, 1983.
———. *Cosmology and the Self in the Apostle Paul: The Material Spirit*. Oxford: Oxford University Press, 2010.
———. *Paul and the Stoics*. Louisville: Westminster John Knox, 2000.

Escobar, Arturo. *Encountering Development: The Making and Unmaking of the Third World*. Princeton: Princeton University Press, 2012 [1995].
Escrig, M. T. *Qualitative Spatial Reasoning: Theory and Practice*. Frontiers in Artificial Intelligence and Applications 47. Amsterdam: IOS Press, 1998.
Fee, Gordon D. *Paul's Letter to the Philippians*. New International Commentary on the New Testament. Grand Rapids: Eerdmans, 1995.
Fitzgerald, John T. "Philippians in the Light of Some Ancient Discussions of Friendship." Pages 141–62 in *Friendship, Flattery, and Frankness of Speech: Studies on Friendship in the New Testament World*. Novum Testamentum Supplements 82. Edited by J. T. Fitzgerald. Leiden: Brill, 1996.
Fortna, Robert. "Paul's Most Egocentric Letter." Pages 219–30 in *The Conversation Continues*. Edited by Beverly Gaventa and Robert Fortna. Philadelphia: Fortress, 1999.
Foucault, Michel. *Abnormal: Lectures at the Collège de France 1974–1975*. Translated by Graham Burchell. New York: Picador, 2003 [1999].
Fowl, Stephen E. *Philippians*. Two Horizons New Testament Commentary. Grand Rapids: Eerdmans, 2005.
Freyburger-Galland, Marie-Laure. "Political and Religious Propaganda between 44 and 27BC." *Vergilius* 55 (2009): 17–30.
Gadamer, Hans-Georg. *Heidegger's Ways*. Translated by John W. Stanley. Albany: SUNY Press, 1994).
———. *Philosophical Hermeneutics*. Translated by David E. Linge. Berkeley: University of California Press, 1976.
———. *Truth and Method*. London: Continuum, 2011 [1975].
Giddens, Anthony. *The Constitution of Society: Outline of the Theory of Structuration*. Berkeley: University of California Press, 1986.
Gieryn, Thomas F. "A Space for Place in Sociology." *Annual Review of Sociology* 26 (2000): 463–96.
Ginouvès, René. *Macedonia: From Philip II to the Roman Conquest*. Translated by David Hardy. Princeton: Princeton University Press, 1994 [1993].
Goonewardena, Kanishka, et. al., eds. *Space, Difference, Everyday Life: Reading Henri Lefebvre*. London: Routledge, 2008.
Gorman, Michael J. *Apostle of the Crucified Lord: A Theological Introduction to Paul and His Letters*. Grand Rapids: Eerdmans, 2003.
———. *Cruciformity: Paul's Narrative Spirituality of the Cross*. Grand Rapids: Eerdmans, 2001.
———. *Inhabiting the Cruciform God: Kenosis, Justification, and Theosis in Paul's Narrative Soteriology*. Grand Rapids: Eerdmans, 2009.
Hammond, N. G. L. *Philip of Macedon*. London: Duckworth, 1994.
Hansen, G. Walter *The Letter to the Philippians*. Pillar New Testament Commentary. Grand Rapids: Eerdmans, 2009.
Harrison, James R. *Paul's Language of Grace in its Graeco-Roman Context*. Wissenschaftliche Uuntersuchungen zum Neuen Testament 2/172 Tübingen: Mohr Siebeck, 2003.
Hatzopoulos, Miltiades B., and Louisa D. Loukopoulos, eds. *Philip of Macédon*. Paris: Bibliothèque des Arts, 1982.
Hawthorn, Gerald F. *Philippians*. Rev. ed. Word Biblical Commentary 43. Waco: Word Books, 2004.
Heil, John Paul. *Philippians: Let Us Rejoice in being Conformed to Christ*. Early Christianity and its Literature 3. Atlanta: SBL, 2010.

Heiland, Paul Hermann. *Untersuchungen zur Geschichte des Königs Perseus von Makedonien, 179–168BCE.* Jena: Neuenhahn, 1913.

Hellerman, Joseph H. *Reconstructing Honor in Roman Philippi: Carmen Christi as Cursus Pudorum.* Cambridge: Cambridge University Press, 2005.

Hengel, Martin. "Hymns and Christology." Pages 78–96 in *Between Jesus and Paul: Studies in the Earliest History of Christianty.* Philadelphia: Fortress, 1983.

Holloway, Paul A. "*Alius Paulus*: Paul's Promise to Send Timothy at Philippians 2.19–24." *New Testament Studies* 54 (2008): 542–65.

———. "*Bona Cogitare*: An Epicurean Consolation in Phil 4:8–9." *Harvard Theological Review* 91.1 (1998): 89–96.

———. *Consolation in Philippians.* Cambridge: Cambridge University Press, 2001.

———. "Paul as Hellenistic Philosopher: The Evidence of Philippians." Pages 52–68 in *Paul and the Philosophers.* Edited by Ward Blanton and Hent De Vries. New York: Fordham University Press, 2013.

———. "Thanks for the Memories: On the Translation of Phil 1.3." *New Testament Studies* 52.3 (2006): 419–32.

Holloway, S., S. Rice, and G. Valentine, eds. *Key Concepts in Geography.* London: Sage, 2003.

Hooker, M.D. "Philippians 2:6–11." Pages 151–64 in *Jesus und Paulus.* Edited by E. Ellis and E. Grasser. Goettingen: Vandenhoeck & Ruprecht, 1975.

hooks, bell. *Yearning: Race, Gender and Cultural Politics.* Boston: South End Press, 1990.

Hubbard, P., R. Kitchin, and G. Valentine, eds. *Key Thinkers on Space and Place.* London: Sage, 2004.

Hubbard, P., R. Kitchin, B. Bartley, and D. Fuller, eds. *Thinking Geographically: Space, Theory and Contemporary Human Geography.* London: Continuum, 2002.

Hyde, Michael J. ed. *The Ethos of Rhetoric.* Columbia: University of South Caroline Press, 2004.

Jameson, F. *The Ideologies of Theory: Essays 1971–1986.* Minneapolis: University of Minnesota Press, 1988.

Jipp, Joshua W. *Christ is King: Paul's Royal Christology.* Minneapolis: Fortress, forthcoming.

Johnson, Luke Timothy. "The New Testament's Anti-Jewish Slander and the Conventions of Ancient Polemic," *Journal of Biblical Literature* 108 (1989): 419–41.

———. "Transformation of the Mind and Moral Discernment in Paul." Pages 215–36 in *Early Christianity and Classical Culture: Comparative Studies in Honor of Abraham J. Malherbe.* Edited by John T. Fitzgerald, Thomas H. Olbricht, and L. Michael White. Leiden: Brill, 2003.

———. "II Timothy and the Polemic Against False Teachers: A Reexamination." *Journal of Roman Studies* 6/7 (1978–79): 1–26.

Keppie, Lawrence. *Colonisation and Veteran Settlement in Italy: 47–14BC.* London: British School at Rome, 1983.

Kisiel, Theodore J. *The Genesis of Heidegger's "Being and Time."* Berkeley: University of California Press, 1995.

Koperski, Veronica. *The Knowledge of Jesus Christ My Lord: The High Christology of Philippians 3:7–11.* Contributions to Biblical Exegesis and Theology 16. Kampen: Pharos, 1996.

Koukouli-Chrysantaki, Chaido. "Colonia Iulia Augusta Philippensis." Pages 5–25 in *Philippi at the Time of Paul and After His death.* Edited by Charalambos Bakirtzis and Helmut Koester. Harrisburg: Trinity Press International, 1998.

Kraftchick, Steven J. "Self-Presentation and Community Construction in Philippians." Pages 239–62 in *Scripture and Traditions: Essays on Early Judaism and Christianity in Honor of Carl R. Holladay*. Edited by Patrick Gray and Gail R. O'Day. Leiden: Brill, 2008.

Krentz, Edgar M. "Military Language and Metaphors in Philippians." Pages 105–27 in *Origins and Method: Towards a New Understanding of Judaism and Christianity*. Edited by Bradley H. McLean. Sheffield: JSOT Press, 1993.

Kurz, W. S. "Kenotic Imitation of Paul and Christ in Phil 2 and 3." Pages 103–26 in *Discipleship in the New Testament*. Edited by F. Segovia. Philadelphia: Fortress, 1985.

Lampe, G. W. H. ed. *A Patristic Greek Lexicon*. Oxford: Clarendon Press, 1961.

Lang, Helen S. *The Order of Nature in Aristotle's* Physics: *Place and the Elements*. Cambridge: Cambridge University Press, 1998.

Lefebvre, Henri. *Critique of Everyday Life*. 3 vols. London: Verso, 2014.

———. *Rythmanalysis: Space, Time and Everyday Life*. New York: Bloomsbury Academic, 2004.

———. *The Production of Space*. Translated by Donald Nicholson-Smith. Oxford: Wiley-Blackwell, 1992.

Lohfink, Gerhard. *Jesus and Community: The Social Dimensions of Christian Faith*. Translated by John P. Galvin. Philadelphia: Fortress, 1984 [1982].

Lohmeyer, Ernst. *Kyrios Jesus: Eine Untersuchung zu Phil. 2,5–11*. Darmstadt: Wissenschaftliche Buchgesellschaft, 1961 [1928].

MacMullen, R. *Romanization in the Time of Augustus*. New Haven, Conn.: Yale University Press, 2000.

Malherbe, Abraham J. *Paul and the Popular Philosophers*. Minneapolis: Fortress, 1989.

Malpas, Jeff. "Hans-Georg Gadamer." *The Stanford Encyclopedia of Philosophy*. Winter 2013 Edition. Edited by Edward N. Zalta. Cited 8 June 2014. Online: http://plato.stanford.edu/entries/gadamer/#DiaPhr.

Marchal, Joseph A. *Hierarchy, Unity, and Imitation: A Feminist Rhetorical Analysis of Power Dynamics in Paul's Letter to the Philippians*. Leiden: Brill, 2006.

Marquis, Timothy L. *Transient Apostle: Paul, Travel, and the Rhetoric of Empire*. New Haven, Conn.: Yale University Press, 2013.

Martin, Dale B. *The Corinthian Body*. New Haven, Conn.: Yale University Press, 1995.

Martin, Ralph. *The Epistle of Paul to the Philippians*. Grand Rapids: Eerdmans, 1959.

Massey, Doreen B. "A Global Sense of Place." *Marxism Today* June (1991): 24–29.

———. "Politics and Space/Time." *New Left Review* 196 (1992): 65–84.

———. *Spatial Divisions of Labor: Social Structures and the Geography of Production*. New York: Methuen, 1984.

Mayer, T. "Gender Ironies of Nationalism: Setting the Stage." Pages 1–22 in *Gender Ironies of Nationalism: Sexing the Nation*. Edited by T. Mayer. London: Routledge, 2000.

McClintock, Anne. *Double Crossings: Madness, Sexuality, and Imperialism*. Vancouver: Ronsdale Press, 2001.

———. *Imperial Leather: Race, Gender and Sexuality in the Colonial Contest*. London: Routledge, 1995.

McDowell, L. *Gender Identity, and Place: Introducing Feminist Geographies*. Minneapolis: University of Minnesota Press, 1999.

Meeks, Wayne. "The Man from Heaven in Johannine Sectarianism." *Journal of Biblical Literature* 91 (1972): 44–72.

———. "The Man from Heaven in Paul's Letter to the Philippians." Pages 329–36 in *The Future of Early Christianity*. Edited by Birger A. Pearson. Minneapolis: Fortress, 1991.

Melanie Johnson-DeBaufre. *I'll Fly Away: Making Space in the Letters of Paul*. Place: Publisher, forthcoming.

Meloni, Piero. *Perseo e la fine della monarchia Macedone*. Roma: "L'Erma" di Bretschneider, 1953.

Mendell, H. "*Topoi* on *topos*: The development of Aristotle's concept of space." *Phronesis* 32 (1987): 206–31.

Mignolo, Walter D. "Delinking: The Rhetoric of Modernity, the Logic of Coloniality, and the Grammar of De-coloniality." *Cultural Studies* 21.2–3 (2007): 449–514.

———. *Local Histories / Global Designs: Coloniality, Subaltern Knowledges, and Border Thinking*. 2d ed. Princeton Studies in Culture/Power/History. Princeton: Princeton University Press, 2012.

———. "On Pluriversality." *Walter Mignolo* (blog). October 20, 2013. http://waltermignolo.com/on-pluriversality/.

Mitchel, Katharyne. "Different Diasporas and the Hype of Hybridity." *Environment and Planning D: Society and Space* 15 (1997): 533–53.

Mitchell, D. *Cultural Geography: A Critical Introduction*. Oxford: Blackwell, 2000.

Momigliano, A. *On Pagans, Jews, and Christians*. Middletown: Wesleyan University Press, 1987.

———. "Some Preliminary Remarks on the 'Religious Opposition' to the Roman Empire." Pages 103–33 in *Opposition et resistances à l'empire d'Auguste à Trajan*. Edited by A. Giovannini and K. A. Raaflaub. Entretiens sur l'Antiquité classique 33. Vandoeuvres-Genève: Foundation Hardt, 1987.

N. Clifford, and G. Valentine, eds. *Key Methods in Geography*. London, Sage, 2003.

Nasrallah, Laura Salah. *Christian Responses to Roman Art and Architecture: The Second-Century Church Amid the Spaces of Empire*. Cambridge: Cambridge University Press, 2010.

———. "Spatial Perspectives: Space and Archaeology in Roman Philippi." Pages 53–74 in *Studying Paul's Letters: Contemporary Perspectives and Methods*. Edited by Joseph A. Marchal. Minneapolis: Fortress, 2012.

Nicolet, Claude. *Space, Geography, and Politics in the Early Roman Empire*. Ann Arbor: University of Michigan Press, 1991 [1988].

Nongbri, Brent. *Before Religion: A History of a Modern Concept*. New Haven, Conn.: Yale University Press, 2013.

O'Brien, P. T. *The Epistle to the Philippians*. New International Greek Testament Commentary. Grand Rapids: Eerdmans, 1991.

O'Neill, Onora. "Practical Reason and Ethics." Pages 7.613–20 in *Routledge Encyclopedia of Philosophy*. Edited by Edward Craig. London: Routledge, 1998.

Oakes, Peter. *Philippians: From People to Letter*. Society for New Testament Studies Monograph Series 110. Cambridge: Cambridge University Press, 2001.

———. "Re-mapping the Universe: Paul and the Emperor in 1 Thessalonians and Philippians." *Journal for the Study of the New Testament* 27.3 (2005): 301–22.

Økland, Jorunn, J. Cornelis de Vos, and Karen J. Wenell. Constructions of Space III: Biblical Spatiality and the Sacred. The Library of Hebrew Bible/Old Testament Studies; London: T&T Clark, 2014.

Peterson, E. "Das Problem des Nationalismus im alten Christentum." Pages 51–63 in *Frühkirche, Judentum und Gnosis*. Freiburg: Herder, 1959.

Pile, Steve. "Introduction: Opposition, Political Identities, and Spaces of Resistance," Pages 1–32 *Geographies of Resistance*. Edited by Steve Pile and Michael Keith. London: Routledge, 1997.
Pilhofer, Peter. *Philippi: Die erste christliche Gemeinde Europas*. Vol. 1. Tübingen: Mohr, 1995.
———. *Philippi: Katalog der Inschriften von Philippi*. Band 2. Wissenschaftliche Uuntersuchungen zum Neuen Testament 119. Tübingen: Mohr Siebeck, 2000.
Polansky, Ronald M. ed. *The Cambridge Companion to Aristotle's* Nicomachean Ethics. Cambridge: Cambridge University Press, 2014.
Porter, Stanley E., and Sean A. Adams, eds. *Paul and the Ancient Letter Form*. Pauline Studies 6; Leiden: Brill, 2010.
Reeve, C. D. C. *Action, Contemplation, and Happiness: An Essay on Aristotle*. Cambridge, Mass.: Harvard University Press, 2012.
———. *Aristotle on Practical Wisdom: Nicomachean Ethics VI*. Cambridge, Mass.: Harvard University Press, 2013.
Reumann, John. *Philippians*. Anchor Bible 33B. New Haven, Conn.: Yale University Press, 2008.
Romm, James S.*The Edges of the Earth in Ancient Thought*. Princeton: Princeton University Press, 1994.
Rose, Gillians. *Feminism and Geography*. Minneapolis: University of Minnesota Press, 1993.
Roy, Arundhati. *The God of Small Things*. London: Fourth Estate, 1997.
Said, Edward. *Culture and Imperialism*. New York: Vintage, 1993.
Salmon, E. T. *Roman Colonization under the Republic*. London: Thames & Hudson, 1969.
Sampley, J. Paul. *Pauline Partnership in Christ*. Philadelphia: Fortress, 1980.
Schrag, Calvin O. *Communicative Praxis and the Space of Subjectivity*. Bloomington: Indiana University Press, 1986.
Scott, Michael. *Space and Society in the Greek and Roman Worlds*. Cambridge: Cambridge University Press, 2012.
Sève, Michel. "Le coté nord du forum de Philippes," *Bulletin de correspondance hellénique* 112.1 (1988): 467–79.
Sève M., and P. Weber. 'Un monument honorifique au forum de Philippes.' *Bulletin de Correspondance Hellénique* 112 (1988): 467–79.
Shavit, Uriya. *The New Imagined Community: Global Media and the Construction of National and Muslim Identities of Migrants*. Eastbourne: Sussex Academic Press, 2009.
Sloterdijk, Peter. *Bubbles*. Spheres 1. Translated by Wieland Hoban. Semiotext(e). Cambridge: MIT Press, 2011 [1998].
Smith, Jonathan Z. *To Take Place: Toward Theory in Ritual*. Chicago: Chicago University Press, 1987.
Soja, Edward W. *Postmodern Geographies: The Reassertion of Space in Critical Social Theory*. 2d ed. London: Verso, 2011.
———. *Thirdspace: Journeys to Los Angeles and Other Real-and-Imagined Places*. Oxford: Blackwell, 1996.
Spicq, Celsas. *Theological Lexicon of the New Testament*. Translated by James D. Ernest. 3 vols. Peabody, Mass.: Hendrickson, 1994.
Stirewalt, M. Luther. *Paul, the Letter Writer*. Grand Rapids: Eerdmans, 2003.

Stowers, Stanley K. "Friends and Enemies in the Politics of Heaven: Reading Theology in Philippians." Pages 105–21 in *Thessalonians, Philippians, Galatians, Philemon*. Pauline Theology 1. Edited by Jouette M. Bassler. Minneapolis: Fortress, 1991.

———. *Letter Writing in Greco-Roman Antiquity*. Library of Early Christianity 5. Louisville: Westminster John Knox, 1986.

Studtmann, Paul. "Aristotle's Categorial Scheme." Pages 63–80 in *The Oxford Handbook of Aristotle*. Edited by Christopher Shields. Oxford: Oxford University Press, 2012.

Tally, Robert T., Jr. *Spatiality*. London: Routledge, 2012.

Tanner, Kathryn. *Theories of Culture: A New Agenda for Theology*. Minneapolis: Fortress, 1997.

Thrift, Nigel. "Space: The Fundamental Stuff of Geography." Pages 95–108 in *Key Concepts in Geography*. Edited by S. L. Holloway, S. Rice, and G. Valentine. London: Sage, 2003.

———. "Time and Theory in Human Geography Part One." *Progress in Human Geography* 1 (1977): 65–101.

———. "Time and Theology in Human Geography Part Two." *Progress in Human Geography* 1 (1977): 415–57.

Thurston, Bonnie B., and Judith M. Ryan. *Philippians and Philemon*. Sacra Pagina Series 10. Collegeville: Liturgical Press, 2005.

Touratsoglou, I. *Die Münzstätte von Thessaloniki in der römischen Kaiserzeit (32/31 v. Chr. Bis 268 n. Chr.)*. Antike Münzen und geschnittene Steine 12. Berlin: de Gruyter, 1998.

Tsing, Anna. "The Global Situation." Pages 66–98 in *The Anthropology of Globalization: A Reader*. 2d ed. Edited by Jonathan Xavier Inda and Renato Rosaldo. Oxford: Blackwell, 2008.

Tuinen, Sjoerd van, and Niamh McDonnell, eds. *Deleuze and the Fold: A Critical Reader*. New York: Palgrave Macmillan, 2010.

Van Buren, James. *The Young Heidegger: Rumor of a Hidden King*. Studies in Continental Thought. Bloomington: Indiana University Press, 1994.

Vimercati, E. "Phronesis," Pages 8595–96 in *Enciclopedia Filosofica*. Edited by Virgilio Melchiorre. Milano: Bompianii, 2006.

Vittinghoff, F. *Römische Kolonisation und Bürgerrechtspolitikunter Caesar und Augustus*. Mainz, Akademie der Wissenschaft und der Literatur, Abhandlungen der Geistes- und Socialwissenschaftlichen Klasse Jahrgang 1951, Nr 14; Wiesbaden: Steiner Verlag, 1952.

Vollenweider, Samuel. "Der 'Raub' der Gottgleichheit: Ein religionsgeschichtlicher Vorschlag zu Phil 2.6(11)." *New Testament Studies* 45 (1999): 413–33.

Walbank, F. W. *Philip V of Macedon*. Cambridge: Cambridge University Press, 1940.

Warf, Barney, and Santa Arias, eds. *Spatial Turn: Interdisciplinary Perspectives*. London: Routledge, 2009.

White, L. Michael. "Morality between Two Worlds: A Paradigm of Friendship in Philippians." Pages 201–15 in *Greeks, Romans, and Christians: Essays in Honor of Abraham J. Malherbe*. Edited by D. L. Balch, E. Ferguson, and W. A. Meeks. Philadelphia: Fortress, 1990.

Winter, Bruce. *Seek the Welfare of the City: Christians as Benefactors and Citizens*. Grand Rapids: Eerdmans, 1994.

Yarbro Collins, Adela. "Psalms, Philippians 2:6–11, and the Origins of Christology." *Biblical Interpretation* 11.3 (2002): 361–72.

———. "The Worship of Jesus and the Imperial Cult" Pages 234–57 in *The Jewish Roots of Christological Monotheism: Papers from the St Andrews Conference on the Histor-*

ical Origins of the Worship of Jesus. Edited by in Carey C. Newman, James R. Davila, and Gladys S. Lewis. Leiden: Brill, 1999.

Yeğenoğlu, Meyda. *Colonial Fantasies: Towards a Feminist Reading of Orientalism.* Cambridge: Cambridge University Press, 1998.

Zanker, Paul. *The Power of Images in the Age of Augustus.* Translated by Alan Shapiro. Ann Arbor: University of Michigan Press, 1988.

Zusak, Markus. *The Book Thief.* New York: Alfred A Knopf, 2005.

Part Two: Some Highlights from Reception History

Two Early Perspectives on Participation in Paul

Irenaeus and Clement of Alexandria

BEN C. BLACKWELL

A. Introduction

As we consider the topic of participation in Christ in Paul's letters, E. P. Sanders' work stands out because he helped raise the discussion to the fore within contemporary scholarship. Though he gives a brief but substantial treatment of what he calls Paul's "participationist eschatology," he also concedes that we do not have the categories with which to understand Paul's argument fully.[1] In response to this perceived quandary, Richard Hays rejoins:

> E.P. Sanders has rightly emphasized that participatory soteriology stands at the center of Paul's thought... and he confesses himself unable to explain what Paul means by this "real participation in Christ." My own guess is that Sanders's insights would be supported and clarified by a careful study of participation motifs in patristic theology, particularly the thought of the Eastern Fathers.[2]

With Hays' suggestion in mind, this essay will explore the topic of participation through the lens of Paul's Greek patristic interpreters.[3] The Fathers are not homogeneous in their perspective on the world and the Bible, so we will explore two Greek interpreters who represent some of the diversity in

---

[1] E. P. Sanders, *Paul and Palestinian Judaism: A Comparison of Patterns of Religion* (Minneapolis: Fortress, 1977), 431–523, esp. 522–23.

[2] Richard B. Hays, *The Faith of Jesus Christ: The Narrative Substructure of Galatians 3:1–4:11* (2d ed.; Grand Rapids: Eerdmans, 2002), xxxii.

[3] On the rising interest in and need for reception-historical studies, see my *Christosis: Pauline Soteriology in light of Deification in Irenaeus and Cyril of Alexandria* (WUNT 2/314; Tübingen: Mohr Siebeck, 2011), 14–25. For some works which explore the reception history of Paul, in particular, see William S. Babcock, ed., *Paul and the Legacies of Paul* (Dallas: Southern Methodist University Press, 1990); Michael F. Bird and Joseph R. Dodson, eds., *Paul in the Second Century* (LNTS 412; London: T&T Clark, 2011); and the series edited by Todd D. Still and David E. Wilhite, *Paul Among the Fathers: Pauline and Patristic Scholars in Debate* (London: T&T Clark, 2013–).

the ancient church – Irenaeus (c. 130–200) and Clement of Alexandria (c. 150–215). They are helpful because their bodies of work are early and substantial enough to gain a holistic view of their approach. In addition, Clement and Irenaeus consider Paul "the apostle," so they regularly interact with his letters.[4] As we study how these Eastern Fathers might enlighten our understanding of Paul, we will see that both describe salvation as *a restoration of the image and likeness of God through participation in Christ and the Spirit*, but their different views on the image color their understanding of participation. Before exploring these two interpreters, we will first situate them in their second- and third-century contexts in order to give us a better perspective on their distinct theological approaches.

B. Irenaeus and Clement: Setting the Stage

Irenaeus was raised in Asia Minor and eventually moved west to Lugdunum (Lyons) in Gaul. As bishop of Lyons, Irenaeus penned his major extant work *The Detection and Overthrow of So-called Knowledge*, better known as *Against Heresies* (AH). Clement was raised in Italy and ultimately settled in Alexandria. While the purpose of Clement's writing is more focused on Christian spiritual progress, he is no less polemical in his primary works,[5] which form a triology of sorts: *Protrepticus*, *Paedagogus*, and *Stromateis*.

As churchmen of their time, their writings represent the ecclesial struggles of their day. Rather than unbelieving outsiders, it is the "insiders," those who profess some kind of faith in Christ, who concern Irenaeus and Clement. These insiders are primarily known to us through the polemical title "gnostics," though it is unlikely that this is a self-moniker.[6] Though Irenaeus and Clement address these insiders from different vantage points, the two share a common theological perspective that unites them. Accordingly, Osborn writes:

---

[4] I have realized that my initial characterization of Clement in *Christosis* (26–27) did not adequately give him his due as a biblical interpreter.

[5] The polemical nature of his work is not just set against his gnostic opponents, as Michael J. Thate has shown in his "Identity Construction as Resistance: Figuring Hegemony, Biopolitics, and Martyrdom as an Approach to Clement of Alexandria," in *Studia Patristica* 66 (ed. Markus Vinzent; Leuven: Peeters, 2013), 14.69–85.

[6] For a helpful recent treatment, see David Brakke, *The Gnostics: Myth, Ritual, and Diversity in Early Christianity* (Cambridge: Harvard University Press, 2010). For all its weakness, I continue to use "gnosticism" for simplicity's sake, especially since any interaction I have with gnosticism in this essay is concerned only with the way Irenaeus and Clement present their opponents' theology. It is important to note that Clement goes to lengths to redeem this term, claiming it back for the church.

They both begin from the God who is universal, spiritual and omnipresent. Their next concern is the divine economy, or history of salvation. Then follow the climax of history and the apex of the universe as it is found in Christ, who sums all things up. Their final questions are again the same, as they ask how humans participate in the new dispensation inaugurated by Christ, what is it like and how will it end.[7]

Over against their opponents who separated creation and salvation as the work of different gods, Irenaeus and Clement both argue for God's united action in the world as creator and savior. They also rebut their opponents' view that humans are determined by nature, as spiritual, natural (psychical), or carnal.[8] Though they share these similar over-arching concerns, their views on anthropology and participation diverge.

Several scholars have helpfully provided taxonomies to describe the differences between Irenaeus and Clement and other larger traditions they represent (see Table 1).[9] I offer these heuristic categories not to enclose these writers in a box but to provide an initial consideration about their different perspectives.[10]

---

[7] Eric Osborn, *Clement of Alexandria* (Cambridge: Cambridge University Press, 2005), 269, cf. 282–92. See also, L. G. Patterson, "The Divine Became Human: Irenaean Themes in Clement of Alexandria," *Studia Patristica* 31 (Leuven: Peeters, 1997): 497–516. For a greater emphasis on their diversity, see John Behr, *Asceticism and Anthropology in Irenaeus and Clement* (Oxford: Oxford University Press, 2000).

[8] Cf. Irenaeus, AH 2.14.4; Clement, *Excerpta ex Theodoto* 56–57. See D. Jeffrey Bingham, "Irenaeus Reads Romans 8: Resurrection and Renovation," in *Early Patristic Readings of Romans* (ed. Kathy L. Gaca and L. L. Welborn; New York: T&T Clark, 2005), 121.

[9] Justo L. González, *Christian Thought Revisited: Three Types of Theology* (rev. ed.; New York: Maryknoll, 1999); Norman Russell, *The Doctrine of Deification in the Greek Patristic Tradition* (Oxford: Oxford University Press, 2004), 2–3; Ivan V. Popov, "The Idea of Deification in the Early Eastern Church," in *Theosis: Deification in Christian Theology*, vol 2 (ed. Vladimir Kharlamov; Eugene, Ore.: Pickwick, 2011), 42–82; Donald Fairbairn, "Patristic Soteriology: Three Trajectories," *JETS* 50 (2007): 289–310.

[10] I previously (*Christosis*, 103) labeled the "mystical" as "likeness," and the "incarnational" as "participation" following the lead of Russell, but these terms relate to both traditions and are not helpful for distinguishing between them.

Table 1: Analysis of Traditions

Scholar	Clement	Irenaeus
González	Type B	Type C
Russell	Ethical	Realistic
Popov	Idealist	Realist
Fairbairn	Mystical	Personal
Blackwell	Mystical	Incarnational

A variety of scholars note the existence of the more Platonic "Christian mystical tradition," which includes writers like Clement of Alexandria, Origen, Gregory of Nyssa, and Pseudo-Dionysius.[11] (These writers emphasize the Platonic tradition, but we should note that a Platonic perspective highly influences most other Greek patristic theologians to one degree or another.) The mystical tradition accentuates the rational and situates the image of God in the soul alone. Russell labels this subgroup "ethical" because *virtue* and inner mastery of the passions is a primary aspect of the believers' transformative experience.[12] Clement's role in what is later termed the "mystical" tradition is evident, particularly through the significant influence of Origen, his successor in Alexandria.

There is much less consensus on how to categorize the other group or even if it represents a cohesive tradition at all. I have labeled Irenaeus and his stream of thought "incarnational" because of his emphasis on embodiment.[13] The combination of the soul and body together (not just the soul) is the locus of the image of God for Irenaeus. While he might be less influenced by philosophical concerns, recent work shows that he is not unaware of philosophical, particularly Stoic, arguments.[14] In contrast to Clement, Irenaeus' specific influence on later writers is not as easy to ascertain. We might see resonances of his theology in others, but the fact that we only have full manuscripts for his *Against Heresies* in Latin is evidence that he

---

[11] See especially, Andrew Louth, *The Origins of the Christian Mystical Tradition: From Plato to Denys* (2d ed.; Oxford: Oxford University Press, 2007).

[12] Russell, The Doctrine of Deification, 2–3.

[13] Other Alexandrians, like Athanasius and (more so) Cyril of Alexandria have affinities for this incarnational theology, but both of these later writers also have distinct correspondences with the mystical tradition.

[14] Popov, "The Idea of Deification"; Anthony Briggman, "Irenaeus' Chistology of Mixture," *JTS ns* 64 (2013): 516–55.

was not widely popular among the Greek fathers.[15] With Smyrna as Irenaeus' hometown, González links Irenaeus to the Antiochene traditions that follow him,[16] though Irenaeus does not play a significant role in their theological constructions.[17] One particular commonality between Irenaeus and the Antiochene tradition is the use of hermeneutical methods taken from the grammatical handbooks.[18]

As we will see, the sometimes overblown distinction between the Antiochene and Alexandrian methods (especially between typology and allegory) has little direct impact on our discussion. The difference we will see here is not so much related to hermeneutical methodologies but rather to perspectives on theological anthropology and the process of participation. With these distinctions in mind, we are better prepared to read Irenaeus and Clement closely to see how they understand participation in light of their readings of Paul.

C. Irenaeus: Communion between God and Humans

Rather than giving a synthetic account of participation in Irenaeus, I will explore two passages that highlight central aspects of his theology – AH 3.17–19 and AH 5.6–14 – in order to allow his own interests to shape our understanding of his theology.[19] We will see that participation centers on

---

[15] That only Book 1 of AH is fully extant in Greek shows that the fathers found his description of the various types of heretics more interesting than Irenaeus' own theological construction.

[16] González, *Christian Thought Revisited*, 15.

[17] Theophilus and Lucian both of Antioch may be the better roots of the later Antiochene tradition than Irenaeus. See, e.g., David S. Wallace-Hadrill, *Christian Antioch: A Study of Early Christian Thought in the East* (Cambridge: Cambridge University Press, 1982), 43–45.

[18] Robert M. Grant, *Irenaeus of Lyons* (New York: Routledge, 1997), 46–53; John Behr, "Irenaeus on the Word of God" in *Studia Patristica*, vol 36 (ed. M. F. Wiles and E. J. Yarnold; Leuven: Peeters, 2001), 163–67; Frances Young, *Biblical Exegesis and the Formation of Christian Culture* (Cambridge: Cambridge University Press, 1997), 161–85; John O'Keefe, "'A Letter that Killeth': Toward a Reassessment of Antiochene Exegesis, or Diodore, Theodore, and Theodoret on the Psalms," *JECS* 8 (2000): 83–104. O'Keefe critiques the Antiochenes for overdependence on their methodology, but this would not be applicable to Irenaeus in the same way.

[19] For a more general treatment, see Ben C. Blackwell, "Paul and Irenaeus," in *Paul and the Second Century* (ed. Michael F. Bird and Joseph R. Dodson; London: T&T Clark, 2011), 190–206; Rolf Noormann, *Irenäus als Paulusinterpret* (WUNT 2/66; Tübingen: Mohr Siebeck, 1994).

communion with the Triune God and results in the restoration of the divine image and likeness. We will first treat a passage from Book 3.[20]

I. Union of Divine and Human in Christ (AH 3.17–19)

In Book 3 Irenaeus employs various NT texts to demonstrate how there is only one God who, through Christ and the Spirit, both creates the world and saves it. In AH 3.17–19 he refutes two alternative positions regarding Christ: the first is that the divine "Christ" did not become truly human (AH 3.17–18) and the second is that the human Jesus was not also divine (AH 3.19). By disputing these two alternate perspectives, he forges a middle ground that Christ is the God-man. Accordingly, a union of divinity and humanity is perfectly acceptable in Christ, and believers too may be united with God.

1. Divine Christ as Human (AH 3.17–18)

In response to a gnostic teaching that held that the man Jesus was merely empowered by the divine Christ or the Holy Spirit (cf. AH 1.7.2), Irenaeus argues that the Holy Spirit came down upon the God-man Christ. This argument about Christ has two important components: 1) the Spirit's presence is necessary for humans to be joined to God (AH 3.17), and 2) Christ's experience as the God-man enables humans to be united with God (AH 3.18). Thus, Irenaeus' line of reasoning depends on an incipient Trinitarianism with both the Spirit and Christ joining believers to God.[21]

As Irenaeus explores the Spirit's presence with Christ and believers in AH 3.17, he points first to OT promises about the coming of the Spirit and then explores a variety of NT passages relating to the Spirit and to Christ, such as the baptisms of Christ and of believers. He then gives this purpose for the Spirit's presence:

[The Spirit] descended on the Son of God, when he had been made the Son of man, becoming accustomed to dwell (*assuescens habitare*) with him in the human race, and to rest (*requiescere*) among human beings, and to dwell (*habitare*) in God's handiwork, thus fulfilling the Father's will in them and renewing them from their old selves for the newness of Christ. (AH 3.17.1)

The presence of the Spirit with Christ was not so much for Christ's sake but for other humans, that the Spirit would dwell in them and enable their obedience (with allusions to Rom 6:4 and 7:6). Indeed, the Spirit must be-

---

[20] The English translations are taken from the Ancient Christian Writers volumes for Books 1–3 and the Ante-Nicene Fathers for Books 4–5, with emendations based on the original languages. Where the Greek portions are extant, I cite those first; otherwise, we must depend on the Latin translation.

[21] Michel René Barnes, "Irenaeus' Trinitarian Theology," *NV* 7/1 (2009): 67–106.

come accustomed to dwell again with humanity (as humans need to become accustomed to dwell with God).²² Throughout this passage Irenaeus uses various phrases to clarify the relationship: the Spirit, "the Comforter who should join (*aptaret*) us to God" (AH 3.17.2), is the water that unites believers and is conferred "upon those who are partakers (*participantur*) of himself" (AH 3.17.2). Weaving together the Good Samaritan story with other parables, he says that believers "receive the image and inscription of the Father and the Son by the Spirit" (AH 3.17.3). Rather than the Spirit bringing divine power to Jesus, he descends on the already divine Son who has become incarnate "in the fullness of time" (AH 3.17.4) in order to transform Christians morally. Though Irenaeus is addressing the issue of Christology, he turns the discussion to soteriology because of the Spirit's role in uniting Christians with God, which at the same time unites believers with one another.

As he transitions to AH 3.18, Irenaeus turns his focus to Christ rather than the Holy Spirit, yet he is still arguing against his opponents' division between the spiritual Christ and the human Jesus. He thus writes:

The Son of God did not begin to exist at that time, having been always with the Father; but when he became incarnate and was made man, he recapitulated in himself the long unfolding of humankind, granting salvation by way of abridgement, that in Christ Jesus we might receive what we had lost in Adam, namely, to be according to the image and likeness of God. (AH 3.18.1)

The divine Son has become human in order to restore humanity to the image and likeness of God.²³ With Adam introduced into the discussion, Irenaeus highlights the congruity of eschatology and protology, or salvation and creation. In the midst of many biblical quotations, Irenaeus dwells on the coherence of Peter's confession to the narrative of the Gospels (AH 3.18.4–6). Christ did not merely appear to suffer; he truly suffered, as he promised Peter. So, his followers rightly follow him in suffering and forgive their enemies. Thus, Christians follow Christ in death as well as in life.

This leads us to one of his most powerful paragraphs in Irenaeus' whole work – AH 3.18.7 – where his focus upon Christ's work of salvation is strongly influenced by Romans 5. "Therefore," Irenaeus writes, "[Christ] caused humanity to adhere (*haerere*) to and to be united (ἥνωσεν, *adunivit*) with God" (AH 3.18.7). A human must have defeated death, so Jesus must be a true man. However, for the salvation to be secure, he must have been God: "Unless man had been joined (συνηνώθη, *conjunctus fuisset*) to God,

---

²² Irenaeus held to a prelapsarian presence of the Spirit. Concerning being "accustomed," see Blackwell, *Christosis*, 61–64.

²³ The incarnation alone does not save: Fundamental to Irenaeus' argument is that the *Christ* suffered death, not just the human *Jesus*, to achieve salvation.

he could have never be a partaker (μεταχεῖν, *particeps fieri*) of incorruptibility" (AH 3.18.7). Irenaeus describes the incarnation as necessary for becoming "partakers (*participes*) of filial adoption," which brings "communion (*communionem*) with God" (AH 3.18.7). The union of divine and human was not in itself salvific because death must be defeated, yet this union in Christ begins to restore the division caused by sin. With the variety of terms – joining, participation, adoption, communion – we see that no one way of speaking of this multifaceted union predominates.

Though no particular Pauline passage is in focus with his initial discussion, Romans 5 eventually comes to take central stage. Adam sinned and the law was powerless to defeat death. Thus, a man obedient and born of a virgin must bring justification and salvation to those under death, a death deriving from the disobedient man molded from virgin soil. Irenaeus concludes: "God...recapitulated in himself the ancient handiwork of man [Adam], that he might kill sin, destroy death and give life to humankind" (AH 3.18.7). Life and death, as in Romans 5, are the focus here. Since sin introduced death and mortality, salvation is cast primarily as life and incorruption. This incorruption is not merely an item transferred from God to humans, nor death merely something destroyed. Only through union with God, communion with God, and participation in God are the divine attributes of life and incorruption enjoyed. Similar themes are explored as the argument progresses in AH 3.19.

2. Human Christ as Divine (AH 3.19)

Continuing his discussion of the God-man Jesus Christ, in AH 3.19 Irenaeus focuses on Christ's true deity. He styles Christ as God, the incorruptible Word, and the Son of God, which all point to his deity. Fundamental to his argument in AH 3.19.1 is that becoming an adopted son of God is necessary for humans to experience incorruption and immortality. Reading Psalm 82:6–7 in light of Gal 4:4, he identifies those experiencing death in the Psalm passage as "those who have not received the gift of adoption, but who despise the incarnation of the pure generation of the Word of God [and] defraud human nature of its ascent to God" (AH 3.19.1). Irenaeus employs an interchange argument very similar to Gal 4:4 in AH 3.19.1: the Son of God became the son of man so that humans, through adoption, become sons of God.[24] This "son of God" experience is then explained as receiving (*percipere*) and being united (*adunare*) to incorruptibility and immortality, an explicit citation of 2 Cor 5:4 and 1 Cor 15:53. Through a reconstituted relationship with God as sons, believers take on the divine at-

---

[24] On the connections between Irenaeus and Paul on the topic of interchange, see Morna D. Hooker, *From Adam to Christ* (Eugene, Ore.: Wipf & Stock, 2008), 13–69.

tributes of incorruption and immortality, such that they can even be (metaphorically) called gods.[25] Interestingly, the connection between *adoption* and *incorruption* is most directly found in Rom 8:14–23, a text Irenaeus does not cite here but which likely links for him the texts he explicitly cites from Galatians and the Corinthian letters.[26]

We see then that Irenaeus combines Pauline texts and concepts with other texts and concepts, creating a new web of meaning. As before, the language of "union" is the basis of this restored divine-human relationship. But now Irenaeus adds the term "adoption," an integrative metaphor where the reconstituted divine-human relationship (becoming sons of God) entails an anthropological experience of incorruption and immortality. This experience of incorruption will also be central to our next passage in AH 5, where Irenaeus clarifies the nature of being in the image and likeness of God.

II. Union of the Flesh with the Life-Giving Spirit (AH 5.6–14)

The primary focus of Book 5 is the restoration of humans (AH 5.1–14) and the world (AH 5.15–36) as the climax of God's economy. Irenaeus thus correlates these two aspects of salvation – anthropological and cosmic – showing that the restoration of both is in continuity with God's original creational intention. In the first section (AH 5.1–14), Irenaeus gives a full account of his understanding of the flesh and s/Spirit. Since the creator God made the flesh, it will not by default be excluded from salvation because of its nature. Fundamental to his reasoning is that Christ became human, taking on flesh, in order to share his salvation with the whole person. Thus, believers share in the immortality granted by Christ in body *and* soul by the presence of the vivifying Spirit. However, due to his polemical setting, Irenaeus' primary focus is the resurrection of the *body*. We will not treat this whole section of AH 5 exhaustively, but a few key passages are worthy of comment.

In AH 5.3 Irenaeus turns his attention to 2 Corinthians 12 and the issue of suffering after addressing Christology and the Eucharist. Instead of being a sign that the flesh is inherently weak and thus unable to experience life, Irenaeus argues that present suffering serves a didactic function: it teaches humans about mortality and humility.[27] Irenaeus repeatedly uses

---

[25] This is clearly a metaphor because in AH 3.19.2 Irenaeus clarifies that only the Son and Father are truly called God, and "no one of the sons of Adam is as to everything and absolutely called God, or named Lord."

[26] Noormann, *Irenäus*, 149–50.

[27] Irenaeus argued similarly in AH 4.38–39 that in a state of immaturity Adam and Eve fell from grace, and that they needed to grow in knowledge of God and their place in

the verb μετέχω (*participere*) to speak of "participating" in life, wisdom, power, incorruption, etc. Accordingly, participation in Christ through the Eucharist (cf. AH 5.2) and participation in divine attributes is not segregated in Irenaeus' theology.

Irenaeus explores the foundation of his theological anthropology in AH 5.6. To explain the spiritual, natural (psychical), and carnal distinctions from 1 Corinthians 2–3, Irenaeus distinguishes between being in the image and being in the likeness of God. A human with the union of soul and body together exists in the *image* of God. However, when the Spirit of God is also joined, the believer is formed into the *likeness* of God, being conformed to Christ's image:

> Now God shall be glorified in his handiwork, fitting it so as to be conformed (*conforme*) to and modelled (*adaptans*) after His own Son. For by the hands of the Father, that is, by the Son and the Holy Spirit, a person, and not [merely] a part of a person, was made in the likeness of God. Now the soul and the spirit are certainly a part of the person, but certainly not the person; for the perfect person consists in the commingling (*commixtio*) and the union (*adunitio*) of the soul receiving the Spirit of the Father and the mixture (*admixta*) of that fleshly nature which was molded after the image of God. (AH 5.6.1)

Just as the soul and body are united to form the image, the soul is united and even commingled with the Spirit for divine likeness. Though the focus is the work of the Holy Spirit, Irenaeus continually notes the Trinitarian shape of salvation: the Father conforms Christians to the image of his Son through the presence of the Holy Spirit. Those who receive the Spirit are "spiritual because they participate in the Spirit" (*secundum participationem Spiritus exsistentes spiritales*, AH 5.6.1), not because the flesh has been removed.[28]

The rest of this first half of Book 5 is an extended treatment of 1 Corinthians 15 (AH 5.7–14). A distinct line of argument in AH 5.9–14 regards the interpretation of 1 Cor 15:50 ("Flesh and blood cannot inherit the kingdom of God"), a key text used by his opponents to dispute the resurrection of the body (cf. AH 5.9.1). Irenaeus' rebuttal follows two lines of argument. First, by citing the numerous cases where Paul describes resurrection of the body, both of Christ and of believers, Irenaeus argues that Paul here cannot be talking about the inability of flesh itself to be raised. Second, he interprets Paul's use of "flesh" in 1 Cor 15:50 to be a moral description of flesh rather than a primarily physical or material one (cf. AH

---

creation. Sin and its effects, while horrible, also serve a pedagogical function to serve God's purposes to increase human knowledge.

[28] For further explanation about how the body and soul relate, see AH 2.33.1 and 2.33.4 where he "speaks of the participation (*participare*) of the soul with the body." Briggman, "Irenaeus' Christology of Mixture," 533. Briggman argues that Irenaeus sees the soul as material, in accordance with Stoic thought.

5.14.4). Making use of Pauline parallels, he highlights passages that oppose flesh and Spirit. As a result, living in immorality (i.e., living according to flesh and blood) is the means of death and not life, but flesh vivified by the Spirit can inherit the kingdom, or rather the flesh is inherited by the Spirit (AH 5.9.3–4).

Since his primary dispute is over a Pauline passage, his engagement with Pauline material in the passage is rich, meaning we can only scratch the surface in our treatment here. Irenaeus balances continuity of the body with the discontinuity of transformation in the context of a partially-realized eschatology.[29] Though 1 Corinthians 15 is the disputed text, Irenaeus draws from a web of other texts to support his interpretation, not least Romans 8. The presence of the Spirit brings about a future resurrection as well as a present transformation, both of which are part of shaping believers into the image and likeness of God:

For if the earnest [the Spirit] even now causes him to cry, "Abba, Father" when he gathers a person into himself, what shall the complete grace of the Spirit effect, which will be given to people by God? He will render us like (*similes*) him and accomplish the will of the Father; for he will make the person after the image and likeness of God (*secundum imaginem et similitudinem Dei*). (AH 5.8.1)

Irenaeus highlights the Spirit's role in adoption (Rom 8:15), but also in conformation to God's image and likeness. He combines readings of Romans 8 and Genesis 1, following but also extending how Paul himself alludes to Gen 1:26 with his language of being conformed to the "image of the Son."

Though Irenaeus shifts the primary discussion to the resurrection of the flesh, the presence of the Spirit recasts believers' perspective about the present and the future:

The person in whom [the Spirit comes] cannot in that case be carnal, but spiritual, because of the fellowship of the Spirit (*propter Spiritus communionem*). Thus it is, therefore, that the martyrs bear their witness, and despise death, not because of the weakness of the flesh, but because of the readiness of the Spirit. For when the weakness of the flesh is swallowed up, it exhibits the Spirit as powerful; and again, when the Spirit swallows up the weakness [of the flesh], it possesses the flesh as an inheritance in itself, and from both of these is formed a living human, – *living* because of participation in the Spirit (*propter participationem Spiritus*), but *human* because of the substance of flesh. (AH 5.9.2)

Irenaeus intertwines a number of Pauline passages here as he associates the Spirit with inheritance (Ephesians 1), power and weakness language (2 Corinthians 12), and being swallowed up (1 Corinthians 15/2 Corinthians 5). The physical flesh can be transformed by the Spirit, and thus martyrs are not merely motivated to rid themselves of the flesh because of its weak-

---

[29] For more detail, see Bingham, "Irenaeus Reads Romans 8."

ness.³⁰ The basis for that transformation is the fellowship of and participation in the Spirit.

In the latter half of AH 5, Irenaeus correlates the restoration of humans with the restoration of creation. He reiterates that the fallenness presently experienced does not entail a nullification of the material aspect of creation but rather the need for restitution according to the original intention. Accordingly, he quotes Rom 8:21 (along with other passages) in support of this creational restoration (AH 5.32.1). Irenaeus ultimately concludes *Against Heresies* by reiterating the importance of humans being restored to the image and likeness of God (AH 5.36.3).

III. Conclusion: Participation according to Irenaeus

While Irenaeus' *Against Heresies* is a polemical work, we gain a clear understanding of his vision. The importance of participation for his theological construction and his polemical purpose is evident, not least as he introduces Book 5:

> All the doctrines of the heretics fall to ruin because the Lord thus has redeemed us through his own blood, giving his soul for our souls, and his flesh for our flesh, and has also poured out (*effundente*) the Spirit of the Father for the union (*adunitionem*) and communion (*communionem*) of God and humans, imparting (*deponente*) God to humans by means of the Spirit, and, on the other hand, attaching (*imponente*) humans to God by His own incarnation, and bestowing upon us immortality durably and truly at his coming, by means of communion (*communionem*) with God. (AH 5.1.1)

A transforming participation in the Father, Son, and Spirit is at the heart of Irenaeus' view of God's economy. Grasping this union demands a proper understanding of God and of humanity, topics which are at the center of Irenaeus' polemic but also his theological vision.

The clear Trinitarian structure we see in AH 5.1.1 also reflects our discussions about AH 3.17–19 and AH 5.6–14. With his view of participation in the Trinitarian God, Irenaeus walks the middle ground against his opponents who argue that God is ultimately unknowable and who also hold that the "spiritual" have a connatural affinity with God. He argues for the necessity of a close unity with God through Christ and the Spirit, but he also maintains a distinction between humans and divine. God is infinite, eternal, and perfect, whereas humans are finite, have a beginning, and can only move towards perfection.³¹ This distinction is fundamental, but it also does not prohibit a transformative relationship between God and believers. Irenaeus presents his soteriological transformation through a wide variety of overlapping terms and concepts, such as union, communion, participation,

---

³⁰ When Clement addresses martyrdom, he will disagree with Irenaeus on this point.
³¹ Cf. AH 4.11.2.

possession, indwelling, adoption, vision, deification, and commingling.[32] None appears to be the orienting concept; rather, they are employed variously in his work.

The anthropological experience resulting from this communion with God is primarily expressed in terms of immortality and incorruption, through which believers are restored to the image and likeness of God. For Irenaeus the union of the soul and the body constitutes the image of God, and likeness to God is established by the presence of the Spirit.[33] A future anthropological transformation that does not include somatic resurrection through the Spirit is inadequate for him. At the same time, this future consummation corresponds to the moral and noetic transformation in the present.[34] Casting this in terms of image and likeness allows him to show connections between the creational intention of God and the Pauline focus on restoration of the image of God expressed in Christ. We will see a similar structure in Clement, but with a modified foundation.

D. Clement of Alexandria: Assimilation to God

Clement spent the majority of his theological career in Alexandria, that urban center of learning and trade in the eastern Mediterranean. He is decidedly more integrative in his theological approach than Irenaeus, evidenced by his attempts to show the coherence between the Christian scriptures and Greek philosophy. Though he argues against the ideas represented in Valentinus, Basilides, and Marcion, Clement's key works are more directly shaped by his own concerns. He is known for reclaiming the term "Gnostic" as the description of the ideal Christian and for emphasizing "paideia" as central to Christian spirituality. We will focus our attention on key passages from his *Stromateis*, a work that details various elements of the Gnostic life, that highlight his theological perspective on participation with a view to his use of Pauline texts – *Strom* 2.22; 4.6–7; and 4.26.[35] Participation is just as important for Clement for as Irenaeus, but Clement emphasizes the purification of the soul as central to being like God.

---

[32] Though not explored here, Irenaeus discusses at length union with God through a vision of him in AH 4.20.

[33] However, Irenaeus does, at times, treat image and likeness synonymously as a hendiadys. Cf. Blackwell, *Christosis*, 40, 65–6.

[34] With his focus on physical salvation, scholars sometimes neglect the noetic growth towards maturity in Irenaeus' thought (cf. AH 4.38–39).

[35] The English translations are modified from the Ante-Nicene Fathers based on the Greek text.

I. Likeness to God as the Chief "End" of Humans (Strom 2.22)

The majority of Book 2 is a discussion of various biblical virtues and how they relate to Greek philosophical perspectives on virtue.[36] In *Strom* 2.21–22 Clement shows how his vision of Christian theology relates to an ongoing debate in the Greek philosophical traditions about the "chief end" of humans. After surveying a variety of options, Clement shows that his own position coheres most closely to that of Plato in *Strom* 2.22.

The achievement of the *telos* is determined by the Forms (the Good), which are communicable (μεθεκτόν), and those things that participate (μετέχον) in them become like (ὁμοιότητα) them (*Strom* 2.22.131.2). Humans who appropriate virtue (ἀρετή), which is the true likeness to God though the soul ruling the body, achieve well-being (εὐδαιμονία), the "most perfect and complete good" (*Strom* 2.22.131.4). Clement asserts that this assimilation (ὁμοίωσις) to God is none other than sharing in both the image and in the likeness (ὁμοίωσις) of God (Gen 1:26–28).[37] Since like is friend to like,[38] those who are like God (particularly through self–control [σώφρων]) are his friends. Ultimately, Clement affirms that this coheres with Plato's argument in the *Theaetetus* 176B that humans should pursue "likeness to God as far as possible. And likeness is to become holy and just with wisdom" (*Strom* 2.22.133.3). After summarizing the key points of Plato, Clement explains how this fits with Christian theology:

> It is incumbent to reach the unaccomplished end, obeying the commands – that is, God – and living according to them irreproachably and intelligently through knowledge (γνώσεως) of God's will. In accordance with right reason (λόγον), likeness (ἐξομοίωσις) as far as possible is the end. It is the restoration to perfect adoption (υἱοθεσίαν) by the Son, eternally glorifying the Father by the great High Priest who has deigned to call us siblings and co-heirs. (*Strom* 2.22.134.1–2)

With the language of adoption and co-heirs, this is surely an allusion to Rom 8:14–30, where Paul associates adoption, being co-heirs, and being conformed to the glorious image of the Son, as Clement does here.

Clement also explains the experience of freedom (from sin), sanctification, and eternal life by quoting Rom 6:22 and 5:4–5, thus teasing out how one's present experience is congruent with the future hope. Rom 6:22 is fitting for Clement's purpose because Paul describes the τέλος of Christians in terms of the virtue of sanctification (ἁγιασμός). Rom 5:4–5 also speaks of virtue in light of eschatological hope. The use of Rom 5:4–5 in

---

[36] See L. L. Welborn, "The Soteriology of Romans in Clement of Alexandria, *Stromateis* 2: Faith, Fear, and Assimilation to God," in *Early Patristic Readings of Romans* (ed. Kathy L. Gaca and L. L. Welborn; New York: T&T Clark, 2005), 66–83.

[37] "Likeness" (ὁμοίωσις) is also often glossed as "assimilation."

[38] Cf. Plato's *Lysis* 214 and Homer's *Odyssey* 17.218.

the context of Rom 8:14–30 is interesting because modern scholars often note how these two passages form an inclusio. In these verses, many tend to emphasize the present age of suffering as the time for moral formation and the eschatological age as emphasizing somatic restoration (glory), but Clement is pushing his readers to consider the future age as an extension of the present moral transformation.

Clement then expresses how believers should follow Paul's model of faith and love (Gal 5:5–6) by becoming imitators (μιμηταί) of God through Christ via Paul (1 Cor 11:1). Paul, therefore, presents "assimilation to God as the aim of faith, so that as far as possible a person becomes righteous and holy with wisdom" (*Strom* 2.22.136.1–6). This direct reference to Plato shows how Clement sees the NT (even Pauline) vision for transformation as directly congruent with Plato's perspective.

Clement uses the language of participation (μετέχω), likeness ([ἐξ]ομοίωσις), adoption (υἱοθεσία), and imitation (μιμητής) to describe the nature and means of human transformation. The focus, importantly, is solely on moral transformation, as believers share in divine virtues and thus share the likeness of God, attaining to their *telos* of eternal life. Not mentioning a later somatic experience, Clement sees a direct congruity between present and future transformation primarily, even solely, as noetic and moral. The next passage we discuss will strengthen this perspective as Clement engages even more deeply with Pauline texts.

*II. Gnostic Martyrdom: The Soul Drawn to God (*Strom *4.6–7)*

In Book 4 of the *Stromateis*, Clement addresses the issue of martyrdom (μαρτύριον) in relation to the "perfect person" (τέλειος), with the focus on a gnostic martyrdom as the renunciation of the world. As an extended reflection on the nature of the τέλειος, this book contains a wealth of information related to Clement's theological anthropology and his perspective on salvation. After some preliminary material in *Strom* 4.1–2, he lays out in *Strom* 4.3 the topics of virtue, contemplation, and the freedom of the soul from sin and death in the body (using an extended quotation of Rom 6:20–23). The ability of Gnostic Christians to sever "the soul from the body" allows them to live a life of martyrdom, a discussion that sets the stage for the rest of Book 4.

In *Strom* 4.6 the treatment of "seeing God" in the Beatitudes shows the importance of knowledge and contemplation for sharing the image and likeness of God. This form of martyrdom can be described as the Lord "draw[ing] the soul away gladly from the body," such that believers find the "knowledge (ἐπίγνωσις) of God, which is the communication of incorruption (κοινωνία ἀφθαρσίας)" (*Strom* 4.6.27.2). Later, showing his important role in the mystical tradition, he describes how contemplation (θεωρία) and participation (μετέχω) lead one impassibly beyond "having" (ἔχειν) ἐπιστήμη and γνῶσις to "being" (εἶναι) ἐπιστήμη and γνῶσις.

As we turn our attention to *Strom* 4.7, we see these themes expressed through engagement with other NT, particularly Pauline, texts. Further exploring martyrdom, he treats the issue of suffering for others out of love and then addresses obedience to Christ as crucifying the flesh and following the Spirit, citing Gal 5:24–25 and 6:8. Clement then compares Greek philosophical opinions about honors and punishments in the afterlife to Paul's promise of recompense relating to the flesh and the Spirit in Gal 6:8. He uses a litany of verses from Romans 8 to expound the flesh-Spirit contrast. I will quote his selection in full because his selectivity is telling:

"The mind set on the flesh is hostile to God," explains the apostle: "for it does not submit to God's law, nor can it. And those in the flesh cannot please God." And in further explanation he continues, that no one may like Marcion regard the creature as evil: "But if Christ is in you, though the body is dead because of sin, the Spirit is life because of righteousness." And again: "For if you live according to the flesh, you will die. I consider that the sufferings of this present time are not worth comparing with the glory about to be revealed in us, if we suffer with him so that we also may be glorified with him as coheirs of Christ. And we know that all things work together for good for those who love God, who are called according to his purpose. For those whom he foreknew he also predestined to be conformed to the image of his Son, in order that he might be the firstborn among many brothers and sisters. And those whom he predestined he also called; and those whom he called he also justified; and those whom he justified he also glorified.... For in hope we were saved. Now hope that is seen is not hope. Who hopes for what is seen? But if we hope for what we do not see, we wait for it with patience." (*Strom* 4.7.45.4–46.2)[39]

Though he primarily focuses on verses that highlight the present experience of life through the Spirit, Clement also notes the role of hope for a future consummation. As with *Strom* 2.22, he again treats Romans 5:4–5 in the context of Romans 8 and describes this martyrdom as motivated by love and hope in the midst of suffering. Unlike some texts that celebrate the future bodily restoration to reframe martyrdom, Clement conspicuously skips over the verses in his quotation above that relate to the resurrection of the body, namely Rom 8:11 and 8:23, where Paul himself situates the hope of creational and anthropological restoration.[40] For Clement, the martyr willingly suffers with Christ because she has the hope of a divinely orchestrated eschatological restoration, but the anticipated restoration is not a

---

[39] Specifically, he quotes Rom 8:7, 8, 10, 13, 17, 18, 24–25, 28–30, though not in that order.

[40] In fact, Clement has little in his corpus that promotes a resurrection of the body besides his discussion of Jesus' resurrection in *Strom* 6.9. This, of course, is a significant distinction from Irenaeus, who spends several chapters arguing on behalf of the resurrection of the body.

resurrection of the body but a purification of the soul. At the same time, Clement explicitly excludes Marcion's negative views of the (material) creation, that is, the body.

Martyrdom helps believers separate themselves from bodily lusts, as Clement's quote from Rom 6:6 shows: "We know that our old self was crucified with him so that the body of sin might be destroyed, and we might no longer be enslaved to sin" (*Strom* 4.7.51.1). He interweaves a variety of texts from 1 Corinthians (4:9–13; 13:7; 11:1; 13:13; 10:26–31) to support his assertion that love is at the heart of this gnostic martyrdom. Ending with Col 3:12–15 and its love command, Clement holds out the expectation that those "still in the body [can], like the just men of old, enjoy impassibility (ἀπάθεια) and freedom from worry (ἀταραξία) in the soul" (*Strom* 4.7.55.4). The gnostic martyr, being motivated by love, will give up the (pleasures of the) body because she knows the soul is purified by this renunciation. Thus, a present martyrdom allows the believer to experience ἀπάθεια and ἀταραξία, states of being that will characterize eternal life. In our next passage, Clement's argument about martyrdom in the context of attaining likeness to God will come to a climax.

III. Likeness to the Creator God (Strom 4.26)

Clement's argument in *Strom* 4.26 treats the soul vis-à-vis the body; we will, however, better understand his discussion here by first noting distinctions he makes elsewhere. In Book 5 he sets the soul above the body because "the image of God is the divine and royal Word, the impassible (ἀπαθής) man [Jesus]; and the image of the image is the human mind (νοῦς)" (*Strom* 5.14). The Son is the true image of God, and humans reflect his image noetically by living impassibly. In another passage he writes: "Is not man, then, rightly said 'to have been made in the image of God?' – not in the form of his [corporeal] structure; but inasmuch as God creates all things by the Word (Λόγῳ), the man who has become a Gnostic performs good actions by the faculty of reason (τῷ λογικῷ)" (*Strom* 6.16.136.3). Clement again directly links the Word with the soul and specifically with its rational faculties.

Though he holds the soul in this special place as the image of God, as we turn to our primary passage in *Strom* 4.26, we see that he distinguishes his position from more radical forms of gnosticism:

Those, then, who run down created existence and vilify the body are wrong. They do not consider that the frame of man was formed erect for the contemplation (θέαν) of heaven, and that the organization of the senses tends to knowledge (γνῶσιν), and that the members and parts are arranged for good, not for pleasure. Therefore this dwelling becomes receptive of the soul which is most precious to God and is dignified with the Holy Spirit through the sanctification of soul and body, with the complete perfection of the Savior.

And the succession of the three virtues is found in the Gnostic, who morally, physically, and logically occupies himself with God. (*Strom* 4.26.163.1–3)

Since the primary role of the body is to serve as an aid for contemplation and knowledge, its function is subsidiary (but not antithetical) to that of the soul. Offering an argument like that of Irenaeus, Clement clarifies that living by the flesh refers not to existing in the body but to following the sinful desires of the flesh. We see the Trinitarian structure of Clement's theology here: The Holy Spirit sanctifies believers in order to form them according to the model of Christ, being transformed holistically in body and soul according to God's will.

Clement vigorously disputes the determinism of his opponents who distinguished between the created states of different type of people. As a part of his defense, he clarifies what makes a person sinful or spiritual:

For he who, being in a state of ignorance, is sinful, "is earth and ashes" (cf. Job 42:6); while he who is in a state of knowledge, being assimilated as far as possible to God, is already spiritual, and so elect.... For the Gnostic must, as far as is possible, imitate God. And the poets call the elect in their pages godlike and gods, and equal to the gods, and equal in sagacity to Zeus, and having counsels like the gods, and resembling the gods, – nibbling, as seems to me, at the expression, "in the image and likeness." (*Strom* 4.26.168.2; 171.3–4)

Placing the creation account in the context of philosophical conceptions, he notes the correspondence between being in the image and likeness of God (Gen 1:26–28) and being gods. Earlier in *Strom* 4.23.149.8 Clement applied Psalm 82 to believers, calling them gods because of their imitation of God. Since God is impassible, when believers through contemplation and participation become like him in virtue (though still personally distinct), they can be called gods. This, as Clement reinforces here, is a fulfillment of the human vocation to live according to the image and likeness of God. We should note his focus on the realized nature of this transformation, in that deification and assimilation are experienced in the present. This passage further extends his argument that likeness to God through imitation of God is at the heart of his theological vision. Though NT passages are not as prominent here, this climactic passage displays his main themes on participation and his eclectic use of sources.

IV. Conclusion: Participation according to Clement

Clement, like Irenaeus, situates his description of human transformation in a polemical context; however, Clement is not willing to cede the moniker "Gnostic," and it becomes the catchword for his perfect Christian. In our three passages from Clement (*Strom* 2.22; 4.6–7; and 4.26), we have gained a progressively clearer picture of how believers participate in God and are transformed into his likeness.

In Clement's theology God holds the place of the Platonic Forms. That is, he is the one who is "being," the one who is communicable and the one to whom believers are drawn. In distinction, Christians are "becoming," as they seek to be like him. However, God is not merely a philosophical principle; rather, he is an active agent and is experienced in Trinitarian terms. The Holy Spirit is the one through whom believers experience sanctification and virtue. The Son is the Word (Λόγος) in and through whom humans experience rationality (λογικός), and he is the image into which the Spirit transforms believers.

Though currently existing in the body, humans have the closest affinity with God through the soul and their rational faculties. Thus, through purification of the soul, humans share more fully in God's likeness. Things that are like one another are thus able to know one another more fully, and as believers are transformed and purified, they are drawn closer to God. Clement employs a variety of terms to explore this transformative relationship, but participation, assimilation (becoming like), imitation, adoption, and deification are primary, with union and communion employed less frequently.[41]

The anthropological experience resulting from participation in God through Christ and the Holy Spirit is expressed in terms of eternal life and immortality, with restoration of the image and likeness of God the end result. Since Clement situates the image of God in the soul, the primary locus of divine likeness is expressed through the experience of virtues. In distinction to Irenaeus, there is almost no discussion of the body in the afterlife. Since believers model Christ, who exists in ἀπάθεια and ἀταραξία, as believers become more like him, they too will experience this divine state of being. Thus, the future life of the Gnostic Christian directly parallels the transformation of the soul presently available.

Having provided readings of Irenaeus and Clement, we are now able to draw together our results and to assess how their readings of Paul might enlighten our own.

E. Conclusion

Some scholars have not found Irenaeus and Clement as the best models for engaging Paul. These patristic writers are seen as "early catholic" readers of Paul,[42] and as intolerant of theological diversity.[43] Although no later in-

---

[41] "Union," however, does become more important in the mystical tradition after Clement.

[42] J. Christiaan Beker (*Paul the Apostle: The Triumph of God in Life and Thought* [Minneapolis: Fortress, 1984]) reflects wider sentiments that these readers de-

terpreter captures all or even most of the emphases of a previous text (much less an author's corpus), that does not mean we should ignore these later interpreters or merely use them as a foil for our more enlightened position. Once we get beyond the veneer of these critiques, we see a depth and complexity to these ancient readings that introduce new vistas that our more recent traditions might not consider. Both writers are constantly engaging the scriptures (and other sources) to build and support their theological arguments. Of course, neither merely parrots the biblical texts, and they also use the texts selectively based upon their rhetorical and polemical purposes. However, the topics and passages they address give us an interesting window into ways of reading Paul. We can argue which are better or worse readings of Paul, but we also must consider the *underdetermined* nature of Paul's letters, particularly on this issue of participation.[44] Paul uses a variety of overlapping but distinct terms and concepts to describe the transformative divine-human relationship, but none seems to be a controlling metaphor for him.[45] Paul's pluriform vision for participation is robust but not easily definable, which has led to the quandary that Sanders has noted. This underdetermination invites further clarification, which both Irenaeus and Clement provide for their audiences.

From our readings of Irenaeus and Clement, we see important similarities and differences in their perspectives on participation with regard to the Pauline letters. For both, the basis of participation is the Trinitarian God who engages humans and allows them to share not merely his attributes (immortality, incorruption, sanctification) but first and primarily in himself.[46] This allows Christians to live according to the image and likeness of

---

apocalypticized Paul. His statement that "Paul's theological influence on the patristic period was minimal" (29–30) is obviously fantastic and unsupportable. However, the contingency of the letters does get minimized at times by later interpreters.

[43] Jouette M. Bassler concedes that we all come to the text with particular perspectives, but she critiques Irenaeus' perspective because of his supposed totalizing claims. Bassler overstates the case regarding Irenaeus. He did not exclude all readings that did not cohere with his own. For example, he is known for promoting a rapprochement between those with differing positions on Quartodeciman controversy; Jouette M. Bassler, "A Response to Jeffrey Bingham and Susan Graham: Networks and Noah's Sons," in *Early Patristic Readings of Romans* (ed. Kathy L. Gaca and L. L. Welborn; New York: T&T Clark, 2005), 133–51.

[44] Cf. Stephen E. Fowl, *Engaging Scripture: A Model for Theological Interpretation* (Oxford: Blackwell, 1998).

[45] Cf. Blackwell, *Christosis*, 239–45.

[46] They do not present believers as independent agents creating their own transformation because these divine attributes are only communicated through participation in God.

God, the climax of the human vocation.⁴⁷ The two writers use much of the same language – participation, likeness, adoption, vision, imitation, and deification – but Irenaeus uses the language of union and communion more frequently. I have previously argued, and still agree, that Paul shares the same basic construction as that found in Irenaeus and Clement: participation in the triune God results in believers being reconstituted to the image of Christ through the Spirit.⁴⁸ Like Paul, these interpreters use a variety of terms and concepts (most from Paul himself) to describe the nature of this participation. In order to bring more clarity to their audience, they also add other phrases and neglect phrases he uses, namely, his ubiquitous "in Christ" language. With this in mind we can rightly speak of a common *relational ontology* that informs all of their perspectives on the divine-human encounter, in that to be fully human demands participation in God.⁴⁹ Of course, this raises thorny questions about Paul's view of the divinity of Christ and the Spirit, of creation *ex nihilo*, and of divine and human agency, issues that we cannot explore here.⁵⁰

While sharing this similar basic construct, Irenaeus and Clement differ on the locus of the image of God in humans and therefore on how humans experience restoration of that image. Irenaeus locates the image in the conjunction of the soul and body together, whereas Clement situates the image in the soul alone. Accordingly, Irenaeus makes an extended argument for the resurrection of the body as central for human restoration, though a noetic maturing and a present moral transformation are no less important for his theology. While not vilifying the body, Clement highlights the purification of the soul from its desires as it participates in divine virtues and achieves ἀπάθεια like God. While not the only source, Paul likely serves as the basis for their use of this image language because he is unique in the NT in his regular use of iconic and morphic language to describe salvation. Conformation to the image of Christ is employed in primarily moral and noetic settings (2 Cor 3:6–18, 4:4–6) as well as primarily somatic settings (1 Cor 15:49; Rom 8:29–30),⁵¹ such that both patristic writers have material on which to draw. Because Paul does not fully specify what the image of

---

⁴⁷ Though space precluded a discussion here, both writers use the language of deification, believers becoming "gods," because of this participation in God. Though both use the language metaphorically, the transforming relationship is no less real.

⁴⁸ Blackwell, *Christosis*, esp. 251–72.

⁴⁹ Cf. Emmanuel L. Rehfeld, *Relationale Ontologie bei Paulus: Die ontische Wirksamkeit der Christusbezogenheit im Denken des Heidenapostels* (WUNT 2/326; Tübingen: Mohr Siebeck, 2012).

⁵⁰ I address some of these issues in "You Are Filled in Him: Theosis and Colossians 2–3," *JTI* 8.1 (2014): 103–24.

⁵¹ I would argue, however, that we can see moral/noetic and somatic intimations in all of these passages.

Christ specifically entails, this underdetermination provides room for later interpreters to appropriate and clarify his language.

In addition to the topic of image, we also see distinct emphases in how Irenaeus and Clement treat other issues. With regard to incorruption, Clement accentuates *moral* incorruption. Thus, when he speaks of experiencing eternal life, he quotes Rom 6:22 (*Strom* 2.22; 4.3) and focuses upon sanctification. Irenaeus also speaks of moral incorruption as the Spirit overcomes the flesh, but as the Spirit "inherits" the flesh at the resurrection, his primary focus is *somatic* incorruption. We also see how they deemphasize certain aspects in distinction to one another. Clement is conspicuously silent on the topic of somatic incorruption. When he extensively quotes from Romans 8 (*Strom* 4.7), a Pauline passage where ἀφθαρσία is directly correlated to resurrection of the body (Rom 8:21–23), Clement leaves out verses that mention resurrection. At the same time, Irenaeus only lightly treats cruciformity, the current embodiment of Christ's death, a topic central to Clement's and Paul's theology.[52] Irenaeus only addresses suffering in the pattern of Christ in AH 3.18.5 (though he also notes suffering's pedagogical function in relation to 2 Corinthians 12 in AH 3.20.1–3 and 5.3.1–3). In distinction, Clement makes cruciformity a primary topic of discussion. For example, most of *Stromateis* 4 is a discussion of gnostic martyrdom, which entails the believer mortifying the desires of the body through suffering.[53] Of course, the nature of present suffering, the resurrection body, and eschatology are topics of debate in current Pauline scholarship as well.[54]

Thus, as we consider these two writers we see that both give interesting and distinct perspectives on the Pauline letters and the topic of participation. A looming question is whether and to what extent Paul engaged or reflected Greek philosophical traditions represented by these interpreters, whether Stoic or Platonic (realizing that these are not always distinct in the first century). This will influence how helpful the readings given by these later writers are perceived to be. I confess that scholarship that ties Paul too closely to (Middle) Platonic or Stoic categories has not been as convincing to me and others, and so these later constructions that have strong affinities to the philosophical traditions might be perceived as biased or misguided by some. However, the questions and answers provided by these

---

[52] This is all the more striking because of the intense persecution in Lyons that likely contributed to Irenaeus becoming bishop.

[53] Irenaeus and Clement also have differing perspectives on the atonement: Irenaeus most frequently employs a *Christus Victor* model, whereas Clement emphasizes Christ's role as pedagogue.

[54] My previous reading of Paul (*Christosis*, 251–72) has more affinities to that of Irenaeus than Clement, but I concede that I too easily dismissed Clement. In fact, my critiques of Irenaeus are issues that Clement highlights.

readers often provide a helpful lens even if one does not accept all their premises. It is interesting to note that some of the most robust and convincing "participationist" readings of Paul from Albert Schweitzer and E. P. Sanders place him primarily (or even solely in Schweitzer's case) in a Jewish context.[55] Of course, in Paul's diaspora setting Judaism cannot be so easily distilled from its Hellenistic context, which Irenaeus and Clement give us windows to.

Rather than trying to assess the growing number of monographs and essays on participation in Paul, I will, in closing, focus my attention on an essay that Richard Hays wrote in dialogue with Sanders.[56] Hays discusses four different models of participation in Paul arising from different spheres: the family, political/military authority, the ecclesia, and Christ's story. Among these Hays gives priority to the latter two: ecclesial participation and narrative participation in Christ's story.[57] These are also important paradigms offered by Irenaeus and Clement. With regard to living out Christ's narrative, we mightnote, however, that certain *attributes* (e.g., incorruption), at times, become more prominent than the *story*. With the incorporation of adoption and communal themes, we also see an important ecclesial emphasis in our writers, particularly Irenaeus.

Interestingly, Hays uses Gregory of Nyssa as a positive example of how *metousia* (participation) in the Eastern tradition can be a helpful window on Paul. Gregory reflects the mystical tradition (as the quote that Hays provides makes clear). Thus, we would do well to read Paul with those in the mystical tradition like Gregory and Clement, as well as with others like Irenaeus, Cyril of Alexandria or John Chrysostom who emphasize other themes. Since various traditions give light on the topic of participation, the much later Maximus the Confessor (c. 580–662) might be of interest to readers since he serves an important role in uniting the two streams of tradition that Irenaeus and Clement represent – the mystical (later influenced by Neoplatonism) and incarnational (due to Maximus' nuanced perspectives on the church and Christology) emphases. His synthesis strongly influences later Byzantine and Orthodox theology, and his description of an

---

[55] Albert Schweitzer, *The Mysticism of Paul the Apostle* (trans. William Montgomery; Baltimore: Johns Hopkins University Press, 1998); E. P. Sanders, *Paul and Palestinian Judaism*. Cf. Douglas A. Campbell, *The Deliverance of God: An Apocalyptic Rereading of Justification in Paul* (Grand Rapids: Eerdmans, 2009).

[56] Richard B. Hays, "What is 'Real Participation in Christ'? A Dialogue with E. P. Sanders on Pauline Soteriology," in *Redefining First-Century Jewish and Christian Identities* (ed. Fabian E. Udoh et al.; CJAS 16; Notre Dame: University of Notre Dame Press, 2008), 336–51.

[57] Hays, "What is 'Real Participation in Christ'?" 347.

unconfused union with God by using an illustration of a sword in a fire is quite helpful.[58]

With Hays I would heartily endorse engaging the Greek fathers for helping us better understand participation in Paul. Whether one finds them convincing or not, they at least have other concerns than those that our Latin-based tradition offers us and thus allow us to expand our horizons as we merge them with those of the text.[59]

Bibliography

Babcock, William S., ed. *Paul and the Legacies of Paul*. Dallas: Southern Methodist University Press, 1990.
Barnes, Michel René. "Irenaeus' Trinitarian Theology." *Nova et Vetera* 7/1 (2009): 67–106.
Behr, John. *Asceticism and Anthropology in Irenaeus and Clement*. Oxford: Oxford University Press, 2000.
———. "Irenaeus on the Word of God." Vol. 36. Edited by M. F. Wiles and E. J. Yarnold. Leuven: Peeters, 2001.
Beker, J. Christiaan. *Paul the Apostle: The Triumph of God in Life and Thought*. Minneapolis: Fortress, 1984.
Bird, Michael F. and Joseph R. Dodson, eds. *Paul in the Second Century*. Library of New Testament Studies 412. London: T&T Clark, 2011.
Blackwell, Ben C. *Christosis: Pauline Soteriology in light of Deification in Irenaeus and Cyril of Alexandria*. Wissenschaftliche Untersuchungen zum Neuen Testament 2/314. Tübingen: Mohr Siebeck, 2011.
———. "You Are Filled in Him: Theosis and Colossians 2–3." *Journal of Theological Interpretation* 8/1 (2014): 103–24.
Blackwell, Ben C., and Kris Miller. "Theosis and Theological Anthropology." N.p. in *Ashgate Research Companion to Theological Anthropology*. Edited by Joshua R. Farris and Charles Taliaferro. Burlington: Ashgate, forthcoming 2014.
Brakke, David. *The Gnostics: Myth, Ritual, and Diversity in Early Christianity*. Cambridge: Harvard University Press, 2010.
Briggman, Anthony. "Irenaeus' Chistology of Mixture." *Journal of Theological Studies* New Series 64 (2013): 516–55.
Campbell, Douglas A. *The Deliverance of God: An Apocalyptic Rereading of Justification in Paul*. Grand Rapids: Eerdmans, 2009.
Fairbairn, Donald. "Patristic Soteriology: Three Trajectories." *Journal of the Evangelical Theological Society* 50 (2007): 289–310.
Fowl, Stephen E. *Engaging Scripture: A Model for Theological Interpretation*. Oxford: Blackwell, 1998.

---

[58] I along with Kris Miller provide a treatment of Maximus here: "Theosis and Theological Anthropology," in *Ashgate Research Companion to Theological Anthropology* (ed. Joshua R. Farris and Charles Taliaferro; Burlington: Ashgate, forthcoming 2014).

[59] I would like to thank Mike Gorman, Jason Maston, and John Goodrich for their comments to improve this essay.

Gaca, Kathy L. and L. L. Welborn, eds. *Early Patristic Readings of Romans*. New York: T&T Clark, 2005.
González, Justo L. *Christian Thought Revisited: Three Types of Theology*. Rev. ed. New York: Maryknoll, 1999.
Grant, Robert M. *Irenaeus of Lyons*. New York: Routledge, 1997.
Hays, Richard B. *The Faith of Jesus Christ: The Narrative Substructure of Galatians 3:1–4:11*. 2d ed. Grand Rapids: Eerdmans, 2002.
———. "What is 'Real Participation in Christ'? A Dialogue with E. P. Sanders on Pauline Soteriology." Pages 336–51 in *Redefining First-Century Jewish and Christian Identities*. Christainity and Judaism in Antiquity Series 16. Edited by Fabian E. Udoh et al. Notre Dame: University of Notre Dame Press, 2008.
Hooker, Morna D. *From Adam to Christ*. Eugene, Ore.: Wipf & Stock, 2008.
Louth, Andrew. *The Origins of the Christian Mystical Tradition: From Plato to Denys*. 2d ed. Oxford: Oxford University Press, 2007.
Noormann, Rolf. *Irenäus als Paulusinterpret*. Wissenschaftliche Untersuchungen zum Neuen Testament 2/66. Tübingen: Mohr Siebeck, 1994.
O'Keefe, John. "'A Letter that Killeth': Toward a Reassessment of Antiochene Exegesis, or Diodore, Theodore, and Theodoret on the Psalms." *Journal of Early Christian Studies* 8 (2000): 83–104.
Osborn, Eric. *Clement of Alexandria*. Cambridge: Cambridge University Press, 2005.
Patterson, L. G. "The Divine Became Human: Irenaean Themes in Clement of Alexandria." Pages 497–516 in *Studia Patristica*. Vol. 31. Edited by E. A. Livingstone. Leuven: Peeters, 1997.
Popov, Ivan V. "The Idea of Deification in the Early Eastern Church." Pages 42–82 in *Theosis: Deification in Christian Theology*. Vol. 2. Edited by Vladimir Kharlamov. Eugene, Ore.: Pickwick, 2011.
Rehfeld, Emmanuel L. *Relationale Ontologie bei Paulus: Die ontische Wirksamkeit der Christusbezogenheit im Denken des Heidenapostels*. Wissenschaftliche Untersuchungen zum Neuen Testament 2/326. Tübingen: Mohr Siebeck, 2012.
Russell, Norman. *The Doctrine of Deification in the Greek Patristic Tradition*. Oxford: Oxford University Press, 2004.
Sanders, E. P. *Paul and Palestinian Judaism: A Comparison of Patterns of Religion*. Minneapolis: Fortress, 1977.
Still, Todd D. and David E. Wilhite, eds. *Paul Among the Fathers: Pauline and Patristic Scholars in Debate*. London: T&T Clark, 2013–.
Schweitzer, Albert. *The Mysticism of Paul the Apostle*. Translated by William Montgomery. Baltimore: Johns Hopkins University Press, 1998.
Thate, Michael J. "Identity Construction as Resistance: Figuring Hegemony, Biopolitics, and Martyrdom as an Approach to Clement of Alexandria." Pages 69–85 in vol. 14 of *Studia Patristica* 66. Edited by Markus Vinzent. Leuven: Peeters, 2013.
Wallace-Hadrill, David S. *Christian Antioch: A Study of Early Christian Thought in the East*. Cambridge: Cambridge University Press, 1982.
Welborn, L. L. "The Soteriology of Romans in Clement of Alexandria, *Stromateis* 2: Faith, Fear, and Assimilation to God." Pages 66–83 in *Early Patristic Readings of Romans*. Edited by Kathy L. Gaca and L. L. Welborn. New York: T&T Clark, 2005.
Young, Frances. *Biblical Exegesis and the Formation of Christian Culture*. Cambridge: Cambridge University Press, 1997.

Augustine and Participation

Some Reflections on his Exegesis of Romans

DARREN SARISKY

I

In the second half of the twentieth century, critical questions have arisen from a couple of different quarters about whether the Western Christian traditions, and especially Protestantism, have marginalized or ignored a valuable theological notion, namely, participation, which aims to express the union of believers and God. Eastern Orthodox theologians such as Vladimir Lossky press this issue in polemical engagements with the West, charging the West with neglecting the teaching of the Eastern Fathers, who portray Christ's work as bearing its ultimate fruit in the believer's participation in God, or the deification of the human person.[1] This critique presupposes that there is a fairly stark contrast between the theological positions of the Eastern and Western Fathers, and that subsequent Western traditions have followed sources that offer relatively meager resources for depicting the depth of the transformation that is brought about in human beings. From the point of view of some in the East, Western soteriologies have done this by limiting themselves to notions such as justification, which falls short of communicating the richness of an intimate union.

A query from a different source dovetails with the first. Recent Pauline scholarship reassessing the apostle's stance toward "the Jews" claims that justification has proven all too central in how the West has read Paul's writings and, thus, that the West has missed participation, which is the true center of gravity for Paul's theology. For instance, according to E. P. Sanders, it is not that justification is entirely absent from Paul's texts, but that it does not mean precisely what Martin Luther thought it meant, that

---

[1] Vladimir Lossky, "Redemption and Deification," in *In the Image and Likeness of God* (Tuchahoe: St. Vladimir's Seminary Press, 1974), 71–110.

is, God's declaring one righteous when one is actually not.² Nor does justification, according to Sanders, have the centrality in Paul that Luther attributed to it.³ Presupposing the correctness of Luther blinds contemporary interpreters as they read, keeping them from seeing to the heart of what epistles such as Romans actually teach. Luther represented Paul's Jewish adversaries as standing for a form of works righteousness that resembled what Luther saw as the position of the decadent Roman Catholicism of his own day. Sanders, however, rereads the Jewish texts that formed the backcloth for Paul's theology, concluding that Luther was wrong to see Judaism as revolving around works, and likewise wrong to see Paul's gospel as essentially to do with the justification of those who cannot become righteous through performing good deeds, but can only become right with God by divine declaration. The West's preoccupation with a certain view of justification means that participation again receives short shrift.

Sanders is not alone in his suspicion that Western theologians have misread Paul. While Sanders's influential study says very little about Augustine, other New Testament scholars working along similar lines do make an explicit link with Augustine and raise critical questions about his theology.⁴ For Krister Stendahl, Augustine served as a powerful early voice in perpetuating a misreading of Paul that was problematic in some of the same respects as Luther's was in the eyes of Sanders. Augustine is, on this interpretation, foremost among the early Christian readers in the West who "found the common denominator between Paul and the experiences of man, since Paul's statements about 'justification by faith' have been hailed as the answer to the problem which faces the ruthlessly honest man in his practice of *introspection*."⁵ The idea is that Augustine so worried about the correctness of his own conduct, never ceasing to examine and re-examine himself, that he projects these questions onto Paul, in whom they are not truly present.⁶ Augustine thus sets in motion many of the dynamics that

---

² For a sample Lutheran response, see Stephen Westerholm, *Perspectives Old and New on Paul: The "Lutheran" Paul and His Critics* (Grand Rapids: Eerdmans, 2003).

³ E. P. Sanders, *Paul and Palestinian Judaism: A Comparison of Patterns of Religion* (Philadelphia: Fortress, 1977).

⁴ Krister Stendahl, "The Apostle Paul and the Introspective Conscience of the West," *HTR* 56 (1963): 203–5.

⁵ Stendahl, "Introspective Conscience," 200; emphasis added.

⁶ It is worth clarifying at this juncture that what Sanders thinks has been missed in Paul (the centrality of participation) is not precisely the same as what Stendahl thinks has been missed (the status of the law after the arrival of Jesus and the ramifications of Jesus' coming for relations between Jews and Gentiles). But in both cases, a re-reading of Judaism is important for how Paul is to be understood, and a certain view of justification needs to be rejected.

reached a climax in Luther's interpretation of the apostle. For both, justification is the answer to a deeply troubled conscience.

This whole recent discussion has taken place with certain notions in the foreground – participation, Paul, and a new assessment of the Judaism of Paul's day – and other notions in the background – how different strands within the Christian tradition have construed these issues. One way of attempting to take the discussion forward a step is by moving what has hovered in the background into focus and asking, in light of the concerns that have been raised, what Augustine thought about participation. How does he understand it – assuming he actually has something to say about it? This essay takes stock of how current scholarship on Augustine handles this question, and it reflects on some of Augustine's exegesis of Romans where participation conceptualities surface, all in an effort better to discern his role in the history of interpretation. What emerges from a close reading of Augustine is that there are reasons to think he does not display the negligence with which some have charged him.

II

What Gerald Bonner says in a seminal essay published thirty years is arguably false today, though it was certainly true when he originally issued the statement: "Augustine's use of the concept of deification tends to be neglected by students of his theology. Not only do general works on patristics ignore it, but even specialized studies pass it by."[7] Though works that survey the ground sometimes still marginalize Augustine,[8] a number of specialist studies have now emerged – not the least of which are Bonner's own contributions – and, as I argue in this section of the essay, a broader surge of scholarly interest in participation has given rise to insights that prove illuminating for readers of Augustine. In much of this literature, there is a benign conflation of "deification" and "participation," both of which signify in some way the union that exists, or that can exist, between God and human creatures. Scholarly literature usually does not labor to distinguish analytically between these two terms, as Augustine himself us-

---

[7] Gerald Bonner, "Augustine's Conception of Deification," *JTS* 37 (1986): 369.

[8] Augustine does not factor into Grant Macaskill's generally quite insightful canvasing of the patristic literature on participation; Grant Macaskill, *Union with Christ in the New Testament* (Oxford: Oxford University Press, 2014), 42–76. Macaskill follows the lead of a major study from Norman Russell, *The Doctrine of Deification in the Greek Patristic Tradition* (Oxford: Oxford University Press, 2004). Russell aims to interpret only the Greek tradition; he provides a concise summary of Augustine's position in an appendix.

es a variety of linguistic forms to refer to the unity that obtains between Christ and Christians.[9] Especially because Augustine does not use these terms with technical precision, it has been important for recent scholars to expound Augustine's thinking about divine-human unity not simply by tracking his usage of certain verbal forms, but also by expounding texts where he is manifestly discussing the relevant themes without using words that are usually translated into English as "deification" or "participation." Terms like adoption and filiation are also crucial in this connection, as is indwelling. This essay capitalizes on a number of insights that have grown out of recent debates about these themes in Augustine's works.

First, though some older studies categorically deny that Augustine has a notion of participation or deification, claiming instead that these concepts are the exclusive possession of Eastern theologians, in recent research the tide has turned against this judgment and toward an affirmation that Augustine does indeed have something important to say on these topics. In broad terms, the argument that the older literature often makes is that Augustine has such a strong sense of how creatures and their divine creator are distinct from one another, and relatedly a belief that humans are so deeply sinful and depraved, that it becomes impossible for him to conceive of the sort of the intimate union that is signaled by participation and/or deification.[10] In this respect, Augustine sets the basic pattern for Western soteriology. On this view, what he does have is a more cautious conception of what is actually possible for human beings:

[L]'esprit augustinien tend de toute la force de ses ailes vers la grâce de la *vision béatifique*, que seule peut lui accorder la «lumière de glorie». Il se sent et se saint ordonné à la *béatitude*, – mais non à la *déification* ; celle-ci lui reste interdite, puisqu'il ne peut y avoir, pour Augustin, consubstantialité, donc compénétration, de la nature divine et de la nature humaine.[11]

Yet, more than fifty years ago, some scholarly literature took a different tack.[12] This literature recognized that Augustine does not give these notions the same obvious prominence that some theologians in the East do.

---

[9] David Vincent Meconi, *The One Christ: St. Augustine's Theology of Deification* (Washington: Catholic University of America Press, 2013), xviii.

[10] Myrrha Lot-Borodine, *La déification de l'homme, selon la doctrine des Pères grecs* Paris: Cerf, 1970); Joseph Mausbauch, *Thomas von Aquin als Meister christlicher Sittenlehre unter Berücksichtigung seiner Willenslehre* (Munich: Theatiner Verlag, 1925). See also Ben Drewery, "Deification," in *Christian Spirituality: Essays in Honour of Gordon Rupp* (ed. Peter Newman Brooks; London: SCM Press, 1975), 33–62.

[11] Lot-Borodine, *Déification de l'homme*: 39–40.

[12] Victorino Capánaga, "La deificación en la soteriología Augustina," *Augustinus Magister* 2 (1954): 745–54; M. Viller, Ferdinand Cavallera, and J. de Guibert, *Dictionnaire de spiritualitâe ascâetique et mystique, doctrine et histoire* (Paris: Beauchesne, 1937), s.v. "divinization."

So it would be more difficult to write a study on these topics in Augustine than it would be for the Greek Fathers, as one finds in Jules Gross.[13] In spite of that, it is still true that Augustine uses these notions in his own distinctive way. His theology ought to be seen for what it is: simply because he is not identical with the East does not mean that notions of participation and deification are not present in his theology. There is, many scholars now argue, a real sense in which participation and deification are actually central to the theological outlook of Augustine.[14] For instance, Henry Chadwick comments: "La participation à la vie divine est, pour Augustin, le coeur même de la Rédemption."[15]

How, more precisely, are themes like participation central? It is possible to explore this question further using a second insight from the current literature. Andrew Louth draws a helpful distinction between conceptual analysis of a key theological term, on the one hand, and, on the other, the work it does within an entire framework of thought, or, to put another gloss on it, the "place" it has within a cohesive theological outlook.[16] A conceptual analysis of participation would essentially be a semantic exercise, an attempt to determine the meaning that a concept bears for Augustine. More fully, this would involve breaking the concept down into its various parts and putting them back together again.[17] Studies that take this form obviously have value, insofar as they clarify how an author uses a term, yet they can end up failing to grasp the wider significance that a term has by neglecting to note what other notions are tied up with it. This brings us to what Louth means by the "place" a notion has within a theology. The question of the location of participation asks not about what the concept means but about the work that a theologian asks it to perform. What function does it have in the author's overall outlook? To what other concepts is

---

[13] Jules Gross, *La divinisation du chrétien d'après les Pères grecs: contribution historique à la doctrine de la grâce* (Paris: J. Gabalda et Cie, 1938).

[14] Bonner, "Augustine's Conception of Deification" 369–86; Gerald Bonner, "Augustine's Doctrine of Man: Image of God and Sinner," in *God's Decree and Man's Destiny: Studies on the Thought of Augustine of Hippo* (London: Variorum Reprints, 1987), 495–514; Gerald Bonner, "God, Christ and Man in the Thought of St Augustine," in *God's Decree and Man's Destiny: Studies on the Thought of Augustine of Hippo* (London: Variorum Reprints, 1987), 268–94; Henry Chadwick, "Note sur la divinisation chez saint Augustin," *RevScRel* 76 (2002): 246–48; Meconi, *One Christ*.

[15] Chadwick, "Note sur la divinisation," 247.

[16] Andrew Louth, "The Place of *Theosis* in Orthodox Theology," in *Partakers of the Divine Nature: The History and Development of Deification in the Christian Traditions* (ed. Michael J. Christensen and Jeffery A. Wittung; Madison: Fairleigh Dickinson University Press, 2007), 32–44. Cf. the discussion of "systematic significance" in A. N. Williams, *The Ground of Union: Deification in Aquinas and Palamas* (Oxford: Oxford University Press, 1999), 7.

[17] Louth, "Place of *Theosis*," 32.

it most closely related? Where does it stand in the "mosaic, as it were, that emerges when the various doctrines of the faith are fitted together"?[18] This second question is distinct from the first and is certainly worth asking.

The special value of some of the recent research on Augustine's conception of the union that exists between God and creation lies in the analysis it provides of the place that concepts like participation and deification have in his thought. This is true for Bonner's research and also for that of David Meconi, who has recently published the first monograph on deification in Augustine.[19] Meconi by no means dispenses with conceptual analysis: he surveys all the texts in which forms of the word *deificare* occur in Augustine's corpus.[20] This study is comprehensive, though the amount of data is modest because Augustine uses this word only eighteen times in an *oeuvre* that consists of over five million words. In so doing, he uses the term more than all other Western authors before him combined:[21] this raises questions about the relative importance of the term in Eastern and Western theologies. This issue will be revisited below. While Meconi analyzes his leading concept, he is especially eager to avoid presenting his theme as one that is isolated from Augustine's other major theological commitments. He argues that this would be profoundly misleading, for deification is anything but a solitary notion in Augustine's theological outlook. It actually serves as a nexus for many of the most important structural features of his theology. The work proceeds by looking at how Augustine explicates the differentiated union between God and creation even in contexts where the term *deificare* itself never surfaces. A discussion of Augustine's understanding of creation *ex nihilo* and of the human being as the image of God serve as a backdrop for Meconi's treatment of deification by situating people in relationship to God: they are dependent on him, even for their very existence; they have fallen; and they are in the process of being restored by divine grace. God's grace comes to humanity as the Son of God descends to be part of the created world, effecting the "great exchange," whereby the Son of God became a son of man so that the sons of men might become sons of God.[22] This process is mediated by the agency of the Holy Spirit in the so-

---

[18] Louth, "Place of *Theosis*," 33.

[19] Meconi, *One Christ*. Prior to the Meconi's work coming into print, probably the closest thing to a monograph on the subject was a thesis: Jan A. A. Stoop, *Die Deificatio Hominis in die Sermones en Epistulae van Augustinus* (Leiden: Drukkerij Luctor et Emergo, 1952).

[20] Meconi, *One Christ*, 79–134.

[21] Meconi, *One Christ*, xv.

[22] See, for instance, Augustine's Tractates on John 23.6. Latin text from Augustine, *In Iohannis Evangelium Tractatus CXXIV* (Corpus Christianorum Series Latina; ed. D. R. Willems; Turnhout, 1954).

cial context of the church, the *totus Christus*. The most original of the connections Meconi makes is that between deification and pneumatology.

A boon of both Meconi's expansive exposition, and Bonner's essays on which he is building, is that while it is true that Augustine has a notion of deification or participation, it becomes clear that it is wrong to assume that he has the *same* understanding of the union between God and creatures that exists in Eastern patristic theologians, or for that matter in modern Orthodox theologies. Notions expressing union differ at least insofar as they are connected to very different doctrines.[23] For instance, Augustine's development of the *totus Christus*, according to which Christ and Christians are united as head and body via the sacraments, is in some measure distinctive to him. In addition, Augustine's understanding of the *imago Dei* is not identical to the anthropology found in many Eastern Fathers and in much later Orthodox theology, for it does not follow the structure where image refers to original condition and likeness to the eschatological vocation of human beings. As Meconi explains with reference to Augustine's *Questions on the Heptateuch*, "Image has to do with a common source resulting in shared qualities, but likeness and equality are relational terms having nothing to do with origin or the relationship between existents."[24] In this essay, my discussion of participation concentrates more on semantic analysis than on placing participation within Augustine's "system" of theology, since work falling into the latter category has performed its task admirably well.

The third point worth registering from recent discussion is another distinction, this time between two different types of participation. This next distinction is the one that Norman Russell makes between ontological and dynamic participation.[25] Ontological participation is a type of predication

---

[23] Cf. the distinction between "theme" and "doctrine" in Gösta Hallonsten, "*Theosis* in Recent Research: A Renewal of Interest and a Need for Clarity," in *Partakers of the Divine Nature: The History and Development of Deificiation in the Christian Traditions* (ed. Michael J. Christensen and Jeffery A. Wittung; Madison: Fairleigh Dickinson University Press, 2007), 281–93. He says, "By a doctrine I mean here a rather well-defined complex of thought that centers on one or more technical terms." "*Theosis* in Recent Research," 283. By theme, he means a treatment that is looser, less rigid, and more small-scale, something like a simple gloss of deification with terms like "union" or "indwelling."

[24] Meconi, *One Christ*, 38. The source is *Questions on the Heptateuch* 3.4. See Augustine, *Quaestionum in Heptateuchum Libri VII* (Corpus Christianorum Series Latina; ed. J. Fraipont and D. De Bruyne; Turnhout, 1958).

[25] Russell, *Deification in the Greek Patristic Tradition*, 147 n. 55. This conceptual division is quite similar to Meconi's distinction between participation as it applies to all of creation and participation as it applies to human beings: David Vincent Meconi, "St. Augustine's Early Theory of Participation," *AugStud* 27 (1996): 87–88. It also bears a strong resemblance to Kathryn Tanner's distinction between weak and strong participa-

that can be made of all instances of created being, which is to say, of all the things that exist, apart from God. Anything in the created world participates ontologically in God in the sense that it is a being that depends on God in order to exist and to have the qualities it possesses. It is not an autonomous existent, nor does it generate from within itself the type of thing that it is. Kathryn Tanner puts it eloquently: "Not just human beings, but everything in the world gets all it is – inclusive of its existence, good qualities and capacities, and well-performed acts, over the whole of its existence – from what it is not – God. This is simply what it means to be a creature."[26] Ontological participation points to the asymmetrical dependence that exists between God and all else: everything depends on God, while God depends in no way on anything. The perfections that God has are his in the strongest possible sense – he is never without them, and they belong to him properly – while the virtues that exist in the created order exist there by means of participations in perfections that are God's in the first instance. As an example of how divine qualities are God's own in this way, consider what Augustine says about the unity of the spirit and the bond of peace that are shared by the Father and the Son: they exist not by participation, but by their own essence (*non participatione sed essentia sua*), that is, by virtue of the Spirit who proceeds from both of them and is of the same substance as them.[27] Dynamic participation, by contrast, is a category that pertains particularly to human beings and functions as an application to the domain of soteriology of the broader heading of ontological participation. Because of the human person's status as a member of the created world, entirely dependent on God, the holiness or Christ-likeness that a human being demonstrates is precisely a derived virtue. It exists in the person, but it does so as a function of divine grace. The dynamic aspect of human participation in God accentuates human existence in time: humans are mutable beings, who can change as time passes, and they ought to progress in their participation in God as their lives unfold. This essay concentrates particularly on dynamic participation as a soteriological category in Augustine.

---

tion: Kathryn Tanner, *Christ the Key* (Current Issues in Theology; Cambridge: Cambridge University Press, 2010), 8–14. Tanner's text is a work of contemporary systematic theology, but she makes reference to many patristic authors, including Augustine, as she is explicating her terms. For a pointer to Augustine, see Tanner, *Christ the Key*, 14 n. 28.

[26] Tanner, *Christ the Key*, 8.

[27] *De Trinitate* 6.5.7. Augustine, *De Trinitate Libri XV (Libri I-XII)* (Corpus Christianorum Series Latina; ed. W. J. Mountain; Turnhout, 1968). I owe this reference to Lewis Ayres, *Augustine and the Trinity* (Cambridge: Cambridge University Press, 2010), 245.

This essay builds on recent advances that scholars have made, yet it proceeds against the background of a couple of contentions that both seem like hangovers from the scholarly habit of denying that Augustine grants scope to participation. The balance of this essay assumes, in line with the consensus of the current scholarly literature, that Augustine does have something to say about participation; the essay deals mainly with what it means to participate in God, rather than trying to sketch how Augustine situates participation in relation to other theological notions; and it centers on participation as a perspective on human salvation, instead of handling the broader issue of the meaning of creaturely existence as such. But the essay aims to unsettle two lingering criticisms of Augustine. The first comes from John Riches as he ruminates on the recent rereadings of Paul by Sanders and Stendahl.[28] Riches finds in Augustine, including in his first commentary on Romans, *Propositions from the Epistle to the Romans* (hereafter *Propositions*), [29] one of the early points on the trajectory that worries Sanders and Stendahl, that is, the line of thinking that construes Paul as operating with legal or forensic notions as his central theological categories. On Riches's reading, Augustine becomes something of a proto-Luther in that he fails to give participatory concepts their due as he engages with the apostle. In the first part of section III below, I respond by offering an interpretation of Augustine's commentary on Romans 8 that presents participation as present there. The second critique is Gösta Hallonsten's assertion that Augustine "clearly uses the *theosis* theme, together with adoption and filiation, in his sermons. Yet in his treatises on grace it is almost absent."[30] Perhaps the operative word is the qualifier *almost.* It is true that in his controversy with the Pelagians, Augustine avoids deploying terminology that play into the hands of his opposition: deification for instance might do so by suggesting that humans can reach a point in their spiritual progress, even in this life, where they might cease sinning, a position held by some of Augustine's adversaries. Still, there is a sense in

---

[28] John K. Riches, "Readings of Augustine on Paul: Their Impact on Critical Studies of Paul," in *Engaging Augustine on Romans: Self, Context, and Theology in Interpretation.* (ed. Daniel Patte and Eugene TeSelle; Harrisburg: Trinity Press International, 2002), 171–98.

[29] Latin text from Augustine, *Expositio quarundam Propositionum ex Epistola ad Romanos* (Corpus Scriptorum Ecclesiasticorum Latinorum; ed. Ioannes Divjak;Vindabonae, 1971). Translation from Paula Fredriksen Landes, *Augustine on Romans: Propositions from the Epistle to the Romans, Unfinished Commentary on the Epistle to the Romans* (Chico: Scholars Press, 1982).

[30] Hallonsten, *"Theosis* in Recent Research," 283. Cf. Augustine Casiday, "St Augustine on Deification: His Homily on Psalm 81," *Sobornost* 23 (2001): 23–44. Casiday provides a translation and introduction to Augustine's most important sermon on deification.

which participation is evident even in Augustine's formal theological reflection on grace. By examining the treatise *Grace of Christ*,[31] a work in which Augustine makes frequent reference to Romans, I attempt to specify the way in which participation factors into this work. The overall force of the following exposition of Augustine's use of Romans is to suggest that it is crucial to be sensitive to the different forms that participation takes in Augustine and that, if this is done, it becomes evident that it is not a marginal topic in his interpretation of Romans.

III

I. Propositions from the Epistle to the Romans

Scholars typically turn to the *Propositions* for one of two reasons: either to demonstrate how Augustine in the mid-390s was gradually assimilating more and more biblical, and specifically Pauline, teaching and was moving away from a philosophical mode of thought,[32] or to establish an initial point of reference on the basis of which to plot the evolution of his view of the interrelationship between human free will and divine grace.[33] Yet for the purpose of this essay, what is most important about this brief and unfinished commentary on Paul's text is what Augustine says in it about participation. The exposition within the commentary is an exercise in anti-Manichean polemics, a point which is evident from the four-part summary of the history of salvation that Augustine uses to structure much of what he says in the commentary (*Propositions* 12). Prior to the law (*ante legem*), human beings are simply led wherever their appetites or desires take them, for they are lacking the definitive guidance the law provides. Once under

---

[31] Latin text from Augustine, *De Gratia Christi et de Peccato Originali Libri Duo* (Corpus Scriptorum Ecclesiasticorum Latinorum; ed. C. F. Vrba and J. Zycha; Vindobonae, 1902). Translation from Augustine, *Answer to the Pelagians* (The Works of Saint Augustine; trans. Roland J. Teske; Hyde Park: New City Press, 1997).

[32] For instance, see Paula Fredriksen Landes, "Introduction," in *Augustine on Romans: Propositions from the Epistle to the Romans, Unfinished Commentary on the Epistle to the Romans* (Chico: Scholars Press, 1982), xii; Michael Cameron, *Christ Meets Me Everywhere: Augustine's Early Figurative Exegesis* (Oxford: Oxford University Press, 2012), 133–64.

[33] This literature tends to focus especially on chapters 7 and 9 of Romans. See William S. Babcock, "Augustine's Interpretation of Romans (A.D. 394–396)," *AugStud* 10 (1979): 55–74; J. Patout Burns, "The Interpretation of Romans in the Pelagian Controversey," *AugStud* 10 (1979): 43–54; Eugene TeSelle, "Exploring the Inner Conflict: Augustine's Sermons on Romans 7 and 8," in *Engaging Augustine on Romans: Self, Context, and Theology in Interpretation* (ed. Daniel Patte and Eugene TeSelle; Harrisburg: Trinity Press International, 2002), 111–46.

the law (*sub lege*), people become aware that their conduct does not measure up to the divinely-given standard, and so they gain a knowledge of their own sin. But awareness of this problem does not suffice to solve it. It is only by grace (*sub gratia*) that any solution becomes possible: human beings turn to Christ and receive the transforming grace that he offers. Though conversion constitutes a far-reaching, fundamental change in a person's orientation, as long as people continue to live in the present world and in their current bodies, they are still caught in the struggle of whether or not to sin: the impulse to give in to the desire to do wrong never entirely goes away. But in the final stage (*in pace*), after one's death and resurrection with a new body, the saints will finally be free from the pull of sin and will thus be at peace in this sense. The entire structure of this scheme runs counter to Manichaean views, because it incorporates the law *within* the history of salvation, rather than portraying it as fundamentally opposed to a new dispensation that arrived with Christ. Even in the midst of trying to overcome his opponents, Augustine does not overcorrect in the way that Riches suggests.

Riches censures Augustine for misreading Romans because, in his determined effort to vanquish the Manichees, he overlooks the way Paul depicts salvation as a cosmological battle in which human beings overcome their bondage to evil forces. Augustine cannot simultaneously do justice to the apostle and fully put to rout the idea that evil is a principle that is hostile to God and does not depend on him for its existence.[34] What does Augustine say in his commentary? There are two sides to this issue. On the negative side, Augustine does face something of a challenge when he comments upon Rom 8:7, "For the wisdom of the flesh is hostile to God; it is not subject to the Law of God, nor can it be (*nec enim potest*) (*Propositions* 41). Because he is combating the Manichees, Augustine is eager to ward off the idea that by saying the flesh cannot submit to God, or that this is fundamentally impossible for it, he implies the existence of an autonomous entity capable of counteracting God. So he clarifies: being hostile to God means not submitting to God's law and acting, instead, in accord with the wisdom of the flesh, which is to say, seeking worldly goods and failing to choose higher things (*Propositions* 41). The flesh is not something that exists apart from the self, but is rather a state of the self – a state in which the human subject has given in to temptation and has chosen that which is inherently worse rather than what is better. In Augustine's own words, "For the soul has a single nature, and it has both the wisdom of the flesh when it follows inferior things, and the wisdom of the Spirit when choosing the superior, just as water's single nature both freezes from cold and melts from heat" (*Propositions* 41). So it is true, in a sense, that acting in a

---

[34] Riches, "Readings of Augustine on Paul," 182–87.

fleshly manner entails being in the power of, or giving in to, something that exerts a pull on oneself. But that which exerts this influence is part (specifically, a lower part) of a created order that nevertheless depends on God. Pursuing worldly goods is tied, later in the commentary, to having the spirit of slavery (*Propositions* 44). This is the spirit that those who seek primarily after worldly goods receive. Those who pursue this course are ultimately in the power of the Devil (*Propositions* 44). Thus, Augustine discusses salvation in the commentary as a sort of cosmological struggle between good and evil forces. At the same time, these evil forces are not equally ultimate with God, and the sense that human beings are genuinely in thrall to them is softened in that Augustine holds, at this stage in his career, that people have the power to turn to God: their choice of him is prior to his choice of them.

Although Augustine will reverse this judgment quite explicitly in his dispute with the Pelagians, for the Augustine of the *Propositions*, nothing within Romans undermines this stance on freedom of the will. There are texts that pose a *prima facie* difficulty, especially Paul's reflections on God's choice of Jacob, not his brother Esau (9:11–13), and the hardening of Pharaoh's heart (9:17). Yet it is possible to reconcile these texts with a robust view of human self-determination by insisting that God foreknows the course that human choices will take in time, once they are allowed to happen, and to conceive of divine choice as being contingent upon the free decisions that God can foresee unfolding in the future (*Propositions* 53–54). On this view, God chooses human beings for the faith they will exhibit, not due to good works they will perform. A bit more than two decades after authoring the *Propositions*, Augustine forcefully condemns his own previous view, and takes pains – partly because of how he comes to understand Romans in this part of his career – to link all spiritual progress with divine agency, thus depicting it as a function of divine grace. When preaching on Rom 8:13 ("But if with the spirit you put to death the doings of the flesh, you shall live"), Augustine pauses over an ambiguity: when the text refers to "the spirit" triumphing over the flesh and establishing one in spiritual life, does the apostle have in mind the Holy Spirit or the human spirit (*Sermon* 156.10)?[35] It is not entirely clear. While v. 13 by itself might allow for either interpretation, the following verse makes it clear that human effort alone is feckless. Paul undercuts the temptation that people may feel to put too much stock in their own resources. "To stop the human spirit swaggering and boasting that it is fit and strong for this work,

---

[35] Latin text from Augustine, *Sermones de Novo Testamento* (Corpus Christianorum Series Latina; Turnhout: Brepols, 1976). Translation from Augustine, *Sermons III/5 (148–183)* (The Works of Saint Augustine; trans. Edmund Hill; Hyde Park: New City Press, 1992).

he [Paul] went on to add, *For as many as are led by the Spirit of God, these are God's sons* (Rom 8:14)" (*Sermon* 156.10). In hindsight, the late Augustine sees his earlier view of freedom as betraying what might be called an insufficiently participatory understanding of human nature and agency, a sense that people have at least a circumscribed autonomy on the basis of which they have the potential to act apart from God. I return to this point below with reference to the treatise *Grace of Christ*.

The opposite of being in slavery to sin is participation through the Spirit. Augustine explicates participation essentially as a form of adoption. In expounding Rom 8:23, which says, "Not only creation but we ourselves who have the first fruits of the Spirit groan inwardly," Augustine explains the text as follows: "In other words, not only does that creaturely part of those not yet faithful, and hence not yet among the sons of God, groan and sorrow, but also we who believe and have the first fruits of the spirit, since we now cling by our spirit to God through faith and hence are called not 'creation' but 'sons of God,' even we 'groan inwardly as we await adoption, the redemption of our bodies'" (*Propositions* 45). Sonship is, therefore, in one way already a present reality (spiritually), but in another way (physically) a promised future reality, for which one must continue to wait and hope. One's spirit has been changed already by clinging to God in faith, though the body has not been reconstituted by the resurrection from the dead (*Propositions* 45). So adoption in the full sense occurs only *in pace*, not *sub gratia*. Though human beings can, through the Spirit, become sons of God, this does not compromise the uniqueness of Jesus' sonship, for his status is original to him rather than derived from another. Sonship is not conferred upon him, but is his by nature. He alone is the only-begotten; he alone is the Word in the beginning through whom all things were made (*Propositions* 48). Those who are adopted as God's children still, however, count as Jesus' brothers and sisters, despite this being a status to which they were raised. Insofar as the saints are elevated to this position, they are brothers and sisters with the one who assumed their flesh and became the incarnate Son of God.

II. Grace of Christ

Notwithstanding Hallonsten's claim that in Augustine's treatises on grace some of his most striking language to express the union between God and human beings, together with terms such as adoption and filiation that gloss its meaning, is nearly entirely missing, there is a sense in which participation in God lies at the heart of what divides Augustine from the Pelagians. Even in this controversy – *especially* in this controversy – what Augustine deems indispensable, but what his opponents scrupulously avoid on principle (at least as Augustine understands and presents them), is that human life participates in God, or depends on him, in a way that is enduring, continuous, and utterly without interruption at any point. Augustine lays out a three-fold distinction as a hermeneutical key to Pelagius' entire theological outlook: the three-part framework includes human ability, will, and action. By ability he means the capacity or potential to perform good actions and to be righteous before God, whereas willing indicates the choice to do so, and action the actual performance of anything virtuous (*Grace of Christ* 4). Crucially, Pelagius views the ability to do good as something with which God has permanently endowed human beings: they always have this capacity (*Grace of Christ* 4). But for this reason, any given human choice or act does not depend on a further discrete dispensation of divine grace in order to follow its proper path. People do not need God's aid in absolute terms, though they may receive it and be assisted by it. If so, that assistance consists in teaching about the nature of the good or serves as an inspiring example of it, with Christ himself serving as the ultimate paradigm of righteousness (*Grace of Christ* 2.2). In addition, it is certainly the case that it is due to grace that one's sins are forgiven. God manifests his grace by putting teaching forward and by sending Christ to earth to serve as a model of rectitude: that differs, however, from grace being indispensable for the reception of such instruction or the emulation of the Lord's life. The latter is not necessary, on Pelagius's view.

Romans is important for Augustine's rebuttal. According to the epistle, grace is necessary at every point along the line, not just at isolated intervals in the process whereby humans act rightly. As Augustine says, "If the help of grace is lacking, the knowledge of the law can only bring about the transgression of the commandment. The apostle says, *For where there is no law, there is no transgression* (Rom 4:15) and *I would not have known desire if the law had not said, 'You shall not desire'* (Rom 7:7)" (*Grace of Christ* 8.9). Just awareness of the law is not enough; indeed, knowledge of the law, apart from the grace needed to fulfill its command, can incite disobedience that would not have occurred without awareness of this binding standard. What is needed in order to will and to do what God requires is a specific sort of divine agency. "Those who want truly to confess the grace of God, by which *the love of God is poured out in our hearts by the Holy Spirit who has been given to us* (Rom 5:5), should confess it so that they have no doubt that without it we can do nothing good pertaining to true piety and righteousness" (*Grace of Christ* 26.27). Apart from this transformative divine indwelling, obedience is impossible. In one of his sermons on Romans, Augustine provides his listeners with a vivid illustration of the respect in which God's grace is necessary for humans to do what they ought to do. It is not that one's dependence on God is limited such that one can get along without grace, while it is still helpful. Absent divine grace, good actions simply cannot occur. The Pelagian view is like imagining that a man in a boat can get where he wants to go simply by rowing, even if there is no wind to assist him (*Sermon* 156.12). He would get there more quickly if there were wind, but he can get to his destination unaided if he exerts himself enough to make up for the lack of an external boost. That is Augustine's point: if, on Pelagius' view, grace seems extrinsic to human conduct, then that action or choice is not being thought of as participating in God's grace for its goodness.

As will already be clear, Augustine wants to reorient Pelagius' theological thinking by supplementing it with a notion that will have significant implications: that human life at every point depends on something external to it that must be assimilated into oneself. In his treatise on the *Grace of Christ*, Augustine does not consistently use a fixed form of language to express both that human life is ecstatic, oriented toward something outside of itself, and that human beings must become utterly at one with that which is inalienably other. Yet he does stress both aspects of this assertion, and he often deploys biblical language to do so. Alluding to Paul's correspondence with the Corinthians, Augustine describes how teaching must both be understood, and be taken deep within oneself by means of God's grace. "If we are to call this grace 'teaching,' we should certainly mean by it the teaching which we believe God pours out with an ineffable sweetness in the depths and interior of the soul, not merely through those who externally plant and water, but also through himself who gives the increase secretly" (*Grace of Christ* 14). To deny the claim that any act of human virtue takes place in complete dependence on God is to deny, or at least to limit, what Russell calls dynamic participation. It should be evident, however, that backing off of a commitment to dynamic participation is simultaneously to back off of ontological participation, insofar as it depends on establishing a space in which something might exist on its own, or from itself. At least as Augustine portrays Pelagius' position, he holds that human beings were given by God a set of capabilities that do not subsequently depend on God for their continuing actuation. The root suggestion that Augustine is making here is that his view of the primacy of grace is, at least in part, a product of thinking through the implications of the view that human creatures can at no point break out of their dependence on God.

IV

This essay takes to task a couple of readings of Augustine that de-emphasize the place of participation in his exegesis of Romans. These focal queries exist against the broader background of contemporary questions about whether Augustine, as a crucial figure in the Western tradition, neglects participation. Contra Riches, it is not the case that Augustine pushes Paul in an overly forensic direction in his early interpretation of the epistle. He does preserve a sense that human beings either subject themselves to the power of the flesh and other evil forces, or they indwell and participate in the Spirit. If Hallonsten means to speak only about where the explicit language of *deificare* shows up, that is especially in Augustine's sermons and much less in his treatises on grace, then he has a point. But that should not mislead readers of Augustine into missing a related point, namely, that precisely what is missing from Pelagius' theology is a certain type of participation. The relevant sense here might be called a thoroughgoing dynamic participation, meaning that salvation is at every point dependent on divine action, though not in such a way as to exclude human involvement.

Bibliography

Augustine. *De Gratia Christi et de Peccato Originali Libri Duo.* Corpus Scriptorum Ecclesiasticorum Latinorum. Edited by C. F. Vrba and J. Zycha. Vindabonae, 1902.

———. *De Trinitate Libri XV (Libri I-XII).* Corpus Christianorum Series Latina. Edited by W. J. Mountain. Turnhout, 1968.

———. *In Iohannis Evangelium Tractatus CXXIV.* Corpus Christianorum Series Latina. Edited by D. R. Willems. Turnhout, 1954.

———. *Quaestionum in Heptateuchum Libri VII.* Corpus Christianorum Series Latina. Edited by J. Fraipont and D. De Bruyne; Turnhout, 1958.

———. *Sermones de Novo Testamento.* Corpus Christianorum Series Latina. Turnhout: Brepols, 1976.

Ayres, Lewis. *Augustine and the Trinity.* Cambridge: Cambridge University Press, 2010.

Babcock, William S. "Augustine's Interpretation of Romans (A.D. 394–396)." *Augustinian Studies* 10 (1979): 55–74.

Bonner, Gerald. "Augustine's Conception of Deification." *Journal of Theological Studies* 37 (1986): 369–86.

———. "Augustine's Doctrine of Man: Image of God and Sinner." Pages 495–514 in *God's Decree and Man's Destiny: Studies on the Thought of Augustine of Hippo.* London: Variorum Reprints, 1987.

———. "God, Christ and Man in the Thought of St Augustine." Pages 268–94 in *God's Decree and Man's Destiny: Studies on the Thought of Augustine of Hippo.* London: Variorum Reprints, 1987.

Burns, J. Patout. "The Interpretation of Romans in the Pelagian Controversey." *Augustinian Studies* 10 (1979): 43–54.

Cameron, Michael. *Christ Meets Me Everywhere: Augustine's Early Figurative Exegesis.* Oxford: Oxford University Press, 2012

Capánaga, Victorino. "La deificación en la soteriología Augustina." *Augustinus Magister* 2 (1954): 745–54.

Casiday, Augustine. "St Augustine on Deification: His Homily on Psalm 81." *Sobornost* 23 (2001): 23–44.

Chadwick, Henry. "Note sur la divinisation chez saint Augustin," *Revue des sciences religieuses* 76 (2002): 246–48.
Drewery, Ben. "Deification." Pages 33–62 in *Christian Spirituality: Essays in Honour of Gordon Rupp*. Edited by Peter Newman Brooks. London: SCM Press, 1975.
Fredriksen Landes, Paula. *Augustine on Romans: Propositions from the Epistle to the Romans, Unfinished Commentary on the Epistle to the Romans*. Chico: Scholars Press, 1982.
Gross, Jules. *La divinisation du chrétien d'après les Pères grecs: contribution historique à la doctrine de la grâce*. Paris: J. Gabalda et Cie, 1938.
Hallonsten, Gösta. "*Theosis* in Recent Research: A Renewal of Interest and a Need for Clarity." Pages 281–93 in *Partakers of the Divine Nature: The History and Development of Deification in the Christian Traditions*. Edited by Michael J. Christensen and Jeffery A. Wittung. Madison: Fairleigh Dickinson University Press, 2007.
Lossky, Vladimir. "Redemption and Deification." Pages 71–110 in *In the Image and Likeness of God*. Tuchahoe: St. Vladimir's Seminary Press, 1974.
Lot-Borodine, Myrrha. *La déification de l'homme, selon la doctrine des Pères grecs*. Paris: Cerf, 1970.
Louth, Andrew. "The Place of *Theosis* in Orthodox Theology." Pages 32–44 in *Partakers of the Divine Nature: The History and Development of Deification in the Christian Traditions*. Edited by Michael J. Christensen and Jeffery A. Wittung. Madison: Fairleigh Dickinson University Press, 2007.
Macaskill, Grant. *Union with Christ in the New Testament*. Oxford: Oxford University Press, 2014.
Mausbauch, Joseph. *Thomas von Aquin als Meister christlicher Sittenlehre unter Berücksichtigung seiner Willenslehre*. Munich: Theatiner Verlag, 1925.
Meconi, David Vincent. "St. Augustine's Early Theory of Participation." *Augustinian Studies* 27 (1996): 79–96.
———. *The One Christ: St. Augustine's Theology of Deification*. Washington: Catholic University of America Press, 2013.
Riches, John K. "Readings of Augustine on Paul: Their Impact on Critical Studies of Paul." Pages 171–98 in *Engaging Augustine on Romans: Self, Context, and Theology in Interpretation*. Edited by Daniel Patte and Eugene TeSelle. Harrisburg: Trinity Press International, 2002.
Russell, Norman. *The Doctrine of Deification in the Greek Patristic Tradition*. Oxford: Oxford University Press, 2004.
Sanders, E. P. *Paul and Palestinian Judaism: A Comparison of Patterns of Religion*. Philadelphia: Fortress, 1977.
Stendahl, Krister "The Apostle Paul and the Introspective Conscience of the West," *Harvard Theological Review* 56 (1963): 199–215.
Stoop, Jan A. A. A. *Die Deificatio Hominis in die Sermones en Epistulae van Augustinus*. Leiden: Drukkerij Luctor et Emergo, 1952.
Tanner, Kathryn. *Christ the Key*. Current Issues in Theology. Cambridge: Cambridge University Press, 2010.
TeSelle, Eugene. "Exploring the Inner Conflict: Augustine's Sermons on Romans 7 and 8." Pages 111–46 in *Engaging Augustine on Romans: Self, Context, and Theology in Interpretation*. Edited by Daniel Patte and Eugene TeSelle. Harrisburg: Trinity Press International, 2002.
Viller, M., Ferdinand Cavallera, and J. de Guibert. *Dictionnaire de spiritualitâe ascâetique et mystique, doctrine et histoire*. Paris: Beauchesne, 1937.

Westerholm, Stephen. *Perspectives Old and New on Paul: The "Lutheran" Paul and His Critics.* Grand Rapids: Eerdmans, 2003.

Williams, A. N. *The Ground of Union: Deification in Aquinas and Palamas.* Oxford: Oxford University Press, 1999.

Apocalyptic Union

Martin Luther's Account of Faith in Christ

STEPHEN CHESTER

A. Introduction

Much of the appeal of the history of exegesis lies in its capacity to help us to see interpretative issues from a different perspective. Through dialog with past interpreters we return to our own examination of the same texts enabled to configure the interpretative possibilities differently. Certainly this is true of Martin Luther's handling of the theme of union with Christ. For popular misconceptions notwithstanding, Schweitzer's famous dictum that the doctrine of righteousness by faith is "a subsidiary crater, which has formed within the rim of the main crater – the mystical doctrine of redemption through being-in-Christ,"[1] is not a reversal of Luther's priorities. Luther simply does not conform to the assumption of much twentieth and twenty-first century scholarship, powerfully shaped by Schweitzer's work, that union with Christ and justification by faith are to be understood in contrast with each other. Union with Christ is vitally important to Luther, but this does not imply that it matters more than justification by faith. To emphasize the significance of one is for Luther not thereby to decrease that of the other. Union with Christ is vital to Luther because of its integrative force, and can only itself be understood in relation to justification by faith and to apocalyptic themes in Paul's theology. Luther of course does not pursue a quest for Paul's theology in the manner of modern and postmodern interpreters, but his explanations of union with Christ push us less to ask which of the categories of Paul's thought are most important and more to ask how the different categories of Paul's thought are related. To write of union with Christ alone is to miss its significance.

Similarly, Luther simply does not fit the categories of E.P. Sanders' insistence that union with Christ is ultimately inexplicable: "We seem to lack

---

[1] Albert Schweitzer, *The Mysticism of Paul the Apostle* (trans. W. Montgomery; London: Adam & Charles Black, 1931), 225.

a category of 'reality' – real participation in Christ, real possession of the Spirit – which lies between naïve cosmological speculation and belief in magical transference on the one hand and a revised self-understanding on the other."[2] Luther is indeed conscious of the mystery of union with Christ and therefore of the limits of possible explanation: "faith is a sort of knowledge or darkness that nothing can see. Yet the Christ of whom faith takes hold sits in this darkness as God sat in the midst of darkness on Sinai and in the temple."[3] However, Luther's account of what Paul means by faith in which Christ is present cannot easily be characterized as either naïve and magical or as simply a revised self-understanding. It fits neither with the existential accounts of faith typical of Bultmann and other mid-twentieth century interpreters nor with Sanders' interpretative pessimism.[4] As Pauline scholarship moves beyond Sanders' counsel of despair and makes renewed attempts to explore the nature of union with Christ,[5] Luther has valuable resources to offer.

B. The Human Plight: Luther's Apocalyptic Anthropology

There is no way to understand the positive value of union with Christ for Luther if we do not first understand the human plight in contrast to which it stands. Union with Christ functions within an apocalyptic dualism which configures the gulf between those who are being saved and those who are perishing in absolute terms. To be a fallen human being is to be like "a sick man whose mortal illness is not only the loss of health of one of his members, but it is, in addition to the lack of health in all his members, the weakness of all of his senses and powers, culminating even in his disdain for those things which are healthful and in his desire for those things which

---

[2] E. P. Sanders, *Paul and Palestinian Judaism* (London: SCM, 1977), 522.

[3] *LW* 26:129–30 = *WA* 40:229, 15–18. References to Luther's texts are to the English translation Philadelphia Edition, *Luther's Works*, (ed. J. Pelikan and H.T. Lehmann; Philadelphia: Concordia, 1955–86) and to the Latin and German Weimar Edition, *D. Martin Luthers Werke: Kritische Gesamtausgabe* (Weimar: H. Böhlau, 1883–2009). References to *WA* DB are to the sub-section within the Weimar edition dealing with the German Bible (deutsche Bibel).

[4] "Faith is the acceptance of the kerygma not as mere cognizance of it and agreement with it but as that genuine obedience to it which includes a new understanding of one's self." Rudolf Bultmann, *Theology of the New Testament Vol. I* (New York: Charles Scribner's Sons, 1951), 324.

[5] See, for example, Constantine R. Campbell, *Paul and Union with Christ: An Exegetical and Theological Study* (Grand Rapids: Zondervan, 2012); Michael J. Gorman, *Inhabiting the Cruciform God: Kenosis, Justification, and Theosis in Paul's Narrative Soteriology* (Grand Rapids: Eerdmans, 2009); Grant Macaskill, *Union with Christ in the New Testament* (Oxford: Oxford University Press, 2013).

make him sick."[6] It is this sense of original sin as completely rampant misdirected desire that gives rise to Luther's new and famous description of sin as "the person turned in upon the self" (*homo incurvatus in se*).[7] The fallen human being therefore has no resources to apply to salvation but is in bondage to the self, in love with sin, and incapable of loving God.

Having reached this view, it is scarcely surprising that Luther rejected the nominalist soteriology in which he had been schooled as a young theologian. For while holding that God could have chosen to justify human beings in any number of ways, the nominalist account argues that God actually does so in response to humble self-judgment. As part of a covenant (*pactum*) with humanity, God graciously grants acts of repentance an ascribed value much greater than their inherent worth. If human beings perform the acts of repentance that are within their power, with each individual doing *quod in se est* ("what lies within him"), God will justify despite the feeble nature of such repentance. Luther's difficulty is that, given his view of sin, he simply does not believe that even the limited required level of repentance is possible for anyone. The view that human beings can offer such repentance is for Luther at odds with the enslavement to sin of which Paul speaks. Repentance is not the gateway to union with Christ but is instead only possible if a person is in Christ. If the nominalist position were accurately to describe how God justifies it would be nothing other than an announcement of universal damnation.[8]

Other perspectives within medieval Pauline interpretation did not share the nominalist optimism about the capacity of fallen human beings to repent. For example, Thomas Aquinas is clear that the power to do so is a divine gift. The idea that God will justify the person who does what lies within that individual means simply "that God will not deny grace to those who do their best, in so far as they are moved by God to do this."[9] Yet whatever the position adopted on this question of initial justification, Lu-

---

[6] *LW* 25:300 = *WA* 56:313, 6–10.

[7] *LW* 25:345 = *WA* 56:356, 5–6. See also *LW* 25:291 = *WA* 56:304, 25–29.

[8] The young Luther initially connected the requirement that an individual do *quod in se est* with the humility of faith. Yet while this emphasis can be seen in the *Lectures on Romans* (1515–16), it has been left behind by 1519–20. Luther insists on divine unilateralism, but the nominalist theology of justification defines covenant as a bilateral agreement. See Alister E. McGrath, *Luther's Theology of the Cross* (2d edition; Oxford: Wiley-Blackwell, 2011), 127–200.

[9] Alister E. McGrath, *Iustitia Dei: A History of the Christian Doctrine of Justification* (2d ed.; Cambridge: Cambridge University Press, 1998), 86. However, Aquinas' position was not well understood in the early sixteenth century. Whether as a result of misreading of Aquinas' *Summa*, or as a result of reliance on his earlier commentary on Peter Lombard's *Sentences* where he did countenance such a view, Aquinas was widely understood to affirm that a sinner can merit initial justification and Luther may have shared this misconception.

ther's apocalyptic dualism ultimately contradicts the entire medieval paradigm for interpreting Paul. For medieval soteriology characteristically understands the Christian life as a pathway for the meritorious transformation of each individual. Having received grace from God, the human being is obliged to co-operate in a process of renewal. Christ in his righteousness enters into individuals and, with their co-operation, produces a righteousness that is inherent to them such that they can eventually stand before God on the basis of their own merits.[10] Such merits can only ever be gained when rooted in the grace of God (i.e. medieval soteriology is not pelagian), but they are truly a person's own. It is within this co-operative framework of the pilgrim's progress towards righteousness that union with Christ is located.

In contrast, Luther knows nothing of such gradual transformation through co-operation. He rejects not only the view that repentance is an efficient cause of justification but also the view that subsequent works are justifying. All works without exception, before or after baptism, are excluded. In his *Commentary on Galatians* (1531/1535),[11] Luther comments on Paul's assertion that having been crucified with Christ he no longer lives but Christ lives in him (Gal 2:19–20). Luther identifies union with Christ not with the gradual healing of the self but with its death. Far from being gradually changed into the likeness of Christ through co-operation with infused grace, the Christian must leave behind his or her own life for that of Christ:

Christian righteousness is, namely, that righteousness by which Christ lives in us, not the righteousness that is in our own person. Therefore when it is necessary to discuss Christian righteousness, the person must be completely rejected. For if I pay attention to the person or speak of the person, then, whether intentionally or unintentionally on my part, the person becomes a doer of works who is subject to the Law. But here Christ and my conscience must become one body, so that nothing remains in my sight but Christ, crucified and risen ...By paying attention to myself ...I lose sight of Christ, who alone is my righteousness and life.[12]

Luther rams the point home again, cautioning that "when it comes to justification, therefore, if you divide Christ's person from your own, you are in

---

[10] H. A. Oberman, "Iustitia Christi and Iustitia Dei: Luther and the Scholastic Doctrines of Justification," *HTR* 59.1 (1966): 1–26 (19): "According to this tradition the 'iustitia Christi' is granted in justification to the sinner as gratia or caritas. But the 'iustitia Dei' is not granted together with or attached to the 'iustitia Christi' ...The 'iustitia Dei' is the standard according to which the degree of appropriation and the effects of the 'iustitia Christi' are measured and will be measured in the Last Judgment."

[11] Many of Luther's "commentaries" have their origins in lecture series delivered at Wittenberg which were later published. The first date given is that of the lecture series, the second date that of publication.

[12] *LW* 26:166 = *WA* 40:282, 17–28.

the Law; you remain in it and live in yourself, which means that you are dead in the sight of God and damned by the law."[13] For Paul to continue to live as Paul would be death for him, but to die and for Christ to live in him is life. The old person and the new creation, the self under sin and the individual in Christ are opposite possibilities. To think at all of meritorious human co-operation in reaching the goal of righteousness is a delusion. Union with Christ cannot be reduced to an aspect of this transition, even if it is the aspect on which the whole transition depends and which makes possible human merit. Rather for Luther the person of Christ encompasses the whole of salvation. For this reason, to be united with Christ is simply to be identified with salvation just as justification by faith in Christ is simply to be identified with salvation. One cannot in Luther's view be partially united with Christ or partially righteous.

Yet, of course, Luther knows well that believers continue to sin. In his *Lectures on Romans* (1515–16), when commenting on Rom 7:25 ("with my mind I am a slave to the law of God, but with my flesh I am a slave to the law of sin"), Luther argues that Paul does not divide the self into two compartments. Instead he says that there are two different servitudes which are both characteristic of the self: "Note that one and the same man at the same time serves the law of God and the law of sin, at the same time is righteous and sins! For he does not say: 'My mind serves the law of God,' nor does he say: 'My flesh serves the law of sin,' but: 'I, the whole man, the same person, I serve a twofold servitude.'"[14] In Luther's view, the flesh is not part of a person but the entire person as he or she stands in opposition to God through sin. He thus eliminates the possibility of interpreting Paul's term "the flesh" as part of a hierarchical dichotomy between body and soul in which the unruly desires of the body refuse to give proper submission to the soul. In his first *Commentary on Galatians* (1516–17/1519), Paul's diverse list of the works of the flesh at 5:19–21 prompts Luther to comment that "flesh is understood not only in the sense of lustful desires but as absolutely everything that is contrary to the spirit of grace ... by flesh the whole man is meant ... the inward and the outward man, or the new man and the old, are not distinguished according to the difference between soul and body but according to their dispositions."[15]

---

[13] *LW* 26:168 = *WA* 40:285, 15–17.

[14] *LW* 25:336 = *WA* 56:347, 2–6. The NRSV rather obscures Luther's point by using the English personal pronoun 'I' twice, once in respect to the mind and once in respect to the flesh. Paul's Greek uses the pronoun once emphatically at the outset (αὐτός ἐγὼ, "I myself") before describing the two aspects of the self's servitude. Luther interprets all of Romans 7 as a discussion of the Christian life.

[15] *LW* 27:367 = *WA* 2:588, 26–32.

This insistence that "the flesh" refers to the whole person has profound consequences for understanding the Christian life. Unsurprisingly, if in the flesh sin infects the whole person, and if the flesh is not necessarily typified by sexual or other bodily desires, then there cannot be a 'higher' religious life which corresponds to the higher parts or faculties of a person and which is therefore necessarily effective in battling sin. To restrain bodily desires through ascetic discipline cannot be identified with mastery over the flesh, for the flesh refers to the whole person and not merely to bodily desires. Luther's exegesis thus undercuts a crucial aspect of the rationale of monasticism. He does so precisely because he construes Paul's anthropology in apocalyptic terms. The believer is not gradually becoming righteous by co-operating with grace in order to subdue desire. Rather, the believer faces constant strife between two modes of existence occupying the same body. When the believer lives out of union with Christ (the Christ-life not the Paul-life), the Christian is then truly and wholly righteous because Christ is truly and wholly righteous. But when faith falters, and the Christian lives from the self (the Paul-life not the Christ-life), the Christian is then truly and wholly a sinner. Whereas the person apart from Christ, whatever he or she perceives to be the case, in fact has only the possibility of enslavement to sin; the believer also has the possibility of obedience to Christ. As the notion of a twofold competing servitude makes clear, the Christian daily dwells victoriously in Christ and under his lordship or falls back defeated into captivity to sin. The Christian lives on an apocalyptic battlefield.

C. Christ Present in Faith: Justification and Union with Christ

It is within this apocalyptic dualism of Christian existence that Luther's famous assertion that the believer is "simultaneously justified and a sinner" (*simul iustus et peccator*) is to be understood. Contrary to popular misinterpretation, this slogan is not a shorthand summary of an exclusively forensic account of justification that grants to the believer a merely fictional righteousness. On this misconceived but widespread account of Luther's views, God acquits the believer because cloaked in Christ's righteousness he or she appears in God's sight as a righteous person even while remaining largely in fact a sinner. While justification brings eternal security, in this life the believer is at best stalled early in a process of transformation that will never move more than marginally forwards. On occasion Luther can express himself in ways that, viewed in isolation, could be taken to support this caricature. When commenting on Gal 3:6, "Abraham believed God and it was reckoned to him as righteousness," Luther suggests that its application to the believer is that God reckons "imperfect faith as perfect righteousness for the sake of Christ."[16] This works in the following way:

> Christ protects me under the shadow of His wings and spreads over me the wide heaven of the forgiveness of sins, under which I live in safety. This prevents God from seeing the sins that still cling to my flesh. My flesh distrusts God, is angry with Him, does not rejoice in Him etc. But God overlooks these sins, and in His sight they are as though they were not sins. This is accomplished by imputation on account of the faith by which I begin to take hold of Christ; and on His account God reckons imperfect righteousness as perfect righteousness and sin as not sin, even though it really is sin.[17]

To understand Luther's intentions fully, however, requires careful attention to what he means by "the faith by which I begin to take hold of Christ." It is in his account of faith that Luther's integration of union with Christ and justification by faith can be seen most clearly. For Luther presents a rich understanding of faith that itself has several dimensions. Each time Paul uses this one word, it carries multiple connotations for Luther. Indeed, if one reads through the later *Commentary on Galatians* (1531/1535) alongside the earlier *Commentary on Galatians* (1516–17/1519), it is perhaps the transformation in his concept of faith that forms the most significant development in Luther's understanding of Galatians. The nature of faith receives little reflection in the earlier commentary, but by 1535 it is a major topic.

When commenting on Paul's use of Gen 15:6 in Gal 3:6 and the words "Abraham believed God," Luther understands faith as trust in God's promises. Abraham believed against reason that God would keep his promise that the aged Sarah would have a son. Similarly, the Christian is called upon to embrace "the foolishness of the cross" (1 Cor 1:18–25), and so "faith slaughters reason and kills the beast that the whole world and all the creatures cannot kill."[18] However, this is not all. In thus believing God's promises, faith acknowledges God for who He is. It regards him as "truthful, wise, righteous, merciful, and almighty …as the author and donor of every good."[19] God has been given his place by his creatures, his glory affirmed, and so "faith justifies because it renders to God what is due him; whoever does this is righteous."[20] Further, by this giving to God of his glory, faith "consummates the deity; and, if I may put it this way, it is the creator of the deity, not in the substance of God but in us."[21] Luther goes so far as to

---

[16] *LW* 26:231 = *WA* 40:366, 29–30.
[17] *LW* 26:231–2 = *WA* 40:367, 13–21.
[18] *LW* 26:228 = *WA* 40:362, 15–16.
[19] *LW* 26:227 = *WA* 40:360, 22–23.
[20] *LW* 26:227 = *WA* 40:361, 12–13.
[21] *LW* 26:227 = *WA* 40:360, 24–25.

compare faith, in its relationship with works, to the divinity of Christ in relation to his humanity:

> Let faith always be the divinity of works, diffused throughout the works in the same way that the divinity is throughout the humanity of Christ. Anyone who touches the heat in the heated iron touches the iron; and whoever has touched the skin of Christ has actually touched God. Therefore faith is the 'do-all' (*fac totum*) in works, if I may use this expression. Thus Abraham is called faithful because faith is diffused throughout all of Abraham. When I look at Abraham doing works, therefore, I see nothing of the physical Abraham or of the Abraham who does works, but only Abraham the believer.[22]

However, Luther does not only discern the relationship between faith and the person of Christ as analogical. In his previous comments on Gal 2:15–16, where Paul asserts that justification is by faith in Christ and not by works of the law, Luther emphasizes that Christ himself is present in faith. "Faith justifies because it takes hold of and possesses this treasure, the present Christ …the Christ who is grasped by faith and who lives in the heart is the true Christian righteousness."[23] In an important passage, Luther uses another image:

> Here it is to be noted that these three things are joined together: faith, Christ, and acceptance or imputation. Faith takes hold of Christ and has him present, enclosing him as the ring encloses the gem. And whoever is found having this faith in the Christ who is grasped in the heart, him God accounts as righteous.[24]

Thus, faith takes hold of Christ and has him present, and because the righteous one is present in faith, imputation is possible. When Luther says, "Christian righteousness consists in two things, namely, faith in the heart and the imputation of God,"[25] it is important to recognize that faith itself is to be identified with union with Christ. Luther makes clear, again in his comments on Gal 3:6, that it is faith's capacity to grasp hold of Christ that is vital to its justifying nature: "to take hold of the Son and to believe in him with the heart as the gift of God causes God to reckon that faith, however imperfect it may be, as perfect righteousness."[26] Christ himself is the gift received by the believer. It is therefore clear that imputation of Christ's righteousness to the believer is not defined over and against, or even in indifference to, union with Christ. Rather, imputation itself in-

---

[22] *LW* 26:266 = *WA* 40:417, 15–21.

[23] *LW* 26:130 = *WA* 40:229, 22–29.

[24] *LW* 26:132 = *WA* 40:233, 16–19. I. D. K. Siggins, *Martin Luther's Doctrine of Christ* (New Haven, Conn.: Yale University Press, 1970), 147 comments, "Luther loves to illustrate the character of faith by the figure of an empty container. Faith is merely a husk, but Christ is the kernel. It is a purse or coffer for the eternal treasure, an empty vessel, a poor little monstrance or pyx for gems of infinite worth."

[25] *LW* 26:229 = *WA* 40:364, 11–12.

[26] *LW* 26:234 = *WA* 40:371, 18–21.

volves union with Christ. God imputes because the Christian believes, but the faith of the Christian is itself a divine gift in which Christ is present.[27]

Further, it is this presence of Christ in the faith of the believer that creates the possibility of living the life of Christ. The Christian is only able to engage in the apocalyptic struggle between opposing modes of existence and live as righteous because his or her life has been invaded by Christ, and the self has been crucified with Christ, in order that there might be a new creation. Obedience results from justification and not vice versa. Works "should be done as fruits of righteousness, not in order to bring righteousness into being. Having been made righteous, we must do them; but it is not the other way around: that when we are unrighteous, we become righteous by doing them. The tree produces fruit; the fruit does not produce the tree."[28] To describe the believer as simultaneously justified and a sinner is not for Luther a pessimistic estimation of the possibilities of the Christian life but instead a battle cry. It summons those liberated from the previous certainty of defeat to the struggle to live in union with Christ and therefore within Christ's victory over sin, death, and the devil.

D. Union with Christ: Receiving Christ's Righteousness

It is, of course, axiomatic for Luther that this victory is Christ's victory and that the believer receives it and lives into it but contributes to it nothing from his or her own resources and works. In union with Christ the believer is not so much empowered to live another life but rather inserted into the life of a victorious other. Set free from all and any reliance on a self that is doomed to defeat, the Christian seeks not to co-operate with divine grace in order to come to merit justification but rather relies solely on the righteousness of Christ granted to those united with him by faith. This reliance on Christ alone is partly a matter of freedom from anxiety about salvation. The Christian need not fear that his or her continuing sins result in a loss of grace that calls justification into question. Such sins are blotted out by the righteousness of Christ. Yet Luther's assertion of reliance on Christ alone does not simply serve the cause of personal serenity. For anyone who receives Christ's righteousness can join battle against the flesh with gusto, ultimate victory secure.[29] There is not only assurance of salva-

---

[27] Indeed, Luther is explicit that Christ is more than the object of faith. See *LW* 26:129 = *WA* 40:228, 31–229, 15: "It takes hold of Christ in such a way that Christ is the object of faith, or rather not the object but, so to speak, the One who is present in faith itself."

[28] *LW* 26:169 = *WA* 40:287, 20–23.

[29] There is thus a temporal aspect to *simul iustus et peccator*. On the one hand sin will cling to the flesh of the Christian throughout earthly life, the conflict between the flesh

tion but also assurance that the relationship between being justified and a sinner is asymmetrical: "righteousness is supreme and sin is a servant."[30] For Luther, confident engagement in the struggle of the Christian life stems from his certainty that the Christ grasped hold of by faith is for us righteousness from God and that to be united with Christ by faith is therefore to receive this infinite righteousness. It is thus clear that when Luther speaks of imputation he is not speaking of a righteousness that is transferred from Christ to the believer apart from Christ's person, but instead of a righteousness that is received by the believer because in being united with Christ the believer is joined with one who personifies righteousness.

It is therefore a serious misunderstanding to think that Luther's rejection of works as in any sense a contributory cause of justification stands in contrast to a bare declaration of acquittal. Rather, it stands in contrast to his particular account of union with Christ. Luther rejects concepts of justification based in part on the merits of what a person becomes because he perceives any element of self-reliance, even in cooperation with grace, as standing in contrast to exclusive reliance on sharing in the person and deeds of Christ. Human beings need to live not a new, improved version of their existing life but instead as new creations to live the life of Christ. The justification of the individual is therefore an apocalyptic event that participates in and relies upon God's larger apocalyptic intervention in Christ for the redemption of the world. God's act of justification for the individual Christian is rooted in God's wider action in the world. It depends on incarnation,[31] and flows from the life, death and resurrection of Jesus. This can be seen particularly clearly in Luther's frequent assertions that between Christ and the believer there is a "joyous exchange" in which, having taken upon himself the sins of the world, Christ gives to the believer his righteousness.[32] What is ours becomes his, while what is his becomes ours. In

---

and the Spirit ceasing only with death. On the other, God's act of justification determines the whole of existence such that the Christian lives now from the future on the basis of promise and hope. See Daphne Hampson, *Christian Contradictions: The Structures of Lutheran and Catholic Thought* (Cambridge: Cambridge University Press, 2001), 27 and Eberhard Jüngel, *Justification: The Heart of the Christian Faith* (Edinburgh: T&T Clark, 2001), 218–19.

[30] *LW* 27:74 = *WA* 40.2:93, 21.

[31] For a helpful general discussion of this relationship, see G. Yule, "Luther's Understanding of Justification by Grace Alone in Terms of Catholic Christology," G. Yule (ed.), *Luther: Theologian for Catholics and Protestants* (Edinburgh: T&T Clark, 1985), 87–112.

[32] The understanding that justification is effected through joyous exchange is vital to a proper appreciation of the exegetical basis of imputation. Luther reads all texts that contain the idea of exchange (e.g. Rom 8:3, Gal 3:13, Phil 2:5–11) as supporting the view that Christ's righteousness is given to believers. Taking the idea from the Fathers, especially Athanasius and Augustine, Luther concentrates on righteousness as it provides the

the *Commentary on Galatians* (1531/1535), this is expressed particularly clearly in Luther's lengthy comments on Gal 3:13, "Christ redeemed us from the curse of the law by becoming a curse for us." Luther rages against those, especially Jerome, who are nervous at the apparent impiety of the idea that Christ was cursed by God. Instead, Luther thinks it absolutely necessary to emphasize that, although innocent in his own person, Christ became "the greatest thief, murderer, adulterer, robber, desecrator, blasphemer etc., there has ever been anywhere in the world."[33] If he is not, then his righteousness cannot become the Christian's righteousness, and salvation is lost. As it is, having taken on himself the sins of the world, Christ is able to give to the believer his righteousness. "By this fortunate exchange with us He took upon Himself our sinful person and granted us His innocent and victorious Person."[34]

Luther links this exchange with Christ's emptying of himself (Phil 2:7), a text that he also used to express the same idea years previously in an important sermon entitled *Two Kinds of Righteousness* (preached late 1518 / early 1519). Because of Christ's willingness to empty himself by taking upon himself all sins, the believer "can with confidence boast in Christ and say: 'Mine are Christ's living, doing and speaking, his suffering and dying, mine as much as if I had lived, done, spoken, suffered and died as he did.'"[35] It is not merely that Christ accomplishes something on the believer's behalf but rather that the believer shares in what Christ does. Luther inserts "the believer directly into the history of Christ."[36] We can see once again that the exchange is not an exchange of detachable qualities between those who have sin as a component of their identities and someone who has righteousness as a component of his identity. Rather it is an exchange of persons between those whose existence is currently constituted by enslavement to sin and the one who personifies righteousness. It is the same Christ, the incarnate son of God, human and divine, who fought and conquered sin and death in his person, who exchanges his righteousness with the believer's sinfulness, who is present in the believer's faith, and whose life the believer now lives.

---

answer to sin and is prominent in Paul's vocabulary. However, he does also include other properties of Christ in the exchange.

[33] *LW* 26:277 = *WA* 40:433, 27–8. Unsurprisingly, Luther uses Gal 3:3 and 2 Cor 5:21 to expound the idea of joyous exchange in his *Lectures on Deuteronomy* (1523–24/1525) when commenting on 27:26. See *LW* 9:215–16 = *WA* 14:699, 18–700, 18.

[34] *LW* 26:284 = *WA* 40:443, 23–24.

[35] *LW* 31:297 = *WA* 2:145, 16–18.

[36] Marc Lienhard, *Luther: Witness to Jesus Christ: Stages and Themes of the Reformer's Christology* (Minneapolis: Augsburg, 1982), 273 referring to K. Bornkamm, *Luthers Auslegungen des Galaterbriefs von 1519 bis 1531 – Ein Vergleich* (Berlin: de Gruyter, 1963), 166–67.

E. Union with Christ: Living an Alien Life

As we have already seen, a similar pattern of thought is prompted by Paul's statement that he has been crucified with Christ and that he no longer lives but Christ in him (Gal 2:19–20). Luther emphasizes that the righteousness received by the believer is not the believer's own but is instead that of Christ. It remains an alien righteousness even in relation to the justified person. Yet that it remains alien does not result in it being a fictional righteousness because, united with Christ, the believer lives an alien life:

> I am not living as Paul now, for Paul is dead. Who then is living? 'The Christian.' Paul, living in himself, is utterly dead through the Law but living in Christ, or rather with Christ living in him, he lives an alien life. Christ is speaking, acting, and performing all actions in him; these belong not to the Paul-life, but to the Christ-life ... 'By my own life I am not living, for if I were, the Law would have dominion over me and hold me captive. To keep it from holding me, I am dead to it by another Law. And this death acquires an alien life for me, namely, the life of Christ, which is not inborn in me but is granted to me in faith through Christ.'[37]

The Christian has Christ's righteousness through union with him, but that union does not work on the basis of a transformation of the self of the Christian. It works rather on the basis of the leaving behind and abandonment of that self. As one contemporary Lutheran theologian expresses it, "faith as self-forgetfulness is the most intensive form of certainty of God."[38]

To speak of union with Christ understood in this way as involving a changed or renewed life is therefore potentially misleading. It is simply not radical enough to capture Luther's sense that union with Christ involves the re-creation of the person. If we are to speak of a restoration or healing of the self in this regard, then it can only be on the basis that the Christian has to come out of him- or herself in order to come to him- or herself. In this sense that faith "places us outside ourselves,"[39] Luther is repeating an idea that had long been central to his theology, for in 1520, in his famous tract *The Freedom of the Christian*, Luther had written that, "a Christian lives not in himself, but in Christ and his neighbor. Otherwise he is not a Christian."[40] This soteriological necessity to live an alien life means that

---

[37] *LW* 26:170 = *WA* 40:287, 30–288, 2.

[38] E. Jüngel, *Justification*, 243.

[39] See *LW* 26:387 = *WA* 40:589, 25–8: "This is the reason why our theology is so certain: it snatches us away from ourselves and places us outside ourselves, so that we do not depend on our own strength, conscience, experience, person, or works but depend on that which is outside ourselves, that is, on the promise and truth of God, which cannot deceive." Luther is here commenting on the cry "Abba, Father" in Gal 4:6.

[40] *LW* 31:371 = *WA* 7:69, 12–13.

There is no linear progress from being a sinner to being justified. It is not that that which is given in creation is transformed through grace. It is only through a discontinuity, through repentance and failure, that in response to the good news of the gospel the human being can come to gain a sense of himself through trusting not in himself but in God.[41]

Luther knows well that this radical discontinuity between a person's own life and his or her life in Christ is open to an obvious objection. To the charge that Paul still appears as Paul with no apparent change, Luther affirms that to the casual, surface level observer Paul still indeed appears as Paul. He uses physical things such as food and clothing just like any other human being. However, this is only "a mask of life,"[42] for although Paul lives in the flesh, it is not on the basis of his own self. Before his conversion, Paul spoke blasphemy, but after it words of faith. Before, Paul spoke, but after, Christ speaks. The voice and tongue were the same in each case, but the words came from an entirely different source. Luther himself cannot teach, preach, write, pray or give thanks except by using the physical instruments of the flesh, but "these activities do not come from the flesh and do not originate there; they are given and revealed divinely from heaven."[43] This alien and spiritual life cannot be perceived by the unspiritual person, who does not recognize its true source. The unspiritual person remains ignorant of the fact that, "This life is not the life of the flesh, although it is a life in the flesh; but it is the life of Christ, the Son of God, whom the Christian possesses by faith."[44]

F. Union with Christ: Faith and Good Works

Perhaps unsurprisingly, if the believer lives the alien life of Christ, then good works inevitably follow. Context is everything here. Whereas Luther never tires of asserting that justification is not by works of the law and that human works cannot merit anything before God, he also places considera-

---

[41] Hampson, *Christian Contradictions*, 101. For Luther, salvation does reinstate what creation was intended to be so that we relate to God in the manner first intended (hence my use of the term re-creation above). The radical discontinuity stems from the fact that through sin what was intended for creation was so grievously and entirely lost (35).

[42] *LW* 26:170 = *WA* 40:288, 25.

[43] *LW* 26:171 = *WA* 40:289, 25–27.

[44] *LW* 26:172 = *WA* 40:290, 30–31. Oberman, "Iustitia Christi and Iustitia Dei," 21–22, 25–26 finds significant the vocabulary used here by Luther. Justifying righteousness is different understood as *possessio* than as *proprietas*. The former term denotes legal occupancy and enjoyment of something, the latter ownership proper. As it is *possessio*, "the righteousness granted is not one's property but one's possession." Hampson, *Christian Contradictions*, 24 draws an analogy with a library book. Once it is borrowed from the library I have it legitimately in my possession, but I am not its owner.

ble emphasis on the works that flow from justifying faith in which Christ is present. Both these emphases can be seen together in Luther's famous introduction to the argument of the epistle with which the *Commentary on Galatians* (1531/1535) begins. This Luther organizes around the distinction between active and passive righteousness, in which righteousness by faith is not the active righteousness that strives to do what lies within (*quod in se est*) but instead passive righteousness "which we do not perform but receive, which we do not have but accept."[45] The active righteousness which does not justify, which Luther can also term civic or political righteousness, comprises every other kind of righteousness, including the Mosaic Law. It is to be highly valued in its rightful sphere but appalling consequences follow from any confusion between the two kinds of righteousness. In 1532, when commenting on Ps 51:16, a verse that expresses Yahweh's refusal to delight in animal sacrifices, Luther asserts that

Political righteousness is a very delightful and good thing for its purpose, that there might be peace and mutual association among men. But if you want to be righteous before God because you are a good citizen, a chaste spouse, or an honest merchant, you make a most delightful thing into an abomination which God cannot stand.[46]

This is another apocalyptic dualism, with political or active righteousness a possibility for fallen human beings but passive righteousness possible only through faith in Christ. Nevertheless, this dualism too often is interpreted exclusively in relation to the activity or passivity involved with the conscience of the believer as its sole arena. Luther's focus is not on the contrast between activity or passivity *per se* as if to be active is a human disposition angering to God and to be passive a human disposition that secures God's favor.[47] Rather, Luther also applies the dualism to the radical discontinuity between the believer's own life and life in Christ: "Christian righteousness applies to the new man, the righteousness of the Law applies to the old man, who is born of flesh and blood."[48] He is also explicit that "We set forth two worlds, as it were, one of them heavenly and the other earthly. Into these we place these two kinds of righteousness, which are distinct and separated from each other."[49] That righteousness by faith ex-

---

[45] *LW* 26:6 = *WA* 40:43, 15–16.

[46] *LW* 12:400 = *WA* 40.2:455, 39–456, 1. On political or civic righteousness, see also *LW* 12:363–4 = *WA* 40.2:402, 26–404, 24; *LW* 17:63 = *WA* 31.2:309, 31–310, 4; *LW* 25:86 = *WA* 56:96, 12–13; *LW* 25:410–11 = *WA* 56:418, 22–419, 18.

[47] That the active nature of the concept of faith appears throughout the commentary, and especially in the discussion of Gal 5:6, shows that in using the term "passive righteousness" Luther is pointing to the nature of grace as *favor* and to the nature of true righteousness as sheer gift, not to the gift of faith as itself essentially passive.

[48] *LW* 26:7 = *WA* 40:45, 27–28.

[49] *LW* 26:8 = *WA* 40:46, 19–21.

ists in the context of these sharp contrasts between active and passive, old and new, earthly and heavenly means that when the believer is united with Christ by faith he or she is empowered actively to live an alien life for the sake of the world: "When I have this righteousness within me, I descend from heaven like the rain that makes the earth fertile. That is, I come forth into another kingdom, and I perform good works whenever the opportunity arises."[50] As Luther will express the same idea in his *Preface to the New Testament (1522)*:

> Faith, however, is a divine work in us which changes us and makes us to be born anew of God ... It kills the Old Adam, makes us entirely different people in heart, spirit, mind, and all our powers, and brings the Holy Spirit with it. Oh, faith is a living, busy, active, mighty thing, so that it is impossible for it not to be constantly doing what is good. Likewise, faith does not ask if good works are to be done, but before one can ask, faith has already done them and is constantly active.[51]

It is therefore apparent that while righteousness is passive (nothing a human being can do will kill the Old Adam, but only an act of God), justifying faith in which Christ is present is inherently active (it is the act of God that makes us entirely different people). Luther makes it clear that, aside from this righteousness of faith he does not accord any general valuation to working or not working in his comment that, "Whatever there is in us besides Him (Christ) – whether it be intellect or will, activity or passivity etc. – is flesh not Spirit."[52] What matters as regards human conduct is not any particular quality as a disposition but rather whether the person is united with Christ. Then good works will inevitably result. Luther thus will celebrate good works but only when they are placed in their proper apocalyptic context of Christian righteousness as new creation. There is a necessary righteousness of works, but:

> It is necessary, however, not by a legal necessity, or one of compulsion, but by a gratuitous necessity, or one of consequence, or an unalterable condition. As the sun shines by necessity, if it is a sun, and yet does not shine by demand, but by its nature and its unalterable will, so to speak, because it was created for the purpose that it should shine so a person created righteous performs new works by an unalterable necessity, not by legal compulsion. For to the righteous no law is given. Further, we are created, says Paul, unto good works... it is impossible to be a believer and not a doer.[53]

---

[50] *LW* 26:11 = *WA* 40:51, 21–23.

[51] *LW* 35:370 = *WA* DB 7:11, 7–12. The Preface was originally written in 1522, but the version presented in *LW* 35 is that found in the Bible of 1546.

[52] *LW* 27:25 = *WA* 40.2:30, 20–21.

[53] Anonymous, "Cordatus' Controversy with Melanchthon," *Theological Quarterly* 11/4 (1907), 193–207 (199) = *Philippi Melanchthonis Epistolae, Iudicia, Consilia, Testimonia Aliorumque ad eum Epistolae quae in Corpore Reformatorum Desiderantur* (ed. H. E. Bindseil; Halle: Gustav Schwetske, 1874), 344–48 (346). This quotation comes from a 1536 dialog between Luther and Melanchthon concerning justification and good

G. Union with Christ: Faith and Love

That righteousness by faith is for Luther an apocalyptic concept is vital to understanding the way in which he expresses the relationship between faith and love. The love of God and neighbor which pleases heaven is not a possibility for human beings apart from faith in Christ. The good works which express such love flow from justifying faith and not vice versa. Even when Luther uses the imagery of marriage to explain justification, he is clear that there is only love before marriage on the divine side of the relationship. For the believer, love results from being united with Christ. He comments on Gal 2:16 that the faith which unites a person with Christ the savior:

> justifies without love and before love... By faith we are in Him, and He is in us (John 6:56). The Bridegroom, Christ, must be alone with his bride in His private chamber, and all the family and household must be shunted away. But later on, when the Bridegroom opens the door and comes out, then let the servants return to take care of them and serve them food and drink. Then let works and love begin.[54]

Works and love are not the consummation of the believer's union with Christ but are instead a new possibility opened up only because in justifying faith that consummation has taken place.[55]

It is for this reason that Luther utterly rejects the widespread medieval interpretation of Paul's statement in Gal 5:6 that "in Christ Jesus neither circumcision nor uncircumcision counts for anything; the only thing that counts is faith working through love." Confronted by the need to coordinate the statements of the book of James that faith without works is dead (2:17) and that even the demons believe and tremble (2:19) with Paul's statements here in Gal 5:6, medieval interpreters do not refuse to categorize solely factual knowledge of God as faith or term such knowledge dead faith. Instead, they develop a distinction between two different kinds of faith: formed and unformed. From Peter Lombard in the twelfth century

---

works. For further commentary on the dialog see Mark Seifrid, "Luther, Melanchthon, and Paul on the Question of Imputation," in *Justification: What's at Stake in the Current Debates?* (ed. M. Husbands and D. Treier; Downers Grove: InterVarsity Press, 2004), 137–52.

[54] *LW* 26:137–8 = *WA* 40:240, 16–241, 16.

[55] It is precisely this apocalyptic context of Luther's use of marital imagery for justification, with its insistence that the believer's love flows from union with Christ rather than constituting part of its basis, that goes unrecognized by Michael Waldstein, "The Trinitarian, Spousal, and Ecclesial Logic of Justification," in *Reading Romans with St. Thomas Aquinas* (ed. Matthew Levering and Michael Dauphinais; Washington DC: Catholic University of America Press, 2012), 274–87. Waldstein sees Luther's use of marital imagery for justification as inconsistent with his rejection of faith formed by love, arguing that such marital imagery ought to imply a role for love in justification: "Does not the primary meaning of spousal love lie precisely in taking hold of the beloved?" (284).

onwards, unformed faith is understood as a cognitive acceptance of the facts of the gospel which does not of itself justify. It is "a 'quality of mind' (*qualitas mentis*) but one that remains 'unformed' because it lacks the shaping effect of love or charity."[56] This unformed faith soon becomes identified with what is received in the sacrament of baptism and the transition to a formed faith is identified with the sacrament of penance: "Forming faith meant persuading people to put the faith into practice by way of charity or penance, and restraining or absolving them from mortal sin."[57] On this view it is only faith formed by love that can justify since it is only faith so formed that can co-operate with grace in producing the good works necessary for the believer eventually to merit heaven.

For his part, Luther finds it monstrous that his opponents teach that unformed faith is at once both a divine gift and yet not able to justify since it requires to be formed by love: "Who could stand for the teaching that faith, the gift of God that is infused in the heart by the Holy Spirit, can coexist with mortal sin ... to believe this way about infused faith is to admit openly that they understand nothing about faith."[58] He also appeals to what he regards as the basic sense of Paul's words: "Paul does not make faith unformed here, as though it were a shapeless chaos without the power to be or to do anything; but he attributes the working itself to faith rather than to love ... He does not say 'Love is effective.' No, he says: 'Faith is effective.' He does not say: 'Love works.' No, he says: 'Faith works.' He makes love the tool through which faith works."[59] Although Luther does not say so, these points clearly rely on taking the participle *energoumenē* as middle rather than passive. If passive it could be taken as saying that faith "is made effective through love." Yet while some patristic writers do take the participle as passive the majority of commentators in all eras, including most pertinently the Latin of the Vulgate itself, and therefore also many medieval advocates of the doctrine of faith formed by love, take it as middle.[60] Luther's argument is that when the participle is so taken as middle in voice, Paul's words do not easily speak of faith as something passive or unformed but as something active and working.

Luther thus considers it essential to hold that faith works or it is not faith. It is faith which justifies and which unites with Christ and leads to love, not love that justifies and unites with Christ and leads to faith. As Lu-

---

[56] John Van Engen, "Faith as a Concept of Order in Medieval Christendom," in *Belief in History: Innovative Approaches to European and American Religion*, (ed. Thomas Kselman; Notre Dame: University of Notre Dame Press, 1991), 19–67 (33). See 31–36 for a fuller account of the distinction between unformed and formed faith.

[57] Van Engen, "Faith as a Concept of Order in Medieval Christendom," 35.

[58] *LW* 27:28 = *WA* 40.2:35, 14–19.

[59] *LW* 27:29 = *WA* 40.2:36, 8–14.

[60] John K. Riches, *Galatians through the Centuries* (Oxford: Blackwell, 2008), 262.

ther reads Paul, there is no place for human love which justifies. Luther's apocalyptic dualism here leads him sharply to distinguish faith and love in an attempt rightly to order their relationship, for confusion between the two can only obscure in deluded and dangerous ways the necessity of new creation. Nevertheless, the relationship between faith and love matters profoundly for Luther. While faith and love must be distinguished, it is equally important that they are not separated. For if faith justifies and unites with Christ and thereby makes a new creation, then love must follow. The cliché that faith alone justifies but that justifying faith is never alone is true to Luther. The believer who produces no works of love is not a believer. Moreover, since Paul teaches both that faith justifies and that faith works through love there is for Luther no sharp separation possible between justification and sanctification. For some, both in Luther's own lifetime and subsequently, the lack of such separation courted the danger of reintroducing justification by works. Luther's distinction between justification as encompassing works of righteousness but not in any degree obtained by them would seem too subtle to be sustainable.[61] Yet for Luther himself the danger of reintroducing justification by works is posed more seriously by separating good works from justification:

> It is, therefore, an unhappy distinction to divide a person (as far as he is a believer) into beginning, middle, and end. Accordingly, a person's works shine because they are rays of his faith, and are accepted because of his faith, not vice versa. Otherwise, in the matter of justification, the works which follow faith would be more excellent, and thus, faith would be justifying faith only in the beginning, afterwards it would step aside and cease and would leave the distinction (of justifying a person) to works, and become void and defunct.[62]

Yet again the fundamentally apocalyptic nature of Luther's interpretation of Paul's texts is clear. Discontinuity is not to be located between different phases of a person's existence as a Christian but rather between existence before faith and justified existence in Christ through faith. If, for Luther, Christ is present in justifying faith and the believer must live not his or her

---

[61] Here there is a significant point of difference between Luther and Lutheran orthodoxy. The *Formula of Concord* states that "neither renewal, sanctification, virtues, nor good works are to be viewed or presented *tanquam forma aut pars aut causa iustificationis* (that is, as our righteousness before God or as a part or a cause of our righteousness). They are also not to be mixed into the article of justification under any other pretense, pretext, or terminology. Instead, the righteousness of faith consists alone in the forgiveness of sins by sheer grace, because of Christ's merit alone." See "The Solid Declaration, Article III: Righteousness," in *The Book of Concord: The Confessions of the Evangelical Lutheran Church* (ed. R. Kolb and T. J. Wengert; Minneapolis: Fortress, 2000), 562–73 (Par. 39).

[62] "Cordatus' Controversy with Melanchthon," 200 = Bindseil (ed.), 347.

own life but the life of Christ, then such justification must pertain to the whole of the Christian life.

H. Conclusion and Implications

As we have seen, Luther's integrates in his exegesis of Paul union with Christ, justification by faith, and the apocalyptic themes of Paul's theology.[63] That he does so serves to dispel some common misapprehensions about his exegesis of Paul:

1. Luther offers an account of Paul's soteriology in which making justification by faith central does not imply any neglect of Christology. That Christ's presence within faith is central to what Luther understands Paul to mean by faith makes it impossible for Luther to construe justification and union with Christ as contrasting categories. To be justified requires union with Christ, since it is only united with him that his righteousness is received, and to be united with Christ requires justification since it is in justifying faith that Christ is present.

2. The charge that by imputed righteousness Luther means fictional righteousness is simply erroneous. While extremely concerned to insist that works are not an efficient cause of justification, Luther does not separate them from justification.[64] If faith justifies because it grasps hold of Christ and unites the believer with him so that his righteousness is received, then it is simply impossible to Luther that such faith will not produce works. The righteousness received is not the believer's own and remains alien, but it is not fictional since through Christ's presence in faith the believer must live an alien life.

3. Luther does not establish a contractual view of justification. Faith does not justify because it is the appropriate response to God's grace and is the right kind of religious disposition to fulfill the human side of a contract between God and humanity. Instead faith justifies because it grasps hold of Christ.

Luther's integrative exegetical approach to central themes in Paul's letters also provides a perspective from which to assess some recent developments in Luther studies. Over a period of several decades, the Finnish school of Luther interpreters have conceived union with Christ as central

---

[63] These themes are also integrated with Luther's theology of the Word. The faith in which Christ is present is received through the preaching of the Word, and, just as the believer receives an alien righteousness and must live an alien life, so God's transforming Word of promise always comes from outside.

[64] Hampson, *Christian Contradictions*, 122: "It is of course a complete farce to say that according to Luther God leaves man corrupt!"

to Luther's explanations of justification. Emphasizing the presence of Christ in faith, and working in the context of ecumenical exchanges between Lutheranism and Russian Orthodoxy, the Finns regard Luther's explanations of justification as fruitful in dialogue with Orthodox notions of salvation as *theosis* or divinization.[65] As Tuomo Mannermaa, the patriarch of the Finnish school, expresses it, "because faith means a real union with Christ, and because in Christ the Logos is of the same essence as God the Father, therefore the believer's participation in the essence of God is also real."[66] This idea of the believer's participation in the essence of God has proved particularly controversial because "the idea of Christ's presence is 'real-ontic,' not just a subjective experience or God's 'effect' on the believer."[67] Unsurprisingly such statements have raised anxieties about the erosion of a proper distinction between God as Creator and the believer as creature.[68] They have also served to direct the debate into the realm of on-

---

[65] See Carl E. Braaten, and Robert W. Jenson, eds.,*Union with Christ: The New Finnish Interpretation of Luther* (Grand Rapids: Eerdmans, 1998) and Tuomo Mannermaa, *Christ Present in Faith: Luther's View of Justification* (Minneapolis: Fortress, 2005). I am not equipped properly to assess the claims made by the Finns about Luther and *theosis*, which would require both a careful analysis of Orthodox concepts of *theosis* and a careful comparison of them with Luther. I am not aware of studies by either the Finns or their opponents providing this. Luther does occasionally use the term *theosis* and his Christology is deeply indebted to the Alexandrian Church Fathers for whom *theosis* certainly was a central concern. Writing before the Finns, Lienhard, *Luther: Witness to Jesus Christ*, 54, 386–7 twice mentions the possible significance of the theme of divinization for Luther on the basis of his familiarity with patristic writings. It seems likely that further study will reveal that there are certain senses in which the term can legitimately be applied to Luther but that his concept of *theosis* is different in very significant ways from those found in the Orthodox tradition.

[66] Mannermaa, *Christ Present in Faith*, 19.

[67] Veli-Matti Kärkkäinen, "Deification View," in *Justification: Five Views* (ed. J. K. Beilby and P. R. Eddy; Downers Grove, Ill.: InterVarsity Press, 2011), 219–43 (225).

[68] Dennis Bielfeldt, "Response to S. Juntunen," in Braaten and Jensen, *Union with Christ*, 161–6 (165) worries that the Finns' claims imply that for Luther the finite human being participates in the substance of the infinite. This leads Bielfeldt to propose a more precise definition of participation using the image of *perichoresis*: "It is not that the inifinte can be predicated of the substance of the finite, but rather that the infinite is present in, permeating the substance of the finite in a nonaccidental way." That Bielfeldt is close to Luther's intention is suggested by a crucial passage quoted in Tuomo Mannermaa, *Two Kinds of Love: Martin Luther's Religious World* (Minneapolis: Fortress, 2010), 65 in which Luther, speaking of Christ as the Word of God, both affirms that because believers are united with the Word by faith they can properly be said to be the Word and denies that this involves their substance changing into that of the Word. See *WA* 1:28, 39–41. Note also Olli-pekka Vainio, *Justification and Participation in Christ* (Leiden: Brill, 2008), 35: "The parties to this conjunction participate in each other's attributes without changing or losing their own essence... The relation between Christ and the believer must be examined according to the rules of christology."

tology, focusing on the implications of what Luther says about union with Christ for his understanding of the nature of being. There is something unsatisfactory about this debate. This is in part because it distracts from the overwhelming exegetical evidence that the Finns are correct that union with Christ is indeed central to Luther's understanding of justification. However, it is also because Luther is not himself primarily concerned to pursue the ontological implications of union with Christ. He is focused rather upon biblical categories and terminology and therefore upon where union with Christ fits within his reflections upon Scripture and upon salvation. The work of both the Finnish school and its critics has somewhat neglected this, and, in particular, said far too little about how Luther relates union with Christ to the apocalyptic themes of Paul's theology.[69]

Luther's exegesis also provides some potential guidance for the attempts of contemporary Pauline scholarship to explore the nature of union with Christ. Partly this is a matter of the imagery that Luther uses. Although not himself concerned with the historical origins of Paul's language, Luther does employ biblical imagery to describe the presence of Christ in faith. He draws on images of divine presence such as on Mt Sinai or in the Jerusalem temple. These images are themselves mysterious and scarcely susceptible to complete explanation, but they do provide a biblical background that can be explored.[70] Further, Luther's reflections on the apocalyptic nature of faith offer some assistance in understanding what it means for the believer to live in union with Christ. The struggle to live by trust in God's promises in the midst of a world marred by sin and death is not entirely beyond our understanding. We know what it is to trust or to fail to trust another. To trust in God's promises is to look to a future reality beyond the present and to live on its basis. Nevertheless, Luther locates the presence of Christ and of that future hope precisely in the present reality of the struggle of faith, and not in the transcendence of it.[71]

---

[69] This omission is especially striking given that a different strand within Luther scholarship in recent decades has strongly emphasized the apocalyptic dimension of Luther's theology. See especially Heiko A. Oberman, *Luther: Man between God and the Devil* (New Haven, Conn.: Yale University Press, 1989).

[70] See, for example, the prominence given to the theme of the temple in Macaskill, *Union with Christ*, 147–59.

[71] Douglas Campbell, *The Quest for Paul's Gospel: A Suggested Strategy* (London: T&T Clark, 2005), 54 makes it plain that in stressing the participation of the Christian in the faithfulness of Christ he is not calling for mere imitation of Christ. Paul "is finding in his own life the experience and life of Christ figuring forth. He is *participating* in Christ ... in particular, he is participating in Christ's weakness" (his emphasis). This is helpful, as is Campbell's emphasis on the role of the Holy Spirit in participation in Christ. However, there is lacking an explanation of how this participation takes place in a way that it is not primarily imitative. In his emphasis on the presence of Christ in faith Luther potentially allows us to say more about this missing step of analysis.

Finally. Luther's insistence on the presence of Christ in faith serves to clarify the relationship between faith and other aspects of Paul's theology. In recent Pauline scholarship a strong emphasis on the apocalyptic nature of Paul's thought has often stood in contrast to an emphasis on faith, a matter of asserting the proper priority of divine initiative over human response. Yet precisely because Luther interprets faith in primarily christological terms he offers exegetical resources which may help us to reconnect the two, offering a strong account of the significance of faith in Paul's theology that stands in continuity with its apocalyptic themes.[72] The presence of Christ in faith grants to faith a very different significance from that of a revised human self-understanding. In union with Christ through faith, the believer shares in Christ's victory. Commenting on Gal 2:16, Luther says of the believer:

> For to the extent that he is a Christian, he is above the Law and sin, because in his heart he has Christ, the Lord of the Law, as a ring has a gem. Therefore when the Law accuses and sin troubles, he looks to Christ; and when he has taken hold of Him by faith, he has present with him the Victor over the Law, sin, death, and the devil – the Victor whose rule over all these prevents them from harming him.[73]

Bibliography

Anonymous, "Cordatus' Controversy with Melanchthon." *Theological Quarterly* 11/4 (1907): 193–207.

Bindseil, H. E. *Philippi Melanchthonis Epistolae, Iudicia, Consilia, Testimonia Aliorumque ad eum Epistolae quae in Corpore Reformatorum Desiderantur*. Halle: Gustav Schwetske, 1874.

Bornkamm, K. *Luthers Auslegungen des Galaterbriefs von 1519 bis 1531 – Ein Vergleich*. Berlin: Walter de Gruyter, 1963.

---

[72] To say this is to highlight the often ignored or unrecognized influence of Luther upon recent apocalyptic interpretations of Paul. Given that so Lutheran a figure as Ernst Käsemann is often regarded as the progenitor of such apocalyptic interpretations this influence should not be surprising. However, it also true that Luther's apocalyptic thought has its own distinctive patterns. Heiko A. Oberman, "Teufelsdreck: Eschatology and Scatology in the 'Old' Luther," in *The Impact of the Reformation* (Edinburgh: T&T Clark, 1994), 51–68, points out that Luther believed God and the devil to be engaged in a struggle now reaching its climax in the last days. However, based on his reading of Augustine and Bernard, Luther believed that in this final phase the devil's characteristic mode of operation was to infiltrate the church and present diabolical distortion as catholic truth. The consequence is that 'the gospel's *primary* function is not – as assumed today, and as was indeed the case in the City Reformation – to change *obvious* injustice by introducing social legislation to establish *biblical* justice, but to unmask *hidden* injustice, thus saving the souls of duped Christians and opening the eyes of the secular authorities for their mandate to establish *civil* justice' (62, his emphasis).

[73] *LW* 26:134 = *WA* 40: 235, 21–25.

Braaten, Carl E. and Robert W. Jenson, eds. *Union with Christ: The New Finnish Interpretation of Luther*. Grand Rapids: Eerdmans, 1998.
Bultmann, Rudolf. *Theology of the New Testament Vol. I*. New York: Charles Scribner's Sons, 1951.
Campbell, Constantine R. *Paul and Union with Christ: An Exegetical and Theological Study*. Grand Rapids: Zondervan, 2012.
Campbell, Douglas. *The Quest for Paul's Gospel: A Suggested Strategy*. London: T&T Clark, 2005.
Gorman, Michael J. *Inhabiting the Cruciform God: Kenosis, Justification, and Theosis in Paul's Narrative Soteriology*. Grand Rapids: Eerdmans, 2009.
Hampson, Daphne. *Christian Contradictions: The Structures of Lutheran and Catholic Thought*. Cambridge: Cambridge University Press, 2001.
Jüngel, Eberhard. *Justification: The Heart of the Christian Faith*. Edinburgh: T&T Clark, 2001.
Kärkkäinen, Veli-Matti. "Deification View." Pages 219–43 in *Justification: Five Views*. Edited by J. K. Beilby and P. R. Eddy. Downers Grove, Ill.: InterVarsity Press, 2011.
Kolb, R. and T. J. Wengert, eds. *The Book of Concord: The Confessions of the Evangelical Lutheran Church*. Minneapolis: Fortress, 2000.
Lienhard, Marc. *Luther: Witness to Jesus Christ: Stages and Themes of the Reformer's Christology*. Minneapolis: Augsburg, 1982.
Luther, Martin. *D. Martin Luthers Werke: Kritische Gesamtausgabe. Die deutsche Bibel*. WA DB. 15 Volumes. Weimar: H. Böhlau, 1883–2009.
———. *D. Martin Luthers Werke: Kritische Gesamtausgabe. Schriften / Werke*. WA. 73 Volumes. Weimar: H. Böhlau, 1883–2009.
———. *Luther's Works*. 54 volumes. Edited by J. Pelikan and H. T. Lehmann. Philadelphia: Concordia, 1955–86.
Macaskill, Grant. *Union with Christ in the New Testament*. Oxford: Oxford University Press, 2013.
Mannermaa, Tuomo. *Christ Present in Faith: Luther's View of Justification*. Minneapolis: Fortress, 2005.
———. *Two Kinds of Love: Martin Luther's Religious World*. Minneapolis: Fortress, 2010.
McGrath, Alister E. *Iustitia Dei: A History of the Christian Doctrine of Justification*. 2d ed. Cambridge: Cambridge University Press, 1998.
———. *Luther's Theology of the Cross*. 2d ed. Oxford: Wiley-Blackwell, 2011.
Oberman, Heiko A. "Iustitia Christi and Iustitia Dei: Luther and the Scholastic Doctrines of Justification." *Harvard Theological Review* 59/1 (1966): 1–26.
———. *Luther: Man between God and the Devil*. New Haven: Yale University Press, 1989.
———. "Teufelsdreck: Eschatology and Scatology in the 'Old' Luther." Pages 51–68 in *The Impact of the Reformation*. Edinburgh: T&T Clark, 1994.
Riches, John K. *Galatians through the Centuries*. Oxford: Blackwell, 2008.
Sanders, E. P. *Paul and Palestinian Judaism*. London: SCM, 1977.
Schweitzer, Albert. *The Mysticism of Paul the Apostle*. Translated by W. Montgomery. London: Adam & Charles Black, 1931.
Seifrid, Mark. "Luther, Melanchthon, and Paul on the Question of Imputation." Pages 137–52 in *Justification: What's at Stake in the Current Debates?* Edited by M. Husbands and D. Treier. Downers Grove: InterVarsity Press, 2004.
Siggins, I. D. K. *Martin Luther's Doctrine of Christ*. New Haven: Yale University Press, 1970.

Vainio, Olli-Pekka. *Justification and Participation in Christ: The Development of the Lutheran Doctrine of Justification from Luther to the Formula of Concord (1598)*. Studies in the Medieval and Reformation Traditions 130. Leiden: Brill, 2008.

Van Engen, John. "Faith as a Concept of Order in Medieval Christendom." Pages 19–67 in *Belief in History: Innovative Approaches to European and American Religion*. Edited by Thomas Kselman. Notre Dame: University of Notre Dame Press, 1991.

Waldstein, Michael. "The Trinitarian, Spousal, and Ecclesial Logic of Justification." Pages 274–87 in *Reading Romans with St. Thomas Aquinas*. Edited by Matthew Levering and Michael Dauphinais. Washington D.C.: Catholic University of America Press, 2012.

Yule, G. "Luther's Understanding of Justification by Grace Alone in Terms of Catholic Christology." Pages 87–112 in *Luther: Theologian for Catholics and Protestants*. Edited by G. Yule. Edinburgh: T&T Clark, 1985.

The Fatherhood of God and Union with Christ in Calvin

JULIE CANLIS

Neil Gunn's *The Silver Darlings* captures well an old Scottish caricature of Calvinist doctrine. Seated in Widow Grant's stone hut is a circle of thirty gathered villagers who have come together for their cross-examination in the Shorter Catechism. All present in this Highland parish are tense or even excited, wondering how they will fare during the ordeal of 'the Questions.' Principal to this venture is Sandy Ware, the catechist, who impartially fires questions round the circle to young and old.

> As he went deeper into the mysteries there were momentary hesitations here and there, but the first real break came with Simple Sanny, who was in his thirties, with a brown hairy face and small acute eyes.
> 'What is adoption?' Mr. Ware asked him.
> Sanny opened his mouth thoughtfully and scratched his chin. 'I know the *justification* one better,' he said.[1]

Simple Sanny is humorously portrayed as being more familiar with the forensic aspect (justification) of Calvin's theology than with the familial (adoption), a familiarity that stretches straight into the present. J. I. Packer is simply the most widely known of those who have noticed the "strange fact that the truth of adoption has been little regarded in Christian history. Apart from two last-century books, now scarcely known ... there is no evangelical writing on it, nor has there been at any time since the Reformation."[2] What both justification and adoption have in common is that they are both treated by Calvin in relation to union with Christ (*unio cum*

---

[1] The extract continues: "We have just had WHAT IS JUSTIFICATION?" remarked the catechist.
"Oh ay," said Sanny, "so we had." His quick eye turned upon a faint noise suspiciously like young laughter at Mr. Ware's back. Encouraged by this, Sanny said, "I'll give you the first commandment instead – if that will suit you."
"We are some way from the commandments yet," replied the catechist, with some severity, "and we do not bargain in these matters as we do over a stirk at a drunken market. A very drunken market, from what I have heard." Neil Gunn, *The Silver Darlings* (London: Faber, 1978), 149.

[2] I'm sure there are those who would take issue with Packer's sweeping statement, but the point is well taken. See J. I. Packer, *Knowing God* (Downers Grove, Ill.: InterVarsity Press, 1994), 228.

Christo). Any Calvin scholar worth their salt will agree with this. But, like Sanny, there is confusion (to put it mildly) as to *how* union relates to these themes that were once spoken of in relative isolation. This very debate, of late, is tearing Calvin studies to pieces.[3]

Most treatments of Calvin's doctrine of union with Christ begin where Calvin apparently began, in the very opening line of the *Institutes*, Book III:

> We must now examine this question. How do we receive those benefits which the Father bestowed on his only-begotten Son – not for Christ's own private use, but that he might enrich poor and needy men? First, we must understand that *as long as Christ remains outside of us, and we are separated from him, all that he has suffered and done for the salvation of the human race remains useless and of no value for us*. ... the Holy Spirit is the bond by which Christ unites us to himself.[4]

However, by beginning here, one risks giving the impression that union with Christ came from nowhere, Athena-like, leaping fully armed from Calvin's forehead only in Book III. It is not the case that God (who had been distant) suddenly decided to come close to us in redemption; nor is it the case that God suddenly decided to change tactics with us, by showing his best paternal face. Calvin's writings shimmer with the conviction that these things have always been in the character of the triune God, who has been after humanity from the start.

Since the Reformation, theologians have time and time again been caught off-guard by Calvin's breathtaking vision of the Christian life. Even giants such as Barth confess their inadequacy, "I lack completely the means, the suction cups, even to assimilate this phenomenon [of Calvin], not to speak of presenting it adequately. What I receive is only a thin little stream and what I can then give out again is only a yet thinner extract of this little stream."[5] What most struck Barth about Calvin was the way in

---

[3] Provocatively, William Evans has noted the presence of this internal tension among Calvin followers for centuries, in his article appropriately titled, *"Déjà Vu All Over Again*: The Contemporary Reformed Soteriological Controversy in Historical Perspective," *WTJ* 72 (2010): 135–51. For an example of the current controversy, simply follow the back-and-forth responses between Evans and Fesko in WTJ in the months that followed.

[4] Calvin, *Institutes*, III.1.1, italics mine. All references to Calvin's *Institutes of the Christian Religion* are to the 1559 edition, unless noted. I am working from John Calvin, *Institutes of the Christian Religion* (LCC 20–21; 2 vols.; ed. John T. McNeil; trans. Ford Lewis Battles; Philadelphia: Westminster, 1960).

[5] Karl Barth to Thurneysen, 8 June 1922, in *Revolutionary Theology in the Making: The Barth-Thurneysen Correspondence, 1914–1925* (ed. Eduard Thurneysen; London: Epworth, 1964), 101. Barth counseled that it is "singularly worth while to become Calvin's free pupil" (though, he quickly mentioned, not necessarily a Calvinist!) Do we see here, already, the embryonic split between "Calvin" and the "Calvinists"? Karl Barth,

which union with Christ functioned in the *Institutes of the Christian Religion* – not as a step – but as the "common denominator,"[6] observes Barth, for all of Calvin's theology. Whether or not Barth read Calvin truly (and this itself is a sore spot in the Reformed world), Barth certainly expressed (as only Barth could) a wonder, awe, and even yearning envy in the face of this comprehensive theologian.

Calvin's theology is comprehensive because of his relentless drive to read all theology, all of Scripture, and all of the Christian life through the person of Christ. He sees Christ as the mediator even before the beginning of creation.[7] He sees Christ as the one through whom "Adam, Abel, Noah, Abraham and the rest of the fathers cleaved to God ... For they had a genuine participation"[8] and "union."[9] He sees Christ as containing within himself everything for our salvation, for "we must seek in Christ not the half, or merely a part, but the entire completion."[10] On the flip side, if we pick apart the reality of salvation (for example, divorcing justification from sanctification), we are culpable of "rending Christ to pieces"[11] – a shocking and graphic accusation, only if we neglect Calvin's perception that the theological categories with which we tinker have an organic connection to the person of Christ. In this vein, Calvin even goes so far as to call Christ "mutilated" if he does not achieve his primary goal, which is to lead us to the Father.[12] We are inexplicably, indissolubly linked to Christ.

At the risk of being too blunt, and not hedging my statement with the usual thousand qualifications, I want to argue that Calvin's much-celebrated (and much debated) doctrine of union with Christ is not an end in itself. This bucks a trend in Calvin studies, which is mirrored in New Testament studies, that considers union with Christ exclusively from the

---

Fragments Grave and Gay (trans. Martin Rumscheidt; Eugene, Ore.: Wipf & Stock, 2011), 110.

[6] For Barth's appreciation of Calvin's formulation of union with Christ, see Barth, *Church Dogmatics* IV/3.2.

[7] For more on this, see Julie Canlis, *Calvin's Ladder: A Spiritual Theology of Ascent and Ascension* (Grand Rapids: Eerdmans, 2010), 53–88 (ch 2).

[8] Calvin, *Institutes*, II.10.7.

[9] Calvin, *Institutes*, II.10.8. For more on this, see T. H. L. Parker, *Calvin's Old Testament Commentaries* (Edinburgh: T&T Clark, 1986), 42–82.

[10] Calvin, *Commentary on 1 Corinthians* 1:30. All references to Calvin's *Commentaries* are from the Calvin Translation Society (Edinburgh: 1843–55), reprinted by Baker, 1979.

[11] For Calvin's extensive usage of this metaphor, see Mark Garcia, *Life in Christ: Union with Christ and Twofold Grace in Calvin's Theology* (Milton Keynes: Paternoster, 2008); and Todd Billings, *Calvin, Participation, and the Gift: The Activity of Believers in Union with Christ* (Oxford: Oxford University Press, 2007).

[12] Calvin, *Commentary on John* 14:28.

perspective of humanity and the saving benefits that Christ procures.[13] Constantine Campbell argues similarly for New Testament studies, "Consequently, it is appropriate to regard union with Christ as dealing with more than just humanity and Christ; indeed, it may well be a significant mistake to do so. The Pauline theme of union with Christ is as much about the Father and the Spirit's union with him as it is about ours."[14] Perhaps if we take a step back and widen out our lens, to not only Christ's union with us but to include aspects of Christ's union with the Father in the Spirit, then we have a larger horizon in which to live and move and have our theological being. Although we will never know "what is the sacred and mystical union between us and him, and again between him and the Father," Calvin is certain that we will experience it "when he diffuses his life in us by the secret efficacy of the Spirit."[15] So it is perchance wiser to begin 'in the beginning' with Calvin's understanding of God as triune. It is from this place, I want to argue, that we can properly appreciate Calvin's theology of union with Christ, as fitting into this prior familial picture.

A. Fatherhood in Calvin: literary theme or cosmic reality?

It is no secret that Calvin's God is primarily a *Father*,[16] a poignant theme given that Calvin himself lost his mother at an early age, only to be followed by his undemonstrative father a decade later. Yet as his father was buried outside the sacrosanct ground of the church, Calvin too excommunicated and buried his own abortive notions of human fatherhood.[17] He discovered that the true referent for fatherhood is God himself:

---

[13] Perhaps this is an unfair generalization, but it does strike me that most of the fighting has to do with *how* the "benefits" of Christ relate to the believer. The fighting continues around whether or not one believes that Reformed Scholasticism carried this (sacred) balance forward or not, in the *ordo salutis* or otherwise. There has been excellent scholarship on all sides of the debate – Gaffin, Horton, Fesko, Evans, Muller, Johnson, Hunsinger – excellent particularly when it is conducted in a humble manner.

[14] Constantine R. Campbell, *Paul and Union with Christ* (Grand Rapids: Zondervan, 2012), 357.

[15] Calvin, *Commentary on John* 14:20.

[16] Brian Gerrish is conceivably the first in recent decades to give extended treatment to Calvin's notion of God's fatherly character (though for Gerrish, it tends to function more as a metaphor for provision and care than as a referent to the divine *Father*). See his wonderful treatment in Brian Gerrish, *Grace and Gratitude: The Eucharistic Theology of John Calvin* (Minneapolis: Fortress, 1993), esp. 22–31.

[17] Calvin muses that earthly fatherhood is a shadowy reflection of God's divine fatherhood (from which it takes its name), not the other way around. If there is any metaphorical "accommodation" to human capacity in Calvin's use of the term "Father," it is an accommodation, Calvin says, in allowing human fathers also to appropriate such a

God, of his own nature, is inclined to allure us to Himself by gentle and loving means. God is like a father going about to win his children, by being merry with them and by giving them all that they desire. If a father could always laugh with his children and fulfill their desires, all his delight would be in them. Such does God show Himself to be toward us....[18]

God's fatherhood is not an abstract, universal truth for Calvin. Rather, it confronts the horror and anguish of our broken world. It has the power to calm terror. It is the golden thread out of the labyrinth. It calls to us in our abyss.[19] For Calvin, God's fatherhood is not merely a sentiment that "frees us from all distrust."[20] Nor is it a "matter of figures"[21] or images or symbols. It is a concrete reality that stretches forward from the dawn of time, from the eternal Fatherhood of God and its reception in the Word, the Son. "Rather, they could not actually be sons of God unless their adoption was founded upon the Head."[22] It is founded upon reality of God the Father himself, as revealed in Christ the Son, and offered to us in the Spirit.

Calvin understands this primary relationship – that of Father and Son – to be at the root of all reality. It took me multiple reads of the *Institutes* and commentaries to realize what Calvin is doing: he is painting the whole biblical story in terms of a *father and son*. We humans fit into this prior dynamic. The human story does not unfold within God generally, but the story of humanity unfolds within a particular, concrete aspect of God's communion, of Father and Son. Although Calvin refused to speculate on the triune "essence" of God, warning that those who "indulge their curiosity ... enter into a labyrinth,"[23] the trinity unquestionably forms the background of Calvin's understanding of God's dealings with humanity, for Calvin is emphatic that there are aspects of it that have been flung open to us in Christ. "He is the bond whereby God may be found to us in fatherly faithfulness."[24] Calvin believes that the relationship of Christ with his Fa-

---

glorious title, rather than in God's own paternity himself (Calvin, *Sermon* on 1 Timothy 9).

[18] Calvin, *Sermon* 160, Deuteronomy 28:46–50.

[19] Many will recognize my use of Calvin's repetitive images of the "labyrinth" and the "abyss," as explored in William Bouwsma, *John Calvin: A Sixteenth-Century Portrait* (New York: Oxford University Press, 1988).

[20] Calvin, *Institutes*, III.20.37.

[21] "For here it is not a matter of figures, such as when atonement was set forth in the blood of beasts." Calvin, *Institutes* II.14.5.

[22] Calvin, *Institutes*, II.14.5.

[23] Calvin, *Institutes*, I.13.21.

[24] Calvin, *Institutes*, III.2.32. He also says, "We shall find our advantage in directing our views to Christ, that in him, as in a mirror, we may see the glorious treasures of Divine grace ... which has not yet been manifested in ourselves." *Commentary on Ephesians* 1:20.

ther frames God's dealings with humanity, both in Christ's role as eternal mediator and Christ's role as Son.

In the first half of this paper, I am going to sketch how Calvin's understanding of God as *Father* and of Christ's offer of *sonship* shapes his understanding of the story of the Old Covenant and the New Covenant.[25] In the second half of this paper, I am going to discuss how union with Christ fits into this larger Trinitarian reality and is only properly understood therein.

B. The Old Covenant: The Father's Search for a Son

In the garden, Adam is portrayed by Calvin as the loving son, surrounded with signs of the "paternal goodness"[26] of God, "excelling the lower animals' in one thing: 'spiritual communion with God.'"[27] Adam has no fear at the sight of God, whom he is able to identify as *Father*. Yet even in the garden, Adam's rich existence is due to the presence of the Mediator, whose presence there guaranteed Adam's union with God.[28] Mediation through the *logos* has always been God's Trinitarian way of being with that which is not God. Adam's perfection is not based on his unfallen "natural" capacities or gifts, but on union with God – who shared with Adam from his own storehouse wisdom, justice, and goodness.[29]

Much is broken in the Fall.[30] But the capital effect that Calvin emphasizes over and over again is that we can no longer, "from a mere survey of the world, infer that he is father."[31] In fact, worse – we now feel *terror*. [32]

---

[25] I am unwilling to drop the gendered term "sonship," as our "sonship" is founded upon Christ's own Sonship. For those who find the term suspect, I do think it can be interchanged with all sorts of terms like "becoming children of God" or "being adopted," but these lose the christological clarity that Calvin intended.

[26] Calvin, *Institutes*, I.14.2.

[27] John Calvin, *A Reformation Debate: Sadoleto's Letter to the Genevans and Calvin's Reply* (ed. John C. Olin; New York: Harper & Row, 1966), 59.

[28] In his letters to the Polish Nobles, Calvin discusses mediation first and foremost as *union*, and only secondarily as *expiation*. See the translation by Joseph Tylenda, "The Controversy on Christ the Mediator: Calvin's Second Reply to Stancaro," *CTJ* 8 (1973): 147.

[29] John Calvin, *Psychopannychia* in *Tracts and Treatises in Defense of the Reformed Faith* (vol. 3; 3 vols.; ed. Henry Beveridge; Grand Rapids: Eerdmans, 1958), 424.

[30] Sidenote: as I was researching Calvin's commentaries online, being in the middle of a transatlantic move and having no books, I attempted to open up Calvin's *Commentary on Genesis*. This, however, proved futile as my web content-filtering program prevented me from doing so, as it was a site classified as having too much violence. Need we say anything more poignant about the Fall?

[31] Calvin, *Institutes*, II.6.1.

Although one American literature professor indicts that it is 'the Calvinist [who] feels himself surrounded by naught but hostile powers,'[33] Calvin's theological insight is that it is the newfound state of humanity (not to mention literature professors!) to transfer these feelings of terror onto God.[34] For Calvin, it is the sinful human perspective that interprets God as, "so to speak, hostile to us..."[35] for "no one now experiences God as Father."[36] Calvin's interpretation of salvation history is a response to this psychological terror, unfolding as the journey toward knowing God's Fatherhood once again.[37] "Since our fall from life unto death, all that knowledge of God the Creator, of which we have discoursed [for 396 pages!], would be useless, were it not followed up by faith, holding forth God to us as a Father in Christ."[38] Whereas Adam was surrounded by signs of paternity that he can no longer discern, the future of humanity is to "embrace the cross so he can again be our Father."[39]

The story thus unfolds through the Old Testament as the pursuit of a Father for a loving son.[40] Calvin sketches the story in broad brushstrokes familiar to us all: Adam refused to be the loving son, but a promise is given to his seed. The story gains complexity as a new son is raised up through the seed of Abraham[41] and expands to include the nation of Israel, who is portrayed as this son:

The Lord had passed by all other nations and selected them as a people peculiar to Himself, and had adopted them as His children, as He often testifies by Moses and the proph-

---

[32] "But who might reach to him? Any one of Adam's children? No, like their father, all of them were terrified at the sight of God [Gen. 3:8]." Calvin, *Institutes*, II.12.1.

[33] The quote continues, "He... is naturally inclined to the belief from the outset that God, who created the world, is a well-meaning but unquestionably a rigorous, cold being who rules the world with some great purpose unknown to the inhabitants of the earth." Leon Kellner, *American Literature* (Garden City, N.Y.: Doubleday, 1915), 40; quoted in Beldon Lane, *Ravished by Beauty* (New York: Oxford University Press, 2011), 3.

[34] Calvin was well acquainted with this existential terror, "I wanted to die to be rid of those fears." Quoted in Herman Selderhuis, *John Calvin, A Pilgrim's Life* (Nottingham: InterVarsity Press, 2009), 33.

[35] Calvin, *Institutes*, II.16.2.

[36] Calvin, *Institutes*, I.2.1.

[37] Heiko Oberman finds Calvin's view of sin to be uniquely psychological for his time. See Heiko A. Oberman, "Subita Conversio: The Conversion of John Calvin," in *Reformiertes Erbe* (vol 2; 2 vols; ed. Heiko A. Oberman; Zurich: Theologischer Verlag, 1993), 279-95.

[38] Calvin, *Institutes*, II.6.1.

[39] Calvin, *Institutes*, II.5.1.

[40] I am deeply indebted to Douglas Kelly for encouraging me to pursue this insight into Calvin.

[41] "For we must hold fast to that statement of St. Paul, that the blessing of Abraham was not promised to his seeds, but to his seed." Calvin, *Commentary on Exodus* 4:22.

ets. And not content to simply name them sons, He sometimes calls them His firstbegotten, and sometimes His beloved. Thus the Lord says in Exodus 4:22, "Israel is my son, my firstborn;" "For I am a father to Israel, and Ephraim is my firstborn" (Jer 31:9) and again, "Is Ephraim my dear son?"[42]

Israel is the new son, raised up by God (through the Exodus)[43] to be the obedient son. Calvin further notes the patriarchs of old invoked God *as Father*.[44] Abraham is a particularly fruitful example of Calvin's filial interpretation, even where it is unwarranted by the biblical text.[45] What is interesting to note is how Calvin interprets the source of Abraham's justification, not due to his laying hold of a 'single word respecting the offspring ... but because he *embraced God as his Father*.'[46] Therefore, Calvin writes, God "made a covenant with Abraham and the adoption of his people was founded upon it."[47] Circumcision, Calvin is quick to note, is Abraham's "pledge of adoption."[48]

This, for Calvin, is the story of the Old Testament. It is the story of a Father who is trying to adopt his son, trying to bless his son, trying to protect his son. Calvin pays exquisite attention to the filial, father-child dimension found throughout the Old Testament because he believes that has always been the pattern of God's relating to humanity for "he was doubtless known even then in the same character in which he is now fully revealed to us."[49] Even the law and the cult (those often opaque and downright difficult portions of Scripture to understand) receive this familial interpretation of shaping into sons. Calvin portrays the law as a provisional mode of relationship that God has with his people, along the lines of a tutor or "grammarian" for a child until the time "appointed by the *father*, after which [the child] enjoys his freedom."[50] The ceremonies are "little ex-

---

[42] Calvin, *Commentary on Romans* 9:4.

[43] Calvin associates the Exodus with redemption and adoption.

[44] Calvin, *Institutes*, II.14.5.

[45] Here Calvin begins to do a curious thing, which is to speak of the adoption of Abraham, curious in that Paul does not associate Abraham with adoption but with inheritance. (Adoption comes hundreds of years later for Paul, in the covenant on Sinai: Romans 9:4 and Exodus 4:22). Thanks to Tim Trumper for this observation, and for graciously allowing me access to Timothy J. R. Trumper, *An Historical Study of the Doctrine of Adoption in the Calvinist Tradition* (Ph.D. diss, University of Edinburgh, 2001), 83.

[46] Calvin, *Commentary on Genesis* 15:6, emphasis mine.

[47] Calvin, *Commentary on Ezekiel* 16:8, Lecture 43 intro.

[48] Calvin, *Commentary on Genesis* 17:8.

[49] Calvin, *Institutes*, II.9.1.

[50] Calvin, *Commentary on Galatians* 4:1, my emphasis. It continues, "The pupil, although he is free and even lord of all his father's family, is still like a slave, for he is under the government of tutors. But this subjection under a guardian lasts only until the time appointed by the father, after which he enjoys his freedom. In this respect the fa-

ternal observances" akin to "rules for children's instruction"[51] that testify to the children that God alone can expiate guilt, forgive sin, and bring about communion. As the nation of Israel could not believe that God was a gracious Father, God had to institute a system to remind them of it! The golden thread leading Calvin through his interpretation of these foreign Old Testament "expiations and sacrifices" is this: that God wanted to "attest that he was Father, and to set apart for himself a chosen people."[52]

Israel is this "son," bound to God in a covenant, "the foundation ... [of which] is the gratuitous promise" and "a declaration of gratuitous love."[53] Calvin speaks as if with God's own voice, "I not only loved him when a child, before he was born I began to love him."[54] Love, however, is returned by obedience, so Calvin says that God, who "cannot lie ... rightly demand[ed] mutual fidelity from his own children."[55] He adopted Israel as his own, that he may obtain the "place and honour of a Father" through their loving obedience to him.[56] This obedience was not to be an external obedience but a filial obedience issuing from the heart.[57]

---

thers under the old covenant, being the sons of God, were free. But they were not in possession of freedom, since the law like a tutor kept them under its yoke. The slavery of the law lasted as long as God pleased and He put an end to it at the coming of Christ. Lawyers enumerate various methods by which guardianship is brought to a close; but of them all, the only one that fits this comparison is that which Paul puts here, the appointment by the father."

[51] "[U]ntil Christ should shine forth." Calvin, *Institutes*, II.6.5. Calvin also associates the theme of "son" with "children" whose "weakness could not bear a full knowledge of heavenly things." Calvin, *Institutes*, II.7.2.

[52] Calvin, *Institutes*, II.9.1.

[53] Calvin, *Commentary on Genesis* 17:1 and 17:2 respectively.

[54] Calvin, *Commentary on Hosea* 11:1. The quote continues, "for the liberation from Egypt was the nativity, and my love preceded that. It then appears, that the people had been loved by me, before they came forth to the light..."

[55] Calvin, *Commentary on Genesis* 17:1.

[56] Calvin, *Commentary on Genesis* 17:1. In the following sentence, Calvin qualifies the obedience of the son as the integrity of the whole person, fidelity "not only of their works, but of their thoughts." Calvin, *Commentary on Genesis* 17:1. Lest this be seen as an impossibility, Calvin says, "Whence also we infer, that there is no other method of living piously and justly than that of depending upon God." (For this reason, Calvin finds it significant that God finds in David a "man after his own heart," and establishes his seed forever through the lineage of this king.)

[57] This is the essence of the unilateral covenant, which does not release the children from obligation, but rather obligates them to obey and also to *enact the forgiveness of God*. Calvin's whole context of election keeps this from being an if/then conditional covenant. Calvin is clear that "the covenant of God with Abram had two parts. The first was a declaration of gratuitous love ... the other was an exhortation to the sincere endeavor to cultivate uprightness.... As if God has said, 'See how kindly I indulge thee: for I do not require integrity from thee simply on account of my uprightness; which I might justly do;

But the son (Israel) would have none of it.[58] Calvin, through the mouth of Hosea, portrays God as the "best and most indulgent Father,"[59] lamenting the loss of communion with his children. "I have not otherwise governed them than as a father his own children; I have been bountiful towards them. I indeed wished to do them good, and, as it was right, required obedience from them."[60] It is in the framework of the faithful Father, and the wandering children, that Calvin most clearly articulates the relationship of salvation and union with Christ.

C. The New Covenant: The Sonship of Christ

Even as the cult and the law pointed to sonship (never overturning the covenant but *renewing* it[61]), the "ancient people" are still dependent upon someone who will unite them to God. "God never showed himself propitious to his ancient people," Calvin reminds, "nor gave them any hope of grace without a Mediator."[62] Just as Adam, that first "son" (Luke 3:38) in the garden was related to God through a Mediator, so too was the son Israel. But now, because of the first son's rebellion, it is necessary that the Mediator be always seen "together with his sacrifice."[63] In words redolent of the first son Adam, Calvin writes of the son Israel as "those whom God adopts to himself from among a people – seeing that he makes them partakers of *his* righteousness and all good things – he also constitutes heirs of celestial life."[64] Participating in God's gifts is the *modus operandi* of all of God's children – whether the first "son" Adam, the "son" of the Old Covenant – Israel, or we children of the New. But Calvin also must emphasize the shadowy, "not yet" aspects of the law, and so he notes, "The fathers under the old covenant were sure of their adoption, but did not as yet so fully enjoy their privilege."[65]

At last, in the fullness of time, God brings forth *the* Son.[66]

---

but whereas I owe thee nothing, I condescend graciously to engage in mutual covenant.'" Calvin, *Commentary on Genesis* 17:2.

[58] Calvin, *Commentary on Ezekiel* 2:3. "The discourse does not relate to individuals, but to the whole people ... God no longer thinks of them as sons."

[59] Calvin, *Commentary on Hosea* 11:3.

[60] Calvin, *Commentary on Hosea* 11:4.

[61] "[T]he covenant of free adoption is comprehended under [the Law]." Calvin, *Institutes*, II.7.1.

[62] Calvin, *Institutes*, II.7.2.

[63] Tylenda's translation of Calvin's *Second Letter to the Polish Nobles*, 147.

[64] Calvin, *Commentary on Genesis* 17:8, italics mine.

[65] Calvin, *Commentary on Galatians* 4:5.

[66] Jesus is the true seed; Calvin, *Institutes*, II.6.2.

Our Lord came forth as true man and took the person and the name of Adam in order to take Adam's place in obeying the Father, to present our flesh as the price of satisfaction to God's righteous judgment, and, in the same flesh, to pay the penalty that we had deserved.[67]

The son in the garden failed; the son in the covenanted nation failed; but this Son who took "Adam's place in obeying the Father" does not fail. Calvin approves of St. Matthew's sensitive quoting of Hosea "*out of Egypt I called my son*" as referring to *the* Son who, "in this second redemption was concealed there, and carried the salvation and life of all shut up in his own person."[68] This Son offers back total obedience – of both exterior action *and* inner thought (as Calvin earlier stipulated) – to the loving Father who rightly required the reciprocated "mutual fidelity" of his children.

When exegeting the life of Christ in Book II of the *Institutes*, Calvin is able to emphasize two things that lay the groundwork for his doctrine of *unio cum Christo* in Book III: Christ's substitutionary (for us) and representative (on our behalf as one of us, for our participation) roles. "For in [his flesh] was accomplished the redemption of man, in it a sacrifice was offered to atone for sins, and an obedience yielded to God, to reconcile him to us; it was also filled with the sanctification of the Spirit, and at length, having vanquished death, it was received into the heavenly glory."[69] Calvin is clear that there are things that Christ did for us in which we cannot participate; yet – and this is the critical point – he is equally clear that these open up the possibility for human participation in him. [70] In Christ's unique death, taking our place, we discover that we are bound up in his death. We can now participate in what happened *for us*. By taking on our humanity, the Son becomes the locus where all this happens. Even in Calvin's portrayal of the forensic, substitutionary nature of redemption, this is reflective of the Son's unity with the Father.[71] His work is neither external to the Godhead nor is it external to us, for even in his substitutionary role, Christ takes our place in such a way that we are brought to God.[72]

---

[67] Calvin, *Institutes*, II.12.3.

[68] Calvin, *Commentary on Matthew* 2:15.

[69] Calvin, *Commentary on Genesis* 6:51.

[70] Substitution and representation are neither mutually exclusive categories in Paul, and nor are they in Calvin.

[71] Atonement is the united work of Father (*causam*), Son (*materiam*), and Spirit (*effectum*) for our salvation. This is also communicated in the descriptive title of *Institutes* II.16.4: "The work of atonement derives from God's love; therefore it has not established the latter."

[72] "It is the proper function of the mediator to unite us to God" – Tylenda's translation of Calvin's *Second Letter to the Polish Nobles*, 148. It is only "man's rebellion that brought it about that expiation was necessary to reconcile us to God" (p. 147).

If Christ is united to the Father in his substitutionary role (expressive of the Father's love and will toward us), Christ is in union with the Father in his representative role where he, as the second Adam, takes our place in obeying the Father. Unlike substitution, representation is inclusive and Calvin waxes eloquent upon this point: "For this is a point we must know, that nothing was given to Jesus Christ in vain. Now He does not need it for His own use. But it is for His members, in order that all of us may draw upon His fullness..."[73] Calvin is clear that every event in Jesus' life was done with the intent that humanity be able to draw from it and be made new by it.[74] In Calvin's eyes, nothing Christ did was in isolation – whether it be his baptism, his obedience, his crucifixion, resurrection, or ascension. Calvin's favorite imagery is of Christ stockpiling treasures for us *in his own person* as he goes about life on earth, living it vicariously for us.[75] So convinced is Calvin of this, that he believes the earthly Jesus to be self-conscious about his identity as the *Son* from whom all of humanity would be able to draw their sonship. For this reason, the baptism narrative in the gospels is of supreme importance, as it contains the "pledge of *our* adoption."[76] As the voice of God thunders, "this is my Beloved son," Calvin tells us that this is not for Christ alone, but *for us*. At the baptism, "it was the design of Christ to lay, as it were, in our bosom a sure pledge of God's love for us."[77] This is God's declaration of *our belovedness*, for his plan is for sonship to come to all of us through this true Son.

In surveying the life of Christ, Calvin shows a further sensitivity to the relational dynamics between Father and Son, in places where the text does not even merit it.[78] Calvin frames Jesus' earthly life of obedience in terms of his love for the Father and the Father's love of him. This is the obedience *of a Son*.[79] In his analysis of Christ's baptism, Calvin knowingly goes

---

[73] Calvin, *Sermon on Acts* 1:4–5.

[74] One of the most important insights Calvin had was that if Christ is going to offer us the hard-won benefits of his obedient life and death, then these benefits must be *human*, not divine – lest we be unable to participate in them. (Our ongoing gratitude goes to Osiander for forcing Calvin to think through this!) The "benefits" of Christ were achieved *not by virtue of his superhuman divinity but by virtue of his obedient humanity,* dependent – as we ever are. For this reason, Christ had to experience God the Father as a human man, not through the divine nature: "The Son of God became man in such a manner, that God was his God as well as ours." Calvin, *Commentary on Ephesians* 1:17.

[75] See his imagery of the "fountain" in particular.

[76] Calvin, *Commentary on Matthew* 3:17, emphasis mine.

[77] Calvin, *Commentary on John* 15:9.

[78] See Gerrish's explication of Jesus' cry of dereliction to "My Father!" on the cross (where in the gospel it is "My God!"); Gerrish, *Grace and Gratitude*, 61.

[79] Although this obedience has been divided into "active" and "passive," I am not sure that is the best way to go about describing it (apologies here to the Reformed tradition). It is a whole self-offering, in life and death and resurrection. The temptation is to think of

against the interpretations of his day that held that Christ had to undergo baptism primarily to uphold the law. No, Calvin remarks, it is not the fact but the *quality* of his upholding the law, as faithful filial obedience.[80] (Thus, it is as important to stress that Christ fulfilled all the aspects of the law on our behalf, as it is to stress the filial character of this fulfillment – reflective of Christ's union with the Father. Calvin reminds us that it is not an abstract righteousness that is offered in the gospel, but the Son's righteousness, in a specifically human, filial shape. "[Paul] at the same time shows what sort of righteousness it is, by calling it *obedience*."[81]) Even passages regarding the atonement are given this gloss: "as if he could atone for our sins in any other way than by obeying the Father!"[82] All of this co-exists with Calvin's emphasis upon substitution (both mediatorial and penal) – but it is the *filial character* of atonement that is equally consistent for Calvin and cannot be underplayed.

D. Union with the Son: "our salvation consists in having God as our Father"

This is where we begin to understand how Calvin's doctrine of union with Christ must be read in this larger narrative of a Father and Son. It is to the *Son* that we are united. If we only study union in Calvin for how it relates to *our* salvation, we miss one of its most important characteristics for Calvin, as being reflective of this ongoing reality of Father and Son. "Neither has Christ any thing, which may not be applied to our benefit."[83] We are not simply united to one who has numerous salvific benefits to give to a bereft humanity; we are united to one whose primary "benefit" is his own union with the Father. This too, Calvin says, is "for us." Calvin argued "but we shall not be satisfied with having Christ, if we do not know that we possess God in him. We must therefore believe that there is such a uni-

---

our justification only in terms of what Christ went through "passively" on the cross, with our sanctification residing in his "active" life. The resurrection is usually left out of the picture.

[80] Calvin specifies, "The general reason why Christ received baptism was, that he might render full obedience to the Father; and the special reason was, that he might consecrate baptism in his own body." Calvin, *Commentary on Matthew* 3:13. See also, "Thus in his very baptism, also, he asserted that he fulfilled a part of the righteousness in obediently carrying out his Father's commandment. In short, from the time when he took on the form of a servant, he began to pay the price of liberation in order to redeem us." Calvin, *Institutes*, II.16.5.

[81] Calvin, *Commentary on Romans* 5:19.

[82] Calvin, *Institutes*, II.16.2.

[83] Calvin, *Commentary on Hebrews* 7:25.

ty between Father and Son as makes it impossible that they shall have anything separate from each other."[84] It is important to note that the storyline from the "son" Adam, to the wandering "son" Israel, to the true Son, Christ, does not stop here. This, says Calvin, is only the "middle of the course." It continues on to *sons*. "We too imagine to ourselves but a half-Christ, and a mutilated Christ, if he does not lead us to God…. for he was not appointed to be our guide, merely to raise us to the sphere of the moon or of the sun, but to make us one with God the Father."[85]

For Calvin, God becoming our Father is perhaps the best summary of the gospel. "[Paul] proves that our salvation consists in having God as our Father."[86] He writes in his *Commentary on John*, "There are innumerable other ways, indeed, in which God daily testifies his fatherly love toward us, but the mark of adoption is justly preferred to them all."[87] Calvin rarely, if ever, speaks of union with God. (Calvin notes that even Plato could speak eloquently of union with God!)[88] Instead, our union with God happens in and through the person of the Mediator, *who is also the Son*. Calvin carefully reflects on Christ's eternal relationship with his Father, knowing that there are portions of it that are "incomprehensible"[89] and parts of it that, as Mediator, are "not as he is himself, but as he is toward us."[90] Calvin tackles this in his *Commentary on John* 17,

> Again, it ought to be understood, that, in every instance in which Christ declares, in this chapter, that he is *one with the Father,* he does not speak simply of his Divine essence, but that he is called *one* as regards his mediatorial office, and in so far as he is our Head.[91]

Calvin clearly is not focusing on a hidden immanent relation in God, but rather Christ's experience of sonship as human, that our adoption might be secure.[92] Christian "union with God" takes the shape of Christ: in adoption,

---

[84] Calvin, *Commentary on John* 17:10.
[85] Calvin, *Commentary on John* 14:28.
[86] Calvin, *Commentary on Romans* 8:17.
[87] Calvin, *Commentary on John* 17:23.
[88] Calvin, *Institutes* III.25.2.
[89] Calvin, *Institutes* I.2.3.
[90] Calvin, *Institutes* I.10.2.
[91] Calvin, *Commentary on John* 17:21. See also how Calvin calls divine-divine as "unitas" (unity) while he speaks of divine-human as "unio" (union). From his "Dedication" in his *Commentary on Jeremiah*.
[92] Calvin is not sloppy, reasoning from the Trinity that, because the Father and Christ are one, and we are one with Christ, then we are one with the Father. (Those of us writing on union with Christ could certainly avoid much trouble, were we to be as careful as Calvin to delineate between the perichoretic union (in the Trinity), the hypostatic union (of the two natures), and our mystical union!) Calvin has a very strict method for speaking of our union with God, and bringing in the perichoretic unity between the members of the

we are joined by the Spirit to Jesus who in turn *opens up to us his earthly relationship to his Father*.[93] With the coming of the Son, and our incorporation into his atoning life of obedience and propitiation, we have been remade into the sons that God desired all along. This is no different than "the ancients [who] were also sons of God and heirs of Christ, but we hold the same character in a different manner; for we have Christ present with us, and enjoy his benefits."[94]

When Calvin says that our adoption is in a "different manner" than the ancients, we move from christology to pneumatology – and it is here that we must stay for the rest of this paper. Although the ancients were "adopted" in Christ, it is the Spirit who has inaugurated the sphere in which we can now taste God as *Father*.[95] When we approach the Lord in faith, Calvin insists on the pneumatological nature of our union: "the Spirit is the bond by which Christ effectually unites us to himself."[96] There is no salvation known to Calvin outside of union with Christ. Christ *is* the context, the 'mechanism' (to put it crassly), the location where we receive all the benefits of salvation – for they are *in him*. But it is the Spirit who is the central player in this union, "Nothing, therefore, is bestowed on us by the Spirit apart from Christ, but he takes it from Christ, that he may communicate it to us ... for he does not enlighten us to draw us away in the smallest degree from Christ ... In a word, the Spirit enriches us with no other than the riches of Christ, that he may display his glory in all things."[97] This is not the application of the 'finished work of Christ' or even the 'benefits of Christ' but entry into the risen Christ.[98] In this way, we are "different"

---

godhead is certainly not it. In fact, Calvin never uses the term *perichoresis*. Not that it can't be applied to Calvin's trinitarian theology and can be very helpful at times but, strictly speaking, Calvin does not use it.

[93] For "to this name [Son] only Christ has a right, because he is by nature *the only Son of God*; [yet] he communicates this honor to us by adoption, when we are engrafted into his body." Calvin, *Commentary on John* 3:16.

[94] Calvin, *Commentary on Galatians* 4:7.

[95] The content of the Old and New Covenants is the same – God as Father, Christ as Mediator, and the same Spirit; "all this," says Calvin, "leads to the conclusion that the difference between us and the ancient fathers lies in accidents, not substance." Calvin, *Commentary on Galatians* 4:1. But the character of our adoption is different, Calvin explains in his *Commentary on Galatians* 4:5; whereas the patriarchs "were certain of their adoption, [they] did not so fully as yet enjoy their privilege."

[96] Calvin, *Institutes*, III.1.1; see also III.11.5, III.11.10, IV.17.10.

[97] Calvin, *Commentary on John* 16:14.

[98] It is not that we "apply Christ's work" to ourselves, or garner "benefits" for our salvation – this is far too individualistic, not to mention that it de-personalizes the Spirit. Rather, the Spirit is the new eschatological reality in which we live. Our union with the Son is made real not by an impersonal sharing in Christ's human substance, but by the

from the ancients who, though united to the Mediator, were not able to participate in his specific, earthly character as Son, nor in the filial benefits worked out through the course of his vicarious life. For the Spirit does not link humanity to the abstract benefits of Christ; the Spirit brings us *into* Christ and his benefits for it is only "through [the Spirit] we come into communion with God" (I.13.14). More specifically, without the Spirit, Calvin argues, "no one can taste either the fatherly favor of God or the beneficence of Christ" (III.1.2). Jesus is our way that we know God as loving Father, but it is only *in the Spirit* that we are led into Jesus' concrete experience of this. "We are the sons of God, because we have received the same Spirit as his only Son."[99]

For this reason, Calvin is adamant that translations of the New Testament uphold and preserve this proper Pauline emphasis on being *in Christ*; he would not allow the language to stray toward any extrinsic or functional relationship. Every time Calvin came across one of Paul's phrases such as "in Christ," he knew he was standing on holy ground ... particularly as many of his contemporaries could translate the same verse without realizing that this preposition altered everything. From his *Commentary on Romans* 6:11, he insists:

> But I prefer to retain the words of Paul, *[alive to God] in Christ Jesus*, rather than to translate with Erasmus, *[alive to God] through Christ Jesus;* for thus the grafting, which makes us one with Christ, is better expressed.

Also from his Commentary on 1 Corinthians 1:4:

> The phrase *in ipso* (*in him*) I have preferred to retain, rather than render it *per ipsum* (*by him*), because it has in my opinion more expressiveness and force. For we are *enriched in Christ*, inasmuch as we are members of his body, and are engrafted into him: nay more, being made one with him, he makes us share with him in everything that he has received from the Father.

For Calvin, that little phrase "in Christ" signals an altered identity.[100] Not a religious platitude, this phrase requires a new self-understanding in which the Christian can no longer separate his or her identity from being "in Christ" or, indeed, from those who join together forming Christ's body. Calvin's term "adoption" can be seen as shorthand for this pneumatological sphere in which we, *en Christo*, are relating to God from the transformed reality of adoptive sonship, able to cry *"Abba"* like the Son. Our cry of "Abba" is not sentimental but pneumatological, as "the Spirit testi-

---

personalizing and creative work of the Holy Spirit who allows us to taste the benefits of our adoption.

[99] Calvin, *Commentary on Galatians* 4:6.

[100] See Calvin's discussion of "and the two shall be one flesh" in Calvin, *Commentary on Ephesians* 5:30–31.

fies to our heart respecting the paternal love of God."[101] Calvin insists that the self can only be understood in its *relation* to God, and thus fights for prepositions that maintain the Christian's position as participating *in Christ*, rather than accomplishing things 'for' Christ or 'on behalf of' Christ or even "by" Christ. For Calvin, it was essential to preserve the central character of the "in," locating all of the Christian life in Christ himself. The real danger is that Christ would be used for some other goal – e.g. a holy life – which would somehow occur not "in Christ" but instrumentally "by Christ" or "through Christ" or "like Christ."[102]

Even as he insists on the mysterious reality of our being *en Christo*, Calvin is always careful – so careful – that there is no blending or fusion of our human nature with the divine nature. This is a covenantal union, a personal union so real because its bond is the *person* of the Spirit – not an impersonal union of "natures." (Calvin has no time for people who look to "nature" to do the Spirit's work for Him, whether that be Heshusius, Westphal, or Osiander.)[103] Calvin separates *in order to join* in an even more profound way. Mystical union is not achieved through the erasing of divine/human categories, but through strengthening them … and leaving the rest, as Calvin does, to the reconciling work of the Holy Spirit. When the Spirit governs the union between divine and human, there can be no blurring of the lines because the Spirit's work is to "not merely bring together, but join in one, things that are separated by distance of place, and far remote."[104] The Spirit allows things that are different to be in a relation of total intimacy, while remaining separate. This is a distinctive aspect of Reformed spirituality, that the separateness of natures is in order – not to denigrate human nature, but – to honor it. Calvin's shorthand for this is to speak of our union with the "human nature of Christ" or the "substance" of Christ's incarnate humanity as a way to fend off notions that this is an ab-

---

[101] Calvin, *Commentary on Romans* 8:16. It continues, "But Paul means, that the Spirit of God gives us such a testimony, that when he is our guide and teacher, our spirit is made assured of the adoption of God: for our mind of its own self, without the preceding testimony of the Spirit, could not convey to us this assurance."

[102] An article entitled, This dissociation of Christ's benefits from his person is certainly reflected in R. T. Magnum, "Is There a Reformed Way to get the Benefits of the Atonement to 'Those Who Have Never Heard'?" *JETS* 47 (2004): 121–36.

[103] Heshusius's neglect of the Spirit (Calvin, *True Partaking* in *Tracts and Treatises on the Doctrine and Worship of the Church* [vol. 2; 3 vols.; ed. Henry Beveridge; Grand Rapids: Eerdmans, 1958], 520); Westphal's neglect (Calvin, *Last Admonition* in *Tracts and Treatises on the Doctrine and Worship of the Church* [vol. 2; 3 vols.; ed. Henry Beveridge; Grand Rapids: Eerdmans, 1958], 387); Osiander's neglect (Calvin, *Institutes*, III.11.10).

[104] Calvin, *Commentary on 1 Corinthians* 11:24; see also *Institutes*, IV.17.10.

sorption into the divine nature *per se*.[105] Rather, we are saved by Christ's vicarious life lived on our behalf – his filial obedience, sin-atoning death, and triumphant resurrection. It is *this life* to which we are united, by the Spirit, for our salvation – a life which now is full of treasures for our taking. But these 'treasures' are not abstract things or concepts. Rather, they bear the character of his life; they bear his imprint which is the imprint of the *Son*. We do not receive them incrementally but through personally dwelling in him – for he refuses to give us things in which he is not personally involved.[106]

Despite the fact that there is no blending of natures, no divine deposit given to humanity, Calvin believed that union with Christ involved real change. Although Calvin was not working with any articulated ontology, it appears that Calvin took seriously the regenerative impact of the human life being drawn into the life of God. Once "united with Christ," Calvin leaves no room for thinking of ourselves as autonomous individuals who happen to also be Christians.[107] No, says Calvin, we have become "one person" with Christ. "'We are bone of his bone, and flesh of his flesh' (Gen 2:23); not because, like ourselves, he has a human nature, but because, by the power of his Spirit, he makes us part of his body, so that from him we derive our life."[108] We have been so united with the Son by the Spirit that we now possess the one thing that makes us Christian: the ability to call God, *Father*. "No man is a Christian who has not learned, by the teaching of the Holy Spirit, to call God his Father."[109] We now have been so united to Christ, that we are stepping into the human Christ's place as Son before his Father. Yet even "marks" of transformation are not necessarily indicative of our true status *en Christo*; better – Calvin would counsel – to simply look for evidence of our salvation elsewhere. The locus (and evidence) of salvation is not in ourselves, by ourselves. (Although I hesitate to speak of it as "outside us," for the same reasons that Calvin

---

[105] We must be careful that when we speak of our union with the human *nature* of Christ, we are not using his human nature in a way that somehow "protects" us from the divine. (Is a subtle doctrine of divine simplicity at play?) No, we are in union with the *person* of Christ who is both human and divine but our "entry," Calvin insists, is through his vicarious humanity.

[106] It is the opinion of many Calvin scholars that we are not "first" forgiven, and "then" transformed – although there is a "logical" priority in this. Calvin says that the mystery of our faith is that they are all bound in Christ – not to be untangled, separated out, or systematized. This is not to say that the *ordo salutis* has no pedagogical use, as long as it does not come at the expense of seeing the gifts separate from the One in whom they exist, and in whom we exist for their enjoyment and participation.

[107] This was perhaps not so much a danger in Calvin's era, as it is now for us whose consciousness is so vastly different.

[108] Calvin, *Commentary on Ephesians* 5:30–31.

[109] Calvin, *Commentary on Galatians* 4:6.

did, in that it places a false distance between Christ and ourselves).[110] As Vermigli, a colleague of Calvin's, wrote, "it is possible to say that we are more perfectly in Christ than He is in us."[111] Transformation is the process of us inhabiting Christ and him inhabiting us. "That Christ should be formed in us is the same thing with our being formed in Christ; for we are born so as to become new creatures in him; and he, on the other hand, is born in us, so that we live his life."[112] However, he is sensitive to the eschatological aspect of Christ "in us" as that which is "not completed in a day in which it is begun in us; but gradually it goes on, and by daily advances is brought by degrees to its end."[113]

One modern problem not confronted by Calvin is that, in our ears, "union" language can sound suspiciously like the destruction of the self, for the sake of the presence of God in our lives. In the presence of Christ and union with Him, can one's personal distinctiveness be maintained? Should it be maintained? Calvin has ample resources to combat these concerns, particularly because his doctrine of union is grounded firmly upon the Spirit. Just as the Spirit preserves our human nature from being dissolved into the divine nature, so the Spirit is the guardian of our own personal distinctiveness and uniqueness. Our true identity is only discovered the more we live in another: *en Christo*, and correspondingly in others. With the Spirit as the "bond," there is a far more profound relationship between *different things* than either assimilation or fusion could ever maintain. Union with Christ is not the dissolving of the self in Christ but the finding of one's true self in Christ, because we are only truly "human" as we exist in the one who rescues us from the alienation of Adam. For this reason, adoption must always govern our understanding of union with Christ, for through it, Calvin expresses not just the fact of our salvation but its character, which is marked by knowing God's fatherhood and by becoming children in the Son, able to cry *Abba* (II.14.5).[114]

But where is this Christ to whom we are united? Calvin takes it quite literally that if we are *in Christ* – the Christ who has ascended – then we

---

[110] "We do not, therefore, contemplate him outside ourselves from afar." Calvin, *Institutes*, III.11.10.

[111] *Defensio* 752, quoted in Joseph C. McLelland, *The Visible Words of God* (Edinburgh: Oliver & Boyd, 1957), 148.

[112] Calvin, *Commentary on Galatians* 4:19.

[113] Calvin, *Commentary on Romans* 6:7.

[114] Calvin"s doctrine of union rarely dips into the nuptial imagery of Luther or the High Middle Ages, for he is more comfortable with the breadth and boundaries offered by the Trinitarian language of adoption. "As to the second clause, in which he says that he *ascends to his Father and our Father*, there is also a diversity between him and us; for he is the Son of God by nature, while we are the sons of God only by adoption." *Commentary on John* 20:18.

have one foot on earth, and one already in heaven. His ascent was unique, but his mission was to include us in his ascending return to the Father – for being with the Father is "the ultimate object at which you ought to aim."[115] From his *Commentary on Ephesians* 2:6:

> It is as if we had been brought from the deepest hell to heaven itself. And certainly, although with respects ourselves, our salvation is still the object of hope, yet in Christ we already possess a blessed immortality and glory; and therefore [Paul] adds *in Christ Jesus*. Hitherto, it does not appear in the members, but only in the head; yet in consequence of the secret union, it belongs truly to the members. Some render it *through Christ*, but for the reason which has been mentioned, it is better to retain the usual rendering *in Christ*.[116]

This is not an escape from the world, but the grounding of our identity in *another*. Calvin explains that "Paul's writings are full of similar assertions, that, while we live in the world, we at the same time live in heaven; not only because our Head is there, but because, in virtue of union, we enjoy a life in common with him."[117] For this reason, Calvin's language about the Christian life takes on an "ascending" tone – which is less indebted to Platonism as it is to christology and eschatology.[118] "Ascension follows resurrection: hence if we are members of Christ we must ascend into Heaven, because He, on being raised up from the dead was received up into Heaven that He might draw us with Him."[119] The ascending motif in Calvin is ubiquitous: the sacraments are "comparable to the steps of a ladder;"[120] the Lord's Supper – "if we refuse not to raise our hearts upwards" – is a "feeding on Christ entire;"[121] idolatry and superstition are to be combated by an ascent of the mind and an "elevation of the senses above the world"[122] to the living God; public worship is a ladder by which God "raises his own folk upward step by step;"[123] and not least, Calvin's favoured liturgical cry is the *sursum corda* – "lift up your hearts."

The ascension represented the culminating stage of the Father's search for sons: the reality of our union with Christ, our communion with the Father, and the necessary work of the Spirit. "Christ, for this reason, is said to send the Spirit from his Father (John 16:7) to raise us, by degrees, up to

---

[115] Calvin, *Commentary on John* 14:28.

[116] Calvin, *Commentary on Ephesians* 2:6.

[117] Calvin, *Commentary on Galatians* 2:20.

[118] Though it would be impossible to argue that the wraith of Platonism has been exorcised completely from Calvin.

[119] Calvin, *Commentary on Colossians* 3:1.

[120] Calvin, *Sermon* on 2 Samuel 6:1–7.

[121] Calvin, "True Partaking," II.516.

[122] Calvin, *Sermon* on 2 Samuel 6:1–7.

[123] Calvin, *Institutes*, IV.1.5.

the Father."[124] Spiritual ascent can only be interpreted by Christ's own ascent to communion with the Father, bringing humanity "up" to the Father as *sons* in him. It is for this reason that the Spirit is the crucial player in our adoption, allowing us to participate in Christ who communicates himself to us "through the secret virtue of his Holy Spirit, which can not merely bring together, but join in one, things that are separated by distance of place, and far remote."[125] Here we are reminded that the Spirit's work is not to give us a benign feeling of God's love, but to place us *in Christ* and his Sonship ... a Sonship that is part of his ongoing ministry to us at his Father's right hand. Furthermore, the ascension has a negative function, providing a safeguard from the human tendency to instrumentalize Christ – the Christ who is 'other' than us, even as we are united to him. As such, Calvin would prefer that we speak of "ascending" to this reality (than "dragging" Christ down to our realm). Calvin always expressed a haggard impatience with other theologians who did not understand the Spirit's role in this, "To them Christ does not seem present unless he comes down to us. As though, if he should lift us to himself, we should not just as much enjoy his presence!"[126] Calvin's language of going "up"' always signals that he takes seriously the Holy Spirit's activity to join us to Christ and all his benefits. It is his metaphor for participation.

E. Fatherhood, Union, and the Church

Following Calvin, I've reserved the sacraments for the end – though I am unconvinced that this is the best place for them, in that it can give the lie that one can have a spiritual *unio cum Christo* without the "messier" (secondary) bits such as church, the sacraments and one another. For Calvin, these were not optional add-ons but the sphere in which union with Christ actually existed. In words reminiscent of St. Cyprian, Calvin writes that the church is the one "into whose bosom God is pleased to gather his sons."[127] Not surprisingly, Calvin continues this familial imagery right into his discussion of the sacraments. If baptism is our "adoption," so the Lord's Supper is offered by a "provident householder" who supplies us with the food of life:

---

[124] Calvin, in Tylenda"s translation of his *First Letter to the Polish Nobles*, 12.
[125] Calvin, *Commentary on 1 Corinthians* 11:24.
[126] Calvin, *Institutes*, IV.17.31.
[127] Calvin, *Institutes*, IV.1.1.

God has received us, once for all, into his family, to hold us not only as servants but as sons. Thereafter, to fulfill the duties of a most excellent Father concerned for his offspring, he undertakes also to nourish us throughout the course of our life.[128]

The Lord's Supper is where the entirety of Calvin's theology of the Fatherhood of God, union with Christ, and participation in the Spirit is "on display." It is where we both receive union with Christ and actively participate in it in the concrete, physical realm – for in the Supper, we are able to join ourselves to Christ over and over again.[129] His task is to "feed" us, ours is to come to him "to be fed with such food"[130] – and not just symbolically, but *really*. "It would be extreme madness to recognize no communion of believers with the flesh and blood of the Lord."

The ascension signaled to Calvin that the eucharistic question had to involve both substance and Spirit. Just as Christ maintains his creaturely integrity as human at the right hand of the Father, so the bread and wine must be allowed to maintain their creaturely character as *meal*, or "supper." And yet, as testimony to the work of the Spirit, these very elemental things are taken up, transfigured, brought nearer to their intended end by their participation in the Spirit.

> It seems incredible that we should be nourished by Christ's flesh, which is at so great a distance from us. Let us bear in mind, that it is a secret and wonderful work of the Holy Spirit, which it were criminal to measure by the standard of our understanding.... Allow [Jesus] to remain in his heavenly glory, and aspire thou thither, that he may thence communicate himself to thee.[131]

The radical – even watershed – role that Calvin gave to the Spirit in the Lord's Supper cannot be overstated, for he (like the patristic fathers before him) attempted to take seriously the pneumatological dimensions of the presence of Christ. Just as it is the Spirit who brings us into Christ's relation to his Father, so it is the Spirit who brings humanity into the presence of Christ as the Lord's Supper is celebrated. Thus, for Calvin, the "miracle" of the Lord's Supper is not some transformation of materiality but our being invited continually into that miracle of the Father-Son relation. This in no way, however, makes the Supper *less* material. The Spirit, rather than 'spiritualizing' things (and thus often is interpreted as making them *less* physical, *less* concrete) is the very condition for their reality.[132] In fact, the

---

[128] Calvin, *Institutes*, IV.17.1.

[129] 'Rather, we ought to hold fast bravely with both hands to that fellowship by which he has bound himself to us." Calvin, *Institutes*, III.2.24.

[130] Calvin, *Institutes*, IV.17.32.

[131] Calvin, *Commentary on 1 Corinthians* 11:24.

[132] "We are truly made partakers of the proper substance of the body and blood of Jesus Christ ... [which] is made effectual by the secret and miraculous power of God, and that the Spirit of God is the bond of participation, this being the reason why it is called

Spirit's role is to ensure that we are fed just as "sumptuously and elegantly" as those who "draw Christ away from heaven."[133]

For this reason, the Supper is spoken in terms of the "steps of a ladder,"[134] bringing humanity 'up' into the concrete communion of Father and Son:

> For although the faithful come into this Communion on the very first day of their calling; nevertheless, inasmuch as the life of Christ increases in them, He daily offers Himself to be enjoyed by them. This is the Communion which they receive in the Sacred Supper.[135]

What do Christians receive in the Supper? They receive the very life of Christ – which they received on the first day of "their calling" – but which is an ongoing, ever-deepening reality.[136] Thus the Supper, far from being dispensable, is an essential part of the new creation self – that pneumatological miracle in which we are living more and more deeply into our corporate union with Christ. It is an identity-grounding praxis in which we are brought truly "out" of ourselves, and yet more deeply "into" ourselves and the others who make up our new identity as people *en Christo*. "What is the source of the *koinonia* or communion which exists among us," asks Calvin, "but the fact that we are united to Christ so that we are 'flesh of his flesh, and bone of His bones?' For it is necessary for us to be incorporated, as it were, into Christ, in order to be united to each other."[137] And this is the final miracle of our union with Christ: having the bounds of our identity stretched to include not only Jesus, but those whom he claims as his own. This is perhaps the truest, most practical (and painful) test of our "union with Christ" because adoption, by its very connotation, obligates us to being part of a family. Calvin says, "in order to prevent the *unity* of the Son with the Father from being fruitless and unavailing, the power of that *unity* must be diffused through the whole body of believers."[138] There are no "only children," no private franchises on *unio cum Christo*. If we are to take our union with Christ seriously, it must take the form of – not doctrinal correctness – but of unity in the Spirit.

---

spiritual." Calvin, *Short Treatise* in *Tracts and Treatises on the Doctrine and Worship of the Church* (vol. 2; 3 vols.; ed. Henry Beveridge; Grand Rapids: Eerdmans, 1958), 197.

[133] Calvin, *Institutes*, IV.17.2.

[134] Calvin, *Commentary on 1 Corinthians* 11:24.

[135] Calvin's Letter to Peter Martyr, 8 August 1555.

[136] Calvin interprets the four ritual acts of the Eucharistic rite in terms of Christ's vicarious humanity. See *Institutes*, IV.17.2.

[137] Calvin, *Commentary on 1 Corinthians* 10:16.

[138] Calvin, *Commentary on John* 17:21.

F. Conclusion

Anyone who has read the recent explosion of material in Calvin studies concerning union with Christ realizes that this consoling doctrine is now being consumed by controversy. A number of recent studies have highlighted Calvin's unusual terminology of the "Christ torn to pieces,"[139] a favorite saying of his to emphasize that one can no more separate justification from sanctification than tear Christ to pieces. It is my concern that it is actually Calvin studies that are being "torn to pieces" by fierce infighting over union with Christ. And this isn't anything new. William B. Evans reminds us that "Calvin's view of union with Christ and soteriology in general involved a matrix of realistic, personal, and forensic categories which was never fully developed and explained."[140] And as Calvin's successors attempted to secure the forensic from works righteousness, it was at the expense of making the forensic "rather abstract."[141] There are those who see this as a logical, even commendable extension of Calvin particularly given the theological and pastoral needs of the time.[142] There are others who want to return to a "naked Calvin" whose theology is clothed only in a mystical Christ. There are plenty in between. But the poles of perception are widening by the minute, such that *unio cum Christo* is becoming the "sorting hat" (of Harry Potter fame) to separate Reformed scholars out into their own houses, loyalties, lineages, and yes – inherited grudges.[143]

The purpose of this paper has been to open up windows and to seek vistas in the midst of the current controversy surrounding Calvin's doctrine of union with Christ, by focusing on the larger adoptive narrative within Calvin. This itself will be perceived to be controversial – as perhaps not giving enough space to the forensic, or the substitutionary, within Calvin. That is not my purpose. Yet I would like to argue that we cannot afford *not* to pay attention to this larger narrative flow. (Furthermore, I contend that our discussion of the very real forensic and substitutionary aspects within Calvin become *distorted* when not kept in check by this larger vision. For this purpose, I have attempted to script the larger drama that governs Calvin's theology, in which *unio cum Christo*, as well as the renowned forensic and substitutionary elements, play an indispensable part. My read is

---

[139] Mark Garcia, *Life in Christ*; Todd Billings, *Calvin, Participation, and the Gift*.

[140] Evans, "*Déjà Vu*," 136.

[141] Evans, "*Déjà Vu*," 136.

[142] Richard Muller, "Union with Christ and the *Ordo Salutis*: Reflections on Developments in Early Modern Reformed Thought," in *Calvin and the Reformed Tradition: On the Work of Christ and the Order of Salvation* (Grand Rapids: Baker, 2012), 202–43.

[143] See Julie Canlis, "Beyond Tearing One Another to Pieces: Union with Christ in Reformed Scholarship," *Journal of Reformed Theology* 8 (2014): 79–88.

that, for Calvin, there is no need to "reconcile" the forensic and participatory – this is a modern dilemma; rather, Calvin is "torn to pieces" when either is read without the other.[144] More specifically, participationist categories do not destroy, undermine, or call the forensic into question. They simply renegotiate the forensic, by insisting that it always be drawn it into the larger arena of the person of Christ and incorporation into him.). My hope is that within this larger vista, Reformed scholars will be able to make room for one another (rather than make union dependent upon uniformity); for has not Calvin taught us that true union is a work of the Holy Spirit, who can "join in one, things that are separated by distance of place" – or harder yet, distance of doctrine? By faithfully rooting union with Christ in the larger picture of Father and Son, my hope is to create an organic and fruitful rehabilitation of Calvin's doctrine of union with Christ for the current debate.

My brief summary of the "big picture" is this: Calvin believed that in the incarnation something drastic occurred. The God, who had been hidden and feared, suddenly revealed himself to humanity as the Father he had been all along. But because humanity has never been able to grasp this, or bring itself to believe the goodness of God (the Old Testament is always seen by Calvin as God testifying to an unbelieving Israel that *he is their Father*), God reveals his fatherhood through *one Man* who is able to truly receive him, relate to him, and obey him as a son. The Son. Even as this Son follows his Father to a cross, to atone for the sins of a world which cannot and will not receive him as Father, this Son is ever united to his Father in will and love. It is only in this Father-Son relationship that God's true identity as *Father*, and our true identity as *children,* are offered to us for our participation. Calvin's theology, for all its clarity and polemic usefulness, loses its narrative flow when it is pulled away from sonship – both the Sonship of Jesus and, consequently, our own adoptive sonship. "Adoption ... is not the cause merely of a partial salvation, but bestows salvation entire."[145]

In Calvin, adoption and union with Christ mutually reinforce one another. Union shows us the broad, marvelous mystery with which we are dealing, while adoption refines it, gives it precision, and takes on the character of Christ himself. Under Calvin's pen, the term "adoption" is used to speak of humanity's election, justification, regeneration, sanctification, and even

---

[144] See, for example, Calvin's *Commentary on Romans* 6:2, "Christ indeed does not cleanse us by his blood, nor render God propitious to us by his expiation, in other way than by making us partakers of his Spirit, who renews us to a holy life..."

[145] Calvin, *True Method of Obtaining Concord* in *Tracts and Treatises in Defense of the Reformed Faith* (vol. 3; 3 vols.; ed. Henry Beveridge; Grand Rapids: Eerdmans, 1958), 275.

glorification. Calvin does not use it consistently as a precise category but rather as one interrelated with many theological loci, perhaps for the obvious reason that these are not concepts, nor things, but aspects of *one* personhood. For Calvin, adoption is such that we are brought, by the "Spirit of adoption,"[146] to live out of the risen Son in his relationship to the Father. The identity and life of the Christian is transposed into a new realm "in Christ," where union is both achieved and a calling. This is our identity in light of the resurrection – it is received, and it is safely in Christ. But far from being ethereal, this new familial identity is nurtured continually at the "bosom" of our mother, the Church, who offers us the sacrament of the Supper and the "sacrament" of our brothers and sisters who now – and this is hard to stomach – form part of my "new creation" self.[147] Perhaps Calvin scholars can begin to allow this unity to sink into our bones, instead of (as Calvin lamented) "hiring ourselves, both hand and tongue, to the ungodly, that we may afford them sport and pastime by tearing one another to pieces."[148]

Bibliography

Barth, Karl. *Church Dogmatics*. 13 vols. 2d ed. Translated by Geoffrey William Bromiley and T. F. Torrance. Edinburgh: T&T Clark, 1957–1961

———. *Fragments Grave and Gay*. Translated by Martin Rumscheidt. Eugene, Ore.: Wipf & Stock, 2011.

———. *Revolutionary Theology in the Making: The Barth-Thurneysen Correspondence, 1914–1925*. Edited by Eduard Thurneysen. London: Epworth, 1964.

Billings, Todd. *Calvin, Participation, and the Gift: The Activity of Believers in Union with Christ*. Oxford: Oxford University Press, 2007.

Bouwsma, William. *John Calvin: A Sixteenth-Century Portrait*. New York: Oxford University Press, 1988.

Calvin, John. *A Reformation Debate: Sadoleto's Letter to the Genevans and Calvin's Reply*. Edited by John C. Olin. New York: Harper & Row, 1966.

———. *Old and New Testament Commentaries*. 22 volumes. Grand Rapids: Baker, 1979 (Calvin Translation Society, Edinburgh 1843–55).

———. *Institutes of the Christian Religion*. Library of Christian Classics 20–21. 2 vols. Edited by John T. McNeil. Translated by Ford Lewis Battles; Philadelphia: Westminster, 1960.

———. *Last Admonition to Joachim Westphal*. Pages 345b–94 in *On the Doctrine and Worship of the Church*. Volume 2 of *Tracts and Treatises*. 3 vols. Edited by Henry Beveridge. Grand Rapids: Eerdmans, 1958

---

[146] Calvin, *Institutes*, III.1.3.

[147] Calvin associates the self of the new creation with the church, *Commentary on 2 Corinthians* 5:17.

[148] John Calvin to an unknown recipient, January 1545, in *Letters of John Calvin I* (ed. Jules Bonnet; New York: Burt Franklin Reprints, 1972), 445.

———. *Letters of John Calvin I*. Edited by Jules Bonnet. New York: Burt Franklin Reprints, 1972.
———. *Psychopannychia*. Pages 413–90 in *In Defense of the Reformed Faith*. Volume 3 of *Tracts and Treatises*. 3 vols. Edited by Henry Beveridge. Grand Rapids: Eerdmans, 1958.
———. *Short Treatise on the Supper of Our Lord*. Pages 163–98 in *On the Doctrine and Worship of the Church*. Volume 2 of *Tracts and Treatises*. 3 vols. Edited by Henry Beveridge. Grand Rapids: Eerdmans, 1958.
———. *True Method of Obtaining Concord*. Pages 240–358 in *In Defense of the Reformed* Faith. Volume 3 of *Tracts and Treatises*. 3 vols. Edited by Henry Beveridge. Grand Rapids: Eerdmans, 1958.
———. *True Partaking of the Flesh and Blood of Christ*. Pages 495–572 in *On the Doctrine and Worship of the Church*. Volume 2 of *Tracts and Treatises*. 3 vols. Edited by Henry Beveridge. Grand Rapids: Eerdmans, 1958
Campbell, Constantine R. *Paul and Union with Christ: An Exegetical and Theological Study*. Grand Rapids: Zondervan, 2012.
Canlis, Julie. "Beyond Tearing One Another to Pieces: Union with Christ in Reformed Scholarship." *Journal of Reformed Theology* 8 (2014): 79–88.
———. *Calvin's Ladder: A Spiritual Theology of Ascent and Ascension*. Grand Rapids: Eerdmans, 2010.
Evans, William. "*Déjà Vu All Over Again*: The Contemporary Reformed Soteriological Controversy in Historical Perspective." *Westminster Theological Journal* 72 (2010): 135–51.
Garcia, Mark. *Life in Christ: Union with Christ and Twofold Grace in Calvin's Theology*. Milton Keynes: Paternoster, 2008.
Gerrish, Brian. *Grace and Gratitude: The Eucharistic Theology of John Calvin*. Minneapolis: Fortress, 1993.
Gunn, Neil. *The Silver Darlings*. London: Faber, 1978.
Kellner, Leon. *American Literature*. Garden City, N.Y.: Doubleday, 1915.
Lane, Beldon. *Ravished by Beauty*. New York: Oxford University Press, 2011.
Magnum, R. T. "Is There a Reformed Way to get the Benefits of the Atonement to 'Those Who Have Never Heard'?" *Journal of the Evangelical Theological Society* 47 (2004): 121–46.
McLelland, Joseph C. *The Visible Words of God*. Edinburgh: Oliver & Boyd, 1957.
Muller, Richard. "Union with Christ and the *Ordo Salutis*: Reflections on Developments in Early Modern Reformed Thought." Pages 202–43 in *Calvin and the Reformed Tradition: On the Work of Christ and the Order of Salvation*. Grand Rapids: Baker, 2012.
Oberman, Heiko A. "Subita Conversio: The Conversion of John Calvin." Pages 279–95 in *Reformiertes Erbe*. Vol 2. 2 vols. Edited by Heiko A. Oberman et al. Zurich: Theologischer Verlag, 1993.
Packer, J. I. *Knowing God*. Downers Grove, Ill.: InetrVarsity Press, 1994.
Parker, T. H. L. *Calvin's Old Testament Commentaries*. Edinburgh: T&T Clark, 1986.
Selderhuis, Herman. *John Calvin, A Pilgrim's Life*. Nottingham: InterVarsity Press, 2009.
Trumper, Timothy J. R. *An Historical Study of the Doctrine of Adoption in the Calvinist Tradition*. Ph.D. diss, University of Edinburgh, 2001
Tylenda, Joseph. "The Controversy on Christ the Mediator: Calvin's Second Reply to Stancaro." *Calvin Theological Journal* 8 (1973): 131–57.

"One with Him in Spirit"

Mystical Union and the Humanity of Christ in the Theology of John Owen

T. ROBERT BAYLOR

". . . whoever is united with the Lord is one with him in spirit."
1 Cor. 6:17 NIV11

The theme of union with Christ has recently been the object of renewed interest and debate within Reformed theology, in no small part because of critiques leveled by the New Perspective on Paul and Radical Orthodoxy, which have tended to find Reformed soteriology either unduly unilateral or overly invested in forensic registers. Under the weight of these criticisms, recent works in Calvin studies,[1] like those of Todd Billings and Julie Canlis, have sought to rehabilitate Calvin's theology of participation in Christ. The function which Calvin assigns to Christ's exalted human nature is pivotal for these readings, not only because Calvin's theology of participation developed alongside of his eucharistic theology, but also because it is in Calvin's doctrine of the eucharist that his theology of participation is most metaphysically specific.

These readings which find a strong theology of participation in Calvin renew the interpretive tradition of the nineteenth-century, American, Presbyterian theologian, John Williamson Nevin, whose work, *The Mystical Presence*,[2] sparked a lengthy and very public dispute with Princeton's Charles Hodge on the nature of participation in Christ. The central thesis of Nevin's work was that participation in Christ's humanity is basic, not only to Reformed eucharistic theology, but to Reformed soteriology as a whole. Not even a tenth of *The Mystical Presence* actually engages Calvin's thought directly - for the most part Calvin functions as a foil for

---

[1] J. Todd Billings, *Calvin, Participation, and the Gift* (Oxford: Oxford University Press, 2007); Julie Canlis, *Calvin's Ladder: A Spiritual Theology of Ascent and Ascension* (Grand Rapids: Eerdmans, 2010).

[2] John W. Nevin, *The Mystical Presence: A Vindication of the Reformed or Calvinistic Doctrine of the Holy Eucharist* (Philadelphia: S. R. Fisher & Co., 1867).

Nevin's polemic against exclusively forensic or moral accounts of union with Christ. But Nevin's reading of Calvin leads him to reject Reformed Scholastic and Puritan accounts of union with Christ as discontinuous with the Reformed tradition, dependent on a form of rationalism, and promoting a kind of "abstract spirituality."[3]

The renewal of Nevin's reading of Calvin has sparked fresh debate concerning the nature of Reformed Orthodoxy and its relation to Calvin on the matter of participation in Christ, resurrecting longstanding intra-mural disputes about the substance of Reformed identity and the nature of salvation. For example, in his book *Imputation and Impartation,* William Evans argues that the Reformed Scholastics divided union with Christ into distinctly federal and moral dimensions, displacing the doctrine's more traditional (and objective) attachments to Christology and sacramentology, and instead distributing the virtue of Christ's benefits across other "successive and discrete acts" of the *ordo salutis*.[4] According to Evans, this exchanged the more authentically Reformed doctrine of participation in Christ's humanity articulated in Calvin, for a fictive doctrine of justification on the one hand and a pietistic vision of the Christian life on the other. In response, defenders of Reformed Orthodoxy, like J. V. Fesko, and more recently Richard Muller, have criticized Evans' depiction as inattentive to the diversity within Reformed Orthodoxy, the nuance of its theological idiom, and the sizable role that union with Christ plays within it.[5]

In these debates, John Owen has often been a convenient figure to cast in a supporting role in the narrative. Not only is he generally regarded as a theological high-watermark of Reformed Orthodoxy, but he also produced one of the most comprehensive and fully developed visions of Reformed soteriology on offer. From the atonement and justification, to sanctification and the work of the Spirit, among the canon of Reformed theologians working prior to Modernity, few gave such focused attention to the economy of redemption. And, as C. F. Allison has rightly noted, with respect to the doctrine of union with Christ, almost no one in the period places more emphasis upon it than Owen.[6]

---

[3] *Mystical Presence*, 152; *cf.* John W. Nevin, "Puritanism and the Creed," *The Mercersburg Review* 1 (1849): 585–607.

[4] William Evans, *Imputation and Impartation: Union with Christ in American Reformed Theology* (Milton Keynes: Paternoster, 2008), 43–83. See also, William Evans, "Déja vu All Over Again? The Contemporary Reformed Soteriological Controversy in Historical Perspective," *WTJ* 72 (2010): 135–51.

[5] J.V. Fesko, "Methodology, Myth, and Misperception: A Response to William B. Evans," *WTJ* 72 (2010): 391–402; Richard Muller, *Calvin and the Reformed Tradition: On the Work of Christ and the Order of Salvation* (Grand Rapids: Baker, 2013), 202–43.

[6] C. F. Allison, *The Rise of Moralism: The Proclamation of the Gospel from Hooker to Baxter* (London: SPCK, 1966), 262.

And yet, depending on the author, Owen's role in the narrative is subject to change. Evans, for example, uses Owen's sacramental theology to illustrate the diminished role of union with Christ within Puritanism and the virtualizing tendency that ultimately reduces union with Christ to forensic or moral categories.[7] George Hunsinger's essay appears to contest this, arguing that, continuous with Calvin, Owen makes mystical union the "necessary precondition" of double-imputation and thus endorses a "moderate forensic" doctrine of justification rather than a "thoroughgoing" forensicism, where justification might be detailed exclusively in law-court imagery.[8] Fesko, on the other hand, argues that Owen's doctrine of union with Christ is quite fulsome, even if it is finally subordinate to forensic themes, which precede it logically and temporally in the form of the covenant of redemption. In that respect, Fesko argues, Owen's view is generally rather "mainstream and mundane."[9]

These analyses of Owen's thought yield conflicting accounts in part because they have failed to set Owen's theology of union with Christ in the context of his larger Christology, where the concept of "union" has a much more variegated and expansive application. In what follows, I will offer a very brief sketch of Owen's doctrine of mystical union with Christ. The mystical character of the church's union with Christ is necessitated by Christ's ascension and bodily absence, therefore the nexus between Owen's christology and pneumatology, particularly as they relate to his theology of the incarnation and the redemptive function of Christ's humanity, are of particular importance to his theology of mystical union. I will argue that the substitutionary nature of Owen's atonement theology introduces several irregularities into his generally Thomist[10] theology of nature and grace, irregularities which he is forced to confront at the point of the believer's incorporation into Christ. Rather than expanding his christology and adjusting his theology of nature, Owen alternately attempts to address these concerns through his theology of the covenant, but mainly through his pneumatology, drawing on Paul's image of the Church as being "one in

---

[7] Evans, *Imputation*, 79–80.

[8] George Hunsinger, "Justification and Mystical Union with Christ: Where Does Owen Stand?" in *The Ashgate Research Companion to John Owen's Theology* (ed. Kelly Kapic and Mark Jones; Burlington, Vt.: Ashgate, 2012), 199–211. In the main, Hunsinger's agrees with that of Kelly Kapic, *Communion with God: The Divine and the Human in the Theology of John Owen* (Grand Rapids: Baker, 2007), 107–47.

[9] J. V. Fesko, "John Owen on Union with Christ and Justification," *Themelios* 37/1 (2012): 7–9; cf. Carl Trueman, *John Owen: Reformed Catholic, Renaissance Man* (Great Theologians Series; Burlington, Vt.: Ashgate), 101–21; and Sinclair Ferguson, *John Owen on the Christian Life* (Edinburgh: Banner of Truth, 1987), 32–36.

[10] For more on the influence of Thomism in Owen's thought, see Christopher Cleveland, *Thomism in John Owen* (Burlington, Vt.: Ashgate, 2013).

spirit" with Christ (1 Cor. 6:17). This leads Owen to seek a more narrow function for Christ's human nature than other Reformed alternatives, and this gives his account of union with Christ a strongly "spiritual" character.

Union with Christ is a dimension of the new creation in Christ, and Owen typically organizes his treatment of the new creation around a distinction between Christ's personal and capital grace, treating first the graces peculiar to Christ's person, and subsequently the operations by which Christ communicates his grace as Head (*caput*) of the church.[11] This is, in the first place, a trinitarian conviction. For in the peace and perfection of God's immanent life, the Son has eternally proceeded from the Father, and the Spirit from the Father and the Son. These trinitarian processions ground the missions of the Father, Son, and Spirit within the economy of grace. It is therefore fitting that the regenerative mission of the Spirit should follow on the redemptive mission of the Son, both because the Son's redemptive work is its cause, but also because the Spirit's work perfects the redemptive mission of the Son by bringing it to its proper fulfillment. Thus, Owen's theology of the new creation carefully reflects his trinitarian theology.

Yet Owen's organization at this point also reflects a series of christological distinctions which he borrowed from Aquinas, who described Christ's person as endued with a three-fold grace: i) the "grace of union," which refers to the virtue that accrues to his person as a consequence of the union of his two natures; ii) habitual or personal grace, which consists in the created graces infused into his humanity by the Spirit; and iii) the grace of headship or capital grace, which is not distinct from his personal grace, but is really only a modality of it as it is exercised for the benefit of the church.[12] For Aquinas, this three-fold distinction served a primarily analytical function, enabling him to closely relate Christ's person and works by tracing the various causes of Christ's works to some antecedent aspect of his person. In particular, this distinction enabled Aquinas to identify the manner in which Christ's two natures served as causes of the church's redemption. Consequently, the doctrine also had a hand in shaping Aquinas' theology of Christ's headship over the church, enabling him to offer a complex account of the church's participation in the work of Christ.[13]

Though by no means identical in every respect, Owen's own account of Christ's headship follows a similar pattern. Therefore, in order to understand Owen's theology of union with Christ, particularly as it relates to the

---

[11] John Owen, *The Works of John Owen* (*Works*), (ed. William H. Goold; Edinburgh: T&T Clark), 2:46–54; 3:160; 5:180.

[12] *Cf.* Aquinas, *Summa Theologiae* (*ST*), (61 vols.; Cambridge: Cambridge University Press, 2006), IIIa, q. 6, a. 6.

[13] *Cf. ST* IIIa, q. 8, a. 1.

church's mystical union with Christ in the time of his exaltation and ascension, it is important for us to locate it within this threefold grace, which enables Owen to distinguish between the different aspects of Christ's headship over the church, and thus the different modes of the church's participation in him.

A. Grace of Union

In the first instance, Christ is the Head of the new creation as he acquires its benefits by the grace of union. The grace which Christ communicates to the church is first and foremost the grace *of Christ*. It is "peculiar unto himself," existing eminently in his person prior to and independently from his loving communication of it to the saints.[14] Owen thus refers to the work of Christ – and his person as the principle of that work – as the *procuring cause* of redemption, because it is by his holy life and obedient death that Christ merits the church's redemption.

This work is rendered necessary by the dictates of divine justice. In 1653, with the publication of his *Dissertation on Divine Justice*, Owen makes an important alteration to his atonement theology. Six years earlier, in *The Death of Death*, Owen had argued that punishment for sin was merely a function of the divine will, that the suggestion that God punishes sin of necessity is "an unwritten tradition, the Scripture affirming no such thing," and one which cannot be deduced from "any good consequence."[15] Owen reverses this position in his *Dissertation on Divine Justice*, making the argument that divine justice is God's active affirmation of the perfection of his own life, and is therefore an essential attribute of God, which directs every operation of the divine will.[16] Owen draws an analogy here between the place of justice and truthfulness in the divine nature – just as God cannot will to be untrue because truthfulness is essential to God's nature, so God cannot will that which is unjust, for justice is essential to God.[17] But by its very nature sin usurps the divine right and despoils God of his glory. And while there can be no question of creaturely sin finally dispensing with God's Lordship, if the creature's insubordination were permitted to stand without punishment, "it might be possible that God should lose his natural right and dominion over his creatures, and thus he

---

[14] Owen, *Works*, 5:180.

[15] Owen, *Works*, 10:205.

[16] Creaturely justice, which is the will or act of "assigning to everyone his due," is an analogue to divine justice, God's affirmation of his own perfection; Owen, *Works*, 10:503–4.

[17] Owen, *Works*, 10:508.

would not be God."[18] This use of the counterfactual and others throughout the *Dissertation* indicate the full investment of the divine nature in the proper order of creation. Sin is not simply the derangement of a relatively arbitrary order, for Owen; for God's nature identifies so closely with creation's original constitution that there is a strict antithesis between creaturely sin and divine perfection. Since God's justice is the active affirmation of his perfection, God cannot be both just and indifferent to the breaking of the law, for this would necessarily entail an absurdity, namely, God's denial of himself.

In order for God to forgive sinners, a proportional satisfaction must be rendered on their behalf. The concept of "proportion" was a critical element of scholastic theologies that, like Owen's, employed a concept of natural law. "Justice" is the act of giving to everyone his due, and therefore that act is "just" which bears a kind of natural proportion to its object.[19] And while the object of creaturely sin is the infinite God, to whom no created thing can possibly be proportionate, like Aquinas, Owen argues that there is an inherent proportion between the work of Christ and the church's salvation, a proportion which is grounded in the grace of union.[20] For as Christ is both God and man, he is of infinitely greater dignity[21] than all other creatures, and therefore his active and passive obedience infinitely exceeds all their demerits by proportion. As such, his work possesses an inherent proportion to its object, namely, to divine justice, and therefore is truly capable of making restitution for the church.

At the same time, however, Owen urges that the relation between Christ and the church that enables Christ to make satisfaction on its behalf does not arise merely "from the nature of the things themselves."[22] That is, though not absolutely contradictory to the order of nature, the mediation of Christ is not native to the original order of nature, as such.

There was no such thing, nothing of that nature or kind, in the first constitution of that relation and obedience by the law of our creation. We were made in a state of immediate relation unto God in our own persons as our creator, preserver, and rewarder . . . nothing of the interposition of a mediator with respect unto our righteousness before God, and

---

[18] Owen, *Works*, 10:509.

[19] See John Finnis, *Natural Law and Natural Rights* (2d ed.; Oxford: Oxford University Press, 2011), 162–63.

[20] Owen, *Works*, 19:94.

[21] "Dignity" has a semi-technical function in classical moral philosophy as a way of mapping the proportionality, and hence justice, of any arrangement between two parties, particularly in cases concerning the act of restitution. This element plays a central role in scholastic moral theology (e.g., *ST* IIaIIae, q. 61, a. 3), and especially in atonement theologies indebted to Anselm.

[22] Owen, *Works*, 19:94.

acceptance with him; which is at present the life and soul of religion, the substance of the gospel, and the centre of all the truths revealed in it.[23]

Under the natural order of things, one must merit exclusively for oneself. As was the case with Adam under the law of nature, each person stands in an "immediate relation unto God" with respect to the virtue and merit of their own actions. The relation that enables Christ to merit on behalf of the church is an augmentation to this order – a kind of emergency measure occasioned only by the fall.

For Owen, the relation that enables Christ to merit for the church is grounded in the *pactum salutis*, that eternally gracious and free determination of God in himself to elect and redeem sinners to the praise of his glory. In this eternal and ineffable *pactum*, the Son voluntarily assumes the call of the Father, who is the principle of this covenant, agreeing to take on flesh and serve as the "surety" of the church's redemption.[24] As Owen defines it, a surety is one who voluntary undertakes for another person or group of people by an oath, and "thereon is justly and *legally* to answer what is due to them, or from them."[25] Thus, against the Socinian argument that Christ is surety from God to the elect – a kind of sign or assurance that God will keep his promise, Owen maintains that Christ is principally a surety *for us* to God, since he undertakes to make restitution for the debt of sin and to endow us with his righteousness. According to Owen, wherever a surety assumes this duty, a union is formalized between the surety and those he represents – they "coalesce into one person, as unto the ends of that suretyship."[26] This union with Christ in the covenant is, for Owen, the basis of Christ's ability to merit on behalf of the elect. As this union is *federal* in nature, it is strictly *forensic*. But because Owen holds to a definite atonement, it is not merely a nameless multitude but the very identities of the elect persons themselves which are incorporated into his person. Christ does not give his life to obtain merely a deposit of grace, but to redeem and sanctify the persons of the elect. For this reason Christ took on flesh, in order that he might fulfill in his person all that God had required of the church, and in this way procure her freedom.

---

[23] Owen, *Works*, 5:44–45.

[24] Though a kind of dramatization of what is ultimately an ineffable determination in the life of God, Owen urges that the *pactum salutis* in no way suggests that the economy of grace was the consequence of a discursive or deliberative process. Only that God's works of redemption were a *free* act of the Father, Son and Spirit, and that these works are logically *ordered* to one another in the mind of God as the fitting conditions and effects attending the redemption of creatures; Owen, *Works*, 19:77–97.

[25] Owen, *Works*, 5:182.

[26] Owen, *Works*, 5:181.

Given the somewhat Thomist framework of Owen's theology of nature, it is instructive to note the differences between Aquinas and Owen at this point. Aquinas understands Christ's work of atonement as congruent with the natural order of friendship, according to which a person may bear the debt of another when the two parties are joined together by love.[27] Yet critically, for Aquinas, Christ's work is not, strictly speaking, a *substitution* for the sinner – Christ does not suffer or merit *in the sinner's place*. Indeed, this could not be the case since, on Aquinas' account, merit is intrinsic to the natural order as the means by which creatures attain their end. To suggest that Christ could suffer or merit as a substitute for the church, would undermine either the order of creation or the nature of divine government, for it would imply that creatures might be justly related to God without being *just* – that is, properly ordered in themselves.[28] Sin is a disruption of the natural order; and the guilt and stain of sin are incommunicable from the person in which they originate and can finally be removed only as a person is properly ordered to the good, acquiring justice only by their union with God in the sacrament of penance. Aquinas thus speaks of the atonement as an "exterior act" (*actu exteriori*), an "instrument" by which Christ offers to the church the kind of aid and support that one might lend to a friend. But this cannot replace or curtail the necessity of Christian confession and contrition, which are *interior* acts by which the church both appropriates Christ's work and merits eternal life.[29]

---

[27] For Aquinas, Christ is appointed by God to be the friend of sinners, and the graciousness of Christ's work consists in the fact that he merits on behalf of the church by his death, which is a supererogatory work. Christ's passion makes satisfaction for the church in the sense that the superabundance of his merit fills up what is lacking in their own merit. Christ's work is universal in scope, in virtue of the abundance of Christ's merit and the potential of any and all men and women to be incorporated into his body (*ST* IIIa, q. 8, a. 3); but his friendship with the church is formalized in the gift of baptism, as the church is mystically united to Christ, becoming one in charity with him (*ST* IIIa, q. 48, a. 2, ad. 1). By virtue of this bond, Christ is able to merit on behalf of the church, and in turn *restores* the church's power to merit, sanctifying and elevating her works so that she might lay hold of her end – eternal life. *Cf. ST* IaIIae, q. 87, a. 7; also Daniel Schwartz, *Aquinas on Friendship* (Oxford: Oxford University Press, 2007), 142–61.

[28] *ST* IaIIae, q. 87, a. 6–8.

[29] *Ad primum ergo dicendum quod caput et membra sunt quasi una persona mystica. Et ideo satisfactio Christi ad omnes fideles pertinet sicut ad sua membra. Inquantum etiam duo homines sunt unum in caritate, unus pro alio satisfacere potest, ut infra patebit. Non autem est similis ratio de confessione et contritione, quia satisfactio consistit in actu exteriori, ad quem assumi possunt instrumenta; inter quae computantur etiam amici; ST* IIIa, q. 48, a. 2, ad. 1.

As we noted above, Owen, like Aquinas, regards merit to be in some sense intrinsic to the natural order between God and creatures.[30] But Owen's theology of definite atonement entitles him to an especially realistic conception of the church's participation in Christ's work such that Christ both suffers the penalty due to the elect by virtue of their sin (the *idem*, as Owen calls it in contrast to Baxter's *tantidem*) and also imputes to them the righteousness of his active obedience, that they might have a right and title to eternal life. It is precisely the *substitutionary* character of Christ's work that constitutes it as gracious, so much so that Owen can contrast grace and merit absolutely, as things "which God had everlastingly separated and opposed," for grace *just is* a gift received on the merit of another.[31] So, while both can speak of the church being incorporated in the very *person* of Christ, the church's relation to the person of Christ is much more intimate on Owen's account than it is on Aquinas'. Owen cannot appeal, as Aquinas does, to the natural order of friendship as a way of grounding Christ's ability to merit for the church, for the substitutionary nature of Christ's work requires a union that is incomparable with anything in the natural order. Owen finds the ground of this relation in something above nature, namely, in the eternal will of the Son to take on flesh and become our substitute – the grace of union.

The grace of union, therefore, is necessary for Christ's procurement of the graces of the new creation. Owen's move to make the incarnation necessary in order for God to forgive sin has several important ramifications for his theology of redemption as a whole. In the first place, it tends to focus Owen's Christology and the soteriological function of the incarnation somewhat more exclusively on his vicarious death within the economy of grace. Consequently, while Owen affirms that the incarnation constitutes Christ as the Mediator according to both natures in the threefold office of prophet, priest, and king, the incarnation is also *heavily* determined for the purpose of Christ's *priestly* work. So much so that Owen not only maintains that Christ became incarnate strictly for the purpose of redeeming sinners, but even that Christ became a man strictly for the purpose of his death.[32] This has the effect of restricting the redemptive virtue of Christ's humanity *primarily* to its penal dimensions, giving Owen's account of participation in Christ's human nature a strongly forensic character.

The second effect of Owen's theology of divine justice is that it tends toward an intensification in his theology of the new creation. Because

---

[30] Because of their infinite ontological difference, any friendship between God and creatures cannot stem from nature *qua* nature, but from the gratuity of God's promise. Cf. Owen, *Works*, 2:8; 10:468.

[31] Owen, *Works*, 3:379–80; 19:95.

[32] Owen, *Works*, 1:356.

God's perfection is itself implicated in the form of creation, the work of redemption must bring about a genuinely *new* creature, one which is fully reflective of God's own peace and perfection. This places a great deal of urgency on the doctrines of regeneration and sanctification as the works by which God leads creatures to peace. It is perhaps no surprise, therefore, that Owen developed a massive and massively detailed account of these works in *Pneumatologia*, his 1,200 page treatise on the person and works of the Holy Spirit. An account of the work of new creation is what Owen "principally intended" when he set out to write *Pneumatologia*.[33]

B. Personal Grace

Christ is the Head of the new creation not only as he is the *cause* of grace by virtue of *the grace of union*, but also as he is the *exemplar* of all those *personal* and *habitual* graces that God works in his church by the Spirit. The gifts and graces of the new creation existed in him as to their first pattern and origin. Accordingly, Owen opens up his discussion of the new creation in *Pneumatologia* by focusing on the Spirit's work of forming and sanctifying Christ's human nature in the womb of the virgin, for by this mysterious work Christ truly *is* in his humanity that which he has come to *give* to his church.[34] So, Owen speaks of Christ's humanity as "a repository and treasury of all that goodness, grace, life, light, power, and mercy, which were necessary for the constitution and preservation of the new creation."[35]

The foundation for this work, too, was laid in the *pactum salutis*, where the Father committed to support the Son in his mission to redeem the church by endowing him with all those graces which were intended for them. Therefore, as the Son voluntarily assumes the law and work of the Mediator in eternity, he is constituted the *prōton dektikon* – that is, the first object to whom the benefits of the covenant accrue. This point is somewhat easy to pass over too quickly as a dramatic feature of Owen's covenantal thought, but it is actually a point of some importance, as it makes the incarnate person of Christ the sole heir of all the benefits of the new creation. It is, in that sense, a kind of gloss, identifying the divine will as the eternal basis of Paul's teaching in Galatians 3:16 – that the promises of the covenant were made to Abraham's seed, "who is *Christ*." The benefits of the new creation are annexed to Christ, in the first instance, because of the grace of union; because by his grace, the Son elected to take on flesh and

---

[33] Owen, *Works*, 3:152.
[34] Owen, *Works*, 3:159–67.
[35] Owen, *Works*, 1:362.

be made a surety on behalf of the church. And because it was the Son who elected this work, it is the Son who shall be made the heir of all things according to the promise.

Thus, the Father sends the Spirit to form in Mary a temple fit for the indwelling of the Son and the fulfillment of his mission.[36] Owen lays considerable emphasis on this as an act of *new creation*, not because the humanity of Christ was produced out of nothing, but because, by the operation of the Holy Spirit, it received a form for which it otherwise had no "active disposition."[37] For while all Adam's descendants were corrupted by original sin, and thus depraved by nature, the humanity of Christ was formed apart from natural generation – it was a miracle, wrought by God in a truly new creation. As the Spirit first moved upon the face of the waters, adorning creation with order and form; and as the Spirit was the breath that first brought Adam to life, crowning all his faculties with the original righteousness which directed him in the holy love and service of God; so also the Spirit moved upon the womb of the virgin, adorning Christ's human nature with every grace. From the very first Christ was sanctified and eminently prepared to perform that work to which he had been called. In this sense, the humanity of Christ was indeed the first and most eminent recipient of all those graces of the Spirit which God had laid up for the church in the promise of new covenant. The church is truly blessed "with every spiritual blessing *in Christ*" (Eph. 1:3).

It is true, of course, that Christ's eminent fullness of grace necessarily distinguishes him from all other persons who contend with the unruly desires of a disordered and depraved nature. But this does not mean that Christ was exempted from the suffering and temptation that afflicts the church, or that his was not a truly human existence. It means only that the afflictions which he suffered advanced on him from "without."[38] At the same time, however, that does not render the moral orientation of Christ's "inner" life automatic. To the contrary! His temptations, like those which Adam faced, were real and true temptations. Nor was their force lessened by the grace of union. Owen urges that apart from the Logos' assumption of his human nature into a personal subsistence with himself, all other communications to Christ's human nature are performed by the Holy Spirit. Owen's stated concern in this is to avoid any hint of Apollinarianism that might abridge Christ's full humanity in common with us.[39] This is a pivotal point for Owen to secure, since Christ atones for sin *as a man,* and

---

[36] Following Aquinas, *ST* Ia, q. 45, a. 3.
[37] Owen, *Works*, 3:164.
[38] Owen, *Works*, 20:467–68.
[39] Owen, *Works*, 3:169.

particularly in virtue of the integrity of his *soul*.[40] Consequently, Owen stresses that the divine nature did not operate directly on the humanity of Christ, as if to cut short its fully human character. Rather, in accordance with the indivisible order of the trinitarian operations, and in keeping with the nature of the Spirit's works in creation and redemption more generally, having assumed flesh, the *Logos* operated upon his human nature only in and by the Holy Spirit.

It is precisely in virtue of Christ's fully human existence that he can fulfill his prophetic office. For as Christ bears his affliction in faith, he not only instructs the church in holiness, and teaches it to suffer patiently – but he also exemplifies those graces which are available to the church, those graces that take hold of the inner life of the soul and compose it even in the face of great hostility. And furthermore, the glorious transformation of Christ's person evidenced in his resurrection is a sign of the certainty of Christian hope and the glory into which the faithful will be welcomed on Christ's account. For not only did Christ merit his own exaltation by his obedient life and death, but also that of his church. Just as Christ was raised to life and glorified in the very body in which he died, so by his divine power he will lift up the church and usher her into a state of perfection and peace. The church need only endure with patience, following the example of her Lord. Thus, the *grace of union* is the final ground of Christ's procurement of the graces of the new creation, but Christ's *personal grace* serves as an *exemplary cause* of the church's redemption, instructing her in holiness and guiding her in the path of truth.

C. Capital Grace

Christ is Head of the new creation as he *procures* grace by the grace of union, and as he *exemplifies* grace by his personal and habitual graces. But Christ is also the Head of the new creation as he *communicates* his benefits to the church by his *capital* grace. Capital grace is thus an operative mode[41] of Christ's personal grace, in its action upon and communication to the church. Unlike much of modern Reformed dogmatics, Owen does not ground this communication in some form of ontological participation established in the incarnation. For Owen, human nature is a created kind – a universal – of which the Son of God has assumed a *particular* instantiation. As such, Christ's humanity does not form, as it does in Barth, a kind of ontological co-principle which either perfects or constitutes human nature. Rather, for Owen, human nature is an ontologically discrete thing by

---

[40] Owen, *Works*, 9:531.
[41] *Cf. ST* IIIa, q. 8, a. 5, ad. 1.

virtue of having an "individual subsistence" which is exclusive to itself as a gift of God, and is therefore both uncompounded with and incommunicable to others.[42]

As a matter of principle, Owen is generally quite reticent to speculate on the finer matters of metaphysics. But this is not merely an abstract principle derived from observations about the metaphysics of nature more generally. Rather, it is an outworking of Owen's theology of creation. Barth's suggestion that the incarnation is in some sense ontologically necessary for the fulfillment of human nature would imply, to Owen at any rate, the imperfection of the created order. For God called creation "good," and the collective witness of Scripture is that the incarnation was necessitated not by *creation* but by *sin*. Therefore, the incarnation was not intended to perfect creation *per se*, but to perfect the natures of fallen creatures. The original perfection of creation thus implies to Owen that human created nature must have been complete in and of itself at the time of its creation.[43]

The work of Christ thus entails no immediate or necessary alteration to creatures or creation more generally, nor even does it effect an immediate alteration in the elect in particular. This distinction on the metaphysics of human nature proves quite pivotal for Owen at several points, especially in his applied soteriology, where it carves out space for distinguishing between redemption accomplished and redemption applied. As we mentioned above, Owen's theology of definite atonement entitles him to a very intimate account of the substitutionary nature of Christ's work such that, in order to receive Christ's benefits, believers must be incorporated into Christ's very *person*. Owen's metaphysics of the incarnation supports him at this point by enabling him to draw a distinction between Christ's *natural* person and his *public* person, and in this way to specify the *nature* of the Christian's union with Christ's person.[44]

This distinction between natural and public persons was a means of differentiating between subjective rights and obligations which were natural to a person, and those which were possessed *ex officio*. Legal historians like F. W. Maitland, Otto von Gierke, and Ernst Kantorowicz have traced the origin of this distinction, unsurprisingly, to principles of Roman law, the influence of which had been on the rise throughout the 16th and early

---

[42] Owen, *Works*, 17:567 (Banner Edition: 16:499).

[43] Owen, *Works*, 19:15–42.

[44] Hunsinger argues that Owen's theology of incorporation into Christ's person moderates the forensic element of his theology of justification; Hunsinger, "Justification and Mystical Union," 199–211. But this distinction would indicate that when Owen speaks of incorporation into Christ's person, he does so to specify a federal relation, rather than a natural relation. A "person," in this context, is a legal agent, suggesting that incorporation into Christ's person does not so much moderate Owen's forensicism, as point to the union of personal and forensic elements within the covenant.

17th centuries, especially among jurists and political theorists. Kantorowicz in particular has shown the wide utility of the concept in early modern England, where jurists often conceptualized the crown as a kind of corporation, analyzing the rights and responsibilities which attended the crown according to the legal fiction of the "King's two-bodies" – that is, his natural or personal body, and his "body politic."[45] The "body politic" was effectively a legal abstraction to which the rights and privileges of the Sovereign were annexed, and which entailed a kind of limitation on the forms of action that the Sovereign might undertake *ex officio*. Among many Reformed thinkers, speaking of Christ as a "public person" became a way to designate Christ in his appointment as the Sponsor of the covenant and Head of the new creation. Richard Sibbes, John Flavel, and William Perkins all refer to Adam and Christ as "public persons," in contrast with "natural" or "private persons," as a way of designating their special federal office.[46] This language is also used in the *Westminster Larger Catechism* in conjunction with q. 22, on the fall of humankind in Adam's sin (citing Gen. 2:16–17; Rom. 5:12–20; 1 Cor. 15:21–22), and q. 52, on Christ's exaltation in the resurrection (citing 1 Cor 15:21–22). In both cases, the term "public person" indicates the headship of Adam and Christ as representatives of the human race, and the corporate solidarity of humankind in them, which forms the basis for participation in their work. As such, it recalls the *pactum salutis* under which Christ assumed the role of a surety for the church.

Owen appeals to this distinction in defending the doctrine of justification against the Socinian objection that imputation confuses the righteousness of Christ with the sinner, making the sinner truly righteous, and Christ truly a sinner, and therefore hated by God. Owen argues that this criticism fails because justification does not finally depend upon incorporation into Christ's *natural* person, but upon participation in Christ as he is a "common person," that is, in the exercise of his office as a federal head.[47] Likewise, it is this distinction which ultimately allows Owen to skirt the charges of Baxter who claimed that his atonement theology was inherently antinomian. Baxter alleged that Owen's theology of substitution effectively

---

[45] Ersnt Hartwig Kantorowicz, *The King's Two Bodies: A Study in Mediaeval Political Theology* (Princeton: Princeton University Press, 1957).

[46] Richard Sibbes, *A Commentary on the First Chapter of the Second Epistle to the Corinthians* (vol. 3 of *The Complete Works of Richard Sibbes*; 7 vols.; Edinburgh: James Nichol, 1862), 418; John Flavel, *The Fountain of Life Opened* (London: The Religious Tract Society, 1836), 399; William Perkins, *A Golden Chaine* (London: Iohn Legatte, 1616), 78.

[47] "Our sin was imputed unto him . . . not absolutely, but as he was a surety." *Works*, 5:203, *cf.* 5:219–23. See also where Owen speaks of the church as "seated in heavenly realms with Christ" according to his public person, by virtue of the covenant of the Mediator; Owen, *Works*, 2:176–80).

conflated the person of Christ with the person of the sinner. For if before their conversion Christ both suffered the very punishment due for the sin of the elect (the *idem*), and by the imputation of his righteousness endowed the elect with a right and title to eternal life, then conversion does not really effect a change in the Christian's standing. Thus, Baxter concluded that Owen had tacitly committed himself to a version of eternal justification by conflating Christ's person and ours. In response, Owen argues that believers are incorporated into Christ's person, not naturally, but as he is their Sponsor in the covenant.[48] So, borrowing a distinction from Grotius, Owen states that the elect possess a right to eternal life prior to their conversion, but that they do not possess this right *actively,* as a "faculty," but only *passively,* as an "aptitude."[49]

The intent of the distinction between Christ's public and private person is thus to avoid some pretty damaging criticisms of the doctrine of justification by relocating discussion of the *application* of Christ's benefits away from the locus of the incarnation and Christ's human nature. At the same time however, this distinction would appear to introduce a separation between Christ's personal and capital grace at a very critical moment, potentially undermining the real union between Christ and the church and thus threatening not only Owen's doctrine of justification, but also the coherence of his doctrine of substitutionary atonement as a whole. This is fundamentally a problem for Owen's theology of nature and grace. For "righteousness" is a predicate of created nature that is properly ordered toward its end; and to be a sinner *just is* to be disordered with respect to one's end. So if the sinner has no real union with Christ's *natural* person by virtue of the incarnation, how can we understand the sinner's participation in Christ's righteousness without appealing to some kind of legal fiction? Or without separating Christ's person and work?

Aquinas addresses a similar problem in the *Summa*, when he considers whether or not Christ's personal grace and capital grace are really separate. It is instructive for us to note how this develops in Aquinas's first reply,[50]

---

[48] Owen, *Works*, 12:614; concerning a similar scuffle with William Sherlock, see Paul C. H. Lim, *Mystery Unveiled: The Crisis of the Trinity in Early Modern England* (Oxford: Oxford University Press, 2012), 204–16.

[49] Owen, *Works*, 12:609–11; Grotius uses the language of "faculty" and "aptitude" to distinguish different ways of holding a subjective right. Under the former, the agent employs and makes active use of his right, while under the latter the agent possesses the moral quality to "have or do something justly," but does not make active use of this quality; Grotius, *The Rights of War and Peace* (ed. Richard Tuck; Indianapolis: Liberty Fund, 2005), I.i.4. *Cf.* Hans Boersma, *A Hot Pepper Corn: Richard Baxter's Doctrine of Justification in Its Seventeenth-Century Context of Controversy* (Vancouver: Regent College Publishing, 2004), 219–56.

[50] *ST* IIIa, q. 8, a. 5, ad. 1.

where he addresses the suggestion that since the *actual* sin of Adam is distinct from the *original* sin which he passed on to his posterity, the *capital* grace that Christ communicates to the church must be distinct from his *habitual* or *personal* grace. Aquinas has already argued that Christ's power to merit on behalf of the church consists in his union with them as "one mystical person."[51] He thus wishes to deny that Christ's personal grace is really distinct from his capital grace because that would create a separation between Christ's person and his work on behalf of the church. Yet, rather than denying the difference between the actual sin of Adam and the original sin which Adam passed to his posterity, Aquinas draws a modal distinction between the manner of the church's *participation* in Adam and Christ. The corruption of Adam's nature was communicated to humankind by means of participation in a common human *nature*; but the grace of Christ is not communicated by means of a common nature. Rather, Christ communicates his grace by continued, personal *action* in and upon the church.

This modal distinction guarantees the progressive character of the Christian life for Aquinas, since participation in Christ's humanity would involve a kind of immediate alteration to our own humanity. It also maintains the unity of Christ's person and work in the gift of his grace. For Christ's person and gracious action are only notionally distinct in his act, since Christ's person is the principle of all his gracious action. At the same time, however, it also carries with it a somewhat unusual implication – namely, that the communication of one's own nature implies a personal distinction between the nature and *donum* of the agent, which a communication by action does not. In other words, Adam remains personally distinct from the *donum* which he communicates to humankind, though the *donum* is his very nature, while Christ is not personally distinct from the *donum* which he communicates to the church, though it is *not* his nature, but his *act*.[52] Thus, Aquinas concludes his reply stating, "Grace, however, is not passed on to us from Christ by means of his human nature, but by Christ's own personal action on us."[53] That is, the union between Christ and the church consists in Christ's action upon the church by the Spirit. This answer is sufficient for Aquinas because his atonement theology is cooperative in nature. Christ's work is an act of friendship – an external act which supports the Christian in meriting for herself. But as Owen's

---

[51] *Cf. ST* IIIa, q. 19, a. 4; q., 48, a. 1–2.

[52] This is one application of a metaphysical principle Aquinas regularly employs according to which a nature is only logically distinct from a person, as that by which a person acts.

[53] "*Sed gratia non derivatur a Christo in nos mediante natura humana, sed per solam personalem actionem ipsius Christi.*" *ST* IIIa, q. 8, a. 5, ad. 1.

atonement theology is substitutionary in character, he must lean considerably harder on his pneumatology in order to deliver a version of the church's incorporation into Christ with a realism sufficient to ground the substitutionary character of Christ's work.

D. Mystical Union

As in Calvin before him, the ascension signals for Owen a definitive alteration in the form of Christ's mediatorial work and inaugurates the dispensation of the Holy Spirit. For in his exaltation to the right hand of the Father, Christ concludes his earthly ministry, having fulfilled the work to which he had been called. From heaven, Christ now extends the virtue of that work to his people by communications of the Spirit. This transition between the *historia salutis* and the *applicatio salutis* was distinctly designed by God to glorify the Holy Spirit, who is exalted precisely as the bond of union between Christ and the church. Thus, participation in the new creation consists in the fact that "one and self-same Spirit dwells in him and in us."[54] This is the correlate to the function of the Spirit in Owen's christology.[55] We have noted already that, as an adjunct of his atonement theology, Owen argues that Christ lived a fully human life, and therefore that his form of existence as a man was in no way discontinuous with our own by virtue of its subsistence in the eternal Son of God. For all divine actings upon the humanity of Christ were the immediate operations of the Holy Spirit. The Head of the new creation lived unto God in faith and by the power of the Holy Spirit. Owen's point here is that the church lives unto God by the same power, and this is what constitutes its mystical union with Christ – that both the head and the members share in the same life-giving power of the Spirit.

While this by no means exhausts his eschatology, it does sufficiently indicate that Pentecost is, for Owen, a deeply eschatological event. It represents the inbreaking of a form of communion with God hitherto unparalleled. For even while the Spirit endowed Adam with every kind of supernatural grace, Owen posits a modal distinction between the manner in which Adam and the church experience the Spirit's work. Adam did not have the Spirit "by especial inhabitation, for the whole world was then the temple of God."[56] The principle of his life before God, "was left to grow on no other root but what was in man himself. It was wholly implanted in

---

[54] Owen, *Works* 11:336f.
[55] Owen, *Works* 11:336; Apollonarianism is an immediate concern in Owen's Spirit-Christology.
[56] Owen, *Works*, 3:102.

his nature, and therein did its springs lie." And as a consequence, it was possible for Adam to fall from grace and be wholly abandoned by the Spirit. "But in the life whereunto we are renewed by Jesus Christ, the fountain and principle of [life] is not in ourselves, but in him, as one common head unto all that are made partakers of him."[57]

Therefore, the Spirit's is "not an original, but a perfecting work."[58] He is the Spirit *of Christ*, and ministers "the things of Christ" (John 16:14), i.e., those graces and benefits which Christ has procured by his death and heavenly intercession, and to which the elect are entitled by virtue of their election in the covenant of grace.[59] Mystical union is, itself, one of these graces and in this sense, it is the actualizing of a relation established between Christ and the church by divine election in eternity past. So, while Owen typically reserves the language of "mystical" for the work of the Spirit in the application of redemption to the church, he can speak of Christ's "voluntary susception" of the office of Mediator as the event in which the church was "constituted one mystical person" with Christ, because mystical union is the actualizing and perfecting of a relation which the church has had with Christ in eternity past by their election to the covenant of grace.[60] But while the elect possess a "right and title" to the benefits of the new covenant as an immediate consequence of Christ's death, their union with Christ remains strictly *federal*, and his benefits strictly *virtual*, until they are made partakers with Christ of his Spirit. It is only as the elect receive the gift of the Holy Spirit that Christ consummates their union and renders it *actual*.[61]

Owen draws on many Scriptural images to convey the intimate nature of the union between Christ and the church – the organic themes found in John or the marital imagery found in the Song of Songs and Ephesians 5 – but the Pauline image of the church as Christ's body is far and away the most frequent and determinative, because it enables Owen to stress the in-

---

[57] Owen, *Works*, 3:286.

[58] Owen, *Works*, 3:189.

[59] Owen, *Works*, 3:195–200; cf. 2:239–40.

[60] Owen, *Works* 5:200; *cf.* 11:308*f.* Fesko points to 5:353–54 in order to argue that, in a sense, imputation precedes mystical union for Owen by virtue of Christ being the surety of the covenant; thus, mystical union is finally grounded in "the forensic." "John Owen," 16–19. Fesko is, of course, correct that the covenant undergirds Christ's work and precedes all creaturely participation in it. But this misses the fact that, for Owen, Christ's suretyship is logically oriented to the order of nature, according to which persons normally merit for themselves. Thus, as a surety, Christ is enabled to merit on behalf of the elect *only with reference* to his union with the elect in one mystical person. This is why Owen grounds the imputation of Christ's righteousness immediately in *mystical* union rather than in federal union, because Christ can be a surety on behalf of the elect only by virtue of their mystical conjunction with him and not otherwise; *cf.* Owen, *Works*, 11:339–40.

[61] Owen, *Works*, 1:352–59; 5:178*f.*

timate nature of the church's union with Christ in *personal* terms. Particularly interesting in this regard is Owen's reading of 1 Corinthians 6:17 – "whoever is united with the Lord is one with him in spirit." In its context, the verse is an indictment of Christians having sex with temple prostitutes, a rumored practice of the Corinthian church. The verse condemns the practice by drawing a comparison between the bodily union of two people in the act of sex, and the spiritual union between Christ and his church. The force of the comparison is to suggest that the spiritual union between Christ and the church renders the Christian's body a real member of Christ. Sexual union with prostitutes is immoral, therefore, because the Christian's body is not excluded from union with Christ, but will be transformed and renewed in the resurrection. The Christian body is "for the Lord." Though its primary function within its context is to advance a theology of the body as a site of God's grace, Owen tends to use this text without its attachments to the theology of the natural body, and instead uses it to stress the intimate connection between Christ and the *mystical* body of his church or the soul of the believer. Linking this text with Colossians 2:9 and Ephesians 4:15–16, he argues that the union between Christ and the church does not consist in any of the gifts which Christ communicates to the church, but principally in the fact that the same Holy Spirit indwells and animates both the Head and the members.[62]

This funds one of Owen's most evocative images of the church's union with Christ – the Holy Spirit as the *soul* uniting Christ and the church into one person.[63] This image enables Owen to speak with an astonishing level of realism about the intimacy of the church's participation in Christ.

There is a twofold union between Christ and us; – the one, by his taking upon him our nature; the other, by bestowing on us his Spirit: for as in his incarnation he took upon him our flesh and blood by the work of the Spirit, so in our regeneration he bestoweth on us his flesh and blood by the operation of the same Spirit. Yea, so strict is this latter union which we have with Christ, that as the former is truly said to be a union of two natures into one person, so this of many persons into one nature; for by it we are "made partakers of the divine nature," 2 Pet. 1:4, becoming "members of his body, of his flesh, and of his bones," Eph. 5:30. We are so parts of him, of his mystical body, that we and he become thereby, as it were, one Christ . . . And the ground of this is, because the same Spirit is in him and us. In him, indeed, dwelleth the *fullness* of it, when it is bestowed upon us only by *measure*; but yet it is still the *same* Spirit, and so makes us, according to his own prayer, one with him, as the soul of man, being one, makes the whole body with

---

[62] "Our union with Christ cannot consist in the communication of any thing to us as members, from him the head; but it must be in that which constitutes him and us in the relation of head and members. He is our head antecedently in order of nature to any communication of grace from him as a head, and yet not antecedently to our union with him." Owen, *Works*, 11:339. *Cf.* Hans Burger, *Being in Christ: A Biblical and Systematic Investigation in Reformed Perspective* (Eugene, Ore.: Wipf & Stock, 2008), 30–86.

[63] Owen, *Works*, 1:365; 8:304; 11:340; 13:22; *cf.* Lim, *Mystery Unveiled*, 193–200.

it to be but one man. Two men cannot be one, because they have two souls; no more could we be one with Christ were it not the same Spirit in him and us. Now, let a man be never so big or tall, so that his feet rest upon the earth and his head reach to heaven, yet, having but one soul, he is still but one man. Now, though Christ for the present, in respect of our nature assumed, be never so far remote and distant from us in heaven, yet, by the effectual energy and inhabitation of the same Spirit, he is still the head of that one body whereof we are partakers, still but one with us.[64]

That Owen compares the Spirit's function in the mystical body to the function of the soul in the natural body is significant because, on a classical conception of the human person, the soul is that which makes an individual the person that he or she is. Functionally, it is a way of indicating creaturely identity within a broadly Thomist theology of creation. Thus, to speak of the church as being one in soul with Christ by the Spirit is to make a claim about the nature of the church's identity in Christ. Owen even speaks here of the church and Christ growing together to become "one Christ" – a clear allusion to the medieval notion of the church as the *totus Christus*,[65] but here relocated within a distinctly Congregationalist ecclesiology.

It is also interesting to note that Owen treats the relationship between Christ's "two bodies" by an analogy between the incarnation and Spirit-baptism. Though Christ first descended to take on flesh, following his ascension, he is now spatially removed from the church as it regards his natural body. Yet, by the "effectual energy and inhabitation of the same Spirit," Christ, in a sense, descends again and "bestoweth on us his flesh and blood." Of course, when Owen speaks in this way, he does not envision a real participation in Christ's human nature *per se*. Owen principally has in mind here the Spirit's work of *regeneration*, by which the Spirit infuses a new spiritual principle into the soul and in this way replicates in the body of the church those same habits, dispositions, and graces which distinguished the person of Christ. This is not, strictly speaking, a participation in Christ's humanity *as such*, for habits are the properties of *particular* human natures, and thus the church participates in Christ's human nature only as it is the exemplary and procuring cause of its own redemption. Yet, the church virtually possesses the substance of Christ's flesh and blood and becomes one with his very person, as it becomes a partaker in the divine nature by the indwelling of the Holy Spirit, whose power first formed Christ's human nature and invested it with its many virtues.

Since all the benefits of Christ are virtually contained in the gift of the Holy Spirit, Owen can make the transition from christology to pneumatol-

---

[64] Owen, *Works*, 13:22; *cf.* Lim, *Mystery Unveiled*, 200–216.

[65] On the concept of the church as the *totus Christus*, see Henri de Lubac, *Corpus Mysticum: The Eucharist and the Church in the Middle Ages* (2d ed.; Notre Dame: University of Notre Dame Press, 2006).

ogy quite definitively. In fact, Owen emphasizes that the transition to pneumatology was distinctly designed by God to glorify the Holy Spirit, who is exalted precisely as the bond of union between Christ, the Head, and the church, his body.[66] In the time of Christ's exaltation, the Spirit, "represents the person, and supplies the bodily absence of Christ." Indeed, the presence of the Spirit is of "more advantage and benefit" than Christ's bodily presence. For the Spirit performs and fulfills those works which Christ has taken to himself as Mediator. In each of his operations, the Spirit works "as if it were wrought immediately by the Lord Christ himself in his own person."[67] Owen can even refer to the Spirit as the true "Vicar of Christ" in the new creation.[68] This is why one does not find in Owen the language that features so prominently in Calvin concerning the believer's ascent by the Spirit and participation in Christ's heavenly flesh.[69] For Owen, Christ's human nature is the instrument by which the *beneficia Christi* are procured, but it is not an instrument by which they are made over to the church – this is the work of the Holy Spirit.[70]

Accordingly, Owen argues that it is the work of the Spirit that grants the church a share in the *status* and *power* of Christ's exaltation. The Spirit grants the church a share in Christ's *status,* because by the bond of the Spirit formally established in faith, Christ and the church coalesce into one mystical person. In this way, sinners are elevated, lifted above themselves, and lay hold of that righteousness by which they may stand justified before the throne of God. Owen insists that this justification is not merely a legal fiction according to which God adjusts the law to accommodate sinners, but a declaration fully in keeping with the law and its holy standard. Nor is

---

[66] Owen, *Works* 2:179, 3:189–90.

[67] Owen, *Works*, 3:193.

[68] Owen, *Works,* 3:193.

[69] Participation in Christ's humanity is clearly a theme of particular ecumenical importance for Calvin, as Thomas J. Davis has shown; Thomas J. Davis, *The Clearest Promises of God: The Development of Calvin's Eucharistic Teaching* (New York: AMS Press, 1995). Though, one need not go as far as Davis does, arguing that Calvin posited a "transfer" of righteousness from Christ's deity to his humanity, in order to speak of participation in Christ's flesh as life-giving; Thomas J. Davis, *This is My Body: The Presence of Christ in Reformation Thought* (Grand Rapids: Baker Academic, 2008), 85.

[70] We cannot treat Owen's eucharistic sermons meaningfully, here. However, we should note that there are texts that appear to buck this trend, especially toward the end of Owen's life. For example, in Discourse XXV, Owen uses the language of "participation," describing the eucharist as a "mysterious reception" and "a real substantial incorporation" of Christ's body and blood by a "spiritual communication." *Works*, 9:620. Proportionally, these texts are clearly in the minority, and in any case they can be understood quite comfortably within the framework outlined above; *cf.* Jon Payne, *John Owen on the Lord's Supper* (Edinburgh: Banner of Truth, 2004), 18–50; Stephen Mayor, "The Teaching of John Owen concerning the Lord's Supper," *SJT* 18/2 (1965): 170–81.

it a bald decree, by which God re-creates the sinner in righteousness *ex nihilo*. For the righteousness by which the sinner satisfies the law of God is the righteousness of Christ, which remains external to him. Rather, the mystical bond of the Holy Spirit forms the "immediate foundation" and real basis for the imputation Christ's righteousness to the church.[71] And it *can* do this, because by the work of the Spirit the persons of the elect are *really* incorporated into one mystical person with Christ. And so, even as the body shares in the honor of its head, so the church shares in the righteousness of her Lord.[72]

Likewise, the church also shares in the *power* of Christ's exaltation by the indwelling and activity of the Holy Spirit. For as Christ unites himself to the church by the Spirit, he truly and definitively washes and sanctifies her, breaking sin's power and cleansing sin's guilt. By the secret work of the Spirit, Christ really changes the nature of the church, infusing her with a new spiritual principle by which she is rendered fit and ready in the service of God. Owen variously describes this grace as an infused *habit*, *power*, or *disposition*, because it enables the creature to perform those spiritual works of service to which it was previously dead. Indeed, by virtue of the Spirit's regenerative work, the church is so fully equipped with the power to do good deeds, that it possesses both a readiness for good works as well as a kind of easiness in the performance of them. At the same time, however, the church is not so furnished with the grace of Christ that it might activate this new nature of itself and spontaneously, apart from the constant assistance of actual grace. For while naturally acquired habits "have a natural efficacy to preserve themselves," the infused habits conveyed in regeneration are preserved in the church by, "the constant powerful actings and influence of the Holy Ghost." This is a consequence, Owen argues, of the fact that the church's participation in the Spirit derives of its union with Christ: "the spring of it [habitual grace] is in our head, Christ Jesus, it being only an emanation of virtue and power from him unto us by the Holy

---

[71] Owen, *Works*, 5:217–21; cf. 2:179–80; 5:200–205.

[72] A full evaluation of Owen's doctrine of justification is beyond the scope of this paper, but we might simply point out here that, because Owen denies that the church participates in Christ's human nature as such, his doctrine of imputation seems to involve some kind of abstraction of righteousness from Christ's concrete person. This would appear to equivocate on the nature of "justice," which Owen appeals to elsewhere in more traditionally Thomist terms as a property inhering in the nature of a thing, according to which it is properly ordered to its end. To the degree that this is the case, it is not finally clear whether Owen can avoid the charge that justification is a legal fiction. In this respect at least, Hunsinger's appraisal of Owen's doctrine of justification underplays the forensic character of Owen's theology of incorporation into Christ's person.

Ghost. If this be not actually and always continued, whatever is in us would die and wither of itself."[73]

This definitive move toward pneumatology is not without significance in Owen's political context.[74] Ecclesiology quickly became a matter of principle concern after the death of Charles I, and as a Non-conformist, much of Owen's public life was devoted to the establishment of a church settlement and religious toleration. Owen's strongly pneumatological account of union with Christ creates space for a kind of critique against religion, which resists the identification of the authority of Christ with a particular set of religious practices or institutions (like the Roman Catholic church).[75] This, in a sense, "democratizes" Christ's authority, for Christ ministers to his people by the Spirit, whose works are, to a significant degree, "internal." As such, the Spirit's work is discernible only on the basis of general "signs" set forward in Scripture. In this way – under the authority of Scripture and by the secret work of the Spirit – the Christian conscience is made the immediate subject of Christ's lordship. A lordship which no government has the right either to transgress or coerce.

E. Conclusion

In the sketch above, we have seen that the doctrine of union with Christ is, for Owen, complex and variegated. The believer is united to Christ in a variety of modes – federal, natural, and mystical – locating the Christian's redemption in a plexus of causes of which Christ is the Head. This enables Owen to give a very complex and conceptually rich account of union with Christ that draws on a variety of themes with a great deal of flexibility. In light of this, it is not surprising that Owen's readers have presented very different accounts of his thought on this score. I have argued that the strongly *substitutionary* character of Owen's atonement theology entails irregularities for his broadly Thomist doctrine of nature and grace. I have also argued that, as a consequence of this theology of nature, Owen makes a less expansive use of the doctrine of the incarnation in his theology of union with Christ than other Reformed alternatives. For Owen, Christ's humanity serves primarily as the exemplary and procuring cause of the church's redemption. Therefore, in describing the church's participation in

---

[73] Owen, *Works*, 3:475; cf. 3:529.

[74] See especially Jeffery R. Collins, *The Allegiance of Thomas Hobbes* (Oxford: Oxford University Press, 2007), 207–41. Also Tim Cooper, *John Owen, Richard Baxter, and the Formation of Nonconformity* (Burlington, Vt.: Ashgate, 2011).

[75] Owen, *Works*, 13:124–53.

the *beneficia Christi*, Owen attempts to correct these irregularities by appealing to forensic and pneumatological themes.

Fesko picks up on the forensic element of Owen's theology of union – the manner in which union with Christ is, as it were, nested within the covenant – and thus argues that, for Owen, redemption rests upon "the forensic."[76] This is true, of course, but the priority of the forensic over the personal that Fesko posits betrays a reading of Owen's atonement theology that is too remote from Owen's theology of nature. For the central problem of Owen's doctrine of penal substitution is one of nature and grace – how a person might live of the merit of another when every person is by nature obligated to merit for themselves. The covenant frames and conceives this work, but Owen finally locates the basis for the imputation of Christ's righteousness in *mystical* union with Christ because he thinks it is only on this basis that one can overcome the problem of *nature* that is fundamental to substitutionary atonement – namely, the coalescence of the person of Christ with the persons of the elect into one mystical person before the just judgment of God. We might say that, for Owen, the indwelling of the Spirit is *more* than super-natural. In a sense, the Spirit is more internal to nature, than nature is to itself.

And this is why one does not find in Owen the language that is often so conspicuous in Calvin regarding the Spirit's work of leading believers in a spiritual ascent to participate in Christ's heavenly flesh. It seems that this is what Evans has in mind when he speaks of the tendency in Owen to "virtualize" union with Christ – that is, Owen tends to exclude a real participation in Christ's human nature from that union and instead identifies it with a mode of the Spirit's agency in the believer which most typically takes form in acts of piety. Evans is certainly correct to see a tendency in Owen to move more definitively from the second article to the third article of the creed, and to marginalize Christ's human nature as the instrument by which redemption is applied. This is not because Owen has no theology of union with Christ – as we have seen here, Owen's theology of union with Christ is quite complex and accommodating of various modes of union. Rather, it is simply that Owen's theology of nature and grace is generally much more Thomist in character than Calvin's, and this leads him to distribute his doctrine of union with Christ more exclusively along pneumatological lines. Whether for better or for worse, this is part of the diversity which comprises the Reformed tradition. And while one might be able to construct a taxonomy of Reformed doctrines of union with Christ based on family resemblances, it could only ever exist as variations on a theme.

A full critical assessment of Owen's theology of union with Christ is a task for another time, yet, at minimum, the sketch above demonstrates the

---

[76] Fesko, "John Owen," 18.

urgent necessity of attending to the relationship between nature and grace for any Reformed theology of union with Christ. Recent scholarly evaluation of the place of union with Christ in the Reformed tradition has tended to circulate too narrowly around the *ordo salutis* and the relationship between regeneration and justification, without examining how the doctrine of creation underwrites these discourses. But if constructive dialogue on these matters is to advance, it will require a larger compass. For the conceptual registers that support these discourses are often, themselves, dispositive, insofar as they entail an implicit metaphysic.

As scholars return to evaluate the full coherence of Reformed theologies of union with Christ, it is essential that they attend not only to the immediate context of the doctrine within applied soteriology, but that they consider its wider relation to the divine works of creation and government more generally. For if the test of any theology is ultimately its power to guide Christian contemplation of God, then any sufficient theology of union with Christ must press in to consider the unity of God's works, and finally, God as the Principle of all things and the Fountain from which every good gift flows.

Bibliography

Allison, C. F. *The Rise of Moralism: The Proclamation of the Gospel from Hooker to Baxter*. London: SPCK, 1966.

Aquinas, Thomas. *Summa Theologiae*. 61 vols. Cambridge: Cambridge University Press, 2006.

Billings, J. Todd. *Calvin, Participation, and the Gift*. Oxford: Oxford University Press, 2007.

Boersma, Hans. *A Hot Pepper Corn: Richard Baxter's Doctrine of Justification in Its Seventeenth-Century Context of Controversy*. Vancouver: Regent College Publishing, 2004.

Burger, Hans. *Being in Christ: A Biblical and Systematic Investigation in Reformed Perspective*. Eugene, Ore.: Wipf & Stock, 2008.

Canlis, Julie. *Calvin's Ladder: A Spiritual Theology of Ascent and Ascension*. Grand Rapids: Eerdmans, 2010.

Cleveland, Christopher. *Thomism in John Owen*. Burlington, Vt.: Ashgate, 2013.

Collins, Jeffery R. *The Allegiance of Thomas Hobbes*. Oxford: Oxford University Press, 2007.

Cooper, Tim. *John Owen, Richard Baxter, and the Formation of Nonconformity*. Burlington, Vt.: Ashgate, 2011.

Davis, Thomas J. *The Clearest Promises of God: The Development of Calvin's Eucharistic Teaching*. New York: AMS Press, 1995.

———. *This is My Body: The Presence of Christ in Reformation Thought*. Grand Rapids: Baker Academic, 2008.

Evans, William. "Déja vu All Over Again? The Contemporary Reformed Soteriological Controversy in Historical Perspective." *Westminster Theological Journal* 72 (2010): 135–51.

———. *Imputation and Impartation: Union with Christ in American Reformed Theology.* Milton Keynes: Paternoster, 2008.

Ferguson, Sinclair. *John Owen on the Christian Life.* Edinburgh: Banner of Truth, 1987.

Fesko, J. V. "John Owen on Union with Christ and Justification." *Themelios* 37/1 (2012): 7–19.

———. "Methodology, Myth, and Misperception: A Response to William B. Evans." *Westminster Theological Journal* 72 (2010): 391–402;

Finnis, John. *Natural Law and Natural Rights.* 2d ed. Oxford: Oxford University Press, 2011.

Flavel, John. *The Fountain of Life Opened.* London: The Religious Tract Society, 1836.

Grotius, *The Rights of War and Peace.* Edited by Richard Tuck. Indianapolis: Liberty Fund, 2005.

Hunsinger, George. "Justification and Mystical Union with Christ: Where Does Owen Stand?" Pages 199–211 in *The Ashgate Research Companion to John Owen's Theology.* Edited by Kelly Kapic and Mark Jones. Burlington, Vt.: Ashgate, 2012.

Kantorowicz, Ersnt Hartwig. *The King's Two Bodies: A Study in Mediaeval Political Theology.* Princeton: Princeton University Press, 1957.

Kapic, Kelly. *Communion with God: The Divine and the Human in the Theology of John Owen.* Grand Rapids: Baker, 2007.

Lim, Paul C. H. *Mystery Unveiled: The Crisis of the Trinity in Early Modern England,* Oxford: Oxford University Press, 2012.

Lubac, Henri de. *Corpus Mysticum: The Eucharist and the Church in the Middle Ages.* 2d ed. Notre Dame: University of Notre Dame Press, 2006.

Mayor, Stephen. "The Teaching of John Owen concerning the Lord's Supper." *Scottish Journal of Theology* 18/2 (1965): 170–81.

Muller, Richard. *Calvin and the Reformed Tradition: On the Work of Christ and the Order of Salvation.* Grand Rapids: Baker, 2013.

Nevin, John W. *The Mystical Presence: A Vindication of the Reformed or Calvinistic Doctrine of the Holy Eucharist.* Philadelphia: S. R. Fisher & Co., 1867.

———. "Puritanism and the Creed." *The Mercersburg Review* 1 (1849): 585–607.

Owen, John. *The Works of John Owen.* Edited by William H. Goold. Edinburgh: T&T Clark.

Payne, Jon. *John Owen on the Lord's Supper.* Edinburgh: Banner of Truth, 2004.

Perkins, William. *A Golden Chaine.* London: Iohn Legatte, 1616.

Schwartz, Daniel. *Aquinas on Friendship.* Oxford: Oxford University Press, 2007.

Sibbes, Richard. *A Commentary on the First Chapter of the Second Epistle to the Corinthians.* Volume 3 of *The Complete Works of Richard Sibbes.* 7 vols. Edinburgh: James Nichol, 1862.

Trueman, Carl. *John Owen: Reformed Catholic, Renaissance Man.* Great Theologians Series. Burlington, Vt.: Ashgate, 2007.

Karl Barth's Reading of Paul's Union with Christ

KEITH L. JOHNSON

Karl Barth approaches Paul's category of union with Christ from the starting point of the living Jesus Christ, the resurrected and ascended Lord. He does so because he believes the link between Paul's claim that "I have been crucified with Christ" and his claim that "it is no longer I who live but Christ who lives in me" (Gal 2:19–20) is *Jesus Christ himself* in the ongoing history of his fulfillment of God's covenant of grace. Barth sees this covenant as God's working out of his eternal plan to adopt us in Christ so that we might be "holy and blameless before him in love" (Eph 1:4). His central presupposition is that Christ's perfect and finished work to unite us to himself through his death and resurrection is ordered toward the goal of creating a human correspondence to God that follows in the pattern of Christ's own obedience to the covenant. Barth adopts this approach because he believes it is the only way to do justice both to Paul's claim that believers already have a share in Christ's Sonship (Gal 4:6–7) and to Paul's description of the concrete implications of this Sonship for our life in the church lived through the power of the Holy Spirit.

The goal of this chapter is to explain how and why Barth adopts this particular approach to union with Christ within his *Church Dogmatics*. The explanation will proceed in three sections. First, we will situate Barth by showing how Barth's core doctrinal commitments led him to explain the relationship between Christ's perfect saving work and the realization of this work in our lives in terms of a distinctly-ordered narrative unity. Second, we will explore Barth's unique formulations of the doctrines of election, Christology, and humanity to see how these doctrines inform the connection Barth draws between the eternal Son, Jesus Christ, and human beings. These two sections form the background of the third section, which will delineate Barth's mature account of union with Christ by means of his description of the concrete form that this union takes in the life of the believer as he or she participates in the living Christ's own prophetic vocation in and through the church.

A. Objectivity and Subjectivity in Covenantal Perspective

In one sense, Barth sees his account of Paul's categories of union and participation as standing firmly within the broader theological tradition. One of the central tasks facing any theologian as he or she considers Paul's letters is to explain how human beings adopted as children of God can be included in God's own life even as they do not live this life in the same way God does. This kind of explanation is precisely what a doctrine of participation is designed to accomplish: it provides an account of how the ontological distinction between God and the human remains intact even as the human is united to God through the saving work of Christ and the Spirit. The differences between the various approaches to participation over the course of theological history stem from the variety of ways theologians have explained the nature of this union-in-distinction. Some, for example, have explained it sacramentally, with baptism and the Eucharist serving as the means by which Christ joins himself to the believer while remaining other than the believer; others have explained it mystically by turning to spiritual exercises or the practices of discipleship. Barth's account is simply his own version of this same kind of explanation.[1] Like much of the tradition, he begins with the conviction that believers have "a share in the Word of God and therefore in God himself – a creaturely share in a creaturely manner, but nevertheless a real share" – and then he seeks to explain how this conviction can be maintained without undermining the distinction between God and creature.[2] He offers his explanation in conversation with thinkers from across the spectrum of the church's theological tradition while retaining his own distinctively Protestant and Reformed theological commitments.[3]

Yet, even as he adopts the same starting point and goal of much of the church's theological tradition, Barth sees himself as consciously standing

---

[1] This comparison is drawn from Daniel L. Migliore, who emphasizes the importance of reading Barth doctrine of participation on Barth's own terms. If one reads Barth "with the expectation of finding confirmation of one or more of these understandings of participation in Christ," he argues, "one will either be disappointed or will impose one's biases on the text." See Daniel L. Migliore, "*Participatio Christi*: The Central Theme of Barth's Doctrine of Sanctification," *Zeitschrift für dialektische Theologie* 18 (2002): 286–307.

[2] Karl Barth, *Church Dogmatics* III/2 (Edinburgh: T&T Clark, 1960), 177. Each volume will be cited fully the first time, and thereafter simply with a *CD* followed by the volume and part number. In line with contemporary practice, I have changed the translators' use of uppercase pronouns to God to lowercase throughout. I have retained Barth's masculine pronouns for human beings as in the original English translation.

[3] Barth sees his approach to Paul as standing specifically in the trajectory of John Calvin: "we have merely taken seriously what Calvin called the *participatio Christi*." See Karl Barth, *Church Dogmatics* IV/2 (Edinburgh: T&T Clark, 1958), 581.

apart from it. He does so because he believes he accounts for a factor that most other approaches ignore: the reality that our union with Christ takes the form of an ongoing covenantal history as we are made "alive to God in Christ Jesus" (Rom 6:11) as Christ himself continues his vocation in the covenant. This extra dimension, for example, explains how and why Barth distances his account of union and participation from those centered around a doctrine of deification or *theosis*.[4] While he thinks *theosis* may capture the metaphysical *effects* of Christ's saving work by explaining how this work leads to the elevation or exaltation of human nature, this doctrine can give us only a partial picture of how the Bible describes our salvation. We cannot do justice to the full scope of Christ's saving work, Barth believes, unless we also ask a further question: "Exaltation to what?"[5] He insists that we will rightly understand the effects of our union with Christ upon our human nature only when we also ask about the specific end or purpose toward which our nature is being elevated. This means we have to talk about our human nature as it exists in union with Christ as Christ continues to act as the resurrected Lord. Barth thus sees his question as simply another form of Paul's question: "Do you not realize that Jesus Christ is in you?" (2 Cor 13:5) – and he believes that any account of Christ's saving work that focuses primarily on the elevation of human nature inevitably leaves this question at least partially unanswered. While such an account may rightly capture the difference that a believer's union with Christ makes for the believer's human nature, it will fail to describe adequately what this union means for Christ and the believer as Christ works in and through the believer joined to him as his partner. Barth sees this point as absolutely critical: to be incorporated into Christ is to be both changed in one's nature *and* to be made a partner with Christ as he continues to act in the ongoing history of God's covenant.

Barth's decision to focus his account of union and participation upon the believer's partnership with the living Christ has its origins in his theological method. From the writing of his book on Anselm onward, Barth holds that our knowledge of God must be grounded in the correspondence between the Son's eternal procession from the Father and his saving mission in time.[6] As "the power of God and the wisdom of God" (1 Cor 1:24),

---

[4] For a fuller comparison of Barth's approach to participation with traditional approaches to deification, see Bruce L. McCormack, "Participation in God, Yes; Deification, No: Two Modern Protestant Responses to an Ancient Question," in *Orthodox and Modern: Studies in the Theology of Karl Barth* (Grand Rapids: Baker Academic, 2008), 235–60.

[5] Karl Barth, *Church Dogmatics* IV/1 (Edinburgh: T&T Clark, 1958), 91.

[6] Karl Barth, *Anselm: Fides Quaerens Intellectum: Anselm's Proof of the Existence of God in the Context of his Theological Scheme* (trans. Ian W. Robertson; Richmond, Va.: John Knox, 1960), 45. For an account of how Barth came to this methodological decision

this saving mission includes the restoration our minds so that, in and through Christ, we may have a creaturely share in God's own reason.[7] Barth insists that Christ does not merely create the possibility that we might know him, as if the realization of this knowledge were the result of two actions – Christ's act and then our response to it. Rather, our knowledge of God in Christ is included within Christ's own act of revealing himself to us, since this revelation has its origin in God's eternal wisdom and has our participation in this wisdom as its intrinsic goal or *telos*. In other words, Christ's objective work (his revelation of himself to us) includes within itself the subjective realization of this work (our knowledge of him), and both aspects are the result of God's action in correspondence to his eternal being. For Barth, the payoff of this method is that the content of our theological knowledge is determined solely by God's own being and action, and not by ourselves, even as we are given a real creaturely participation in God's self-knowledge.

Barth's broader account of the human relationship to God follows the template set in and by this methodology. He begins with the presupposition that the whole of the created order, including human being itself, is intrinsically determined by God's covenant of grace. God's covenant of grace is his plan to save sinful human beings so that we might live in partnership with him, with this partnership constituting our creaturely share in his divine being. Barth sees this participation-as-partnership as the content of "God's wisdom, secret and hidden, which God decreed before the ages for our glory" (1 Cor 2:7). God executes his covenantal decision in and through the mission of the eternal Son, Jesus Christ. This is the lens through which Barth interprets Paul's statement that "all things have been created through him and for him; he himself is before all things, and in him all things hold together" (Col 1:16–17). Since Christ himself is the agent who makes the covenant happen, his own life and action is identical to the covenant and thus the intrinsic meaning of created history itself. As Barth puts it, the covenant takes place as "the history in which God himself became and was and is and will be very man in His Son, Jesus of Nazareth, the Son of Man. And the force of his history is the raising, the exaltation of human essence by the fact that God himself lent it his own existence in his Son thus uniting it with his own divine essence."[8] Or, to put it in Pauline terms: Christ himself is the meaning of history because the joining of hu-

---

and its effect on the *Church Dogmatics*, see Keith L. Johnson, "A Reappraisal of Karl Barth's Theological Development and His Dialogue with Catholicism," *International Journal of Systematic Theology* 14/1 (2012): 1–23.

[7] Barth describes this as an "indirect" participation in God's own self-knowledge. See Karl Barth, *Church Dogmatics* II/1 (Edinburgh: T&T Clark, 1957), 59.

[8] *CD* IV/2, 69.

man beings to God that happens in him is the fulfillment of God's plan for history, a "plan for the fullness of time, to gather up all things in him, things in heaven and things on earth" (Eph 1:10).

Based upon these central assumptions, Barth argues that since God's plan for history is for human beings to live in fellowship with him as his partners, his covenant of grace has within itself the goal of fashioning free human subjects who can actually *be* his partners. Barth describes this partnership as the human "being by the side of God, the participation of man in the being and life of God, a willing of what he wills and a doing of what he does. It will be a being not only as object, but as active subject in the fellowship of God."[9] He approaches this idea through the lens of Paul's term *koinonia*, which Barth defines as "a relationship between two persons in which these are brought into perfect mutual coordination within the framework of a definite order, yet with no destruction of their two-sided identity and particularity, but rather in its confirmation and expression."[10] With the content of Paul's claim that God calls the believer "into the fellowship (*koinonia*) of his Son" (1 Cor 1:9) working in the background, Barth argues that God establishes *koinonia* between Christ and the believer by bringing them into coordination with one another within the history of the covenant. He also draws from Paul's description of the "communion (*koinonia*) of the Holy Spirit (2 Cor 13:13) as well as the connection between the unity of believers and their "sharing (*koinoinia*) of the Spirit" (Phil 2:1) in order to argue that the Spirit is the agent who establishes this relationship between Christ and the believer. "The work of the Holy Spirit," he explains, "is to bring and to hold together that which is different . . . not to identify, intermingle, nor confound them, not to change the one into the other nor to merge the one into the other, but to coordinate them, to make them parallel, to bring them into harmony and therefore bind them into a true unity."[11] The Spirit accomplishes this work by creating "the unity in which Jesus Christ is at one and the same time the heavenly head with God and the earthly body with his community."[12]

---

[9] *CD* IV/1, 113.

[10] *CD* IV/3.2, 535. George Hunsinger has offered the definitive treatment of this theme in Barth's theology. See George Hunsinger, "The Mediator of Communion: Karl Barth's Doctrine of the Holy Spirit," in *Disruptive Grace: Studies in the Theology of Karl Barth* (Grand Rapids: Eerdmans, 2000), 168–73. My description of Barth's approach to *koinonia* is indebted to his insights.

[11] *CD* IV/3.2, 761.

[12] *CD* IV/3.2, 760. Barth always sees the Holy Spirit as the Spirit of *Christ*, with an emphasis that in the Spirit, Christ himself "is present and active among and with and in certain men." See Karl Barth, *Church Dogmatics* IV/3.1 (Edinburgh: T&T Clark, 1961), 52.

The product of this unity is a true partnership between the believer and Christ, one in which the believer's actions truly are coordinated with and correspond to God's own actions in Christ in covenant history. This correspondence marks the believer's creaturely participation in the fellowship that Christ himself shares with his Father. "As Jesus Christ calls us and is heard by us," Barth says, "he gives us his Holy Spirit in order that his own relationship to his Father may be repeated in us. He then knows us, and we know him, as the Father knows him and he the Father. Those who live in this repetition live in the Holy Spirit."[13] Barth thinks this dynamic account of the relationship between Christ and Christian – one centered on the correspondence of being and activity – is the best way to account for both the state of our exalted human nature *and* the ongoing history of our nature as it is caught up in Christ's own history as he continues to fulfill God's covenantal plan.

This vision sets the context from which Barth understands Christ's saving work both in terms of its objective perfection and its subjective realization. Since the creation of a free human subject in partnership with God is the goal of the covenant, the events of Christ's death and resurrection that stand at the center of this covenant are understood in light of this goal. As Barth puts it, the "meaning and purpose of the atonement made in Jesus Christ is that man should not cease to be a subject in relation to God but that he should be maintained as such . . . That he should be newly created and grounded as such, from above."[14] In other words, Christ's perfect and complete saving work accomplished in his death and resurrection has as its goal the establishment of the corresponding effects of this work in human being and action. "This creating and grounding of a human subject which is new in relation to God and therefore in itself is, in fact, the event of the atonement made in Jesus Christ. This is what was altered in him. This is what was accomplished by the grace of God effective and revealed in him."[15] Barth sees this claim as standing directly in line with Paul's statement that "if anyone is in Christ, there is a new creation: the old has passed away; see, everything has become new!" (2 Cor 5:17). The objective work (Christ's saving actions) has our own subjective realization of this work (our new being in Christ) as its primary goal and consequence.[16]

The key to holding these two aspects together is to recognize that Christ himself accomplishes this work on both sides. We cannot "split up" the

---

[13] Karl Barth, *Church Dogmatics* II/2 (Edinburgh: T&T Clark, 1957), 780.

[14] *CD* IV/1, 89.

[15] *CD* IV/1, 89.

[16] For further developments on this theme, see Adam Neder, *Participation in Christ: An Entry into Karl Barth's* Church Dogmatics (Louisville: Westminster John Knox, 2009), 16–28. Neder's volume is the best book-length treatment on this topic.

grace of Christ, Barth insists, as if Christ's past work of grace needs a second, further actualization to become effective for us. "If it is a matter of the grace of the one God and the one Christ," Barth says, "there can only be one grace."[17] Rather, in the history of Christ's ongoing fulfillment of God's covenant, the "objective becomes subjective" as Christ personally guarantees that the consequences of his death and resurrection are realized in the life of the believer through the work of his Holy Spirit.[18] Barth thinks this approach captures both aspects of Christ's work without surrendering either one's integrity.[19] The fact that Christ's saving work has the creation of a free human subject as its goal means that the subjective realization of this work cannot be collapsed into the objective: this subjective realization follows from the objective work as its consequence, but it is not identical to this objective work. At the same time, the fact that *Christ himself* brings about our subjective realization of the effects of his saving work as its intended consequence means that there is no weakening of the objectivity, as if Christ's work in the past were incomplete or insufficient. Instead, the two aspects of this work stand together in an ordered, narrative relationship that corresponds to the narrative history of the covenant itself.[20] Christ reconciles us to God by uniting us to himself through his life, death, and resurrection precisely so we can live *with* him and *in* him as God's partners into eternity. Barth thinks that Paul draws the same sort of connection when he links our present "life in Christ Jesus" directly to the "righteousness and sanctification and redemption" that we have *in* him (1 Cor 1:30). Such a connection means that God's grace to us in Christ must be seen as "subjectively strong in its divine objectivity."[21] Our salvation happens apart from us by Christ alone even as this salvation makes us new and enables us to become human participants in God's own life. Barth sees

---

[17] *CD* IV/1, 88.

[18] *CD* IV/1, 119.

[19] Barth sees this approach as transcending the traditional theological divisions related to determinism. He has "no time either for the arrogance of the indeterminists or the pusillanimity or melancholy or idle dissuasions of the determinists. In view of the one to whom they look – however well or badly – in their *participatio Christi*, everything is in good order as regards their freedom." *CD* IV/2, 532.

[20] John Webster describes this as an "inclusive perfection," where the completeness of Christ's work "is not only its 'being finished,' but its effective power in renewing human life by bringing about human response to itself. Consequently, the relation of 'objective' and 'subjective' shifts. The objective is not a complete realm, separate from the subjective and, therefore, standing in need of 'translation' into the subjective. Rather, the objective includes the subjective within itself, and is efficacious without reliance on a quasi-independent realm of mediating created agencies." See John B. Webster, *Barth's Ethics of Reconciliation* (Cambridge: Cambridge University Press, 1995), 127–28.

[21] *CD* IV/1, 88. For a development of this point, see Hunsinger, "The Mediator of Communion," 162–67.

this description of participation corresponding directly to Paul's remarks about the "life of Jesus" being "made visible on our bodies" (2 Cor 4:10). And, as we will see below, he thinks that this visibility – in line with the connection Paul himself draws between our being in Christ and God's act of "entrusting the message of reconciliation to us" (2 Cor 5:18–19) – takes the concrete form of our partnership with Christ in the task of proclaiming the gospel to the world in and through the church.

B. Election, Christology, and Humanity

Barth's claim about the intrinsic narrative relationship between Christ's perfectly completed saving work and its subjective realization in our lives has its roots in his belief that God's decision to share his life does not stand at a remove from his divine being but instead reflects his own self-determination and eternal plan. Barth develops this claim in his doctrine of election, and its effects are felt especially in his unique approaches to the doctrines of Christology and humanity. A clear account of the relationship between these three doctrines will enable us to better understand both how Barth supports his particular approach to the objective and subjective aspects of Christ's saving work and why he describes Paul's union with Christ in the specific manner he does.

With respect to election, Barth's core conviction is that Jesus Christ's historical fulfillment of God's covenantal plan is a function of his election by God for this particular service. "For God's eternal election of grace," Barth says, "is concretely the election of Jesus Christ."[22] As he sees it, to say with Paul that God "chose us in Christ before the foundation of the world" (Eph 1:4) is to say nothing other than God elects Christ himself to fulfill his covenant of grace on both the divine and human side in and through his own personal history. "From all eternity," Barth says, "God elected and determined that he himself would become man for us men. From all eternity, he determined that men would be those for whom he is God: his fellow-men. In willing this, in willing Jesus Christ, he wills to be our God and he wills that we should be his people."[23] As the true God, Christ fulfills God's determination to be God for us; and as the true human, Christ fulfills God's determination that human beings would live in true partnership with God. The incarnation is thus the actualization of the entire covenant, an "*operatio* between God and man, fulfilled in Jesus Christ, as the union of God with men."[24]

---

[22] *CD* IV/2, 45.
[23] *CD* IV/1, 45.
[24] *CD* IV/2, 105.

Barth's line of thought here is guided by the basic shape of God's covenantal promise: that God will be our God and we will be his people (cf. Jer 31:33). Since this promise involves both God and human beings, Barth thinks its fulfillment must take place, not as a state or a singular transaction, but as a *history* – an ongoing relationship between God and humans in space and time. "The divine being and life and act takes place with ours," Barth says, "and it is only as the divine takes place that ours takes place . . . He does not allow his history to be his and ours, but causes them to take place as a common history."[25] This history takes place as *salvation* history because the specific kind of relationship God wills to have with us is "not proper to created being as such" but involves our having "a part in the being of God" and thus having "a being which is hidden in God, and in that sense (distinct from God and secondary) *eternal* being."[26] Jesus Christ stands at the center of salvation history because he is the one who makes us creaturely participants in God's eternal being. He does so by obediently taking human nature upon himself so that it may be exalted in him. This reflects God's goal to make us *like* him, holy and blameless free subjects who are capable of living in partnership with God as Christ's "joint heirs" (Rom 8:17). "As God condescends and humbles Himself to man and becomes man," Barth explains, "man himself is exalted, not as God or like God, but to God, being placed at his side, not in identity, but in true fellowship with him, and becoming a new man in this exaltation and fellowship."[27]

A core commitment underlying this account of the exaltation of human nature is the inseparability of Jesus Christ's saving work from his person: because human nature is exalted in and through Christ's own life of covenantal obedience, our doctrinal description of this exaltation cannot be divorced from his specific covenantal history. Barth supports this conviction by arguing that the union of Christ's two natures must be approached *historically* rather than statically.[28] If we are truly to understand Christ's saving work, we cannot think of his two natures "like two planks lashed or glued together . . . as if each retained its separate identity in this union and the two remained mutually alien in a neutral proximity." Rather, each of Christ's two natures, "without being either destroyed or altered, acquires and has its own determination" in and through its union with the other. The

---

[25] *CD* IV/1, 7.
[26] *CD* IV/1, 8, emphasis added.
[27] *CD* IV/2, 6.
[28] One of the clearest expositions of this aspect of Barth's theology is found in Bruce L. McCormack, "Karl Barth's Historicized Christology: Just How 'Chalcedonian' Is it?" in *Orthodox and Modern: Studies in the Theology of Karl Barth* (Grand Rapids: Baker Academic, 2008), 201–33.

distinction of each nature's determination follows the order of being as unfolded within the narrative of the covenant. Specifically, the divine nature is determined *toward* the human as the Son fulfills God's eternal plan to share his own being with humans; and the human nature receives its determination *from* the divine nature as the incarnate Son lives his human life as the true covenant partner of God. Throughout the history of his incarnate life, Barth explains, Jesus Christ himself "grasps and has and maintains the leadership in what his divine essence is and means for his human, and his human for his divine, in their mutual participation." The "twofold differentiation" of their participation – with the divine giving to the human and the human receiving from the divine – is not reversible or interchangeable, and so always reflects the ontological distinction between Creator and creature.[29] This participation thus occurs "as a real history. It takes place both from above to below and from below to above. But it takes place from above to below first, and only then from below to above."[30] In the context of this ordered movement, Christ's personal history leads to salvation because, in and through it, Christ's human nature receives "a part in his divine essence."[31]

Sinful human beings are incorporated into Christ's saving history through his death on the cross, which marks our atonement and justification. On the cross, Barth says, Jesus "rendered that obedience which is required of the covenant partner of God . . . by taking to himself the sins of all men."[32] He sees this act of bearing our sin as a penal substitution, one verified by a concurrent declaration of righteousness for sinful human beings. This declaration creates a new reality for sinners, because it is a "declaration about man which is fulfilled and therefore effective in this event, which corresponds to an actuality because it creates and therefore reveals the actuality." That is, because Jesus Christ *lives* as the judged and yet vindicated savior who has united sinners to himself, God's declaration of the sinner's righteousness is absolutely effective: the sinful human being "is not merely called righteous before God, but *is* righteous before God" in

---

[29] Barth develops this point further: "He himself is always the subject of this history. It is not merely because they are different by definition, but because they have a different relationship to this subject, that the divine and human essence bear a different character in their mutual participation." *CD* IV/1, 71.

[30] Barth argues that this approach to the incarnation leaves no for "anything static at the broad center of concepts of *unio, communio,* and *communicatio* – or in the traditional doctrine of the two states." Rather, he says, "we have retranslated the whole phenomenology into the sphere of history. And we have done this because originally the theme of it is not a phenomenon, or a complex of phenomena, but a history." *CD* IV/2, 105–6.

[31] *CD* IV/2, 70.

[32] *CD* IV/1, 94–95.

Christ.³³ This new objective existence changes not only our status before God but also our determination as human beings. "In the death which the Son of God has died for them," Barth says, "they themselves have died as sinners. And that means their radical sanctification, separation, and purification for participation in a truly creaturely independence, and more than that, for the divine sonship of the creature which is the grace for which from all eternity they are elected in the election of the man Jesus."³⁴ Barth's argument here draws from Paul's insistence that, because believers have "died with Christ," they are now "dead to sin" and can pursue a life of righteousness (Rom 6:5–14). Barth takes this idea to indicate that our new existence in Christ is an objectively perfect work even as there is an ongoing realization of this newness in the life of the sinner, because this realization is included within the perfect work as its intended consequence. This is the frame of reference from which he understands Paul's claim that God made Christ "to be sin" so that "in him we might become the righteousness of God" (2 Cor 5:21).

Barth sees this new existence not merely in individual terms, as it if were applied only to specific human beings, but in terms of the creation of true human being itself. Here he simply works out the implications of his doctrines of election and Christology for the status of human nature. He argues that if Jesus Christ is eternally elected to be the human being who lives in perfect fellowship with God within the context of the covenant, then Jesus' own human nature is *the* "concrete possibility of human existence as determined and elected and prepared by God."³⁵ Jesus does not *have* human nature, as if true human nature exists already as "something different and earlier and more intrinsic, a deeper stratum or more original substance of being."³⁶ Instead, Jesus *creates* human nature as he fulfills God's plan for human nature through his covenant partnership. The "humanity of the Son of God," Barth insists, is "humanity as such, the humanity for which every man is ordained."³⁷ He believes this way of under-

---

[33] *CD* IV/1, 95, emphasis added.

[34] *CD* II/2, 125.

[35] *CD* IV/2, 48.

[36] *CD* III/2, 150.

[37] *CD* IV/2, 519. In this sense, Barth thinks that Jesus is "the pledge of what we ourselves will be." See *CD* IV/1, 115. McCormack aptly summarizes the implications of this claim: "what it means to be human has been decided in eternity by means or our election in Jesus Christ. We are 'chosen in him' – this is a statement pregnant with ontological significance. We are who are 'in him.' We can decide to live in conformity with our true being or not – we are free to do that. But whether we do the one or the other changes nothing with respect to the 'in him' of the divine election by which our true being – our 'essence' – has been established." See Bruce L. McCormack, "Participation in God, Yes; Deification, No," 239–40.

standing the implications of Christ's human nature fits the meaning of Paul's claim that "our lives are hidden with Christ in God" (Col 3:3), and he also thinks it flows directly from Paul's argument that Jesus Christ is the "firstborn of a large family" (Rom 8:29). God's eternally foreknown and predestined plan for human beings – and thus his true intention for human nature – is not realized strictly in our creation by God but in our future conformity to the image of his Son that happens as we are saved. Created human being has always been intrinsically determined by God's plan that *this* specific human life would be actualized in space and time and that humans would be united to it for their salvation. "The basic divine decision concerning man is embodied in Jesus," Barth says. "The determination in which man is directed to as his promised future, and set in motion toward this future, is given in him."[38] Barth thinks this stands in line with the link Paul draws between the "image of the invisible God" and Christ's status as the "firstborn of all creation" (Col 1:16). Christ's own human nature quite simply *is* the fulfillment God's eternal plan for what human beings should and will be in their partnership with him.

All of this means that, for Barth, Jesus Christ's human life marks the "creation of a new form of existence for man in which he can live as the loyal covenant-partner of God who is well-pleasing to and blessed by him."[39] The coming of this "new creation" to human beings does not mean "the extinguishing of our humanity," Barth insists, "but its establishment."[40] In the same way Paul linked our changed perception of Christ – "even though we once knew Christ from a human point of view, we no longer know him this way" – to our changed perception of ourselves – "from now on, therefore, we regard no one from a human point of view" (2 Cor 5:16) – so too does our understanding of what it means to be human change in light of our knowledge of Christ's human nature as it has been actualized in the history of the covenant and now in its exalted form at the right hand of God. The fact that this change is prompted by Christ's personal history means that it is not merely an actualization drawn from the capacities of human nature itself, as if this realization of true human nature was within "the sphere of the specific possibilities characteristic to human existence." Rather, it occurs as the "transcending of such a sphere," as a movement of grace, from God to us, from above to below.[41] And since the

---

[38] *CD* II/2, 567.

[39] *CD* IV/2, 514. "For in him, in this man," Barth says, "we have to do with the exaltation of the essence common to all men." *CD* IV/2, 69.

[40] *CD* IV/1, 15.

[41] *CD* III/2, 159. This means that Jesus is "the one Archimedian point given us beyond humanity, and therefore the one possibility of discovering the ontological determination of man." *CD* III/2, 132.

goal of God's grace is the creation of a human being who can live as God's partner, this movement is ordered toward the realization of the capacities of this partnership in the lives of the believers who receive this grace. Christ becomes truly human so that *we* might become the truly human partners of God. This does not mean the divination of human nature but its *determination*: human nature is determined in Christ and by Christ in such a way that it now can exist in "full harmony with the divine essence common to the Father, Son, and Holy Spirit" even while it "remains human."[42] God moves from above to below so that humans can move from below to above and live in partnership with God.

Believers are caught up in this movement when they are united to Christ and begin to live in harmony with the divine essence in and through him. The beginning of this movement occurs with their faith in Christ. When Christ calls the believer to have faith in him, Barth says, "the history inaugurated by God becomes man's own subjective history."[43] And this call to faith always comes also as a call to *obedience*. "When the reality of human nature is in question," Barth says, "the word 'real' is simply equivalent to 'summoned'."[44] To be truly human is not simply to exist in relationship with God, but to engage in "a task for which I am commissioned."[45] This claim provides the lens through which Barth approaches the doctrine of sanctification: he sees it as the actualization of Christ's saving work here and now as we hear Christ's call and respond to it in "the obedience of faith" (Rom 1:5). Our obedience takes the form of our concrete realization of our new being in Christ through the power of the Spirit as our being is given a determination that corresponds to Christ's own human life of covenant obedience. The fact that this realization is actualized as an event, Barth insists, does not detract from the reality that Christ's saving work is perfect and definitive. Even as we affirm that the salvation won by Christ happened "once and for all in the birth and life and death of Jesus Christ" and was verified by his resurrection, this work "has not ceased to be history and therefore to happen. As this history, it is not enclosed and confined in that given time."[46] The present realization our sanctification stands in an intrinsic relationship to Christ's saving work into the past because Christ himself is the primary actor in *both* moments in the context of his personal history.

Barth argues that this priority of Christ's action in the realization of our new human being in Christ means that we remain distinct from Christ even

---

[42] *CD* IV/2, 72.
[43] *CD* III/2, 176.
[44] *CD* III/2, 150.
[45] *CD* III/2, 180.
[46] *CD* IV/2, 107.

while we live in correspondence to him. Christ's action unconditionally precedes our own: there are "two very different active subjects," Barth explains, who "are obviously at work together in different ways, but with a clear differentiation of function."[47] At the same time, there is a difference between our actions of obedience and other human actions. Any action performed in correspondence to Christ remains distinct from every other human action, because these actions cannot and do not "arise from our own heart or emotions or spontaneity" but rather have their "origin in the power of the direction" that has come to us from Christ himself.[48] As a result, on the one hand, it is correct to talk about a "real alteration" of our being; we are transformed in such a way that our own human being "becomes and is conformable to [Christ's] being."[49] On the other hand, this alteration takes the form, once again, of a new determination rather than a state: we are transformed in the sense that there is now a "claiming of all human life and being and activity by the will of God for the active fulfillment of that will."[50] Believers are those humans, Barth says, who live "different from others in relation to the divine verdict and direction when the Holy Spirit awakens them to faith and love. They do not merely live under the promise, which could be said of all men. They live in and with and by the promise. They seize it. They apprehend it. They conform themselves to it. And therefore in their present life they live as those who belong to the future."[51] Barth describes this altered life as the arrival of a "temporal future," his particular way of describing a life lived in the "hope of sharing the glory of God" (Rom 5:2).[52] As believers, we begin to live into our eschatological future now, not because we transcend our creaturely being, but because "we find the essence of all creaturely glory in serving him, actively siding with him and helping him and in this way . . . being clothed with all the honor and also with all the joy and peace of eternal life."[53] This vision of a

---

[47] *CD* IV/3.2, 601. Adam Neder provides a clarifying summary of this point: "To be God is to be the one who is always gracious; to be properly human is to be the corresponding active recipient of God's grace. This ordering of giving and receiving, preceding and following, lordship and grateful obedience, constitutes the basic difference between the parties within their fellowship. To confuse God and human beings would mean to reverse, weaken, or misunderstand the nature and ordering of these distinct actions." See Neder, *Participation in Christ*, 7.

[48] *CD* IV/2, 528.

[49] *CD* IV/2, 529.

[50] *CD* IV/1, 101.

[51] *CD* IV/1, 120.

[52] *CD* IV/3.1, 351. Barth historical approach to God's covenant leads him to see a close alignment between the life of the present and that of the *eschaton*: "What 'will be' there and then in the *eschaton* is in visibility that which really is here and now in virtue of the reconciling action of God." *CD* IV/3.2, 489.

[53] *CD* IV/1, 116.

truly *human* life – a concrete, embodied life lived in obedience to God in anticipation of an eternal covenantal partnership with God – provides the context into which Barth places his particular account of union with Christ.

C. Union with Christ as Vocation

As we have seen, Barth believes that God's determination of human being originates as a movement of sovereign grace from God to us, from above to below, and proceeds with the goal of establishing a union between God and human agents. "God has the freedom to be present with that which is not God," Barth says, "to communicate himself and unite himself with the other, and the other with himself."[54] God's free and loving act establishes a correspondingly free act of gratitude and love on the part of the human. This second act, enclosed within the first one, moves from the human to God, from below to above. The enclosure of this human act within the prior divine act means that *both* acts occur as a single history, one wholly determined by God's grace even as it includes free human actions. The divine and human actions remain distinct even in their unity because the *actors* are utterly distinct from one another. "The grace of God and the gratitude of man, the Word of God and the response of man, the knowledge and act of God and those of man, take place on two very different levels and two very different ways which even in the content of this history are not the same and not interchangeable."[55] The end result is a true partnership between God and human beings, a correspondence of divine and human agents who remain distinct even as the human participates in the being of God. Jesus Christ is the key to this partnership because he sets the human correspondence to God in motion through his own obedience as the true God and true human; he also is the one who, through his own eternal life as the mediator between God and human beings (1 Tim 2:5), establishes and guarantees that this partnership will be *eternal*.

This particular vision for the participation of human beings in the life of God within a single covenant history centered on Christ is the context from which Barth describes the believer's union with Christ. Since he sees the category of union as the lens through which the Christian life can be described in its present-tense existence, he depicts it not as a state of being but as a dynamic history of corresponding movement between two sub-

---

[54] *CD* II/1, 313.

[55] *CD* III/2, 180. He repeatedly emphasizes, however, that even with the distinction of grace and gratitude, the unity of the covenant is not in any way diminished: "grace is divine giving and human receiving. It can be 'had' only in the course of this history." *CD* IV/2, 90. Also see his remarks on the *concursus Dei* in *CD* III/3, 90–154.

jects, with the divine movement from above to below preceding and enabling the human movement from below to above. For Barth, union with Christ *happens*. This must be the case, he thinks, because even to speak of the idea of a union "is already to suggest an act or movement."[56] It happens as we are taken up "in the sphere of God" by Christ through his act of joining us to himself through his own life, death, and resurrection so that we may have a real share in his own ongoing partnership with God as the true human being.[57] God has "made us alive together with Christ" (Eph 2:5), Barth thinks, as Christ continues to live as the resurrected and ascended Lord. To be *in* Christ means that "objectively we can no longer be remote from him in a private sphere but that we are drawn into his sphere, into what takes place in him. This occurrence becomes objectively our own experience."[58] The result is not our dissolution into Christ but our *activation* by him. As true God and the "subject who initiates and acts decisively in this union," Christ remains distinct from us even as he joins us to himself and himself to us.[59] We are simply drawn into his own covenantal life as co-participants in it, with both Christ and us maintaining our personal identities even as "the spatial distance between Christ and [us] disappears."[60]

Christ lives in and through us as he "speaks, acts, and rules . . . as the Lord of [our] thinking speech, and action."[61] We are determined by him in the sense that our being and action is directed by him as he goes about his own covenant life: as a "recipient and bearer of the divine promise" activated in Christ, we stand "in relation to God as one who can only respond or correspond" to him.[62] This union is enacted through Christ's call to us and our obedient response to it. This call comes to us as the Word of God, and we hear and respond to it through the power of Christ's own Spirit. Barth believes that our obedience to Christ's call brings us into correspondence to the objective reality of the true human being Christ himself actualized in his own personal covenantal history as well as his ongoing obedience as the living Lord. The call itself thus becomes "our bond to the person of Jesus."[63] It is precisely by uniting us to himself through his call to us, Barth thinks, that "Christ has set us free" (Gal 5:1). We are freed for

---

[56] *CD* IV/2, 109.

[57] *CD* IV/1, 7.

[58] *CD* IV/3.1, 182. This happens as an unconditional election: believers have "no option but to attach themselves to him with their own action." *CD* IV/3.2, 606.

[59] *CD* IV/3.2, 541.

[60] *CD* IV/3.2, 547.

[61] *CD* IV/3.2, 547.

[62] *CD* IV/1, 113.

[63] *CD* II/2, 613.

covenantal obedience as Christ joins us to himself in his command "in order that, in this bond, our life may be liberated."[64]

Our free obedience to Christ's call is not divorced from Christ's personal action – as if our obedience were our own work – but rather, it arises as the consequence of Christ's action, since his call is "effective with divine power."[65] He determines us "by giving [us] direction," Barth says, and this direction has a twofold effect.[66] At one moment, it sets limits to our fallen existence by moving us away from the false sphere of sinful human being and action. It thus comes to us as a form of judgment, disturbing us in our sinful rebellion and prompting our repentance.[67] We are given a new determination in the sense that we are "made a partisan of God even against [ourselves] and the world."[68] At the same time, Christ's call propels us into true covenant partnership here and now with him. Believers "are not merely called out," Barth explains. "They are also called *in*. They are called into the fellowship of their existence with his."[69] This fellowship, a true *koinonia* with Christ by the Spirit, does not cancel out our humanity but makes it anew. We are "awakened to genuine humanity," Barth says, as the Spirit transforms our reason to bring it into correspondence to "the mind of Christ," which is itself the revelation of the wisdom of God (1 Cor 2:16).[70]

Barth holds that this correspondence to God's own reason – revealed in Christ and understood by us through the Spirit – exists together with embodied actions that stand in line with Paul's own account of the embodied dynamic of the Christian life. Christ's call leads us ever more deeply into "the knowledge of God's will in all spiritual wisdom and understanding" and prompts us to "lead lives worthy of the Lord" and "grow in the knowledge of God" (Col 1:9–10). As we hear this call through the power of the Spirit, who awakens and enlivens us to it, we realize we cannot simply be "hearers and spectators who are left to [ourselves] and ordained for pure passivity."[71] Rather, we are prompted to active obedience, and this activity *is* our union: it happens in and through our "attachment to Christ, co-ordination and fellowship with him, discipleship, appropriation to him with the corresponding expropriation, life of and by the Holy Spirit."[72] To be united to Christ is thus to be tasked to perform a "definite action," one that takes the form of a "repetition, confirmation and revelation not only of

---

[64] *CD* II/2, 609.
[65] *CD* IV/2, 523.
[66] *CD* IV/2, 523.
[67] *CD* IV/2, 524.
[68] *CD* IV/2, 525.
[69] *CD* IV/3.2, 527, emphasis added.
[70] *CD* IV/3.2, 548.
[71] *CD* IV/3.2, 542.
[72] *CD* IV/3.2, 549.

the manner but also of the will and act of God."[73] We do not add something new to what Christ has done through this action; rather, this action is simply a summons to believe and confess what he has done, first to ourselves and then to the world, and then "lead a life worthy of the calling" we have received (Eph 4:1). We act by seeking to be "imitators of God, as beloved children, and live in love as Christ loved us and gave himself up for us" (Eph 5:1).

This imitation is the concrete form of our covenantal service, and it leads us to develop in obedience as we present our bodies as a "living sacrifice" while seeking the transformation and renewal of our minds so that we "may discern what is the will of God" (Rom 12:1–2). We grow as we remove "every proud obstacle raised up against the knowledge of God" and become more and more able to "take every thought captive to obey Christ" (2 Cor 10:5).[74] The result is that we live more and more in alignment with the goal toward which God has ordered us: to be "created in Christ Jesus for good works, which God prepared beforehand to be our way of life" (Eph 2:10). Barth sees this life of good works – that is, our life of covenant partnership with God in correspondence to Christ through the power of the Spirit – in terms of the *vocation* Christ himself gives us as we participate in his own life with him. As we are joined with the living Christ, Barth argues, we "become and are a single totality, a fluid and differentiated but genuine and solid unity, in which [God] is with his people."[75] We participate in Christ as he fulfills his specific vocation as the risen and ascended Lord while in union with us. Barth describes Christ's vocation in terms of his prophetic office. He explains that Christ does not "find himself indolently resting at his place," but rather, "he strides through the ages still left to the world until his final return in its final form."[76] As he strides, he proclaims himself. That he does so stems from the fact that his own life is determined by God's decision that he would reconcile human beings to himself through Christ so that they might live as his partners. Since this reconciliation is a complete and finished work even

---

[73] *CD* IV/3.2, 533.

[74] Paul Nimmo offers a helpful description of the nature of this development: "Self-determination is thus an ongoing event for the ethical agent, yet it is not an activity that occurs independently of God, for her history remains 'under the transcendent leadership of God, in which decisions are made first by God and then also by man.'…There is no question that the ethical agent can directly be the covenant partner of God that Jesus Christ alone is: rather her destiny is to *become* a true covenant partner of God, and this *becoming* depends directly on the Self-determination of God in Jesus Christ to be for her." See Paul Nimmo, *Being in Action: The Theological Shape of Barth's Ethical Vision* (London: T&T Clark, 2007), 96–97, citing *CD* III/2, 124.

[75] *CD* IV/3.2, 540.

[76] *CD* IV/3.2, 663.

as its effects are still being unfolded in history, it cannot remained undeclared: a reconciliation that remained hidden would be no true reconciliation at all. And so God himself *proclaims* what he has done. "A mute and obscure God would be an idol," Barth insists. "The true and living God is eloquent and radiant."[77] As the one who accomplished the reconciliation, Jesus also is the one who proclaims it. This task of bearing testimony to himself in human history – of proclaiming the gospel of who he is and what he has done in and through his life, death, and resurrection – is his ongoing vocation.[78] Christ "speaks for himself" in human history, Barth says, and he thus serves as "his own authentic witness."[79] He does so through the power of his Spirit, who is the form of his own personal presence and the means by which human beings can be joined to him: "The Holy Spirit is he himself in the action in which he reveals and makes himself known to other men as the one he is, placing them under his direction, claiming them as his own, as the witnesses of his holiness."[80] He also speaks through the Spirit by means of his people, the church. "The Holy Spirit is the living Lord Jesus Christ himself in the work of the sanctification of his particular people in the world, of his community and all its members."[81] This idea corresponds to the link Paul draws between the message of the gospel and God's plan to reveal his eternal purpose and wisdom, executed through the saving work of Jesus Christ, "through the church" (Eph 3:10). As Barth puts it: "[t]here is no vocation, and therefore no *unio cum Christo*, which does not lead as such directly into the communion of the saints, i.e., the *communio vocatorum*."[82]

Barth sees the church as a "living people awakened and gathered by Jesus Christ as the Lord for the fulfillment of a specific task."[83] This task is the vocation the church shares with Christ himself: the proclamation of the gospel. Barth holds that, as Christ himself declares that he has accomplished the reconciliation God and human beings in and through his life, death, and resurrection, he calls together a church with the "intention and commission that it for its part should speak to the world, that it should be his messenger within it."[84] Since this church exists through Christ's saving work and as the fulfillment of this work, the church has its being when it lives in active correspondence to his call. "The church is when it takes

---

[77] *CD* IV/3.1, 279.

[78] On this point, Barth remarks: "The real goal and end of the resurrection of Jesus and its attestation was [Christ's] going out into the world." *CD* IV/3.1, 303.

[79] *CD* IV/3.1, 46.
[80] *CD* IV/2, 522.
[81] *CD* IV/2, 522.
[82] *CD* IV/3.2, 682.
[83] *CD* III/4, 488.
[84] *CD* IV/3.1, 18.

place that God lets certain people live as his servants, his friends, his children, the witnesses of the reconciliation of the world with himself as it has taken place in Jesus Christ."[85] We participate in Christ, therefore, as Christ enlists us as participants in his own vocation. As Barth sees it, this way of accounting for *participatio Christi* stands directly in line with God's original goal in the covenant of grace for which Christ was elected. As the one who lived an obedient human life in order to create free human subjects able to join with God in covenant partnership, it makes sense that the living and ascended Christ "cannot and will not remain alone" but rather "wills to be what he is and do what he does in company with others whom he calls for the purpose . . . making common cause and conjoining himself with them.[86] In other words, this act of making us participants in his ongoing prophetic work is simply the present anticipatory realization of the eschatological consequences of his perfect saving work. Because of what he did in the past – and because of what this past work guarantees about our future – we live in union with Christ in the present as his co-workers within the context of God's eternal plan. This is the lens through which Barth understands Paul's description of the church as the "body of Christ" (1 Cor 12:12), and it means that the history of the church is one and the same as "the history of the Christian in connection with that of Jesus Christ himself as engaged in his prophetic work."[87] Christ lives and acts in and through his church which constitutes "his earthly-historical form of existence" as he fulfills his prophetic mission.[88]

This prophetic ministry determines the specific form of the church's communal life. The church's practices are not ordered internally toward the church's own members, as if the Christian were called to a private life of self-enrichment or spiritual growth.[89] Rather, every Christian is called to a "personal participation in the ministry of the Christian community sent into the world."[90] This participation takes place as a public ministry, because Christ himself lives publicly: he is the living and active Lord who works in the world visibly through his Spirit. Our union with Christ manifests itself in our visible witness to Christ, centering primarily on our proclamation of his gospel through his Word. The church's task is "to attest Jesus Christ as

---

[85] *CD* IV/1, 650.

[86] *CD* IV/3.2, 541–42.

[87] *CD* IV/3.2, 663.

[88] *CD* IV/2, 60. The fullest treatment of these theme in Barth's theology is found in John G. Flett, *The Witness of God: The Trinity, Missio Dei, Karl Barth, and the Nature of Christian Community* (Grand Rapids: Eerdmans, 2010).

[89] As Barth puts it: "But all this is not a private arrangement between him and us. He is not merely our Lord and Representative. As he takes our own place, he takes also that of our fellows and brothers." *CD* IV/2, 519.

[90] *CD* IV/3.2, 932.

the Savior of the world who is also the great prophet speaking to the world." This act occurs as the fulfillment of our election and vocation in Christ: the believer "has no option but to spring into the breach between Jesus Christ, whom it is given him to know, and those to whom it is not yet given to know him."[91] The church's action does not take place apart from Christ, but is its "actual fellowship with Christ."[92] It thus entails, not only proclamation but a life lived "in a manner worthy of the gospel" (Phil 1:17), which means – as Paul himself argues – a life lived in the pattern of the obedience of Christ himself (Phil 2:5–8). Or, as Barth puts it, the church engages in an "unqualified participation in the cause of God and therefore in the cause of the world and humanity."[93] To be *for* the world in this vocation – in the pattern of Christ who lived his own history for the world and lives this way still in his ongoing vocation – is what it means to participate in, and thus be united with, him.

Bibliography

Barth, Karl. *Anselm: Fides Quaerens Intellectum: Anselm's Proof of the Existence of God in the Context of his Theological Scheme*. Translated by Ian W. Robertson. Richmond, Va.: John Knox, 1960.

———. *Church Dogmatics*. 13 vols. 2d ed. Translated by Geoffrey William Bromiley and T. F. Torrance. Edinburgh: T&T Clark, 1957–1961.

Flett, John G. *The Witness of God: The Trinity, Missio Dei, Karl Barth, and the Nature of Christian Community*. Grand Rapids: Eerdmans, 2010.

Hunsinger, George. "The Mediator of Communion: Karl Barth's Doctrine of the Holy Spirit." Pages 168–73 in *Disruptive Grace: Studies in the Theology of Karl Barth*. Grand Rapids: Eerdmans, 2000.

Johnson, Keith L. "A Reappraisal of Karl Barth's Theological Development and His Dialogue with Catholicism." *International Journal of Systematic Theology* 14/1 (2012): 1–23.

McCormack, Bruce L. "Karl Barth's Historicized Christology: Just How 'Chalcedonian' Is it?" Pages 201–33 in *Orthodox and Modern: Studies in the Theology of Karl Barth*. Grand Rapids: Baker Academic, 2008.

———. "Participation in God, Yes; Deification, No: Two Modern Protestant Responses to an Ancient Question." Pages 235–60 in *Orthodox and Modern: Studies in the Theology of Karl Barth*. Grand Rapids: Baker Academic, 2008.

Migliore, Daniel L. "*Participatio Christi*: The Central Theme of Barth's Doctrine of Sanctification." *Zeitschrift für dialektische Theologie* 18 (2002): 286–307.

Neder, Adam. *Participation in Christ: An Entry into Karl Barth's* Church Dogmatics. Louisville: Westminster John Knox, 2009.

---

[91] *CD* IV/3.2, 933.
[92] *CD* IV/3.2, 482.
[93] *CD* IV/3.1, 248.

Nimmo, Paul. *Being in Action: The Theological Shape of Barth's Ethical Vision*. London: T&T Clark, 2007.

Webster, John B. *Barth's Ethics of Reconciliation*. Cambridge: Cambridge University Press, 1995.

Part Three: Theological Reflection

Fitting Participation

From the Holy Trinity to Christian Virtue

ASHISH VARMA

"If then you have been raised with Christ, seek the things that are above, where Christ is seated at the right hand of God" (Col. 3:1). The Apostle Paul begins this section in Colossians on the vices of "what is earthly" (3:5) and the virtues of the things of God "above" with a reminder of identity: "if then you have been raised with Christ."[1] The implication is that those who are *in Christ* are to "put on" things (3:12) and think on things (3:2) that belong to the realm of God.[2] On one hand, identity is key, for Paul's exhortation belongs to those who are in Christ, buried and raised together with him (2:11–12). On the other hand, this identity entails a responsibility, namely to think and live rightly, even virtuously. Paul's clothing metaphor of taking off and putting on implies a way of life, for one's clothes are befitting of one's identity and commensurate actions: a busi-

---

[1] Scholars debate whether Paul was in fact responsible for the writing of Colossians. For an overview of the options, see R. McL Wilson, *A Critical and Exegetical Commentary on Colossians and Philemon* (London: T&T Clark, 2005), 30–35. Wilson seems to conclude that there is no straight forward answer. For the sake of the present essay, I will follow Church tradition and assume Pauline authorship. However, my argument does not hinge upon this assumption.

[2] The identification of Paul's use of being raised with Christ and union with Christ should not be a controversial decision since there is abundant precedent. For a few examples, see Richard B. Gaffin Jr., *Resurrection and Redemption: A Study in Paul's Soteriology* (2d ed.; Phillipsburg, N.J.: Presbyterian & Reformed, 1987), esp. 49–50; James R. Edwards, *Romans* (NIBCNT 6; Peabody, Mass.: Hendrickson, 1992), 160; Constantine R. Campbell, *Paul and Union with Christ: An Exegetical and Theological Study* (Grand Rapids: Zondervan, 2012), 333–43; Hans Burger, *Being in Christ: A Biblical and Systematic Investigation in a Reformed Perspective* (Eugene, Ore.: Wipf & Stock, 2009), 218–19; Marianne Meye Thompson, *Colossians and Philemon* (Grand Rapids: Eerdmans, 2005), 123, 149; Richard B. Hays, *The Moral Vision of the New Testament: Community, Cross, New Creation: A Contemporary Introduction to New Testament Ethics* (San Francisco: HarperCollins, 1996), 38; Lane G. Tipton, "Union with Christ and Justification," in *Justified in Christ: God's Plan for Us in Justification*, (ed. K. Scott Oliphint; Fearn, Scotland: Mentor, 2007), 37–38.

nessman puts on a suit in order to enact his duties during the day in a manner befitting of his employment while an Olympic speed skater dawns apparel appropriate to the task of helping her skate swiftly.[3] Paul commends the clothes most fitting of the Christian life, clothes that reflect being in Christ, even as he identifies the clothing contrary to identity in Christ.[4] Yet taken in isolation, Col. 3 may seem as merely an urging to correct oneself in light of one's self identification. However, Col. 1–2 reveals a more complete reality, one in which Christ is the one who makes right living possible in his own person and acts of redemption and reconciliation (1:11, 15–23), and apart from whom lies folly, the "appearance of wisdom" (2:18–23). For Paul, "putting on virtue" is really about "putting on Christ." That is, being virtuous is about union and fitting participation with Christ.

A tension arises, though, in that Paul does not actually use the word "virtue" (*aretē*) in this context. Is the idea of virtue foreign to Paul's purposes here? If Jennifer Herdt is correct, it would seem so, for she thinks that virtue must involve a gradual transformation independent of the sort of decisive divine initiative presented in soteriologies that begin in union with Christ. She writes, "Luther's insistence that union with Christ is precondition rather than culmination of justification radically changes its meaning [from medieval predecessors]; participation in the divine life is no longer understood as requiring transformation of the human person, but is understood . . . as Christ's presence 'inside' the sinner, who is otherwise alien to, and alienated from, God."[5] For Herdt, the problem is Luther's positing union with Christ as a "prerequisite" for the Christian life means a "displacement of human agency" that "threatens the intelligibility of any account of growth in faith as gradual transformation."[6] A front-loading of union with Christ through faith "suggests [that] a clear recognition of our dependence on God and despair over our independent agency" is necessary precondition for virtue, as opposed to Herdt's insistence that "God's grace,

---

[3] One may contend that clothes do not necessarily say something about an individual. After all, the businessman would don shorts for a trip to the beach and a tuxedo for a wedding. However, even here, his choice of clothing is telling of his identity amid the occasion. People in other cultures would dress in a manner commensurate with their cultural identity. For instance, what a person wears to a traditional Indian wedding not only speaks for the occasion but also his or her status at the wedding (Groom/Bride? Parent of the groom? Parent of the bride? Extended family? Friend?). The point to be taken from Colossians is that the clothes of Christ are befitting of identity in Christ and are not seasonal wear that may be discarded when on holiday.

[4] For a more protracted defense of understanding Paul's use of the clothing metaphor in this way, see Grant Macaskill, *Union with Christ in the New Testament* (Oxford: Oxford University Press, 2013), 196–97.

[5] Jennifer A. Herdt, *Putting on Virtue: The Legacy of the Splendid Vices* (Chicago: University Of Chicago Press, 2008), 178–79.

[6] Herdt, *Putting on Virtue*, 194.

not our acknowledgment of grace," enables virtue.[7] She is concerned that Luther's theology creates a "competitive understanding of human and divine agency" and "requires human passivity."[8] However, as she states earlier, "If true goodness is a pure gift that excludes human agency, then any virtue acquired by human effort is necessarily tainted."[9] That is, it would not be virtue since, for her, "Christian virtue and piety, like 'pagan' virtue, result from a gradual process of imitation and habituation, even as this is understood as a process in which God is actively luring us toward divine goodness."[10] If Herdt is right, it would seem that the tension between Paul's grounding virtuous living in one's union with Christ and Herdt's insistence that an initial decisive grace in union with Christ cannot create a truly virtuous person is insurmountable. The idea of virtue would be in conflict with Pauline theology.

In what follows, I will argue to the contrary. Herdt's complaint is specifically against Luther, with added distrust of Calvin and the Reformed tradition(s).[11] The present essay is not an attempt to defend Luther or any other single theologian from Herdt's charge. That could be an essay of its own. Rather, I will make a positive case for theological virtue as a fitting and important reality that follows from one's gracious union with Christ. A byproduct of this argument will be a vindication of seeing Paul's language in such passages as Col. 3 as virtue language, especially since it is apparent that he grounds his call in the Christians' union with Christ.[12]

---

[7] Herdt, *Putting on Virtue*, 195–96.

[8] Herdt, *Putting on Virtue*, 188.

[9] Herdt, *Putting on Virtue*, 164.

[10] Herdt, *Putting on Virtue*, 163. Again, Herdt affirms what seems to be a problem, by her account, for a union with Christ that brings a decisive act of grace unto justification and sanctification: "Human agency and divine agency do not compete for control, and human agency need not step aside in order for divine agency to enter in."

[11] See Herdt, *Putting on Virtue*, 198–202.

[12] Since Paul does not appeal to the category of virtue, it is difficult to argue that he intended to utilize the category. The contention here is theological, namely that Paul's description of the moral life flowing from identity and life in Christ are fitting with the idea of Christian virtue. Ellen Charry argues this well when she coins the terms "aretology" and "aretegenic," meaning "conducive to virtue;" Ellen Charry, *By the Renewing of Your Minds: The Pastoral Function of Christian Doctrine* (New York: Oxford University Press, 1997), 19. Paul's language in Colossians and elsewhere is "conducive to virtue" in that, for Paul, "Christian excellence is based in divine action" (i.e., participation), it "comes from adjusting to ontological realities," and it is "public and social" (58). Elsewhere, Harrington and Keenan notice teleological, participatory, and practical features in Philippians 3:10–11 that attest the "basic concerns and contours of Christian virtue ethics." J. Daniel S. J. Harrington and James Keenan, *Paul and Virtue Ethics: Building Bridges Between New Testament Studies and Moral Theology* (Lanham, Md.: Rowman & Littlefield, 2010), 17.

Before proceeding, a point of clarification: in the Thomistic traditions – the most widely propagated Christian model of virtue – "theological virtue" has been used to refer to faith, hope, and love, those virtues that direct toward a "happiness surpassing man's nature, and which man can obtain by the power of God alone, by a kind of participation of the Godhead."[13] This is in direct contrast to those "cardinal virtues" that are "human virtues" directed at natural ends and attainable apart from a special divine – or "supernatural" – act of grace.[14] Attainment of the two kinds of virtues is wholly other, for in this scheme, it is impossible to attain to theological virtue apart from grace precisely because the end is supernatural. There is discontinuity, then, between the character development that aims at cardinal virtue and the graciously directed development of faith, hope, and love.[15] Herdt rejects this Thomistic model in favor of a single kind of virtue that she models after Erasmus; Herdt's proposal seeks to "make room for pagan virtue . . . [through which] we can take baby steps toward conformity with Christ even when we do not yet even explicitly desire this conformity."[16] The Thomistic approach posits two kinds of *teloi* distinguished by natural and gracious means of attainment while Herdt's approach argues for a single *telos* toward which some progress may be made through natural pursuits though ultimately cannot be reached apart from grace. The present project lays aside this important question and instead uses "virtue," "theological virtue," and "Christian virtue" synonymously to refer to that kind of virtue to which Christians are called in Christ and by the Spirit. My use will necessarily impinge upon the kinds-and-number-of-virtue debate in that part of Herdt's contention with traditional Protestant theology is its front-loading (as opposed to culminating) soteriology with union with Christ and thereby interrupting virtue formation with a divine act that necessitates at least a moment of human passivity. Nevertheless, the question of kind and number must be taken up separately.

---

[13] Thomas Aquinas, *Summa theologica* (trans. Fathers of the English Dominican Province; New York: Ave Maria, 1948), 1–2ae.62.1.

[14] Aquinas, *ST*, 1–2ae.61.1. See also 1–2ae.62.1.

[15] There is some debate as to whether Aquinas himself intended two kinds of virtue with different ends or whether this reading of Aquinas is due to Cajetan's sixteenth century misinterpretation of Aquinas. See D. Stephen Long, "Moral Theology," in *The Oxford Handbook of Systematic Theology* (New York: Oxford University Press, 2007), 471–72.

[16] Herdt, Putting on Virtue, 126.

A. Ontology of Virtue

The heart of the traditional Protestant proclamation of union with Christ is the soteriological problem of human fallenness and inability to do what is right before the Lord. Implicit (and often made explicit) in this is the holiness of God, the ontological grounds of our own being made holy. Indeed, Lev. 11:44–45 testifies to an ontology of the priority of God's holiness, and 1 Peter 1:15–16 capitalizes on this proclamation: "just as he who called you is holy, so be holy in all you do; for it is written: 'Be holy, because I am holy.'" So it is with the holiness of God that an ontology of Christian virtue must begin.

I. Holiness of God

The holiness of God is an aspect of the glory of God, which – at least for those rightly situated before God – "generates awe and worship."[17] God's own holiness is the precondition for our creaturely holiness, to which virtue ("excellence") strives. Holiness is the way God is, the corollary to which is unholiness, as John Webster rightly identifies: "[t]he unholy is that which lies beyond the will of God. The unholy is the absurd affair in which the creature seeks to be creature in a way other than that which is purposed by God."[18] Christian virtue, as a striving toward holiness, requires attention to who God is, what he is doing, and what our part is in response. To separate Christian virtue from the holiness of God is to forge a new path, one that is inherently opposed to God's purposes and to our own identity as redeemed creatures of God. However, as Henri Blocher reminds, this forging of a new path independently of God's ways is what lies at the heart of sin, for "in its generality sin is defined by nothing except a negative and definite way; the positive is always another side, the side of God and of his creation."[19] At the heart of Christian virtue, then, is participation with the God who is holy and the ways of his holiness.

For Christians to speak of the holiness of God is not to speak of God's holiness in the abstract but rather of the holiness of the triune God and in

---

[17] Pierre Berthoud, "The Compassion of God: Exodus 34:5–9 in the Light of Exodus 32–34," in *Engaging the Doctrine of God: Contemporary Protestant Perspectives*, ed. Bruce L. McCormack (Grand Rapids: Baker Academic, 2008), 159–60. The right posturing before God is life in union with Christ by the Spirit, as I shall show below.

[18] John B. Webster, *Holiness* (Grand Rapids: Eerdmans, 2003), 49.

[19] "Le péché dans sa généralité ne se définit que d'une façon négative et formelle ; le positif est toujours de l'autre côté, du côté de Dieu et de sa création." Henri Blocher, *La Doctrine Du Péché et de La Rédemption*. (3d ed.; Vaux-sur-Seine, France: Edifac, 2000), 36. Translation mine.

the ways of the triune God.[20] That is, it is not just God but the *triune God* who is our holiness principle, directing and empowering us.[21] Webster identifies the general ways in which the holiness of God reveals the triune being of God, pointing to the Father as the electing one who "wills and purposes" the setting apart of a people to be holy, the Son who "achieves this separation of humankind by rescuing humanity from its pollution and bondage to unholiness," and the Spirit who "completes or perfects that separation by sanctifying humankind and drawing it into righteous fellowship with the holy God."[22] Properly situated Christian or theological virtue demands attention to God's triune way of being, for it establishes the way in which our being made virtuous involves not vain strivings on a path of our making but participation in the ways of the triune God in Christ by the Spirit.

Indeed, the triune God is "the good" toward which Christian virtue strives, for, as Augustine confessed, the good "is nothing else but God Himself. For how can any thing be man's chief good but that in cleaving to which he is blessed? Now this is nothing but God, to whom we can cleave only by affection, desire, and love."[23] The idea of "cleaving" is beautifully vivid in its depiction of the level of commitment true Christian virtue has to the Creator, finding its source and *eudaimonia* in the triune God. The purest of Christian virtue, or the height of cleaving to God, says Augustine, is "perfect love of God," from which flows all the other cardinal virtues.[24] Joining Augustine's image of virtue as cleaving to the ontological priority of God's holiness, we might add that the love of God that comes only from cleaving to him is the height of virtue that comes only from the outpouring of God's own holiness. God's holiness in action alone enables the Christian to turn to him and cleave and, therein, to be transformed.

---

[20] Webster eloquently writes, "The doctrine of the Trinity is the Christian understanding of God; and so the doctrine of the Trinity shapes and determines the entirety of how we think of God's nature, including how we think of God's holiness;" Webster, *Holiness*, 36.

[21] The triune God as our holiness principle is a deliberate adaptation of Vanhoozer's "the Trinity is our Scripture Principle." The borrowing of language is meant to highlight a similar theme in what Vanhoozer wishes to say of Scripture as I wish to say of holiness. He grounds the vitality of Scripture in the life and communicative act of the Triune God while my aim is to ground holiness in the same way. However, the analogy of the phrases should not be pressed too hard since Scripture is ultimately an instrument of God's work while holiness is an aspect of God's being. See Kevin J. Vanhoozer, "Triune Discourse: Theological Reflections on the Claim That God Speaks (Part 2)," in *Trinitarian Theology for the Church: Scripture, Community, Worship* (ed. Daniel J. Treier and David Lauber; Downers Grove: IVP Academic, 2009), 75–76.

[22] Webster, *Holiness*, 48.

[23] Augustine, *On the Morals of the Catholic Church* xv.24 (*NPNF*[1] 4:48).

[24] Augustine, *On the Morals of the Catholic Church* xv.25.

II. The Economy of Virtue: Holiness of Christ

If theological virtue is a predicate of the holiness of God and – as Paul seems to indicate – a function of our identity in Christ, then it is only fitting to speak of the God-man as the place where humanity sees the holiness of God. Paul Althaus writes that for Luther "whoever seeks God outside of Jesus finds the devil. This means that such autonomous attempts can, in every case, result only in something completely contrary to God and produced by the devil."[25] As we have already seen, holiness is an aspect of God's being and cannot be grasped for oneself but rather is seen only in God's triune ways and revealed to us in Jesus Christ. Thus, following Luther, we may boldly proclaim that whoever seeks holiness outside of Jesus finds the devil. As the Holy One of the Father, Jesus Christ manifests the economy of virtue: the holiness of God as the grounds of the Christian's fitting participation. The economy of virtue describes the procession of holiness from wholly other to God-in-action with the result of creaturely participation just as the economy of the Trinity relates the life of God *en se* to the life of God in the world: Son and Spirit as sent by the Father to complete the divine mission. The economy of virtue is caught up in the economy of the Trinity.

The holiness of the God-man is not only the holiness of the triune God but also holiness realized in the flesh. Bavinck writes that "according to his human nature" holiness is "infused" and that "Christ had to manifest his innate holiness through temptation and struggle."[26] The holiness of the Son is divine, but in taking on human flesh, the holiness of God comes to man in a creaturely way, being confirmed in the life of Jesus Christ through his life of holiness. Calvin somewhat scandalously speaks of the creaturely element of Christ's holiness in terms of "merit" working under and in obedience to God's mercy.[27] Christ's own life of faithfulness and

---

[25] Paul Althaus, *The Theology of Martin Luther* (trans. Robert C. Schultz; Philadelphia: Fortress, 1966), 23.

[26] Herman Bavinck, *Reformed Dogmatics, Volume 3: Sin and Salvation in Christ*, (trans. John Vriend; Grand Rapids: Baker Academic, 2006), 315. The controversy over the idea of "infusion" is not one that I wish to take up here. For the present purposes, it should suffice to note that Bavinck's language of infusion helps underscore that creaturely holiness is enacted by Jesus Christ in and through the Incarnation. That is, the Incarnation makes possible creaturely holiness after the fall by joining the human to the divine, with the latter the source of holiness.

[27] John Calvin, *Institutes of the Christian Religion* (LCC 20–21; ed. John T. McNeill; trans. Ford Lewis Battles; Louisville: Westminster John Knox, 1960), II.xvii.1. It is apparent that Calvin is responding to some controversy over the idea that no one, not even Christ, could merit anything of effect for salvation. Calvin calls these people "perversely subtle men." Nevertheless, he does (rightly) concede that some qualification must be giv-

obedience is the manifestation of God's self-holiness and is the creaturely reflection of the divine holiness by which believers are "clothed." Thus Calvin could joyfully preach the gift of grace that "believers are united with Christ and 'clothed' with Christ's righteousness."[28] This clothing in Christ's creaturely righteousness or holiness is the basis of the Christian's justification,[29] but it also becomes the means of a Christian being made holy/sanctified. This is true in two senses: *imitatio Christi* and transformation by the Spirit.[30] *Imitatio* follows upon transformation as an important element in virtue formation, but the key movement for the development of the present ontology is the latter.

III. Situating Our Holiness: In Christ

On a basic level, we may affirm Herdt's insistence that "God's grace, not our acknowledgment of grace . . . allows the process of our restoration in God's image to get underway."[31] After all, it is God's grace alone apart from (or even in spite of) our strivings that turns us to him and his boundless love. Specifically, the genesis of our transformation and the coming and manifestation of God's holiness all occur in a single place: Jesus Christ. Calvin famously insisted,

[A]s long as Christ remains outside of us, and we are separated from him, all that he has suffered and done for the salvation of the human race remains useless and of no value for us. Therefore, to share with us what he has received from the Father, he had to become ours and to dwell within us. . . . [F]or, as I have said, all that he possesses is nothing to us until we grow into one body with him.[32]

In this oft-quoted declaration of the centrality of union with Christ for soteriology, at least two things come to the fore. First, union with Christ prioritizes God's work. The purity and primacy of God's holiness worked out in the person and life of Jesus Christ means that as long as Christ is distant from us, all that he has accomplished remains separate from us. Invariably,

---

en with such language as he affirms, "In discussing Christ's merit, we do not consider the beginning of merit to be in him, but we go back to God's ordinance, the first cause."

[28] Dawn DeVries, "Calvin's Preaching," in *The Cambridge Companion to John Calvin* (ed. Donald K. McKim; Cambridge: Cambridge University Press, 2004), 117.

[29] See T. F. Torrance, "Justification: Its Radical Nature and Place in Reformed Doctrine and Life," in *Theology in Reconstruction* (London: SCM, 1965), 153–55: "justification means not simply the non-imputation of our sins through the pardon of Christ, but the positive sharing in his divine-human righteousness" (155).

[30] Michael Allen draws upon and moves beyond T. F. Torrance to argue for *imitatio Christi* as the "second function" of Christ's faith. Michael Allen, *The Christ's Faith: A Dogmatic Account* (New York: T&T Clark, 2009), 195–98.

[31] Herdt, *Putting on Virtue*, 196.

[32] Calvin, *Institutes*, III.i.1.

this includes both the clothing of Christ's holiness and the impetus for our own growth in holiness. As Calvin eloquently puts it, amid such distance, God's confirmed holiness in Jesus Christ remains "useless" to us. Conversely, in union with Christ, the all that "he had" has "become ours." Of note for the present essay, in Christ the holiness of God comes to us as the economy of virtue.

Second, all of the blessings found in Christ, including growth into his body "become ours." Surely, some of these blessings are more immediately felt (justification, adoption) while others begin as a mustard seed and slowly sprout (sanctification, glorification). Nevertheless, in Christ, the latter process immediately begins to transform the Christian, for union with Christ is necessary condition and invitation for fitting participation in the economy of virtue. Paul's language of union indicates the often painstaking process, for sometimes – as in the appeal with which we began the essay (Col. 3:1) – Paul speaks of an already realized resurrection with Christ ("having been raised with Christ") while at other times Paul indicates an eschatologically realized resurrection ("if we have been united with him in a death like his, we shall certainly be united with him in a resurrection like his" – Rom. 6:5). Yet even in the case of Romans, Paul speaks of the sense in which Christians have already been united to Christ (i.e., in his death). In both settings, union with Christ becomes the grounds for Paul's exhortation unto excellence of life ("we too might walk in newness of life" – Rom. 6:5; "let not sin therefore reign in your mortal bodies" – Rom. 6:12). On the surface, then, it would seem that the task of ontologically rooting the Christian's growth in virtue in God's holiness is complete.

However, to stop here would be to omit the life of union wherein and whereby the Christian grows in holiness. Furthermore, the ontological sketch would fall short of a Trinitarian grounding of holiness. After all, if the triune God's holiness is enacted by God and confirmed in the flesh by the Son, whence the role of the Spirit in the revelation of God's holiness? It is the Spirit that joins Christians to Christ.[33] In short, our union is a Spirit-union, and it is on account of the nature of this union that Calvin calls the Holy Spirit "not only the beginning or source" of the benefits of Christ and gifts of God in believers, "but also the author," for apart from the Spirit who completes the economy of virtue, the benefits of Christ, including his holiness, remain apart from us.[34] The Spirit joins the Christian to Christ and his manifestation of divine holiness in the flesh and enacts transformation in the Christian, enabling her to participate actively in the life of

---

[33] Calvin, *Institutes*, III.xi.5. Calvin writes, "For we hold ourselves to be united with Christ by the secret power of his Spirit."

[34] Calvin, *Institutes*, I.xiii.14.

Christ and grow in holiness.[35] That is, the life of Christian enactment of virtue is in Christ by the Spirit.

The life-giving role of the Spirit helps nuance Augustine's notion of the virtuous life as one of cleaving to God. The Holy Father is the electing God who sets apart his people to be holy. The Son reveals the Father and confirms this divine holiness in the person and life of Jesus Christ, to whom we cleave. The cleaving takes place both on account of the Spirit actually joining us to the holy Christ and at the impetus of the Spirit, who leads us in the life of Christ and teaches us to love the Father in Christ. Amid this participation in the Trinitarian economy, the "Spirit's mediation of Christ's person and work, not an immediate participation in the divine essence, is a critical aspect" of this ontology.[36] Indeed, it ensures, at least in response to part of Herdt's concern, that the life of Christ remains our own life in a crucial sense, for we maintain our individual identity and conscious participation even as Christ lives in us.

Todd Billings notes the importance of this active participation in Christ in the theology of Calvin. In asserting the active nature of participation through union with Christ, Billings even alludes to the type of ontology for which I have argued: "In sanctification, all of the human faculties are, in fact, utilized – but if one views humanity as fundamentally related to God, indeed as truly flourishing only in union with God, then one must not speak of a good human action in separation from God's action."[37] The priority of God's action does not negate human action but rather is the context of virtuous human action. Just as God's holiness grounds and effects holiness – via Incarnation and Spirit-union – in those whom the Father has called to himself, so also God's own action grounds and effects action in those who are called by the name of the Incarnate Son. Human action directed by the Spirit in this way is a "flourishing" action that grows in likeness to God's own action, and it is precisely this sort of action that is able to be called excellent, that is, virtuous. The Christian who consistently and faithfully thinks and acts in this flourishing way is the person who is said to be virtuous.

---

[35] Mark Achtemeier wonderfully summarizes the Christian life in the light of the Trinity: "In trinitarian terms, the whole of the Christian life can be seen as the process of our coming to the Father, through the Son, in the Holy Spirit; and of our sharing by the same Spirit in the life and ministry of the Son given from the Father for the sake of the world." Mark Achtemeier, "The Union with Christ Doctrine in Renewal: Movements of the Presbyterian Church (USA)," in *Reformed Theology: Identity and Ecumenicity* (ed. Wallace M. Alston Jr. and Michael Welker; Grand Rapids: Eerdmans, 2003), 337.

[36] Michael Scott Horton, *Christian Faith: A Systematic Theology for Pilgrims on the Way* (Grand Rapids: Zondervan, 2011), 596.

[37] J. Todd Billings, *Calvin, Participation, and the Gift: The Activity of Believers in Union with Christ* (Oxford: Oxford University Press, 2007), 48.

The significance of this ontology should now be evident, for it situates Christian virtue within the economy of God's own holiness. God's holiness grounds the Christian's holiness by making one holy in Christ by the Spirit. Living, moving, and having one's own being in Christ – participation in Christ – is in fact living, moving, and having one's own being. That is, the life in which the Spirit directs Christians is a life in which Christians think and act, and it is life lived in the economy of virtue: from and by God's own holiness as confirmed in the person, life, death, and resurrection of Jesus Christ by the Spirit. Growth in this way of being is growth in living by the Spirit, which increasingly leads to a flourishing life. This excellently lived life is the theologically virtuous life. What, then, is entailed by the "virtuous" element, the life in Christ? It is to this question that we now turn.

B. Excellence in Christ

To be theologically virtuous is intimately bound with the holiness of the triune God. Towards the end of the description of ontology, a glimpse was given of the Christian's life amid the triune economy. However, the emphasis laid on the ontology, for therein lies proper situating of a virtuous life. The purpose was to show that apart from right attention to who God is and who the human creature – particularly the Christian – is in light of its Creator, we have insufficient ability and understanding of what is entailed by being virtuous. After all, the virtuous one lives excellently within the bounds of a particular way of understanding who she is.

The second section of this essay attends to reorientation in light of the preceding ontology. Life in Christ is a process of growth in which the Christian responds faithfully to the direction of the Spirit. This involves a cycle of steady realization of reorientation to the ways and purposes of God, a life of gratitude and obedience, and the formation of habits that increasingly incline the Christian to right thought and action. In other words, this is a life of transformation that is directed by God into the ways of God so that we may live worthily of the Lord (Col. 1:9–10). These components of reorientation, faithful response, and habit formation fill in the Christian's life of virtue in Christ.

I. Right Orientation: Simulacra vs. Participation in God's Action

The above ontology of holiness sought to situate the Christian – and thus Christian thought and action – in the order of the cosmos through participation in the triune economy. A problem of ontology will inevitably make way for a problem of orientation for a thinking and acting subject. A closer examination of what is at stake in right orientation will clarify an aspect of virtue and what distinguishes virtuous action from some form of *simulacra* of that action. Right orientation makes Christian virtue possible because it situates the Christian's action in participation with God's actions in the world whereas *simulacra* become the context for the appearance of Christian virtue since they misunderstand the priority of divine action and the Christian's life of thankful response.

Traditionally, the antonym for virtue is vice, and in the sense that vice is failure of action through love of a wrongly elevated object while virtue is right action through rightly directed love, virtue and vice are in fact opposed. For instance, gluttony would be a vice that is opposed to temperance in that the former is directed toward love of food or taste whereas temperance does not oppose food but rather views it proportionately with respect to love of God. Rebecca DeYoung astutely notes the way in which gluttony blocks a theological rendering of temperance: gluttony is "about being able to find our happiness in a pleasure we think we can provide for ourselves. Rather than accepting food as a gift from God, and looking to God to fill our spiritual hungers as well as our bodily ones, we take on God's responsibility for ourselves."[38] The temperate Christian, then, would follow Jesus in recognizing the validity and necessity of food for the body even as he prioritizes loving obedience and devotion to God and trust in him. Thus, in the wilderness Jesus displays temperance when tempted by Satan to turn stones to bread: "Man shall not live on bread alone, but on every word that comes from the mouth of God" (Matt. 4:1–4). The opposing posture to that of Jesus – vice – would be the result of disoriented love, specifically in the way of aiming at and loving proximal goods – in this case, food.[39] Few would argue that the vice in question ought to be the final good, as if the vicious person could be considered virtuous if his context were understood; it is merely adopted for the sake of or self-fulfillment of one's own pleasure. If Christian virtue is fitting participation, then vice is a rejection of participation in the ways of God in favor of the ways of self.

In another sense, though, the opposite of virtue is the appearance of virtue.[40] Augustine ascribed this version to the "pagan virtues." Since the pre-

---

[38] Rebecca Konyndyk DeYoung, *Glittering Vices: A New Look at the Seven Deadly Sins and Their Remedies* (Grand Rapids: Brazos, 2009), 156.

[39] DeYoung describes this disorientation of vice toward proximal goods in terms of "subtle and deceptive imitations of the fullness of the human good." DeYoung, *Glittering Vices*, 38. This disorientation of good through shift to a proximal good as the focal point "subverts other goods in order to achieve it (or a semblance of it). When good things are wrongly pursued, sin happens" (39).

[40] Kent Dunnington offers another potential antonym to virtue in his examination of addiction. In distinction from the vicious person who loves the proximal object of his

sent study is limited specifically to Christian virtue, the debate as to whether or not Augustine was right to dismiss the possibility of natural virtue (if he in fact did so)[41] will be left to the side. Instead, I will consider another facet of the same question: the appearance of Christian virtue, or unfitting participation. As with vice, this unfitting participation is also a case of disorientation. Unlike vice, the appearance of virtue does not direct its love toward a proximal good but rather toward a *simulacrum* of the way things are. That is, while vice is an overindulgence in what otherwise would be good, albeit proximally, the appearance of virtue has a misconception of what the good is. In this alternate universe, an ontological problem arises, for the priority of God and his action are overturned for either an anthropologically directed approach (Pelagianism) or a cooperative system (where no priority is granted to either side). Both variations make way for *simulacra* that encompass Christians into false conceptions of reality that are disoriented precisely because of their ontological inadequacies.

Twentieth century French philosopher of media Jean Baudrillard helpfully articulates the nature of *simulacra*, an understanding that will guide the project of rightly orienting theological virtue. In his seminal *Simulacra and Simulation*, Baudrillard differentiates *simulacra* from mere pretending (or, perhaps, what Herdt would call "play acting"). He contends that "pretending, or dissimulating, leaves the principle of reality intact: the difference is always clear, it is simply masked, whereas simulation threatens the difference between the 'true' and the 'false,' the 'real' and the 'imaginary.'" In medical terms, he notes that the pretender "stays in bed" but does not actually display symptoms of the alleged illness while the "simulator" does. Seemingly symptoms would demand medicine, but the gap between *simulacra* and reality render the medicine ineffective since there is no actual sickness. Even with medicine, the symptoms persist.[42] We may take this a step further and add that the *simulacrum* is the illness and, thus, needs a different prescription – one that reorients – than the symptoms suggest. The nature of the illness is abstraction from reality, such that Baudrillard may characterize *simulacra* as that which sits at the end of transition from signs that are "reflection of a profound reality" to (eventu-

---

vice, Dunnington argues that the addict resembles the incontinent moral agent in that the latter does not love the proximal object of addiction but instead is stuck in its habits. Kent Dunnington, *Addiction and Virtue: Beyond the Models of Disease and Choice* (Downers Grove, Ill.: IVP Academic, 2011), 38–41.

[41] T. H. Irwin contends that Romans 2:14–16 provides Augustine a basis from which to acknowledge a chastened sense of "pagan virtues." See T. H. Irwin, "Splendid Vices? Augustine For and Against Pagan Virtues," *Medieval Philosophy and Theology* 8 (1999): 117–19.

[42] Jean Baudrillard, *Simulacra and Simulation* (trans. Sheila Faria Glaser; Ann Arbor: University of Michigan Press, 1994), 3.

ally) signs with "no relation to any reality whatsoever." In the middle is a move of "sorcery" wherein a sign "plays at being an appearance." The final stage, *simulacra*, has not even the concern of "play"; it is its own world but with no relation to the actual. At best it is "nostalgia."[43] In terms of participation, it is not fitting because it has no bearing on the actual. On the other hand, it remains participation on account of its attempt of conformity to the simulation of reality that it is.[44] *Simulacra* is unfitting participation because in the end, it is merely participation in the world of signs sans referent.

In the setting of Christian holiness, a sort of Christian *simulacra* falls short of virtue in that it neglects the ontology of the Holy One made known in Jesus Christ. Paul identifies this semblance of virtue in Colossians just prior to his exhortation to those who have been united with Christ "to seek the things that are above" (3:1). The passage is replete with the proper ontology of Christians – who have been buried and raised with Christ (2:12–13, 20) – and markers of orientation ("if with Christ you died to the elemental spirits of the world," 2:20). In opposition to ontology and, thus, right orientation are those with false qualifications of worship and ideas about the Christian message. Indeed, the implication is that these are not nourished by Christ, the "head" (2:19), but rather flout "an appearance of wisdom" (2:23), the treasures of which Paul has already confessed rest in Christ himself (2:2–3). The participation advocated by these false practitioners is a disorienting one, distracting from the person of Jesus Christ and the gifts offered to Christians only through him.

Paul's indictment of these false teachings and accompanying practices fits the nature of *simulacra*, particularly as he designates them as "self-made religion" (2:23). Some have hypothesized that the heresies in view in Colossians were Judaistic, merging traditional Jewish thought with a sort of proto-Gnosticism.[45] This would certainly satisfy Baudrillard's claim that *simulacra* at best is "nostalgia" since the heresy in view seems to have affinity for the stipulations of the old covenant but fails to understand the nature of the old covenant in light of new identity in Christ. Yet the most prominent characteristic shared between Paul's adversary and the general appearance of Christian virtue is the failure of each to bear witness to the orthodox order of Christian action. Indeed, this significant commonality shows that the two are really of a single kind. As Stanley Hauerwas ex-

---

[43] Baudrillard, *Simularca and Simulation*, 6.

[44] A prime example of just such a "reality" for Baudrillard is Disney World, which bears resemblance to the world but has its own rules and has no self-existence. It is inherently a façade with its own parking lot. When entering Disney World, one leaves her car behind in this depository of cars and enters a world of symbols without referents.

[45] Wilson, *Colossians and Philemon*, 57–8.

plains, "Christian practice and theology are neither self-referential nor self-justifying. Christian practices and beliefs . . . must be witnesses to the God who is Father, Son, and Holy Spirit." Hauerwas continues by connecting Christian action directly to its ontology in Christ and by the Spirit: "Just as the Son witnesses to the Father so the Spirit makes us witnesses to the Son so that the world may know the Father."[46] Paul counters the appearance of virtue laid within a nostalgic simulation of reality and the Christian's place therein with a reorientation: "if with Christ you died to the elemental spirits of the world . . . [and] if then you have been raised with Christ, seek the things that are above" (Col. 2:20; 3:1). Whereas *simulacra* provides a false reality in which to participate to the end of disoriented semblances of virtue, Paul advocates a fitting participation in the ways of the triune God through recognition of union with Christ, an identity and impulse that fills out in Paul in a robustly Trinitarian understanding of union, participation, and ethics.[47] Christian virtue witnesses to the Holy One by putting on the clothes of Christ and rejects *simulacra*'s promise of new "clothing" that only leaves one exposed.[48]

If Christian virtue is about right orientation, entailed in virtue as witness is both right acting *and* right knowing since right knowing means directing one's gaze toward Christian identity (in Christ) within Christian ontology (the Triune Holy God and Creator).[49] This knowing, too, depends upon givenness, for apart from grace and due to sinfulness, humanity is stuck in a mode of "misknowledge." Oliver O'Donovan sees this mode of knowing apart from revelation and transformation in Christ as lacking in that it is "fragmentary knowledge of the way things are," a kind of knowledge with a basic level of explanatory power but ultimately lacking a "true understanding" of the way the cosmos is.[50] This sort of "misknowledge" proves

---

[46] Stanley Hauerwas, *With the Grain of the Universe: The Church's Witness and Natural Theology* (Grand Rapids: Brazos, 2001), 207.

[47] Burger captures the inseparability of Christ and Spirit in Paul's articulation of union with Christ. Burger, *Being in Christ*, 261–63.

[48] Cf. Hans Christian Andersen's "The Emperor's New Clothes," which – like the illusion of *simulacra* – were not clothes at all.

[49] In an interesting corollary, Blocher refers even to fallen humanity as witness. In contrast to Christian virtue witnessing to the Holy One, sinful humanity is "witness against himself" and thus a "caricature" of the witness that ought to characterize humanity as image bearers of God. Henri Blocher, *In the Beginning: The Opening Chapters of Genesis* (Leicester: InterVarsity Press, 1984), 94.

[50] Oliver O'Donovan, *Resurrection and Moral Order: An Outline for Evangelical Ethics* (2d ed.; Grand Rapids: Eerdmans, 1994), 89. O'Donovan's aim is to describe a gracious shift from non-Christian to Christian ways of knowing, understanding, and ethics. Since the present essay leaves that shift to the side, my use of O'Donovan is an adaptation to Christian virtue where the contrast is between those purported forms of Christian virtue already discussed and Christian virtue in Christ by the Spirit.

debilitating to Christian virtue in that it harbors the disorientation that allows *simulacra* to flourish. It is a kind of knowledge in need of continual transformation and refinement into an understanding of the cosmos as the creation of the triune God and the life of God's image bearers as life in the ways of God.

That this knowing includes understanding demonstrates a rift from the *simulacrum* of modernity (and strictly modern Christianity) and its myth of knowledge. Robert Roberts and Jay Wood helpfully clarify what *understanding* adds to typical propositional ways of rendering knowledge: while propositional knowledge is "relatively isolated" and "does not come in degrees" – meaning it is context-free and either true or false – knowledge as understanding involves "complex bodies of propositions (stories, theories, books) or things other than propositions (a drawing, a symphony), and which does come in degrees (a person can increase in his understanding of a proposition or a text or a symphony)."[51] Understanding is a "complex" of knowledge that requires right orientation, the capacity to know, a view of the way things are, and the habits of mind to seek right things in excellent ways, all of which come progressively in Christ. Right orientation is a turning to Christ and grasping him in faith. The creaturely capacity to know is a gift to rightly oriented, good creation and is in the process of renewal through resurrection with Christ. The turn to Christ is the turn to the economy of the triune God and, therein, to increasing noetic and experiential clarity in the way things are. The recasting of the habits of the mind is a work of transformation in which the Spirit progressively renews our mind in accord with the mind of Christ through life with Christ.

Becoming virtuous Christians cannot be a Spirit-led task apart from union with Christ, for it is only in Christ that believers participate in the economy of holiness. Failure to be within this ontology and subsequent orientation, as seen in Paul, is the nature of *simulacra*. That is to say that apart from Christ, creaturely understanding of holiness is lacking since the triune God draws near in Christ. Herdt's conception of virtue that culminates in union with Christ is vulnerable at precisely this point. Amid the collapse of the development of virtue into a state of being prior to union with Christ, Herdt loses Paul's reorienting appeal for virtue predicated upon death and resurrection with Christ. Indeed, one is left precisely with the *simulacrum* Paul identifies as due to autonomy from Christ. Further, apart from following Paul's reorientation of Christian virtue, we lose the posture of Christian virtue.

---

[51] Robert C. Roberts and W. Jay Wood, *Intellectual Virtues: An Essay in Regulative Epistemology* (New York: Oxford University Press, 2010), 43.

II. Gratitude and Faithful Obedience

The orientation of Christian virtue necessarily makes way for participation in the economy of virtue. While the nature of Christian virtue includes understanding God's ways and fittingly participating with God's actions in the world, it begins with fitting response of gratitude to God, which in turn makes way for faithful obedience. Virtue is recognition of dependence upon the giver of life. Just as the created state of humanity was and properly is one of life in dependence upon God,[52] the Christian life – as redeemed and reconciled life before the Creator – finds the source of its actions in the person of Jesus Christ, the revelation of the triune God. Calvin perceptively understood both sides of this, the creaturely and the redemptive. Concerning human being as image bearing, Calvin writes that Scripture's testimony of the bestowal of *imago dei* upon people indicates "that man was blessed, not because of his own good actions, but by participation in God."[53] Later in the *Institutes*, he will speak similarly of the Christian, this time in relation specifically to Christ: "We ought not to separate Christ from ourselves or ourselves from him. Rather we ought to hold fast bravely with both hands to that fellowship by which he has bound himself to us. So the apostle teaches us: 'Now your body is dead because of sin; but the Spirit of Christ which dwells in you is life because of righteousness' [Rom. 8:10p.]."[54] The Christian life is a turning to the revealed Holy One to whom the Christian is united just as the rightly oriented life of the human creature in general is a turning to the Holy One who created. Apart from this recognition and turning, Christian virtue remains untenable.

The realization and recognition of dependence upon the Holy One in Christ necessarily requires gratitude, for the subjective aspect of dependence is a function of thankfulness. Any attempt to turn to the Lord without it is, in fact, not turning at all but rather a state of hostility or resentment. Conversely, true gratitude releases claim to self-sufficiency and asks of God the wisdom and strength to live in the ways given in Christ. John Ow-

---

[52] Blocher argues that this is contained in the fact of bearing the image of God: "An image *is only an image*. . . . Mankind's being an image stresses the radical nature of his dependence." *In the Beginning*, 82; in an equally elegant and more ontological fashion, Webster describes humanity in creation properly "from, for, and with God": "Humanity is *from* God, in that to be created is to be absolutely derivative, brought into being by an action which precedes the creature unconditionally. . . . Having this nature, humankind also has an end, and so is *for* God, existing in a distinctive teleology, ordered toward relation to God. And so humankind is also *with* God, that is, created for participation in the history of covenantal fellowship between God and his creatures." John Webster, "The Human Person," in *The Cambridge Companion to Postmodern Theology* (ed. Kevin J. Vanhoozer; New York: Cambridge University Press, 2003), 224–25.

[53] Calvin, *Institutes*, II.ii.1.

[54] Calvin, *Institutes*, III.ii.24.

en calls this subjective response to union with Christ a step of communion with Christ by the Spirit. Kelly Kapic explains Owen's understanding of the relation of subjective communion to objective union by noting that in the former Christians "*respond* to God's loving embrace. While union with Christ is something that does not ebb and flow, one's experience of communion with Christ can fluctuate."[55] When the response is one of gratitude, the second step of communion follows: faithfulness. Gratitude makes way for faithfulness because the response of gratitude itself is a response of faith, cleaving to God. This is possible only through the purely gracious call of the Father and union of the Christian to Christ by the Spirit, an objective bringing of the Christian into fellowship with the Holy Trinity. Subsequent faithfulness becomes the form of fitting participation because it is life in the economy of virtue, a participatory cycle of returning to the Lord with gratitude and further empowerment to live in faithful obedience to the ways of God.[56]

Just as virtue is recognition of dependence upon God, it is also an act of trust in the ways of God. In a sense faithful obedience itself is a response of gratitude, since it turns to God in Christ as the source of life in order to live wisely and faithfully in the tasks the Lord sets before us. Faith permeates the process as the occasion of fitting participation, the subjective instrument of union with Christ, the turn of gratitude to Christ in communion, and the act of joyful obedience that lives in the ways of the Holy God. Virtue is the development and solidification of Christian character amid this orientation, response of gratitude, and faithful obedience. Virtuous character becomes visible through the progressive transformation of the intellect (ways of thinking) and acts (morality) of faithful Christians.

III. Habits of Excellence

As the final piece of the puzzle of Christian virtue, the notion of habit describes maturity in the transformation of a fallen person into redeemed Christian living in the resurrection of Christ. The cycle of communion in which the Christian continually returns to Christ as the fount of life helps orient Christians rightly so that they may live faithfully. Persistent repetition of this cycle is only possible in the power of the Spirit, who has joined us to Christ, enables us to turn to him with gratitude, and directs us in joy-

---

[55] Kelly M. Kapic, "Introduction: Worshiping the Triune God: The Shape of John Owen's Trinitarian Spirituality," in *Communion with the Triune God*, by John Owen (ed. Kelly M. Kapic and Justin Taylor; Wheaton: Crossway, 2007), 21.

[56] Indeed, David Wells identifies virtue as that which lives in the space between obedience to the law of God and the freedom of a life with abundant possibilities. See David Wells, *Losing Our Virtue: Why the Church Must Recover Its Moral Vision* (Grand Rapids: Eerdmans, 1998), 63.

ful and faithful obedience. Through the combination of right orientation and faithful acting, the Spirit begins to form holy habits in Christians whereby they become inclined toward looking to Christ for strength and wisdom. These holy habits are the essence of Christian virtue.[57] Indeed, by developing holy habits in Christians, the Holy Spirit unpacks Christ's own virtues in those united to Christ, making Christians increasingly more like Christ.

All things being equal, habits provide humanity the opportunity to live abundantly. They are a "useful, precious 'mechanism' of creation."[58] The most obvious examples of their utility are the habits of skill: musicians who spend years perfecting their craft are able to perform complicated pieces without agonizing over the basic movements of their hands or feet; professional athletes unrelentingly practice their moves so that during game time they worry less about their mechanics and more about recognizing the schemes of the opposing team. The formation of habits helps them act fluidly in a variety of environments by allowing them to concentrate on the particulars of a situation. As Dunnington rightly notes, to maintain mental concentration on the mechanics of action for a long period time is quite simply "exhausting."[59] This is especially evident in the early stages of learning a craft. The basketball player learning the correct form of a jump shot expends much energy training his arms and legs to move in concert and in the most useful manner. It is only after he becomes comfortable with the basic movements of a jump shot that he can spend hours in the gym just shooting, honing and perfecting his skill. Similarly, the young piano player expends much energy identifying the correct key that corresponds with the sheet music; initially, this proves too draining and time consuming to endure a full pass through an intermediate song. Eventually, though, she begins to master the keystrokes and is then able to concentrate on increasingly complicated scores. In each of these cases, as habit develops and becomes perfected through persistent practice, the beauty of a complex task begins to emerge, even as the athlete and musician make their tasks look easy.

Some describe habits as those actions that have become "second nature." There is truth in this: the beauty of habits as a "mechanism of creation" is that attentive repetition makes the given actions easier, even nearly

---

[57] Aquinas, *ST*, 1–2ae.55.1.

[58] Henri Blocher, "Agnus Victor: The Atonement as Victory and Vicarious Punishment," in *What Does It Mean to Be Saved? Broadening Evangelical Horizons of Salvation* (ed. John. G. Stackhouse Jr.; Grand Rapids: Baker Academic, 2002), 80.

[59] Dunnington writes, "Deliberative action is inherently fragile and unstable because it requires an agent with finite powers to engage in an activity that tends to deplete those powers." Dunnington, *Addiction and Virtue*, 58.

to the point of being automatic. Yet there is a distinction between habits and nature, such that "second nature" can only approximate what is meant when referring to those habits that belong to virtue. Dunnington explains the roles of imagination and desire in the formation of habits. Whereas nature is basic to one's experience on account of one's ontological identity, imagination is shaped by orientation. Thus Dunnington may say, "Because a person comes to 'see' his or her world a certain way, his or her memory records the world a certain way and represents it to the agent as informed by the agent's habituated imagination."[60] The way in which one perceives the world shapes the possibilities for being in the world. Perception itself becomes habitual so that those trained by the Word and body of Christ and the Spirit of Christ are directed to understand their identity in Christ and see the world as the place where the church lives in faithful obedience to the gospel of Jesus Christ. As the Spirit perfects the habits of perception, the Christian imagination takes shape, presenting possibilities for living in the world that are fitting for participation in Christ. The similarities with the professional musician and athlete are significant, for when perception or skill is perfected through right habit, creativity in the field of action abounds.[61] In the case of the virtuous Christian, this creativity takes the form of wisdom (Col. 1:9) – the wisdom of Christ (Col. 2:2–3) – to live in the resurrection of Christ and to discern right action amid the variety of sometimes unpredictable circumstances.

Whereas habit conditions the possibilities of imagination, desire shapes habit. Amid the reality of sin, habits tend toward disorientation because of the prior disorientation of desire. Vice and *simulacra* thrive on the disorientation of the desire, directing it toward proximal goods or the appearance of good, respectively. Habits develop accordingly, inclining perception and action toward these partial or illusory ends; these disoriented habits give "sinful behavior a contagious power."[62] However, in union with Christ, the Spirit begins sanctifying the totality of the Christian, including the desire. The Spirit unpacks Christ's own life – including desires – in the life of the Christian, enabling the possibility of progressively renewed desire for Christ, expressed through gratitude and faithful obedience. The continual return to Christ through the direction of the Spirit and faithful response by the power of the Spirit who renews desire makes way for the development

---

[60] Dunnington, *Addiction and Virtue*, 76.

[61] Samuel Wells distinguishes between "creative" and "ordinary" imagination. The former pertains to the improvisational way in which we interact with ever new scenarios. The latter refers to the formation of habit in "ordinary" (i.e., non-crisis) moments. The language of "ordinary" versus "creative" imagination emphasizes that habits are formed on the practice field, that is, the "ordinary." Samuel Wells, *Improvisation: The Drama of Christian Ethics* (Grand Rapids: Brazos, 2004), 74–76.

[62] Blocher, "Agnus Victor," 80.

of faithful habits. Apart from union with Christ, fitting habits – the essence of Christian virtue – are impossible because of the absence of regenerated desires.

What, then, does this mean for Herdt's critique of Christian virtue that begins with (rather than culminates in) union with Christ? Her concern is that this would eliminate an Erasmian understanding of play acting that includes the formation of Christian habits before explicit faith and apart from an initially passive posture to the grace of God through union with Christ. If we are to follow Paul in Colossians, it would seem that Herdt's critique is unfounded since Paul himself begins with the work of God through union with Christ. This does not preclude the Lord providentially preparing people through various life circumstances – even play acting – to bring them to the place of his decisive grace. Indeed, the sort of non-combative approach to divine and human action that Herdt rightly espouses demands a rich understanding of God's providential ways. Nevertheless, the decisive grace of union with Christ is unilaterally God's own work, and it is in the setting of this union that the habits of Christian virtue develop since they are ultimately the desires and habits of Jesus himself that the Spirit unpacks.

Vanhoozer recognizes a biblical example of what could be called the pre-Christian habits of play acting in his recounting of Peter chopping off the ear of the guard in Gethsemane. This provides helpful contrast to the model sketched here, showing the weakness of Herdt's version of the formation of true virtue through play acting apart from union with Christ. Vanhoozer is particularly interested in demonstrating the "fittingness" of action to the "[p]atterns of speech, thought, and action" in the "Christ-drama." Peter's failure to act fittingly "displayed his misunderstanding of the true nature of Christ's kingdom," something Vanhoozer expounds from the four parallel accounts of the event in each of the canonical gospels. Or, stated in terms of Peter's own moment of action instead of our present post-canon situation, "he could not follow what was happening [in the garden]."[63] Extended to a discussion of habits, Peter's failed recognition of fittingness may be seen as a cumulative failure to see rightly the historical unfolding of significant Christological events – for which he not only had front row seats but of which he was also an active participant (e.g., Matt. 17:1–13; Mk. 6:30–44; Lk. 9:1–6 and the respective parallels). He was certainly close, as in his declaration of Jesus as the Christ (Matt. 16:13–17), yet he was in just enough ignorance so as to miss "what was happening," as is evidenced in Jesus' rebuke of Peter's well-intentioned misunderstanding in the next passage: "get behind me, Satan!" (Matt. 16:21–23; interest-

---

[63] Kevin J. Vanhoozer, *The Drama of Doctrine: A Canonical-Linguistic Approach to Christian Theology* (Louisville: Westminster John Knox, 2005), 263.

ingly enough, most of these biblical events to which Peter is privy but ultimately ignorant occur in succession in Lk. 9).

Peter's failure of understanding, even of Jesus' words, resulted in the formation of the wrong kind of habits, for evidently, he placed the ministry of Jesus Christ within a different sort of "Christ-drama," one that did not follow the actual one. The wrong kinds of habits culminate, then, not only in Peter's wrong (though pious) act of taking a sword to the guard's ear but also of denying Jesus after the arrest. Peter's habits were apparently the result of his embodying *a* Christ-drama but not *the* Christ-drama, a problem that ultimately could not be overcome until Jesus ascended and sent his Spirit, through whom Peter was united to Christ. It is worth noting that Peter's proximity to and hearing from Jesus was discontinuous from his being joined to Christ, at least in the significant way of forming right habits. As with Peter, not even piety can overcome the wrong habits that result from disorientation, much less play acting. The Christian habits that characterize Christian virtue come only through union with Christ.

C. Conclusion

Paul's epistle to the Colossians directly calls for virtue subsequent to and based upon union with Christ. Indeed, the first half of the letter is saturated with references of the importance of union for Christian holiness. This claim itself already casts doubt over Herdt's suspicion of traditional Protestant soteriologies that prioritize union with Christ. For Herdt, such theologies undermine claims to virtue since they posit passiveness of Christians, at least initially. While a broadly Reformed doctrine of union with Christ does, in fact, confess an initial passiveness, the Christian life is thoroughly active in participation with Christ by the Spirit. Despite the concerns of Herdt, the initial passivity does not necessarily create a problem for soteriologies that begin with union. On the contrary, the nature of the ontology inferred by Paul calls for a vision of virtue that begins not only with divine, gracious impetus but also transformation of the fallen, disoriented sinner. This vision attends to the ontology of the person as created for fellowship and dependence upon the Holy Trinity. The holiness of God is the only basis for creaturely holiness – the state of Christian virtue. The holiness of God is manifest in Jesus Christ, and it is through union with Christ that the Christian has access to true virtue, a holiness unpacked in the life of the Christian by the Spirit.

Christian virtue is ultimately fitting participation in the economy of holiness through Jesus Christ. The Trinitarian character of virtue is evident in the persistent direction of the Spirit and is realized in the Christian through reorientation into true understanding of the world as the place of the ways of God, the Christian's response of gratitude and subsequent faithful obedience, and the development of holy habits. Fitting participation involves habits that incline believers to think and act virtuously, something that only occurs as the Spirit transforms us by unpacking the life of Christ in the Christian. Fitting participation – Christian virtue – truly is, then, "Christ in you, the hope of glory" (Col. 1:27).

Bibliography

Achtemeier, Mark "The Union with Christ Doctrine in Renewal: Movements of the Presbyterian Church (USA)." Pages 336–50 in *Reformed Theology: Identity and Ecumenicity*. Edited by Wallace M. Alston Jr. and Michael Welker. Grand Rapids: Eerdmans, 2003.

Allen, Michael. *The Christ's Faith: A Dogmatic Account*. New York: T&T Clark, 2009.

Althaus, Paul. *The Theology of Martin Luther*. Translated by Robert C. Schultz. Philadelphia: Fortress, 1966.

Aquinas, Thomas. *Summa theologica*. Translated by the Fathers of the English Dominican Province. New York: Ave Maria, 1948.

Augustine. *On the Morals of the Catholic Church*. In vol. 4 of *The Nicene and Post-Nicene Fathers*, Series 1. Edited by Philip Schaff. 1886–1889. 14 vols. Repr: Peabody, Mass. Hendrickson, 1994

Baudrillard, Jean. *Simulacra and Simulation*. Translated by Sheila Faria Glaser. Ann Arbor: University of Michigan Press, 1994.

Bavinck, Herman. *Reformed Dogmatics, Volume 3: Sin and Salvation in Christ*. Translated by John Vriend. Grand Rapids: Baker Academic, 2006.

Berthoud, Pierre. "The Compassion of God: Exodus 34:5–9 in the Light of Exodus 32–34." Pages 142–67 in *Engaging the Doctrine of God: Contemporary Protestant Perspectives*. Edited by Bruce L. McCormack. Grand Rapids: Baker Academic, 2008.

Billings, J. Todd. *Calvin, Participation, and the Gift: The Activity of Believers in Union with Christ*. Oxford: Oxford University Press, 2007.

Blocher, Henri. "Agnus Victor: The Atonement as Victory and Vicarious Punishment." Pages 67–91 in *What Does It Mean to Be Saved? Broadening Evangelical Horizons of Salvation*. Edited by John. G. Stackhouse Jr. Grand Rapids: Baker Academic, 2002.

———. *In the Beginning: The Opening Chapters of Genesis*. Leicester: InterVarsity Press, 1984.

———. *La Doctrine Du Péché et de La Rédemption*. 3d ed. Vaux-sur-Seine, France: Edifac, 2000.

Burger, Hans. *Being in Christ: A Biblical and Systematic Investigation in a Reformed Perspective*. Eugene, Ore.: Wipf & Stock, 2009.

Calvin, John. *Institutes of the Christian Religion*. Library of Christian Classics 20–21. Edited by John T. McNeill. Translated by Ford Lewis Battles. Louisville: Westminster John Knox, 1960.

Campbell, Constantine R. *Paul and Union with Christ: An Exegetical and Theological Study*. Grand Rapids: Zondervan, 2012.

Charry, Ellen. *By the Renewing of Your Minds: The Pastoral Function of Christian Doctrine*. New York: Oxford University Press, 1997.

DeVries, Dawn. "Calvin's Preaching." Pages 106–24 in *The Cambridge Companion to John Calvin*. Edited by Donald K. McKim. Cambridge: Cambridge University Press, 2004.

DeYoung, Rebecca Konyndyk. *Glittering Vices: A New Look at the Seven Deadly Sins and Their Remedies*. Grand Rapids: Brazos, 2009.

Dunnington, Kent. *Addiction and Virtue: Beyond the Models of Disease and Choice*. Downers Grove, Ill.: IVP Academic, 2011.

Edwards, James R. *Romans*. New International Biblical Commentary on the New Testament 6. Peabody, Mass.: Hendrickson, 1992.

Gaffin, Richard B., Jr. *Resurrection and Redemption: A Study in Paul's Soteriology*. Second edition. Phillipsburg, N.J.: Presbyterian & Reformed, 1987.

Harrington, J.Daniel, S.J., and James Keenan. *Paul and Virtue Ethics: Building Bridges Between New Testament Studies and Moral Theology*. Lanham, Md.: Rowman & Littlefield, 2010.

Hauerwas, Stanley. *With the Grain of the Universe: The Church's Witness and Natural Theology*. Grand Rapids: Brazos, 2001.

Hays, Richard B. *The Moral Vision of the New Testament: Community, Cross, New Creation: A Contemporary Introduction to New Testament Ethics*. San Francisco: HarperCollins, 1996.

Herdt, Jennifer A. *Putting on Virtue: The Legacy of the Splendid Vices*. Chicago: University Of Chicago Press, 2008.

Horton, Michael Scott. *Christian Faith: A Systematic Theology for Pilgrims on the Way*. Grand Rapids: Zondervan, 2011.

Irwin, T. H. "Splendid Vices? Augustine For and Against Pagan Virtues." *Medieval Philosophy and Theology* 8 (1999): 105–27.

Kapic, Kelly M. "Introduction: Worshiping the Truine God: The Shape of John Owen's Trinitarian Spirituality." Pages 17–46 in *Communion with the Triune God*, by John Owen. Edited by Kelly M. Kapic and Justin Taylor. Wheaton: Crossway, 2007.

Long, D. Stephen. "Moral Theology." Pages 456–75 in *The Oxford Handbook of Systematic Theology*. Edited by XXX. New York: Oxford University Press, 2007.

Macaskill, Grant. *Union with Christ in the New Testament*. Oxford: Oxford University Press, 2013.

O'Donovan, Oliver. *Resurrection and Moral Order: An Outline for Evangelical Ethics*. 2d ed. Grand Rapids: Eerdmans, 1994.

Roberts, Robert C., and W. Jay Wood. *Intellectual Virtues: An Essay in Regulative Epistemology*. New York: Oxford University Press, 2010.

Thompson, Marianne Meye. *Colossians and Philemon*. Grand Rapids: Eerdmans, 2005.

Tipton, Lane G. "Union with Christ and Justification." Pages 23–49 in *Justified in Christ: God's Plan for Us in Justification*. Edited by K. Scott Oliphint. Fearn, Scotland: Mentor, 2007.

Torrance, T. F. "Justification: Its Radical Nature and Place in Reformed Doctrine and Life." Pages 150–68 in *Theology in Reconstruction*. London: SCM, 1965.

Vanhoozer, Kevin J. *The Drama of Doctrine: A Canonical-Linguistic Approach to Christian Theology*. Louisville: Westminster John Knox, 2005.

———. "Triune Discourse: Theological Reflections on the Claim That God Speaks (Part 2)." Pages 50–78 in *Trinitarian Theology for the Church: Scripture, Community, Worship*. Edited by Daniel J. Treier and David Lauber. Downers Grove: IVP Academic, 2009.

Webster, John B. *Holiness*. Grand Rapids: Eerdmans, 2003.

———. "The Human Person." Pages 219–34 in *The Cambridge Companion to Postmodern Theology*. Cambridge Companions to Religion. Edited by Kevin J. Vanhoozer. New York: Cambridge University Press, 2003.

Wells, David. *Losing Our Virtue: Why the Church Must Recover Its Moral Vision*. Grand Rapids: Eerdmans, 1998.

Wells, Samuel. *Improvisation: The Drama of Christian Ethics*. Grand Rapids: Brazos, 2004.

Wilson, R. McL. *A Critical and Exegetical Commentary on Colossians and Philemon*. London: T&T Clark, 2005.

Participating in the Body and Blood of Christ

Christian Κοινωνία and the Lord's Supper

MARY PATTON BAKER

In the middle of his discourse concerning Christians eating meat sacrificed to idols, the Apostle Paul interjects a striking statement about the food that is eaten in the Lord's Supper: "Is not the cup of thanksgiving for which we give thanks a participation (κοινωνία) in the blood of Christ? And is not the bread that we break a participation in the body of Christ?" (1 Cor 10:16).[1] On the one hand this appears to be a straight forward statement, consistent with Paul's soteriology: the shedding of Christ's blood and the offering of his body secured an eternal union with Christ for those who believe in his name. Thus, in the Lord's Supper we enjoy the fellowship made possible by Christ's eternal sacrifice. But, upon closer examination, we might ask what kind of fellowship or participation in Christ does Paul have in mind? What are the sacrificial connotations of sharing in the body and blood of Jesus? Is this fellowship with God or among worshippers, or both?

Paul's statement provides an important implication for eucharistic theology: that is, Paul's attention is not focused on what happens to the physical elements of the communion celebration, but rather on what happens when believers share in the Lord's Supper. Traditionally, eucharistic theology has focused on how the wine and bread become the body and blood of Christ. However, neither here in 1 Cor 10:14–22 nor later in 1 Cor 11:17–31 does Paul appear to be preoccupied by such a question. Rather, he focuses on the nature and quality of Christian κοινωνία that is experienced in eucharistic celebration while contrasting it with being participants (κοινωνός) with demons in a pagan sacrifice (1 Cor: 10:20).

In this essay I will examine Paul's statement in 1 Cor 10:16 in light of Paul's overall conception of Christian κοινωνία found in the Pauline corpus, as well as his teachings on participating in pagan meals (1 Cor 8 and 10) and the proper celebration of the Lord's Supper expressed in 1 Cor

---

[1] All English scripture quotations are from the New International Version (Grand Rapids: Zondervan, 2011), unless noted otherwise.

11:17–34. I will also provide a canonical analysis of what participation in a sacrificial meal entails. I will conclude by exploring the implications of this study for understanding Paul's theology of participation in general and eucharistic theology in particular, namely what happens in the celebration of the Lord's Supper.

It is Paul who primarily uses the word κοινωνία in the New Testament to describe participation or fellowship in Christ.[2] My first task in this essay is to examine the various contexts in which Paul employs κοινωνία, as well as other cognates from the κοινων- group. I do not presume that Paul only uses this one word to communicate his conceptions of sharing in the life of the triune God, a sharing of the benefits of being found in Christ, or the fellowship of the church. However, I do believe there is theological and exegetical value in paying attention to the ways in which Paul specifically employs κοινωνία as a way into beginning to understand his broader conceptual understanding of κοινωνία.[3]

Paul's use of κοινωνία in the texts I examined indicates the idea of sharing: a sharing of something with someone in something.[4] Accordingly, the operative questions in my study were: who is doing the sharing, what is being shared, and how is it being shared? A particular pattern of usage did

---

[2] Κοινωνία occurs nineteen times in the New Testament, and thirteen of those occurrences are in the Pauline corpus. Additionally, it occurs once in Acts and Hebrews, and four times in 1 John. Paul uses the verb κοινωνέω in seven out of the nine New Testament occurrences, and the noun κοινωνός seven out of the ten New Testament occurrences.

[3] My methodology follows closely that of Constantine R. Campbell, *Paul and Union with Christ: An Exegetical and Theological Study* (Grand Rapids: Zondervan, 2012), wherein he surveys the various idioms used to express union with Christ in Paul, such as ἐν Χριστῷ and εἰς Χριστὸν. Campbell describes his method as first "to observe all the uses of [a] phrase," to discover "the unifying features of the usage," and then secondly to "move out beyond this phrase to detect other phrases or indicators of the theme..." (25) Unfortunately, the word limit of this essay prevents me from moving into the second step he describes. Additionally, I would describe my reading of these texts as theological, in that I bring a passage's literary, historical, and grammatical contexts into canonical focus. Biblical reasoning is viewed through the larger dogmatic concerns of a theologian. Further, a theological reading addresses the Biblical readership of the church, and the demands of Christian discipleship.

[4] Both the TDNT and BDAG must be used cautiously. Nevertheless, the lexical data gleaned from both is helpful here. The lexical definition for the κοινων- word group given by in TDNT is "to share with someone in something." Friedrich Hauck, "κοινων-," *TDNT* 3:804. The BDAG entry for κοινωνία indicates four categories of the range of meaning in the New Testament: 1) "close association involving mutual interests and sharing, association, communion fellowship" 2) "an attitude of good will that manifests an interest in a close relationship," i.e. generosity, altruism 3) "a sign of fellowship," usually a gift or contribution 4) "participation, sharing in something." Bauer, "κοινωνία," *BDAG*, 552–53. My study bore out this semantic range of meaning in the Pauline corpus.

emerge. Paul primarily uses κοινωνία to portray three types of sharing: (1) a sharing "in the Spirit," constituted primarily as communion with the triune God, and a sharing of the Spirit among those who are found in Christ; (2) a sharing in the personal history of Jesus Christ through self-denial and identification with the sufferings of other Christians; and, (3) this self-denial and identification is demonstrated when Christians share their material goods with those in need. Moreover, throughout these passages, Paul concerns himself with the quality of the Corinthians' κοινωνία: it must reflect the love of Christ. These Pauline themes require teasing out to help us better understand the full context of his description of the Lord's Supper as κοινωνία. I will examine each theme within the context of the Corinthian correspondence as well as other Pauline letters.

The social context of Paul's letter to the Corinthians frames Paul's teaching about κοινωνία, and also must be taken into consideration in our reading of the Corinthian texts.[5] The primary motivation for Paul writing to the Corinthians grew out of his concern over the quality and type of κοινωνία the Corinthians were experiencing in their entire life together in Corinth, including the quality of κοινωνία in their Lord's Suppers. Paul definitely had a church discipline problem in Corinth. Various factions were following different leaders who boasted of their own personal power, position, and gifting, rather than the power of the Gospel, and the results were devastating. Instances of gross sinful behavior were occurring in the community. In his Corinthian correspondence Paul addresses divisions over leadership, worship, and social class, and disagreements over what was appropriate behavior for Christians. He challenges the Corinthians to reform their behavior by valuing unity in holiness as the highest priority in their life together. Throughout the Corinthian epistles and even in the opening address of 1 Cor, Paul reminds the Corinthians the source of this unity can only be found in the sharing of Christ.

---

[5] The socio-economic situation in Corinth and its effect on the Christian community has been the subject of numerous monographs over the past several decades. The interdisciplinary collection of essays found in Daniel N. Schowalter and Steven J. Friesen, eds., *Urban Religion in Roman Corinth: Interdisciplinary Approaches* (HTS 53; Cambridge, Mass.: Harvard University Press, 2005) provides an overview of the state of scholarship in the fields of New Testament scholarship, archeology, and social sciences. Four other noted monographs in this area are: Wayne A. Meeks, *The First Urban Christians: The Social World of the Apostle Paul* (New Haven, Conn.: Yale University Press, 1983); Ben Witherington, *Conflict and Community in Corinth: A Socio-Rhetorical Commentary on 1 and 2 Corinthians* (Grand Rapids: Eerdmans, 1995); Bruce W. Winter, *After Paul Left Corinth: The Influence of Secular Ethics and Social Change* (Grand Rapids: Eerdmans, 2001) and Dale B. Martin, *The Corinthian Body* (New Haven, Conn.: Yale University Press, 1995).

A. A Mutual Communion with the Triune God through the Holy Spirit

Paul's opening greeting hints at what is to come later, by first reminding the church at Corinth that they are called to be God's holy people:

Paul, called to be an apostle of Christ Jesus by the will of God [. . .] to the church of God that is in Corinth, to those sanctified in Christ Jesus, and called to be his holy people, together with all those everywhere who call on the name of our Lord Jesus Christ–their Lord and ours: Grace and peace to you from God our Father and the Lord Jesus Christ. (1 Cor 1:1–3)

In this opening greeting, Paul provides parameters for thinking about the church and his own apostolic authority. The church is composed of those who are called out by God to be set apart as a holy people through sanctification in Christ Jesus.[6] But he also reminds the Corinthians that the church encompasses a community that is larger than their own: it is all those everywhere who reciprocate God's call by calling upon his name.

Paul first describes the church according to its juridical existence: it is composed of the elect who are made holy in Christ Jesus, and their holiness is attained in their union with Christ through justification and sanctification. God also brings each of these called-out ones into community: by virtue of their shared sanctification in Christ, believers are brought into a holy community with others who also share this new existence in the Spirit. "When accepted, the saving call of God brings the believer into a new mode of existence whose dominant characteristic is the sharing of a common life in an organic unity."[7] Accordingly, Paul extends to them the grace and peace which flows from God the Father and from the Lord Jesus Christ. These gifts are not separate gifts, one from God and one from Jesus Christ but should be viewed as one "gift which is inseparable from the self-giving of God's own presence and God's own self in and through Christ."[8]

---

[6] Theiselton notes that ἐν could be translated as "in" or "by," and reviews the grammatical grounds for either translation in Anthony C. Thiselton, *The First Epistle to the Corinthians* (NIGTC; Grand Rapids: Eerdmans, 2000), 76. Conzelmann states that ἐν "can merge into the instrumental sense (διά)" because in these two senses the "expression refers to the objective work of salvation which God accomplishes in Christ" but also merges into the "converse statement that Christ is in us." Hans Conzelmann, *First Corinthians: A Commentary on the First Epistle to the Corinthians* (Hermeneia; Philadelphia: Fortress, 1988), 21.

[7] Jerome Murphy-O'Connor, "Eucharist and Community in First Corinthians," in *Living Bread, Saving Cup: Readings on the Eucharist* (ed. R. Kevin Seasoltz; Collegeville, Minn.: Liturgical Press, 1982), 19.

[8] Thiselton, *Corinthians*, 56.

In concluding his greeting, Paul declares that those who have been called are in κοινωνία: "God is faithful, who has called you into fellowship (κοινωνία) with his Son, Jesus Christ our Lord (1 Cor 1: 9)." Thiselton observes that "it is not simply or primarily the experience of being together as Christians which is shared, but the status of being-in-Christ and of being shareholders in a sonship derived from the sonship of Christ."[9] The Corinthians have not created their κοινωνία with God or each other; it has been accomplished for them by being found in Christ.

A correlative verse to this opening greeting is found in Paul's closing benediction in 2 Cor 13:13: "May the grace of the Lord Jesus Christ, and the love of God, and the communion [κοινωνία] of the Holy Spirit be with you all." In the Trinitarian shape of this benediction Paul supremely expresses his belief that God's love for his people, demonstrated in the redemptive work of Christ, is imparted to believers through the Spirit. Fee summarizes Paul's words: "God has now arrived in the new creation as an abiding, empowering presence – so that what most characterizes the Holy Spirit is κοινωνία..."[10] The Holy Spirit, conjoined to God the Father and God the Son, is the source of sharing in Christ. By delineating the Trinitarian gifting as the "grace of the Lord Jesus Christ," the "love of God [the Father]," and the κοινωνία of the Holy Spirit, Paul is emphasizing that sharing in the Spirit flows out of the *intra* and *ad extra* Trinitarian life of God. As Thornton observes, "fellowship in the Spirit involves a reciprocal relationship of mutual interchanges."[11] Our relationship to the Spirit flows from Christ's union with the Father and the Father and the Son's union with the Holy Spirit. Being found in union with Christ means that we share *with Christ* a mutual indwelling of the Spirit. Kevin Vanhoozer describes this as being placed into the "thick of the Trinitarian action," or to be inserted into "what the Father is doing in Christ through the Spirit."[12] Further, this κοινωνία of the Holy Spirit is what constitutes the distinctive character of the Christian community; no other community is comprised of triune sharing with humanity.

It is important to understand this fellowship with the Spirit is a fellowship with the third person of the Trinity. The Spirit is not an aid or instrument. Nor is the Spirit some sort of commodity, but a person. Again, in

---

[9] Thiselton, *Corinthians*, 104.

[10] Gordon D. Fee, *God's Empowering Presence: The Holy Spirit in the Letters of Paul*, (Peabody, Mass.: Hendrickson, 1994; repr., Grand Rapids: Baker Academic, 2009), 363.

[11] Lionel Spencer Thornton, *The Common Life in the Body of Chirst* (4th ed.; London: Dacre, 1963), 71.

[12] Kevin J. Vanhoozer, *Remythologizing Theology: Divine Action, Passion, and Authorship* (Cambridge Studies in Christian Doctrine; Cambridge: Cambridge University Press, 2010), 293.

this benediction Paul makes profoundly Trinitarian statement. Fee argues, "that Paul would include the Holy Spirit as an equal member of this triadic formula, and that he would pray to the Spirit in their behalf, says as much about his understating of the Spirit both as person and as deity as any direction statement of this kind ever could." [13] In simpler terms, sharing the fellowship of the Spirit means that believers are not sharing in *some thing*, but with a divine *someone*. The person of the Spirit binds us to Christ in a divine-human relationship, in a κοινωνία relationship that grows out of the κοινωνία relationship shared in the Godhead.[14]

In Eph 2:18 Paul states that it is through the Son that all believers, Jewish and Gentile, "have access to the Father by one Spirit." Paul later tells the Romans: "some of the branches have been broken off, and you, though a wild olive shoot, have been grafted in among the others and now share [συγκοινωνὸς . . . ἐγένου; lit., "have become co-sharers"] in the nourishing sap from the olive root" (Rom 11:17).[15] Access to the Father by one Spirit is then "co-experienced" with others. Our new legal identity as adopted children, which is granted through our union with Christ, leads to a new life of sharing together the one Spirit.

B. The Quality of Κοινωνία

Paul's repeated exhortations to "walk in the Spirit," indicates that active sharing in the Spirit is not forced upon the believer, but is a choice. For the power of Christ to be active in our lives, we must choose to embrace the fellowship extended to us by the Spirit for our mutual growth and find ways to make that fellowship a concrete reality.[16] In other words, the quality of the shared κοινωνία is affected by the choices each member of the family of God makes.

Paul states at the close of 1 Cor 1, that God, in Christ Jesus, is to be the very source of the Corinthians' life (1 Cor 1:30). To commune properly with each other they need to be communing with God. This can be the only

---

[13] Fee, *God's Empowering Presence*, 364–65.

[14] However, it must be understood that there is an asymmetry inherent in any comparison of relations between the persons of the Godhead and the relations between God and his children.

[15] When σύν, a preposition that denotes union (with, beside) is joined to cognates from the κοινων- group, it "indicates participation with Christ and has clear implications for Christian living." Campbell, *Union with Christ*, 372.

[16] Also 1 Cor 3:7. Also Paul adds this admonition in Phil 2:12–13: "continue to work out your salvation with fear and trembling, for it is God who works in you to will and to act in order to fulfill his good purpose." In Rom 12:11 Paul exhorts his listeners to be "fervent in the Spirit." (NRSV)

basis for their sharing together: their κοινωνία is not constituted by a shared social status. The breaking down of social barriers was just as radical in the first century as the breaking down of the barriers between Jew and Gentile.[17] The society Paul envisioned in his Corinthian correspondence was a different vision of society than the one dominant in the Greco-Roman world and represented a clear alternative to the imperial order and culture.[18]

Thus Paul's arguments fly in the face of the cultural status quo. The people of God are to live in a community wherein social boundaries have been broken down. He declares that the basis for Christian fellowship is the mutual identity found in Christ and the active sharing in Christ by his Spirit. The Spirit of Christ will enable the Corinthians to share in this new way: through sharing love. Paul writes in his letter to the Philippians: "Therefore if you have any encouragement from being united with Christ, if any comfort from his love, if any common sharing (κοινωνία) in the Spirit, if any tenderness and compassion, then make my joy complete by being like–minded, having the same love, being one in spirit and of one mind (Phil 2:1–4). Authentic sharing in the Spirit results in a κοινωνία of like-mindedness and love.

Therefore, following his opening greeting in 1 Cor, Paul cuts right to the chase: "you are still wordly" (1 Cor 3:3). The Corinthians are not living lives that reflect the loving κοινωνία of the Spirit. In fact, they are having an identity crisis. Rather than finding their identification in being joint-sharers in Christ, they are choosing to identify with one leader or another.[19] Most likely, the factions arose due to the Corinthian obsession with pres-

---

[17] Meeks suggests that social status was determined not only by economic status but by several other factors as well: "ethnic origins, *ordo*, citizenship, personal liberty, occupation, age, sex, and public offices or honors." See Meeks, *First Urban Christians*, 55. See also "Social Stratification in the Corinthian Community," in Gerd Theissen, *The Social Setting of Pauline Christianity: Essays on Corinth* (Philadelphia: Fortress, 1982), 69–119. However, descriptions of the Corinthian assembly derived from sociological analysis can be overstated, as the actual social and economic make-up of the Corinthian assembly is largely based upon conjecture. Steven Friesen examines the textual evidence of those groups or individuals named in the Corinthian letters against what is known about the demographics of Corinth in Steven J. Friesen, "Prospects for a Demography of the Pauline Mission: Corinth Among the Churches," in *Urban Religion in Roman Corinth: Interdisciplinary Approaches* (HTS 53; ed. Daniel N. Schowalter and Steven J. Friesen; Cambridge, Mass.: Harvard University Press, 2005), 367–70.

[18] Thus argues Richard A. Horsley, "Paul's Assembly in Corinth: An Alternative Society," in *Urban Religion in Roman Corinth: Interdisciplinary Approaches* (HTS 53; ed. Daniel N. Schowalter and Steven J. Friesen; Cambridge, Mass.: Harvard University Press, 2005), 371–95.

[19] Winter discusses the professional competition among teachers in Winter, *After Paul Left Corinth*, 36–38.

tige, with members of the community attaching themselves to leaders, just as the upwardly mobile in their society attached themselves to powerful patrons. In the upwardly mobile climate of Corinth, where a small percentage of merchants, minor government officials, and soldiers were intent on reaching the highest social class, appearances were everything.[20] Those few members of the Corinthian body that belonged to this upwardly mobile social class were threatened by Paul's teaching that they accommodate their lifestyle and needs to those lower on the economic ladder. Dale Martin has suggested that the intense struggle at the heart of the Corinthian church lay in the desire of the wealthier members of the community to adhere to and preserve the hierarchical arrangement of the "body politic" in the body of Christ.[21]

Indeed, suffering such as Paul was encountering, was shameful to these believers oriented towards the world's wisdom and acceptance. To suggest that they actually identify with suffering was a completely new idea. And yet, this is the second type of κοινωνία Paul emphasizes: one of the ways believers embrace the life of the Spirit is by embracing Jesus' personal history as their own.

---

[20] Aspiration to a higher social class may have played as large a role as social status itself. Corinth was re-founded in 44 BCE, and as a newer Roman city the social situation was more mobile than in other cities. Steven Freisen provides approximate demographical statistics based on historical data in Friesen, "Prospects for a Demography of the Pauline Mission," 351–70. His statistical analysis of Corinth provides a context for understanding the economic conditions in Corinth. He provides data that demonstrates that .04% of the population was comprised of the imperial Roman senatorial elite; only 3–4 percent of the population were considered wealthy, an additional 7 per cent were minor officials, merchants, artisans who employed others, or military veterans who aspired to reach the higher two social classes, either through earning more money or gaining social prestige, while the remaining 90% of population remained at subsistence level or below (364–67). Some members of the Corinthian church most likely were among those 7 per cent aspiring to higher social status. Therefore, Friesen reasons, we cannot assume that "if someone in Paul's churches was not as poor as someone else, they must have been rich" (366).

[21] Martin argues that "by calling on any Corinthians who consider themselves to be of high status to imitate his own position of low status, Paul implicitly advocates what upper-class ideology feared the most: the disruption of the stable hierarch of the political and cosmic body." Martin, *The Corinthian Body*, 68. He sums up the differences between the competing groups in Corinth as "Those who controlled their economic destiny and those who did not" (xvii). Martin's imposition of a "socio-ideological" hermeneutic upon the entire text (through an analysis of Greco-Roman texts on the theoretical constructions of the body), reduces the conflicts in 1 Cor entirely to divisions between Christians of "higher and lower status" (74). It is hard to imagine that all of Paul's opponents were of a higher social status; for if the economic make-up of the assembly paralleled the larger population, most of the Corinthian assembly was most likely poor, as Friesen's study bears out.

C. Participation in the Personal History of Jesus Christ

For Paul, Christian identity can be found only through identification with the crucified Christ. He appeals to the Corinthians to consider the power of the cross, which is utter foolishness and shame to the world (1 Cor 1: 18–25).[22] Paul states, "I resolved to know nothing while I was with you except Jesus Christ, and him crucified (1 Cor 2:2)." Paul continues to elaborate, throughout the following two chapters, the many ways in which he personally, as well as his companions, suffered for the cross of Christ. In appealing to them to be imitators of him, he appeals to them to be willing to embrace suffering, for our sharing *with* Christ is only complete when we share in his suffering and death. Michael Gorman calls this sharing "cruciformity" and has demonstrated that it is a strong theme throughout the Pauline corpus.[23]

In Rom 8:17, Paul declares that we will be co-sharers [συγκληρονόμος] in the inheritance of Christ "if, indeed, we share in his sufferings in order that we may also share in his glory."[24] Hauck observes: "fellowship with Christ means that present participation in one phase, namely, that of humility and suffering assures us of winning through to participation in the other, namely, that of glory."[25] Jesus' life of self-sacrifice to God and others was fulfilled in his death, a death in perfect accordance with the life he lived. For believers to participate in Christ's death involves embracing a life of self-denial and self-sacrifice, consumed not by comfort or power, but by the needs of others. Paul's own life exemplified such dedication to the Father's will, no matter how costly the sacrifice, even the threat of death.

---

[22] Martin Hengel's classic study on crucifixion, utilizing primary sources from the ancient world, gives readers an understanding the degree of cruelty and torture endured in Roman crucifixion. Crucifixion was considered the most publicly humiliating punishment, especially for Jews, since the victim was hung naked, and it held connotations of human sacrifice. Additionally, it was a punishment reserved only for the most dangerous criminals, slaves, and those of the lowest social classes. See Martin Hengel, *Crucifixion in the Ancient World and the Folly of the Message of the Cross* (Philadelphia: Fortress, 1977).

[23] Gorman describes participation in Christ (or *theosis*) fundamentally as "the transformative participation in the kenotic, cruciform character of God through Spirit-enabled conformity to the incarnate, crucified, and resurrected/glorified Christ." Michael J. Gorman, *Inhabiting the Cruciform God: Kenosis, Justification, and Theosis in Paul's Narrative Soteriology* (Grand Rapids: Eerdmans, 2009), 7.

[24] Additionally, in Phil 3:10 Paul teaches that the key to knowing Christ and the power of his resurrection is to possess a share [κοινωνία] in his sufferings "by becoming like him in his death."

[25] Hauck, *TDNT* 3:806.

Paul's exhortation to the Corinthians to embrace the cross was to serve as the antidote to their divisions, the source of which was the pursuit of power, popularity, and social status. Paul also teaches that sharing in the sufferings of Christ also involves sharing in the sufferings of fellow Christians. His second letter to that community continues in the same vein when he encourages the Corinthians to share in the sufferings of others: "because we know that just as you share [κοινωνοί ἐστε; lit., "are sharers"] in our sufferings, so also you share in our comfort" (2 Cor 1:7). He was not asking of them anything he had not also experienced, as indicated in the autobiographical material in 1 Cor: 8–13 and 2 Cor 4:8–12. He tells the Corinthians: "I do all this [referencing the hardships of his apostolic ministry] for the sake of the gospel, that I may share [συγκοινωνὸς . . . γένωμαι; lit., "become a co-sharer"] with them [the weak and the strong] in its blessings" (1 Cor 9:23, ESV)."[26] Elsewhere, Paul says something very similar when he expresses thanksgiving that the Philippians share with him in the κοινωνία of the Gospel, and that they are also co-sharers [συγκοινωνός] "in God's grace" with him (Phil 1:7).

D. Fellowship Embodied in Generosity

Experiencing solidarity with those who suffer was part of the purpose behind Paul's call for the collection for the Jewish Christians in Jerusalem. In 2 Cor, Paul encourages that community to join the Macedonians in a collection for the poor in Jerusalem. Paul praises the Macedonians for their desire to participate in the sufferings of the poor in Jerusalem through their active offering of both monies and personnel.[27] The Macedonians even viewed their participation in the collection as a sign of favor (2 Cor 8:4). Paul's third primary use of κοινωνία in pertaining to these collections indi-

---

[26] Thiselton believes that Paul's meaning here "is neither that of bringing benefits to others (NJB), nor that of sharing in these benefits as a missionary-pastor" (NRSV and NIV) but rather to emphasize that "to stand alongside the Jew, the Gentile, the socially dependent and vulnerable, or to live and act in solidarity with every kind of person in every kind of situation is to have a share [with them] in the nature of the gospel., i.e., *to instantiate what the gospel is and how it operates*." Thiselton, *Corinthians*, 707. The ESV translation is compatible with Thiselton's interpretation.

[27] See Acts 18:5; 2 Cor 8:1–4 and 11:9; Rom. 15:26; Phil. 2:25 and 4:18. Those who offered the money were most likely poor themselves. Horsley describes these collections as a "horizontal international movement of economic resources from one assembly of poor people to another, dramatically different from the vertical movement of resources—in the form of tribute to Rome and patronage pyramids—that structured the larger Roman imperial order." Horsely, "Paul's Assembly in Corinth," 393.

cates an active, not a passive, participation.²⁸ For instance, in Rom 15:26, where Paul calls the contribution a κοινωνία, he is indicating the money was not a "soulless gift, but the outward expression of the deep love that binds Christian believers in one body, the church."²⁹ Here it is important to note that Paul's desire that the Corinthians share in the suffering of Christ by sharing in the suffering of others is embodied in these collections. In other words, Paul encourages practices that enable believers to practice an outward focused, loving κοινωνία.

In conclusion, Paul believes that Christian κοινωνία is first founded in a sharing of the reality of being in Christ, the radical new existence given to all who have been justified by faith and sanctified by the Holy Spirit. What is shared among those who are in Christ is something that is uniquely given to those found in him—the life of the Holy Spirit. In the life of the Spirit, each believer shares in a communion between the persons of the Godhead and his brothers and sisters in Christ. Paul further teaches that the authentic sharing in the Spirit of Christ, which produces love, is made visible through sharing in the experiences of Christ: humility, sacrificial love, suffering, enduring persecution, and caring for the poor.

As I shall demonstrate below, Paul understands the Lord's Supper must also embody the loving κοινωνία of a shared life together in the Spirit, which in turn brings the believer into a deeper awareness of all the aspects of κοινωνία I have described above. Apropos here is Lionel Thornton's observation that there are two "fundamental factors" of a "complex yet simple whole," involved in κοινωνία: viz., *"the divine and the human."*³⁰ The common life the early Christians shared with each other, described more extensively in Acts, "transcended the community because in essence it was a communion with Christ and with the Holy Spirit. On the divine side it was a mystical union and participation in the life of Christ through receiving the gift of the Spirit. On the human side it consisted in a fellowship of brethren, whose mutual relations were transformed in quality and significance through the gift which they shared."³¹ Therefore, the social setting of the eucharistic celebration must reflect the loving, self-effacing quality true Christian κοινωνία demands.

---

²⁸ Murray J. Harris, *The Second Epistle to the Corinthians* (NIGTC; Grand Rapids: Eerdmans, 2005), 566–67.

²⁹ Leon Morris, *The Epistle to the Romans*, PNTC (Grand Rapids: Eerdmans, 1988), 520. Instances of κοινων- cognates concerning these collections are found in 2 Cor 8:4 and 9:13; and Rom 12:13.

³⁰ Thornton, *The Common Life*, 77.

³¹ Thornton, *The Common Life*, 76.

E. Meals with Idols Versus a Meal with Christ

In 1 Cor 8, Paul begins a long discourse on another issue that has divided their κοινωνία: the participation by some of their community in pagan meals.[32] There can be no mistake about the placement of his later discussion of the Lord's Supper within the context of his exposition on pagan sacrificial meals. Paul warns the Corinthians not to participate in pagan meals by demonstrating an antithetical relationship between pagan meals and the Christian holy meal. The Lord's Supper consists of fellowship with the Lord and the pagan meals consist of fellowship with demons. Paul argued against those who offered well-known "slogans" that the pagan meals were of no consequence.[33] Their desire to engage socially in these meals was an affront to the weaker brothers and sisters, either in terms of conscience or the flaunting of their higher social position.[34] Ultimately, Paul argues that neither meal is simply a conceptuality—but an experience of a spiritual reality.[35]

---

[32] These meals would have taken place in pagan temples. In addition to the works cited in note 5 above, studies consulted per the nature of the pagan meals were: Wendell Lee Willis, *Idol Meat in Corinth: The Pauline Argument in 1 Corinthians 8 and 10* (Chico, Calif.: Scholars Press, 1985); Derek Newton, *Deity and Diet: The Dilemma of Sacrificial Food at Corinth* (Sheffield: Sheffield Academic Press, 1998); Ben Witherington, "Not So Idle Thoughts About Eidolothuton," *TynBul* 44/2 (1993): 237–54.

[33] After quoting various Corinthian slogans which were used as justification for participation in the pagan meal (1 Cor 8:4–5) Paul dismisses their so called "knowledge" in vs. 11: "So this weak brother or sister, for whom Christ died, is destroyed by your knowledge." Thiselton paraphrases Paul's meaning: "What a way to "build" them! This is where all this propaganda [knowledge] about "the right to choose leads." Thiselton, *Corinthians*, 654. Moreover, earlier theories relating γνῶσις to a form of proto-gnostism (such as in Conzelmann, *First Corinthians*) are no longer considered valid. Rather, Paul is disparaging the inflated conceit of the educated elite who use their knowledge to assert their right to participate in idolatrous meals. See Thiselton, 620–28 for a review of the literature, as well as his conclusion that Paul is simply engaging in the "utmost irony and word-play: it is love that "builds"; "knowledge" merely inflates!"

[34] The issue also had socio-economic considerations, in that only the wealthier classes could afford meat, and the vast majority of the population was nourished by food from flour, such as porridges or bread. Additionally, the wealthier members of the Corinthian society may have been participating in these meals to increase their social standing. See Theissen, *The Social Setting of Pauline Christianity*, 126. Martin asserts: "Corinthians interested in status or social advancement could scarcely avoid such situations, to do so would have amounted to social suicide." Martin, *The Corinthian Body*, 75.

[35] In light of Paul's teaching, scholars have examined the social and religious context of pagan meals in the first century. Willis takes the extreme position that the pagan meals were no more than social occasions, "normative features of Hellenistic cults and associations . . . occasions of good company, good food, and good fun makes it obvious why the Corinthian Christians would not have wanted to miss out." Willis, *Idol Meat in Corinth*, 63. Witherington and Newton, contra Willis, affirm the religious context of pagan meals.

Some might argue that little should be read into 1 Cor 10:15–17 because "Paul's focus is *only* on what is genuinely similar between the two meals."[36] But others, such as N. T. Wright, believe Paul's comparison between the two actually "speaks volumes" about what Paul thinks is happening in the Lord's Supper.[37] Wright finds that Paul's entire exposition concerning the Lord's Supper and pagan meals tells us that for Paul the Lord's Supper is: (1) firmly anchored in salvation history, the Exodus and Passover narratives, as well as Jewish sacrificial worship, which has found new fulfillment in Jesus; (2) to be "understood as the intimate sharing of life and presence between the Lord and his people;" and, (3) "designed to express the unity, solidarity, and holiness of the community."[38] I will use Wright's three points as a framework for my own interpretation of these chapters that follows, and also provide some needed amplification.[39]

Paul begins by relating the meal controversy to the experiences of the Israelites in the desert (1 Cor 10:1–3). He speaks of the Israelite's crossing the Red Sea as a baptism and the eating of the manna and drinking from the rock of Christ as spiritual food and drink, a possible illusion to both sacraments of Baptism and the Lord's Supper.[40] By calling these gifts in the desert spiritual food, he is not referring to something immaterial, but

---

Witherington describes the sacrificial procedures of the pagan meals, citing primary sources in Witherington, "Not So Idle Thoughts," 242–46. He concludes: "Even when a club (*collegium*) or society, or trade guild held a meal in the temple precincts this would have been preceded by a specific sacrificial event of worship." (245) Newton, in *Deity and Diet*, presents an extensive survey of the primary source material. His survey of evidential material on pagan sacrifices is found on 185–257. He concludes: "at every point of our analysis what did emerge was the inseparable presence of what we would call social and religious ingredients." (255) I agree with his statement: "The social and religious setting of any ancient context were inseparable." (197)

[36] Gordon D. Fee, *The First Epistle to the Corinthians* (NICNT; Grand Rapids: Eerdmans, 1987), 465.

[37] N. T. Wright, *Paul and the Faithfulness of God* (Christian Origins and the Question of God 4, Minneapolis: Fortress, 2013), 1344.

[38] Wright, Paul and the Faithfulness of God, 1344.

[39] In particular, Wright makes no mention of the pneumatological dimension of the "intimate sharing of life and presence between the Lord and his people."

[40] Thiselton states: "Paul finds it appropriate to denote this as a baptismal-like redemptive experience of grace. The significance of baptized in relation to Moses is not least to identify the participating nature of their status and experience." (723) Concerning the manna illusions: "the parallel "visible signs" of the old and new covenants are set alongside each other: manna is said to imply (either typologically or in some other way) the spiritual food of the Lord's Supper or Eucharist, while the water from the rock is said to signify further the spiritual drink of the eucharistic wine of the Lord's Supper. Paul does move explicitly to the Eucharist or Lord's Supper in 10:14–22." (726) However, there are also other rabbinic traditions Thiselton considers. See Thiselton, *Corinthians*, 723–26.

rather that these gifts are, like the feeding in the Lord's Supper, a miraculous gift of the Spirit. He is also trying to move forward his argument concerning the danger of Christians engaging in pagan sacrifices.

Paul's primary objective in employing a typological reinterpretation of Israel's experience in the desert is to draw a correspondence between the behavior of the Israelites and the Corinthians. He is warning the Corinthians not to replicate the patterns of the Israelites.[41] Frances Young offers some guidance here. She states that the term *typos* "may be used for any 'model' or 'pattern' or 'parable' foreshadowing its fulfillment, whether an event or an oft repeated ritual. It is not its character as historical event which makes it a 'type,' what matters is its mimetic quality."[42] Thus, "it is not the 'historical event' as such which makes typology what it is; it is the sense of recapitulation, the 'impress' of one narrative or symbol on another, 'fulfilling it' and so giving it meaning."[43] Accordingly, Paul instructs the Corinthians, "do not be idolaters as some of them were" (1 Cor 10:7) with further references to the failure of the Israelites at covenant keeping as witnessed in Exodus and Numbers.[44] Those who participate in Christ must reflect the moral living of a redeemed community at which the Israelites failed. Therefore, the Corinthians must "flee from idolatry" (1 Cor 10:15).

It is at this point in his argument, that Paul interjects his statement about what happens in the Christian cultic meal (1 Cor 10: 16–17). What does Paul mean by stating that those who bless the cup and break the bread possess a share (κοινωνία) in the body and blood of Jesus? The reference to the body and blood of Jesus clearly points to his broken body and shed blood on the cross. Paul then asks the Corinthians: "Consider the people of Israel; are not those who eat the sacrifices partners (κοινωνός) in the altar?" (1 Cor 10:18, NRSV). What is being shared and with whom?

---

[41] Richard Briggs also makes this point in Richard Briggs, "'The Rock Was Christ': Paul's Reading of Numbers and the Significance of the Old Testament for Theological Hermeneutics," in *Horizons in Hermeneutics* (ed. Stanley E. Porter and Matthew R. Malcolm; Grand Rapids: Eerdmans, 2013), 90–116.

[42] Frances Young, *Biblical Exegesis and the Formation of Christian Culture* (New York: Cambridge University Press, 1997), 153.

[43] Young, *Biblical Exegesis*, 152.

[44] In 1 Cor 10:1–10 Paul alludes to scenes from Exodus 13, 16, and 17, and Num 21: 5–6; 14: 29–37; 25:9 and 26:65–65. Paul goes so far as to compare their fall into sexual idolatry with the Israelites whoredom with the daughters of Moab and making sacrifices to their gods and eating the Moabite sacrificial meals, which resulted in the death of 23,000 in one day (1 Cor 10:8). "These things," Paul warns, "happened to them to serve as an example, and they were written down to instruct us, on whom the ends of the ages have come (1 Cor 10:11)."

The connection between sacrifice and participation in the Lord's Supper is much more difficult to grasp in the twenty-first century than it would have been in the first century. Sacrifice was the central feature of all the religions of the day, and a practice significantly embedded in the Greco-Roman social structures. As Wright observes "one was never far away either from an animal about to be killed or from the smell of a recently sacrificed animal being cooked and eaten."[45]

Paul views the experience of the altar in the history and life of the Jewish people as the *typos* for understanding the sharing in the body and blood of Jesus. Yet it is not only a matter of Christ's fulfillment of the sacrificial system, but also discerning the mimetic behavior that took place at Israel's altar, which is then recapitulated in participation in the Lord's Supper.

When the Israelites offered sacrifices at the tabernacle site in the wilderness or the temple, they understood they were fellowshipping with God. Averbeck presents the purpose of the sacrificial system as "a means of approaching the Lord in his place of manifest presence in Israel (e.g., Lev 1:2) and to maintain that presence by preserving the purity and holiness of the sanctuary."[46] Presence denotes fellowship, and the sacrificial system upheld "the value of communion between the people and their God."[47]

An important aspect of sacrificial worship that warrants typological significance is that an expiatory offering in Israel was always accompanied by a celebratory sacrificial meal. When the Mosaic covenant was presented before the Israelites, Moses first offered a sacrifice of oxen to the Lord. He spread the blood on the altar and then read the covenant to the people. As they cried out their assent, Moses threw more blood on the gathered community as a sign of the blood of the covenant that the Lord made with them. Then a most amazing thing happened: Moses and Aaron, Nadab, and Abihu, and seventy of the elders of Israel went up the mountain, "they saw God and they ate and drank" with him (Exod 24:3–11). The sealing of the covenant between God and Israel was marked by a meal. This event is recapitulated in Christ's last meal before his sacrificial death, when looking ahead to the sacrificial offering he was about to accomplish on the cross, he stated to his disciples: "This cup is the new covenant in my blood, which is poured out for you" (Luke 22:20).

When the Levitical sacrificial requirements were instituted, the peace offering was mandated (Lev 3:1). This type of offering stands apart from

---

[45] Wright, *Paul and the Faithfulness of God*, 1340.
[46] Richard E. Averbeck, "Sacrifices and Offering," in *Dictionary of the Old Testament: Pentateuch* (ed. T. Desmond Alexander; Downers Grove, Ill.: InterVarsity Press, 2003), 706.
[47] Paul R. House, *Old Testament Theology* (Downers Grove, Ill.: IVP Academic, 1998), 119.

the other types of offerings because, in this ritual, the entire community ate the sacrificed meat, with certain portions reserved for the priests. "It was a 'fellowship,' or 'communion,' offering that indicated and enacted the fact that there was 'peace' between God and his people."[48] Participation in the peace offering provided a way of enjoying fellowship with the Lord since a portion of the offered meat was eaten at the sanctuary in his presence.[49] The peace offering was always the last offering performed in the sacrificial ritual. It was preceded by the expiatory offerings such as the whole burnt offerings, sin and guilt offerings, followed by the grain offerings. The purpose of the grain offerings was largely remembrance and what was to be remembered may have depended on the type of offering, but the general intent was to remember "the Lord and his blessings."[50]

Averbeck explains that the order of the offerings from sin and guilt to burnt and grain offerings to the final peace offerings and banquet "leads the worshiper along a *ritual path* from one stage to the next. It begins with expiatory atonement for sin, impurity, or trespass . . . which leads to the person's presentation of him or herself to the LORD . . . and eventually to a celebration of sacrificial communion.[51] The peace offering was the culminating offering, "an expression of harmonious relation with God, the ultimate goal of worship."[52]

In light of Young's explanation of typological *mimesis*, a typological pattern for worship emerges from the Israelites' sacrificial worship: *repentance, self-offering, remembrance, and thanksgiving for atonement, resulting in communion.* One can begin to see how the celebration of the Eucharist fulfills Israel's multiple modes of sacrificial worship."[53]

Therefore, when Paul asks the Corinthians to consider the people of Israel and their participation in the altar, there is a shared history behind his statement.[54] The cultic system of the second Temple continued to follow

---

[48] Averbeck, "Sacrifices and Offering," 715.

[49] See Lev 2:1–6 and 3:1–17.

[50] Averbeck, "Sacrifices and Offering," 714. Other instances included remembering the iniquity, such as in Num 5:15.

[51] Averbeck, "Sacrifices and Offering," 722.

[52] Philip P. Jenson, "The Levitical Sacrificial System," in *Sacrifice in the Bible* (ed. Roger T. Beckwith; Carlisle, UK: Paternoster, 2004), 31.

[53] Matthew Levering, in his substantial volume on the Eucharist and sacrifice, also affirms that in Israel's mode of sacrificial worship, "sacrifice and communion are inextricably integrated." Matthew Levering, *Sacrifice and Community: Jewish Offering and Christian Eucharist* (Malden, Mass.: Blackwell, 2005), 27–28.

[54] Even the Gentile members of the community understood sacrificial worship, albeit through their own lens of pagan experience. There were in fact similar features in the pagan rituals of Paul's day. A portion of the food was burned upon the altar, another portion placed upon the 'table of the God' and a third was allotted to the worshippers. You

these procedures, including "communion-sacrifices," in which a portion of the sacrificed animal was returned to the offerers, so that they shared a sacred meal with God.[55]

The similarity between the celebrations at the altars of Israel and the eucharistic κοινωνία in Christ's body and blood can be understood in different aspects. First, the sacrifice resulted in divine and human communion. Secondly, God required from the participants an attitude of repentance and faith in the covenantal promises of the Lord. Finally, sacrificial worship also involved communion and solidarity with the other worshippers. It therefore was the vehicle for community formation and identification for the Israelites. All of these aspects are replicated in the new sacrificial meal of Christ's people and point us to Paul's understanding of the nature of participation in Christ's sacrifice in the Lord' Supper. The Lord's Supper is a celebration of the ultimate sacrifice of Jesus Christ, participants offer their thanksgivings (εὐχαριστία) with hearts of faith and repentance, and participants share together in the fellowship (κοινωνία) of Father, Son, and Holy Spirit.

Paul's emphasis in 1 Cor 10:16–17 on the liturgical actions of the celebration of the Lord's Supper is telling. The emphasis is not upon what happens to the actual bread and wine, but upon the acts of blessing and breaking. These actions harkened back to the Jewish custom at the beginning of a Jewish formal meal, such as the Passover meal or the Sabbath meal, when the head of a household gave thanks, broke bread, and handed the pieces to those who were at table with him. Likewise, at the conclusion of the meal, the head of household gave thanks over the final cup of wine.[56] At his last supper with his disciples, Jesus faithfully followed these customs, but he radically changed the meaning of the liturgy by indicating these elements were now his body and blood, and he commanded his disciples to repeat his very actions as a commemoration of his sacrifice, the new covenant sealed by his blood.

Paul's point in 1 Cor: 16–17 precisely emphasizes that it is *in* the blessing and *in* the breaking that we participate with Christ in his sacrifice. In

---

did not "eat" the god, you communed with it. "Eating [in pagan meals] . . . was in fact the successful climax of the act of worship." Witherington, "Not So Idle Thoughts," 245.

[55] Paul F. Bradshaw and Maxwell E. Johnson, *The Eucharistic Liturgies: Their Evolution and Interpretation* (Collegeville, Minn.: Liturgical Press, 2012), 7–8.

[56] It is unlikely that the descriptions of the Passover Meal and the Sabbath supper in the *Mishna* were as fully developed in the first century. However, other primary sources such as the Qumran texts, Philo, and Josephus describe the Jewish custom of blessings over bread and wine at the beginning and end of their communal meals. On the relationship between early eucharistic prayers and Jewish prayers, including original sources and other scholarship, see Bradshaw and Johnson, *Eucharistic Liturgies*, 4–8.

the actions of the Lord's Supper, according to Paul, the narrative of Christ's sacrifice is invoked, made present and effective, and shared.

If the eating and drinking is a real participation, it is because the remembrance (ἀνάμνησις) is more than a simple recollection. The Jewish people understood remembrance as a way of appropriating stories of God's salvific acts into the present to affirm his presence and power in their lives. For example, through the invoking of the narrative of the Passover, the Jews inserted themselves into the story so that it became their story as well. In the active remembrance of Christ's sacrifice "the past is made real in the present and its power is released to shape the future."[57]

The Jewish sacrificial meal tradition also comes into play here: the communal *share* in the sacrifice was completed only when the sacrificial meal was celebrated among the worshippers. By eating the flesh of the sacrifice, the worshippers participated in not only the benefits of the offering (forgiveness) but in a mutual celebration of the Lord's presence with Israel. Paul understood this and that is perhaps partly why he called the Christian holy meal a participation in the sacrifice of Christ for the participants in the Lord's Supper celebrate the forgiveness achieved by Christ's sacrifice, while enjoying his presence.

This is why Paul also feared the consequence of partaking at the pagan table. Because he understood Christian partaking at the Lord's Table meant partaking of Christ, it was anathema to him that the Corinthians would partake with demons (1 Cor 10:20–21). There was nothing magical about the meat itself. In fact, Paul indicates that merely purchasing sacrificed meat in the market will bring no harm (v. 25). The significance is not in the object per se, but in the spiritual reality that is invoked through the liturgical actions and words of the religious meal. So just as there is nothing magical about bread and wine, there is nothing magical about sacrificed meat. Rather, it is the fellowship that is real. Κοινωνία with Christ or κοινωνία with demons is the choice before the Corinthians. The sacrificial table is a meeting place for fellowship with God.[58]

Two aspects of Paul's understanding of Christ's sacrifice are foundational to understanding Paul's argument. First, that redemption and justification are given in salvation through Jesus' once-for-all "sacrifice of atonement by his blood" (Rom 3:21–26; 1 Cor 5:7; Rom 8:3–4); and, secondly, Christ's sacrifice is an eternal one, thus its efficacy is past, present,

---

[57] Murphy-O'Connor, "Eucharist and Community in First Corinthians," 21.

[58] Witherington comments that "The reference to the 'table of demons' (cf. 1 Cor. 10:20–21) probably suggests that in Paul's mind dining in the temple dining room was itself putting oneself into the presence of demons, whether or not one was actually present for the preceding rituals and sacrifice." Witherington, "Not So Idle Thoughts," 246, n22.

and future (Rom 5:9–11). In the Lord's Supper, the ongoing and eternal efficacy of Christ's offering is invoked. He is both priest and victim. However, participation in Christ's sacrifice demands self-offering: a life lived for God and others. As explained above, participation in Christ is found in participating in his personal history, his brokenness and self-offering, as well as being attentive to the needs of others.

Paul was not afraid to use the language of sacrifice to express the Christian's primary obligation back to God in our participation in his life. Just as the Israelites offered their gifts at the altar, Paul commands his flock to "offer your bodies as a living sacrifice, holy and pleasing to God––this is your true and proper worship" (Rom 12:1). He exhorts the Ephesians to "walk in the way of love just as Christ loved us and gave himself up for us as a fragrant offering and sacrifice to God" (Eph 5:1). Participation in the sacrifice of Christ, the Lord's Supper, must be done in such a way as to emulate his self-sacrifice and love. Considering Paul's frequent admonishments to believers to participate in the death of Christ through their own self-sacrifice for the welfare of others, it is clear that Paul understands that participation in the sacrifice of Christ in the Lord's Supper needs to express this central feature of Christian κοινωνία: sharing self-sacrificially with others.

F. The Lord's Supper in Corinth: 1 Cor 11: 7–34

However, in 1 Cor 11, we read that a very different experience is occurring in Corinth. The disagreement over the propriety of participating in pagan meals is not the only factor in Paul's teaching concerning the Lord's Supper. We learn that the Corinthians' worldly social habits were marring their shared meals. The boundaries and social distinctions present in the formal meals of the wider Hellenistic culture were present in the Corinthian suppers.[59] When the Corinthian church "came together" to share meals, there

---

[59] The prime function of meal fellowship in Hellenistic culture was to establish ones' social rank and identity. Hal Tausigg focuses his study on the multitude of aspects in which the "social value of community/*kononia* was reinforced through the appropriate arrangements of food, reclining order, shared leadership, and finances of the meal itself." Hal Tausigg, *In the Beginning Was the Meal: Social Experimentation and Early Christian Identity* (Minneapolis: Fortress, 2009), 27. Paul Bradshaw provides documentary evidence that formal non-religious meals among Jews in the first century did not differ largely from the social customs of the Hellenistic culture. For instance, participants were often seated according to their social status. See Bradshaw and Johnson, *Eucharistic Liturgies*, 4–5. Accordingly, the gospel accounts that portray Jesus eating with "tax collectors and sinners" (Matt 11:19; Luke 7:34) indicate Jesus challenged the meal culture of

were "divisions," (v. 19) created by social distinctions and outright exclusions. Many remained hungry, while others became drunk and rowdy.[60] The church's meals were being treated as private celebratory dinners in which the privileged members were served first. Considering some of the members of the Corinthian church had no resources for food, Paul finds this practice reprehensible. It is certainly not in keeping with the provision of sustenance to the poor and widows that characterized the community meals in Jerusalem described in Acts 6.

Paul's rebuke to the Corinthians about the disintegration of true Christian fellowship caused him to declare: "When you come together, it is not really to eat the Lord's Supper" (11:20). Christ's actions of blessing and breaking may have been performed, but Christ's voice was not heard. Christ could not be the host of such a meal. The imitation of the behavior of pagans, as well as the inattention to the needs of others is certainly not fitting for a meal designed to commemorate Christ's sacrifice. Those that considered themselves worthy were in fact unworthy because they did not "discern the body of Christ," i.e. the needs of those present (1 Cor 11:29).[61]

This brings us back to Paul's statements concerning the Lord's meal in 1 Cor 10:17: "Because there is one bread, we who are many are one body, for we all partake of the one bread." The communal participation in the body of Christ (v.16) is the referent for the "one bread." In this analogical

---

his day, and Paul was simply following his example by challenging the Corinthians to not act as unbelievers in their communal meals.

[60] See Tausigg, *In the Beginning Was the Meal*, 72–74, for documentation from Hellenistic literature that may explain what was happening in the Corinthian meals. It was a common practice for "some people to receive more than others in recognition of their status" (72). Tausigg's work is representative of the body of work that focuses on the similarities between the early Christian meals and the Roman *symposium* meals/gatherings. However, this popular method of "social coding" the early Christian meals based solely upon Greco-Roman meal customs is overdrawn. Early Christian formal meals also grew out of the traditions of Jewish religious meals, such as the Jewish Passover and the Sabbath meal, attendant with specific religious content and meaning. Thus argues Bradshaw and Johnson, *The Eucharistic Liturgies*, 8–24. For example, liturgical actions such as blessing the wine and bread before the meal was a practice in keeping with Jewish meals and differed from the standard practices in the Roman symposium (17). See also "'Private' Dinners and Christian Divisiveness (1 Corinthians 11:17–34)," in Winter, *After Paul Left Corinth: The Influence of Secular Ethics and Social Change* (Grand Rapids: Eerdmans, 2001), 142–63, wherein he provides a plausible reconstruction of the Lord's Supper at Corinth in keeping with the Sabbath and Passover customs, as well as demonstrating the negative influences of pagan meals upon these celebrations.

[61] Since Paul has already referred to the body as the assembly gathered for the meal in 10:17, the context would suggest "body" is referring to the body of Christ as the assembled community. See Fee, *Corinthians*, 563–64, for a review of the possible interpretations for body. Fee agrees it refers to the assembly.

play on words, Paul is commenting further on what happens in the Lord's Supper when the Spirit is the mode of participation.

Because there is one loaf (Christ's body)
We who are many are one body (the church)
For we partake of the one loaf (Christ's body)

The dual identification of the body as *both* Christ's sacrificial presence and those who partake of his body is stunning. By partaking of the one loaf together, Christ's body, worshippers celebrate and make manifest their κοινωνία of shared fellowship as Christ's body.

Paul's statement in 1 Cor 12:13 provides an interpretative link: "For we were all baptized by one Spirit so as to form one body – whether Jews or Gentiles, slave or free – and we were all given the one Spirit to drink." This verse illustrates Paul's understanding of the juridical aspects of union with Christ sealed in baptism, as well as the active participatory bond made visible in the Lord's Supper. It is the Spirit who brings believers together to form one body in the κοινωνία of the Supper. As participants drink from one cup, they are also drinking from one Spirit. God's design for participation in the Lord's Supper is to confirm for believers the reality of their union in Christ. The church does not become the church in the Lord's Supper; it simply realizes it is the church as the Spirit makes manifest her unity. Through the mutual sharing in the Spirit, participants are united to each other. In the Lord's Supper vertical and horizontal meet.

The necessity then for a unified community celebrating together without regard to social class or the needs of the poor is essential. As Thiselton rightly observes, "the 'vertical' dimension of communal participation in the Lord's Supper, underlined by both themes, naturally spills over into the 'horizontal' dimensions of lifestyle."[62] Paul recognizes the weaknesses of the Corinthians when they come together to celebrate. That is why he offers them a different pattern for eucharistic celebration that will be a worthy imitation of the Lord's words and actions "on the night he was betrayed."

Paul's instructions concern the form and the manner of the Lord's sacrificial meal. The Corinthians are to consider the needs of others before they even come to the weekly meal. Those who can afford meals that are more elaborate need to celebrate them in their private homes (1 Cor 11:34). When they do come together they must wait for each other, so that all are properly fed. Paul's warnings about the spiritual and physical consequences for not correctly perceiving the body, i.e. not considering first the whole body of Christ, speaks volumes about the spiritual reality of the Lord's meal.

---

[62] Thiselton, *Corinthians*, 770.

Liturgically, Paul commands personal recollection and reflection before eating and drinking (11:28). These preparations are typological parallels to the Old Testament actions of the Israelites: repentance and self-offering. Paul recites Jesus' institutional words and actions, which may have been repeated at some point during the meal: "the Lord Jesus on the night when he was betrayed took bread, and when he had given thanks, he broke it and said, 'This is my body that is for you. Do this in remembrance of me'" (1 Cor 11:23–24).[63] Remembering the narrative of the Lord's last night with his disciples embeds the meal in the personal history of Jesus: his death that effected the salvation of the world. As discussed initially above, the Lukan formula "This cup is the new covenant in my blood," points to the Exodus narrative of the Sinai covenant where Moses threw the blood upon the people and declared "This is the blood of the covenant that the Lord has made with you in accordance with all these words" (Exod 24:8). There could not be a covenant without bloodshed. Paul reminds the participants that when they drink the cup of wine they are participating in the new covenant of the Lord accomplished through Christ's sacrifice.

Further, Paul states "whenever you eat this bread and drink this cup, you proclaim the Lord's death until he comes" (1 Cor 11:26). In other words, participation in the Lord's Supper involves looking back to Christ's death and looking forward to his second coming, while proclaiming the power of his gospel in the present. Accordingly, their behavior should reflect the eschatological expectation of a community that will be found ready and waiting for their Lord's παρουσία.

Paul offers the proper celebration of the Lord's Supper as a model for their life in Christian community and as a means of strengthening their unity as a people. Murphy-O'Conner affirms the significance of right practice of the Lord's Supper: "Only the profound conviction that all believers shared the common life of the body could restrain and eventually destroy the centrifugal tendencies that were the residue of their previous self-

---

[63] See Andrew B. McGowan, "'Is There a Liturgical Text in This Gospel?': The Institution Narratives and Their Early Interpretive Communities," *JBL* 118/1 (1999): 77–80. Paul's repetition of Jesus' words certainly has liturgical significance here, and for later eucharistic liturgical developments, but the 1 Corinthian texts only clearly indicate the liturgical actions of blessing and breaking (10:16) and the liturgical eating of bread and drinking of wine ("the bread" [τὸν ἄρτον] and "the cup" [τὸ ποτήριον] in 11:29). McGowan states that "it is in this sense that the liturgical action is repeating even if read prescriptively or performatively for liturgical purposes, the narrative and the call to 'do this in memory of me' would seem to lead to 'thanksgiving' (or 'blessing,' which was often equivalent) over bread and cup, which is what Jesus is said to have done, more easily than to recitation of the words 'this is my body that is for you' and 'this cup is the new covenant in my blood' or similar" (80).

centered mode of existence."⁶⁴ It is through *practicing* the celebration of the Lord's Supper in the manner Paul prescribes, that their community will be transformed from one of division and bickering, to one of love and unity. Then the Lord's Supper will be a meal worthy of its divine host, a meal where the hungry and the well fed, Jew and Gentile, men and women, slave and free, sit together at table with their Lord in a radical demonstration of true Christian κοινωνία.

G. Conclusion

The implications that can be gleaned for eucharistic theology from this study are significant. Additionally, understanding how the eucharistic celebration embodies Paul's understanding of Christian κοινωνία may promote better appreciation for how eucharistic participation also nurtures its emergence in the Christian church.

First, understanding the nature of κοινωνία as a divine and human participatory fellowship in the Holy Spirit, opens up the possibility for regarding the Eucharist as an event in which the triune God moves towards his people in love as they open up their spirits to receive his life. Through the agency of the Holy Spirit, Christ presents himself in the breaking of the bread and the pouring out of the wine, and when he is received through faith, a life-giving encounter results. It is the role of the Holy Spirit to impart the life of Christ, crucified, risen, and glorified to the faithful as well as to unite Christ's people into one body.

Secondly, just as the sacrificial worship of Israel served to sanctify and form the identity of the congregation of Israel, Paul understood the celebration of the Lord's Supper is integral to the church's formation and identity as a Christ-like community. In the Lord's Supper, the power of Christ's κοινωνία is realized and lived by the community who rightly celebrates this meal of unity. Just as Paul designates eucharistic sharing as a sharing in the body and blood of Christ, participating in a liturgy of breaking bread and blessing wine reminds participants of the importance of sharing in the life of Christ's personal history of suffering, death, and resurrection. Participation in the body and blood of Christ is experienced through a community who loves and cares for each other, and at the same time this love and care for each other is strengthened by the Lord who presents himself to his church in his meal.

Thirdly, an understanding of the *mimetic* features of the sacrificial worship of Israel helps in understanding how the Eucharist is a participation in

---

⁶⁴ Murphy-O'Connor, "Eucharist and Community in First Corinthians," 29.

the sacrifice of Christ. The patterns of sacrificial worship mandated by the Lord required repentance, self-offering, remembrance, and thanksgiving for atonement, resulting in communion. In the traditional eucharistic liturgies of the church, the congregants recite a prayer of confession before the eucharistic prayer commences. Christ's words of Institution are recited, prompting congregants to enter into an ἀνάμνησις of Christ's offering, realizing its present efficacy for all who come to the altar. The giving of thanks over the elements, in the power of the Holy Spirit, is an opportunity for each worshipper to offer thanksgiving for forgiveness and redemption, and renew their covenant with the Father in Christ by offering up their own life as a living sacrifice to the Father. As the Spirit joins the assembly in a sharing of the triune presence, Christ reveals himself in the meal which celebrates his sacrifice, and a κοινωνία with the living God of the new covenant meal takes place.

The intent of this volume is to explore the relationship between union and participation. I have attempted to show that Paul understood that the κοινωνία of the Spirit is only shared by those who are found in Christ. Similarly, the Eucharist is a celebration of the sacrifice of Christ that secured this union. And yet, the sharing itself is an event in the present. An understanding of κοινωνία as an active participation in a sharing of the Holy Spirit fits the distinction that Campbell makes between the concept of union and participation. Union is *static*, and conveys our state of being in Christ: our location, identity, and incorporation into his sonship, achieved juridically by Christ's redemptive work and the believer's faith in its efficacy for salvation. However, while union reflects our spiritual state, participation or κοινωνία, on the other hand, conveys our ongoing sharing in the life of the Spirit. "To *participate* is a doing word, while *union* is a being word."[65] The "doing" that takes place in the κοινωνία of the Lord's Supper consists of the human acts of repentance, remembering, and thanksgiving. The repetition of the Lord's words and actions on the night before his ultimate sacrifice invokes Christ's presence, while the "co-sharers in Christ" present themselves as the church of Christ in a living sacrifice offered to her Lord. But the ultimate part of the "doing" is the receiving: a mutual receiving of the κοινωνία of Father, Son, and Holy Spirit as participants experience and celebrate together their union with Christ.

---

[65] Campbell, *Paul and Union with Christ*, 413. Campbell identifies union, participation, identification, and incorporation as the four "umbrella concepts," which cover the full spectrum of Pauline language, ideas, and themes that are bound up in the metatheme of 'union with Christ.'" His exploration of this "metatheme" has shown that no "single-idea" term is broad enough to "encapsulate all that Paul envisions by our relatedness to Christ," 413.

Bibliography

Averbeck, Richard E. "Sacrifices and Offering." Pages 706–33 in *Dictionary of the Old Testament: Pentateuch*. Edited by T. Desmond Alexander. Downers Grove, Ill.: InterVarsity Press, 2003.

Bauer, Walter. *A Greek-English Lexicon of the New Testament and other Early Christian Literature*. 3d ed. Revised and edited by Frederick William Danker. Chicago: University of Chicago Press: 2000.

Bradshaw, Paul F., and Maxwell E. Johnson. *The Eucharistic Liturgies: Their Evolution and Interpretation*. Collegeville, Minn.: Liturgical Press, 2012.

Briggs, Richard. "'The Rock Was Christ': Paul's Reading of Numbers and the Significance of the Old Testament for Theological Hermeneutics." Pages 90–116 in *Horizons in Hermeneutics*. Edited by Stanley E. Porter and Matthew R. Malcolm. Grand Rapids: Eerdmans, 2013.

Campbell, Constantine R. *Paul and Union with Christ: An Exegetical and Theological Study*. Grand Rapids: Zondervan, 2012.

Conzelmann, Hans. *First Corinthians: A Commentary on the First Epistle to the Corinthians*. Hermeneia. Philadelphia: Fortress, 1988.

Fee, Gordon D. *God's Empowering Presence: The Holy Spirit in the Letters of Paul*. Peabody, Mass.: Hendrickson, 1994. Repr., Grand Rapids: Baker Academic, 2009.

———. *The First Epistle to the Corinthians*. New International Commentary on the New Testament. Grand Rapids: Eerdmans, 1987.

Gorman, Michael J. *Inhabiting the Cruciform God: Kenosis, Justification, and Theosis in Paul's Narrative Soteriology*. Grand Rapids: Eerdmans, 2009.

Harris, Murray J. *The Second Epistle to the Corinthians*. New International Greek Testament Commentary. Grand Rapids: Eerdmans, 2005.

Kittel, G., and G. Friedrich, eds. *Theological Dictionary of the New Testament*. Translated by G. W. Bromiley. 10 vols. Grand Rapids: Eerdmans, 1964–1976.

Hengel, Martin. *Crucifixion in the Ancient World and the Folly of the Message of the Cross*. Philadelphia: Fortress, 1977.

House, Paul R. *Old Testament Theology*. Downers Grove, Ill.: IVP Academic, 1998.

Jenson, Philip P. "The Levitical Sacrificial System." Pages 25–40 in *Sacrifice in the Bible*. Edited by Roger T. Beckwith. Carlisle, UK: Paternoster, 2004.

Levering, Matthew. *Sacrifice and Community: Jewish Offering and Christian Eucharist*. Malden, Mass.: Blackwell, 2005.

Martin, Dale B. *The Corinthian Body*. New Haven, Conn.: Yale University Press, 1995.

McGowan, Andrew B. "'Is There a Liturgical Text in This Gospel?': The Institution Narratives and Their Early Interpretive Communities." *Journal of Biblical Literature* 118/1 (1999): 73–87.

Meeks, Wayne A. *The First Urban Christians: The Social World of the Apostle Paul*. New Haven, Conn.: Yale University Press, 1983.

Murphy-O'Connor, Jerome. "Eucharist and Community in First Corinthians." Pages 1–30 in *Living Bread, Saving Cup: Readings on the Eucharist*. Edited by R. Kevin Seasoltz. Collegeville, Minn.: Liturgical Press, 1982.

Newton, Derek. *Deity and Diet: The Dilemma of Sacrificial Food at Corinth*. Sheffield: Sheffield Academic Press, 1998.

Schowalter, Daniel N., and Steven J. Friesen, eds. *Urban Religion in Roman Corinth: Interdisciplinary Approaches*. Harvard Theological Studies 53. Cambridge, Mass.: Harvard University Press, 2005.

Tausigg, Hal. *In the Beginning Was the Meal: Social Experimentation and Early Christian Identity*. Minneapolis: Fortress, 2009.

Theissen, Gerd. *The Social Setting of Pauline Christianity: Essays on Corinth*. Philadelphia: Fortress, 1982.

Thiselton, Anthony C. *The First Epistle to the Corinthians*. New International Greek Testament Commentary. Grand Rapids: Eerdmans, 2000.

Thornton, Lionel Spencer. *The Common Life in the Body of Christ*. 4th ed. London: Dacre, 1963.

Vanhoozer, Kevin J. *Remythologizing Theology: Divine Action, Passion, and Authorship*. Cambridge Studies in Christian Doctrine. Cambridge: Cambridge University Press, 2010.

Willis, Wendell Lee. *Idol Meat in Corinth: The Pauline Argument in 1 Corinthians 8 and 10*. Chico, Calif.: Scholars Press, 1985.

Winter, Bruce W. *After Paul Left Corinth: The Influence of Secular Ethics and Social Change*. Grand Rapids: Eerdmans, 2001.

Witherington, Ben. *Conflict and Community in Corinth: A Socio-Rhetorical Commentary on 1 and 2 Corinthians*. Grand Rapids: Eerdmans, 1995.

———. "Not So Idle Thoughts About Eidolothuton." *Tyndale Bulletin* 44/2 (1993): 237–54.

Wright, N. T. *Paul and the Faithfulness of God*. Christian Origins and the Question of God 4. Minneapolis: Fortress, 2013.

Young, Frances. *Biblical Exegesis and the Formation of Christian Culture*. New York: Cambridge University Press, 1997.

Until We Are One?

Biopolitics and the United Body

DEVIN P. SINGH

...until all of us come to the unity of the faith and of the knowledge of the Son of God, to maturity, to the measure of the full stature of Christ. We must no longer be children... we must grow up in every way into him who is the head, into Christ, from whom the whole body, joined and knitted together by every ligament with which it is equipped, as each part is working properly, promotes the body's growth in building itself up in love.
(Eph 4:13–16, NRSV)

The body is not a minor matter; rather, it is the main attraction.[1]

Metaphysical, ontological, and theological speculations about union with Christ notwithstanding, practices of unity in the world are where its effects are felt and history is made.[2] Of course, this is not to say that conceptualization is secondary or of less import, for how one thinks about the nature of union will have a bearing on how it is embodied. For good reason this volume has pursued the question of participation "in Christ," to consider various attempts at understanding what it means, partly to grasp how it may be performed and what the implications of its performance over time have been. For life in the world is where a legacy is made. Union in Christ is a lived reality, a reality hazarded. The church, called to be or to become the united body of Christ, makes unity known in some way, for better or for worse, to a variety of onlookers, individual and institutional, material and spiritual.[3] As an institution that is fully a part of this world and its cul-

---

[1] Sallie McFague, *The Body of God: An Ecological Theology* (Minneapolis: Fortress, 1993), 16.

[2] I write not as a biblical scholar but as one trained primarily in theology and sociopolitical theory. While some of the questions I pursue and methodologies I employ may appear dissonant to those rooted in the former discipline, I trust that such dissonance will be productive nonetheless. In addition to the editors of this volume, I wish to thank Stephen Fowl and Dale Martin for feedback on and critique of an earlier draft.

[3] On unity as a witness to the powers, see, e.g., Stephen Fowl, "Scripture and the Divided Church," in *Horizons in Hermeneutics* (ed. Stanley E. Porter and Matthew R. Malcolm; Grand Rapids: Eerdmans, 2013), 217–33.

tures (despite many hopes and intentions to the contrary), it draws upon language, models, and concepts of union from the wider culture and gives back its own interpretations and transformed practices.[4] Somewhat paradoxically, in fact, unity actually includes – even depends upon – interaction with the world. Unity cannot be conceived of in isolation from whatever it is that is posited as outside the union. Through the give and take of this performance, a witness both intentional and unintentional, concrete practices are exchanged, and what union means is deeply shaped by and comes to shape meaning in other registers. In our case this means, in particular, the sphere of the political.

Forging a unity of diverse members under a single concept, system, set of practices, or authority is certainly not a concern restricted to the purview of the church. It is central to the problem of politics, and is a site of reflection that long precedes the first centuries C.E. when the church began to make its history. If anything, the emerging *ecclesia* inserted itself into this longer narrative – or set of competing and conflicting narratives – about the nature of social union. Such insertion was a process of cooptation, adaptation, appropriation, and innovation, in ways both supportive of, oppositional, or indifferent toward surrounding ideas of unity and the nature of community. Conversation partners, both explicit and implicit, included not only Greco-Roman thought systems but also a long tradition of Jewish reflection on communal formation and the nature and scope of the political. Such a dialogue, in turn, has been fundamental to the directions of ecclesial and political thought in the West. Voices within ecclesial and political spheres have shaped each other's perspectives on tactics of governance and direction of their respective communities. Despite our ostensibly secular moment, political philosophers and theorists continually return to major Christian tropes of community for resources to think through various contemporary crises of unity.[5]

This essay pursues a line of inquiry about the nature of one such biblical trope – that of the united body of Christ – in relation to contemporary con-

---

[4] This process is explored in, e.g, Kathryn Tanner, *Theories of Culture: A New Agenda for Theology* (Minneapolis: Fortress, 1997).

[5] Of the litany of examples, we might include Derrida's reflections on attempts at (linguistic) unity and translation in light of the Babel trope in Jacques Derrida, "De Tours de Babel," *Semeia* 54 (1991): 3–34. Noteworthy as well is Badiou's attempt to think Pauline universalism – and a basis for social unity – in the face of a politics of difference in Alain Badiou, *Saint Paul: The Foundation of Universalism* (Stanford: Stanford University Press, 2003). See the outstanding collection of essays analyzing this philosophical turn to Paul, in particular, in Ward Blanton and Hent de Vries, eds., *Paul and the Philosophers* (New York: Fordham University Press, 2013); Douglas Harink, ed., *Paul, Philosophy, and the Theopolitical Vision: Critical Engagements with Agamben, Badiou, Žižek and Others* (Eugene, Ore.: Cascade, 2010).

cerns about governmental attempts at defining and policing the social body or body politic. Paul's injunctions toward unity as a corporate body, set forth most extensively in his correspondence with the Corinthians, have served as a touchstone for reflection on ecclesial identity. Such vision has also made itself felt in a broader social imaginary, in societies influenced or to whatever degree impacted by Christian tradition, for better or for worse. Thinking about bodies – individual and corporate, material and spiritual – permeates Pauline discourse in this letter and elsewhere. Likewise, conceptualizing and managing bodies figure centrally in contemporary political projects. What remains is to draw out potential links between such Christian tradition and *biopolitics*, understood as these tactics of management of bodies and lives in the furtherance of political aims and of the life of the state.

Many connections have been drawn between biopolitics and Christian notions of pastoral oversight, a trajectory that I will review. To add to this conversation, I will consider Christian concerns about preserving the purity of the body – both in conceptions of the actual human body and in its "metaphorical" or extended application to the church as body.[6] As we think about modern attempts to police the boundaries and internal purity of the body politic, what insights might be gained by considering the ancient ecclesial concerns about preserving the unity and sanctity of the body of Christ? To contextualize my study, I first explore discussions of biopolitics and questions of contagion and immunity in terms of the body politic. I turn then to the notion of the body – both individual and social – in ancient and biblical perspective, and follow how the idea of the church as the body of Christ may have influenced notions of the social body in the medieval world. Here we see biblical themes of concern for pollution and the permeability of the body worked out politically. I then consider the transition to modernity and transformation in ideas of the social body. The hope is that my genealogical sketch, however preliminary, might contribute to analyses of the past trajectories and future directions of attempts to manage bodies in relation to communal aims, whether in the church or society at large.

As we will see, it is not sufficient to draw a hard and fast line between the church and the world, and with this to claim that secular notions of the united body are simply the result of secular reason and concepts. Those

---

[6] As we will see, whether or not the application of "body" to a corporate form is literal or metaphorical is at the heart of the ambiguity and productivity of such a notion. For the significant slippage between metaphor and reality in Pauline discourse, see Constantine R. Campbell, "Metaphor, Reality, and Union with Christ," in this volume. For exploration of an idea of material bodies as corporately conceived in biological discourse, see Matthew Croasmun "'Real Participation': The Body of Christ and Body of Sin in Evolutionary Perspective," in this volume.

operating from a sense of location inside the church cannot simply claim two clear lines of development, an ecclesial tradition of ideas of the body of Christ and a secular political legacy of the body politic. The two are intertwined. Not only is this clearly the case in the medieval world of Christendom, which has left an ambiguous legacy for modernity, but it also becomes clear in Pauline explorations of the church as the body of Christ. Paul draws on a contemporary political metaphor to depict Christ's body. Furthermore, we find in Paul an awareness of and concern for the permeability of the body, the thinness of the layer separating church from world and hence the necessity of policing this corporate "skin" and its orifices. Whatever one thinks about the merits or faults of these injunctions to boundary maintenance, the foundational assumption is one of a porous membrane between church and world, between body and cosmos. The body is penetrable. It is not yet conceived as "buffered," to invoke Charles Taylor's much touted demarcation of the secular subject.[7]

Indeed, there is a correlation between the new, secular, buffered self and changes in ideas of the human and social body. The rise of anatomy and physiology, viewing the body as a self-contained organism, functioning like a machine, exhibits correspondences with the Hobbesian view of the political body as automaton, as machine, which provides the grounding fiction for Leviathan to assume control of individuated human bodies. Yet, even in this modern vision, earlier concerns for bodily integrity and purity persist and have arguably become radicalized. How might modern notions of policing the purity of the body politic, with anxieties about pollution and contagion, result from the peculiar transferal and transmutation of ancient concerns about the body as mediated through Christian tradition? How does the Pauline vision for the body of Christ, itself a unique incorporation of ancient scriptural, philosophical, and cultural assumptions about literal and figurative bodies, convey to later Christian and eventually modern society its own peculiar set of assumptions about the nature, scope, and composition of the social body and the techniques necessary for its preservation and maintenance?

A. Of bodies and biopolitics

Discourse on biopolitics examines the ways modern political rationality takes individual and social bodies seriously as sites of policing and control. Modes of governance have moved from a paradigm concerned primarily with obedience, where the threat of death operated as centralized power's

---

[7] Charles Taylor, *A Secular Age* (Cambridge, Mass.: Belknap Press of Harvard University Press, 2007).

chief intervention into the lives of subjects.[8] Arguably, of course, such a paradigm of sovereignty is still operative, but it has shifted forms and emphases. What we find, instead, in modernity is that state and governmental power now exert significant efforts toward observing, analyzing, organizing, directing, and nurturing the details and directions of human lives and populations. Authority is concerned with life content and quality in a way that appears distinct from classical models of rule. Why this is so and the implications of this shift in focus are of interest to our exploration. Furthermore, the relation of a particular Christian theological and ecclesial legacy to these broader social and ostensibly secular practices must be considered. This helps shed light on how Christianity has influenced the development of statecraft in the West, how its ideas may continue to operate implicitly, and what the church's relation to secularized forms of Christian practice might be. As we will see, the idea of the body is central in biopolitical governance. The legacy of the church as a body may have a role to play in this development.

Biopolitics, as explored famously by Michel Foucault and elaborated by thinkers such as Giorgio Agamben and Roberto Esposito, speaks to a new direction of power and control glimpsed in modern statecraft.[9] Typical models of authority and social organization in Antiquity and the Middle Ages emphasize forms of centralized sovereignty, with the focal point being the ruler whose power over life is absolute. This power manifests itself in "the right to kill or let live."[10] Oversight and policing of the nature and content of the life lived under sovereign power's purview are minimal – what is important is this boundary that the authority guards between life and death. The citizen or subject's life choices, aside from their bearing on matters of law, are of little concern. What we take for granted today and often accept uncritically as a governmental and institutional concern for matters of health, work, (re)productivity, and other internal and personalized life choices is part of a new configuration of power and governance, claims Foucault.

---

[8] Michel Foucault, *Society Must be Defended: Lectures at the Collège de France, 1975–76* (New York: Picador, 2003), 25–26.

[9] See, e.g., Michel Foucault, *The History of Sexuality. Vol. 1: An Introduction* (trans. Robert Hurley; New York: Pantheon, 1978); Michel Foucault, *Security, Territory, Population: Lectures at the Collège de France, 1977–1978* (New York: Palgrave Macmillan, 2007); Giorgio Agamben, *Homo Sacer: Sovereign Power and Bare Life* (trans. Daniel Heller-Roazen; Stanford: Stanford University Press, 1998); Giorgio Agamben, *State of Exception* (trans. Kevin Attell; Chicago: University of Chicago Press, 2005); Roberto Esposito, *Bíos: Biopolitics and Philosophy* (trans. Timothy Campbell; Minneapolis: University of Minnesota Press, 2008).

[10] Foucault, *The History of Sexuality. Vol. 1*, 133–60.

To be sure, there are multiple sources of this new orientation and emergence of governmental rationality. One influence that Foucault highlights, which is of interest to my exploration, is the emergence of pastoral power as a new mode of authority in the West. The Christian pastorate marks a novel arrangement of authority, obedience, oversight, and formation of subjects.[11] The pastorate is shaped by an understanding of God as shepherd, a model of leadership conveyed through the Hebrew scriptures that draws upon ancient Near Eastern ideals of kingship. God as the shepherd king is a caretaker of a mobile flock, who attends intimately to the welfare of each member as well as simultaneously to the whole. Foucault claims this differs significantly from predominant Greco-Roman models of the gods and the postures of political authority in the polis and empire.[12] The Greco-Roman importance of place, such as the city-state, and its demarcation of citizenship as the preeminent mark of membership, are displaced by a focus on the co-identification of leader with those who are led, as well as by ideas of group belonging detached from a specific locale.[13] While it would take some time before this model of the shepherd would influence political leadership within the Christian empire, its more immediate manifestation was the pastorate. The bishop was the caretaker of the church as flock. This authority, after the model of Christ, was to engage in servant leadership authenticated by self-sacrifice. Practically, this facilitated pastoral attention to the details of Christian lives, and to practices of confession, penance, and repentance, which, Foucault claims, helped Christianity's unique contribution to the idea of "conscience" in Western tradition.[14]

Foucault suggests a genealogical relation between the idea of the pastoral leader, who cares for, oversees, and stewards the lives of the flock and an eventual centrality within governmental practice of methods of managerial concern for the populace. This is not a linear form of direct causation.

---

[11] On these points see esp. Foucault, *Security, Territory, Population*, lectures 5 and 6.

[12] Foucault's dichotomy may be overblown. There are examples of strong co-identification and rhetoric of affection between ruler and ruled in Greco-Roman context as well. The trope of emperor as father to the people is one such obvious example. On this, see, e.g., Michael Peppard, *The Son of God in the Roman World: Divine Sonship in its Social and Political Context* (New York: Oxford University Press, 2011).

[13] Certainly in Hebraic tradition there is an identification with the land of Israel. But YHWH is presented as a God not linked to a territory, in contrast to neighboring deities, and who calls out and forms a people rather than defines and sanctifies a space. The land is significant because it is given to God's people. For one classic development of this theme of God drawing a people forward in movement and promise, delinked from place, see Jürgen Moltmann, *Theology of Hope: On the Ground and the Implications of a Christian Eschatology* (trans. James W. Leitch; London: SCM Press, 1967).

[14] Cf. Charles Taylor, *Sources of the Self: The Making of the Modern Identity* (Cambridge: Harvard University Press, 1989); Krister Stendahl, "The Apostle Paul and the Introspective Conscience of the West," *HTR* 56/3 (1963): 199–215.

Rather, a series of diffuse permutations of various practices and mentalities eventually produces echoes and analogues in other registers. While pastoral power exists as a kind of "prelude" to modern biopolitics, the transition from a regime of sovereignty to one of governmentality does not occur until early modernity. Again, we take for granted today that the state to some extent bears responsibility to protect the lives of its populations as well as to direct such lives toward greater levels of productivity and flourishing, however defined. Yet, this has not always been the case. The modern state concerns itself with matters of sexual practice, public hygiene, vaccination campaigns, rates of birth, aging, and death, as well as fuzzy "quality of life" measures, while tying these metrics to economic indicators like employment levels and gross national product, for instance. The state seeks to take care of its citizens and ensure the flourishing of its population, through various tactics of surveillance, discipline, and life management in a manner distinct from the rule of ancient sovereigns.[15] Such management is also more decentralized, such that it becomes difficult at various junctures to speak of the state itself as directing or overseeing such procedures, or to ascribe agency to discrete sites of control. Ongoing debates about the boundaries of state and civil society signal the tensions between state attempts at bodily management and ways other social bodies – corporations, businesses, media and educational institutions, and other non-governmental organizations, for instance – each take up the charge of corporeal and life direction in their particular ways.

The development of a biopolitical regime indexes the body on two levels. At one stage, Foucault claims, disciplinary practices and new governmental techniques in the 17th and 18th centuries work to forge habits and practices in the figure of the citizen. Manuals for personal hygiene and sexual conduct are two of many potential examples circulating in this early modern period. A history of conscience formation through Christian penitential practices and habits of confession provides a backdrop to forms of modern self-policing. Law and punishment become internalized modes of control. A self is shaped in part through habits and bodily practices. At this level, the target is the body and its movements, postures, and desires. Mechanisms of power appear diffuse and decentered, with techniques of the self as the active sites of enforcement. In this stage of biopolitics, control is not exerted so much from a sovereign center, but instead becomes internalized in the individual bodies of subjects. Such bodies become self-governing according to such new disciplinary mechanisms.

---

[15] Cf. Mika Ojakangas, "Impossible Dialogue on Bio-power: Agamben and Foucault," *Foucault Studies* 2 (May 2005): 5–28; Graham Burchell, Colin Gordon, and Peter Miller, eds., *The Foucault Effect: Studies in Governmentality* (Chicago: University of Chicago Press, 1991).

A second stage involves regulation and control at the level of the population. Whereas previously the target was micro-practices of individual bodies and attitudes, governmental rationality zooms out, as it were, to take on management of entire social bodies. Species life and corporate identity become factors, as new metrics of statistical measurement and economic policy are employed. Individual bodies have not quite disappeared, but now governance is a numbers game, where group survival and societal flourishing mean that individual bodies are expendable for the sake of the whole. Techniques of power and administration thus exhibit sensitivity to the reality and flourishing of the corporate body, while doing so still through the management of bodies. A peculiar resonance between individual and social bodies is evident, as the metaphorical body politic becomes the conceptual site of control, all the while mediated through the fate of "statistically significant" numbers of actual human bodies.[16] This double orientation, to the particular and the whole, is something that Foucault discerns in pastoral power as well. The shepherd will both leave the flock in search of one lost sheep and at times remove a sick sheep lest it corrupt the whole.

This theme of corruption, of elements threatening to the health of the group, is a concept pursued in depth by Italian philosopher Roberto Esposito.[17] Esposito has drawn attention to ideas of immunity and concerns about contamination that undergird modern notions of community and invoke this biopolitical paradigm. Modern ideas of political community are rife with the desire to police and protect boundaries and identity. For Esposito, the immunity paradigm defines modernity, underlying the development of political models centered on protection of the self (whether individual or communal) from its other. The chief theorist of this transition is Hobbes, whose theory of state sovereignty is predicated upon the protection of the individual from other individuals.[18] Esposito notes the tenuous grounds upon which the modern polis is formed, seen somewhat paradoxi-

---

[16] This is in part why a theorist like Agamben can make the striking claim that the concentration camp is the *"nomos* of the modern." The camp is the dark underside, the exceptional moment when the overlay to modern society is stripped away, revealing its governing logic. Such a logic is one of both the centrality and superfluity of bodies, where bare human flesh is policed and managed toward productivity while being fully disposable. Furthermore, "the separation of the Jewish body is the immediate production of the specifically German body," revealing the dual necessity and exclusion of bodies in nation state – and hence body politic – formation. See Agamben, *Homo Sacer*, 174.

[17] Roberto Esposito, *Communitas: The Origin and Destiny of Community* (trans. Timothy Campbell; Stanford: Stanford University Press, 2010); Roberto Esposito, *Immunitas: The Protection and Negation of Life* (trans. Zakiya Hanafi; Cambridge: Polity, 2011).

[18] Esposito, *Communitas*, 13.

cally as a community justified by its protection of each from the other. It is community founded upon negation, community in which immunity and self-enclosure are the guiding logic. Leviathan serves to immunize the modern self from others. This dynamic is then extrapolated and becomes writ large across the body politic, for emerging, early modern nation states are of course constructed and maintained on the basis of immunity from other states. Borders, as well as arguments for national identity based upon religion, language, and race, are techniques of communal immunization. The horizon of such modern hope is to render the edges or "skin" of the social body impregnable, even as internal cleansing attempts to rid the body of foreign contaminants.

The immunity paradigm is noteworthy for my purposes because it invokes a metaphor associated with the physical, individual body and applies it socially. We can see the body metaphor at work here in dialogue with modern science and new paradigms of contagion, infection, and immune response. The social body, or body politic, is conceived of as a bounded entity that is at risk of infiltration and contamination. Thus, not only is the population managed toward aims of productivity and growth, as Foucault highlights, but, as Esposito's exploration claims, it is protected and policed in the interests of its health, both literal and figurative.

As Esposito and many other theorists of political community are careful to note, Christian tradition has made a decisive impact upon theories of community in the West. Central in such tradition is Pauline reflection on the church, which has bequeathed a legacy of concepts, social patterns, and institutions that have shaped the course of Western politics. As Eric Santner claims, "[i]n Paul's writings on these matters, we find some of the first statements that inaugurate in the West the political theology of sovereignty, the biopolitics of states, and the rhetorical figures that organize their reciprocal exchange of properties and energies."[19] It is to Paul that Esposito turns for a touchstone of thinking about the social body. Paul's reflections on the church as the body of Christ catalyzed a political metaphor and ensured its transmission and reactivation in a variety of future contexts.

Central to community (*communitas*) is a notion of gifting and of self-donation. Esposito arrives at this position through etymological exploration of the *munus* at the heart of *communitas*. Having to do with exchange and gifting, *munus* and its cognate *donum* (gift), hint that community is constituted by certain types of exchanges and an openness to relation.[20]

---

[19] Eric L. Santner, *The Royal Remains: The People's Two Bodies and the Endgames of Sovereignty* (Chicago: University of Chicago Press, 2011), 29.

[20] Esposito here employs a philosophical-cum-philological method that has remained popular among post-Heideggerian approaches to genealogy. While it may appear to bibli-

What is gifted, claims Esposito, is the self, given to the community in a relinquishing of total enclosure, isolated independence, and exclusive right to property. *Communio* is characterized by a type of sharing, and what is shared is the "lack," the debt or obligation that each has imposed upon him- or herself through participation in the community.[21] For Esposito, Paul's invocation of a community created as a gift from God and through the death of Christ signals a critical loss of self that is recuperated in the communal subject. The Pauline notion of unity in the body of Christ thus takes up this Greco-Roman notion of gifting and radicalizes it through an idea of community created through divine giving. Dying with Christ signifies the loss that founds community, the necessary death to self that enables sharing of the mutual lack or debt in common.

It is precisely this loss, this openness to the other and lack of total self-enclosure, that the modern paradigm neutralizes though immunity. The Hobbesian sovereign founds an order based on the myth of contract, of reciprocal obligation among and between isolated individuals. It marks an attempt at community that eliminates the lack and absence that, in Esposito's view, makes *communitas* possible. It signals the loss of gift. Through the policing of borders and through the demarcation of radically isolated, buffered selves, modern immunity becomes a kind of autoimmunity, an undoing and attacking of community at its heart. Its attempt at protection mounts an offensive against the social body and, ultimately, against the bodies of which it is comprised.

While Esposito finds in Augustine certain precursors for the declension toward Hobbes, immunity and autoimmunity in his reading are a distinctly modern emergence. I want to suggest, however, that themes of immunity are present within the Pauline ideal of community that Esposito invokes. As Esposito would no doubt admit, scriptural discursive tradition is complex and ambivalent, and the idealized language of unity in Christ and a death to self operate alongside concerns about social purity and boundary maintenance that resonate with a paradigm of immunity. That such Pauline discourse is linked explicitly to bodies, both material, fleshly bodies and the figurative, social body, betrays further the dynamics that may be at work that prefigure the biopolitical. Esposito perceives this in inchoate form in an elision of the flesh in favor of the body in Paul's discourse.[22] As

---

cal scholars and linguists as flirting with an etymological fallacy, the intent is less to pin down an original or fixed meaning based on root forms, and more to suggest hints and traces of parallel meanings and deployments of terms in new contexts. This type of allusive word play highlights layers of meaning in a term as well as possible new uses, rather than delimiting what a word "means" in a given register, since both "sense" and "reference" appear continually on the move.

[21] Esposito, *Communitas*, 6.
[22] Esposito, *Bíos: Biopolitics and Philosophy*, 164–65.

we will see, it is not just a denial of the flesh but a policing of the body that is bequeathed to Western legacy. The remainder of this essay explores the discourse of the body and its links with concerns about contamination, tracing Paul's language and the legacy it may have conveyed to modernity. A complex and vivid imaginary is at work informing notions of corporeal boundaries and destinies in both Christian and later secular moments. Sketching some of these movements is essential for diagnosing the ways biopolitical management of social and individual bodies may have developed.

B. Ancient bodies and the body of Christ

Paul displays significant concern for bodies, both individual and corporate. In his correspondence with the Corinthians, he takes up and reworks a popular metaphor of the polis as a body politic, with interdependent members, and applies it famously to the church (1 Cor 12:12–27). This metaphor undertakes much work, appearing to call the Corinthians to a unity and common goal, while distinguishing diverse parts, noting their interdependence and equality of value. An apparent division of labor exists. The letter also engages a tension between "strong" and "weak" members of Christ's body, and makes repeated appeals to notions of purity, morality, and bodily integrity. Paul fluctuates between direct appeals that church members "honor God in [their] bod[ies]" (1 Cor 6:20) as well as maintain the honor, unity, and sanctity of the church itself as Christ's body. A resonance and discursive fluidity appear at work, as Paul moves back and forth between literal and metaphorical bodies.

Indeed, as Dale Martin persuasively demonstrates, Paul's letter to the Corinthians is all about bodies.[23] Furthermore, Paul's invocation of a social body, the community of the church, relies upon his understanding of material bodies. In this way, Martin's exploration reveals that Paul does not just speak figuratively about the church as a body, but conceives of it as an organic unity, such that members' material, bodily conduct has a direct impact upon the life and health of the whole. The body of Christ is a real body. The vision that Paul sets forth is one to which theologians, ecclesial leaders, and philosophers have turned over the centuries, making it one of the most influential texts on community in Western tradition. Dwelling here on Pauline tropes of embodiment and the perils and possibilities that attend to the bodily and fleshly life, both individual and social, is critical to grasping the legacy of biopolitics in the West.

---

[23] Dale B. Martin, *The Corinthian Body* (New Haven, Conn.: Yale University Press, 1995).

Martin retrieves a number of contextual factors from Greco-Roman cosmology and medicine that are at work in Paul's discussion of bodily conduct and the social body metaphor. Broadly speaking, ancient bodies are both hierarchically ordered and permeable, two major themes Martin develops in this work. In terms of hierarchy, bodies display governance by the head, mind, or soul, with other members playing indispensible supportive or executive roles. While the head is given a type of precedence, other members are deemed absolutely necessary to make this headship meaningful and even to sustain it. Such internal arrangement of the body reflects a larger cosmological whole, into which the body is placed. The body itself is part of a larger body of the world, for instance. And bodies, too, like the organs and members that comprise them, can be diversely and hierarchically arranged in the world. Greco-Roman ideology posited as natural a certain distribution of status and prestige among bodies and classes of bodies in the ancient world. Perhaps not unlike the Hindu caste system (whose own origin myths draw directly on a bodily metaphor), social ordering in the ancient Greco-Roman world reflected a cosmic arrangement. Just as various members of a body have differing levels of honor, even if all are essential, so various classes of people in a society might be attributed different levels of status and power in the functioning of the whole.

As Martin and other scholars note, Paul's reflections on the united body of Christ make use of a popular political metaphor, a possible adaptation of one of Aesop's fables about the belly and other members of the body.[24] In his *History of Rome* (2.32), Livy recounts a version told by Menenius Agrippa during a time of civil unrest. Agrippa equates the belly with the senate, which may be misrecognized and critiqued as idle by more active members, i.e., the limbs or laboring classes. Yet the belly, or the leadership of the senate, provides a crucial if at times imperceptible nourishment and sustenance to the body politic. The fable thus becomes a metaphor for the interdependence of various sites within the political body, invoking a necessary division of labor for the smooth functioning of the polis or empire. It also invokes as natural the hierarchical arrangement of parts, functioning to legitimate and sanction a particular arrangement of status and power.

With regard to permeability, Martin notes that bodies were not conceived of as completely self-enclosed wholes. The body's location within a cosmic network meant its interaction with that broader reality in various

---

[24] See, e.g., David George Hale, *The Body Politic: A Political Metaphor in Renaissance English Literature* (The Hague: Mouton, 1971), 18–32; Bruno Blumenfeld, *The Political Paul: Justice, Democracy and Kingship in a Hellenistic Framework* (JSNTSup 210; London: T&T Clark, 2003), 383–84; A. D. Harvey, *Body Politic: Political Metaphor and Political Violence* (Newcastle, U.K.: Cambridge Scholars Publishing, 2007), 4–22.

ways. Whether in personified and agential forces, or notions of power and energy transfer, the body could be penetrated and its boundaries crossed. The body was a microcosm of the wider world, and material forces moved both into and out from the individual body through its pores, channels (*poroi*), and orifices. Indeed,

> for most people of Greco-Roman culture the human body was of a piece with its environment. The self was a precarious, temporary state of affairs, constituted by forces surrounding and pervading the body, like the radio waves that bounce around and through the bodies of modern urbanites. In such a maelstrom of cosmological forces, the individualism of modern conceptions disappears, and the body is perceived as a location in a continuum of cosmic movement. The body or the "self" is an unstable point of transition, not a discrete, permanent, solid entity.[25]

Closely following on this understanding of the body is discourse on illness and disease. Martin identifies two dominant paradigms for conceiving of disease etiology: imbalance and invasion. Imbalance etiology, the dominant paradigm for illness among the upper classes and educated elites, was one of disequilibrium in bodily humors. Healing came through restoring harmony of hot and cold, wet and dry, and other continua inside the body. Such a perspective saw as superstitious an older as well as stubbornly persistent popular etiology of disease as invasion or pollution from without. Such contamination was often seen as demonic in origin, with magical prescriptions and talismanic objects and rituals designed to ward off such assaults.

Discourses like Menenius Agrippa's emphasizing social cohesion, harmony, and stability were known as *homonoia* speeches. As Martin and others recognize, Paul follows many *homonoia* speech rhetorical conventions in this letter, shaping it into his own type of appeal to social unity, in this case ecclesial.[26] In making his case, however, Paul, Martin claims, subverts elements related to the dominant ideologies of the body in his day. Taking the "strong" of Corinth as exemplifying a high status and elite worldview, Martin views Paul as challenging their assumptions about the hierarchical organization of the social body, as well as the respectable theory of bodily health that rejected ideas of invasion and pollution. Paul claims that status, class, and occupational hierarchies accepted as natural by the elite were upended within Christ's body.[27] The relation of the various members to

---

[25] Martin, *Corinthian Body*, 25.

[26] Martin, *Corinthian Body*, 38–39. Cf. Margaret Mary Mitchell, *Paul and the Rhetoric of Reconciliation: An Exegetical Investigation of the Language and Composition of 1 Corinthians* (HUT 28; Tübingen: Mohr, 1991), 65–66.

[27] Martin more fully explores the Pauline challenge to and inversion of many assumed hierarchies in Greco-Roman context in Dale B. Martin, *Slavery as Salvation: The Metaphor of Slavery in Pauline Christianity* (New Haven, Conn.: Yale University Press, 1990).

each other is reconfigured, and the entire body is subjected to Christ, who is conceived of as its head (cf. Eph 1:22, Col 1:18).

Paul also challenges the "strong's" view that bodily health and purity are maintained through balance and (presumably) through forms of hierarchy, rendering them less susceptible to pollution from without. Paul appears, on the contrary, to regard pollution via angelic or other agential penetration as a real threat to Christian bodies and to the Christian body.[28] Sexual immorality unites bodies with a fallen cosmos and its (albeit unmasked) principalities. Christian bodies engaging in such practices implicate Christ's body in the very same acts, something unthinkable for Paul (1 Cor 6:15–16). As Martin claims, each of the concerns Paul addresses – the man sleeping with his stepmother, Christians visiting prostitutes, eating food sacrificed to idols, and injustices at the Lord's Supper – all "are particular instances of what is essentially a single conflict regarding the boundaries of the body."[29] In policing the permeability of the body, Paul seeks to preserve its unique identity and underscore distinctions with the world. In doing this he accentuates or underscores the fluidity and instability of corporeal boundaries.[30]

One ideal mark of the political or ecclesial leader is as one who sees to it that the whole remains "healthy," that the body thrives. In the Pauline case, this united flourishing is tied directly to the health of individual bodies. Here we can descry the basic biopolitical template of authoritative concern for the whole, for all parts functioning well to the benefit of the whole, as well as the curious but potent intermeshing of injunctions addressing the literal, physical body and how it is cared for, on one hand, and the effects and implications of such bodily concern on the social body, on the other. This may relate to literal sickness and health and the concern over epidemics, as well as control over the attitudes and beliefs of the body, and hence ideological maintenance.[31] What one does in the flesh, in

---

[28] Paul exhibits far more concern about fallen angels and their interference in human affairs than he does about demons. The two were distinct species in the ancient world, and only later conflated in the Christian imaginary. On this see Dale B. Martin, "When did Angels become Demons?" *JBL* 129/4 (2010): 657–77.

[29] Martin, *Corinthian Body*, 163.

[30] Paul's discourse on purity and contamination is of course not only informed by pagan philosophy in the Greco-Roman world but by a long Judaic tradition of reflection on such themes, seen perhaps most poignantly in Levitical codes. It remains a matter of debate, however, to what extent the views espoused by Paul reveal a radical difference between Jewish and broader Hellenistic views on corporeality, illness, and pollution, or whether the traditions during his time in fact shared much more in common.

[31] It is striking that Pliny in his report to the emperor Trajan refers to the "spread" of Christianity as a "contagion" and efforts at persecution and suppression are given an epidemiological twist. The infected parts of the social body must be cut off – exterminated – or else somehow purified and healed. And just as the knife or fire might be used to re-

one's physical body, now quite plainly does matter for the body politic, and the eyes of power turn from a concern to maintain supremacy through the threat of death as the limit of life, to the concern to police and shape the quality and content of life – including bodily functions like sexuality, reproduction, health, labor, and leisure. These now matter as discrete sites of control, as elements to be managed. Centrally operative in such policing is what takes place at the boundaries of each body and the body politic, since permeability persists and hence the possibilities of penetration and contagion abound.

Thus, a number of issues related to the body (individual and social) are indexed and taken up in the Pauline trope of unity in Christ. Bodies are permeable, with boundaries constantly in contention and flux, able to be penetrated and polluted. This produces an instability of identity, with practices remaining critical for shoring up and demarcating where the body resides and what comprises it. Furthermore, what happens in physical bodies has direct consequences for the social body. The material health and practices of each body impacts the whole. There are no bounded selves. Here we see that what is done in the flesh matters for the larger, corporate body. Even as the flesh of Christ is lost to Christians after the ascension, it is retained in their bodies, so to speak, as their physical acts impact upon and reflect Christ's body on earth in the church. A certain continuity and discontinuity – materially and spiritually – are presumed between Christ's body, the bodies of Christians, and the church as the body of Christ.

John Milbank takes up this theme of how the body of the Christian, rooted in the *ecclesia*, persists as placeholder and embodiment of the reign of the risen Christ.[32] Milbank sees Paul as advocating a form of just dealings in community founded upon a trust (*pistis*) made possible by the sacrifice and resurrection of Christ as king. In fact, such justice requires the displacement and removal of Christ's body: "there can be justice for Paul only if we all act as surrogates for the king who is resurrected and yet also semiremoved and absent."[33] We can see here resonances with Esposito's claim of a lack or founding loss that instantiates community. Congruent as well is a notion of trust that enables "prestation" and "counterprestation," the giving of gifts that ground community in mutuality and reciprocity.[34]

---

move an infected limb or cauterize a wound, with pain being the passageway to health, torture is the means of ensuring the social body's survival. Their correspondence can be found in, e.g., Henry Scowcroft Bettenson and Chris Maunder, eds., *Documents of the Christian Church* (3d ed.; Oxford: Oxford University Press, 1999), 3–4.

[32] John Milbank, "Paul Against Biopolitics," in *Paul's New Moment: Continental Philosophy and the Future of Christian Theology* (ed. John Milbank, Slavoj Žižek, and Creston Davis; Grand Rapids: Brazos, 2010), 21–73.

[33] Milbank, "Paul Against Biopolitics," 62–63.

[34] Milbank, "Paul Against Biopolitics," 65.

Absent in Milbank's reflections, however, as they appear absent in Esposito, is consideration of how Pauline concerns for boundary policing actually evince a type of *dis*trust. Certainly, the internal communal ideal set forth is one of radical openness, such that boundaries separating members are removed. Concerns for immunity and protection from pollution are irrelevant within the body, so much so that we can discern an ideal of nakedness (literal and figurative) between members.[35] But posture toward the *cosmos* is decidedly different. There are no bodily exchanges with the world, for the body's boundaries are to be shored up and its orifices blocked. We might try to maintain a simple and rigid dichotomy between church and world and set forth internal trust and external distrust as an ideal to be pursued.[36] But, as the entire force and anxiety of Paul's letter to the Corinthians reveals, a watchful and concerned eye toward the world doubles back upon the bodies of the community itself. Policing the edges and surfaces of the social body becomes identical with enforcing the same tactics on individual bodies, for where do the boundaries of the body of Christ fall if not at the boundaries of actual (Christian) bodies? Here we see hints of the ironic trend in most modern attempts at social surveillance: vigilance toward the potential impurity of outsiders turns its watchful eye inward to analyze and excise incipient threats within. Anyone can become an agent of contamination and hence an enemy. If anything, radical trust and distrust operate side by side in this Pauline model, as defense against the world requires a micro-management of bodily practices. Put differently, the loss of self required for gift giving is met with a reestablishment of self that follows from the boundary definition needed to designate and maintain this very gifting community.

---

[35] This draws on the archetype of Edenic nakedness without shame. The boundaries of the self and individual body are here destabilized such that the mutual penetration of individual bodies within Christ's body becomes less of a concern. As Milbank claims, "Paul astonishingly suggests (1 Cor. 12:24–25) that our genitalia are *not* socially concealed because of shame but rather because, by christological kenotic reversal (that we only now fully understand in the light of the *euangelion*), we give greater honor (*timē*, which is also lordship, 'the prerogative of a king') to that which in itself possesses the least honor (and is most to be ruled over: the drastic implication is that in the purified, already-resurrected body, it is safe for the passionate genitals also to rule the head)." Milbank, "Paul Against Biopolitics," 63.

[36] Milbank evinces this type of simple idealization of church vs. world, Christianity vs. the secular. His essay's title here, its ambiguity notwithstanding, suggests this: either Milbank intends to use "Paul Against Biopolitics" or to claim that "Paul [is] Against Biopolitics." In the first case, he implies that a Pauline vision is a clear weapon against the biopolitical. In the latter, he risks the anachronism of suggesting that something like biopolitics was a live target of Paul's writings. In reality, the Pauline legacy is much more ambiguous and lent its own contributions to an eventual biopolitical paradigm.

Concerns of social "health" have long preoccupied political theory. Martin's study recalls "a long rhetorical tradition that portrayed the polis, the city-state, as a body, and strife, discord, or any civil disturbance as a disease that must be eradicated from it."[37] A thinker like Esposito is no doubt acquainted with this tradition. What is it, therefore, that marks the uniqueness of the modern moment and its immunity/autoimmunity paradigm? As intimated, part of the transmutation to the modern is the shift to and prioritization of the self-enclosed body, both individual and sociopolitical. Esposito sees radical individualism, as well as notions of contract and of the body as private property, as being central to the immunity paradigm and its march toward autoimmunity.[38] A focus on purity and boundary maintenance becomes ossified and self-referential. Significant as well is a transition out of a medieval moment in which the socio-political and ecclesial boundaries are blurred into a modern distinction of spheres. Paul's use of the social body metaphor drew an image of the polis into the ecclesia, even as he reconfigured its scope and application. Grasping the significance of the modern move out of such a conflation into an ostensibly secular demarcation of political and ecclesial bodies requires tracing its progression through the Middle Ages. A genealogical exploration of the centuries preceding modernity might draw out the conflation of bodies (individual and social, political and ecclesial), a conflation that helps amplify the already existing resonance between individual and corporate bodily maintenance in Pauline discourse.

C. From Christ's body to the king's two bodies

As Martin notes, Livy narrates a fable of the belly to defend and maintain the status quo, to enforce a particular pattern of socio-political hierarchy and stability. The somatic metaphor inscribes a division of labor and a hierarchy of status that was taken as natural and thus good. While Martin claims that Paul appropriates this metaphor and yet also subverts its hierarchical implications, the dynamic that interests me is the broader trajectory of appropriation and its legacy, both intentional and unintentional. Wheth-

---

[37] Martin, *Corinthian Body*, 38.
[38] This coincides with the erosion of the trust (*pistis*) that Milbank sees as central to reciprocal gift giving in the Christian community. See Milbank, "Paul Against Biopolitics," 48–58. Trust implies an openness of self to and for the other. The Hobbesian sovereign trades on and inculcates a lack of trust between now atomized bodies, facilitating the self-enclosure of modern immunity. Yet, as indicated, we must consider whether concerns for communal immunity in a Pauline context are seeds of distrust that germinate and later bloom in this modern shift.

er or not we can agree that Paul was intentionally subversive, we must pause to consider the implications of his usage of a popular political metaphor to describe the *ecclesia*, and also dwell on the effects of the legitimation this brings.

Following the trope of Christ's body takes us in many directions, but a dominant strand of this genealogy is the re-appropriation of the body trope for the political space under Christendom. This suggests that Pauline usage reinvigorates the metaphor, associating it with discourse on Christ and redemption, providing a sacral aura to concepts of social unity. Although we might want to resist this and to claim that a strong demarcation must be made between the church as Christ's body and society as such, the two concepts can certainly blend and have done so. Furthermore, even if conceptual distinction is maintained, associating a trope of the body politic with the body of the savior adds a "weight of glory" to such images of society, particularly when such a society has been influenced by the Christian imaginary. This is indeed the legacy of Western Christendom and its outgrowth in modern, secular society.

Peter Brown recounts how, in the immediate context of the early church and late antiquity, the theme of Christ's body resonated with broader cultural tropes of virginity as critical to a city's defense.[39] Sexual morality was linked to social stability, with the figure of the virgin grounding discourse about the city's boundary maintenance. Protecting bodily orifices somehow correlated to securing the walls of the city. The hymen and the rampart here coincide. Paul's own language of sexual purity resonates with such views, as his concerns about the individual bodies of members of the church at Corinth weave together with an exhortation about the successful function of the ecclesial body.[40]

Such concerns are retained as the church grows and develops a distinct institutional identity vis-à-vis the Roman Empire and in light of persecution.[41] Brown examines, for instance, Cyprian's attempts to shore up and protect what he saw as the church under threat from this broader order. For Cyprian "the body of the Christian emerged as a microcosm of the threat-

---

[39] Peter Brown, *The Body and Society: Men, Women, and Sexual Renunciation in Early Christianity* (Twentieth anniversary ed.; New York: Columbia University Press, 2008), 5–32.

[40] Such associations have not gone away. Invocations in popular, often religiously-inflected rhetoric today of sexual immorality eroding the fabric of the nation, for instance, appear to invoke this age-old association. See, e.g., Erin Runions, *The Babylon Complex: Theopolitical Fantasies of War, Sex, and Sovereignty* (New York: Fordham University Press, 2014).

[41] For exploration of the wider context of the Roman empire as an extension of the emperor's body see Clifford Ando, *Imperial Ideology and Provincial Loyalty in the Roman Empire* (Berkeley: University of California Press, 2000), 398–405.

ened state of the Church, which itself was a compact body, held in firm restraint by the unshakeable, God-given will of its head and guiding mind, the Bishop."[42] For Brown, Cyprian's chief concern is resisting the *saeculum*, interpreted as Roman rule and its pantheon. The body functions as one way to preserve the church in this context. "The great collective body of the Church had to exert constant discipline, lest it be disrupted by the 'blind, uncontrolled urges' of its own unruly members. Church and body alike were both presented in terms of ever-vigilant control, from which the relentless pressure of the *saeculum* gave no respite."[43] Brown notes that these views were influential on both Ambrose and Augustine. For Cyprian the bodily language of resistance is sometimes sexual, with the ideal of virginity set out as the site of resistance to the attacks on the ecclesial body. But more often, Brown notes, Cyprian's imagery invokes the threat of physical punishment and pain inflicted by the world against the body, seen most explicitly in martyrs. Martyrdom signifies in the destruction of the flesh the battle of the *saeculum* against the body of Christ. Concerns of bodily integrity, policing its boundaries and protecting its flesh from penetration and corruption, mark a practice of preserving the church as social body.

The body metaphor was carried forward along a number of trajectories. As noted, Paul's adaptation of the Greco-Roman trope had the effect of associating it with divine life and power through identification with the church. It is no surprise therefore that this trope made inroads back into political application. But this road was long and tortuous. Ernst Kantorowicz's magisterial study of medieval political theology traces, among many themes, the development of this idea in ecclesial and imperial spheres.[44] Through a wide-ranging analysis of a number of textual instances, Kantorowicz documents the variations of the notion of the body of Christ. He shows how, initially, the language of the body of Christ remained in association with the church, which was described as *corpus Christi*. There emerged a new term, *corpus mysticum*, used in discussions of the Eucharist. The host was referred to figuratively as Christ's mystical body in something of a contradistinction to the literal or material body of Christ in the church. Through a variety of factors, including debates about transubstantiation and a resultant literalization of the understanding of the Eucharist, we witness a reversal and transcription of terms. Eventually, the Eucharist was referred to as *corpus Christi* and *corpus verum*, while the church was described as *corpus mysticum*.

---

[42] Brown, *Body and Society*, 195.
[43] Brown, *Body and Society*, 195.
[44] Ernst Kantorowicz, *The King's Two Bodies: A Study in Medieval Political Theology* (Princeton: Princeton University Press, 1957).

The center and ground of the church was now the sacrament, while its group manifestation took on a figurative designation, the precise boundaries of which were resultantly obscured. This accorded well with an Augustinian tradition of speaking of society as a *corpus mixtum*, of the indecipherability of the city of God and city of man during the *saeculum*. Given the rise of Christian empire, literal designations of Christ's body as the church visible became more challenging, and the blurring of medieval church and society invited figurative or mystical ascriptions. Arguably, earlier Pauline concerns about boundary policing of the church as Christ's body, seen for instance in Cyprian, were sublated and displaced. Insider/outsider distinctions were perhaps more easily deployed by early Christian house churches, given their minority status in a pagan, Greco-Roman context. Such a binary became more of a conceptual challenge when Christianity emerged as the official religion of the land. Authentic membership became at once individually and internally marked – the orientation of one's love – and eschatologically defined – true membership to be revealed at the end of time (cf. Matt 13:24–30). Identification of the church as a literal, material, and organic body of Christ – part of the spectrum of individual Christian bodies – was sidelined.

Significant for our exploration is the way in which, according to Kantorowicz, language of a mystical body is taken up in wider political rhetoric in the Middle Ages. An intermediary step facilitating this is Thomas Aquinas' importation of Aristotelian political discourse in the sphere of ecclesiology. Thomas refers to the church as a mystical body in its own right, taking language of incorporation and socio-political organization and applying it spiritually to the church as a social grouping. This marks a departure from previous designations of the church as the mystical body *of Christ*, where ecclesial group identity remained derivative. Its anchoring in a particular transcendent concept muted (while not necessarily Thomas' intention), the church as an independently conceived mystical body becomes a site of theorization for other figurative unions or forms of social organization, the central one being the republic.[45]

It is thus in the high and late Middle Ages, as Kantorowicz documents, that notions of the *corpus ecclesiae mysticum* contribute to conceptualizations of the *corpus reipublicae mysticum*. Key agents in this process are jurists and other theorists in the employ of the king. The development is

---

[45] Kantorowicz, *The King's Two Bodies*, 200–205. Aquinas scholars may no doubt take issue with Kantorowicz's assessment here, a debate into which I have no intention of entering. It would be worthwhile to consider the degree to which Thomas' Aristotelian reconfigurations of theological tradition aided theology's profanation and resultant secularization. Certainly this would provide an interesting counterbalance to attacks on Scotus as the dark forefather of the secular.

motivated in part through struggles between imperial and papal authority (seen in the Investiture Controversy, for instance). Jurists seek to wrest some of the authority from the church in its self-constitution as a political body and apply it to developing notions of territorial sovereignty such as the republic and commonwealth. In this competitive relation, the emerging nation state takes up and reconfigures notions of church polity for broader society, a transfer already made conceivable by the blurring of ecclesial and social boundaries in the medieval era. Perhaps less obvious is that this transfer appears to reactivate the political lineage of the body metaphor itself. A political trope appropriated by Paul to describe the church thus returns to its field with novel theological and sacral legitimation.[46]

Now that the republic is described like the church as a body, parallels between king and Christ as respective heads can be strategically mobilized. Certainly such theopolitical analogies are in no way new here, and a long history of a Christocentrally-grounded divine right of kingship can be traced. What is novel at this juncture are the particular networks of meaning surrounding political, ecclesial, and cosmic headship and figurative/literal constitutions of a body politic. Just as, Paul tells us, the body of Christ takes Christ as its head, and must grow up into fullness and unity under his lordship, so the republic enjoys the king as its head. And just as a type of duality exists between Christ's earthly, embodied presence and his spiritual, enduring omnipresence as the Son of God, so a duality emerges in construals of the king's presence and relation to the state. The king as body, as literal flesh, stands in as head and representative of the people. Yet, the people persist as his figurative, mystical body. Just as the church enjoys a unity under the penumbra of Christ's authority, so the commonwealth finds a source of union in the king.

This notion of the king's two bodies becomes particularly evident and useful in moments of transition, in states of exception where sovereignty might be called into question. In particular, the king's death presented a conundrum for theorists wanting to postulate continuity of the republic. With just a literal, fleshly body as site of authority and political integration, the fragile unity risked dissolution at the passing of the king. Given the mystical body of the king, however, continuity and stability might be ensured. The paradoxical acclamation, "The king is dead; long live the king," gestures toward this tension: the king's fleshly passing is met with a

---

[46] This is not at all to say that the political sphere to which the now theologized trope returned was identitical with the ancient political sphere whence it came. It should also be noted that the church was not the only source of the idea of the body politic for medieval political theorists. Ancient Greek and Greco-Roman political uses of the body metaphor shaped medieval theorization as well. See, e.g., Hale, *The Body Politic*; Harvey, *Body Politic*.

continuity of the socio-political body, as the mystical body of the king. The duality provides for the stability of the republic. Anxieties about the permeability and instability of political identity as its head vanishes are quelled through invocations of a mystical body that persists.[47]

This legacy reveals an ongoing slippage between the different bodies that constitute political and religious orders, as well as between figures and representatives of each. The bishop or pope as vicar of Christ emerges as head of the church, a position that continually struggles with that of the emperor as head of the political body. The boundaries of each are continually observed and policed, even as they merge and overlap throughout the medieval period. While the organic or material emphasis on the ecclesial body of Christ is displaced by a mystical unity, which is then relocated to the republic, concerns about fleshly bodies and materiality are retained in anxieties over the king and dynastic transition. What this period suggests is a significant transferal into the political sphere of biblical and theological motifs concerned with preserving the purity and sanctity of the body of Christ. Again, the body metaphor is not new to the political sphere, nor is concern about the life and destiny of the ruler. But these notions become imbued with new layers of significance, interpreted in light of the ecclesial legacy that came to shape medieval society and polity.

D. The church and the machine

As Eric Santner claims, central to the transition to modernity is the loss of the actual, fleshly king's body and a consequent search for grounding among the bodies of the people. The quest for the "royal remains," as it were, marks the anxiety of modern, liberal regimes in seeking legitimation. Now that the king's head has been cut off, with monarchical sovereignty dissipated and replaced by popular sovereignty, modern statecraft reveals itself to be obsessed with the vanished body and flesh of authority. The loss of the king's flesh means the distribution of the "flesh" on all members of the body. This is partly why biopolitics erupts in significance, as tactics of control and identification make bodies and flesh sites of policing and observation. The state must always have bodies in view, as demo-

---

[47] Agamben explores the ways this medieval tradition invokes earlier Roman imperial funerary practices. An effigy was created to triangulate between the death of the emperor's body and the ongoing life of the empire, signifying an excess of sovereignty revealed in such exceptional moments. See Agamben, *Homo Sacer*, 91–103. Cf. Florence Dupont, "The Emperor-God's Other Body," in *Fragments for a History of the Human Body, Part 3* (ed. Michael Feher, Ramona Nadoff, and Nadia Tazi; New York: Zone Books, 1989), 396–419.

graphic definitions become central to determining the boundaries of and justifications for the nation. In trying to pin down, stabilize, regulate, and codify the flesh (reproductive rights, racial classifications, census and taxation systems, sexual identity and family values regulations, prison industrial complexes, etc.), the modern nation-state evinces an ongoing search for identity and justification. In losing the king's body as ground, it tries to seek it among the people's bodies.

Santner's study merges with elements of Esposito's, for the loss of the king's body coincides with the rigid demarcation of bodily boundaries that Esposito sees in Hobbes. The self-enclosure and fixity of identity that try to render bodies immune to one another and so become a form of destructive, communal autoimmunity are of a piece with the Hobbesian state as fleshless automaton. Indeed, it is striking that in setting out to define and defend Leviathan, Hobbes begins with the mechanical body. Nature, as a fixed pattern of divine governance, is imitated in human statecraft to forge government as "an artificial man...in which sovereignty is an artificial soul."[48] The transition to the mechanical body and the distribution of the flesh among the people work in tandem. When the flesh of the king is stripped away, a skeleton remains, and it becomes the basic framework for a Hobbesian mechanized automaton: "For what is the *heart*, but a *spring*; and the *nerves*, but so many *strings*; and the *joints*, but so many *wheels*; giving motion to the whole body, as was intended by the artificer?"[49] Freed from theological and theopolitical sanction, and in the face of the king's absence, state power now persists as pure state, as bare, fleshless structure. In regularized, repetitive, unseeing motion, with deathlike vacuity, Leviathan functions as pure sovereignty, grounded in nothing beyond its lack of ground and the veneer of legitimation found in the mythical need for flesh to protect itself from other flesh, bodies from neighbor's bodies. The modern state thus lives off the flesh and bodies of the people, in the name of representing them.

While Santner reflects briefly on Pauline tropes and early ecclesial vision, he does not consider the ways the modern anxieties about the royal remains may have been prefigured in Christian tradition.[50] I claimed above that concerns about immunity and boundary policing are present in early Christian tradition in a way left unaddressed by Esposito, and are not simply modern developments. Likewise, we can discern anxieties over the lost body of the king from the beginnings of Christianity. The empty tomb, limited post-resurrection sightings, and eventual ascension all index this

---

[48] Thomas Hobbes, *Leviathan: With Selected Variants from the Latin Edition of 1668* (ed. E. M. Curley; Indianapolis: Hackett, 1994), 3.
[49] Hobbes, *Leviathan*, 3, emphasis original.
[50] Santner, *Royal Remains*, 29–30.

loss. All speak to the reality that the ruler whose "kingdom is not of this world" has vanished. Arthurian and Tolkienian legends of the "return of the king," for instance, while politically inflected, arguably invoke this more perennial longing within Christian tradition. Christianity is marked by perpetual concerns over the body and the flesh – not just the Christian body and what is done in the flesh, nor the identity and protection of the church as Christ's body, but the foundational loss of Christ's earthly body and the legacy that this bequeaths. Paul's struggle to ensure that the Corinthian church conduct itself rightly as bodies and as a body is grounded in a concern to orient it rightly to the resurrected body of its Lord (1 Cor 15:12–58). The loss of Christ's fleshly body initiates a tradition of thinking about how to preserve and maintain the body of Christ, often at the cost of suppressing the flesh. It is this legacy and submerged anxieties that have mingled and melded with political logics of authority and control, rendering post-Christian realities peculiar ones, where we can not speak of a simplistic return to pre-ecclesial society.

The construction of the secular sphere – in connection with the break-up of ecclesial authority and the emergence new Christian traditions – is therefore tied to matters of the body. Not only are ecclesial boundaries redefined vis-à-vis the authority of the pontiff as contested head of Christ's body, but church identity is soon established in relation to the bodies of princes who arise to champion certain communities and persecute others. Church life is shaped according to new configurations called nation-states and ecclesial boundaries suddenly align with the borders of political territories. Furthermore, debates about the nature of the Eucharist and consequently about the location of Christ's flesh are central in this period of transition. This suggests that matters of the flesh and body of Christ index this socio-political and ecclesial transformation. Reconceiving the nature of Christ's flesh figured centrally in this moment when the king's own flesh was being excised from or distributed among the political body, when a fleshless automaton was under construction, and when the limits of ecclesial bodies were being redefined. Attuning ourselves to this longstanding logic of bodily integrity in Christian tradition should enable a better analysis and grasp of the sociopolitical transitions associated with the birth of the modern.

Furthermore, the church in the secular sphere now partakes of the boundedness that marks the modern moment. For if, following Esposito, the modern paradigm is one of fixed self-enclosures and resistance to penetration from others, then embracing the freedoms that the secular sphere affords to the church through a rigid demarcation of spheres provides at least tacit support to the immunity paradigm. Early Pauline ecclesial thinking resonates in peculiar ways with modern, secular immunity and autoimmunity. How might the church, in passing along a theological matrix to be employed by the state in its new self-definition, have also conveyed ecclesial concerns about preserving and policing the body and bodies? In what ways is modern autoimmunity, with its attack upon communities and fleshly bodies, one of the many lives of the body that has developed in part through confluence and interaction with this biblical, theological, and ecclesial legacy?

Issues of body and boundary maintenance in the church with regard to the political community remain central sites for reflection and innovation. The lines have never been clearly defined, and Paul's usage of a political trope to designate Christ's body complicates matters. It is not simply, as some might suggest, that Paul's deployment of the political metaphor of the body, with Christ depicted as its head, displaces Caesar or establishes a competitive *ecclesia* as polis.[51] The process involves co-optation, incorporation, and transformation of a political concept, deployed within a new register and field. The body of Christ does not and never has displaced or usurped the body politic, even in medieval Christendom. The emergence of the secular sphere, which, I suggest, should not be viewed as a return to a pre-Christian pagan body, but as a construction of a post- or, perhaps better, hyper-Christian mechanical body, poses novel conceptual challenges for church-society relations.

What might it mean to embrace the permeability of the church rather than seek to police its boundaries, acknowledging with Paul and the ancients that the body is indeed porous, but choosing instead to allow its penetration? This would be to accept the body as part of a larger whole, in its cosmological placement, just as the church is part of society and cannot be disassociated from it. While this might be seen as in tension with Paul's anxious concern to protect the Christian body (both individual and corporate) from unsanctioned penetration, certainly there are other strands in the Christian imaginary that might provide a vision for this. Christologically, what does it mean for the church as the body of Christ that Christ himself actively yielded to the penetration of thorns, nails, and, albeit more passively, a spear to his side?[52] His body was handed over, and the Eucharistic

---

[51] I refer here obliquely to the "Paul against empire" conversation, which raises many important theopolitical and historical-contextual considerations, but too often trades in simplistic binaries or appears overly optimistic about the subversive vision of the early church. For a trenchant problematization, see, in this volume, Michael J. Thate, "Paul and the Anxieties of (Imperial?) Succession: Galatians and the Politics of Neglect."

[52] Let us not forget that such evidence of penetration and openness functioned to confirm Christ's identity.Indeed, Thomas, for instance, was invited not simply to recollect but to reenact such penetration (John 20:25–27). It might follow that the marks of openness and permeability are epistemologically and missiologically critical to the Christological identity of the church. For one theological exploration of themes of Christologi-

rite at the heart of ecclesial identity celebrates a body that was "given up and broken." In other words, to the tropes of boundary preservation bequeathed by the Pauline legacy one might counterpose themes of ecclesial openness, acknowledging the fragility of the body but responding nondefensively.[53] In the least this would disrupt rather than support the centrality of boundary maintenance and self-enclosure that define the modern moment.[54]

Union with Christ and *embodying* the united *body* of Christ remain critical sites of reflection and interrogation for Christian communities as well as for biblical scholars and theologians. They should also function as points of investigation for broader social and political theory to seek insight into the influences on social formations at various historical junctures. As the essays in this volume display in their remarkable diversity, union and participation "in Christ" are multifaceted concepts, and their ambiguity and polyvalence have resulted in various lines of interpretation and practice. Unity in Christ is a totalizing concept. Its effects are far reaching for its claims are all encompassing. This is what makes it so compelling a vision for many Christians, and what makes it so potentially nefarious for many others, Christian or not. Attempts at such unity are instantiated in the world, however beautifully or brutally and always imperfectly. In either case the discourse of authenticity often dictates responses, whether to hail "true" manifestations of a united body or to distance and declaim "false" attempts as heterodox or secular stillbirths. My intuition is that this line can never be clearly drawn, and that the church needs to claim the many lives of the body as part of its heritage and legacy, for better or for worse. For discourse on the permeability of the body suggests that the

---

cal, corporeal vulnerability, see Graham Ward, *Christ and Culture* (Oxford: Blackwell, 2005).

[53] Arguably, what was so groundbreaking about Vatican II was the church's move in the face of modernity to embrace a certain permeability and a blurring of the boundaries between itself and the world (even as ecclesial identity was championed). Anonymous Christianity marks one controversial flashpoint where *extra ecclesiam nulla salus* was reinterpreted to include certain outsiders. The body's boundaries were made strange.

[54] An example polar opposite to the Vatican II embrace of permeability might be the Dutch Reformed Church's allowance of racially segregated congregations in South Africa. The decision was based on an appeal – using the text of 1 Corinthians – for consideration to be given to "weaker" white Christians who were troubled by the presence of blacks in their congregation. Here we see a remarkable alignment of Pauline ideals of boundary maintenance and protection, as well as unity-in-diversity, with modern racism. The overall unity of the body of Christ was to be maintained through the allowance of this internal, racialized division. The ecclesial decision would of course resonate deeply with and help enforce political decisions under apartheid. See the discussion in J. Todd Billings, *Union with Christ: Reframing Theology and Ministry for the Church* (Grand Rapids: Baker Academic, 2011), 97–100.

body of Christ's history is larger and wider than it might think, since the edges of the body are rendered ambiguous. Such discourse also suggests that closing the body off completely leads to its death, a death in auto-referential isolation, without gift or exchange, detached from the world. This amounts to a denial of the body. To embrace bodily identity, then, is to embrace permeability, which constitutes a kind of vulnerability. This, too, might lead to death, but a death in the manner of the one whose body the church claims to be. Following its own logic, such a death would then be the church's life.

Bibliography

Agamben, Giorgio. *Homo Sacer: Sovereign Power and Bare Life*. Translated by Daniel Heller-Roazen. Stanford: Stanford University Press, 1998.

———. *State of Exception*. Translated by Kevin Attell. Chicago: University of Chicago Press, 2005.

Ando, Clifford. *Imperial Ideology and Provincial Loyalty in the Roman Empire*. Berkeley: University of California Press, 2000.

Badiou, Alain. *Saint Paul: The Foundation of Universalism*. Stanford: Stanford University Press, 2003).

Bettenson, Henry Scowcroft, and Chris Maunder, eds. *Documents of the Christian Church*. 3rd ed. Oxford: Oxford University Press, 1999.

Billings, J. Todd. *Union with Christ: Reframing Theology and Ministry for the Church*. Grand Rapids: Baker Academic, 2011.

Blanton, Ward, and Hent de Vries, eds. *Paul and the Philosophers*. New York: Fordham University Press, 2013.

Blumenfeld, Bruno. *The Political Paul: Justice, Democracy and Kingship in a Hellenistic Framework*. Journal for the Study of the New Testament: Supplement Series 210. London: T&T Clark, 2003.

Brown, Peter. *The Body and Society: Men, Women, and Sexual Renunciation in Early Christianity*. Twentieth anniversary ed. New York: Columbia University Press, 2008.

Burchell, Graham, Colin Gordon, and Peter Miller, eds. *The Foucault Effect: Studies in Governmentality*. Chicago: University of Chicago Press, 1991.

Derrida, Jacques. "De Tours de Babel." *Semeia* 54 (1991): 3–34.

Dupont, Florence. "The Emperor-God's Other Body." Pages 396–419 in *Fragments for a History of the Human Body, Part 3*. Edited by Michael Feher, Ramona Nadoff, and Nadia Tazi. New York: Zone Books, 1989.

Esposito, Roberto. *Bíos: Biopolitics and Philosophy*. Translated by Timothy Campbell. Minneapolis: University of Minnesota Press, 2008.

———. *Communitas: The Origin and Destiny of Community*. Translated by Timothy Campbell. Stanford: Stanford University Press, 2010.

———. *Immunitas: The Protection and Negation of Life*. Translated by Zakiya Hanafi. Cambridge: Polity, 2011.

Foucault, Michel. *Security, Territory, Population: Lectures at the Collège de France, 1977–1978*. New York: Palgrave Macmillan, 2007.

———. *Society Must be Defended: Lectures at the Collège de France, 1975–76*. New York: Picador, 2003.

———. *The History of Sexuality. Vol. 1: An Introduction*. Translated by Robert Hurley; New York: Pantheon, 1978.

Fowl, Stephen. "Scripture and the Divided Church." Pages 217–33 in *Horizons in Hermeneutics*. Edited by Stanley E. Porter and Matthew R. Malcolm. Grand Rapids: Eerdmans, 2013.

Hale, David George. *The Body Politic: A Political Metaphor in Renaissance English Literature*. The Hague: Mouton, 1971.

Harink, Douglas, ed. *Paul, Philosophy, and the Theopolitical Vision: Critical Engagements with Agamben, Badiou, Žižek and Others*. Eugene, Ore.: Cascade, 2010.

Harvey, A. D. *Body Politic: Political Metaphor and Political Violence*. Newcastle, U.K.: Cambridge Scholars Publishing, 2007.

Hobbes, Thomas. *Leviathan: With Selected Variants from the Latin Edition of 1668*. Edited by E. M. Curley. Indianapolis: Hackett, 1994.

Kantorowicz, Ernst. *The King's Two Bodies: A Study in Medieval Political Theology*. Princeton: Princeton University Press, 1957.

Martin, Dale B. *Slavery as Salvation: The Metaphor of Slavery in Pauline Christianity*. New Haven, Conn.: Yale University Press, 1990.

———. *The Corinthian Body*. New Haven, Conn.: Yale University Press, 1995.

———. "When did Angels become Demons?" *Journal of Biblical Literature* 129/4 (2010): 657–77.

McFague, Sallie. *The Body of God: An Ecological Theology*. Minneapolis: Fortress, 1993.

Milbank, John. "Paul Against Biopolitics." Pages 21–73 in *Paul's New Moment: Continental Philosophy and the Future of Christian Theology*. Edited by John Milbank, Slavoj Žižek, and Creston Davis. Grand Rapids: Brazos, 2010.

Mitchell, Margaret Mary. *Paul and the Rhetoric of Reconciliation: An Exegetical Investigation of the Language and Composition of 1 Corinthians*. Hermeneutische Untersuchungen zur Theologie 28. Tübingen: Mohr, 1991.

Moltmann, Jürgen. *Theology of Hope: On the Ground and the Implications of a Christian Eschatology*. Translated by James W. Leitch. London: SCM Press, 1967.

Ojakangas, Mika. "Impossible Dialogue on Bio-power: Agamben and Foucault." *Foucault Studies* 2 (May 2005): 5–28.

Peppard, Michael. *The Son of God in the Roman World: Divine Sonship in its Social and Political Context*. New York: Oxford University Press, 2011.

Runions, Erin. *The Babylon Complex: Theopolitical Fantasies of War, Sex, and Sovereignty*. New York: Fordham University Press, 2014.

Santner, Eric L.. *The Royal Remains: The People's Two Bodies and the Endgames of Sovereignty*. Chicago: University of Chicago Press, 2011.

Stendahl, Krister. "The Apostle Paul and the Introspective Conscience of the West." *Harvard Theological Review* 56/3 (1963): 199–215.

Tanner, Kathryn. *Theories of Culture: A New Agenda for Theology*. Minneapolis: Fortress, 1997.

Taylor, Charles. *A Secular Age*. Cambridge, Mass.: Belknap Press of Harvard University Press, 2007.

———. *Sources of the Self: The Making of the Modern Identity*. Cambridge: Harvard University Press, 1989.

Ward, Graham. *Christ and Culture*. Oxford: Blackwell, 2005.

List of Contributors

MARY PATTON BAKER
PhD in Theology
Trinity Evangelical Divinity School

T. ROBERT BAYLOR
PhD Candidate in Theology
University of St. Andrews

BEN C. BLACKWELL
Assistant Professor of Christianity
Houston Baptist University

CONSTANTINE R. CAMPBELL
Professor of New Testament
Trinity Evangelical Divinity School

DOUGLAS A. CAMPBELL
Professor of New Testament
Duke Divinity School

JULIE CANLIS
PhD in Theology
University of Aberdeen

STEPHEN CHESTER
Academic Dean and Professor of New Testament
North Park University

MATTHEW CROASMUN
Director of Research and Publications
Yale Center for Faith and Culture, Yale University

SUSAN EASTMAN
Associate Research Professor of New Testament
Duke Divinity School

MICHAEL J. GORMAN
Raymond E. Brown Professor of Biblical Studies and Theology
St Mary's Seminary & University

JOSHUA W. JIPP
Assistant Professor of New Testament
Trinity Evangelical Divinity School

KEITH L. JOHNSON
Associate Professor of Theology
Wheaton College

GRANT MACASKILL
Senior Lecturer in New Testament
University of St. Andrews

ISAAC AUGUSTINE MORALES, O.P.
Student Brother
Dominican House of Studies

DARREN SARISKY
Tutor in Doctrine and Ministry
Wycliffe Hall, University of Oxford

DEVIN P. SINGH
Mellon Fellow in the Integrated Humanities and
    Lecturer in Religious Studies
Yale University

MICHAEL J. THATE
Alexander von Humboldt Fellow at the Institute for Ancient Judaism
    and Hellenistic Religion
University of Tübingen

KEVIN J. VANHOOZER
Research Professor of Systematic Theology
Trinity Evangelical Divinity School

ASHISH VARMA
PhD Candidate in Theology
Wheaton College

Index of References

Old Testament

Genesis
1:26–28   344, 348
1:26   341
2:16–17   440
2:23   416
2:24   80, 83
15:5–6   231
15:6–7   233
15:6   381
17:5   46, 231
26:3   231
26:4   17
49:8–12   260

Exodus
4:22–23   230
4:22   406
12–14   94
24:3–11   517
24:8   524
29:45–46   112

Leviticus
1:2   517
3:1   517
11:44–45   481
26:12   73

Numbers
24:17–19   260

Deuteronomy
1:31–32   231
8:5   231
14:2   17
26:5   94
32:18   231

Joshua
24:2   231

1 Samuel
10:6–11   265
11:6–7   265
16:1–13   265
16:13   255, 265
22:20   266

2 Samuel
7:12–14   255, 260, 266
7:14–16   15
7:14   231, 265
7:18   266
22   269
22:44   269
22:51   269

1 Chronicles
17:13–14   265
17:13   231
22:10   231
28:6   231

Psalms
2   261 f., 267
2:1–3   258
2:2–3   259, 262
2:2   258, 265
2:6–9   255
2:6–8   259, 266
2:7   231, 260, 265 f.
2:8–9   260
2:9–10   260
2:11   260
8:7   262
18:4–6   259
18:20–21   259
18:43–48   259
18:51   258
20:8   258
22:20–25   260
22:26   260

22:27–31	260	112	203
23:1	270	112:9	200, 203
45:5	258	115:10	53
46:3–6	259	118:22	20
48:4–8	259	132:11	258
49:12	270	132:17	258
51:6	388	144:11–14	260
68	254		
68:19	274	*Isaiah*	
69:9–10	258	1:2	231
69:9	50	6:1–3	270
72:1–4	260	9:5–6	254, 273
72:3	260	11:1–2	255
72:5–6	260	28:16	20
72:7	260	41:8	17
72:8	260	43:6–7	231
72:9	258	51:2	231
72:12–14	260	52:7	254, 273
72:15	260	53	16
72:16	260	59:17	254, 273
72:17	260	61:1–3	255
82	348	63:16	230
82:6–7	338		
88:4	265	*Jeremiah*	
88:12	270	7:23	28
88:20	265	23:24	270
89:3	258	31:9	230, 406
89:20	258	31:33	461
89:20–37	255	32:38	73
89:21–22	265		
89:23	260	*Ezekiel*	
89:24	260	37:27	73
89:27–27	265		
89:25	260	*Daniel*	
89:26–28	255	7:14	260
8:26–27	260	7:27	262
89:27–28	265		
89:35	258	*Hosea*	
89:39	258	11:1	231
101:5–8	260		
110	259, 261, 263	*Habakkuk*	
110:1–4	255	2:4	40
110:1	261 f.		
110:2–3	262	*Zechariah*	
110:2	260	9:10	260
111	203		

Pseudepigrapha

Psalms of Solomon
17:22	255	17:37	255
17:32	255	18:5–7	255

New Testament

Matthew
4:1–4	488
13:24–30	548
16:13–17	497
16:21–23	497
17:1–13	497
18:20	29

Mark
6:30–44	497
10:26–27	47

Luke
9	498
9:1–6	497
22:20	517

John
1:14	17
16:7	418
17:21	412

Acts
10:42	267
11:26	37
17:31	267
22:16	165

Romans
1:4	266
1:7	302
1:8	302
1:17	40
1:20	150
1:28	120, 144, 146
2:29	116
3:21–31	287
3:21–26	520
3:22	53
3:23	191
3:26	53
3:30	38
4:15	370
4:16–22	46 f., 55
4:18	46
4:19	46 f.
4:20	46
4:21	47
4:23–24	47
4:24	38
5–8	95
5–6	109
5	96, 337
5:1–11	199
5:2	190, 466
5:3–5	118, 123
5:4–5	344, 346
5:5	117 f., 370
5:8	118, 199
5:9–11	521
5:12–21	287
5:12–20	440
5:12–14	47
5:14–15	199
5:21	146
6	98, 111, 164 f., 167, 171, 192
6:1–11	51, 160 f.
6:1–2	51
6:3–4	160, 166
6:3	19, 161
6:4–5	19
6:4	160–162, 336
6:5–14	463
6:5–11	111
6:5–10	161
6:5–7	163 f.
6:5	160–162, 485

6:6	108, 145, 150, 160, 161 f., 164, 172, 174, 347	8:4–8	119
		8:4–5	119
		8:4	108, 119
6:7	163, 166	8:5–8	112
6:8–10	163 f.	8:5	120
6:8	51	8:6	120
6:10	161	8:7–8	149
6:11	3, 52, 111, 160 f., 414, 455	8:7	367
		8:9–11	109–112
6:12	145 f., 485	8:9	111 f.
6:13	146, 192	8:10	111, 493
6:14–15	52	8:11	18, 111, 346
6:14	146	8:13	111, 116, 368
6:16	192	8:14–30	345
6:17	3, 4	8:14–23	339
6:19	192	8:14–17	113, 116
6:20–23	345	8:14	115, 116, 368
6:22–23	176	8:15–17	97, 117
6:22	164, 344, 352	8:15–16	105
7	108	8:15	21, 96–98, 118, 341
7:1–4	20, 74	8:16–17	114 f.
7:1–3	74	8:16	113 f.
7:4	74	8:17–21	190
7:6	336	8:17	17, 114–116, 123, 176, 190, 461, 511
7:7–25	47, 109		
7:7–24	109	8:19–23	137, 150
7:7–20	108	8:21–23	352
7:7–18	147	8:21	342
7:7	370	8:22	121
7:8	147	8:23–25	121
7:15	147	8:23	346, 369
7:17	109, 112, 149	8:24–25	47
7:20	109, 112, 149	8:26–30	113
7:21–23	149	8:26–29	114, 116
7:23	149	8:26–27	114
7:24	106, 108	8:26	111, 121
7:25	149, 150, 379	8:28–29	16, 115
8	11, 91, 95 f., 105, 112, 121, 341, 346, 352, 365	8:28	115, 118
		8:29–30	10, 58, 115, 351
8:1–30	119	8:29	115, 117, 190 f., 267, 464
8:1–29	121		
8:1–4	106 f., 109, 123	8:30	123
8:1–2	149	8:31–39	107
8:1	97	8:32–29	199
8:2–3	116	8:33–34	109
8:2	108	8:34	38, 111
8:3–4	520	8:35–39	118
8:3	108, 112	8:39	109
8:2–9	116	9:4–5	117
8:4–11	119	9:4	99

9:11–13	368	1:17	164
9:17	368	1:18–2:16	241
10:9–10	37, 38	1:18–25	381, 511
11:17	508	1:18	141
12–15	39, 44, 48, 52	1:24	141, 455
12	42, 137, 141, 192	1:28	261
12:1–2	120, 141, 189, 192, 470	1:30	195, 198, 459, 508
12:1	42, 521	2:2	511
12:2	42, 46, 144, 150	2:7	114, 267, 456
12:3	39, 42–44, 120, 123	2:11–12	114
12:4	42	2:12	170
12:3–8	42	2:16	141, 193, 469
12:4–5	20	3:3	509
12:5	305	3:5	170
12:6	39, 43	3:9	74
12:9	118, 124	3:10	72
12:10–13	118	3:16–17	72 f., 83
13:8–10	118, 124	4:9	347
13:12–14	75	4:11–13	192
13:12	118	4:16	316
13:14	195	5	341
14	40, 42	5:7	95
14:1–23	41 f.	6	165–169, 174
14:1	39, 50	6:1–11	200, 203
14:2	39	6:9–20	166
14:22	39 f.	6:9–11	166
14:23	39–41	6:9–10	167
15	49	6:9	165 f.
15:1–2	50	6:10	165
15:3	50	6:11–12	166
15:4	50	6:11	164–168, 203
15:5	50	6:12–20	167
15:6	41, 50	6:13–18	168, 176
15:7	41	6:13–14	167
15:9–12	50	6:15–17	20, 83
15:13	39, 41 f., 46	6:15–16	77, 82, 542
15:26	513	6:15	77, 167 f., 171
16:19	302	6:17	168, 427, 429
		6:19–20	72, 83
1 Corinthians		6:19	167
1–2	140	6:20	539
1	509	7	152
1:1–3	506	7:10–11	152
1:2	38, 193	7:29–31	152
1:4	414	8	503, 514
1:7	203	8:6	38, 58
1:8–13	512	9:10	203
1:9	94, 457, 507	9:23	512
1:13–17	169	10	91, 167, 169, 170, 503
1:13	164, 165	10:1–13	169

Reference	Page(s)
10:1–3	515
10:1	92
10:2	164
10:4	92, 99
10:6	93
10:7	516
10:8	99
10:9	93
10:11	154
10:12	169
10:14–22	503
10:15–17	515
10:16–22	91
10:16–17	69, 77, 93, 516, 519
10:16	78, 94, 503, 522
10:17	78, 522
10:18	516
10:20–21	520
10:20	77, 94, 503
10:21	78, 94
10:25	520
10:26–31	347
11	91, 521
11:1	316, 345, 347
11:7–34	521
11:17–34	91, 503
11:17–31	503
11:19	522
11:20	522
11:23–24	524
11:26	524
11:28	524
11:29	78, 522
11:34	523
12–14	137
12	20, 169, 170
12:4–5	69
12:4	203
12:7	171
12:9	203
12:12–27	69, 82, 539
12:12	69, 82, 167, 472
12:13–26	69, 82
12:13	52, 164 f., 167–171, 176, 523
12:25	176
12:26	168, 171, 175
12:27	69, 82, 305
12:28–31	203
13:7	347
13:13	347
14	141
14:26–31	141
15	341
15:3	38
15:12–28	553
15:12	38
15:20	18
15:21–22	440
15:22	17
15:24–25	261
15:29	164, 169
15:42–44	191
15:44	18
15:49	84, 351
15:50	167, 340
15:51–54	84, 191
15:51	191
15:53–54	75
15:53	338

2 Corinthians

Reference	Page(s)
1:5	317
1:7	512
2	192
2:4	192
2:16	192
3:6–18	351
3:8–9	204
3:16	189
3:18	182, 186–188, 191 f., 197 f., 205 f.
4:4–6	351
4:4	190
4:5–12	191
4:8–12	512
4:8–9	192
4:10–11	191
4:10	30, 191, 460
4:13	53
4:14	53, 191
4:16–5:11	191
5	47
5:4	338
5:7	47
5:14–21	199
5:15	196
5:16	108, 464
5:17	11, 108, 137, 458
5:18–19	460

5:18	108, 204	2:26	21
5:21	108, 182 f., 185–187, 192 f., 195–199, 201, 203–206, 463	3:1	173
		3:2–5	105
		3:2–3	233
6:3	204	3:3	76
6:10	203, 205	3:6	380–382
6:16	73, 79	3:7	232
6:19	79	3:9	232
8–9	200, 201	3:11	40
8:4	203, 204, 512	3:13–14	173
8:7–9	201	3:13	384
8:9	182 f., 185–188, 197, 201–206	3:14	233
		3:16	233, 436
8:19–20	204	3:18	234
9:1	204	3:19	233
9:6–11	203	3:21–4:7	233
9:8–10	205	3:21	233
9:9–10	201	3:24–26	233
9:9	200 f., 203	3:26–29	165, 173
9:12	204	3:26–28	52
9:13	203 f.	3:26–27	75, 76
9:15	201	3:26	80, 230
10:5	470	3:27–28	169, 176
10:12–18	42	3:27	171 f., 195
11:2–3	20, 80	3:28	152, 172, 236
11:8	204	3:29	166, 233 f.
12	339, 341, 352	4	96
12:1–10	189	4:1–7	234
13:5	455	4:4	93, 230, 338
13:13	457, 507	4:5–7	234
		4:5	98
Galatians		4:6–7	453
1:1–5	234–236	4:6	21, 105, 114, 230
1:1	230–232	4:7	230
1:2	230, 235	4:21–5:1	236
1:4	173, 230, 240	5	174
1:11–17	38	5:1	468
1:11–12	232	5:5–6	51, 345
1:14	232	5:5	51
1:16	230, 232	5:6	51, 390
2	171	5:19–21	166, 174, 176, 379
2:4	235	5:20	174
2:13	232	5:21	166, 174
2:15–21	199	5:22–23	175
2:15–16	232, 382	5:22	174
2:16	53, 390, 396	5:24–25	346
2:17	199	5:24	172–174
2:19–20	171, 378, 386, 453	5:25	174 f.
2:19	3, 172	5:26	175
2:20	18, 51, 53, 173, 230	6:8	346

6:10	235	2:16	272 f.
6:12	173	2:17	273
6:14–15	137, 241	2:18	272, 508
6:14	173	2:19	274
6:15	235 f., 240	2:20	20, 73, 274
		2:21–22	20, 67, 73 f.
Ephesians		2:21	73, 274
1	341	2:22	274
1:3–14	58, 265	3:10	471
1:3	16, 19, 256 f., 267, 437	3:18	318
1:4–6	16	3:20	264
1:4	17, 256, 266 f., 453, 460	3:31-32	8
		4:4–5	170
1:5	265, 267	4:5–6	303
1:9	17, 266	4:7–11	254
1:10	19, 254, 256, 266, 457	4:7	274
1:7–10	16	4:8	274
1:11–12	16	4:9	275
1:13–14	17	4:10	270, 274
1:19–20	264	4:11–16	70, 275
1:20–2:22	272	4:11–13	78, 82
1:20–23	254, 257, 261, 263 f., 272	4:12	270
		4:13–16	529
1:20	254, 256, 261–264, 275	4:15–16	70, 270, 445
1:21	254, 261 f.	4:11	70, 274
1:22–23	69, 267–269	4:12	70 f., 73, 274
1:22	261 f., 268, 542	4:13	53, 70, 78, 82, 274
1:23	268, 270	4:15–16	71
2:1–8	272	4:20–24	81
2:1–3	254	4:20	254
2:1	261–263	4:24	81
2:2	261, 264	4:32	256
2:4	267	5:1	521
2:5–6	258, 263 f.	5:5	254, 257
2:5	18, 254, 257, 261–263, 468	5:14	254
		5:21–22	79
2:6	19, 257, 263, 418	5:22–32	74, 80
2:7–8	38	5:22	270
2:7	263	5:22–23	20
2:8	263	5:23	263
2:10	256, 470	5:24	81
2:11–22	271	5:25–27	75
2:11	272	5:25	18, 270
2:12	272	5:29	270
2:13–16	275	5:30	305, 445
2:13	272, 274	5:31	21, 80
2:14–18	254	5:32	80
2:14	272 f.	6:10–20	264
2:15–16	83	6:10	264
2:15	272–274	6:11	264

6:12	264	3:17–21	290
6:13	264	3:17	316
		3:18–19	290
Philippians		3:18	290
1:1	282, 304, 308, 316	3:19	290, 314
1:3–8	313	3:20–21	38, 317
1:5	303 f.	3:20	284, 290 f., 298, 304, 305, 313
1:6	304, 313		
1:7	303 f., 512	3:21	191, 291, 304
1:9–10	121	4:1–4	313
1:10	304, 313	4:1	304
1:12	303	4:2	304, 314
1:17	473	4:3	304
1:25	304	4:4	304
1:26–27	313	4:5	304, 313
1:27–30	290, 305	4:6–7	304
1:27	303–305, 307 f., 313	4:13	304
1:28	314	4:15	305
1:29	317	4:21–23	303
2:1–4	509	4:21	303
2:1	304, 457		
2:2	290, 313	*Colossians*	
2:5–8	473	1–2	478
2:5	193, 284, 290, 313	1:9–10	469, 487
2:6–11	283–285, 287 f., 290, 298, 305, 313, 315, 317	1:9	496
		1:11	478
2:6–8	201	1:12	266
2:6	202, 285	1:13	29, 266
2:7–8	318	1:15–23	478
2:7	385	1:15–17	38, 58
2:9–11	285, 287 f., 317	1:16–17	456
2:9	291	1:16	464
2:12	313	1:18	20, 542
2:15–16	288, 317	1:19	270
2:16	304, 313	1:24	3
2:19–24	287	1:27	499
2:22	304	2:2–3	490, 496
2:24	313	2:9–10	270
2:25–30	287	2:9	445
2:25	307	2:11–12	477
2:30	284	2:12–13	18, 490
3:1–16	287	2:18–23	478
3:1	304, 313	2:19	490
3:2	290	2:20	490 f.
3:3	304, 313	2:23	490
3:4–11	305	3	479
3:8–9	12	3:1	18, 477, 485, 490 f.
3:9	53	3:3	464
3:10	3, 30, 317	3:5	477
3:15	305, 314	3:9–10	76

3:10	84		*2 Thessalonians*	
3:11	52, 169		2:1–15	38
3:12	84, 477			
4:1	470		*1 Timothy*	
4:16	302		2:5	467
5:1	470			
			Hebrews	
1 Thessalonians			10:38–12:2	53
1:1	303			
1:6	316		*James*	
1:8	303		2:17	390
1:10	38		2:19	390
4:13–14	38			
4:15–17	38, 287		*1 Peter*	
5:3	287, 288		1:15–16	481
5:27	302			
			2 Peter	
			1:4	445

Ancient Authors

Aelius Aristides

Orations
26.33   307

Appian

Bella civilia
4.105–38   295
5.12–13   295

Aristotle

Ethica nichomachea
VI   308
VI.1   309, f.
VI.5   310
VI.5.1   287
VI.6   310
VI.8   310, 315

Magna Moralia
1196b27–28   309
1197a3–16   309
1198a32–b8   309

Augustine

Expositio quarumdam quaestionum in epistula ad Romanos
12   366
41   367
44   367
45   369
48   369
53–54   368

De gratia Christi, et de peccato originali
2.2   370
4   369 f.
8.9   370
14   371
26.27   370

Quaestiones in Hepateuchum
3.4   363

Sermones
156.10   368
156.12   370

Basil of Caesarea

On the Holy Spirit
1.1 13

Clement of Alexandria

Stromata
2.21–22	344
2.22	343 f., 346, 348, 352
2.22.131.2	344
2.22.131.4	344
2.22.133.3	344
2.22.134.1–2	344
2.22.136.1–6	345
4	345, 352
4.1–2	345
4.23.149.8	348
4.26	343, 347
4.26.163.1–3	348
4.26.166.1	307
4.26.168.2	348
4.26.171.3–4	348
4.3	345, 352
4.6–7	343, 345, 348
4.6.27.2	345
4.7	346, 352
4.7.45.4–46.2	346
4.7.51.1	347
4.7.55.4	347
4.26	348
6.16.136.3	347
7.12.78.3	307
79.4	307

Dio

Historia Romana
48.4–14	295–296
54.9	296
61.7.4	228
66.4.4	221

Irenaeus

Adversus haereses
1.7.2	336
3.17–19	335 f., 342
3.17–18	336
3.17	336
3.17.2	337
3.17.3	337
3.17.4	337
3.18	336 f.
3.18.1	337
3.18.4–6	337
3.18.5	352
3.18.7	337
3.19	336, 338
3.19.1	338
3.20.1–3	352
5	339, 342
5.1–14	339
5.1.1	342
5.2	340
5.3	339
5.3.1–2	352
5.6–14	342
5.6	340
5.6.1	340
5.7–14	340
5.8.1	341
5.9.2	341
5.9.3–4	341
5.9–14	340
5.14.4	341
5.15–36	339
5.32.1	342
5.36.3	342
6.6–14	335

Livy

Ab Urbe Condita
2.32	540
45.29.5	294

Ovid

Metamorphoses
1.205	229
15.855–60	217

Tristia
2.157	220
2.181	220

Philo

De confusione linguarum
17   305

De gigantibus
61   305

De vita Mosis
2.30   269

Plato

Theaetetus
176B   344

Pliny the Younger

Panergyricus
2.3   222
7.4   222

Plutarch

Moralia
824D   271

Seneca

De Celementia
1.1.2   221
1.2–3   221
1.2   221
1.11–13   221
1.14.1–16.1   221
1.14.2   221
1.3.5   269
1.4.1   269
1.4.2–3   269
2.2.1   269
14.2–3   222
14.2   221

21.2   221

Suetonius

Divus Augustus
28   219
58   218

Divus Claudius
46   227

Nero
7.2   226
33.2   229

Tiberius
14.3   296

Tacitus

Annales
1.2   220
12.41   226, f.
12.68.2   227
12.69.3   227
13.10.3   228
13.12.1   228
13.14.3–6   228
13.15.2   228
13.15.3–5   228
13.15–17   228
13.17.2   228

Thucydidies

History of the Peloponnesian War
2.40.2   241

Anonymous

Res gestae divi Augusti
20   219
35.1   218

Index of Names

Agamben, Giorgio 533
Allan, John 256
Allen, Leslie 266
Allison, C. F. 428
Althaus, Paul 483
Anderson, Benedict 301 f.
Ando, Clifford 221–223, 306
Aquinas, Thomas 184, 377, 430, 432–435, 441 f.

Badiou, Alain 239
Baker, Mary Patton 503–528
Barclay, John 213 f.
Barth, Karl 3, 12, 22, 401, 454–473
Barth, Markus 14
Bataille, Georges 238
Bavinck, Herman 23 f., 483
Baudrillard, Jean 293, 301, 489 f.
Baylor, T. Robert 427–452
Benjamin, Walter 302
Bhabha, Homi 237, 315
Billings, Todd 427
Blackwell, Ben 186 f., 189 f., 331–355
Blocher, Henri 481
Bockmuehl, Markus 305
Bonner, Gerald 359
Bourdieu, Pierre 311 f.
Brown, Peter 546 f.
Bultmann, Rudolf 127 f., 154
Burger, Hans 25f.

Calvin, John 7–12, 22, 184, 399–424, 427–429, 443, 447, 450, 479, 483, 484–486, 493
Campbell, Constantine 14, 24, 26, 61–86, 267, 526
Campbell, Douglas 37–60, 96
Canlis, Julie 399–425
Chadwick, Henry 361
Chester, Stephen 375–425
Chow, Rey 315
Coakley, Sarah 131, 144

Coffey, Davis 89
Collins, Adela Yarbro 284 f., 315
Croasmun, Matthew 127–156
Darwin, Charles 131
Deissmann, Adolf 5
Del Colle, Ralph 89
DeYoung, Rebecca 488
Descartes, René 122
Douglas, Mary 142 f., 147–149, 151
Dunn, James 88–90, 98, 160
Dunnington, Kent 495 f.
Durkheim, Émile 130, 142, 147, 151

Eastman, Susan 103–125
Edwards, Jonathan 22
Engberg-Pedersen, Troels 150
Escrig, M. T. 312, 314
Esposito, Roberto 533, 536–538, 543, 545, 551
Evans, William 422, 428, 450

Favro, Diane 219
Fears, J. Rufus 271
Fee, Gordon 103 f., 112, 115
Fesko, J. V. 428 f.
Finlan, Stephen 187
Fleck, Ludwig 130, 142, 146–148
Foucault, Michel 533–535, 537
Fowl, Stephen 312

Gadamer, Hans-Georg 8, 310–312
Gaffin, Richard 10, 17
Glover, T. R. 231
Gorman, Michael 158, 181–208, 511
Grieb, Katherine 201
Gross, Jules 360
Gunn, Neil 400

Hallonsten, Gösta 365, 369, 371
Harris, Murray 15
Hauck, Friedrich 511
Hauerwas, Stanley 490 f.

Hawkes, Terence 63–65
Hays, Richard 7, 127, 196, 275, 331, 353
Heidegger, Martin 310
Herdt, Jennifer 478–480, 486, 489, 492, 497
Hinkelammert, Franz 147 f.
Hobson, Peter119
Hoekema, Anthony 10
Hooker, Morna 54, 187 f., 196, 205
Horsley, Richard 214
Hunsinger, George 429
Hyde, Michael 291

Jewett, Robert 112, 114–116
Jipp, Joshua 251–279
Johnson, Keith 453–474
Johnson, Luke Timothy 286, 317
Johnson, Marcus 27

Kahl, Brigitte 216
Kant, Immanuel 297
Kantorowicz, Ernst 547 f.
Kapic, Kelly 494
Käsemann, Ernst 112
Keck, Leander 106
Keppie, Lawrence 295
Koester, Helmut 283
Kojève, Alexandre 238
Knausgaard, Karl Ove 209, 235
Knorr Cetina, Karin 139, 142
Kraftchick, Steven 289–291, 308, 318

Lash, Nicholas 122 f.
Lefebvre, Henri 299
Levick, Barbara 227
Litwa, David 189
Lohse, Eduard 158 f.
Lossky, Vladimir 358
Luther, Martin 6, 22, 357 f., 375–396, 478, 483

Macaskill, Grant 27, 87–101, 184
Mackey, James 89
MacQuarrie, John 89
Mannermaa, Tuomo 394
Martin, Dale 136, 539–542, 545
Martyn, J. Louis 123, 151 f.
Massey, Doreen 299
McClintock, Anne 315

Meconi, David 362 f.
Meeks, Wayne 283 f., 308, 314
Meyer, Paul 104 f., 109
Mignolo, Walter 302, 316
Milbank, John 543 f.
Mitchel, Katharyne 315
Morales, Isaac Augustine 157–179
Murphy-O'Connor, Jerome 524
Murray, John 10
Narsallah, Laura 293, 295 f., 298, 304
Nevin, John Williamson 427 f.
Nowak, Martin 132–134
Nygren, Anders 145

Oakes, Peter 287–289, 317
O'Donovan, Oliver 491
Osiander, Andreas 8
Owen, John 22, 427–451, 493f.

Packer, J. I. 400
Pettit, Philip 139, 149
Price, Simon 217

Queneau, Raymond 238

Riches, John 365
Ricoeur, Paul 62
Russell, Norman 363

Sanders, E. P. 6 f., 12, 54, 127 f., 157 f., 168, 181, 252, 331, 350, 353, 357 f., 365, 375 f.
Sarisky, Darren 357–373
Santner, Eric 537, 550 f.
Scathmáry, Eörs 133
Schnelle, Udo 158
Schweitzer, Albert 5, 158, 175, 353, 375
Shakespeare, William 209, 281
Singh, Devin 529–556
Sloterdijk, Peter 281, 300 f.
Smith, John Maynard 133
Smith, Jonathan Z. 297
Spatfora, Andrea 72
Stendahl, Krister 358, 365
Stowers, Stanley 128
Strecker, Christian 158, 160
Stuhlmacher, Peter 273

Tannehill, Robert 160
Tanner, Kathryn 290, 364

Thate, Michael 209–250, 281–327
Thiselton, Anthony 507
Thrift, Nigel 299, 317
Torrance, T. F. 61

Vanhoozer, Kevin 3–33, 497, 507
Varma, Ashish 477–501

Webster, John 481
Wesley, John 199
Wheeler, William Morton 134
Williams, G. C. 131

Wilson, David Sloan 135, 138, 140 f., 143, 149
Wilson, E. O. 132, 144
Wallace-Hadrill, Andrew 271
Weber, Max 223
Wright, N. T. 15, 79, 515, 517

Yeğenoğlu, Meyda 315 f.
Young, Frances 516, 518

Žižek, Slavoj 209
Zusak, Markus 281

Subject Index

Abraham 15–17, 27, 46, 47, 56, 174, 230– 235, 380–382, 401, 405 f., 436
Abrahamic covenant, *see* Covenant, Abrahamic
Adam 16, 23, 27, 75, 97 f., 106, 108, 145, 268, 337 f., 389, 401, 404 f., 408– 410, 412, 417, 433, 437, 440–443
Adam Christology 16, 97, 145, 268, 337, 417, 437, 440–441, 443
Adoption 12, 21 f., 24, 68, 88, 90, 97–99, 118, 209, 223 f., 229, 231, 234 f., 265 f., 338 f., 341, 343, 344 f., 349, 351, 353, 360, 365, 369, 400, 403, 406, 408, 412–415, 417, 419, 421, 423 f.
Apocalyptic
– readings of Paul 48, 88, 92 f., 95 f., 100, 151, 152, 240, 375
– theology 48, 152, 240
– Luther's theology 376–396
Ascension 19, 38, 257, 401, 410, 418–420, 429, 443, 543, 551
Ascent 220, 239, 338, 401, 418 f., 447, 450
Atonement 17, 411, 428–434, 439–442, 449 f., 458, 462, 518, 520, 526

Baptism 12, 19, 24, 52, 80, 97, 98, 145, 150, 152, 157–176, 336, 378, 391, 410 f., 419, 434, 446, 454, 515, 523
Blood 69, 83, 94 f., 99, 225, 231, 272, 273, 340– 342, 388, 403, 420, 423, 445 f., 504, 516 f., 519, 520, 524 f.
Body
– of Christ 4, 8, 15, 20, 25, 66–85, 94 f., 99, 108, 122 f., 127–129, 137, 140 f., 144 f., 151, 167, 171, 191, 268–270, 291, 304, 317 f., 339, 416, 438, 444 f., 472, 485, 516 f., 519, 523–525, 539, 542, 545–547, 550, 552, 553–555

– of a human 3–5, 106, 108–111, 127, 129, 130–132, 134–138, 140 f., 144–147, 152, 154, 162 f., 168, 172, 174, 176, 191 f., 269, 297 f., 317, 334, 340, 343, 345–349, 351 f., 369, 379 f., 439, 445 f., 488, 493, 529, 533, 535, 541–545, 549, 551, 553–555
– eschatological 6, 15, 197, 291, 339, 340 f., 351 f., 367, 369, 552
– the church 20, 29, 42, 61, 63, 65–85, 94, 105, 129, 136–138, 140 f., 144–150, 151, 153 f., 162, 168, 170 f., 175 f., 252, 267–270, 272–274, 307, 318, 363, 414, 421, 446, 448, 457, 496, 503, 510, 513, 522–525, 529–533, 537–543, 546–548, 550, 552–555

Co-crucifixion 160, 172, 199
Communication 27 f., 97, 105, 113–115, 217, 345, 431, 437 f., 442 f.
Communion 13, 22, 24, 27–30, 58, 106, 252, 289, 335 f., 338, 341–343, 349, 351, 403 f., 407 f., 414, 418 f., 421, 429, 443, 457, 494, 503 f., 506 f., 513, 517–519, 526
Corporate solidarity/incorporation 5 f., 15, 19 f., 25, 27, 62 f., 66 f., 72–74, 76, 78, 85, 108, 112, 120, 137, 145 f., 149 f., 153, 164, 182 f., 192, 195, 199, 205, 257, 274 f., 421, 433 f., 435, 439 f., 448, 455, 462, 531 f., 536, 539, 543, 545
Covenant
– Abrahamic 46
– Adamic 16, 23, 27, 106, 108, 145, 268, 337–389, 404–409, 433, 441–443
– and contract 9, 393, 538, 545
– and kinship 116–117, 119
– Davidic 15, 90, 273, 275
– Mosaic 27, 74, 189, 388, 517
– new, *see* new covenant

Subject Index

– partner 91, 96, 298, 303, 455–457, 458–470, 516
Crucifixion 24, 107 f., 172 f., 197, 199, 410
Curse 50, 173, 188, 192, 384 f.
David 15 f., 27, 90, 265 f., 269, 273, 275
Davidic Covenant, *see* Covenant, Davidic
Deification 182 f., 189 f., 198, 343, 348, 349, 351, 358–363, 365, 455
Duplex gratia 21

Election 10–12, 16 f., 19, 24, 58, 99, 253, 265–267, 275, 346, 423, 444, 460, 463, 468, 473
ἐν Χριστῷ 13–15, 52, 96, 160, 199, 201, 233, 256–258, 263, 267, 274, 282, 284, 292, 302–305, 307 f., 312–318, 414–421 504
Eschatology 6, 27, 106, 288, 289, 332, 337, 341, 352, 418, 443
Eucharist/Lord's Supper 12, 19, 22, 69, 77, 78, 91, 93–95, 98 f., 158, 169 f., 175, 339 f., 402, 418–421, 424, 428, 446, 454, 503–505, 513–526, 542, 547, 552 f.
Exchange 28, 187, 202, 362, 384 f.

Faith 6, 8 f., 17–19, 21, 25, 37–59, 70, 78, 80, 82, 91, 95, 170, 175, 200, 203, 229, 232 f., 236, 260, 274, 289, 303, 306, 332, 345, 355, 358, 361, 368 f., 376–396, 405, 408, 411, 413, 438, 443, 447, 465 f., 478, 480, 492, 497, 513, 519, 525 f., 529
Filiation 21, 91, 96 f., 113, 216, 297, 338, 360, 365, 369, 406 f., 411, 414, 416
Flesh 3, 17, 20 f., 23, 30, 38, 67, 75, 83 f., 87–90, 96, 105–110, 112, 116, 119 f., 149, 171–175, 272 f., 339–342, 346, 348, 352, 367–269, 371, 379–381, 383, 387–389, 409, 414, 416, 420 f., 433, 435–437, 445–447, 450, 483, 485, 520, 538 f., 542 f., 547, 549–553

Gift 20, 42–44, 47 f., 50, 52, 54, 56–59, 67, 70 f., 78, 82, 88 f., 92 f., 96–99,
109, 117–119, 121, 171, 188, 200 f., 203 f., 223, 253–255, 260, 265 f., 268, 270 f., 274 f., 338, 377, 382, 388, 391, 401, 404, 408, 435 f., 438, 442, 444–446, 451, 479, 484 f., 488, 490, 492, 505–507, 513, 515 f., 521, 537 f., 543–545, 555
Glorification 11, 17, 114, 116, 121, 123, 190, 193, 198, 206, 424, 485
Glory 19, 38, 52, 97 f., 113, 115, 117, 182 f., 187–192, 198–200, 205 f., 308, 345 f., 381, 413, 418, 420, 431, 438, 456, 466, 481, 499, 511, 546

Headship 15, 20, 23, 67, 69–72, 75, 267–270, 275, 363, 403, 412, 418, 430 f., 436, 438, 440, 443, 445 f., 448 f., 457, 490, 519, 529, 540, 542, 549 f., 552 f.
Hope 16 f., 41 f., 44, 46–48, 51, 116, 118, 121, 123, 161 f., 168, 170, 190, 258, 260, 264, 283, 344, 346, 369, 395, 408, 418, 438, 466, 480, 499

Image/imagery 4 f., 19–21, 29, 67 f., 71, 73 f., 76, 79, 83–85, 92, 94, 98, 115 f., 123, 135, 146, 162, 164, 167, 171–174, 182, 189 f., 195, 197–199, 203, 212, 217, 221 f., 229–232, 237, 267, 332, 334, 336 f., 339–352, 362 f., 382, 390, 395, 410, 419,
Image of Christ/God 4, 76, 84, 115 f., 182, 190, 198 f., 332, 334, 336 f., 339–352, 362 f., 464, 484, 492 f.
Imagery 4 f., 19–21, 67 f., 71, 73 f., 79, 83, 85, 92, 94, 98, 113, 135, 146, 162, 164, 167, 171–174, 189, 195, 197, 203, 212, 217, 221 f., 229 f., 231 f., 237, 267, 382, 390, 395, 403, 410, 419, 429, 444 f., 482, 545–547
Imitation of Christ/God 29, 49 f., 116, 204, 345, 348 f., 351, 470, 479, 484, 523
Incarnation 17 f., 24, 58, 87, 89, 91, 95, 98, 108–110, 182, 187, 196 f., 201, 334, 337 f., 342, 353, 369, 385, 415, 423, 429, 435, 438 f., 441, 445 f., 449, 460, 462, 483, 486
Incorruption 75, 84, 338–340, 343, 350, 352 f.

Infusion 378, 391, 430, 446, 448, 483
Isaianic Servant 16, 273
Israel 15–17, 78, 89–93, 95 f., 99 f., 112, 169, 230 f., 252–255, 258, 261, 263–266, 275, 405–408, 412 f., 515–519, 521, 524 f.
– and church 78, 521, 524 f.
– and identity of Jesus 15–16, 89–90, 95, 252, 254 f., 258, 261, 515–519
– people of 15–17, 89–93, 96, 99 f., 112, 169, 230 f., 253, 263–266, 272, 275, 405–408, 412, 423

Jesus
– heavenly session 16, 19, 27, 29, 38, 55, 84, 199, 252 f., 256–258, 261–264, 267 f., 270, 274 f., 388, 420 f., 443–445, 447, 450, 457
– priestly role 344, 435, 518, 521
– real divinity 8, 87–93, 99 f., 183, 188, 336, 351, 381, 415 f.
– real humanity 415 f., 437, 462
Judgment 18, 26, 415–417, 427, 429, 435–439, 441 f., 446 f., 450, 455, 458, 461–465, 483
Justification 5, 6, 9, 11, 158, 164, 166, 181–183, 195, 198 f., 205 f., 338, 357, 375, 377–384, 387, 390, 392–395, 399, 401, 423, 428 f., 440 f., 447 f., 451, 478, 484 f., 506, 551

Kingship 11, 15, 231, 241, 251–266, 269–276, 285, 318, 340, 435, 534, 543 f., 549–552
Kinship 71, 112 f., 116, 119
κοινωνία 91, 94, 203 f., 304, 345, 421, 457, 503–526

Law 74, 92 f., 95, 99, 105, 106, 108–110, 116, 118 f., 135, 146–150, 153, 173, 181, 232–234, 236, 272, 309, 312, 338, 346, 366 f., 370, 378 f., 382, 384, 386–389, 396, 406, 408, 411, 429, 432 f., 436, 439, 447, 533, 535
Liturgy 141, 170, 233, 418, 519 f., 524, 525
Logos 87, 89, 394, 404, 437
Luther, theology 6 f., 12 f., 184, 357, 358, 365, 375–396, 478 f., 483

Marriage 20 f., 23, 28, 61, 66 f., 74 f., 80–85, 225, 390
Martyr, martyrdom 4, 341, 345–347, 352, 547
Messiah 15–17, 74, 78, 90, 182–184, 194 f., 198, 205, 251–258, 261–270, 272–276
Morality 25, 123, 128 f., 141–154, 163 f., 166, 190, 193, 197, 198, 275, 283 f., 286 f., 337, 340 f., 343, 345, 348, 351 f., 427–429, 432, 437, 445, 494, 516, 539, 542, 546
Mosaic covenant, *see* Covenant, Mosaic
Moses 15, 27, 99, 106, 169, 189, 405, 517, 524

New covenant 27, 90, 182, 408, 437, 444, 517, 519, 524
New creation 11, 23, 27 f., 30, 123, 137 f., 152, 195 f., 236, 241, 379, 383, 389, 392, 421, 424, 430 f., 435–438, 440, 443, 458, 464, 507
'New Perspective on Paul' 428
Noahic covenant, *see* Covenant, Noahic
Noah 401
Noetic transformation 343, 345, 347, 351, 492
Platonism/Platonic influence 22, 26, 94, 136, 334, 344 f., 349, 352 f., 412
Presence 9, 15, 58, 72, 79, 92 f., 95–97, 99, 103–105, 110, 112, 114, 117 f, 121 f., 124, 147, 149, 184, 185, 191, 195, 269 f., 336, 339–341, 343, 383, 393–396, 404, 417, 419 f., 427, 447 f., 506 f., 515, 517 f., 520, 523, 526, 549

Representation 25, 27, 410
Resurrection 5 f., 10 f., 16, 18 f., 24, 27, 29 f., 38, 47, 52 f., 55, 56, 82, 90, 110 f., 157, 160–164, 167 f., 176, 182, 188, 190, 194, 197, 199, 205 f., 239, 253 f., 257 f., 261–264, 267, 275, 283, 339–341, 343, 346 f., 351 f., 369, 384, 410, 416, 424, 428, 438, 440, 445, 453, 455, 458 f., 465, 468, 471, 485, 487, 492, 494, 496, 543, 551 f.

Subject Index

Revelation 56, 141, 150, 182, 189 f., 192, 206, 387, 403, 423, 456, 458, 469, 483, 485, 491, 493, 548

Sacraments 9, 24, 94, 363, 391, 418, 419, 424, 428, 434, 454, 515, 548
Salvation 6, 8, 9–12, 16, 17, 27, 28, 51, 92, 93, 95, 96, 99, 121, 182, 191, 199, 202, 209, 257, 263, 269, 270, 332, 333, 337–340, 351, 365–367, 372, 377, 379, 385, 394, 400, 401, 405, 408, 409, 411–413, 416, 417, 418, 423, 428, 432, 455, 459, 461, 462, 464, 465, 484, 515, 520, 524, 526
Salvation history 405, 461, 515
Sanctification/sanctifying 9–12, 17, 24, 164–166, 184, 192, 197, 344, 347–350, 352, 392, 401, 409, 422 f., 428, 433, 435–437, 448, 459, 463, 465, 471, 482, 484–486, 496, 506, 513, 525
Sin 3, 6, 14, 27, 40 f., 52, 79, 92 f., 95, 105–112, 127, 129, 132, 144–154, 160–164, 166, 172, 174, 188, 193, 195 f., 198 f., 204, 262, 338, 344–347, 366 f., 369, 376 f., 379–381, 383–385, 387, 391, 395 f., 407, 416, 431–435, 437, 439–441, 448, 462 f., 481, 485, 488, 493, 496, 518
Sinai covenant, *see* Covenant, Mosaic
Solidarity 7, 17, 107, 127, 231, 252, 440, 512, 515, 519
Sonship 8, 22, 29, 88f., 91, 95–99, 265–267, 275, 369, 404, 408, 410, 412, 414, 419, 423, 453, 463, 507, 526
Spirit 6, 8 f., 13, 15, 17, 19–22, 24, 26f., 29, 41, 46, 48, 53 f., 56–58, 67, 72–74, 79 f., 83, 88–90, 92, 95–100, 105–124, 127 f., 149, 159, 165–171, 174 f., 182, 184, 189, 192, 203, 205 f., 241, 252, 255, 265, 269, 297, 303, 304, 332, 336, 337, 339–343, 346–352, 362, 367–371, 375, 379, 389, 391, 400, 402 f., 409, 413–424, 427–430, 436 f., 442–450, 453 f., 457, 458, 465 f., 468–472, 480, 482 f., 485–487, 491–499, 504, 506–510, 513, 516, 519, 523, 525 f.

Substitution 25, 409–411, 422, 429, 434 f., 439–442, 449, 450, 462
Suffering
– of believers 121, 147, 175, 288 f., 317, 346, 352, 505
– of Christ 8, 19, 90, 337, 339 f., 434, 484, 525
– shared 3 f., 30, 97, 115 f., 123, 190–192, 346, 352, 385, 437 f., 510 f., 513

Temple
– church and 20 f., 71–74, 79–81, 83–85, 274, 436,
– earthly 61, 66 f., 270, 376, 395, 443, 517 f.
– heavenly 27
– *theosis* 7, 11, 158, 182–206, 365, 394, 455,
– Second Temple Judaism 181, 231, 518
Trinity 26 f., 29, 56, 58, 67, 79, 89, 99 f., 111, 340, 342, 348–350, 403 f., 430, 437, 477, 483, 485 f., 491, 494, 498, 507, 508

Zion 79, 259

www.ingramcontent.com/pod-product-compliance
Lightning Source LLC
Chambersburg PA
CBHW031538300426
44111CB00006BA/101